THE DOUBLEDAY
DEVOTIONAL CLASSICS

VOLUME II

Other books by E. Glenn Hinson

A SERIOUS CALL TO A CONTEMPLATIVE LIFE-STYLE

SEEKERS AFTER A MATURE FAITH

THE DOUBLEDAY
DEVOTIONAL CLASSICS

VOLUME II

———◆———

Edited by E. Glenn Hinson

A DOUBLEDAY-GALILEE ORIGINAL

DOUBLEDAY & COMPANY, INC.
GARDEN CITY, NEW YORK
1978

ISBN: 0-385-13425-8
Library of Congress Catalog Card Number 77-16929

CONTENTS

THE JOURNAL OF
GEORGE FOX

Abridged from THE JOURNAL OF GEORGE FOX
(London: W. and F. G. Cash, 1852)

EDITOR'S INTRODUCTION TO
THE *JOURNAL* OF GEORGE FOX

By the judgment of most persons, George Fox's *Journal* is a re-markable spiritual autobiography, but it has never become a widely read classic, as, for example, John Woolman's *Journal* has. Several factors probably account for this. One is its length, running to two substantial volumes in modern print. A more significant factor is its content. Even as edited by Thomas Ellwood, who took substantial liberties in improving the style and even the content, the *Journal* drags. It contains insightful and informative sections; indeed, for those willing to put forth the effort, the whole leaves one with a profound impression that George Fox was not an ordinary person. Nevertheless, truly lofty passages are set in the midst of many pe-destrian ones, and one can readily understand why Fox's work has not caught on as others' have. For the modern era a third factor may have limited the *Journal*'s appeal; that is, its controversial na-ture. A historian can appreciate Fox's context sufficiently to recog-nize that polemic, debate, apology, and invective belonged to the spirit of his age and culture. But the average reader will not have the same level of tolerance as the historian.

Given such limitations as these, why bother even with a con-densed version? The answer to this question is simple: George Fox. Though comparatively uneducated, Fox was a man of profound religious experience and insight. He hit upon a truth that was to produce a remarkable religious movement. Today, of course, we would entertain serious doubts about many of Fox's ideas, attitudes, and actions. Viewed from several centuries' distance, his refusal to take off his hat in the presence of officials as a sign of honor seems trifling. So also his addressing of all persons with the familiar "thee" or "thou." Who today would suffer imprisonment, whipping, fines, or even death for these? To be fair to Fox, however, we must recall the larger principle that undergirded such actions and that action mattered a great deal to the brilliant but simple man. Fox was, just as William Penn observed, above all a man of action. He, like the Puritans with whom he broke on fundamental theological perspective, wanted deeds to match words, and that if only in minute ways.

FOX'S *JOURNAL*

The condensation of Fox's *Journal* that appears in this series incorporates about half of the Ellwood version, along with a portion of William Penn's characterization of Fox. Fox himself did not keep a day-to-day account of his activities. Rather, in 1674 or 1675 he dictated his autobiography to Thomas Lower, husband of his stepdaughter. This work, interspersed with personal letters, pastoral directives, and other papers, was published in 1911 as *The Journal of George Fox* and is now known as the *Cambridge Journal*. The *Journal* that Ellwood compiled was a more polished and literary composite. Ellwood worked with substantial freedom to put together a more coherent autobiography than the earlier work. Most scholars today would adjudge him a careful editor, notwithstanding the liberties he took.[1] Among other things, he toned down Fox's claims to psychic powers and omitted accounts of miracles, items liable to cause political controversy, and doubtful or unverifiable statements. At the end he added a narrative of the last fifteen years of Fox's life, based upon information in diaries kept for Fox and laden with pastoral letters and treatises. Recently John L. Nickalls published an edition of Fox's *Journal* that uses the earlier *Cambridge Journal* as a base, thus giving preference to Fox's own phraseology and selection, but adds selections from the Ellwood *Journal*.

Selection is always a serious problem in abridgment. In this condensation I have followed as a rule of thumb the selection of materials, chiefly biographical, that illustrate and demonstrate best the religious insights of George Fox. A number of Fox's treatises or letters explain some of these, but I have given preference to the action passages, since Fox was far more a man of action than a writer, even as assisted by Ellwood. He operated more or less consistently on a philosophy of life that centers upon the concept of the Light Within.

In a brilliant exposition of Fox's thought Rachel King has shown that for Fox the Light Within meant two things: (1) "that which shows a man evil" and (2) "that in which is unity." By "evil" he meant breaking the Ten Commandments. To understand this concept in Fox, one needs to remember the vast array of religious thinkers and groups of his day who entertained a similar spirituality: Sebastian Franck, Anne Hutchinson, Gerrard Winstanley, the Familists, the General or Arminian Baptists, the Ranters, Joseph Everard, and Jakob Boehme. Among these Fox would have owed the greatest debt to Franck and the Familists. His bipartite definition of the Light Within, however, helped him to avoid the pitfalls of antinomianism, found, for instance, in Hutchinson, and the anarchism of the Ranters. Indeed, King has argued that "he made a practical synthesis of individual inward spiritual authority and group authority by means of a practical synthesis of the prophetic idea of a morally righteous God who demands moral righteousness of men and the mystical idea of the unity of God and man."[2]

Fox and his followers were often misunderstood in the turbulent era and situation in which they lived. Contrary to what many have thought, he never discarded the Calvinistic dualism that distinguishes the human from the divine. He never called the Light a "spark" of the divine. Indeed, the word Light symbolized to him something that flows constantly from an ultimate source. Furthermore, although rejecting the doctrine of depravity and affirming free will, he described God "as crashing violently into a man's life both at conversion and afterward."[3] The Light is "the divine made sufficiently available to man."[4] Likewise, Fox never identified the Seed with the human soul. By "Seed" he meant the divine essence and potentiality in human beings, which has been oppressed by the seed of the Devil or repressed in them by the Fall. Despite being himself a "once-born" type of religious genius, he maintained a light-darkness dualism. His higher estimate of human nature originated in his view that the soul is created, but he did not equate the soul with the Seed. Rather, in his view, regeneration involves the joining of the soul and the Seed. He even distinguished the Seed and the Light Within. According to King, the Light may be identified with the Holy Spirit in traditional Christian theology; it is thoroughly supernatural. Sometimes it is Christ. But Fox normally reserves the term Seed for Christ after regeneration.

Fox agreed with Calvinists on the need for regeneration. He differed with them on the universal availability of salvation and whether grace can be received or rejected by the natural human being. For him salvation involves turning to the Light, having faith in the Light. If we turn to the Light, we turn to Christ, for Christ *is* the Light. The Light is within, but it is also transcendent. The Light convinces us of sin. We can "feel" it.

Fox retained the covenant theology of Calvin, but he understood it in a different way. God elected the Seed, Christ, from the beginning. When the Seed is united with human nature, one passes from the state of reprobation to that of election. After being regenerated, human beings cannot sin. When pushed in debate, Fox espoused a perfectionist view. In writing to Quakers, however, he took a more realistic and temperate position. He was horrified at James Naylor's demented claims to divinity. Fox himself never blurred the distinction between divine and human. King has concluded that he conserved the idea of progressive sanctification, as other Puritans did, but his greater optimism caused him to telescope the process. Thus he made no distinction between justification and sanctification; they are the same.

The primal emphasis of Fox in his concept of the Light Within, by way of contrast with the light symbolism of traditional Christian mysticism, was moral—that which shows evil. He seldom used the word love either, as it was used by medieval mystics, partly because of his Puritanism. For him the Light Within became to Quakers what Scriptures were to Puritans and the Church to Roman Catholics. He did not deny that Scriptures were inspired, that they are God's *words*. Rather, he insisted that the power is the Word, the Spirit, the Light that produced these. The Light is not contrary to Scriptures; it brings people into unity with Scriptures. It also unites people with one another. If they lack unity, they do not have the Light. Thus, for Fox, the ultimate authority lies in individual inspiration. The Light alone gives the Church infallible authority. Faith in the Light is the one essential for salvation. It is a constant means of revelation.

Despite Fox's emphasis upon unity, his definition of the Light Within as "that in which is unity" was secondary, deriving from the moral definition. Whereas other mystics posited the experience of unity in the emotions and the will, Fox posited it in "intuitive moral discernment and the will."[5] This does not mean he was not emotional; he simply accentuated morality, which helps to explain why he did not record "dryness" in his religious experience. For him the corollary of unity with God is unity of the saints with one another. Because the Light and the Seed are the same in all, all can be in unity with one another. Although Fox took the future life for granted, he expected it to be a prolongation of earthly experience. Heaven would be an extension of the earthly unity of the saints, hell an extension of an earthly hell.

The two-sided definition of the Light Within, according to King, supplied the foundation of Fox's applied Christianity. The definition of it as that which shows evil explains his insistence on sober clothes, the use of "thee" and "thou" in addressing others, his objection to "hat-honor," and his refusal to pay tithes. The definition of it as that in which is unity underlies his permission for women to preach, silent meetings, refusal to take oaths, "speaking to conditions," opposition to violence, and his special interpretation of marriage.

Through the centuries, Fox and his followers have been charged with neglecting the historical Jesus. To some extent this may be a fair charge if considered in theory only. In practice, however, Fox saturated his teaching with and based his deeds upon the Bible. He differed from the Puritans only in the place he gave to direct revelation. He never claimed to hold any beliefs, doctrines, or principles he did not think came from the Bible, even though he claimed to be in the same state as the apostles respecting the Light. He wanted to restore apostolic Christianity. In actuality, he "saturated his mind with the Bible and then gave forth as direct revelation thoughts that came without effort to his mind when he waited quietly upon God."[6]

GEORGE FOX

The subject and ultimately the author of this *Journal* was a luminous figure in an age of luminaries. Despite modest culture, Fox made a powerful impression on persons on all levels of English society, from illiterate farmers to King Charles II. The secret of this remarkable impact no doubt lies deeper than Fox's words and actions, but these played their part. "For in all things he acquitted himself like a man," William Penn, a convert to the Friends movement in 1667, said, "yea, a strong man, a new and heavenly-minded man; a divine and a naturalist, and all of God Almighty's making."[7]

Fox was born in July 1624 at Fenny Drayton or Drayton-in-the-Clay, in Leicestershire, in the English Midlands. His parents were devout and gentle people. His father, Christopher, a weaver, was complimented by his neighbors with the name "Righteous Christer" and by his son with the label of "an honest man" with "a seed of God in him." His mother, Mary Lago, was similarly honored by Fox as "an upright woman" and "of the stock of the martyrs."

Christopher and Mary left an indelible mark on their son. By his own assessment he developed early "a gravity and stayedness of mind and spirit, not usual in children" and a distaste for wantonness in others. Prophetic gravity remained a characteristic and without doubt was a source of George's prophetic ministry. Christopher and Mary also helped their son develop a positive self-estimate. Matter-of-factly, Fox says, "When I came to eleven years of age, I knew pureness and righteousness; for while a child I was taught how to walk to be kept pure." The word "pureness" was connected by Fox with the Puritan covenant concept: acting faithfully "inwardly to God, and outwardly to man" and keeping to "Yea and Nay in all things."

The youth impressed others with his seriousness and sanctity. Some of his relatives encouraged him to become a priest, but others dissuaded him. Instead, he apprenticed himself to a shoemaker, wool dealer, and cattleman named George Gee. He did well, and his employer prospered as long as Fox stayed with him, but went broke when he left his service. In this job young George gained a reputation like his father's. The word went around that "If George say Verily, there is no altering him." Some ridiculed him for his scrupulousness and seriousness, but, by his own account, "people had generally a love to me for my innocency and honesty."

The sensitive, devout Fox's vocation emerged from a disturbing bout with "professors" of religion, Fox's word for superficial believers, at the age of nineteen. Fox, one of his cousins, and a friend attended a fair at Atherstone, near Drayton. The others asked him to drink a jug of beer with them. He was agreeable. But when they had drunk a glass apiece, they began to drink toasts one after another and to chide Fox, saying that the person who did not drink all would have to pay for the whole jug. Fox became so distressed at this game that he got up, plunked a groat down on the table and, after completing his business, went home. That night, unable to sleep, he did not go to bed but paced back and forth and prayed. God spoke to him as to the ancient prophets: "Thou seest how young people go together into vanity, and old people into the earth; thou must forsake all, both young and old, and keep out of all, and be a stranger unto all." In response, Fox records, he left his family and broke off "all familiarity or fellowship with old or young" in September 1643.

Fox spent the next several years, the period of the English Civil War, wandering about the country as a lonely Seeker. Rufus Jones suggested that one of the psychological factors that loosed Fox from his moorings was the extreme Puritan theology of Nathaniel Stephens, curate and then rector at Drayton.[8] Fox himself describes the experience in terms of "some years" of "temptation" almost to the point of despair. For him, however, the crisis was a struggle less with sin than with vocation. Like Francis of Assisi, he no longer fitted into the mold of his age and had to break free even from family connections. Fox, however, did not disown his father, as Francis did.

Fox's own account suggests that for a while he tried hard to make connection with one of the numberless religious groups then flourishing in order that he might properly exercise his vocation. In London an uncle named Pickering tried to bring him into the Baptist fold. Though impressed with their "tender" character, Fox could not subscribe to their views or join them, and returned to Leicestershire. After resisting the persuasion of relatives that he marry, "being a tender youth," he went to Coventry and stayed a time in a "professor's" house. When he returned again to Drayton, he and Nathaniel Stephens, who was evidently impressed with Fox's serious search, began an extended series of discussions. Despite his restricted education, Fox proved a keener "divine" than the Oxford-educated Stephens, for, according to Fox, the latter preached on Sundays what Fox told him in their dialogues. Stephens' plagiarism offended Fox and resulted in an irreparable rift between them. Later Stephens became a persecutor of Fox.

Wherever the serious-minded young man turned, he was disappointed to find superficial Christianity among clergy and people. A priest at Mancetter, in Warwickshire, Richard Abel, probably thinking Fox too serious, advised him to "take tobacco and sing psalms." Then he proceeded to breach Fox's confidences by telling them to his servants. Doctor Cradock of Coventry conversed about theological matters well, but he increased Fox's burgeoning disillusionment when he became enraged because Fox accidentally stepped into his flower bed during a walk. John Macham, a lecturer at Atherstone, only added to Fox's melancholia by giving him a physic and trying unsuccessfully to bleed him.

Early in the year 1646 Fox began to experience revelations or, as he called them, "openings." One conviction was that only the regenerate are true believers, no matter what name they go by, Protestant or Catholic. Another was that "being bred at Oxford or Cambridge was not enough to fit and qualify men to be ministers of Christ. . . ." A third was that "God, who made the world, did not dwell in temples made with hands." A fourth was that Christ alone could unlock the Scriptures.

During these strife-torn years, Fox led a solitary life. Save for his first convert and minister, Elizabeth Hooton, he had no followers. His weighty "exercises" were lifted only occasionally by a joyous experience, a window into his struggle. After realizing that education at Oxford and Cambridge did not fit persons for ministry, he looked increasingly to dissenters, among whom he discerned "some tenderness" and "some openings." In time, however, even these proved disappointing, "for I saw there was none among them all that could speak to my condition." Near despair, he heard a voice saying, "There is one, even Christ Jesus, that can speak to thy condition." Like other saints in other ages, he had come to realize that his life in the end had to serve "God Alone." This experience was reinforced for Fox a short time later by a second. After a meditative walk one day, as he returned home he felt himself "taken up in the love of God" and, in that condition, found the truth "opened unto me by the eternal Light and power," and with it also "all appeared that is out of the Light." Later on in the *Journal,* Fox described how, in other experiences, he saw "an ocean of darkness and death" enveloped by "an infinite ocean of light and love."

This series of "openings," about 1647, prompted Fox to begin his courageous and persistent preaching mission throughout the Midlands, intent on thundering against superficial religion among "professors" in their "steeplehouses." His *modus operandi* was to preach the Truth after priests had finished their sermons. Naturally gifted with a powerful voice that could not be shouted down and with obvious charisma, he quickly attracted a following. His initial success, at Mansfield, filled him with an overwhelming sense of urgency. "I saw the harvest white, and the seed of God lying thick in the ground, as ever did wheat that was sown outwardly," he stated graphically, "and none to gather it; for this I mourned with tears." His fame as a young man with "a discerning spirit" spread far and wide.

Fox's itinerant ministry cannot be outlined in detail here. A crucial factor in his remarkable success was his "conquest," in 1652, of Swarthmore Hall, the home of Thomas Fell, Judge of Assize of the Chester and North Wales Circuit, Vice Chancellor of the Duchy, and Attorney for the County Palatine of Lancaster. Judge Fell's wife, Margaret, sixteen years younger than he, had been a "Seeker" for twenty years before she met Fox. She had kept her Elizabethan home open to ministers and those who had insight into religious matters. When Fox learned this, as he toured the area, he made a beeline for Swarthmore. Despite the efforts of the local minister, William Lampitt, to cast suspicion on Fox, Margaret Fell became "convinced" and, with her, her daughters and most of the family servants. The judge was more reserved, but he kept his home open to Fox until he died, in 1658, and protected those who gathered there. Fox little knew at the time the impact this "conquest" would have, but a huge, pentecostal harvest followed it in the North of England.

Not unexpectedly, while he attracted followers by the thousands everywhere, Fox also aroused critics and opponents. His *manner* probably had much to do with the fury of the opposition. He discharged his calling with all the self-assurance of a prophet—an Amos, a Jeremiah, a John the Baptist. More offensive still, however, were his claims to direct inspiration. "These things I did not see by the help of man, nor by the letter, though they are written in the letter," he insisted, "but I saw them in the Light of the Lord Jesus Christ, and by his immediate Spirit and power, as did the holy men of God, by whom the Holy Scriptures were written." Here was a claim that obviously bordered on blasphemy in the minds of those who attributed authority to the Bible, as Anglicans and Puritans did, and which also threatened "the powers that be."

Fox and his followers suffered intensely. At first the opposition originated in mob action; later it came from the action of courts and magistrates. Popular response to the Quaker use of "thee" or "thou" or their refusal to doff their hats was rage again and again. "O! The rage and scorn, the heat and fury that arose!" Fox wrote. "O! The blows, punchings, beatings, and imprisonments that we underwent, for not putting off our hats to men, for that soon tried all men's patience and sobriety what it was." At Mansfield-Woodhouse in 1649, Fox was put in the stocks. And while there, the mob threw stones at him, bruising his head, arms, breast, shoulders, back, and sides and nearly knocking him senseless. Occasionally Fox obtained better treatment from officials: a sympathetic judge or jailer. But such occasions were rare. It is unquestionable that time spent in cold, damp, unsanitary prisons under the worst possible conditions hastened his death, at age sixty-seven. The most terrible of his imprisonments was an eight-month confinement in Launceston Castle for posting a paper he had written. He and others were fined for contempt of court for refusing to remove their hats. When they refused to pay the fine and also jailer's fees, considering themselves innocent, they were cast into a hole, in the lowest part of the castle prison, called "Doomsdale." Human dung and water came up to the tops of their shoes, but the jailer refused to let them clean out their cell. Townspeople furnished them with bits of straw to burn so as to cover over some of the odors. This so enraged the jailer when smoke came up to his room that he took chamber pots filled by other prisoners and poured the excrement down on their heads in Doomsdale. Only the persistence of Friends enabled them eventually to obtain some relief. Fox's final, his eighth, imprisonment began in Worcester on December 17, 1673, and ended in London fourteen months afterward. By this time the country as a whole was ripe for toleration.

An interesting sidelight on Fox's story is his relationship with Oliver Cromwell, O.P. (Oliver Protector), as Fox called him. The two men had much in common. Both had a mystical temperament. Both were innately gifted, unusual men. They met first in March 1655, when Cromwell gave instructions for Fox to be brought before him at Whitehall after Fox in a letter had denied any Quaker inclination to organize an insurrection, avowing pacifism. In this encounter Fox confidently articulated to Cromwell his prophetic ministry. What he said evidently impressed the Lord Protector, for, according to Fox, he sent Fox away with a handshake and tears in his eyes, with the word, "Come again to my house; for if thou and I were but an hour in a day together, we should be nearer one to the other." This tender early relationship subsequently turned sour as Cromwell was forced by circumstances to assume a more authoritarian command of the Commonwealth. Fox blamed Cromwell for the suffering of the Quaker saints and bitterly opposed his appeals for a national fast in a time of sustained drought. Fox confronted Cromwell with the plight of the Quakers in an unplanned encounter in Hyde Park and again on a second visit to Whitehall. In the latter confrontation Fox sought directly to convert the Protector to Quaker views, but Cromwell made light of his attempt and afterward became more hostile to Quakers. When many urged Cromwell to assume the title of king, Fox again confronted him, threatening that, if he did, he would forfeit his life. Through the remainder of Cromwell's life Fox wrote admonitory letters and could not keep out a trace of rancor in what he said. Shortly before Cromwell died, Fox saw him in Hampton Court and "saw and felt a waft of death go forth against him." He shed no tears when Charles II ordered the Protector's body exhumed and hanged, then buried in common ground.

After the James Naylor tragedy, in 1656, Fox turned his attention increasingly to organization of his movement. Naylor, a cultured and attractive gentleman, had joined the Friends movement in 1651. By all accounts he possessed much charm and rivaled or surpassed Fox in popular appeal. A small group of followers, led by one Martha Simmonds, eventually came to hail him as the Messiah and egged him on into a revolt against Fox. This aberration led to a charge of blasphemy and indescribable punishments for Naylor and a rift that was never healed. Although Naylor eventually came to his senses and sought reconciliation and forgiveness from Fox, the latter did not have sufficient charity to forgive him. Still, the repentant Naylor served Fox's cause effectively until he died, in 1660.[9]

Fox, unlike many other Nonconformist leaders, had a penchant for organization. In his biography, Rufus Jones has pointed out that Fox's organizational efforts proceeded in two phases. The first occurred during the Naylor crisis, of 1656–60, the second after Fox's release from Scarborough Castle, in 1666, lasting until the end of his life. In the first phase, the General Meeting enabled Fox and his followers to formulate plans for holding meetings for worship; conducting simple business matters; collecting funds to care for the poor, the imprisoned, and "the publishers of truth"; disciplining the disorderly; caring for the flock pastorally; and performing marriages "after the manner of Adam and Eve's before the Fall"; that is, without normal legal proceedings. In the second phase, monthly, quarterly, and yearly meetings offered a framework for the movement. Fox himself logged hundreds of miles traveling up and down his own country and to other countries, strengthening and encouraging his followers. He visited Scotland and Wales on several occasions. In 1669 he went to Ireland. In 1671–72 he toured the West Indies, in 1672–73 the American colonies, and in 1677 and 1684 Holland and Germany. His own record of these travels attests the steely determination that motivated him and confirms his immense physical endurance.

An interesting sidelight on Fox's story is his marriage to Margaret Fell, on October 27, 1669. Margaret gave immediate consent, but Fox delayed until "it opened in me from the Lord, that the thing should be accomplished." Afterward he obtained concurrence of her daughters and sons-in-law and renounced any claim to the Fell estate lest the children "suffer loss" by the marriage. To many moderners, the relationship of George and Margaret may appear somewhat strange. It was hardly a romantic one, his references to her as his "dear heart" notwithstanding. She was many years his senior. Moreover, in twenty-one years of marriage, he spent no more than five with her. The other sixteen years, he devoted to his calling. Nevertheless, many things attest the genuine love and gentleness that bound them together. In many ways, one is more impressed with Margaret Fell than with George Fox. She drew her whole family into Fox's entourage. Then, after marriage, she paid a great price for her devotion to him in loss of property and even in imprisonment. She outlived him eleven years.

It was remarkable that Fox, unlettered artisan that he was, attracted the retinue he did. Besides the Fells, he cast his spell upon William Penn, son of Admiral William Penn, in 1667. Not Fox himself, but Thomas Loe, of Oxford, planted the first seed. Sent down from Oxford in disgrace and put in charge of his father's estate in Ireland, young William became thoroughly "convinced." Despite severe opposition from the admiral for several years, he became a devoted follower and "publisher of truth." The firmness of his commitment is reflected in the "holy experiment," the colony of Pennsylvania, which he founded in 1682. This volume contains the kernel of his admiring sketch of Fox's life and character.

Fox also attracted the Barclays, of Scotland, into his fold. Colonel David Barclay (1610–86) became a follower during Fox's visit to Scotland in 1657. His son Robert (1648–90), the greatest of the early apologists for the Friends movement, was "convinced" at age eighteen during a visit to his father and John Swinton, then prisoners for their faith in Edinburgh. Ten years later, he published *The Apology*, first in Latin and two years later in English. According to Rufus Jones,[10] Barclay turned the Quaker movement in quite a different direction from what Fox intended, for his training came from the schools of theology rather than the humanists and mystics in whose stream Fox drank. Elton Trueblood has called the alternative that he offered "rational evangelicalism."[11] It is unquestionable that his mediating position gained for the Quakers a respectability they might never have obtained with George Fox's leadership alone.

The roll of early Quaker notables could be extended. It included Isaac Penington, converted in 1658 after years as a "Seeker," who paid a heavy price for his faith, and Thomas Ellwood, secretary of John Milton, who suggested that he write *Paradise Regained*. During his first visit to Holland and Germany, in 1677, Fox sent a letter to Princess Elizabeth, daughter of Frederick, Elector Palatine, and granddaughter of James I of England, and received a gentle and understanding reply. She did not, however, become a Quaker.

The early Quakers had a profound social impact. Fox was, above all, a prophet and reformer. His tireless efforts to reform Christianity, however, took their toll. Burdened in his last years with heavy leadership responsibilities, suffering as a result of persecution and conflicts within the Quaker fold, he died January 11, 1691, in London. Just as he showed courage in life, so he did in death. His parting words to Friends who came to visit him in the throes of death were just as optimistic as those which bore him through many periods of distress: "All is well. The Seed of God reigns over all, and over death itself. And though I am weak in body, yet the

power of God is over all, and the Seed reigns over all disorderly
spirits."

—E. Glenn Hinson

NOTES

1. Hanna Darlington Monaghan, *"Dear George": George Fox, Man and Prophet* (Philadelphia: Franklin Publishing Co., 1970), pp. 71ff., has judged Ellwood's work harshly, but her concern to establish Fox's healing gifts reveals why. Geoffrey F. Nuttall, in an introduction to *The Journal of George Fox*, rev. ed. by John L. Nickalls (London: Cambridge University Press, 1952), pp. ix–x, is more gracious.

2. Rachel Hadley King, *George Fox and the Light Within, 1650–1660* (Philadelphia: Friends Book Store, 1940), p. 38.

3. Ibid., p. 45.

4. Ibid., p. 47.

5. Ibid., p. 115.

6. Ibid., p. 167.

7. Preface to the *Journal*.

8. *George Fox: Seeker and Friend* (New York & London: Harper & Bros., 1930), pp. 17–18.

9. An excellent description of this tragic affair is given by Vernon Noble, *The Man in Leather Breeches: The Life and Times of George Fox* (London & New York: Elek Books, 1953), pp. 108–43.

10. Op. cit., p. 156.

11. *Robert Barclay* (New York: Harper & Row, 1968), p. 241.

PREFACE TO FOX'S *JOURNAL*

WILLIAM PENN

The blessed instrument of this work in this day of God, of whom I am now about to write, was George Fox, distinguished from another of that name, by that other's addition of Younger to his name in all his writings; not that he was so in years, but that he was so in the truth; but he was also a worthy man, witness, and servant of God in his time.

But this George Fox was born in Leicestershire, about the year 1624. He descended of honest and sufficient parents, who endeavoured to bring him up, as they did the rest of their children, in the way and worship of the nation; especially his mother, who was a woman accomplished above most of her degree in the place where she lived. But from a child he appeared of another frame of mind than the rest of his brethren; being more religious, inward, still, solid, and observing, beyond his years, as the answers he would give, and the questions he would put upon occasion, manifested to the astonishment of those that heard him, especially in divine things.

His mother taking notice of his singular temper, and the gravity, wisdom, and piety that very early shined through him, refusing childish and vain sports and company, when very young, she was tender and indulgent over him, so that from her he met with little difficulty. As to his employment, he was brought up in country business; and as he took most delight in sheep, so he was very skillful in them; an employment that very well suited his mind in several respects, both from its innocency and solitude; and was a just figure of his after ministry and service.

I shall not break in upon his own account, which is by much the best that can be given, and therefore desire, what I can, to avoid saying anything of what is said already, as to the particular passages of his coming forth; but, in general, when he was somewhat above twenty, he left his friends and visited the most retired and religious people in those parts; and some there were, short of few, if any, in this nation, who waited for the consolation of Israel night and day; as Zacharias, Anna, and good old Simeon did of old time.

To these he was sent, and these he sought out in the neighbouring counties, and among them he sojourned till his more ample ministry came upon him. At this time he taught, and was an example of silence, endeavouring to bring them from self-performances, testifying and turning to the Light of Christ within them, and encouraging them to wait in patience to feel the power of it to stir in their hearts, that their knowledge and worship of God might stand in the power of an endless life, which was to be found in the Light, as it was obeyed in the manifestation of it in man. "For in the Word was Life, and that Life is the Light of men," Life in the Word, Light in men—and Life in men too, as the Light is obeyed; the children of the Light living in the Life of the Word, by which the Word begets them again to God, which is the regeneration and new birth, without which there is no coming unto the kingdom of God; and which, whoever comes to, is greater than John, that is, than John's dispensation, which was not that of the kingdom, but the consummation of the legal, and forerunning of the gospel dispensation. Accordingly, several meetings were gathered in those parts; and thus his time was employed for some years.

In 1652, he being in his usual retirement to the Lord upon a very high mountain, in some of the higher parts of Yorkshire, as I take it, his mind exercised toward the Lord, he had a vision of the great work of God in the earth, and of the way that he was to go forth to begin it. He saw people as thick as motes in the sun, that should in time be brought home to the Lord; that there might be but one shepherd and one sheepfold in all the earth. There his eye was directed northward, beholding a great people that should receive him and his message in those parts. Upon this mountain he was moved of the Lord to sound forth his great and notable day, as if he had been in a great auditory, and from thence went north, as the Lord had shown him; and in every place where he came, if not before he came to it, he had his particular exercise and service shown to him, so that the Lord was his leader indeed; for it was not in vain that he travelled, God in most places sealing his commission with the convincement of some of all sorts, as well publicans as sober professors of religion. Some of the first and most eminent of them which are at rest, were Richard Farnsworth, James Naylor, William Dewsbury, Francis Howgill, Edward Burrough, John Camm, John Audland, Richard Hubberthorn, T. Taylor, John

Aldam, T. Homes, Alexander Parker, William Simpson, William Caton, John Stubbs, Robert Widders, John Burnyeat, Robert Lodge, Thomas Salthouse, and many more worthies, that cannot be well here named, together with divers yet living of the first and great convincement, who, after the knowledge of God's purging judgments in themselves, and some time of waiting in silence upon him, to feel and receive power from on high to speak in his name (which none else rightly can, though they may use the same words), felt the divine motions, and were frequently drawn forth, especially to visit the public assemblies, to reprove, inform, and exhort them; sometimes in markets, fairs, streets, and by the high-way-side, calling people to repentance, and to turn to the Lord with their hearts as well as their mouths; directing them to the Light of Christ within them, to see, examine, and consider their ways by, and to eschew the evil, and do the good and acceptable will of God. They suffered great hardships for this their love and good-will, being often put in the stocks, stoned, beaten, whipped, and imprisoned, though honest men and of good report where they lived, that had left wives and children, and houses and lands, to visit them with a living call to repentance. And though the priests generally set themselves to oppose them, and write against them, and insinuated most false and scandalous stories to defame them, stirring up the magistrates to suppress them, especially in those northern parts; yet God was pleased so to fill them with his living power, and give them such an open door of utterance in his service, that there was a mighty convincement over those parts.

And through the tender and singular indulgence of Judge Bradshaw and Judge Fell, who were wont to go that circuit in the infancy of things, the priests were never able to gain the point they laboured for, which was to have proceeded to blood, and, if possible, Herod-like, by a cruel exercise of the civil power, to have cut them off and rooted them out of the country. Especially Judge Fell, who was not only a check to their rage in the course of legal proceedings, but otherwise upon occasion, and finally countenanced this people; for his wife receiving the truth with the first, it had that influence upon his spirit, being a just and wise man, and seeing in his own wife and family a full confutation of all the popular clamours against the way of truth, that he covered them what he could, and freely opened his doors, and gave up his house to his wife and her friends, not valuing the reproach of ignorant or evil-minded people, which I here mention to his and her honour, and which will be, I believe, an honour and a blessing to such of their name and family, as shall be found in that tenderness, humility, love, and zeal for the truth and people of the Lord.

That house was for some years at first, till the truth had opened its way in the southern parts of this island, an eminent receptacle of this people. Others of good note and substance in those northern counties, had also opened their houses with their hearts, to the many publishers, that in a short time the Lord had raised to declare his salvation to the people, and where meetings of the Lord's messengers were frequently held, to communicate their services and exercises, and comfort and edify one another in their blessed ministry.

But lest this may be thought a digression, having touched upon this before, I return to this excellent man; and for his personal qualities, both natural, moral, and divine, as they appeared in his converse with his brethren, and in the church of God, take as follows:

I. He was a man that God endued with a clear and wonderful depth, a discerner of others' spirits, and very much a master of his own. And though the side of his understanding which lay next to the world, and especially the expression of it, might sound uncouth and unfashionable to nice ears, his matter was nevertheless very profound; and would not only bear to be often considered, but the more it was so, the more weighty and instructing it appeared. And as abruptly and brokenly as sometimes his sentences would fall from him, about divine things, it is well known they were often as texts to many fairer declarations. And indeed it showed, beyond all contradiction, that God sent him; that no arts or parts had any share in the matter or manner of his ministry; and that so many great, excellent, and necessary truths as he came forth to preach to mankind, had therefore nothing of man's wit or wisdom to recommend them; so that as to man he was an original, being no man's copy. And his ministry and writings show they are from one that was not taught of man, nor had learned what he said by study. Nor were they notional or speculative, but sensible and practical truths, tending to conversion and regeneration, and the setting up of the kingdom of God in the hearts of men; and the way of it was his work. So that I have many times been overcome in myself, and been made to say, with my Lord and Master upon the like occasion; "I thank thee, O Father, Lord of heaven and earth, that thou hast hid these things from the wise and prudent of this world, and revealed them to babes." For many times hath my soul bowed in an humble thankfulness to the Lord, that he did not choose any of the wise and learned of this world to be the first messenger, in our age, of his blessed truth to men; but that he took one that was not of high degree, or elegant speech, or learned after the way of this world, that his message and work he sent him to do, might come with less suspicion or jealousy of human wisdom and interest, and with more force and clearness upon the consciences of those that sincerely sought the way of truth in the love of it. I say, beholding with the eye of my mind, which the God of heaven had opened in me, the marks of God's finger and hand visibly, in this testimony, from the clearness of the principle, the power and efficacy of it, in the exemplary sobriety, plainness, zeal, steadiness, humility, gravity, punctuality, charity, and circumspect care in the government of church affairs, which shined in his and their life and testimony that God employed in this work, it greatly confirmed me that it was of God, and engaged my soul in a deep love, fear, reverence, and thankfulness for his love and mercy therein to mankind; in which mind I remain, and shall, I hope, to the end of my days.

II. In his testimony or ministry, he much laboured to open truth to the people's understandings, and to bottom them upon the principle and principal, Christ Jesus, the Light of the world, that by bringing them to something that was of God in themselves, they might the better know and judge of him and themselves.

III. He had an extraordinary gift in opening the Scriptures. He would go to the marrow of things, and show the mind, harmony, and fulfilling of them with much plainness, and to great comfort and edification.

IV. The mystery of the first and second Adam, of the fall and restoration, of the law and gospel, of shadows and substance, of the servant's and Son's state, and the fulfilling of the Scriptures in Christ, and by Christ, the true Light, in all that are his through the obedience of faith, were much of the substance and drift of his testimonies. In all which he was witnessed to be of God, being sensibly felt to speak that which he had received of Christ, and which was his own experience, in that which never errs nor fails.

V. But above all he excelled in prayer. The inwardness and weight of his spirit, the reverence and solemnity of his address and behaviour, and the fewness and fulness of his words, have often struck, even strangers, with admiration, as they used to reach others with consolation. The most awful, living, reverent frame I ever felt or beheld, I must say, was his in prayer. And truly it was a testimony he knew and lived nearer to the Lord than other men; for they that know him most, will see most reason to approach him with reverence and fear.

VI. He was of an innocent life, no busy-body, nor self-seeker, neither touchy, nor critical; what fell from him was very inoffensive, if not very sure to be in his company. He exercised no authority but over evil, and that everywhere and in all; but with love, compassion, and long-suffering. A most merciful man, as ready to forgive, as unapt to take or give an offence. Thousands can truly say, he was of an excellent spirit and savour among them, and because thereof, the most excellent spirits loved him with an unfeigned and unfading love.

VII. He was an incessant labourer; for in his younger time, before his many great and deep sufferings and travels had enfeebled his body for itinerant services, he laboured much in the word, and doctrine, and discipline in England, Scotland, and Ireland, turning many to God, and confirming those that were convinced of the truth, and settling good order as to church affairs among them. And towards the conclusion of his travelling services, between the years seventy-one and seventy-seven, he visited the churches of Christ in the plantations in America, and in the United Provinces, and Germany, as his following Journal relates, to the convincement and consolation of many. After that time he chiefly resided in and about the city of London; and besides the services of his ministry, which were frequent and serviceable, he wrote much, both to them that are within, and those that are without, the communion. But the care he took of the affairs of the church in general was very great.

VIII. He was often where the records of the affairs of the church are kept, and the letters from the many meetings of God's people over all the world, where settled, come upon occasions; which letters he had read to him, and communicated them to the meeting that is weekly (Called the Meeting for Sufferings, and now held monthly, except exigencies require more frequent sittings.) held there for such services; and he would be sure to stir them up to discharge them, especially in suffering cases, showing great sympathy and compassion upon all such occasions, carefully looking into the respective cases, and endeavouring speedy relief, according to the nature of them. So that the churches, or any of the suffering members thereof, were sure not to be forgotten or delayed in their desires, if he were there.

IX. As he was unwearied, so he was undaunted in his services for God and his people; he was no more to be moved to fear than to wrath. His behaviour at Derby, Lichfield, Appleby, before Oliver Cromwell, at Launceston, Scarborough, Worcester, and Westminster-Hall, with many other places and exercises, did abundantly evidence it to his enemies as well as his friends.

But as in the primitive times, some rose up against the blessed apostles of our Lord Jesus Christ, even from among those that they had turned to the hope of the gospel, who became their greatest trouble; so this man of God had his share of suffering from some that were convinced by him, who through prejudice or mistake ran against him, as one that sought dominion over conscience; because he pressed, by his presence or epistles, a ready and zealous compliance with such good and wholesome things as tended to an orderly conversation about the affairs of the church, and in their walking before men. That which contributed much to this ill work, was, in some, a begrudging of this meek man the love and esteem he had and deserved in the hearts of the people; and weakness in others, that were taken with their groundless suggestions of imposition and blind obedience.

They would have had every man independent; that as he had the principle in himself, he should only stand and fall to that, and nobody else; not considering that the principle is one in all; and though the measure of light or grace might differ, yet the nature of it was the same; and being so, they struck at the spiritual unity, which a people, guided by the same principle, are naturally led into; so that what is an evil to one, is so to all, and what is virtuous, honest, and of good report to one, is so to all, from the sense and savour of the one universal principle which is common to all, and, which the disaffected also profess to be, the root of all true Christian fellowship, and that Spirit into which the people of God drink, and come to be spiritually-minded, and of one heart and one soul.

Some weakly mistook good order in the government of church affairs for discipline in worship, and that it was pressed or recommended by him and other brethren. And they were ready to reflect the same things that Dissenters had very reasonably objected upon the national churches, that have coercively pressed conformity to their respective creeds and worships. Whereas these things related wholly to conversation, and the outward (and as I may say) civil part of the church, that men should walk up to the principles of their belief, and not be wanting in care and charity. But though some have stumbled and fallen through mistakes, and unreasonable obstinacy, even to a prejudice; yet, blessed be God, the generality have returned to their first love, and seen the work of the enemy, that loses no opportunity or advantage by which he may check or hinder the work of God, disquiet the peace of his church, and chill the love of his people to the truth and one to another; and there is hope of divers of the few that are yet at a distance.

In all these occasions, though there was no person the discontented struck so sharply at as this good man, he bore all their weakness and prejudice, and returned not reflection for reflection; but forgave them their weak and bitter speeches, praying for them that they might have a sense of their hurt, see the subtilty of the enemy to rend and divide, and return into their first love that thought no ill.

And truly, I must say, that though God had visibly clothed him with a divine preference and authority, and indeed his very presence expressed a religious majesty, yet he never abused it; but held his place in the church of God with great meekness, and a most engaging humility and moderation. For upon all occasions, like his blessed Master, he was a servant to all; holding and exercising his eldership, in the invisible power that had gathered them, with reverence to the Head and care over the body; and was received only in that spirit and power of Christ, as the first and chief elder in this age; who, as he was therefore worthy of double honour, so for the same reason it was given by the faithful of this day; because his authority was inward and not outward, and that he got it and kept it by the love of God, and power of an endless life. I write my knowledge and not report, and my witness is true, having been with him for weeks and months together on divers occasions, and those of the nearest and most exercising nature, and that by night and by day, by sea and by land, in this and in foreign countries: and I can say I never saw him out of his place, or not a match for every service or occasion. For in all things he acquitted himself like a man, yea, a strong man, a new and heavenly-minded man; a divine and a naturalist, and all of God Almighty's making. I have been surprised at his questions and answers in natural things; that whilst he was ignorant of useless and sophistical science, he had in him the foundation of useful and commendable knowledge, and cherished it everywhere. Civil, beyond all forms of breeding, in his behaviour; very temperate, eating little, and sleeping less, though a bulky person.

Thus he lived and sojourned among us: and as he lived, so he died; feeling the same eternal power, that had raised and preserved him, in his last moments. So full of assurance was he, that he triumphed over death; and so even in his spirit to the last, as if death were hardly worth notice or a mention; recommending to some with him, the despatch and dispersion of an epistle, just before written to the churches of Christ throughout the world, and his own books; but, above all, Friends, and, of all Friends, those in Ireland and America, twice over saying, "Mind poor Friends in Ireland and America."

And to some that came in and inquired how he found himself, he answered, "Never heed, the Lord's power is over all weakness and death; the Seed reigns, blessed be the Lord": which was about four or five hours before his departure out of this world. He was at the great meeting near Lombard Street on the first day of the week, and it was the third following, about ten at night, when he left us, being at the house of Henry Goldney in the same court. In a good old age he went, after having lived to see his children's children, to many generations, in the truth. He had the comfort of a short illness, and the blessing of a clear sense to the last; and we may truly say, with a man of God of old, that "being dead, he yet speaketh"; and though absent in body, he is present in spirit; neither time nor place being able to interrupt the communion of saints, or dissolve the fellowship of the spirits of the just. His works praise him, because they are to the praise of Him that wrought by him; for which his memorial is, and shall be blessed. I have done, as to this part of my Preface, when I have left this short epitaph to his name: "Many sons have done virtuously in this day; but, dear George, thou excellest them all."

THE JOURNAL OF
GEORGE FOX

CHAPTER I

1624–47

That all may know the dealings of the Lord with me, and the various exercises, trials, and troubles through which he led me, in order to prepare and fit me for the work unto which he had appointed me, and may thereby be drawn to admire and glorify his infinite wisdom and goodness, I think fit (before I proceed to set forth my public travels in the service of Truth) briefly to mention how it was with me in my youth, and how the work of the Lord was begun, and gradually carries on in me, even from my childhood.

I was born in the month called July, 1624, at Drayton-in-the-Clay, in Leicestershire. My father's name was Christopher Fox: he was by profession a weaver, an honest man; and there was a seed of God in him. The neighbours called him Righteous Christer. My mother was an upright woman; her maiden name was Mary Lago, of the family of the Lagos, and of the stock of the martyrs.

In my very young years I had a gravity and stayedness of mind and spirit, not usual in children; insomuch, that when I saw old men behave lightly and wantonly towards each other, I had a dislike thereof raised in my heart, and said within myself, "If ever I come to be a man, surely I shall not do so, nor be so wanton."

When I came to eleven years of age, I knew pureness and righteousness; for while a child I was taught how to walk to be kept pure. The Lord taught me to be faithful in all things, and to act faithfully two ways, viz., inwardly to God, and outwardly to man; and to keep to Yea and Nay in all things. For the Lord showed me, that though the people of the world have mouths full of deceit, and changeable words, yet I was to keep to Yea and Nay in all things; and that my words should be few and savoury, seasoned with grace; and that I might not eat and drink to make myself wanton, but for health, using the creatures in their service, as servants in their places, to the glory of Him that created them; they being in their covenant, and I being brought up into the covenant, and sanctified by the Word which was in the beginning, by which all things are upheld; wherein is unity with the creation.

But people being strangers to the covenant of life with God, they eat and drink to make themselves wanton with the creatures, wasting them upon their own lusts, and living in all filthiness, loving foul ways, and devouring the creation; and all this in the world, in the pollutions thereof, without God: therefore I was to shun all such.

Afterwards, as I grew up, my relations thought to make me a priest; but others persuaded to the contrary: whereupon I was put to a man, a shoemaker by trade, but who dealt in wood, and was a grazier, and sold cattle; and a great deal went through my hands. While I was with him, he was blessed; but after I left him he broke, and came to nothing. I never wronged man or woman in all that time; for the Lord's power was with me, and over me to preserve me. While I was in that service, I used in my dealings the word Verily, and it was a common saying among people that knew me, "If George say Verily, there is no altering him." When boys and rude people would laugh at me, I let them alone, and went my way; but people had generally a love to me for my innocency and honesty.

When I came towards nineteen years of age, being upon business at a fair, one of my cousins, whose name was Bradford, a professor, and having another professor with him, came to me and asked me to drink part of a jug of beer with them, and I, being thirsty, went in with them; for I loved any that had a sense of good, or that sought after the Lord. When we had drunk each a glass, they began to drink healths, calling for more, and agreeing together, that he that would not drink should pay all. I was grieved that any made profession of religion, should do so. They grieved me very much, having never had such a thing put to me before, by any sort of people; wherefore I rose up to go, and putting my hand into my pocket, laid a groat on the table before them, and said, "If it be so, I will leave you." So I went away; and when I had done what business I had to do, I returned home, but did not go to bed that night, nor could I sleep, but sometimes walked up and down, and sometimes prayed and cried to the Lord, who said unto me, "Thou seest how young people go together into vanity, and old people into the earth; thou must forsake all, both young and old, and keep out of all, and be a stranger unto all."

Then at the command of God, on the ninth day of the seventh month, 1643, I left my relations, and broke off all familiarity or fellowship with old or young. I passed to Lutterworth, where I stayed some time; and thence to Northampton, where also I made some stay: then to Newport-Pagnell, whence, after I had stayed a while, I went to Barnet, in the fourth month, called June, in 1644. As I thus travelled through the country, professors took notice, and sought to be acquainted with me; but I was afraid of them, for I was sensible they did not possess what they professed. Now during the time that I was at Barnet, a strong temptation to despair came upon me. Then I saw how Christ was tempted, and mighty troubles I was in; sometimes I kept myself retired in my chamber, and often walked solitary in the chace [open fields], to wait upon the Lord.

I wondered why these things should come to me; and I looked upon myself and said, "Was I ever so before?" Then I thought, because I had forsaken my relations, I had done amiss against them; so I was brought to call to mind all the time that I had thus spent, and to consider whether I had wronged any. But temptations grew more and more, and I was tempted almost to despair; and when Satan could not effect his design upon me that way, he laid snares for me, and baits to draw me to commit some sin, whereby he might take advantage to bring me to despair. I was about twenty years of age when these exercises came upon me; and I continued in that condition some years, in great trouble, and fain would have put it from me. I went to many a priest to look for comfort, but found no comfort from them.

From Barnet I went to London, where I took a lodging, and was under great misery and trouble there; for I looked upon the great professors of the city, and I saw all was dark and under the chain of darkness. I had an uncle there, one Pickering, a Baptist (and they were tender then), yet young and old, where they were. Some tender people would have had me stay, but I was fearful, and returned homewards into Leicestershire again, having a regard upon my mind unto my parents and relations, lest I should grieve them; who, I understood, were troubled at my absence.

When I was come down into Leicestershire, my relations would have had me marry, but I told them I was but a lad, and I must get wisdom. Others would have had me into the auxiliary band among the soldiery, but I refused; and I was grieved that they proffered such things to me, being a tender youth. Then I went to Coventry, where I took a chamber for a while at a professor's house, till people began to be acquainted with me; for there were many tender people in that town. After some time I went into my own country again, and was there about a year, in great sorrows and troubles, and walked many nights by myself.

Then the priest of Drayton, the town of my birth, whose name was Nathaniel Stephens, came often to me, and I went often to him; and another priest sometimes came with him; and they would give place to me to hear me, and I would ask them questions, and reason with them. And this priest Stephens asked me a question, viz., Why Christ cried out upon the cross, "My God, my God, why hast thou forsaken me?" and why he said, "If it be possible, let this cup pass from me; yet not my will, but thine be done"? I told him that at that time the sins of all mankind were upon him, and their iniquities and transgressions with which he was wounded, which he was to bear, and to be an offering for, as he was man, but he died not as he was God; and so, in that he died for all men, and tasted death for every man, he was offering for the sins of the whole world. This I spoke, being at that time in a measure sensible of Christ's sufferings, and what he went through. And the priest said,

"It was a very good, full answer, and such a one as he had not heard." At that time he would applaud and speak highly of me to others; and what I said in discourse to him on the weekdays, he would preach on the First-days; for which I did not like him. This priest afterwards became my great persecutor.

After this I went to another ancient priest at Mancetter, in Warwickshire, and reasoned with him about the ground of despair and temptations; but he was ignorant of my condition; he bade me take tobacco and sing psalms. Tobacco was a thing I did not love, and psalms I was not in state to sing; I could not sing. Then he bid me come again, and he would tell me many things; but when I came he was angry and pettish, for my former words had displeased him. He told my troubles, sorrows, and griefs to his servants; which grieved me that I had opened my mind to such a one. I saw they were all miserable comforters; and this brought my troubles more upon me. Then I heard of a priest living about Tamworth, who was accounted an experienced man, and I went seven miles to him; but I found him only like an empty hollow cask. I heard also of one called Dr. Cradock, of Coventry, and went to him. I asked him the ground of temptations and despair, and how troubles came to be wrought in man? He asked me, Who was Christ's father and mother? I told him, Mary was his mother, and that he was supposed to be the Son of Joseph, but he was the Son of God. Now, as we were walking together in his garden, the alley being narrow, I chanced, in turning, to set my foot on the side of a bed, at which the man was in a rage, as if his house had been on fire. Thus all our discourse was lost, and I went away in sorrow, worse than I was when I came. I thought them miserable comforters, and saw they were all as nothing to me; for they could not reach my condition. After this I went to another, one Macham, a priest in high account. He would needs give me some physic, and I was to have been let blood; but they could not get one drop of blood from me, either in arms or head (though they endeavoured to do so), my body being, as it were, dried up with sorrows, grief and troubles, which were so great upon me that I could have wished I had never been born, or that I had been born blind, that I might never have seen wickedness or vanity; and deaf, that I might never have heard vain and wicked words, or the Lord's name blasphemed. When the time called Christmas came, while others were feasting and sporting themselves, I looked out poor widows from house to house, and gave them some money. When I was invited to marriages (as I sometimes was), I went to none at all, but the next day, or soon after, I would go and visit them; and if they were poor, I gave them some money; for I had wherewith both to keep myself from being chargeable to others, and to administer something to the necessities of those who were in need.

About the beginning of the year 1646, as I was going to Coventry, and approaching towards the gate, a consideration arose in me, how it was said that "all Christians are believers, both Protestants and Papists"; and the Lord opened to me that, if all were believers, then they were all born of God, and passed from death to life, and that none were true believers but such; and though others said they were believers, yet they were not. At another time, as I was walking in a field on a First-day morning, the Lord opened unto me, "that being bred at Oxford or Cambridge was not enough to fit and qualify men to be ministers of Christ"; and I wondered at it, because it was the common belief of people. But I saw it clearly as the Lord opened it to me, and was satisfied, and admired the goodness of the Lord who had opened this thing unto me that morning. This struck at priest Stephens' ministry, namely, "that to be bred at Oxford or Cambridge was not enough to make a man fit to be a minister of Christ." So that which opened in me, I saw struck at the priest's ministry. But my relations were much troubled that I would not go with them to hear the priest; for I would get into the orchards, or the fields, with my Bible, by myself. I asked them, Did not the apostle say to believers, that "they needed no man to teach them, but as the anointing teacheth them"? And though they knew this was Scripture, and that it was true, yet they were grieved because I could not be subject in this matter, to go to hear the priest with them. I saw that to be a true believer was another thing than they looked upon it to be: and I saw that being bred at Oxford or Cambridge did not qualify or fit a man to be a minister of Christ: what then should I follow such for? So neither these, nor any of the Dissenting people, could I join with, but was a stranger to all, relying wholly upon the Lord Jesus Christ.

At another time it was opened in me, "That God, who made the world, did not dwell in temples made with hands." This at first seemed a strange word, because both priests and people used to call their temples or churches, dreadful places, holy ground, and the temples of God. But the Lord showed me clearly, that he did not dwell in these temples which men had commanded and set up, but in people's hearts: for both Stephen and the apostle Paul bore testimony, that he did not dwell in temples made with hands, not even in that which he had once commanded to be built, since he put an end to it; but that his people were his temple, and he dwelt in them. This opened in me as I walked in the fields to my relations' house. When I came there, they told me that Nathaniel Stephens, the priest, had been there, and told them "he was afraid of me, for going after new lights." I smiled in myself, knowing what the Lord had opened in me concerning him and his brethren; but I told not my relations, who though they saw beyond the priests, yet they went to hear them, and were grieved because I would not go also. But I brought them Scriptures, and told them, there was an anointing within man to teach him, and that the Lord would teach his people himself. I had also great openings concerning the things written in the Revelations; and when I spoke of them, the priests and professors would say that was a sealed book, and would have kept me out of it: but I told them, Christ could open the seals, and that they were the nearest things to us; for the epistles were written to the saints that lived in former ages, but the Revelations were written of things to come.

After this, I met with a sort of people that held, women have no souls (adding in a light manner) no more than a goose. But I reproved them, and told them that was not right; for Mary said, "My soul doth magnify the Lord, and my spirit hath rejoiced in God my Saviour."

Removing to another place, I came among a people that relied much on dreams. I told them, except they could distinguish between dream and dream, they would confound all together; for there were three sorts of dreams; multitude of business sometimes caused dreams; and there were whisperings of Satan in man in the night-season; and there were speakings of God to man in dreams. But these people came out of these things, and at last became Friends.

Now though I had great openings, yet great trouble and temptation came many times upon me; so that when it was day, I wished for night, and when it was night, I wished for day: and by reason of the openings I had in my troubles, I could say as David said, "Day unto day uttereth speech, and night unto night showeth knowledge." When I had openings, they answered one another, and answered the Scriptures; for I had great openings of the Scriptures: and when I was in troubles, one trouble also answered to another.

About the beginning of the year 1647, I was moved of the Lord to go into Derbyshire, where I met with some friendly people, and had many discourses with them. Then passing further into the Peak-country, I met with more friendly people, and with some in empty, high notions. Travelling on through some parts of Leicestershire and into Nottinghamshire, I met with a tender people, and a very tender woman, whose name was Elizabeth Hooton; and with these I had some meetings and discourses. But my troubles continued, and I was often under great temptations; I fasted much, and walked abroad in solitary places many days, and often took my Bible, and went and sat in hollow trees and lonesome places till night came on; and frequently, in the night, walked mournfully about by myself: for I was a man of sorrows in the times of the first workings of the Lord in me.

During all this time I was never joined in profession of religion with any, but gave myself up to the Lord, having forsaken all evil company, and taken leave of father and mother and all other relations, and travelled up and down as a stranger in the earth, which way the Lord inclined my heart; taking a chamber to myself in the town where I came, and tarrying sometimes a month, more or less in a place; for I durst not stay long in any place, being afraid both of professor and profane, lest, being a tender young man, I should be hurt by conversing much with either. For which reason I kept myself much as a stranger, seeking heavenly wisdom and getting knowledge from the Lord; and was brought off from outward things, to rely wholly on the Lord alone. Though my exercises and troubles were very great, yet were they not so continual but that I had some intermissions, and was sometimes brought into such a heavenly joy, that I thought I had been in Abraham's bosom. As I cannot declare the misery I was in, it was so great and heavy upon me; so neither can I set forth the mercies of God unto me in all my misery. O, the everlasting love of God to my soul, when I was in great distress! When my troubles and torments were great, then was his love exceedingly great. "Thou, Lord, makest a fruitful field a barren wilderness, and a barren wilderness a fruitful field; thou bringest down and settest up; thou killest and makest alive; all honour and glory be to thee, O Lord of glory; the knowledge of thee in the Spirit, is life; but that knowledge which is fleshly, works death." While there is this knowledge in the flesh, deceit and self-will conform to anything, and will say yes, yes, to that it doth not know. The knowledge which the world hath of what the prophets and apostles spoke, is a fleshly knowledge; and the apostates from the life, in which the prophets and apostles were, have gotten their words, the Holy Scriptures, in a form, but not in their life nor Spirit that gave them forth. So they all lie in confusion, and are making provision for the flesh, to fulfil the lusts thereof; but not to fulfil the law and command of Christ in his power and Spirit: this, they say, they cannot do; but to fulfil the lusts of the flesh, that they can do with delight.

Now after I had received that opening from the Lord, that "to be bred at Oxford or Cambridge was not sufficient to fit a man to be a minister of Christ," I regarded the priests less, and looked more after the Dissenting people. Among them I saw there was some tenderness; and many of them came afterwards to be convinced, for they had some openings. But as I had forsaken the priests, so I left the separate preachers also, and those esteemed the most experienced people; for I saw there was none among them all that could speak to my condition. When all my hopes in them and in all men, were gone, so that I had nothing outwardly to help me, nor could I tell what to do; then, O! Then I heard a voice which said, "There is one, even Christ Jesus, that can speak to thy condition"; and when I heard it, my heart did leap for joy. Then the Lord let me see why there was none upon the earth that could speak to my condition, namely, that I might give Him all the glory; for all are concluded (i.e. shut up) under sin, and shut up in unbelief, as I had been, that Jesus Christ might have the pre-eminence, who enlightens, and gives grace, and faith, and power. Thus when God doth work, who shall hinder it? And this I knew experimentally. My desires after the Lord grew stronger, and zeal in the pure knowledge of God, and of Christ alone, without the help of any man, book, or writing. For though I read the Scriptures that spoke of Christ and of God; yet I knew Him not, but by revelation, as He who hath the key did open, and as the Father of Life drew me to his Son by his

Spirit. Then the Lord gently led me along, and let me see his love, which was endless and eternal, surpassing all the knowledge that men have in the natural state, or can obtain from history or books; and that love let me see myself, as I was without him. I was afraid of all company, for I saw them perfectly where they were, through the love of God, which let me see myself. I had not fellowship with any people, priests or professors, or any sort of separated people, but with Christ, who hath the key, and opened the door of Light and Life unto me. I was afraid of all carnal talk and talkers, for I could see nothing but corruptions, and the life lay under the burden of corruptions. When I myself was in the deep, shut up under all, I could not believe that I should ever overcome; my troubles, my sorrows, and my temptations were so great, that I thought many times I should have despaired, I was so tempted. But when Christ opened to me, how He was tempted by the same devil, and overcame him and bruised his head, and that through him and his power, light, grace, and Spirit, I should overcome also, I had confidence in him; so He it was that opened to me, when I was shut up, and had no hope nor faith. Christ, who had enlightened me, gave me his light to believe in; he gave me hope, which he himself revealed in me, and he gave me his Spirit and grace, which I found sufficient in the deeps and in weakness. Thus, in the deepest miseries, and in the greatest sorrows and temptations, that many times beset me, the Lord in his mercy did keep me. I found that there were two thirsts in me; the one after the creatures, to get help and strength there; and the other after the Lord, the Creator, and his Son Jesus Christ. I saw all the world could do me no good; if I had had a king's diet, palace, and attendance, all would have been as nothing; for nothing gave me comfort, but the Lord by his power. I saw professors, priests, and people, were whole and at ease in that condition which was my misery; and they loved that which I would have been rid of. But the Lord stayed my desires upon himself, from whom came my help, and my care was cast upon him alone. Therefore, all wait patiently upon the Lord, whatsoever condition you be in; wait in the grace and truth that came by Jesus: for if ye so do, there is a promise to you, and the Lord God will fulfil it in you. Blessed are all they that do indeed hunger and thirst after righteousness, they shall be satisfied with it. I have found it so, praised be the Lord who filleth with it, and satisfieth the desires of the hungry soul. O let the house of the spiritual Israel say, "His mercy endureth forever!" It is the great love of God to make a wilderness of that which is pleasant to the outward eye and fleshly mind; and to make a fruitful field of a barren wilderness. This is the great work of God. But while people's minds run in the earthly, after the creatures and changeable things, changeable ways and religions, and changeable, uncertain teachers, their minds are in bondage, they are changeable, tossed up and down with windy doctrines and thoughts, and notions and things; their minds being out of the unchangeable truth in the inward parts, the Light of Jesus Christ, which would keep them to the unchangeable. He is the way to the Father; and in all my troubles he preserved me by his Spirit and power; praised be his holy name forever!

Again, I heard a voice which said, "Thou serpent! Thou dost seek to destroy the life, but canst not; for the sword which keepeth the tree of life, shall destroy thee." So Christ, the Word of God, that bruised the head of the serpent, the destroyer, preserved me; my inward mind being joined to his good Seed, that bruised the head of this serpent, the destroyer. This inward life sprung up in me, to answer all the opposing professors and priests, and brought Scriptures to my memory to refute them with.

At another time, I saw the great love of God, and I was filled with admiration at the infinitude of it; I saw what was cast out from God, and what entered into God's kingdom; and how by Jesus, the opener of the door, with his heavenly key, the entrance was given; and I saw death, how it had passed upon all men, and oppressed the seed of God in man, and in me; and how I in the seed came forth, and what the promise was to. Yet it was so with me, that there seemed to be two pleading in me; questionings arose in my mind about gifts and prophecies; and I was tempted again to despair, as if I had sinned against the Holy Ghost. I was in great perplexity and trouble for many days; yet I gave up myself to the Lord still. One day when I had been walking solitarily abroad, and was come home, I was wrapped up in the love of God, so that I could not but admire the greatness of his love. While I was in that condition, it was opened unto me by the eternal light and power, and I saw clearly therein, "that all was done, and to be done, in and by Christ; and how he conquers and destroys this tempter, the Devil, and all his works, and is above him; and that all these troubles were good for me, and temptations for the trial of my faith, which Christ had given me." The Lord opened me, that I saw through all these troubles and temptations; my living faith was raised, that I saw all was done by Christ, the life, and my belief in Him. When at any time my condition was veiled, my secret belief was stayed firm, and hope underneath held me, as an anchor in the bottom of the sea, and anchored my immortal soul to its Bishop, causing it to swim above the sea, the world, where all the raging waves, foul weather, tempests, and temptations are. But, O! Then did I see my troubles, trials, and temptations, more clearly than ever I had done. As the light appeared, all appeared that is out of the light; darkness, death, temptations, the unrighteous, the ungodly; all was manifest and seen in the light. After this, a pure fire appeared in me; then I saw how he sat as a refiner's fire and as fullers' soap; then the spiritual discerning came into me, by which I did discern my own thoughts, groans, and sighs; and what it was that veiled me, and what it was that opened me. That which could not abide in the patience, nor endure the fire, in the light I found it to be the groans of the flesh, that could not give up to the will of God; which had so veiled me, that I could not be patient in all trials, troubles, and perplexities; could not give up self to die by the cross, the power of God, that the living and quickened might follow him; and that that which would cloud and veil from the presence of Christ—that which the sword of the Spirit cuts down, and which must die, might be kept alive. I discerned also the groans of the Spirit, which opened me, and made intercession to God; in which Spirit is the true waiting upon God, for the redemption of the body and of the whole creation. By this Spirit, in which the true sighing is, I saw over the false sighings and groanings. By this invisible Spirit I discerned all the false hearing, the false seeing, and the false smelling which was above the Spirit, quenching and grieving it; and that all they that were there, were in confusion and deceit, where the false asking and praying is, in deceit, in that nature and tongue that takes God's holy name in vain, wallows in the Egyptian sea, and asketh, but hath not; for they hate his light and resist the Holy Ghost; turn grace into wantonness, and rebel against the Spirit; and are erred from the faith they should ask in, and from the Spirit they should pray by. He that knoweth these things in the true Spirit, can witness them. The divine light of Christ manifesteth all things; the spiritual fire trieth all things, and severeth all things. Several things did I then see as the Lord opened them to me; for he showed me that which can live in his holy refining fire, and that can live to God under his law. He made me sensible how the law and the prophets were until John; and how the least in the everlasting kingdom of God is greater than John. The pure and perfect law of God is over the flesh, to keep it and its works, which are not perfect, under, by the perfect law; and the law of God that is perfect, answers the perfect principle of God in everyone. This law the Jews, and the prophets, and John were to perform and do. None know the giver of this law but by the Spirit of God; neither can any truly read it, or hear its voice, but by the Spirit of God; he that can receive it, let him. John, who was the greatest prophet that was born of a woman, did bear witness to the light, which Christ, the great heavenly prophet, hath enlightened every man that cometh into the world withal; that they might believe in it, and become the children of light, and so have the light of life, and not come into condemnation. For the true belief stands in the light that condemns all evil, and the Devil, who is the prince of darkness, and would draw out of the light into condemnation. They that walk in this light, come to the mountain of the house of God, established above all mountains, and to God's teaching, who will teach them his ways. These things were opened to me in the light.

I saw also the mountains burning up; and the rubbish, the rough and crooked ways and places, made smooth and plain, that the Lord might come into his tabernacle. These things are to be found in man's heart. But to speak of these things being within, seemed strange to the rough, and crooked, and mountainous ones. Yet the Lord saith, "O Earth, hear the word of the Lord!" The law of the Spirit crosseth the fleshly mind, spirit, and will, which lives in disobedience, and doth not keep within the law of Spirit. I saw this law was the pure love of God, which was upon me, and which I must go through though I was troubled while I was under it; for I could not be dead to the law, but through the law which did judge and condemn that, which is to be condemned. I saw many talked of the law, who had never known the law to be their schoolmaster; and many talked of the gospel of Christ, who had never known life and immortality brought to light in them by it. You that have been under that schoolmaster, and the condemnation of it, know these things; for though the Lord in that day opened these things unto me in secret, they have since been published by his eternal Spirit, as on the house top. And as you are brought into the law, and through the law to be dead to it, and witness the righteousness of the law fulfilled in you, ye will afterwards come to know what it is to be brought into the faith, and through faith from under the law; and abiding in the faith, which Christ is the author of, ye will have peace and access to God. But if ye look out from the faith, and from that which would keep you in the victory, and look after fleshly things or words, ye will be brought into bondage to flesh again, and to the law, which takes hold upon the flesh and sin, and worketh wrath, and the works of the flesh will appear again. The law of God takes hold upon the law of sin and death; but the law of faith, or the law of the Spirit of life, which is the love of God, and which comes by Jesus (who is the end of the law for right-eousness' sake), makes free from the law of sin and death. This law of life fleshly-minded men do not know; yet they will tempt you, to draw you from the Spirit into the flesh, and so into bondage. There-fore ye, who know the love of God, and the law of his Spirit, and the freedom that is in Jesus Christ, stand fast in him, in that divine faith which he is the author of in you; and be not entangled with the yoke of bondage. For the ministry of Christ Jesus, and his teaching, bring into liberty and freedom; but the ministry that is of man, and by man, and which stands in the will of man, bringeth into bondage, and under the shadow of death and darkness. There-fore none can be ministers of Christ Jesus but in the eternal Spirit, which was before the Scriptures were given forth; for if they have not his Spirit, they are none of his. Though they may have his light to condemn them that hate it, yet they can never bring any into unity and fellowship in the Spirit, except they be in it; for the Seed of God is a burdensome stone to the selfish, fleshly, earthly will, which reigns in its own knowledge and understanding that must perish, and in its wisdom that is devilish. And the Spirit of God is grieved, and vexed, and quenched with that which brings into the fleshly bondage; and that which wars against the Spirit of God, must be mortified by it; for the flesh lusteth against the Spirit, and the Spirit against the flesh; and these are contrary the one to the other. The flesh would have its liberty, and the Spirit would have its liberty; but the Spirit is to have its liberty and not the flesh. If therefore ye quench the Spirit, and join to the flesh, and be servants of it, then ye are judged and tormented by the Spirit; but if ye join to the Spirit and serve God in it, ye have liberty and victory over the flesh and its works. Therefore keep in the daily cross, the power of God, by which ye may witness all that to be crucified which is contrary to the will of God, and which shall not come into his kingdom. These things are here mentioned and opened for information, exhortation, and comfort to others, as the Lord opened them unto me in that day. In that day I wondered that the children of Israel should murmur for water and victuals, for I could have fasted long without murmuring or minding victuals. But I was judge at other times, that I was not contented to be sometimes without the water and bread of life, that I might learn to know how to want, and how to abound.

I heard of a woman in Lancashire, that had fasted two and twenty days, and I travelled to see her; but when I came to her I saw that she was under a temptation. When I had spoken to her what I had from the Lord, I left her, her father being one high in profession. Passing on, I went among the professors at Duckingfield and Manchester, where I stayed a while, and declared truth among them. There were some convinced, who received the Lord's teaching, by which they were confirmed and stood in the truth. But the professors were in a rage, all pleading for sin and imperfection, and could not endure to hear talk of perfection, and of a holy and sinless life. But the Lord's power was over all; though they were chained under darkness and sin, which they pleaded for, and quenched the tender thing in them.

About this time there was a great meeting of the Baptists, at Broughton, in Leicestershire, with some that had separated from them; and people of other notions went thither, and I went also. Not many of the Baptists came, but many others were there. The Lord opened my mouth, and the everlasting truth was declared amongst them, and the power of the Lord was over them all. For in that day the Lord's power began to spring, and I had great openings in the Scriptures. Several were convinced in those parts, and were turned from darkness to light, from the power of Satan unto God; and many were raised up to praise God. When I reasoned with professors and other people, some became convinced.

I was still under great temptations sometimes, and my inward sufferings were heavy; but I could find none to open my condition to but the Lord alone, unto whom I cried night and day. I went back into Nottinghamshire, and there the Lord showed me that the natures of those things, which were hurtful without, were within, in the hearts and minds of wicked men. The natures of dogs, swine, vipers, of Sodom and Egypt, Pharaoh, Cain, Ishmael, Esau, etc.; the natures of these I saw within, though people had been looking without. I cried to the Lord, saying, "Why should I be thus, seeing I was never addicted to commit those evils?" and the Lord answered, "That it was needful I should have a sense of all conditions, how else should I speak to all conditions!" and in this I saw the infinite love of God. I saw also, that there was an ocean of darkness and death; but an infinite ocean of light and love, which flowed over the ocean of darkness. In that also I saw the infinite love of God, and I had great openings. And as I was walking by the steeplehouse, in Mansfield, the Lord said unto me, "That which people trample upon, must be thy food." And as the Lord spoke he opened it to me, that people and professors trampled upon the life, even the life of Christ; they fed upon words, and fed one another with words; but they trampled upon the life; trampled underfoot the blood of the Son of God, which blood was my life, and lived in their airy notions, talking of him. It seemed strange to me at first, that I should feed on that which the high professors trampled upon; but the Lord opened it clearly to me by his eternal Spirit and Power.

Then came people from far and near to see me; but I was fearful of being drawn out by them; yet I was made to speak, and open things to them. There was one Brown, who had great prophecies and sights upon his deathbed of me. He spoke only of what I should be made instrumental by the Lord to bring forth. And of others he spoke, that they should come to nothing, which was fulfilled on some, who then were something in show. When this man was buried, a great work of the Lord fell upon me, to the admiration of many, who thought I had been dead; and many came to see me for about fourteen days. I was very much altered in countenance and person, as if my body had been new moulded or changed. While I was in that condition, I had a sense and discerning given me by the Lord, through which I saw plainly, that when many people talked of God and of Christ, etc., the serpent spoke in them; but this was hard to be borne. Yet the work of the Lord went on in some, and my sorrows and troubles began to wear off, and tears of joy dropped from me, so that I could have wept night and day with tears of joy to the Lord, in humility and brokenness of heart. I saw into that which was without end, things which cannot be uttered, and of the greatness and infinitude of the love of God, which cannot be expressed by words. For I had been brought through the very ocean of darkness and death, and through and over the power of Satan, by the eternal, glorious power of Christ; even through that darkness was I brought, which covered over all the world, and which chained down all, and shut up all in death. The same eternal power of God, which brought me through these things, was that which afterwards shook the nations, priests, professors, and people. Then could I say I had been in spiritual Babylon, Sodom, Egypt, and the grave; but by the eternal power of God I was come out of it, and was brought over it, and the power of it, into the power of Christ. I saw the harvest white, and the seed of God lying thick in the ground, as ever did wheat that was sown outwardly, and none to gather it; for this I mourned with tears. A report went abroad of me, that I was a young man that had a discerning spirit; whereupon many came to me, from far and near, professors, priests, and people. The Lord's power broke forth; and I had great openings and prophecies; and spoke unto them of the things of God, which they heard with attention and silence, and went away, and spread the fame thereof. Then came the tempter, and set upon me again, charging me, that I had sinned against the Holy Ghost; but I could not tell in what. Then Paul's condition came before me, how, after he had been taken up into the third heavens, and seen things not lawful to be uttered, a messenger of Satan was sent to buffet him. Thus, by the power of Christ, I got over that temptation also.

CHAPTER II

1648–49

In the year 1648, as I was sitting in a friend's house in Nottinghamshire (for by this time the power of God had opened the hearts of some to receive the word of life and reconciliation), I saw there was a great crack to go throughout the earth, and a great smoke to go as the crack went; and that after the crack there should be a great shaking: this was the earth in people's hearts, which was to be shaken before the seed of God was raised out of the earth. And it was so; for the Lord's power began to shake them, and great meetings we began to have, and a mighty power and work of God there was amongst people, to the astonishment of both people and priests.

And there was a meeting of priest and professors at a justice's house, and I went among them. Here they discoursed how Paul said, "He had not known sin, but by the law, which said, Thou shalt not lust": and they held that to be spoken of the outward law. But I told them, Paul spoke that after he was convinced; for he had the outward law before, and was brought up in it, when he was in the lust of persecution; but this was the law of God in his mind, which he served, and which the law in his members warred against; for that which he thought had been life to him, proved death. So the more sober of the priests and professors yielded, and consented that it was not the outward law, but the inward, which showed the inward lust which Paul spoke of after he was convinced: for the outward law took hold upon the outward action; but the inward law upon the inward lust.

After this I went again to Mansfield, where was a great meeting of professors and people; here I was moved to pray; and the Lord's power was so great, that the house seemed to be shaken. When I had done, some of the professors said it was now as in the days of the apostles, when the house was shaken where they were. After I had prayed, one of the professors would pray, which brought deadness and a veil over them: and others of the professors were grieved at him and told him, it was a temptation upon him. Then he came to me, and desired that I would pray again; but I could not pray in man's will.

Soon after there was another great meeting of professors, and a captain, whose name was Amor Stoddard, came in. They were discoursing of the blood of Christ; and as they were discoursing of it, I saw, through the immediate opening of the invisible Spirit, the blood of Christ. And I cried out among them, and said, "Do ye not see the blood of Christ? See it in your hearts, to sprinkle your hearts and consciences from dead works, to serve the living God": for I saw it, the blood of the New Covenant, how it came into the heart. This startled the professors, who would have the blood only without them, and not in them. But Captain Stoddard was reached, and said, "Let the youth speak; hear the youth speak"; when he saw they endeavoured to bear me down with many words.

There was also a company of priests, that were looked upon to be tender; one of their names was Kellett; and several people that were tender, went to hear them. I was moved to go after them, and bid them mind the Lord's teaching in their inward parts. That priest Kellett was against parsonages then; but afterwards he got a great one, and turned a persecutor.

Now, after I had had some service in these parts, I went through Derbyshire into my own county, Leicestershire, again, and several tender people were convinced. Passing thence, I met with a great company of professors in Warwickshire, who were praying, and expounding the Scriptures in the fields. They gave the Bible to me, and I opened the inward state to them, and the outward state; upon which they fell into a fierce contention, and so parted; but the Lord's power got ground.

Then I heard of a great meeting to be at Leicester, for a dispute, wherein Presbyterians, Independents, Baptists, and Common-prayer-men were said to be all concerned. The meeting was in a steeplehouse; and thither I was moved by the Lord God to go, and be amongst them. I heard their discourse and reasonings, some being in pews, and the priest in the pulpit; abundance of people being gathered together. At last one woman asked a question out of Peter, What that birth was, viz., a being born again of incorruptible seed, by the Word of God, that liveth and abideth forever? And the priest said to her, "I permit not a woman to speak in the church"; though he had before given liberty for any to speak. Whereupon I was wrapped up, as in a rapture, in the Lord's power; and I stepped up and asked the priest, "Dost thou call this (the steeple-house) a church? Or dost thou call this mixed multitude a church?" For the woman asking a question, he ought to have answered it, having given liberty for any to speak. But, instead of answering me, he asked me what a church was? I told him "The church was the pillar and ground of truth, made up of living stones, living members, a spiritual household, which Christ was the head of; but he was not the head of a mixed multitude, or of an old house made up of lime, stones, and wood." This set them all on fire: the priest came down out of his pulpit, and others out of their pews, and the dispute there was marred. But I went to a great inn, and there disputed the thing with the priests and professors of all sorts; and they were all on a fire. But I maintained the true church, and the true head thereof, over the heads of them all, till they all gave out and fled away. One man seemed loving, and appeared for a while to join with me; but he soon turned against me, and joined with a priest, in pleading for infants' baptism, though he himself had been a Baptist before; and so left me alone. Howbeit, there were several convinced that day; and the woman that asked the question was convinced, and her family; and the Lord's power and glory shone over all.

After this I returned into Nottinghamshire, and went into the Vale of Beavor. As I went, I preached repentance to the people; and there were many convinced in the Vale of Beavor, in many towns; for I stayed some weeks amongst them. One morning, as I was sitting by the fire, a great cloud came over me, and a temptation beset me; but I sat still. And it was said, "All things come by nature"; and the elements and stars came over me, so that I was in a manner quite clouded with it. But as I sat still, and silent, the people of the house perceived nothing. And as I sat still under it, and let it alone, a living hope arose in me, and a true voice, which said, "There is a living God who made all things." And immediately the cloud and temptation vanished away, and life rose over it all; my heart was glad, and I praised the living God. After some time, I met with some people who had a notion that there was no God, but that all things came by nature. I had a great dispute with them, and overturned them, and made some of them confess that there is a living God. Then I saw that it was good that I had gone through that exercise. We had great meetings in those parts, for the power of the Lord broke through in that part of the country. Returning into Nottinghamshire, I found there a company of shattered Baptists, and others; and the Lord's power wrought mightily, and gathered many of them. Afterwards I went to Mansfield and thereaway, where the Lord's power was wonderfully manifested both at Mansfield and other neighbouring towns. In Derbyshire the mighty power of God wrought in a wonderful manner. At Eton, a town near Derby, there was a meeting of Friends, where there was such a mighty power of God that they were greatly shaken, and many mouths were opened in the power of the Lord God. Many were moved by the Lord to go to steeplehouses, to the priests and to the people, to declare the everlasting truth unto them.

At a certain time, when I was at Mansfield, there was a sitting of the justices about hiring of servants; and it was upon me from the Lord to go and speak to the justices, that they should not oppress the servants in their wages. So I walked toward the inn where they sat; but finding a company of fiddlers there, I did not go in, but thought to come in the morning, they were gone, and I was struck even blind, that I could not see. I inquired of the innkeeper where the justices were to sit that day; and he told me, at a town eight miles off. My sight began to come to me again; and I went and ran thitherward as fast as I could. When I was come to the house where they were, and many servants with them, I exhorted the justices not to oppress the servants in their wages, but to do that which was right and just to them; and I exhorted the servants to do their duties, and serve honestly, etc. They all received my exhortation kindly; for I was moved of the Lord therein.

Moreover, I was moved to go to several courts and steeplehouses at Mansfield, and other places, to warn them to leave off oppression and oaths, and to turn from deceit to the Lord, and do justly. Particularly at Mansfield, after I had been at a court there, I was moved to go and speak to one of the most wicked men in the country, one who was a common drunkard, a noted whoremaster, and a rhymemaker; and I reproved him in the dread of the mighty God, for his evil courses. When I had done speaking, and left him, he came after me, and told me, that he was so smitten when I spoke to him, that he had scarcely any strength left in him. So this man was convinced, and turned from his wickedness, and remained an honest, sober man, to the astonishment of the people who had known him before. Thus the work of the Lord went forward, and many were turned from the darkness to the light, within the compass of these three years, 1646, 1647, and 1648. Divers meetings of Friends, in several places, were then gathered to God's teaching, by his light, Spirit, and power; for the Lord's power broke forth more and more wonderfully.

Now was I come up in Spirit through the flaming sword, into the paradise of God. All things were new; and all the creation gave another smell unto me than before, beyond what words can utter. I knew nothing but pureness, and innocency, and righteousness, being renewed into the image of God by Christ Jesus, to the state of Adam, which he was in before he fell. The creation was opened to me; and it was showed me how all things had their names given them, according to their nature and virtue. I was at a stand in my mind, whether I should practice physic for the good of mankind, seeing the nature and virtues of things were so opened to me by the Lord. But I was immediately taken up in Spirit, to see into another or more steadfast state than Adam's innocency, even into a state in Christ Jesus, that should never fall. And the Lord showed me that such as were faithful to him, in the power and light of Christ, should come up into that state in which Adam was before he fell; in which the admirable works of creation, and the virtues thereof, may be known, through the openings of that divine Word of wisdom and power, by which they were made. Great things did the Lord lead me into, and wonderful depths were opened unto me, beyond what can by words be declared; but as people come into subjection to the Spirit of God, and grow up in the image and power of the Almighty, they may receive the Word of Wisdom, that opens all things, and come to know the hidden unity in the Eternal Being.

Thus I travelled on in the Lord's service, as the Lord led me. And when I came to Nottingham, the mighty power of God was there among Friends. From thence I went to Clawson in Leicestershire, in the Vale of Beavor, and the mighty power of God was there also, in several towns and villages where Friends were gathered. While I was there, the Lord opened to me three things, relating to those three great professions in the world, physic, divinity (so called), and law. He showed me that the physicians were out of the wisdom of God, by which the creatures were made; and so knew not their virtues, because they were out of the Word of Wisdom; by which they were made. He showed me that the priests were out of the true faith, which Christ is the author of; the faith which purifies and gives victory, and brings people to have access to God, by which they please God; which mystery of faith is held in a pure conscience. He showed me also that the lawyers were out of the equity, and out of the true justice, and out of the law of God, which went over the first transgression, and over all sin, and answered the Spirit of God, that was grieved and transgressed in man. And that these three, the physicians, the priests, and the lawyers, ruled the world out of the wisdom, out of the faith, and out of the equity and law of God; the one pretending the cure of the body, the other the cure of the soul, and the third the property of the people. But I saw they were all out of the wisdom, out of the faith, out of the equity and perfect law of God. And as the Lord opened these things unto me, I felt his power went forth over all, by which all might be reformed, if they would receive and bow unto it. The priests might be reformed, and brought into the true faith, which was the gift of God. The lawyers might be reformed, and brought into the law of God, which answers that of God, which is transgressed, in everyone, and brings to love one's neighbour as himself. This lets man see, if he wrongs his neighbour he wrongs himself; and this teaches him to do unto others as he would they should do unto him. The physicians might be reformed, and brought into the wisdom of God, by which all things were made and created; that they might receive a right knowledge of them, and understand their virtues, which the Word of Wisdom, by which they were made and are upheld, hath given them. Abundance was opened concerning these things; how all lay out of the wisdom of God, and out of the righteousness and holiness that man at the first was made in. But as all believe in the light, and walk in the light, which Christ hath enlightened every man that cometh into the world withal, and so become children of the light, and of the day of Christ; in his day all things are seen, visible and invisible, by the divine light of Christ, the spiritual, heavenly man, by whom all things were made and created.

Then I saw concerning the priests, that although they stood in deceit, and acted by the dark power, which both they and their people were kept under; yet they were not the greatest deceivers spoken of in the Scriptures; for these were not come so far as many of them had come. But the Lord opened to me who the greatest deceivers were, and how far they might come; even such as came as far as Cain, to hear the voice of God; and such as came out of Egypt, and through the Red Sea, and to praise God on the banks of the seashore; such as could speak by experience of God's miracles and wonders; such as were come as far as Korah and Dathan, and their company; such as were come as far as Balaam, who could speak the word of the Lord, who heard his voice and knew it, and knew his Spirit, and could see the star of Jacob, and the goodliness of Israel's tent; the second birth, which no enchantment could prevail against: these that could speak so much of their experiences of God, and yet turned from the Spirit and the Word, and went into the gainsaying; these were, and would be, the great deceivers, far beyond the priests. Likewise among the Christians, such as should preach in Christ's name, and should work miracles, cast out devils, and go as far as a Cain, a Korah, and a Balaam, in the gospel times, these were and would be the great deceivers. They that could speak some experiences of Christ and God, but lived not in the life: these were they that led the world after them, who got the form of godliness, but denied the power; who inwardly ravened from the Spirit, and brought people into the form, but persecuted them that were in the power, as Cain did; and ran greedily after the error of Balaam, through covetousness, loving the wages of unrighteousness, as Balaam did. These followers of Cain, Korah, and Balaam have brought the world, since the apostles' days, to be like a sea. And such as these, I saw, might deceive now, as they had in former ages: but it is impossible for them to deceive the elect, who are chosen in Christ, who was before the world began, and before the deceiver was; though others may be deceived in their openings and prophecies, not keeping their minds to the Lord Jesus Christ, who doth open and reveal to his.

I saw the state of those, both priests and people, who, in reading the Scriptures, cry out much against Cain, Esau, and Judas, and other wicked men of former times, mentioned in the Holy Scriptures; but do not see the nature of Cain, of Esau, of Judas, and those others, in themselves. These said, it was they, they, they, that were the bad people; putting it off from themselves: but when some of these came, with the light and Spirit of truth, to see into themselves, then they came to say, I, I, I, it is I myself, that have been the Ishmael, and the Esau, etc. For then they came to see the nature of wild Ishmael in themselves; the nature of Cain, of Esau, of Korah, of Balaam, and of the son of perdition in themselves, sitting above all that is called God in them. Thus I saw it was the fallen man that was got up into the Scriptures, and was finding fault with those before mentioned; and, with the backsliding Jews, calling them the sturdy oaks, and tall cedars, and fat bulls of Bashan, wild heifers, vipers, serpents, etc.; and charging them that it was they that closed their eyes, and stopped their ears, and hardened their hearts, and were dull of hearing: that it was they that hated the light, and rebelled against it; that quenched the Spirit, and vexed, and grieved it; that walked despitefully against the Spirit of grace, and turned the grace of God into wantonness: and that it was they that resisted the Holy Ghost, that got the form of godliness, and turned against the power: and they were the inwardly ravening wolves, that had got the sheep's clothing; they were the wells without water, and clouds without rain, and trees without fruit, etc. But when these, who were so much taken up with finding fault with others, and thought themselves clear from these things, came to look into themselves, and, with the light of Christ, thoroughly to search themselves, they might see enough of this in themselves; and then the cry could not be, it is he, or they, as before; but I, and we are found in these conditions.

I saw also, how people read the Scriptures without a right sense of them, and without duly applying them to their own states. For, when they read that death reigned from Adam to Moses; that the law and the prophets were until John; and that the least in the kingdom is greater than John; they read these things and applied them to others, but they did not turn in to find the truth of these things in themselves. As these things came to be opened in me, I saw death reigned over them from Adam to Moses; from the entrance into transgression, till they came to the ministration of condemnation, which restrains people from sin, that brings death. Then, when the ministration of Moses is passed through, the ministry of the prophets comes to be read and understood, which reaches through the figures, types, and shadows unto John, the greatest prophet born of a woman; whose ministration prepares the way of the Lord, by bringing down the exalted mountains, and making straight paths. And as this ministration is passed through, an entrance comes to be known into the everlasting kingdom. Thus I saw plainly that none could read Moses aright, without Moses' spirit, by which Moses saw how man was in the image of God in Paradise, and how he fell, how death came over him, and how all men have been under his death. I saw how Moses received the pure law, that went over all transgressors; and how the clean beasts, which were figures and types, were offered up, when the people were come into the righteous law that went over the first transgression. Both Moses and the prophets saw through the types and figures, and beyond them, and saw Christ, the great prophet, that was to come to fulfil them. I saw that none could read John's words aright, and with a true understanding of them, but in and with the same divine Spirit by which John spoke them; and by his burning, shining light, which is sent from God. For by that Spirit their crooked natures might be made straight, and their rough natures smooth, and the exacter and violent doer in them might be cast out; and they that had been hypocrites might come to bring forth fruits meet for repentance, and their mountain of sin and earthliness might be laid low, and their valley exalted in them, that there might be a way prepared for the Lord in them: then the least in the kingdom is greater than John. But all must first know the voice crying in their wilderness, in their hearts, which, through transgression, were become as a wilderness. Thus I saw it was an easy matter to say death reigned from Adam to Moses; and that the least in the kingdom is greater than John; but none could know how death reigned from Adam to Moses, etc., but by the same Holy Spirit that Moses, the prophets, and John were in. They could not know the spiritual meaning of Moses', the prophets', and John's words, nor see their path and travels, much less see through them, and to the end of them into the kingdom, unless they had the Spirit and light of Jesus; nor could they know the words of Christ and of his apostles, without his Spirit. But as man comes through, by the Spirit and power of God, to Christ, who fulfils the types, figures, shadows, promises, and prophecies that were of him, and is led by the Holy Ghost into the truth and substance of the Scriptures, sitting down in him who is the author and end of them; then are they read, and understood, with profit and great delight.

Moreover, when I was brought up into his image in righteousness and holiness, and into the paradise of God, He let me see how Adam was made a living soul: and also the stature of Christ, the mystery that had been hid from ages and generations; which things are hard to be uttered, and cannot be borne by many. For, of all the sects in Christendom (so called) that I discoursed withal, I found none that could bear to be told that any should come to Adam's perfection, into that image of God, that righteousness and holiness that Adam was in before he fell; to be clear and pure without sin, as he was. Therefore, how should they be able to bear being told that any should grow up to the measure of the stature of the fulness of Christ, when they cannot bear to hear that any should come, whilst upon earth, into the same power and Spirit that the prophets and apostles were in? Though it is a certain truth, that none can understand their writings aright, without the same Spirit by which they were written.

Now the Lord God opened to me by his invisible power, "that every man was enlightened by the divine light of Christ"; and I saw it shine through all; and that they that believed in it came out of condemnation to the light of life, and became the children of it; but they that hated it, and did not believe in it, were condemned by it, though they made a profession of Christ. This I saw in the pure openings of the light, without the help of any man; neither did I then know where to find it in the Scriptures, though afterwards, searching the Scriptures, I found it. For I saw in that Light and Spirit which was before the Scriptures were given forth, and which led the holy men of God to give them forth, that all must come to that Spirit, if they would know God, or Christ, or the Scriptures aright, which they that gave them forth were led and taught by.

But I observed a dulness and drowsy heaviness upon people, which I wondered at: for sometimes, when I would set myself to sleep, my mind went over all to the beginning, in that which is from everlasting to everlasting. I saw death was to pass over this sleepy, heavy state; and I told people they must come to witness death to that sleepy, heavy nature, and a cross to it in the power of God, that their minds and hearts might be on things above.

On a certain time, as I was walking in the fields, the Lord said unto me: "Thy name is written in the Lamb's book of life, which was before the foundation of the world"; and, as the Lord spoke it, I believed, and saw it in the new birth. Then, some time after, the Lord commanded me to go abroad into the world, which was like a briery, thorny wilderness; and when I came, in the Lord's mighty power, with the word of life into the world, the world swelled, and made a noise, like the great raging waves of the sea. Priests and professors, magistrates and people, were all like a sea, when I came to proclaim the day of the Lord amongst them, and to preach repentance to them.

I was sent to turn people from darkness to the light, that they might receive Christ Jesus: for, to as many as should receive him in his light, I saw that he would give power to become the sons of God; which I had obtained by receiving Christ. I was to direct people to the Spirit, that gave forth the Scriptures, by which they might be led into all truth, and so up to Christ and God, as they had been who gave them forth. I was to turn them to the grace of God, and to the truth in the heart, which came by Jesus; that by this grace they might be taught, which would bring them salvation, that their hearts might be established by it, and their words might be seasoned, and all might come to know their salvation nigh. I saw that Christ died for all men, and was a propitiation for all; and enlightened all men and women with his divine and saving light; and that none could be a true believer, but who believed in it. I saw that the grace of God, which bringeth salvation, had appeared to all men, and that the manifestation of the Spirit of God was given to every man, to profit withal. These things I did not see by help of man, nor by the letter, though they are written in the letter, but I saw them in the light of the Lord Jesus Christ, and by his immediate Spirit and power, as did the holy men of God, by whom the Holy Scriptures were written. Yet I had no slight esteem of the Holy Scriptures, but they were very precious to me, for I was in that Spirit by which they were given forth: and what the Lord opened in me, I afterwards found was agreeable to them. I could speak much of these things, and many volumes might be written, but all would prove too short to set forth the infinite love, wisdom, and power of God, in preparing, fitting, and furnishing me for the service he had appointed me to; letting me see the depths of Satan on the one hand, and opening to me, on the other hand, the divine mysteries of his own everlasting kingdom.

Now, when the Lord God and his Son Jesus Christ sent me forth into the world, to preach his everlasting gospel and kingdom, I was glad that I was commanded to turn people to that inward light, Spirit, and grace, by which all might know their salvation, and their way to God; even that Divine Spirit which would lead them into all truth, and which I infallibly knew would never deceive any.

But with and by this divine power and Spirit of God, and the light of Jesus, I was to bring people off from all their own ways, to Christ, the new and living way; and from their churches, which men had made and gathered, to the church in God, the general assembly written in heaven, which Christ is the head of: and off from the world's teachers, made by men, to learn of Christ, who is the way, the truth, and the life, of whom the Father said, "This is my beloved Son, hear ye Him"; and off from all the world's worships, to know the Spirit of Truth in the inward parts, and to be led thereby; that in it they might worship the Father of spirits, who seeks such to worship him; which Spirit they that worshipped not in, knew not what they worshipped. And I was to bring people off from all the world's religions, which are vain; that they might know the pure religion, might visit the fatherless, the widows, and the strangers, and keep themselves from the spots of the world; then there would not be so many beggars, the sight of whom often grieved my heart, as it denoted so much hard-heartedness amongst them that professed the name of Christ. I was to bring them off from all the world's fellowships, and prayings, and singings, which stood in forms without power; that their fellowship might be in the Holy Ghost, and in the Eternal Spirit of God; that they might pray in the Holy Ghost, and sing in the Spirit, and with the grace that comes by Jesus; making melody in their hearts to the Lord, who hath sent his beloved Son to be their Saviour, and caused his heavenly sun to shine upon all the world, and through them all, and his heavenly rain to fall upon the just and the unjust (as his outward rain doth fall, and his outward sun doth shine on all), which is God's unspeakable love to the world. I was to bring people off from Jewish ceremonies, and from heathenish fables, and from men's inventions and worldly doctrines, by which they blew the people about this way and the other way, from sect to sect; and from all their beggarly rudiments, with their schools and colleges for making ministers of Christ, who are indeed ministers of their own making, but not of Christ's; and from all their images and crosses, and sprinkling of infants, with all their holy days (so called) and all their vain traditions, which they had instituted since the apostles' days, which the Lord's power was against: in the dread and authority of which, I was moved to declare against them all, and against all that preached and not freely, as being such as had not received freely from Christ.

Moreover, when the Lord sent me forth into the world, he forbade me to "put off my hat" to any, high or low; and I was required to Thee and Thou all men and women, without any respect to rich or poor, great or small. And as I travelled up and down, I was not to bid people Good morrow or Good evening; neither might I bow or scrape with my leg to any one; and this made the sects and professions to rage. But the Lord's power carried me over all to his glory, and many came to be turned to God in a little time; for the heavenly day of the Lord sprung from on high, and broke forth apace, by the light of which many come to see where they were.

But O! The rage that then was in the priests, magistrates, professors, and people of all sorts; but especially in priests and professors! For, though Thou, to a single person, was according to their own learning, their accidence, and grammar rules, and according to the Bible, yet they could not bear to hear it: and as to the hat-honour, because I could not put off my hat to them, it set them all into a rage. But the Lord showed me that it was an honour below, which he would lay in the dust, and stain;—an honour which proud flesh looked for, but sought not the honour which came from God only;—an honour invented by men in the fall, and in the alienation from God, who were offended if it were not given them; and yet they would be looked upon as saints, church members, and great Christians: but Christ saith, "How can ye believe, who receive honour one of another, and seek not the honour that cometh from God only?" "And I (saith Christ) receive not honour of men": showing that men have an honour, which men will receive and give; but Christ will have none of it. This is the honour which Christ will not receive, and which must be laid in the dust. O! The rage and scorn, the heat and fury that arose! O! The blows, punchings, beatings, and imprisonments that we underwent, for not putting off our hats to men, for that soon tried all men's patience and sobriety what it was. Some had their hats violently plucked off and thrown away, so that they quite lost them. The bad language and evil usage we received on this account are hard to be expressed, besides the danger we were sometimes in, of losing our lives for this matter, and that by the great professors of Christianity, who thereby evinced that they were not true believers. And though it was but a small thing in the eye of man, yet a wonderful confusion it brought among all professors and priests: but, blessed be the Lord, many came to see the vanity of that custom of putting off the hat to men, and felt the weight of Truth's testimony against it.

About this time I was sorely exercised in going to their courts to cry for justice, and in speaking and writing to judges and justices to do justly; in warning such as kept public houses for entertainment, that they should not let people have more drink than would do them good; and in testifying against their wakes or feasts, may-games, sports, plays, and shows, which trained up people to vanity and looseness, and led them from the fear of God; and the days they had set forth for holy days were usually the times wherein they most dishonoured God by these things. In fairs, also, and in markets, I was made to declare against their deceitful merchandise, cheating, and cozening; warning all to deal justly, to speak the truth, to let their yea be yea, and their nay be nay; and to do unto others as they would have others do unto them; forewarning them of the great and terrible day of the Lord, which would come upon them all. I was moved also to cry against all sorts of music, and against the mountebanks playing tricks on their stages, for they burdened the pure life, and stirred up people's minds to vanity. I was much exercised, too, with school-masters and school-mistresses, warning them to teach their children sobriety in the fear of the Lord, that they might not be nursed and trained up in lightness, vanity, and wantonness. Likewise I was made to warn masters and mistresses, fathers and mothers in private families, to take care that their children and servants might be trained up in the fear of the Lord; and that they themselves should be therein examples and patterns of sobriety and virtue to them. For I saw that as the Jews were to teach their children the law of God and the old covenant, and to train them up in it, and their servants, yea, the very strangers were to keep the Sabbath amongst them, and be circumcised, before they eat of their sacrifices; so all Christians, and all that made a profession of Christianity, ought to train up their children and servants in the new covenant of light, Christ Jesus, who is God's salvation to the ends of the earth, that all may know their salvation: and they ought to train them up in the law of life, the law of the Spirit, the law of love and of faith; that they might be made free from the law of sin and death. And all Christians ought to be circumcised by the Spirit, which puts off the body of the sins of the flesh, that they may come to eat of the heavenly sacrifice, Christ Jesus, that true spiritual food, which none can rightly feed upon but they that are circumcised by the Spirit. Likewise, I was exercised about the stargazers, who drew people's minds from Christ, the bright and the morning star; and from the Sun of righteousness, by whom the sun, and moon, and stars, and all things else were made, who is the wisdom of God, and from whom the right knowledge of all things is received.

But the earthly spirit of the priests wounded my life; and when I heard the bell toll to call people together to the steeplehouse, it struck at my life; for it was just like a marketbell, to gather people together, that the priest might set forth his ware for sale. O! The vast sums of money that are gotten by the trade they make of selling the Scriptures, and by their preaching, from the highest bishop to the lowest priest! What one trade else in the world is comparable to it? Notwithstanding the Scriptures were given forth freely, and Christ commanded his ministers to preach freely, and the prophets and apostles denounced judgment against all covetous hirelings and diviners for money. But in this free Spirit of the Lord Jesus was I sent forth to declare the Word of life and reconciliation freely, that all might come to Christ, who gives freely, and who renews up into the image of God, which man and woman were in before they fell, that they might sit down in heavenly places in Christ Jesus.

CHAPTER III

1649–50

Now as I went towards Nottingham on a First-day in the morning, with Friends to a meeting there, when I came on the top of a hill in sight of the town, I espied the great steeplehouse; and the Lord said unto me, "Thou must go cry against yonder great idol, and against the worshippers therein." I said nothing of this to the Friends that were with me, but went on with them to the meeting, where the mighty power of the Lord was amongst us; in which I left Friends sitting in the meeting, and I went away to the steeple-house. When I came there, all the people looked like fallow-ground, and the priest (like a great lump of earth) stood in his pulpit above. He took for his text these words of Peter, "We have also a more sure Word of prophecy, whereunto ye do well that ye take heed as unto a light that shineth in a dark place, until the day dawn, and the day-star arise in your hearts." And he told the people that this was the Scriptures, by which they were to try all doctrines, religions, and opinions. Now the Lord's power was so mighty upon me, and so strong in me, that I could not hold, but was made to cry out and say, "O no, it is not the Scriptures"; and I told them what it was, namely, the Holy Spirit, by which the holy men of God gave forth the Scriptures, whereby opinions, religions, and judgments were to be tried; for it led into all truth, and so gave the knowledge of all truth. The Jews had the Scriptures, and yet resisted the Holy Ghost, and rejected Christ, the bright morning-star. They persecuted Christ and his apostles, and took upon them to try their doctrines by the Scriptures, but erred in judgment, and did not try them aright, because they tried without the Holy Ghost. As I spoke thus amongst them, the officers came and took me away, and put me into a nasty, stinking prison; the smell whereof got so into my nose and throat, that it very much annoyed me.

But that day the Lord's power sounded so in their ears, that they were amazed at the voice; and could not get it out of their ears for some time after, they were so reached by the Lord's power in the steeplehouse. At night they took me before the mayor, aldermen, and sheriffs of the town; and when I was brought before them, the mayor was in a peevish, fretful temper, but the Lord's power allayed him. They examined me at large; and I told them how the Lord had moved me to come. After some discourse between them and me, they sent me back to prison again; but some time after the head sheriff, whose name was John Reckless, sent for me to his house. When I came in, his wife met me in the hall, and said, "Salvation is come to our house." She took me by the hand, and was much wrought upon by the power of the Lord God; and her husband, and children, and servants were much changed, for the power of the Lord wrought upon them. I lodged at the sheriff's, and great meetings we had in his house. Some persons of considerable condition in the world came to them, and the Lord's power appeared eminently amongst them. This sheriff sent for the other sheriff, and for a woman they had had dealings with in the way of trade; and he told her before the other sheriff, that they had wronged her in their dealings with her (for the other sheriff and he were partners), and that they ought to make her restitution. This he spoke cheerfully; but the other sheriff denied it; and the woman said she knew nothing of it. But the friendly sheriff said it was so, and that the other knew it well enough; and having discovered the matter, and acknowledged the wrong done by them, he made restitution to the woman, and exhorted the other sheriff to do the like. The Lord's power was with this friendly sheriff, and wrought a mighty change in him, and great openings he had. The next marketday, as he was walking with me in the chamber, in his slippers, he said, "I must go into the market, and preach repentance to the people"; and accordingly he went into the market, and into several streets, and preached repentance to the people. Several others also in the town were moved to speak to the mayor and magistrates, and to the people, exhorting them to repent. Hereupon the magistrates grew very angry, and sent for me from the sheriff's house, and committed me to the common prison. When the assize came on, there was one moved to come and offer up himself for me, body for body; yea, life also: but when I should have been brought before the judge, the sheriff's man being somewhat long in fetching me to the sessions house, the judge was risen before I came. At which I understood the judge was somewhat offended, and said, "he would have admonished the youth, if he had been brought before him"; for I was then imprisoned by the name of a Youth. So I was returned to prison again, and put into the common jail. The Lord's power was great among Friends; but the people began to be very rude; wherefore the governor of the castle sent down soldiers, and dispersed them; and after that they were quiet. But both priests and people were astonished at the wonderful power that broke forth; and several of the priests were made tender, and some did confess to the power of the Lord.

Now, after I was released from Nottingham jail, where I had been kept prisoner some time, I travelled as before, in the work of the Lord. Coming to Mansfield-Woodhouse, there was a distracted woman under a doctor's hand, with her hair loose all about her ears. He was about to bleed her, she being first bound, and many people being about her, holding her by violence; but he could get no blood from her. I desired them to unbind her, and let her alone, for they could not touch the spirit in her, by which she was tormented. So they unbound her; and I was moved to speak to her, and in the name of the Lord to bid her be quiet and still; and she was so. The Lord's power settled her mind, and she mended; and afterwards she received the truth, and continued in it to her death. The Lord's name was honoured; to whom the glory of all his works belongs. Many great and wonderful things were wrought by the heavenly power in those days; for the Lord made bare his omnipotent arm, and manifested his power to the astonishment of many, by the healing virtue whereof many have been delivered from great infirmities, and the devils were made subject through his name; of which particular instances might be given, beyond what this unbelieving age is able to receive or bear. But blessed forever be the name of the Lord, and everlastingly honoured, and over all exalted and magnified be the arm of his glorious power, by which he hath wrought gloriously; let the honour and praise of all his works be ascribed to him alone.

Now while I was at Mansfield-Woodhouse, I was moved to go to the steeplehouse there, and declare the truth to the priest and people; but the people fell upon me in great rage, struck me down, and almost stifled and smothered me; and I was cruelly beaten and bruised by them with their hands, Bibles, and sticks. Then they haled me out, though I was hardly able to stand, and put me into the stocks, where I sat some hours; and they brought dog-whips and horse-whips, threatening to whip me. After some time they had me before the magistrate, at a knight's house, where were many great persons; who, seeing how evilly I had been used, after much threatening, set me at liberty. But the rude people stoned me out of the town, for preaching the word of life to them. I was scarcely able to move or stand, by reason of the ill usage I had received; yet with considerable effort I got about a mile from the town, and then I met with some people who gave me something to comfort me, because I was inwardly bruised; but the Lord's power soon healed me again. That day some people were convinced of the Lord's truth, and turned to his teaching, at which I rejoiced.

Then I went into Leicestershire, several Friends accompanying me. There were some Baptists in that country whom I desired to see and speak with, because they were separated from the public worship. So one Oates, who was one of their chief teachers, and others of the heads of them, with several others of their company, came to meet us at Barrow; and there we discoursed with them. One of them said, "What was not of faith was sin." Whereupon I asked them, What faith was? And how it was wrought in man? But they turned off from that, and spoke of their baptism in water. Then I asked them, Whether their mountain of sin was brought down and laid low in them? And their rough and crooked ways made smooth and straight in them? For they looked upon the Scriptures as meaning outward mountains and ways. But I told them they must find them in their own hearts; which they seemed to wonder at. We asked them who baptized John the Baptist? And who baptized Peter, John, and the rest of the apostles? And put them to prove by Scripture that these were baptized in water; but they were silent. Then I asked them, "Seeing Judas, who betrayed Christ, and was called the Son of Perdition, had hanged himself, what Son of Perdition was that which Paul spoke of, that sat in the temple of God, exalted above all that is called God? And what temple of God that was in which this Son of Perdition sat? And whether he, that betrays Christ within in himself, be not one in nature with that Judas, that betrayed Christ without?" But they could not tell what to make of this, nor what to say to it. So after some discourse we parted; and some of them were loving to us.

On the First-day following we came to Bagworth, and went to a steeplehouse, where some Friends were got in; and the people locked them in, and themselves too, with the priest. But after the priest had done, they opened the door, and we went in also, and had a service for the Lord amongst them. Afterwards we had a meeting in the town, amongst several people that were in high notions. Passing from thence, I heard of a people that were in prison in Coventry for religion. And as I walked towards the jail, the word of the Lord came to me saying, "My love was always to thee, and thou art in my love." And I was ravished with the sense of the love of God, and greatly strengthened in my inward man. But when I came into the jail, where the prisoners were, a great power of darkness struck at me, and I sat still, having my spirit gathered into the love of God. At last these prisoners began to rant, and vapour, and blaspheme, at which my soul was greatly grieved. They said they were God; but we could not bear such things. When they were calm, I stood up and asked them, whether they did such things by motion, or from Scripture; and they said, from Scripture. A Bible being at hand, I asked them to point out that Scripture; and they showed me the place where the sheet was let down to Peter, and it was said to him, what was sanctified he should not call common or unclean. When I had showed them that that Scripture proved nothing for their purpose, they brought another, which spoke of God's reconciling all things to himself, things in heaven, and things on earth. I told them I owned that Scripture also, but showed them that that was nothing to their purpose either. Then seeing they said they were God, I asked them, if they knew whether it would rain tomorrow? They said they could not tell. I told them, God could tell. Again, I asked them if they thought they should be always in that condition, or should change? And they answered they could not tell. Then said I unto them, God can tell, and God doth not change. You say you are God; and yet you cannot tell whether you shall change or not. So they were confounded, and quite brought down for the time. After I had reproved them for their blasphemous expressions, I went away; for I perceived they were Ranters. I had met with none before; and I admired the goodness of the Lord in appearing so unto me before I went amongst them. Not long after this, one of these Ranters, whose name was Joseph Salmon, put forth a paper, or book of recantation; upon which they were set at liberty.

While I was in prison, divers professors came to discourse with me; and I had a sense, before they spoke, that they came to plead for sin and perfection. I asked them, Whether they were believers, and had faith? And they said, Yes. I asked them, In whom? And they said, In Christ. I replied, If ye are true believers in Christ, you are passed from death to life; and if passed from death, then from sin that bringeth death. And if your faith be true it will give you victory over sin and the devil, purify your hearts and consciences (for the true faith is held in a pure conscience), and bring you to please God, and give you access to him again. But they could not endure to hear of purity, and of victory over sin and the devil; for they said they could not believe that any could be free from sin on this side the grave. I bid them give over babbling about the Scriptures, which were holy men's words, whilst they pleaded for unholiness. At another time a company of professors came, and they also began to plead for sin. I asked them, Whether they had hope? And they said, Yes: God forbid but we should have hope. I asked them, What hope is it that you have? Is Christ in you the hope of your glory? Doth it purify you, as he is pure? But they could not abide to hear of being made pure here. Then I bid them forbear talking of the Scriptures, which were holy men's words. For the holy men, that wrote the Scriptures, pleaded for holiness in heart, life, and conversation here; but since you plead for impurity and sin, which is of the devil, what have you to do with the holy men's words?

Now the keeper of the prison, being a high professor, was greatly enraged against me, and spoke very wickedly of me: but it pleased the Lord one day to strike him so, that he was in great trouble and under great terror of mind. As I was walking in my chamber I heard a doleful noise; and standing still, I heard him say to his wife, "Wife, I have seen the day of judgment, and I saw George there, and I was afraid of him, because I had done him so much wrong, and spoken so much against him to the ministers and professors, and to the justices, and in taverns and ale-houses." After this, toward the evening, he came up into my chamber, and said to me, "I have been as a lion against you; but now I come like a lamb, and like the jailer that came to Paul and Silas trembling." And he desired that he might lodge with me; I told him that I was in his power, he might do what he would: but he said nay, he would have my leave, and he could desire to be always with me, but not to have me as a prisoner; and he said "he had been plagued, and his house had been plagued for my sake." So I suffered him to lodge with me; and then he told me all his heart, and said he believed what I had said of the true faith and hope to be true; and he wondered that the other man that was put into prison with me did not stand to it; and said, "That man was not right, but I was an honest man." He confessed also to me, that at times when I had asked him to let me go forth to speak the word of the Lord to the people, and he had refused to let me, and I had laid the weight thereof upon him, that he used to be under great trouble, amazed, and almost distracted for some time after; and in such a condition that he had little strength left him. When the morning came, he rose, and went to the justices, and told them, "that he and his house had been plagued for my sake": and one of the justices replied (as he reported to me), that the plagues were on them too for keeping me. This was Justice Bennet of Derby, who was the first that called us Quakers, because I bid them tremble at the word of the Lord. This was in the year 1650.

As my restraint prevented my travelling about, to declare and spread truth through the country, it came upon me to write a paper, and send it forth to be spread abroad both amongst Friends and other tender people, for the opening of their understandings in the way of truth, and directing them to the true teacher in themselves. It was as follows:

"The Lord doth show unto man his thoughts, and discovereth all the secret workings in man. A man may be brought to see his evil thoughts, running mind, and vain imaginations, and may strive to keep them down, and to keep his mind in; but he cannot overcome them, nor keep his mind within, to the Lord. In this state and condition submit to the Spirit of the Lord, which will discover them, and will bring to wait upon Him, and destroy them. Therefore stand in the faith of the Lord Jesus Christ, who is the author of the true faith, and mind Him; for He will discover the root of lusts, evil thoughts, and vain imaginations, and how they are begotten, conceived, and bred; then how they are brought forth, and how every evil member doth work. He will discover every principle from its own nature and root.

"So mind the faith of Christ, and the anointing which is in you, to be taught by it, which will discover all workings in you; and as he teacheth you, so obey and forsake; else you will not grow up in the faith, nor in the life of Christ, where the love of God is received. Now love begetteth love, its own nature and image: and when mercy and truth meet, what joy there is! Mercy triumphs in judgment; and love and mercy bear the judgment of the world in patience. That which cannot bear the world's judgment is not the love of God; for love beareth all things, and is above the world's judgment and practice to cast all the world's filthiness that is among themselves upon the saints, yet their judgment is false. Now the chaste virgins follow Christ, the Lamb that takes away the sins of the world; but they that are of that spirit which is not chaste, will not follow Christ the Lamb in his steps, but are disobedient to him in his commands. So the fleshly mind doth mind the flesh, and talketh of the flesh; its knowledge is fleshly and not spiritual; and savours of death and not of the Spirit of life. Some men have the nature of swine wallowing in the mire. Some the nature of dogs to bite both the sheep and one another. Some of lions, to tear, devour, and destroy. Some of wolves, to tear and devour the lambs and sheep of Christ; and some men have the nature of the serpent (that old adversary), to sting, envenom, and poison. 'He that hath an ear to hear, let him hear,' and learn these things within himself. Some men have the natures of other beasts and creatures, minding nothing but earthly and visible things, and feeding without the fear of God. Some have the nature of a horse, to prance and vapour in their strength, and to be swift in doing evil; and some have the nature of tall, sturdy oaks, to flourish and spread in wisdom and strength; who are strong in evil, which must perish and come to the fire. Thus the evil is but one in all, but worketh many ways; and whatsoever a man's or woman's nature is addicted to, that is outward, the evil one will fit him with that, and will please his nature and appetite to keep his mind in his inventions, and in the creatures from the Creator. O! Therefore, let not the mind go forth from God; for if it do, it will be stained, venomed, and corrupted. If the mind go forth from the Lord it is hard to bring it in again;

therefore take heed of the enemy, and keep in the faith of Christ. O! Therefore mind that which is eternal and invisible, and Him who is the Creator and Mover of all things; for the things that are made are not made of things that do appear; for the visible covereth the invisible sight in you. But as the Lord, who is invisible, opens you by his invisible Power and Spirit, and brings down the carnal mind in you, so the invisible and immortal things are brought to light in you. O! Therefore you, that know the light, walk in the light! For there are children of darkness, that will talk of the light and of the truth, and not walk in it. The children of the light love the light, and walk in the light; but the children of darkness walk in darkness, and hate the light; and in these the earthly lust, and the carnal mind choke the seed of faith; and this bringeth oppression on the seed and death over themselves. O! Therefore, mind the pure Spirit of the everlasting God, which will teach you to use the creatures in their right place, and which judgeth the evil. 'To thee, O God, be all glory and honour, who art Lord of all, visible and invisible! To thee be all praise, who bringest out of the deep, to thyself; O powerful God, who art worthy of all glory!' For the Lord, who created all, and gives life and strength to all, is over all, and merciful to all. 'So thou, who hast made all, and art over all, to thee be all glory! In thee is my strength, my refreshment, and life, my joy and my gladness, my rejoicing and glorying forevermore!' To live and walk in the Spirit of God is joy, and peace, and life; but the mind going forth into the creatures, or into any visible things from the Lord, this bringeth death. Now when the mind is got into the flesh, and into death, the accuser gets within, and the law of sin and death gets into the flesh. Then the life suffers under the law of sin and death; and then there is straitness and failings. For then the good is shut up, and the self-righteousness is exalted. Then man doth work in the outward law, though he cannot justify himself by the law, but is condemned by the light; for he cannot get out of that state, but by abiding in the light, resting in the mercy of God and believing in him, from whom all mercy flows. For there is peace in resting in the Lord Jesus. This is the narrow way that leads to him, the life; but few will abide in it; keep therefore in the innocency, and be obedient to the faith in him; and take heed of conforming to the world, and of reasoning with flesh and blood, for that bringeth disobedience; and then imaginations and questionings arise to draw from obedience to the truth of Christ. But the obedience of faith destroyeth imaginations, and questionings, and all the temptations in the flesh, and buffetings, and lookings forth, and fetching up things that are past. By not keeping in the life and light, and not crossing the corrupt will by the power of God, the evil nature grows up in man, and then burdens will come, and man will be stained with that nature. But Esau's mountain shall be laid waste, and become a wilderness, where the dragons lie: but Jacob, the second birth, shall be fruitful, and shall arise. For Esau is hated, and must not be lord: but Jacob, the second birth, which is perfect and plain, shall be lord; for he is beloved of God.

G.F."

CHAPTER IV

1650–51

While I was yet in the House of Correction, there came unto me a trooper, and said, as he was sitting in the steeplehouse, hearing the priest, exceeding great trouble came upon him; and the voice of the Lord came to him saying, "Dost thou not know that my servant is in prison? Go to him for direction." So I spoke to his condition, and his understanding was opened. I told him, that which showed him his sins, and troubled him for them, would show him his salvation; for he that shows a man his sin, is the same that takes it away. While I was speaking to him, the Lord's power opened him, so that he began to have a good understanding in the Lord's truth, and to be sensible of God's mercies; and began to speak boldly in his quarters amongst the soldiers, and to others, concerning truth (for the Scriptures were very much opened to him), insomuch that he said, "his colonel was as blind as Nebuchadnezzar, to cast the servant of the Lord into prison." Upon this his colonel had a spite against him; and at Worcester fight, the year after, when the two armies were lying near one another, two came out from the king's army, and challenged any two of the Parliament army to fight with them; his colonel made choice of him and another to answer the challenge. And when in the encounter his companion was slain, he drove both his enemies within musket-shot out of the town, without firing a pistol at them. This, when he returned, he told me with his own mouth. But when the fight was over, he saw the deceit and hypocrisy of the officers; and being sensible how wonderfully the Lord had preserved him, and seeing also to the end of fighting, he laid down his arms.

Now the time of my commitment to the house of correction being nearly ended, and there being many new soldiers raised, the commissioners would have made me captain over them; and the soldiers said they would have none but me. So the keeper of the house of correction was commanded to bring me before the commissioners and soldiers in the marketplace; and there they offered me that preferment, as they called it, asking me, if I would not take up arms for the Commonwealth against Charles Stuart? I told them, I knew from whence all wars arose, even from the lust, according to James's doctrine; and that I lived in the virtue of that life and power that took away the occasion of all wars. But they courted me to accept their offer, and thought I did but compliment them. But I told them, I was come into the covenant of peace, which was before wars and strifes were. They said, they offered it in love and kindness to me, because of my virtue; and such like flattering words they used. But I told them, if that was their love and kindness, I trampled it under my feet. Then their rage got up, and they said, "Take him away, jailer, and put him into the dungeon amongst the rogues and felons."

In this time of my imprisonment, I was exceedingly exercised about the proceedings of the judges and magistrates in their courts of judicature. I was moved to write to the judges concerning their putting men to death for cattle, and money, and small matters; and to show them how contrary it was to the law of God in old time; for I was under great suffering in my spirit because of it, and under the very sense of death; but standing in the will of God, a heavenly breathing arose in my soul to the Lord. Then did I see the heavens opened, and I rejoiced, and gave glory to God. So I wrote to the judges as follows:

"I am moved to write unto you to take heed of putting men to death for stealing cattle or money, etc.; for thieves in the old time were to make restitution; and if they had not wherewith, they were to be sold for their theft. Mind the laws of God in the Scriptures, and the Spirit that gave them forth; let them be your rule in executing judgment; and show mercy, that you may receive mercy from God, the judge of all. Take heed of gifts and rewards, and of pride; for God doth forbid them; they blind the eyes of the wise. I do not write to give liberty to sin; God hath forbidden it; but that you should judge according to his laws, and show mercy; for he delighteth in true judgment and in mercy. I beseech you to mind these things, and prize your time, now you have it: fear God, and serve him; for he is a consuming fire."

Besides this, I wrote another letter to the judges, to this effect:

"I am moved to write unto you that ye do true justice to every man; and see that none be oppressed, or wronged, or any oaths imposed; for the land mourneth because of oaths, and adulteries, and sorceries, and drunkenness, and profaneness. O consider, ye that are men set in authority; be moderate, and in lowliness consider these things. Show mercy to the fatherless, to the widows, and to the poor; and take heed of rewards or gifts, for they blind the eyes of the wise; the Lord doth loathe all such. Love mercy and true judgment, justice, and righteousness, for the Lord delighteth therein. Consider these things in time, and take heed how ye spend your time. Now ye have time, prize it; and show mercy, that ye may receive mercy from the Lord; for he is coming to try all things, and will plead with all flesh, as by fire."

While I was here in prison, there was a young woman in the jail for robbing her master of some money. When she was to be tried for her life, I wrote to the judge and to the jury about her, showing them how it was contrary to the law of God in old time to put people to death for stealing, and moving them to show mercy. Yet she was condemned to die, and a grave was made for her; and at the time appointed she was carried forth to execution. Then I wrote a few words, warning all people to beware of greediness or covetousness, for it leads from God; and exhorting all to fear the Lord, to avoid all earthly lusts, and to prize their time while they have it: this I gave to be read at the gallows. And though they had her upon the ladder, with a cloth bound over her face, ready to be turned off, yet they did not put her to death, but brought her back again to prison: and in the prison she afterwards came to be convinced of God's everlasting truth.

At length they were made to turn me out of jail, about the beginning of Winter in the year 1651, after I had been a prisoner in Derby almost a year; six months in the House of Correction, and the rest of the time in the common jail and dungeon.

As I was walking along with several Friends, I lifted up my head, and I saw three steeplehouse spires, and they struck at my life. I asked them what place that was? And they said, Lichfield. Immediately the word of the Lord came to me, that I must go thither. Being come to the house we were going to, I wished the Friends that were with me, to walk into the house, saying nothing to them whether I was to go. As soon as they were gone, I stepped away, and went by my eye over hedge and ditch, till I came within a mile of Lichfield; where, in a great field, there were shepherds keeping their sheep. Then I was commanded by the Lord to pull off my shoes. I stood still, for it was Winter; and the word of the Lord was like a fire in me. So I put off my shoes, and left them with the shepherds; and the poor shepherds trembled and were astonished. Then I walked on about a mile, and as soon as I was within the city, the word of the Lord came to me again, saying, "Cry, Woe unto the bloody city of Lichfield." So I went up and down the streets, crying with a loud voice, "Woe to the bloody city of Lichfield!" It being marketday, I went into the marketplace, and to and fro in the several parts of it, and made stands, crying as before, "Woe to the bloody city of Lichfield!" And no one laid hands on me; but as I went thus crying through the streets, there seemed to me to be a channel of blood running down the streets, and the marketplace appeared like a pool of blood. When I had declared what was upon me, and felt myself clear, I went out of the town in peace; and returning to the shepherds, gave them some money, and took my shoes of them again. But the fire of the Lord was so in my feet, and all over me, that I did not matter to put on my shoes anymore, and was at a stand whether I should or not, till I felt freedom from the Lord so to do; and then, after I had washed my feet, I put on my shoes again. After this a deep consideration came upon me, why, or for what reason, I should be sent to cry against that city, and call it The Bloody City. For though the parliament had the minister one while, and the king another, and much blood had been shed in the town, during the wars between them, yet that was no more than had befallen many other places. But afterwards I came to understand, that in the Emperor Dioclesian's time, a thousand Christians were martyred in Lichfield. So I was to go, without my shoes, through the channel of their blood, and into the pool of their blood in the marketplace, that I might raise up the memorial of the blood of those martyrs which had been shed above a thousand years before, and lay cold in their streets. So the sense of this blood was upon me, and I obeyed the word of the Lord. Ancient records testify how many of the Christian Britons suffered there. Much I could write of the sense I had of the blood of the martyrs that hath been shed in this nation for the name of Christ, both under the ten persecutions and since; but I leave it to the Lord, and to his book, out of which all shall be judged; for his book is a most certain record, and his Spirit a true recorder.

From them I went to Stath, where also I met with many professors, and some Ranters. I had large meetings amongst them, and a great convincement there was. Many received the truth; amongst whom, one was a man of an hundred years of age; another was a chief constable; and a third was a priest, whose name was Philip Scafe. Him the Lord, by his free Spirit, did afterwards make a free minister of his free gospel.

The priest of this town was a lofty one, who much oppressed the people for his tithes. If they went a-fishing many leagues off, he would make them pay the tithe money of what they made of their fish, though they caught them at a great distance, and carried them as far as Yarmouth to sell. I was moved to go to the steeplehouse there, to declare the truth, and expose the priest. When I had spoken to him, and laid his oppression of the people before him, he fled away. The chief of the parish were very light and vain; so after I had spoken the word of life to them, I turned away from them, because they did not receive it, and left them. But the word of the

Lord, which I had declared amongst them, remained with some of them; so that at night some of the heads of the parish came to me, and most of them were convinced and satisfied, and confessed to the truth. Thus the truth began to spread in that country, and great meetings we had; at which the priest began to rage, and the Ranters to be stirred; and they sent me word that they would have a dispute with me, both the oppressing priest, and the leaders of the Ranters. A day was fixed, and the Ranter came with his company; and another priest, a Scotchman, came; but not the oppressing priest of Stath. Philip Scafe, who had been a priest, and was convinced, was with me; and a great number of people met. When we were settled, the Ranter, whose name was T. Bushel, told me he had had a vision of me; that I was sitting in a great chair, and that he was to come and put off his hat, and bow down to the ground before me; and he did so: and many other flattering words he spoke. I told him it was his own figure, and said unto him, "Repent, thou beast." He said it was jealousy in me to say so. Then I asked him the ground of jealousy, and how it came to be bred in man? And the nature of a beast, what made it, and how it was bred in man? For I saw him directly in the nature of the beast; and therefore I wished to know of him how that nature came to be bred in him? I told him he should give me an account of the things done in the body, before we came to discourse of things done out of the body. So I stopped his mouth, and all his fellow Ranters were silenced; for he was the head of them. Then I called for the oppressing priest, but he came not; only the Scotch priest came, whose mouth was soon stopped with a very few words; he being out of the life of what he professed. Then I had a good opportunity with the people. I laid open the Ranters, ranking them with the old Ranters in Sodom. The priests I manifested to be of the same stamp with their fellow-hirelings, the false prophets of old, and the priests that then bore rule over the people by their means, seeking for their gain from their quarter, divining for money, and teaching for filthy lucre. I brought all the prophets, and Christ, and the apostles, over the heads of the priests, showing how the prophets, Christ, and the apostles, had long since discovered them by their marks and fruits. Then I directed the people to their inward teacher, Christ Jesus their Saviour; and I preached up Christ in the hearts of his people, when all these mountains were laid low. The people were all quiet, and the gainsayers' mouths were stopped; for though they broiled inwardly, yet the power bound them down, that they could not break out.

After the meeting, this Scotch priest desired me to walk with him on the top of the cliffs; whereupon I called a brother-in-law of his, who was in some measure convinced, and desired him to go with me, telling him I desired to have somebody by to hear what was said, lest the priest, when I was gone, should report anything of me which I did not say. We went together; and as we walked, the priest asked me many things concerning the light, and concerning the soul; to all which I answered him fully. When he had done questioning, we parted, and he went his way; and meeting with Philip Scafe, he broke his cane against the ground in madness, and said, if ever he met with me again, he would have my life, or I should have his; adding, that he would give his head, if I was not knocked down within a month. By this, Friends suspected that his intent was, in desiring me to walk with him alone, either to thrust me down from off the cliff, or to do me some mischief; and that when he saw himself frustrated in that, by my having one with me, it made him rage. I feared neither his prophecies nor his threats; for I feared God Almighty. But some Friends, through their affection for me, feared much that this priest would do me some mischief, or set on others to do it. Yet after some years this very Scotch priest, and his wife also, came to be convinced of the truth; and about twelve years after this, I was at their house.

After some time, I came to Pickering, where in the steeplehouse the justices held their sessions, Justice Robinson being chairman. I had a meeting in the schoolhouse at the same time; and abundance of priests and professors came to it, asking questions, which were answered to their satisfaction. It being sessions time, four chief constables and many other people were convinced that day; and word was carried to Justice Robinson that his priest was overthrown and convinced, whom he had a love to, more than to all the priests besides. After the meeting, we went to an inn. Justice Robinson's priest was very lowly and loving, and would have paid for my dinner, but I would by no means suffer it. Then he offered that I should have his steeplehouse to preach in, but I refused it, and told him and the people, that I came to bring them off from such things to Christ.

The next morning I went with the four chief constables, and others, to visit Justice Robinson, who met me at his chamber door. I told him, I could not honour him with man's honour. He said he did not look for it. So I went into his chamber, and opened to him the state of the false prophets, and of the true prophets; and set the true prophets, and Christ, and the apostles over the other; and directed his mind to Christ his teacher. I opened to him the parables, and how election and reprobation stood; as that reprobation stood in the first birth, and election stood in the second birth. I showed also what the promise of God was to, and what the judgment of God was against. He confessed to it all; and was so opened with the truth, that when another justice that was present, made some little opposition, he informed him. At our parting, he said it was very well that I exercised that gift, which God had given me. He took the chief constables aside, and would have given them some money for me, saying, he would not have me at any charge in their country; but they told him that they could not persuade me to take any; and so accepting his kindness, I refused his money.

The next day, Friends and friendly people having left me, I travelled alone, declaring the day of the Lord amongst people in the towns where I came, and warning them to repent. One day, I came toward night into a town called Patrington; and as I walked along the town, I warned both priest and people (for the priest was in the street) to repent, and turn to the Lord. It grew dark before I came to the end of the town; and a multitude of people gathered about me, to whom I declared the word of life. When I had cleared myself, I went to an inn, and desired them to let me have a lodging; but they would not. Then I desired them to let me have a little meat, or milk, and I would pay them for it; but they would not. So I walked out of the town, and a company of fellows followed me, and asked me, what news? I bid them repent, and fear the Lord. After I had gone some distance, I came to another house, and desired the people to let me have a little meat and drink, and lodging for my money; but they denied me. Then I went to another house, and desired the same; but they refused me also. By this time it was grown so dark, that I could not see the highway; but I discerned a ditch, and got a little water and refreshed myself. Then I got over the ditch, and being weary with travelling, sat down among the furze-bushes till it was day. About break of day I got up and passed over the fields. A man came after me with a great pikestaff, and went along with me to a town; and he raised the town upon me, with the constable and chief constable, before the sun was up. I declared God's everlasting truth amongst them, warning them of the day of the Lord, that was coming upon all sin and wickedness; and exhorted them to repent. But they seized me, and had me back to Patrington, about three miles, guarding me with pikes, staves, and halberds. Now when I was come back to Patrington, all the town was in an uproar, and the priest and people were consulting together; so I had another opportunity to declare the word of life amongst them, and warn them to repent. At last a professor, a tender man, called me into his house, and there I took a little milk and bread, not having eaten for some days before. Then they guarded me about nine miles to a justice. When I was come near his house, a man came riding after us, and asked me whether I was the man that was apprehended? I asked him wherefore he asked? He said, for no hurt; and I told him I was; so he rode away to the justice before us. The men that guarded me said, It was well if the justice was not drunk, before we got to him; for he used to be drunk early. When I was brought in before him, because I did not put off my hat, and said Thou to him, he asked the man that rode thither before me, whether I was not mazed or fond; but the man told him, no, it was my principle. Then I warned him to repent, and come to the light, which Christ had enlightened him with, that by it he might see all his evil words and actions; and to return to Christ Jesus whilst he had time; and that whilst he had time, he should prize it. "Ay, ay," said he, "the light, that is spoken of in the third of John." I desired him that he would mind it, and obey it. As I admonished him, I laid my hand upon him, and he was brought down by the power of the Lord; and all the watchmen stood amazed. Then he took me into a little parlour with the other man, and desired to see what I had in my pockets, of letters or intelligence. I plucked out my linen, and showed him that I had no letters. He said, He is not a vagrant by his linen; and then he set me at liberty. I went back to Patrington, with the man that had ridden before me to the justice; for he lived at Patrington. When I came there, he would have had me have a meeting at the Cross; but I said, it was no matter, his house would serve. He desired me to go to bed, or lie down upon a bed; which he did, that they might say, they had seen me in a bed, or upon a bed; for a report had been raised that I would not lie on any bed, because at that time I lay many times out of doors. Now when the First-day of the week was come, I went to the steeplehouse, and declared the truth to the priest and people; and the people did not molest me, for the power of God was come over them. Presently after I had a great meeting at the man's house where I lay, and many were convinced of the Lord's everlasting truth, who stand faithful witnesses of it to this day. They were exceedingly grieved that they did not receive me, nor give me lodging, when I was there before.

From hence I travelled through the country, even to the furthest part thereof, warning people, in towns and villages, to repent, and directing them to Christ Jesus, their teacher.

CHAPTER V

1652

The next First-day I went to Tickhill, whither the Friends of that side gathered together, and in the meeting a mighty brokenness by the power of God was amongst the people. I went out of the meeting, being moved of God to go to the steeplehouse; and when I came there, I found the priest and most of the chief of the parish together in the chancel. So I went up to them, and began to speak; but they immediately fell upon me; and the clerk took up his Bible, as I was speaking, and struck me on the face with it, so that it gushed out with blood, and I bled exceedingly in the steeplehouse. Then the people cried, "Let us have him out of the church"; and when they had got me out, they beat me exceedingly, and threw me down, and over a hedge; and afterwards they dragged me through a house into the street, stoning and beating me as they drew me along, so that I was besmeared all over with blood and dirt. They got my hat from me, which I never obtained again. Yet when I was got upon my legs again, I declared to them the word of life, and showed them the fruits of their teacher, and how they dishonoured Christianity. After a while I got into the meeting again amongst Friends; and the priest and people coming by the house, I went forth with Friends into the yard, and there I spoke to the priest and people. The priest scoffed at us, and called us Quakers. But the Lord's power was so over them, that the priest began trembling himself; and one of the people said, "Look how the priest trembles and shakes, he is turned a Quaker also." When the meeting was over, Friends departed; and I went without my hat to Balby, about seven or eight miles. Friends were much abused that day by the priest and his people; insomuch that some moderate justices hearing of it, two or three of them came, and sat at the town, to hear and examine the business. And he that had shed my blood was afraid of having his hand cut off, for striking me in the church (as they called it); but I forgave him, and would not appear against him.

In the same week there was a great fair, at which servants used to be hired; and I declared the day of the Lord through the fair. After I had done so, I went into the steeplehouse yard, and many of the people of the fair came thither to me, and abundance of priests and professors. There "I declared the everlasting truth of the Lord, and the word of life for several hours, showing that the Lord was come to teach his people himself, and to bring them off from all the world's ways and teachers, to Christ the true teacher, and the true way to God. I laid open their teachers, showing that they were like them that were of old condemned by the prophets, and by Christ, and by the apostles. I exhorted the people to come off from the temples made with hands; and wait to receive the Spirit of the Lord, that they might know themselves to be the temples of God." Not one of the priests had power to open his mouth against what I declared: but at last a captain said, "Why will you not go into the church? This is not a fit place to preach in." I told him, I denied their church. Then stood up one Francis Howgill, who was a preacher to a congregation: he had not seen me before, yet he undertook to answer that captain, and soon put him to silence. Then said Francis Howgill of me, "This man speaks with authority, and not as the scribes." After this I opened to the people, that that ground and house was no holier than another place; and that that house was not the church, but the people, whom Christ is the head of. After a while the priests came up to me, and I warned them to repent. One of them said I was mad, and so they turned away. But many people were convinced there that day, and were glad to hear the truth declared, and received it with joy. Amongst these was one Captain Ward, who received the truth in the love of it, and lived and died in it.

The next First-day I came to Firbank Chapel, in Westmorland, where Francis Howgill, before named, and John Audland, had been preaching in the morning. The chapel was full of people, so that many could not get in. Francis Howgill said, he thought I looked into the chapel, and his spirit was ready to fail, the Lord's power did so surprise him; but I did not look in. They made haste, and had quickly done, and they and some of the people went to dinner, but abundance stayed till they came again. Now John Blakelin and others came to me, and desired me not to reprove them publicly; for they were not parish teachers, but pretty tender men. I could not tell them whether I should or not (though I had not at that time any drawings to declare publicly against them), but I said they must leave me to the Lord's movings. While the others were gone to dinner, I went to a brook and got a little water; and then came and sat down on the top of a rock hard by the chapel. In the afternoon the people gathered about me, with several of their preachers. It was judged there were above a thousand people; "amongst whom I declared God's everlasting truth and word of life freely and largely, for about the space of three hours, directing all to the Spirit of God in themselves, that they might be turned from darkness to the light, and believe in it, that they might become the children of it; and might be turned from the power of Satan, which they had been under, unto God; and by the Spirit of truth might be led into all truth, and sensibly understand the words of the prophets, and of Christ, and of the apostles; and might all come to know Christ to be their teacher to instruct them, their counsellor to direct them, their shepherd to feed them, their bishop to oversee them, and their prophet to open divine mysteries to them; and might know their bodies to be prepared, sanctified, and made fit temples for God and Christ to dwell in. In the openings of heavenly life, I explained unto them the prophets, and the figures, and shadows, and directed them to Christ, the substance. Then I opened the par-

ables and sayings of Christ, and things that had been long hid, showing the intent and scope of the apostles' writings, and that their
epistles were written to the elect. When I had opened that state, I
showed also the state of the apostasy since the apostles' days; that
the priests have got the Scriptures, but are not in that Spirit which
gave them forth, and have put them into chapter and verse, to
make a trade of holy men's words; and that the teachers and priests
now are found in the steps of the false prophets, chief priests,
scribes, and Pharisees of old, and are such, as the true prophets,
Christ, and his apostles cried out against, and so are judged and
condemned by the Spirit of the true prophets, and of Christ, and of
his apostles; and that none, who are in that Spirit, and guided by it
now, can own them.

Now there were many old people, who went into the chapel and
looked out at the windows, thinking it a strange thing to see a man
preach on a hill, and not in their church, as they called it; whereupon "I was moved to open to the people, that the steeplehouse,
and the ground whereon it stood, were no more holy than that
mountain; and that those temples, which they called the dreadful
houses of God, were not set up by the command of God and of
Christ; nor their priests called, as Aaron's priesthood was; nor their
tithes appointed by God, as those amongst the Jews were; but that
Christ was come, who ended both the temple and its worship, and
the priests and their tithes; and that all should now hearken unto
him; for he said, 'Learn of me'; and God said of him, 'This is my beloved Son, in whom I am well pleased, hear ye him.' I declared
unto them that the Lord God had sent me to preach the everlasting
gospel and word of life amongst them, and to bring them off from
all these temples, tithes, priests, and rudiments of the world, which
had been instituted since the apostles' days, and had been set up by
such as had erred from the Spirit and power the apostles were in."
Very largely was I opened at this meeting, and the Lord's convincing power accompanied my ministry, and reached the hearts of the
people, whereby many were convinced; and all the teachers of that
congregation (who were many) were convinced of God's everlasting truth.

From thence I went to Underbarrow, to one Miles Bateman's;
and several people going along with me, great reasonings I had

with them, especially with Edward Burrough. At night the priest
and many professors came to the house, and much disputing I had
with them. Supper being provided for the priest and the rest of the
company, I had not freedom to eat with them, but told them, if
they would appoint a meeting for the next day at the steeplehouse,
and acquaint the people with it, I might meet them. They had a
great deal of reasoning about it; some being for it, and some
against it. In the morning I went out, after I had spoken again to
them concerning the meeting; and as I walked upon a bank by the
house, there came several poor people, travellers, asking relief, who
I saw were in necessity; and they gave them nothing, but said they
were cheats. It grieved me to see such hard-heartedness amongst
professors; so, when they were gone in to their breakfast, I ran after
the poor people about a quarter of a mile, and gave them some
money. Meanwhile some of them that were in the house, coming
out again, and seeing me a quarter of a mile off, said I could not
have gone so far in such an instant, if I had not had wings. Hereupon the meeting was like to have been put by; for they were filled
with such strange thoughts concerning me, that many of them were
against having a meeting with me. I told them I ran after those
poor people to give them some money, being grieved at their hard-
heartedness, who gave them nothing. Then came Miles and Stephen Hubbersty, who being more simple-hearted men, would have
the meeting held. So to the chapel I went, and the priest came. A
great meeting there was, and the way of life and salvation was
opened; and after a while the priest fled away. Many of Crook and
Underbarrow were convinced that day, received the word of life,
and stood fast in it under the teaching of Christ Jesus. After I had
declared the truth to them for some hours, and the meeting was
ended, the chief-constable, and some other professors fell to reasoning with me in the chapel-yard; whereupon I took a Bible, and
opened to them the Scriptures, and dealt tenderly with them, as
one would do with a child. They that were in the light of Christ,
and Spirit of God, knew when I spoke Scripture, though I did not
mention chapter and verse, after the priest's form unto them.

From hence I went to Ulverstone, and so to Swarthmore to Judge
Fell's; whither came up one Lampitt, a priest, who was a high no-
tionist. With him I had much reasoning; for he talked of high no-

tions and perfection, and thereby deceived the people. He would have owned me, but I could not own nor join with him, he was so full of filth. He said, he was above John; and made as though he knew all things. But I told him, "Death reigned from Adam to Moses, that he was under death, and knew not Moses, for Moses saw the paradise of God; but he knew neither Moses nor the prophets, nor John." For that crooked and rough nature stood in him, and the mountain of sin and corruption; and the way was not prepared in him for the Lord. He confessed he had been under a cross in things; but now he could sing psalms, and do anything: I told him, "now he could see a thief, and join hand in hand with him, but he could not preach Moses, nor the prophets, nor John, nor Christ, except he were in the same Spirit that they were in." Margaret Fell had been absent in the daytime; and at night her children told her, that priest Lampitt and I had disagreed; which somewhat troubled her, because she was in profession with him; but he hid his dirty actions from them. At night we had much reasoning, and I declared the truth to her and her family. The next day Lampitt came again, and I had much discourse with him before Margaret Fell, who then clearly discerned the priest. A convincement of the Lord's truth came upon her and her family. Soon after a day was to be observed for a humiliation, and Margaret Fell asked me to go with her to the steeplehouse at Ulverstone, for she was not wholly come off from them; I replied, "I must do as I am ordered by the Lord." So I left her, and walked into the fields; and the word of the Lord came to me, saying, "Go to the steeplehouse after them." When I came, Lampitt was singing with his people; but his spirit was so foul, and the matter they sung so unsuitable to their states, that after they had done singing, I was moved of the Lord to speak to him and the people. The word of the Lord to them was, "He is not a Jew that is one outwardly, but he is a Jew that is one inwardly, whose praise is not of man, but of God." Then, as the Lord opened further, I showed them, "that God was come to teach his people by his Spirit, and to bring them off from all their old ways, religions, churches, and worships; for all their religions, worships, and ways, were but talking with other men's words; but they were out of the life and Spirit which they were in who gave them forth." Then cried out one, called Justice Sawrey, "Take him away"; but Judge Fell's wife said to the officers, "Let him alone, why may not he speak as well as any other?" Lampitt also, the priest, in deceit said, "Let him speak." So at length, when I had declared some time, Justice Sawrey caused the constable to put me out; and then I spoke to the people in the graveyard.

Soon after, Judge Fell being come home, Margaret Fell his wife sent to me, desiring me to return thither; and, feeling freedom from the Lord so to do, I went back to Swarthmore. I found the priests and professors, and that envious Justice Sawrey, had much incensed Judge Fell and Captain Sands against the truth by their lies; but when I came to speak with him, I answered all his objections; and so thoroughly satisfied him by the Scriptures, that he was convinced in his judgment. He asked me if I was that George Fox, whom Justice Robinson spoke so much in commendation of amongst many of the parliament men. I told him, I had been with Justice Robinson, and with Justice Hotham in Yorkshire, who were very civil and loving to me, and that they were convinced in their judgment by the Spirit of God, that the principle which I bore testimony to, was the truth, and they saw over and beyond the priests of the nation; so that they, and many others, were now come to be wiser than their teachers. After we had discoursed some time together, Judge Fell himself was satisfied also, and came to see, by the openings of the Spirit of God in his heart, over all the priests and teachers of the world, and did not go to hear them for some years before he died; for he knew it was the truth that I declared, and that Christ was the teacher of his people, and their Saviour. He sometimes wished that I were a while with Judge Bradshaw to discourse with him. There came to Judge Fell's, Captain Sands beforementioned, endeavouring to incense the judge against me; for he was an evil-minded man, and full of envy against me; and yet he could speak high things, and use the Scripture words, and say, "Behold, I make all things new." But I told him, then he must have a new God, for his God was his belly. Besides him, came also that envious justice, John Sawrey. I told him "his heart was rotten, and he was full of hypocrisy to the brim." Several other people also came, whose states the Lord gave me a discerning of; and I spoke to their conditions. While I was in those parts, Richard Farnsworth and James Naylor came to see me and the family; and Judge Fell, being satisfied that it was the way of truth, notwithstanding all their opposition, suffered the meeting to be kept at his house; and a great meeting was settled there in the Lord's power, which continued near forty years, until the year 1690, that a new meeting-house was erected near it.

After this, on a lecture-day, I was moved to go to the steeple-house at Ulverstone, where were abundance of professors, priests, and people. I went up near to priest Lampitt, who was blustering on in his preaching; and after the Lord had opened my mouth to speak, John Sawrey the justice came to me and said, "if I would speak according to the Scriptures, and bring the Scriptures to prove what I had to say; for I had something to speak to Lampitt and to them." Then he said, I should not speak, contradicting himself who had said just before, "I should speak, if I would speak according to the Scriptures." The people were quiet, and heard me gladly, until this Justice Sawrey (who was the first stirrer up of cruel persecution in the North) incensed them against me, and set them on to hale, beat, and bruise me. Suddenly the people were in a rage, and fell upon me in the steeplehouse before his face; knocked me down, kicked me, and trampled upon me; and so great was the uproar, that some tumbled over their seats for fear. At last he came and took me from the people, led me out of the steeplehouse, and put me into the hands of the constables and other officers, bidding them whip me and put me out of the town. They led me about a quarter of a mile, some taking hold of my collar, and some by my arms and shoulders, and shook and dragged me along. Many friendly people being come to the market, and some of them to the steeplehouse to hear me, divers of these they knocked down also, and broke their heads, so that the blood ran down from several of them; and Judge Fell's son running after, to see what they would do with me, they threw him into a ditch of water, some of them crying, "Knock the teeth out of his head." Now when they had haled me to the common moss-side, a multitude of people following, the constables and other officers gave me some blows over my back with their willow-rods, and so thrust me among the rude multitude, who, having furnished themselves, some with staves, some with hedge-stakes, and others with holm or holly-bushes, fell upon me, and beat on my head, arms, and shoulders, till they had deprived me of sense; so that I fell down upon the wet common. When I recovered again, and saw myself lying in a watery common, and the people standing about me, I lay still a little while; and the power of the Lord sprang through me, and the Eternal Refreshings refreshed me, so that I stood up again in the strengthening power of the Eternal God; and stretching out my arms amongst them, I said with a loud voice, "Strike again; here are my arms, my head, and my cheeks." There was in the company a mason, a professor, but a rude fellow; he with his walking rule-staff gave me a blow with all his might, just over the back of my hand, as it was stretched out; with which blow my hand was bruised, and my arm so benumbed, that I could not draw it unto me again; so that some of the people cried out, "He hath spoiled his hand forever having the use of it anymore." But I looked at it in the love of God (for I was in the love of God to them all, that had persecuted me), and after a while the Lord's power sprang through me again, and through my hand and arm, so that in a moment I recovered strength in my hand and arm, in the sight of them all. Then they began to fall out among themselves, and some of them came to me, and said, if I would give them money, they would secure me from the rest. But I was moved of the Lord to declare to them the word of life, and showed them their false Christianity, and the fruits of their priest's ministry; telling them they were more like heathens and Jews, than true Christians. Then was I moved of the Lord to come up again through the midst of the people, and go into Ulverstone market. As I went, there met me a soldier, with his sword by his side; "Sir," said he to me, "I see you are a man, and I am ashamed and grieved that you should be thus abused"; and he offered to assist me in what he could. But I told him the Lord's power was over all; so I walked through the people in the market, and none of them had power to touch me then. But some of the market-people abusing some Friends in the market, I turned me about and saw this soldier among them with his naked rapier, whereupon I ran in amongst them, and catching hold of his hand that his rapier was in, I bid him put up his sword again, if he would go along with me; for I was willing to draw him out from the company, lest some mischief should be done. A few days after seven men fell upon this soldier, and beat him cruelly, because he had taken part with Friends and me; for it was the manner of the persecutors of that country, for twenty or forty people to run upon one man. And they fell so upon

Friends in many places, that they could hardly pass the highways, stoning, beating, and breaking their heads. When I came to Swarthmore, I found the friends there dressing the heads and hands of Friends and friendly people, which had been broken or hurt that day by the professors and hearers of Lampitt, the priest. My body and arms were yellow, black, and blue, with the blows and bruises I received amongst them that day. Now began the priests to prophesy again, that within half a year we should be all put down and gone.

CHAPTER VI

1652–53

I went from the meeting to Grayrigg, and had a meeting there at Alexander Dixon's house, to which the priest (who was a Baptist, and a chapel priest) came to oppose; but the Lord confounded him by his power. Some of the priest's people tumbled down some milkpails which stood upon the side of the house, which was much crowded; whereupon the priest, after he and his company were gone away, raised a slander, "that the Devil frightened him, and took away a side of the house while he was in the meeting." And though this was a known falsehood, yet it served the priests and professors to feed on for a while; and so shameless they were, that they printed and published it.

Another time this priest came to a meeting, and fell to jangling. First he said, "the Scriptures were the word of God." I told him they were the words of God, but were not Christ, who is the Word; and bid him prove by Scripture what he said. Then he said it was not the Scripture that was the word; and setting his foot upon the Bible, he said it was but copies bound up together. Many unsavoury words came from him, but after he was gone we had a blessed meeting, and the Lord's power and presence was preciously manifested and felt amongst us. Soon after he sent me a challenge to meet me at Kendal. I sent him word he need not go so far as Kendal, for I would meet him in his own parish. The hour being fixed, we met, and abundance of rude people gathered together, besides the baptized people who were his own members; and they had intended to do mischief, but God prevented them. When we were met, I declared the day of the Lord to them, and directed them to Christ Jesus. Then the priest out with his Bible, and said it was the word of God. I told him it was the words of God, but not God, the Word. His answer was, he would prove the Scriptures to be the word before all the people. I let him go on, having a man there that could take down in writing both what he said, and what I said. When he could not prove it (for I kept him to Scripture proof, chapter and verse for it), the people gnashed their teeth for anger, and said he would have me anon; but in going about to prove that one error, he ran into many. And when at length he saw he could not prove it, then he said he would prove it to be a God: so he toiled himself afresh, till he perspired again, but could not prove what he had affirmed. And he and his company were full of wrath; for I kept his assertions on the head of him and them all, and told them I owned what the Scriptures said of themselves, namely, that they were the words of God, but Christ was the Word. So the Lord's power came over all, and they being confounded went away. The Lord disappointed their mischievous intentions against me; and Friends were established in Christ, and many of the priest's followers saw the folly of their teacher.

About this time I was in a fast for about ten days, my spirit being greatly exercised on truth's account; for James Milner and Richard Myer went out into imaginations, and a company followed them. This James Milner and some of his company, had true openings at first; but getting into pride and exaltation of spirit, they ran out from truth. I was sent for to them, and was moved of the Lord to go, and show them their outgoings: and they were brought to see their folly, and condemned it, and came into the way of truth again. After some time I went to a meeting at Arn-Side, where Richard Myer was, who had been long lame of one of his arms. I was moved of the Lord to say unto him, amongst all the people, "Stand up on thy legs" (for he was sitting down): and he stood up, and stretched out his arm that had been lame a long time, and said, "Be it known unto you, all people, that this day I am healed." Yet his parents could hardly believe it; but after the meeting was done, they had him aside, took off his doublet, and then saw it was true. He came soon after to Swarthmore meeting, and then declared how that the Lord had healed him. Yet after this the Lord commanded him to go to York with a message from him, but he disobeyed the Lord; and the Lord struck him again, so that he died about three-quarters of a year after.

After this I went to a village, and many people accompanied me. As I was sitting in a house full of people, declaring the word of life unto them, I cast mine eye upon a woman, and discerned an unclean spirit in her. And I was moved of the Lord to speak sharply to her, and told her she was under the influence of an unclean spirit; whereupon she went out of the room. Now, I being a stranger there, and knowing nothing of the woman outwardly, the people wondered at it, and told me afterwards that I had discovered a great thing; for all the country looked upon her to be a wicked person. The Lord had given me a spirit of discerning, by which I many times saw the states and conditions of people, and could try their spirits. For not long before, as I was going to a meeting, I saw some women in a field, and I discerned an evil spirit in them; and I was moved to go out of my way into the field to them, and declare unto them their conditions. At another time there came one into Swarthmore-hall in the meeting time; and I was moved to speak sharply to her, and told her she was under the power of an evil spirit; and the people said afterwards she was generally accounted so. There came also at another time another woman, and stood at a distance from me, and I cast mine eye upon her, and said, "Thou hast been an harlot"; for I perfectly saw the condition and life of the woman. The woman answered and said, many could tell her of her outward sins, but none could tell her of her inward. Then I told her her heart was not right before the Lord, and that from the inward came the outward. This woman came afterwards to be convinced of God's truth, and become a Friend.

CHAPTER VII

1653-54

After my release from Carlisle prison, I was moved to go to priest Wilkinson's steeplehouse again at Brigham; and being got in before him, when he came in, I was declaring the truth to the people, though they were but few; for the most and the best of his hearers were turned to Christ's free teaching; and we had a meeting of Friends hard by, where Thomas Stubbs was declaring the word of life amongst them. As soon as the priest came in, he opposed me; and there we stayed most part of the day; for when I began, he opposed me; so if any law was broken, he broke it. When his people would be haling me out, I manifested his fruits to be such as Christ spoke of when he said, "they shall hale you out of their synagogues"; and then he would be ashamed, and they would let me alone. There he stood till it was almost night, jangling and opposing me, and would not go to his dinner; for he thought to weary me out. But at last, the Lord's power and truth came so over him that he packed away with his people. When he was gone, I went to the meeting of Friends, who were turned to the Lord, and by his power established on Christ, the rock and foundation of the true prophets and apostles, but not of the false.

About this time the priests and professors fell to prophesying against us afresh. They had said long before that we should be destroyed within a month; and after that, they prolonged the time to half a year; but that time being long expired, and we mightily increased in number, they now gave forth, that we would eat out one another. For often after meetings, many tender people having a great way to go tarried at Friends' houses by the way, and sometimes more than there were beds to lodge in; so that some have lain on the hay-mows; hereupon Cain's fear possessed the professors and world's people. For they were afraid that when we had eaten one another out, we would all come to be maintained by the parishes, and be chargeable to them. But after a while, when they saw that the Lord blessed and increased Friends, as he did Abraham, both in the field and in the basket, at their goings forth, and comings in, at their risings up and lyings down, and that all things prospered with them; then they saw the falseness of all their prophecies against us; and that it was in vain to curse, where God had blessed. At the first convincement, when Friends could not put off their hats to people, or say You to a single person, but Thou and Thee;—when they could not bow, or use flattering words in salutations, or adopt the fashions and customs of the world, many Friends that were tradesmen of several sorts lost their customers at first; for the people were shy of them, and would not trade with them; so that for a time some Friends could hardly get money enough to buy bread. But afterwards, when people came to have experience of Friends' honesty and faithfulness, and found that their yea was yea, and their nay was nay; that they kept to word in their dealings, and that they would not cozen and cheat them; but that if they sent a child to their shops for anything, they were as well used as if they had come themselves; the lives and conversation of Friends did preach, and reached to the witness of God in the people. Then things altered so, that all the inquiry was, "where is there a draper, or shopkeeper, or tailor, or shoemaker, or any other tradesman, that is a Quaker?" Insomuch that Friends had more trade than many of their neighbours, and if there was any trading, they had a great part of it. Then the envious professors altered their note, and began to cry out, "if we let these Quakers alone, they will take the trade of the nation out of our hands." This has been the Lord's doing to and for his people! Which my desire is, that all, who profess his holy truth, may be kept truly sensible of, and that all may be preserved, in and by his power and Spirit, faithful to God and man; first to God, in obeying him in all things; and then in doing unto all men that which is just and righteous, to all men and women, in all things, that they have to do or deal with them in; that the Lord God may be glorified in their practicing truth, holiness, godliness, and righteousness, amongst people in all their lives and conversation.

Friends being now grown very numerous in the northern parts of the nation, and many young-convinced ones coming daily in among us, I was moved of the Lord to write the following epistle, and send it forth amongst them, in order to stir up the pure mind, and raise a holy care and watchfulness in them over themselves, and one another, for the honour of truth:

To you all, Friends everywhere, scattered abroad:

"In the measure of the life of God, wait for wisdom from God, even from Him from whom it comes. And all ye, who are children of God, wait for living food from the living God, to be nourished up to eternal life, from the one fountain, from whence life comes, that ye may all be guided and walk in order; servants in your places, young men and women in your places, and rulers of families; that everyone, in your respective places, may adorn the truth, in the measure of it. With it let your minds be kept up to the Lord Jesus, from whom it comes, that ye may be a sweet savour to God, and in wisdom ye may all be ordered and ruled; that a crown and a glory ye may be one to another in the Lord. And that no strife, bitterness, or self-will, may appear amongst you; but with the Light, in which is unity, all these may be condemned. And that everyone in particular, may see to, and take care of, the ordering and ruling of his own family; that in righteousness and wisdom it may be governed, the fear and dread of the Lord being set in everyone's heart; that the secrets of the Lord everyone may come to receive; that stewards of his grace you may come to be, to dispense it to everyone as they have need; and so in savouring and right-discerning you may all be kept; that nothing, that is contrary to the pure life of God, may be brought forth in you, or among you; but all that is contrary to it, may be judged by it; so that in light, in life, and love, ye may all live, and all that is contrary to the light, and life, and love, may be brought to judgment, and by that light condemned. And that no fruitless trees be among you; but all cut down and condemned by the light, and cast into the fire; so that everyone may bear and bring forth fruit unto God, and grow fruitful in his knowledge, and in his wisdom; and that none may appear in words beyond what they are in the life, that be of those trees whose fruit withers; such go in Cain's way, from the light, and by it are condemned. Let none amongst you boast yourselves above your measure; for if you do, out of God's kingdom you are excluded; for in that boasting part gets up the pride, and the strife, which is contrary to the light, that leads to the kingdom of God, and gives an entrance thereinto, and an understanding to know the things that belong to the kingdom of God. There the light and life of man everyone receives, even Him who was, before the world was, by whom it was made, who is the righteousness of God, and his wisdom; to whom all glory, honour, thanks, and praise belong, who is

God blessed forever. Let no image or likeness be made; but wait in the light, which will bring condemnation on that part that would make the images; for that prisons the just. So to the lust yield not the eye, nor the flesh; for the pride of life stands in that which keeps out the love of the Father; and upon which his judgments and wrath remain, where the love of the world is sought after, and a crown that is mortal. In this ground the evil enters, which is cursed; which brings forth briars and thorns, where death reigns, and tribulation and anguish are upon every soul, and the Egyptian tongue is heard; all which is by the light condemned. There the earth is, which must be removed; by the light it is seen, and by the power it is removed, and out of its place it is shaken; to which the thunders utter their voices, before the mysteries of God be opened, and Jesus revealed. Therefore all ye, whose minds are turned to this light, wait upon the Lord Jesus for the crown that is immortal, and that fadeth not away.

G.F."

"This is to be sent amongst all Friends in the truth, the flock of God, to be read at their meetings."

About this time did the Lord move upon the spirits of many, whom he had raised up, and sent forth to labour in his vineyard, to travel southwards, and spread themselves, in the service of the gospel, to the eastern, southern, and western parts of the nation; as Francis Howgill and Edward Burrough to London; John Camm and John Audland to Bristol; Richard Hubberthorn and George Whitehead toward Norwich; Thomas Holmes into Wales, and other different ways; for above sixty ministers had the Lord raised up, and now sent abroad out of the North country.

Then I came again to Thomas Taylor's, within three miles of Halifax, where was a meeting of about two hundred people; amongst which were many rude people, and divers butchers, several of whom had bound themselves with an oath before they came out, that they would kill me (as I was told); one of those butchers had been accused of killing a man and a woman. They came in a very rude manner, and made a great disturbance in the meeting. The meeting being in a field, Thomas Taylor stood up, and said unto them, "If you will be civil, you may stay, but if not, I charge you to be gone from off my ground." But they were the worse, and said they would make it like a common; and they yelled, and made a noise, as if they had been at a bear-baiting. They thrust Friends up and down; and Friends being peaceable, the Lord's power came over them. Several times they thrust me off from the place I stood on, by the crowding of the people together against me; but still I was moved of the Lord to stand up again, as I was thrust down. At last I was moved of the Lord to say unto them, "if they would discourse of the things of God, let them come up to me one by one; and if they had anything to say or to object, I would answer them all, one after another"; but they were all silent, and had nothing to say. And then the Lord's power came so over them all, and answered the witness of God in them, that they were bound by the power of God; and a glorious, powerful meeting we had, and his power went over all, and the minds of the people were turned by the Spirit of God in them to God, and to Christ their teacher. The powerful word of life was largely declared that day; and in the life and power of God we broke up our meeting; and that rude company went their way to Halifax. The people asked them why they did not kill me, according to the oath they had sworn; and they maliciously answered that I had so bewitched them that they could not do it. Thus was the devil chained at that time. Friends told me that they used to come at other times, and be very rude; and sometimes break their stools and seats, and make frightful work amongst them; but the Lord's power had now bound them. Shortly after this, the butcher that had been accused of killing a man and woman before, and who was one of them that had then bound himself by an oath to kill me, killed another man, and was sent to York jail. Another of those rude butchers, who had also sworn to kill me, having accustomed himself to thrust his tongue out of his mouth, in derision of Friends, when they passed by him, had it so swollen out of his mouth, that he could never draw it in again, but died so. Several strange and sudden judgments came upon many of these conspirators against me, which would be too large here to declare. God's vengeance from heaven came upon the blood-thirsty who sought after blood; for all such spirits I laid before the Lord, and left them to him to deal with them, who is stronger than all; in whose power I was preserved, and carried on to do his work. The Lord hath raised a fine people in these parts, whom he hath drawn to Christ, and gathered in his name; who feel Christ amongst them, and sit under his teaching.

After Captain Drury had lodged me at the Mermaid, he left me there, and went to give the Protector an account of me. When he came to me again, he told me, the Protector required that I should promise not to take up a carnal sword or weapon against him or the government, as it then was, and that I should write it in what words I saw good, and set my hand to it. I said little in reply to Captain Drury. But the next morning I was moved of the Lord to write a paper to the Protector, Oliver Cromwell; "where I did in the presence of the Lord God declare, that I denied the wearing or drawing of a carnal sword, or any other outward weapon, against him or any man; and that I was sent of God to stand a witness against all violence, and against the works of darkness; and to turn people from darkness to light; and to bring them from the causes of war and fighting, to the peaceable gospel, and from evildoers, which the magistrates' swords should be a terror to." When I had written what the Lord had given me to write, I set my name to it, and gave it to Captain Drury to hand to Oliver Cromwell, which he did. After some time Captain Drury brought me before the Protector himself at Whitehall. It was in a morning, before he was dressed, and one Harvey, who had come a little among Friends, but was disobedient, waited upon him. When I came in, I was moved to say, "Peace be in this house; and I exhorted him to keep in the fear of God, that he might receive wisdom from him, that by it he might be directed, and order all things under his hand to God's glory." I spoke much to him of truth, and much discourse I had with him about religion; wherein he carried himself very moderately. But he said we quarrelled with priests, whom he called ministers. I told him, "I did not quarrel with them, but they quarrelled with me and my friends. But," said I, "if we own the prophets, Christ, and the apostles, we cannot hold up such teachers, prophets, and shepherds, as the prophets, Christ, and the apostles declared against; but we must declare against them by the same power and Spirit." Then I showed him, "that the prophets, Christ, and the apostles declared freely, and against them that did not declare freely; such as preached for filthy lucre, and divined for money, and preached for hire, and were covetous and greedy, that can never have enough; and that they that have the same Spirit, that Christ, and the prophets, and the apostles had, could not but declare against all such now, as they did then." As I spoke, he several times said, it was very good, and it was truth. I told him, "that all Christendom (so called) possessed the Scriptures, but wanted the power and Spirit that they had, who gave forth the Scriptures, and that was the reason they were not in fellowship with the Son, nor with the Father, nor with the Scriptures, nor one with another." Many more words I had with him, but people coming in, I drew a little back; and as I was turning, he caught me by the hand, and with tears in his eyes, said, "Come again to my house, for if thou and I were but an hour a day together, we should be nearer one to the other"; adding, that he wished me no more ill than he did to his own soul. I told him, "if he did, he wronged his own soul"; and I bid him "hearken to God's voice, that he might stand in his counsel and obey it; and if he did so, that would keep him from hardness of heart; but if he did not hear God's voice, his heart would be hardened." He said it was true. Then I went out; and when Captain Drury came out after me, he told me, "his lord Protector said, I was at liberty, and might go whither I would." Then I was brought into a great hall, where the Protector's gentlemen were to dine; and I asked them, what they brought me thither for? They said, it was by the Protector's order, that I might dine with them. I bid them let the Protector know, I would not eat of his bread, nor drink of his drink. When he heard this, he said, "Now I see there is a people risen and come up that I cannot win either with gifts, honours, offices, or places; but all other sects and people I can." It was told him again, "that we had forsaken our own, and were not likely to look for such things from him."

Being set at liberty I went to the inn again, where Captain Drury had at first lodged me. This Captain Drury, though he sometimes carried fairly, was an enemy to me and to truth, and opposed it; and when professors came to me (while I was under his custody) and he was by, he would scoff at trembling, and call us Quakers, as the Independents and Presbyterians had nicknamed us before. But afterwards he once came to me, and told me, that, as he was lying on his bed to rest himself in the daytime, a sudden trembling seized on him, that his joints knocked together, and his body shook so that he could not rise from his bed; he was so shaken, that he had not

strength enough left to rise. But he felt the power of the Lord was
upon him, and he fell off his bed, and cried to the Lord, and said
he never would speak against the Quakers more, or such as trembled at the word of God.

CHAPTER VIII

1654–55

About two in the morning we took horse for Norwich, where
Christopher Atkins had run out, and brought dishonour upon the
blessed truth and name of the Lord. But he had been denied by
Friends; and afterwards he gave forth a paper of condemnation of
his sin and evil. We came to Yarmouth, and there stayed a while;
where there was a Friend, Thomas Bond, in prison for the truth of
Christ. There we had some service; and some were turned to the
Lord in that town. From thence we rode to another town, about
twenty miles off, where were many tender people; and I was moved
of the Lord to speak to them, as I sat on my horse, in several places
as I passed along. We went to another town about five miles from
thence, and set up our horses at an inn, Richard Hubberthorn and I
having travelled five and forty miles that day. There were some
friendly people in the town; and we had a tender, broken meeting
amongst them, in the Lord's power, to his praise.

We bid the hostler have our horses ready by three in the morning; for we intended to ride to Lynn, about three and thirty miles,
next morning. But when we were in bed at our inn, about eleven at
night, the constable and officers came, with a great rabble of people, into the inn, and said they were come with a hue and cry from
a justice of peace, that lived near the town about five miles off,
where I had spoken to the people in the streets, as I rode along, to
search for two horsemen, that rode upon gray horses, and in gray
clothes; a house having been broken up on the Seventh-day before
at night. We told them "we were honest, innocent men, and abhorred such things"; yet they apprehended us, and set a guard with

halberts and pikes upon us that night; making some of those friendly people, with others, to watch us. Next morning we were up betimes, and the constable with his guard carried us before a justice of peace about five miles off. We took two or three of the sufficient men of the town with us, who had been with us at the great meeting at Captain Lawrence's, and could testify that we lay both the Seventh-day night, and the First-day night, at Captain Lawrence's; and it was the Seventh-day night that they said the house was broken up. The reader is to be informed, that during the time that I was a prisoner at the Mermaid at Charing-Cross, this Captain Lawrence brought several Independent justices to see me there, with whom I had much discourse; which they took offence at. For they pleaded for imperfection, and to sin as long as they lived; but did not like to hear of Christ teaching his people himself, and making people as clear, whilst here upon the earth, as Adam and Eve were before they fell. These justices had plotted together this mischief against me in the country, pretending a house was broken up; that they might send their hue and cry after me. They were vexed also, and troubled, to hear of the great meeting at John Lawrence's aforesaid; for a colonel was convinced there that day, who lived and died in the truth. But Providence so ordered that the constable carried us to a justice about five miles onward in our way towards Lynn, who was not an independent justice, as the rest were. When we were brought before him, he began to be angry, because we did not put off our hats to him. I told him, I had been before the Protector, and he was not offended at my hat; and why should he be offended at it, who was but one of his servants? Then he read the hue and cry; and I told him, "that that night, wherein the house was said to be broken up, we were at Captain Lawrence's house; and that we had several men present who could testify the truth thereof." Thereupon the justice, having examined us and them, said, "he believed we were not the men that had broken the house; but he was sorry," he said, "that he had no more against us." We told him, "he ought not to be sorry for not having evil against us, but rather to be glad; for to rejoice, when he got evil against people, as for housebreaking, or the like, was not a good mind in him." It was good while yet, before he could resolve, whether to let us go, or send us to prison; and the wicked constable stirred him against us, telling him, "we had good horses, and that if it pleased him, he would carry us to Norwich jail." But we took hold of the justice's confession, that "he believed we were not the men that had broken the house"; and after we had admonished him to fear the Lord in his day, the Lord's power came over him, so that he let us go; so their snare was broken. A great people were afterwards gathered to the Lord in that town, where I was moved to speak to them in the street; and from whence the hue and cry came.

This year came out the oath of abjuration, by which many Friends suffered; and several went to speak to the Protector about it; but he began to harden. And sufferings increasing upon Friends, by reason that envious magistrates made use of that oath as a snare to catch Friends in, who, they knew, could not swear at all; I was moved to write to the Protector, as follows:

"The magistrate is not to bear the sword in vain, who ought to be a terror to evildoers; but as the magistrate that doth bear the sword in vain, is not a terror to evildoers, so he is not a praise to them that do well. Now hath God raised up a people by his power, whom people, priests, and magistrates, who are out of the fear of God, scornfully call Quakers, who cry against drunkenness (for drunkards destroy God's creatures), and against oaths (for because of oaths the land mourns), and these drunkards and swearers, to whom the magistrate's sword should be a terror, are, we see, at liberty; but for crying against such, many are cast into prison; as also for testifying against their pride and filthiness, their deceitful merchandise in markets, their cozening and their cheating, their excess and naughtiness, their playing at bowls and shuffleboards, at cards and at dice, and their other vain and wanton pleasures. They who live in pleasures, are dead while they live; and they who live in wantonness, kill the just. This we know by the Spirit of God, which gave forth the Scriptures, which the Father has given to us, and hath placed his righteous law in our hearts; which law is a terror to evildoers, and answers that which is of God in every man's conscience. They who act contrary to the measure of God's Spirit in every man's conscience, cast the law of God behind their backs, and walk despitefully against the Spirit of grace. The magistrate's sword, we see, is borne in vain, whilst the evildoers are at liberty to do evil; and they that cry against such, are for so doing punished by the magistrate, who hath turned his sword backward against the Lord. Now the wicked one fenceth himself, and persecutes the innocent as vaga-

bonds and wanderers, for crying against sin, and against unrighteousness and ungodliness openly, in the markets and in the highways;
or as railers, because they tell them what judgment will come upon
them that follow such practices. Here they that depart from iniquity
are become a prey, and few lay it to heart. But God will thrash the
mountains, beat the hills, cleave the rocks, and cast into his press,
which is trodden without the city, and will bathe his sword in the
blood of the wicked and unrighteous. You that have drunk the cup of
abominations, a hard cup have you had to drink; you are the enemies
of God, and of you he will be avenged.

"Now ye, in whom something of God is remaining, consider; if the
sword was not borne in vain, but turned against the evildoers, then
the righteous would not suffer, and be cast into holes, dungeons,
corners, prisons, and houses of correction, as peace-breakers, for testifying against sin openly, as they are commanded of the Lord, and
against the covetousness of the priests, and their false worships; who
exact money of poor people, whom they do no work for. O! Where
will you appear in the day of the Lord? Or how will you stand in the
day of his righteous judgment? How many jails and houses of correction are now made places to put the lambs of Christ in, for following
him, and obeying his commands, which are too numerous to mention.
The royal law of Christ, 'to do as ye would be done by,' is trodden
down under foot; so that men can profess him in words, but crucify
him wheresoever he appears, and cast him into prison, as the talkers of
him always did in the generations and ages past. The labourers, which
God, the master of the harvest, hath sent into his vineyard, do the
chief of the priests, and the rulers now take counsel together against,
to cast them into prison: and here are the fruits of priests, and people,
and rulers, without the fear of God. The day is come and coming, that
every man's work doth appear, and shall appear; glory be to the Lord
God forever. So see, and consider the days you have spent, and do
spend; for this is your day of visitation. Many have suffered great
fines, because they could not swear, but obey Christ's doctrine, who
saith, 'Swear not at all': and are made a prey upon for abiding in the
command of Christ. Many are cast into prison because they cannot
take the oath of abjuration, tho' they denied all that is abjured in it;
and by that means many of the messengers and ministers of the Lord
Jesus Christ are cast into prison because they will not swear, nor go
out of Christ's command. Therefore, O man, consider; to the measure
of the life of God in thee I speak. Many also lie in jails, because they
cannot pay the priest's tithes; many have their goods spoiled, and tre-
ble damages taken of them; and many are whipped and beaten in the

house of correction, without breach of any law. These things are done in thy name, in order to protect them in these actions. If men fearing God bore the sword, if covetousness were hated, and men of courage for God were set up, then they would be a terror to evildoers, and a praise to them that do well; and not cause them to suffer. Here equity would be heard in our land, and righteousness would stand up and take place; which giveth not place to the unrighteous, but judgeth it. To the measure of God's Spirit in thee I speak, that thou mayest consider, and come to rule for God; that thou mayest answer that which is of God in every man's conscience; for this is that, which bringeth to honour all men in the Lord. Therefore consider for whom thou dost rule, that thou mayest come to receive power from God to rule for him; and all that is contrary to God may by his light be condemned. "From a lover of thy soul, who desires thy eternal good."

But sufferings and imprisonments continuing and increasing, and the Protector (under whose name they were inflicted), hardening himself against the complaints that were made to him, I was moved to issue the following amongst Friends, to bring the weight of their sufferings more heavy upon the heads of the persecutors:

"Who is moved by the power of the Lord to offer himself to the justice for his brother or sister, that lies in prison, and to go lie there in their stead, that his brother or sister may come out of prison, and so offer his life for his brother or sister? Where any lie in prison for tithes, witnessing the priesthood changed, that took tithes, and the unchangeable priesthood come; if any brother in the light, who witnesseth a change of the old priesthood that took tithes, and a disannulling of the commandment for tithes, be moved of the Lord to go to the priest or impropriator, to offer himself to lie in prison for his brother, and to lay down his life, that he may come forth, he may cheerfully do it, and heap up coals of fire upon the head of the adversary of God. Likewise where any suffer for the truth by them who are in the untruth, if any Friends be moved of the Lord to go to the magistrate, judge, general, or protector, and offer up themselves to lay down their lives for the brethren; as Christ hath laid down his life for you, so lay down your lives one for another. Here you may go over the heads of the persecutors, and reach the witness of God in all. And this shall rest a judgment upon them all forever, and be witnessed to by that which is of God in their consciences. Given forth from the Spirit of the Lord through

                                                                G.F."

Besides this, I wrote also a short epistle to Friends, as an encouragement to them in their several exercises; which was as follows:

"My Dear Friends:

"In the power of the everlasting God, which comprehends the power of darkness, and all temptation, and that which comes out of it, in this power of God dwell. It will bring and keep you to the Word in the beginning; it will keep you up to the life, to feed thereupon, in which you are over the power of darkness, and in which you will find and feel dominion and life. And that will let you see, before the tempter was, and over him; and into that the tempter cannot come; for the power and truth he is out of. Therefore in that life dwell, in which you will know dominion; and let your faith be in the power, and over the weakness and temptations, and look not at them: but in the light and power of God look at the Lord's strength, which will be made perfect in your weakest state. In all temptations look at the grace of God to bring you salvation, which is your teacher to teach you: for when you look or hearken to the temptations, you go from your teacher, the grace of God; and so are darkened in going from that teacher, the grace of God, which is sufficient in all temptations, to lead out of them, and to keep over them.

G.F."

CHAPTER IX

1655–56

From Badgley we passed to Swannington and Higham, and so into Northamptonshire and Bedfordshire, having great meetings; and many were turned to the Lord by his power and Spirit. When we came to Baldock in Hertfordshire, I asked, if there was nothing in that town, no profession; and it was answered me, there were some Baptists and a Baptist woman sick. John Rush of Bedfordshire went with me to visit her. When we came in, there were many tender people about her. They told me she was not a woman for this world, but if I had anything to comfort her concerning the world to

come, I might speak to her. I was moved of the Lord God to speak
to her; and the Lord raised her up again to the astonishment of the
town and country. This Baptist woman and her husband, whose
name was Baldock, came to be convinced, and many hundreds of
people have met at their house since. Great meetings and con-
vincements were in those parts afterwards; many received the word
of life, and sat down under the teaching of Christ, their Saviour.

When we had visited this sick woman, we returned to our inn,
where were two desperate fellows fighting so furiously, that none
durst come nigh to part them. But I was moved, in the Lord's
power, to go to them; and when I had loosed their hands, I held
one of them by one hand, and the other by the other, showed them
the evil of their doings, and reconciled them one to the other, and
they were so loving and thankful to me, that people admired at it.

We passed on to Thomas Patchings', of Binscombe in Godalming,
where we had a meeting, to which several Friends came from London, and John Bolton and his wife came on foot in frost and snow.
After this we went towards Horsham Park; and having visited
Friends, passed on to Arundel and Chichester, where we had meetings. At Chichester many professors came in, and made some jangling, but the Lord's power was over them. The woman of the
house where the meeting was, though convinced of truth, yet not
keeping her mind close to that which convinced her, fell in love
with a man of the world, who was there that time. When I knew it,
I took her aside, and was moved to speak to her, and to pray for
her; but a light thing got up in her mind, and she slighted it. Afterwards she married the man, and soon after went distracted; for he
was greatly in debt, and she greatly disappointed. Then was I sent
for to her, and the Lord was entreated, raised her up again, and
settled her mind by his power. Afterwards her husband died; and
she acknowledged the just judgments of God were come upon her,
for slighting the exhortation and counsel I had given her.

There was a captain of horse in the town, who sent to me, and
would fain have had me to stay longer; but I was not to stay. He
and his man rode out of town with me about seven miles, Edward
Pyot also being with me. This captain was the fattest, merriest man,
the most cheerful, and the most given to laughter, that ever I met

with; insomuch that I was several times moved to speak in the dreadful power of the Lord to him; and yet it was become so customary to him, that he would presently laugh at anything he saw. But I still admonished him to come to sobriety, sincerity, and the fear of the Lord. We stayed at an inn that night; and in the morning I was moved to speak to him again, when he parted from us. Next time I saw him, he told me, that when I spoke to him at parting, the power of the Lord so struck him, that before he got home he was serious enough, and had discontinued his laughing. He afterwards was convinced, and became a serious and good man, and died in the truth.

At night we were brought to a town called Smethick then, but since Falmouth. It being the evening of the First-day, there came to our inn the chief constable of the place, and many sober people, some of whom began to inquire concerning us. We told them we were prisoners for truth's sake; and much discourse we had with them concerning the things of God. They were very sober, and loving to us. Some were convinced, and stood faithful ever after.

After the constable and these people were gone, other people came in, who also were very civil, and went away very loving. When all were gone we went to our chamber to go to bed, and about eleven o'clock Edward Pyot said, "I will shut the door, it may be some may come to do us a mischief." Afterwards we understood that Captain Keat, who commanded the party, had purposed to do us some mischief that night; but the door being bolted, he missed his design. Next morning Captain Keat brought a kinsman of his, a rude, wicked man, and put him into the room, he himself standing without. This evil-minded man, walking huffing up and down the room, I bid him fear the Lord; whereupon he ran upon me, struck me with both his hands; and placing his leg behind me, would fain have thrown me down, but he could not, for I stood stiff and still, and let him strike. As I looked toward the door, I saw Captain Keat look on and see his kinsman thus beat and abuse me. Whereupon I said, "Keat, dost thou allow this?" and he said, he did; "Is this manly or civil," said I, "to have us under a guard and put a man to abuse and beat us? Is this manly, civil, or Christian?" I desired one of our friends to send for the constables, and they came. Then I desired the captain to let the constables see his warrant or order, by which he was to carry us; which he did; and his warrant was to conduct us safe to Captain Fox, governor of Pendennis Castle; and if the governor should not be at home, he was to convey us to Launceston jail. I told him, he had broken his order concerning us; for we, who were his prisoners, were to be safely conducted, but he had brought a man to beat and abuse us; so he having broken his order, I wished the constable to keep the warrant. Accordingly he did, and told the soldiers they might go, for he would take charge of the prisoners; and if it cost twenty shillings in charges to carry us up, they should not have the warrant again. I showed the soldiers the baseness of their carriage towards us; and they walked up and down the house, being pitifully blank and down. The constables went to the castle, and told the officers what they had done. The officers showed great dislike of Captain Keat's base carriage towards us; and told the constables that Major-General Desborough was coming to Bodmin, and that we should meet him; and it was likely he would free us. Meanwhile our old guard of soldiers came by way of entreaty to us, and promised that they would be civil to us, if we would go with them. Thus the morning was spent till it was about eleven o'clock; and then upon the soldiers' entreaty, and promise to be more civil, the constables gave them the order again, and we went with them. Great was the civility and courtesy of the constables and people of that town towards us, who kindly entertained us; and the Lord rewarded them with his truth; for many of them have since been convinced thereof, and are gathered into the name of Jesus, and sit under Christ, their teacher and Saviour.

Captain Keat, who commanded our guard, understanding that Captain Fox, who was the governor of Pendennis Castle, was gone to meet Major-General Desborough, did not take us thither; but went with us directly to Bodmin. We met Major-General Desborough on the way; the captain of his troop that rode before him, knew me, and said, "O, Mr. Fox, what do you here?" I replied, "I am a prisoner." "Alack," said he, "for what?" I told him, "I was taken up as I was travelling." "Then," said he, "I will speak to my lord, and he will set you at liberty." So he came from the head of his troop, rode up to the coach, and spoke to the major-general. We also told him how we were taken. He began to speak against the light of Christ, for which I reproved him; then he told the soldiers they might carry us to Launceston; for he could not stay to talk with us, lest his horses should take cold.

So to Bodmin we were conveyed that night; and when we were come to our inn, Captain Keat, who was in before us, put me into a room, and went his way. When I was come in, there stood a man with a naked rapier in his hand. Whereupon I turned out again, called for Captain Keat, and said unto him, "What now, Keat, what trick hast thou played now, to put me into a room where there is a man with his naked rapier? What is thy end in this?" "O," said he, "pray hold your tongue; for if you speak to this man we cannot all rule him, he is so devilish." "Then," said I, "Dost thou put me into a room where there is such a man with a naked rapier, that thou sayest, you cannot rule him? What an unworthy, base trick is this! And to put me singly into this room from the rest of my friends, that were my fellow-prisoners with me!" Thus his plot was discovered, and the mischief they intended was prevented. Afterwards we got another room, where we were together all night; and in the evening we declared the truth to the people; but they were hardened and dark people. The soldiers also, notwithstanding their fair promises, were very rude and wicked to us again, and sat up drinking and roaring all night.

Next day we were brought to Launceston, where Captain Keat delivered us to the jailer. Now was there no friend, nor friendly people near us; and the people of the town were dark and hardened. The jailer required us to pay seven shillings a week for our horsemeat, and seven for our diet a-piece. But after some time, several sober people came to see us, and some of the town were convinced; and many friendly people, out of several parts of the country, came to visit us, and were convinced. Then arose a great rage among the professors and priests against us; and they said, this people Thou and Thee all men without respect, and they will not put off their hats, nor bow the knee to any man: this made them fret. But, said they, we shall see, when the assize comes, whether they will dare to Thou and Thee the judge, and keep on their hats before him. They expected we should be hanged at the assize. But all this was little to us; for we saw how God would stain the world's honour and glory, and were commanded not to seek that honour, nor give it; but we knew the honour that comes from God only, and sought that.

It was nine weeks from the time of our commitment to the assizes, to which abundance of people came from far and near to hear the trial of the Quakers. Captain Bradden lay with his troop of horse there, whose soldiers and the sheriff's men guarded us up to the court through the multitude of people that filled the streets; and much ado they had to get us through them. Besides, the doors and windows were filled with people looking out upon us. When we were brought into the court, we stood sometime with our hats on, and all was quiet; and I was moved to say, "Peace be amongst you!" Judge Glynne, a Welchman, then chief justice of England, said to the jailer, "what be these you have brought here into the court?" "Prisoners, my Lord," said he. "Why do you not put off your hats?" said the judge to us: we said nothing. "Put off your hats," said the judge again. Still we said nothing. Then said the judge, "The court commands you to put off your hats." Then I spoke, and said, "Where did ever any magistrate, king, or judge, from Moses to Daniel, command any to put off their hats, when they came before them in their courts, either amongst the Jews, the people of God, or amongst the heathens? And if the law of England doth command any such thing, show me that law either written or printed." Then the judge grew very angry, and said, "I do not carry my law-books on my back." "But," said I, "tell me where it is printed in any statute-book, that I may read it." Then said the judge, "Take him away, prevaricator! I'll ferk him." So they took us away, and put us among the thieves. Presently after he calls to the jailer, "Bring them up again." "Come," said he, "where had they hats from Moses to Daniel; come, answer me: I have you fast now," said he. I replied, "Thou mayest read in the third of Daniel, that the three children were cast into the fiery furnace by Nebuchadnezzar's command, with their coats, their hose, and their hats on." This plain instance stopped him: so that not having anything else to say to the point, he cried again, "Take them away, jailer." Accordingly we were taken away, and thrust in among the thieves, where we were kept a great while; and then, without being called again, the sheriff's men and the troopers made way for us (but we were almost spent) to get through the crowd of people, and guarded us to the prison again, a multitude of people following us, with whom we had much discourse and reasoning at the jail. We had some good books to set forth our principles, and to inform people of the truth;

which the judge and justices hearing of, they sent Captain Bradden for them, who came into the jail to us, and violently took our books from us, some out of Edward Pyot's hands, and carried them away; so we never got them again.

Now we were kept in prison, and many came from far and near, to see us; of whom some were people of account in the world; for the report of our trial was spread abroad, and our boldness and innocency in our answers to the judge and court were talked of in town and country. Among others came Humphrey Lower to visit us, a grave, sober, old man, who had been a justice of peace; he was very sorry we should lie in prison; telling us how serviceable we might be if we were at liberty. We reasoned with him concerning swearing; and having acquainted him how they tendered the oath of abjuration to us, as a snare, because they knew we could not swear, we showed him that no people could be serviceable to God, if they disobeyed the command of Christ; and that they that imprisoned us for the hat-honour, which was of men, and which men sought for, prisoned the good, and vexed and grieved the Spirit of God in themselves, which should have turned their minds to God. So we directed him to the Spirit of God in his heart, and to the light of Christ Jesus; and he was thoroughly convinced, and continued so to his death, and became very serviceable to us.

There came also to see us one Colonel Rouse, a justice of peace, with a great company with him. He was as full of words and talk as ever I heard any man in my life, so that there was no speaking to him. At length I asked him "whether he had ever been at school, and knew what belonged to questions and answers"; (this I said to stop him). "At school!" said he, "Yes." "At school!" said the soldiers; "doth he say so to our colonel, that is a scholar?" Then said I, "If he be so, let him be still, and receive answers to what he hath said." Then I was moved to speak the word of life to him in God's dreadful power; which came so over him that he could not open his mouth: his face swelled and was red like a turkey; his lips moved, and he mumbled something; but the people thought he would have fallen down. I stepped to him, and he said he was never so in his life before: for the Lord's power stopped the evil power in him; so that he was almost choked. The man was ever after very loving to Friends, and not so full of airy words to us; though he was full of pride; but the Lord's power came over him, and the rest that were with him.

Another time there came an officer of the army, a very malicious, bitter professor, whom I had known in London. He was full of his airy talk also, and spoke slightingly of the light of Christ, and against the truth, and against the Spirit of God being in men, as it was in the apostles' days; till the power of God that bound the evil in him, had almost choked him as it did Colonel Rouse: for he was so full of evil that he could not speak, but blubbered and stuttered. But from the time that the Lord's power struck him, and came over him, he was ever after more loving to us.

The assize being over, and we settled in prison upon such a commitment, that we were not likely to be soon released, we discontinued giving the jailer seven shillings a week each for our horses, and seven for ourselves; and sent our horses out into the country. Upon which he grew very wicked and devilish; and put us down into Doomsdale, a nasty, stinking place, where they put murderers, after they were condemned. The place was so noisome, that it was observed few that went in ever came out again in health. There was no house of office in it; and the excrements of the prisoners that from time to time had been left there, had not been carried out (as we were told) for many years. So that it was all like mire, and in some places to the top of the shoes in water and urine; and he would not let us cleanse it, nor suffer us to have beds or straw to lie on. At night some friendly people of the town brought us a candle and a little straw, and we burnt some of it to take away the stink. The thieves lay over our heads, and the head jailer in a room by them, over us also. It seems the smoke went up into the jailer's room; which put him into such a rage, that he took the pots of excrements of the thieves, and poured them through a hole upon our heads in Doomsdale; whereby we were so bespattered, that we could not touch ourselves nor one another. And the stink under our feet before, but now we had it on our heads and backs also; and he having quenched our straw with the filth he poured down, had made a great smother in the place. Moreover he railed at us most hideously, calling us hatchet-faced dogs, and such strange names as we had never heard. In the manner were we fain to stand all night, for we could not sit down, the place was so full of filthy excrements. A great while he kept us in this manner, before he would let us cleanse it, or suffer us to have any victuals brought in but what we had through the grate. Once a girl brought us a little meat, and he arrested her for breaking his house, and sued her in the town-court for breaking the prison. Much trouble he put her to, whereby others were so discouraged, that we had much to do to get water or victuals. Near this time we sent for a young woman, Ann Downer, from London, that could write, and take things well in short-hand, to buy and dress our meat for us, which she was very willing to do, it being also upon her spirit to come to us in the love of God; and she was very serviceable to us.

After the assizes, the sheriff, with some soldiers, came to guard a woman to execution, that was sentenced to die; and we had much discourse with them. One of them wickedly said, that "Christ was as passionate a man as any that lived upon the earth"; for which we rebuked him. Another time we asked the jailer what doings there were at the sessions; and he said, "Small matters; only about thirty for bastardy." We thought it very strange, that they who professed themselves Christians should make small matters of such things. But this jailer was very bad himself; I often admonished him to sobriety; but he abused people that came to visit us. Edward Pyot had a cheese sent him from Bristol by his wife; and the jailer took it from him, and carried it to the mayor, to search it for treasonable letters, as he said; and though they found no treason in the cheese, they kept it from us. This jailer might have been rich if he had carried himself civilly; but he sought his own ruin; which soon after came upon him; for the next year he was turned out of his place, and for some wickedness cast into the jail himself; and there begged of our Friends. And for some unruliness in his conduct, he was, by the succeeding jailer, put into Doomsdale, locked in irons, and beaten; and bid to "remember how he had abused those good men, whom he had wickedly, without any cause, cast into that nasty dungeon"; and told, "that now he deservedly should suffer for his wickedness; and the same measure he had meted to others, should be meted out to himself." He became very poor, and died in prison; and his wife and family came to misery.

While I was in prison in Launceston, a friend went to Oliver

Cromwell, and offered himself, body for body, to lie in Doomsdale in my stead; if he would take him, and let me have liberty. Which thing so struck him, that he said to his great men and council, "Which of you would do so much for me if I were in the same condition?" And though he did not accept of the Friend's offer, but said, "he could not do it, for that it was contrary to law"; yet the truth thereby came mightily over him. A good while after this he sent down Major-General Desborough, pretending to set us at liberty. When he came, he offered us our liberty, if we could say, "we would go home, and preach no more"; but we could not promise him. . . .

After this Major Desborough came to the Castle-Green, and played at bowls with the justices and others. Several Friends were moved to go, and admonish them not to spend their time so vainly; desiring them to consider, that "though they professed themselves to be Christians, yet they gave themselves up to their pleasures, and kept the servants of God meanwhile in prison"; and telling them, "the Lord would plead with them, and visit them for such things." But notwithstanding what was written or said to him, he went away, and left us in prison. We understood afterwards, that he left the business to Colonel Bennet, who had the command of the jail. For sometime after Bennet would have set us at liberty, if we would have paid his jailer's fees. But we told him, "we could give the jailer no fees, for we were innocent sufferers; and how could they expect fees of us, who had suffered so long wrongfully?" After a while Colonel Bennet coming to town, sent for us to an inn, and insisted again upon fees, which we refused. At last the power of the Lord came so over him, that he freely set us at liberty on the 13th day of the seventh month, 1656. We had been prisoners nine weeks at the first assize, called the Lent-assize, which was in the spring of the year.

CHAPTER X

1656–57

From thence we came to Exeter, where many Friends were in prison; and amongst the rest James Naylor. For a little before we were set at liberty, James had run out into imaginations, and a company with him; which raised up a great darkness in the nation. He came to Bristol, and made a disturbance there: and from thence he was coming to Launceston to see me; but was stopped by the way, and imprisoned at Exeter; as were also several others; one of whom, an honest tender man, died in prison there, whose blood lieth on the heads of his persecutors.

The night we came to Exeter, I spoke with James Naylor; for I saw he was out and wrong; and so was his company. Next day, being First-day, we went to visit the prisoners, and had a meeting with them in the prison; but James Naylor and some of them could not stay the meeting. There came a corporal of horse into the meeting, and was convinced, and remained a very good Friend. The next day I spoke to James Naylor again; and he slighted what I said, and was dark, and much out; yet he would have come and kissed me. But I said, "since he had turned against the power of God, I could not receive his show of kindness"; the Lord moved me to slight him, and to "set the power of God over him." So after I had been warring with the world, there was now a wicked spirit risen up amongst Friends to war against. I admonished him and his company. When he was come to London, his resisting the power of God in me, and the truth that was declared to him by me, became one of his greatest burdens. But he came to see his outgoing, and to condemn it; and after some time he returned to truth again; as in the printed relation of his repentance, condemnation, and recovery, may be more fully seen.

On First-day morning I went to the meeting in Broadmead at Bristol; which was large and quiet. Notice was given of a meeting to be in the afternoon in the orchard. There was at Bristol a rude Baptist, named Paul Gwin, who had before made great disturbance in our meetings, being encouraged and set on by the mayor, who, it was reported, would sometimes give him his dinner to encourage him. Such multitudes of rude people he gathered after him, that it was thought there had been sometimes ten thousand people at our meeting in the orchard. As I was going into the orchard, the people told me, that Paul Gwin, the rude jangling Baptist, was going to the meeting. "I bid them never heed, it was nothing to me who went to it." When I was come into the orchard, I stood upon the stone that Friends used to stand on when they spoke; and I was moved of the Lord to put off my hat, and to stand a pretty while, and let the people look at me; for some thousands of people were there. While I thus stood silent, this rude Baptist began to find fault with my hair; but I said nothing to him. Then he ran on into words; and at last, "Ye wise men of Bristol," said he, "I strange at you, that you will stand here, and hear a man speak and affirm that which he cannot make good." Then the Lord opened my mouth (for as yet I had not spoken a word), and I asked the people, "whether they ever heard me speak; or ever saw me before": and I bid them "take notice what kind of man this was amongst them that should so impudently say, that I spoke and affirmed that which I could not make good; and yet neither he nor they had ever heard me or seen me before. Therefore that was a lying, envious, malicious spirit, that spoke in him; and it was of the Devil, and not of God. I charged him in the dread and power of the Lord to be silent: and the mighty power of God came over him, and all his company. Then a glorious, peaceable meeting we had, and the word of life was divided amongst them; and they were turned from darkness to the light,—to Jesus their Saviour. The Scriptures were largely opened to them; and the traditions, rudiments, ways, and doctrines of men were laid open before the people; and they were turned to the light of Christ, that with it they might see them, and see him to lead them out of them. I opened also to them the types, figures, and shadows of Christ in the time of the law; and showed them that Christ was come, and had ended the types, shadows, tithes, and oaths, and put down swearing; and had set up yea and nay instead of it, and a free ministry; for he was now come to teach people himself, and his heavenly day was springing from on high." For many hours did I declare the word of life amongst them in the eternal power of God, that by him they might come up into the beginning, and be reconciled to him. And having turned them to the Spirit of God in themselves, that would lead into all truth, I was moved to pray in the mighty power of God; and the Lord's power came over all. When I had done, this fellow began to babble again; and John Audland was moved to bid him repent, and fear God. So his own people and followers being ashamed of him, he passed away, and never came again to disturb the meeting. The meeting broke up quietly, and the Lord's power and glory shone over all: a blessed day it was, and the Lord had the praise. After a while this Paul Gwin went beyond the seas; many years after I met with him again at Barbadoes: of which in its place.

About this time many mouths were opened in our meetings, to declare the goodness of the Lord, and some that were young and tender in the truth would sometimes utter a few words in thanksgiving and praises to God. That no disorder might arise from this in our meetings, I was moved to write an epistle to Friends, by way of advice in that matter. And thus it was:

"All my dear friends in the noble Seed of God, who have known his power, life, and presence among you, let it be your joy to hear or see the springs of life break forth in any; through which ye have all unity in the same, feeling life and power. And above all things, take heed of judging anyone openly in your meetings, except they be openly profane or rebellious, such as be out of the truth; that by the power, life, and wisdom ye may stand over them, and by it answer the witness of God in the world, that such, whom ye bear your testimony against, are none of you: that therein the truth may stand clear and single. But such as are tender, if they should be moved to bubble forth a few words, and speak in the Seed and Lamb's power, suffer and bear that; that is the tender. And if they should go beyond their measure, bear it in the meeting for peace and order's sake, and that the spirits of the world be not moved against you. But when the meeting is done, if any be moved to speak to them, between you and them, one or two of you, that feel it in the life, do it in the love and wisdom that is pure and gentle from above: for love is that which edifies, bears all things, suffers long, and fulfils the law. In this ye have order and edification, ye have wisdom to preserve you all wise and in patience; which takes away the occasion of stumbling the weak, and the occasion of the spirits of the world to get up: but in the royal Seed, the heavy stone, ye keep down all that is wrong; and by it answer that of God in all. For ye will hear, see, and feel the power of God preaching, as your faith is all in it (when ye do not hear words), to bind, to chain, to limit, to frustrate; that nothing shall rise, nor come forth but what is in the power: with that ye will hold back, and with that ye will let up, and open every spring, plant, and spark; in which will be your joy and refreshment in the power of God.

"Now ye that know the power of God, and are come to it, which is the cross of Christ, that crucifies you to the state that Adam and Eve were in, in the fall, and so to the world; by this power of God ye come to see the state they were in before they fell; which power of God is the cross, in which stands the everlasting glory; which brings up into the righteousness, holiness, and image of God, and crucifies to the unrighteousness, unholiness, and image of Satan, that Adam and Eve, and their sons and daughters, are in, in the fall. Through this power of God, ye come to see the state they were in before they fell; yea, I say, and to a higher state, to the Seed Christ, the second Adam, by whom all things were made. For man hath been driven from God: all Adam and Eve's sons and daughters, being in the state of the fall, in the earth, are driven from God. But it is said, The church is in God, the Father of our Lord Jesus Christ: so they who come to the church, which is in God the Father of Christ, must come to God again; and so out of the state that Adam and Eve, and his children are in, in the fall, out of the image of God, of righteousness and holiness, and they must come into the righteousness, true holiness, and image of God; and so out of the earth, whither man hath been driven, when they come to the church which is in God. The way to this, is Christ, the Light, the Life, the Truth, the Saviour, the Redeemer, the Sanctifier, and the Justifier; in and through whose power, light, and life, conversion, regeneration, and translation, are known from death to life, from darkness to light, and from the power of Satan to God again. These are members of the true church, who know the work of regeneration in the operation and feeling of it; and being come to be members of the church in God, they are indeed members one of another in the power of God, which was before the power of darkness was. So they that come to the church, that is in God and Christ, must come out of the state that Adam was in, in the fall, driven from God, to know the state that he was in before he fell. But they that live in the state that Adam was in, in the fall, and cannot believe a possibility of coming into the state he was in before he fell, come not to the church, which is in God; but are far from that, and are not passed from death to life;

but are enemies to the cross of Christ, which is the power of God. For they mind earthly things, and serve not Christ, nor love the power, which should bring them up to the state that Adam was in before he fell, and crucify them to the state that man is in in the fall; that through this power they might see to the beginning, the power that man was in before the heavenly image, and holiness, and righteousness was lost; by which power they might come to know the Seed, Christ, which brings out of the old things, and makes all things new; in which life eternal is felt. For all the poorness, emptiness, and barrenness is in the state that man is in, in the fall, out of God's power; by which power he is made rich, and hath strength again; which power is the cross, in which the mystery of the fellowship stands: and in which is the true glorying, which crucifies to all other gloryings.

"And, Friends, though ye may have been convinced, and tasted of the power, and felt the light; yet afterwards ye may feel a winter storm, tempest and hail, frost and cold, and temptation in the wilderness. Be patient and still in the power, and in the light, that doth convince you, to keep your minds to God; in that be quiet, that ye may come to the summer; that your flight be not in the winter. For if ye sit still in the patience, which overcomes in the power of God, there will be no flying. The husbandman, after he hath sowed his seed, is patient. And by the power, being kept in the patience, ye will come by the light to see through, and feel over winter storms and tempests, and all the coldness, barrenness, and emptiness: and the same light and power will go over the tempter's head; which power and light was before he was. So standing still in the light, ye will see your salvation, ye will see the Lord's strength, feel the small rain, and the fresh springs, your minds being kept low in the power and light: for that which is out of the power lifts up. But in the power and light ye will feel God, revealing his secrets, inspiring your minds, and his gifts coming in unto you: through which your hearts will be filled with God's love, and praises to him that lives forevermore: for in his light and power his blessing is received. So in that, the eternal power of the Lord Jesus Christ preserve and keep you! Live everyone in the power of God, that ye may all come to be heirs of that, and know it to be your portion; even the kingdom, that hath no end, and the endless life, which the Seed is heir of. Feel that set over all, which hath the promise and blessing of God forever.

G.F."

At this time there was a great drought; and after this general meeting was ended, there fell so great a rain, that Friends said, they thought we could not travel, the waters would be so risen. But I believed the rain had not extended so far, as they had come that day to the meeting. Next day in the afternoon, when we turned back into some parts of Wales again, the roads were dusty, and no rain had fallen there.

When Oliver Cromwell sent forth a proclamation for a fast throughout the nation, for rain, when there was a very great drought, it was observed, that as far as truth had spread in the north, there were pleasant showers and rain enough, when in the south, in many places, they were almost spoiled for want of rain. At that time I was moved to write an answer to the Protector's proclamation, wherein I told him, "if he had come to own God's truth, he should have had rain; and that drought was a sign unto them of their barrenness, and want of the water of life." About the same time was written the following paper, to distinguish between true and false fasts: "Concerning the true Fast and the false."

"That which gives to know the true fast, and the false fast, is the Light, which gives the eye to see each fast, where the true judgment is, and the iniquity standeth not, nor the transgressor, nor the speaker of lies; but that is judged and condemned with the Light, which makes it manifest. And when they who are in this fast call upon the Lord, the Lord will answer them, Here am I. Here truth is pleaded for, and falsehood flies away. But they who are out of this fast, in the perverseness, whose tongues utter perverse things, who are stumbling and groping like blind men, out of the light, in the iniquity which separates from God, who hides his face from them that he will not hear;— these going from the light, go from the Lord and his face. So this is it which must be fasted from; for it separates from God; and here comes the reward openly, which condemns all that is contrary to the light; injustice, iniquity, transgression, vanity, and that which bringeth forth mischief, which hatcheth the cockatrice eggs, and weaves the spider's web: he that eateth of these eggs dies. Mark, 'that which is crushed breaks out into a viper'; mark again, 'their webs shall not become garments, neither shall they cover themselves with their works of vanity; acts of violence are in their hands.' This is all far from the light. Again, 'the way of peace they know not, there is no judgment in their goings; they have made them crooked paths, whosoever go therein, shall not know peace.' Mark; who go in their way, that know not the way of peace, shall they know peace? 'Whose path is crooked, where there is no judgment in their goings'; take notice, 'no judgment in their goings'; this is all from the light, which manifesteth that which is to be judged; where the covenant of peace is known, where all that which is contrary to it is kept out. All who live in those things contrary to the light, in the false fast, stumbling and groping like blind men, may mark their path, and behold their reward. They that are in the true fast, are separated from all these; from their words and actions, their fruits, and their fast: but of those whose fast breaks the bonds of iniquity, whom the Lord hears, and to whom righteousness springs forth, and goes before them, the glory of the Lord is the rere-ward.

G.F."

Next day, being market day, we were to cross a great water: and not far from the place where we were to take boat, many of the market-people drew to us; amongst whom we had good service for the Lord, "declaring the word of life and everlasting truth unto them, and proclaiming the day of the Lord amongst them, which was coming upon all wickedness; and directing them to the light of Christ, which he had enlightened them with, by which they might see all their sins, and false ways, religions, worships, and teachers: and by the same light might see Christ Jesus, who was come to save them, and lead them to God. After the Lord's truth had been declared to them in the power of God, and Christ the free teacher set over all the hireling teachers, I bid John-ap-John get his horse into the boat, which was then ready. But there being a company of wild gentlemen, as they called them, got into it, whom we found very rude, and far from gentleness, they, with others, kept his horse out of the boat. I rode to the boat's side and spoke to them, showing them "what unmanly and unchristian conduct it was; and told them they showed an unworthy spirit, below Christianity or humanity." As I spoke, I leaped my horse into the boat amongst them, thinking John's horse would have followed, when he had seen mine go in before him; but the water being deep, John could not get his horse into the boat. Wherefore I leaped out again on horseback into the water, and stayed with John on that side till the boat returned. There we tarried from eleven in the forenoon, to two in the afternoon, before the boat came to fetch us; and then we had forty-two miles to ride that evening: and when we had paid for our passage, we had but one groat left between us in money. We rode about sixteen miles, and then got a little hay for our horses. Setting forward again, we came in the night to a little ale-house, where we intended to stay and bait; but finding we could have neither oats nor hay there, we travelled on all night; and about five in the morning got to a place within six miles of Wrexham; where that day we met with many Friends, and had a glorious meeting; and the Lord's everlasting power and truth was over all: and a meeting is continued there to this day. Very weary we were with travelling so hard up and down in Wales; and in many places we found it difficult to get meat either for our horses or ourselves.

CHAPTER XI

1657

Having got a little respite from travel, I was moved to write an epistle to Friends, as follows:

"All Friends of the Lord everywhere, whose minds are turned in towards the Lord, take heed to the light within you, which is the light of Christ; which, as ye love it, will call your minds inward, that are abroad in the creatures: so your minds may be renewed by it, and turned to God in this which is pure, to worship the living God, the Lord of Hosts over all the creatures. That which calls your minds out of the lusts of the world, will call them out of the affections and desires, and turn you to set your affections above. That which calls the mind out of the world, will give judgment upon the world's affections and lusts, and is the same that calls out your minds from the world's teachers, and the creatures, to have your minds renewed. There is your obedience known and found; there the image of God is renewed in you; and ye come to grow up in it. That which calls your minds out of the earth, turns them towards God, where the pure Babe is born of the virgin; and the Babe's food is known, the children's bread, which comes from the living God, and nourishes up to eternal life. These babes and children receive their wisdom from above, from the pure living God, and not from the earthly one: for that is trodden under foot with such. All who hate this light, whose minds are abroad in the creatures, in the earth, and in the image of the devil, get the words of the saints, that received their wisdom from above, into the old nature, and their corrupted minds. Such are murderers of the just, enemies to the cross of Christ, in whom the prince of the air lodgeth: sons of perdition, betrayers of the just. Therefore take heed to that light, which is oppressed with that nature; which light, as it arises, shall condemn all that cursed nature, shall turn it out, and shut it out of the house: and so ye will come to see the candle lighted, and the house sweeping and swept. Then the pure pearl ariseth; then the eternal God is exalted. The same light that calls in your minds out of the world, turns them to God, the Father of lights. Here in the pure mind is the pure God waited upon for wisdom from above; the pure God is seen night and day; and the eternal peace, of which there is no end, enjoyed. People may have openings, and yet their minds go into the lusts of the flesh; but there the affections are not mortified. Therefore hearken to that, and take heed to that, which calls your minds out of the affections and lusts of the world, to have them renewed. The same will turn your minds to God; the same light will set your affections above, and bring you to wait for the pure wisdom of God from on high, that it may be justified in you. Wait all in that, which calls in your minds, and turns them to God; here is the true cross. That mind shall feed upon nothing that is earthly; but be kept in the pure light of God up to God, to feed upon the living food, which comes from the living God. The Lord God Almighty be with you all, dear babes, and keep you all in his strength and power to his glory, over all the world, —you whose minds are called out of it, and turned to God, to worship the Creator, and serve him, and not the creature. The light of God, which calls the mind out of the creatures, and turns it to God, brings into a being of endless joy and peace. Here is always a seeing God present, which is not known to the world, whose hearts are in the creatures, whose knowledge is in the flesh, whose minds are not renewed. Therefore all Friends, the Seed of God mind and dwell in, to reign over the unjust: and the power of the Lord dwell in, to keep you clear in your understandings, that the Seed of God may reign in you all;—the Seed of God, which is but one in all, which is Christ in the male and in the female, which the promise is to. Wait upon the Lord for the just to reign over the unjust, and for the Seed of God to reign over the seed of the serpent, and be the head; and that all that is mortal may die; for out of that will rise presumption. So fare ye well, and God Almighty bless, and guide, and keep you in his wisdom.

G.F."

I was also moved to give forth the following epistle to Friends, to stir them up to be bold and valiant for the truth, and to encourage them in their sufferings for it:

"All Friends and brethren everywhere, now is the day of your trial, now is the time for you to be valiant, and to see that the testimony of the Lord doth not fall. Now is the day for the exercise of your gifts, of your patience, and of your faith. Now is the time to be armed with patience, with the light, with righteousness, and with the helmet of salvation. Now is the trial of the slothful servant, who hides his talent, and will judge Christ hard. Now, happy are they that can say, 'the earth is the Lord's and the fulness thereof, and he gives the increase'; and therefore, who takes it from you? Is it not the Lord still that suffers it? For the Lord can try you as he did Job, whom he made rich, whom he made poor, and whom he made rich again; who still kept his integrity in all conditions. Learn Paul's lesson, 'in all states to be content'; and have his faith, that 'nothing is able to separate us from the love of God, which we have in Christ Jesus.' Therefore be rich in life, and in grace, which will endure, ye who are heirs of life, and born of the womb of eternity, that noble birth, that cannot stoop to that which is born in sin, and conceived in iniquity; who are better bred and born; whose religion is from God, above all the religions that are from below; and who walk by faith, by that which God hath given you, and not by that which men make, who walk by sight, from the Mass-Book to the Directory. Such are subject to stumble and fall, who walk by sight and not by faith. Therefore mind him that destroys the original of sin, the devil and his works, and cuts off the entail of Satan, viz., sin; who would have by entail an inheritance of sin in men and women from generation to generation, and pleads for it by all his lawyers and counsellors. For though the law, which made nothing perfect, did not cut it off; yet Christ being come destroys the devil and his works, and cuts off the entail of sin. This angers all the devil's lawyers and counsellors, that Satan shall not hold sin by entail in thy garden, in thy field, in thy temple, thy tabernacle. So keep your tabernacles, that there ye may see the glory of the Lord appear at the doors thereof. And be faithful; for ye see, what the worthies and valiants of the Lord attained unto by faith. Enoch by faith was translated. Noah by faith was preserved over the waters in his ark. Abraham by faith forsook his father's house and religion, and all the religions of the world. Isaac and Jacob by faith followed his steps. See also how Samuel, with other of the Lord's prophets, and David, by faith were preserved to God, over God's enemies! Daniel and the three children by faith escaped the lions and the fire, and preserved their worship clean, and by it were kept over the worships of the world. The apostles by faith travelled up and down the world, were preserved from all the religions of the world, and held forth the pure religion to the dark world, which they had received from God; and likewise their fellowship was received from above, which is in the gospel that is everlasting. In this, neither powers, principalities, nor thrones, dominions nor angels, things present, nor things to come, nor heights, nor depths, nor death, mockings, nor spoiling of goods, nor prisons, nor fetters, were able to separate them from the love of God, which they had in Christ Jesus. And Friends, 'quench not the Spirit, nor despise prophesying,' where it moves; neither hinder the babes and sucklings from crying Hosanna; for out of their mouths will God ordain strength. There were some in Christ's day that were against such, whom he reproved; and there were some in Moses's day, who would have stopped the prophets in the camp, whom Moses reproved, and said, by way of encouragement to them, 'Would God, that all the Lord's people were prophets!' So I say now to you. Therefore ye, that stop it in yourselves, do not quench it in others, neither in babe nor suckling; for the Lord hears the cries of the needy, and the sighs and groans of the poor. Judge not that, nor the sighs and groans of the Spirit, which cannot be uttered, lest ye judge prayer; for prayer as well lies in sighs and groans to the Lord as otherwise. Let not the sons and daughters, nor the handmaidens be stopped in their prophesyings, nor the young men in their visions, nor the old men in their dreams; but let the Lord be glorified in and through all, who is over all, God blessed forever! So everyone may improve his talents, everyone exercise his gifts, and everyone speak as the Spirit gives him utterance. Thus everyone may minister as he hath received the grace, as a good steward to him that hath given it him; so that all plants may bud and bring forth fruit to the glory of God; 'for the manifestation of the Spirit is given to everyone to profit withal.' See, that everyone hath profited in heavenly things: male and female, look into your own vineyards, and see what fruit ye bear to God; look into your own houses, see how they are decked and trimmed, and see what odours, myrrh, and frankincense ye have therein, and what a smell and savour ye have to ascend to God, that he may be glorified. Bring all your deeds to the light, which ye are taught to believe in by Christ, your Head, the heavenly Man; and see how they are wrought in God. Every male and female, let Christ dwell in your hearts by faith, and let your mouths be opened to the glory of God the Father, that he may rule and reign in you. We must not have Christ Jesus, the Lord of life, put anymore in a stable, amongst the horses and asses; but he must now have the best chamber, the heart, and the rude, debauched spirit must be turned out. Therefore let Him reign, whose right it is, who was conceived by the Holy Ghost, by which ye call him Lord, in which ye pray, and have comfort and fellowship with the Father and with the Son. Therefore know the triumph in it, and in God and his power (which the devil is out of), and in the seed, which is first and last, the beginning and ending, the top and cornerstone; in which is my love to you, and in which I rest— Your friend, G.F.

"Postscript—And, Friends, be careful how ye set your feet among the tender plants, that are springing up out of God's earth; lest ye tread upon them, hurt, bruise, or crush them in God's vineyard."

CHAPTER XII

1657–59

About this time the Lady Claypole [a favorite daughter of Oliver Cromwell] (so called) was sick and much troubled in mind, and could receive no comfort from any that came to her; which when I heard of, I was moved to write to her the following letter:

"Friend:

"Be still and cool in thy own mind and spirit from thy own thoughts, and then thou wilt feel the principle of God to turn thy mind to the Lord, from whom cometh life; whereby thou mayest receive his strength and power to allay all storms, and tempests. That is it which works up into patience, innocency, soberness, into stillness, staidness, quietness up to God, with his power. Therefore mind; that is the word of the Lord God unto thee, that thou mayest feel the authority of God, and thy faith in that, to work down that which troubles thee; for that is it which keeps peace, and brings up the witness in thee, which hath been transgressed, to feel after God with his power and life, who is a God of order and peace. When thou art in the transgression of the life of God in thy own particular, the mind flies up in the air, the creature is led into the night, nature goes out of its course, an old garment goes on, and an uppermost clothing; and thy nature being led out of its course, it comes to be all on fire, in the transgression; and that

defaceth the glory of the first body. Therefore be still a while from thy
own thoughts, searching, seeking, desires, and imaginations, and be
staid in the principle of God in thee, that it may raise thy mind up to
God, and stay it upon God, and thou wilt find strength from him, and
find him to be a God at hand, a present help in the time of trouble,
and of need. And thou being come to the principle of God, which hath
been transgressed, it will keep thee humble; and the humble, God will
teach his way, which is peace, and such he doth exalt. Now as the
principle of God in thee hath been transgressed, come to it, that it
may keep thy mind down low to the Lord God; and deny thyself; for
from thy own will, that is, the earthly, thou must be kept. Then thou
wilt feel the power of God, which will bring nature into its course,
and give thee to see the glory of the first body. There the wisdom of
God will be received, which is Christ, by which all things were made
and created, and thou wilt thereby be preserved and ordered to God's
glory. There thou wilt come to receive and feel the physician of value,
who clothes people in their right mind, whereby they may serve God,
and do his will. For all distractions, unruliness, and confusion are in
the transgression; which transgression must be brought down, before
the principle of God, which hath been transgressed against, be lifted
up: whereby the mind may be seasoned, and stilled, and a right understanding of the Lord may be received; whereby his blessings enter,
and are felt, over all that is contrary, in the power of the Lord God,
which raises up the principle of God within, gives a feeling after God,
and in time gives dominion. Therefore, keep in the fear of the Lord
God; that is the word of the Lord unto thee. For all these things happen to thee for thy good, and for the good of those concerned for thee,
to make you know yourselves, and your own weakness, and that ye
may know the Lord's strength and power, and may trust in him. Let
the time that is past be sufficient to everyone, who in anything hath
been lifted up in transgression out of the power of the Lord; for he
can bring down and abase the mighty, and lay them in the dust of the
earth. Therefore, all keep low in his fear, that thereby ye may receive
the secrets of God and his wisdom, may know the shadow of the Almighty, and sit under it, in all tempests, and storms, and heats. For
God is at hand, and the Most High rules in the children of men. This
then is the word of the Lord God unto you all; whatever temptations,
distractions, confusions, the light doth make manifest and discover, do
not look at these temptations, confusions, corruptions; but look at the
light, which discovers them, and makes them manifest; and with the
same light you may feel over them, to receive power to stand against
them. The same light which lets you see sin and transgression, will let

you see the convenant of God, which blots out your sin and transgression, which gives victory and dominion over it, and brings into
covenant with God. For looking down at sin, and corruption, and distraction, ye are swallowed up in it: but looking at the light, which discovers them, ye will see over them. That will give victory; and ye will
find grace and strength: there is the first step to peace. That will bring
salvation; by it ye may see to the beginning, and the 'glory that was
with the Father before world began'; and so come to know the Seed of
God, which is the heir of the promise of God, and of the world which
hath no end; which bruises the head of the serpent, who stops people
from coming to God. That ye may feel the power of an endless life,
the power of God, which is immortal; which brings the immortal soul
up to the immortal God, in whom it doth rejoice. So in the name and
power of the Lord Jesus Christ, God Almighty strengthen thee.

G.F."

When the foregoing paper was read to Lady Claypole, she said,
it staid her mind for the present. Afterwards many Friends got copies of it, both in England and Ireland, and read it to people that
were troubled in mind; and it was made useful for the settling of
the minds of several.

After a while I went to Reading, where I was under great sufferings and exercises, and in great travail of spirit for about ten weeks.
For I saw there was great confusion and distraction amongst the
people, and that the powers were plucking each other to pieces.
And I saw how many were destroying the simplicity, and betraying
the truth. Much hypocrisy, deceit, and strife, was got uppermost in
the people, so that they were ready to sheath their swords in one
another's bowels. There had been tenderness in many of them formerly, when they were low; but when they were got up, had killed,
and taken possession, they came to be as bad as others; so that we
had much to do with them about our hats, and saying Thou and
Thee to them. They turned their profession of patience and moderation into rage and madness; and many of them were like distracted men for this hat-honour. For they had hardened themselves
by persecuting the innocent, and were at this time crucifying the
Seed, Christ, both in themselves and others; till at last they fell to
biting and devouring one another, until they were consumed one of
another; who had turned against, and judged, that which God had

wrought in them, and showed unto them. So shortly after God overthrew them, turned them upside down, and brought the king over them, who were often surmising that the Quakers met together to bring in King Charles, whereas Friends did not concern themselves with the outward powers, or government. But at last the Lord brought him in, and many of them, when they saw he would be brought in, voted for bringing him in. So with heart and voice praise the name of the Lord, to whom it doth belong; who over all hath the supremacy, and who will rock the nations, for he is over them. I had a sight and sense of the king's return a good while before, and so had some others. I wrote to Oliver several times, and let him know that while he was persecuting God's people, they whom he accounted his enemies were preparing to come upon him. When some forward spirits that came amongst us would have bought Somerset-House that we might have meetings in it, I forbade them to do so: for I then foresaw the king's coming in again. Besides, there came a woman to me in the Strand, who had a prophecy concerning King Charles's coming in, three years before he came: and she told me, she must go to him to declare it. I advised her to wait upon the Lord, and keep it to herself; for if it should be known that she went on such a message, they would look upon it to be treason: but she said, she must go, and tell him, that he should be brought into England again. I saw her prophecy was true, and that a great stroke must come upon them in power; for they that had then got possession were so exceeding high, and such great persecution was acted by them, who called themselves saints, that they would take from Friends their copyhold lands, because they could not swear in their courts. Sometimes when we laid these sufferings before Oliver Cromwell, he would not believe it. Wherefore Thomas Aldam and Anthony Pearson were moved to go through all the jails in England, and to get copies of Friends' commitments under the jailer's hands, that they might lay the weight of their sufferings upon Oliver Cromwell. And when he would not give order for the releasing of them, Thomas Aldam was moved to take his cap from off his head, and to rend it in pieces before him, and to say unto him, "So shall thy government be rent from thee and thy house." Another Friend also, a woman, was moved to go to the parliament (that was envious against Friends) with a pitcher in her hand, which she broke into pieces before them, and told them, "so should they be broken to pieces": which came to pass shortly after. And in my great suffering and travail of spirit for the nation, being grievously burdened with their hypocrisy, treachery, and falsehood, I saw God would bring that over them, which they had been above; and that all must be brought down to that which convinced them, before they could get over that bad spirit within and without: for it is the pure, invisible Spirit, that doth and only can work down all deceit in people.

While I was under that sore travail at Reading, by reason of grief and sorrow of mind, and the great exercise that was upon my spirit, my countenance was altered, and I looked poor and thin; and there came a company of unclean spirits to me, and told me, "the plagues of God were upon me." I told them, it was the same spirit spoke that in them, that said so of Christ, when he was stricken and smitten; they hid their face from him. But when I had travailed with the witness of God, which they had quenched, and had got through with it, and over all that hypocrisy which the outside professors were run into, and saw how that would be brought down, and turned under, and that life would rise over it, I came to have ease, and the light, power, and Spirit shone over all. And then having recovered, and got through my travails and sufferings, my body and face swelled, when I came abroad into the air; and then the bad spirits said, "I was grown fat," and they envied at that also. So I saw, that no condition nor state would please that spirit of theirs. But the Lord preserved me by his power and Spirit through and over all, and in his power I came to London again.

Now was there a great pother made about the image or effigies of Oliver Cromwell lying in state; men standing and sounding with trumpets over his image, after he was dead. At this my spirit was greatly grieved, and the Lord, I found, was highly offended. Then did I write the following lines, and sent among them, to reprove their wickedness, and warn them to repent:

"O friends, what are ye doing! What mean ye to sound before an image! Will not all sober people think ye are like madmen! O how am I grieved with your abominations! O, how am I wearied! My soul is wearied with you, saith the Lord: will I not be avenged of you, think ye, for your abominations? O, how have ye plucked down and set up! How are your hearts made whole, and not rent! How are ye turned to fooleries! Which things in times past, ye stood over. How have ye left

my dread, saith the Lord! Fear therefore, and repent, lest the snare
and the pit take you all. The great day of the Lord is come upon all
your abominations; the swift hand of the Lord is turned against them.
The sober people in these nations stand amazed at your doings, and
are ashamed, as if ye would bring in Popery.

G.F."

About this time great stirs were in the nation, the minds of the
people being unsettled. Much plotting and contriving there was by
the several factions, to carry on their several interests. And a great
care being upon me, lest any young or ignorant people, that might
sometimes come amongst us, should be drawn into that snare, I was
moved to give forth the following epistle as a warning unto all
such:

"All Friends everywhere, keep out of plots and bustling, and the
arm of flesh; for all these are amongst Adam's sons in the fall, where
they are destroying men's lives like dogs, beasts, and swine, goring,
rending, and biting one another, destroying one another, and wrestling
with flesh and blood. Whence arise wars and killing but from the
lusts? Now all this is in Adam in the fall, out of Adam that never fell,
in whom there is peace and life. Ye are called to peace, therefore follow it; and that peace is in Christ, not in Adam in the fall. All that
pretend to fight for Christ, are deceived; for his kingdom is not of this
world, therefore his servants do not fight. Fighters are not of Christ's
kingdom, but are without Christ's kingdom; his kingdom stands in
peace and righteousness, but fighters are in the lust; and all that
would destroy men's lives, are not of Christ's mind, who came to save
men's lives. Christ's kingdom is not of this world; it is peaceable: and
all that are in strife, are not of his kingdom. All that pretend to fight
for the gospel, are deceived; for the gospel is the power of God, which
was before the devil, or fall of man was; and the gospel of peace was
before fighting was. Therefore, they that pretend fighting, are ignorant
of the gospel; and all that talk of fighting for Sion, are in darkness; for
Sion needs no such helpers. All such as profess themselves to be
ministers of Christ, or Christians, and go about to beat down the
whore with outward, carnal weapons, the flesh and the whore are got
up in themselves, and they are in a blind zeal; for the whore got up
by the inward ravening from the Spirit of God; and the beating down
thereof, must be by the inward stroke of the sword of the Spirit
within. All such as pretend Christ Jesus, and confess him, and yet run
into the use of carnal weapons, wrestling with flesh and blood, throw

away the spiritual weapons. They that would be wrestlers with flesh and blood, throw away Christ's doctrine; the flesh is got up in them, and they are weary of their sufferings. Such as would revenge themselves, are out of Christ's doctrine. Such as being stricken on one cheek, would not turn the other, are out of Christ's doctrine: and such as do not love one another, nor love enemies, are out of Christ's doctrine. Therefore, ye that are heirs of the blessings of God, which were before the curse and the fall were, come to inherit your portions; and ye that are heirs of the gospel of peace, which was before the devil was, live in the gospel of peace, seeking the peace of all men, and the good of all men; and live in Christ, who came to save men's lives, out of Adam in the fall, where they destroy men's lives, and live not in Christ. The Jews' sword outwardly, by which they cut down the heathen, was a type of the Spirit of God within, which cuts down the heathenish nature within. So live in the peaceable kingdom of Christ Jesus. Live in the peace of God, and not in the lusts, from whence wars arise. Live in Christ, the Prince of Peace, the way of God, who is the second Adam, that never fell; but live not in Adam in the fall, in the destruction, where they destroy one another. Therefore come out of Adam in the fall, into the second Adam that never fell. Live in love and peace with all men; keep out of all the bustlings in the world; meddle not with the powers of the earth; but mind the kingdom, the way of peace. Ye that are heirs of grace, heirs of the kingdom, heirs of the gospel, heirs of salvation, saints of the Most High, and children of God, whose conversation is in heaven, that is, above the combustions of the earth; let your conversation preach to all men, and your innocent lives, that they who speak evil of you, beholding your godly conversation, may glorify your Father which is in heaven. All Friends everywhere, this I charge you, which is the word of the Lord God unto you all, 'Live in peace, in Christ the way of peace,' and therein seek the peace of all men, and no man's hurt. In Adam in the fall, is no peace; but in Adam out of the fall, is peace: so, ye being in Adam which never fell, it is love that overcomes, and not hatred nor strife with strife. Therefore live all in the peaceable life, doing good to all men, and seeking the good and welfare of all men.

G.F."

CHAPTER XIII

1659–60

I had then also a general meeting at Edward Pyot's, near Bristol, at which it was supposed were several thousands; for besides Friends from many parts thereabouts, some of the Baptists and Independents, with their teachers, came to it, and many of the sober people of Bristol; insomuch that the people that stayed behind said, "the city looked naked," so many were gone out of it to this meeting. It was very quiet, many glorious truths were opened to the people, and the Lord Jesus Christ was set up, who was the end of all figures and shadows of the law, and the first covenant. It was declared to the people that all figures and shadows were given to man, after he fell; and that all the rudiments and inventions of men, which have been set up in Christendom, many of which were Jewish and heathenish, were not set up by the command of Christ; and all images and likenesses man has made to himself, or for himself, whether of things in heaven or things in earth, have been since he lost the image and likeness of God, which God made him in. But now Christ is come to redeem, translate, convert, and regenerate man out of all these things that he hath set up in the fall, out of the true types, figures, and shadows also, and out of death and darkness, into the light, life, and image of God again, which man and woman were in before they fell. Therefore all now should come, and all might come to receive, Christ Jesus, the substance, by his light, Spirit, grace, and faith; and should live and walk in him, the Redeemer and Saviour.

And as we had much work with priests and professors, who pleaded for imperfection, I was opened to declare and manifest unto them, that Adam and Eve were perfect before they fell; and God saw that all that he had made, was good, and he blessed it. But imperfection came in by the fall, through man and woman's hearkening to the devil, who was out of truth, and though the law made nothing perfect, yet it made way for the bringing in of the better hope, which hope is Christ, who destroys the devil and his works, that made man and woman imperfect. Christ saith to his disciples, "Be ye perfect, even as your heavenly Father is perfect": and he, who himself was perfect, comes to make man and woman perfect again, and brings them again to the state which God made them in. So he is the maker up of the breach, and the peace between God and man. That this might the better be understood by the lowest capacities, I used a comparison of two old people, that had their house broken down by an enemy, so that they, with all their children, were liable to all storms and tempests. And there came some to them that pretended to be workmen, and offered to build up their house again, if they would give them so much a year: but when they had got their money, they left their house as they found it. After this manner came a second, third, fourth, fifth, and sixth, each with his several pretence, to build up the old house, and each got the people's money; and then cried, "they could not rear up the house, nor could the breach be made up; for this is no perfection here, cry they; the house can never be perfectly built up again in this life"; though they had taken the people's money for the doing of it. For all the sect-masters in Christendom (so called) have pretended to build up Adam and Eve's fallen house, and when they have got people's money, they tell them the work cannot be perfectly done here; and so their house lies as it did. But I told the people, Christ was come to do it freely, who, by one offering, hath perfected forever all them that are sanctified, and renews them into the image of God, which man and woman were in before they fell, and makes man and woman's house as perfect again as God made them at the first: and this, Christ, the heavenly man, doth freely. Therefore all are to look unto him, and all that have received him, are to walk in him, the life, the substance, the first and the last, the rock of ages, and foundation of many generations. Largely were these, and many other things, opened and declared unto the people, the word of life was preached, which doth live and abide; and all were exhorted to hear and obey that which liveth and abideth, that by it all might be born again of the immortal Seed, and feed on the milk of the Word. A glorious meeting there was, wherein the Lord's everlasting Seed, Christ Jesus, was set over all, and Friends parted in the power and Spirit of the Lord, in peace and in his truth, that is over all.

From Warmsworth I passed in the Lord's power to Barton-Abbey, where I had a great meeting; and thence to Thomas Taylor's, and so to Skipton, where there was a general meeting of men Friends out of many counties, concerning the affairs of the church. A Friend went naked (divested of the upper garments) through the town, declaring truth, and he was much beaten. Some others also came to me all bloody. As I walked in the street, a desperate fellow had an intent to do me a mischief; but he was prevented, and our meeting was quiet. To this meeting came many Friends out of most parts of the nation; for it was about business relating to the church, both in this nation and beyond the seas. Several years before, when I was in the North, I was moved to recommend the setting up of this meeting for that service; for many Friends suffered in divers parts of the nation, their goods were taken from them contrary to the law, and they understood not how to help themselves, or where to seek redress. But after this meeting was set up, several Friends who had been magistrates, and others that understood something of the law, came thither, and were able to inform Friends, and to assist them in gathering up the sufferings, that they might be laid before the justices, judges, or Parliament. This meeting had stood several years, and divers justices and captains had come to break it up; but when they understood the business Friends met about, and saw their books and accounts of collections for relief of the poor, how we took care one county to help another, and to help our friends beyond the seas, and provide for our poor, that none of them should be chargeable to their parishes, etc., the justices and officers confessed we did their work, and passed away peaceably and lovingly, commending Friends' practice. Sometimes there would come two hundred of the poor of other people, and wait there till the meeting was done (for all the country knew we met about the poor) and after the meeting, Friends would send to the bakers for bread, and give everyone of these poor people a loaf, how many soever there were of them; for we were taught to "do good unto all; though especially to the household of faith."

Whilst I was kept in Lancaster jail, I was moved to give forth the following paper, "for staying the minds of any such as might be hurried or troubled about the change of government":

"All Friends, let the dread and majesty of God fill you! And as concerning the changing of times and governments, let not that trouble any of you; for God hath a mighty work and hand therein. He will yet change again, until that come up, which must reign; in vain shall powers and armies withstand the Lord, for his determined work shall come to pass. But it is just with the Lord that what is now come up should be so, and he will be served by it. Therefore let none murmur, nor distrust God; for he will provoke many to zeal against unrighteousness, and for righteousness, through things which are suffered now to work for a season; yea many, whose zeal was even dead, shall revive again, shall see their backslidings, and bewail them bitterly. For God shall thunder from heaven, and break forth in a mighty noise; his enemies shall be astonished, the workers of iniquity confounded, and all that have not the garment of righteousness shall be amazed at the mighty and strange work of the Lord, which shall be certainly brought to pass. But, my babes, look ye not out, but be still in the light of the Lamb; and he shall fight for you. The Almighty Hand, which must break and divide your enemies, and take away peace from them, preserve and keep you whole, in unity and peace with itself, and one with another. Amen.

G.F."

We went next morning to Judge Mallet's chamber, who was putting on his red gown, to go sit upon some more of the king's judges. He was very peevish and froward, and said I might come another time. We went again to his chamber, when Judge Foster was with him, who was called the lord chief justice of England. With me was one called Esquire Marsh, who was one of the bedchamber to the king. When we had delivered to the judges the charge that was against me, and they had read to those words, "that I and my friends were embroiling the nation in blood," etc., they struck their hands on the table. Whereupon I told them, "I was the man whom that charge was against, but I was as innocent of any such thing as a newborn child, and had brought it up myself; and some of my friends came up with me, without any guard." As yet they had not minded my hat, but now seeing it on, they said, "What, did I stand with my hat on!" I told them I did not so in any contempt of them. Then they commanded it to be taken off; and when they called for the marshall of the King's Bench, they said to him, "You must take this man, and secure him; but let him have a chamber, and not put him amongst the prisoners." "My lord," said the marshall, "I have no chamber to put him into; my house is so full I cannot tell where to provide a room for him but amongst the prisoners." "Nay," said the judge, "you must not put him amongst the prisoners." But when he still answered, he had no other place to put me in, Judge Foster said to me, "Will you appear tomorrow about ten o'clock at the King's Bench bar in Westminster-Hall?" I said, "Yes, if the Lord give me strength." Then said Judge Foster to the other judge, "If he says yes, and promises it, you may take his word"; so I was dismissed. Next day I appeared at the King's Bench bar at the hour appointed, Robert Widders, Richard Hubberthorn, and Esquire Marsh going with me. I was brought into the middle of the court; and as soon as I came in, was moved to look around, and turning to the people, said, "Peace be among you"; and the power of the Lord sprang over the court. The charge against me was read openly. The people were moderate, and the judges cool and loving; and the Lord's mercy was to them. But when they came to that part which said, "that I and my friends were embroiling the nation in blood, and raising a new war, and that I was an enemy to the king," etc., they lifted up their hands. Then, stretching out my arms, I said, "I am the man whom that charge is against; but I am as innocent as a child concerning the charge, and have never learned any war postures. And," said I, "do ye think that if I and my friends had been such men as the charge declares, that I would have brought it up myself against myself? Or that I should have been suffered to come up with only one or two of my friends with me? Had I been such a man as this charge sets forth, I had need to have been guarded with a troop or two of horse. But the sheriff and magistrates of Lancashire thought fit to let me and my friends come up with it ourselves, nearly two hundred miles, without any guard at all; which, ye may be sure, they would not have done, had they looked upon me to be such a man." Then the judge asked me, whether it should be filed, or what I would do with it. I answered, "Ye are judges, and able, I hope, to judge in this matter, therefore do with it what ye will; for I am the man these charges are against, and here ye see, I have brought them up myself; do ye what ye will with them, I leave it to you." Then Judge Twisden beginning to speak some angry words, I appealed to Judge Foster and Judge Mallet, who had heard me overnight. Whereupon they said, "They did not accuse me, for they had nothing against me." Then stood up Esquire Marsh, who was of the king's bedchamber, and told the judges, "It was the king's pleasure, that I should be set at liberty, seeing no accuser came up against me." They asked me, "Whether I would put it to the king and council?" I said, "Yes, with a good will." Thereupon they sent the sheriff's return, which he made to the writ of habeas corpus, containing the matter charged against me in the mittimus, to the king, that he might see for what I was committed.

CHAPTER XIV

1660–62

Having lost our former declaration in the press, we hastily drew up another against plots and fighting, got it printed, and sent some copies to the king and council; others were sold in the streets, and at the Exchange. Which declaration was some years after reprinted, and is as follows:

"A Declaration from the harmless and innocent people of God, call Quakers, against all sedition, plotters, and fighters in the world: for removing the ground of jealousy and suspicion from magistrates and people concerning wars and fightings.

"Presented to the King upon the 21st day of the 11th Month, 1660.

"Our principle is, and our practices have always been, to seek peace and ensue it; to follow after righteousness and the knowledge of God; seeking the good and welfare, and doing that which tends to the peace of all. We know that wars and fightings proceed from the lusts of men, as James iv. 1–3, out of which the Lord hath redeemed us, and so out of the occasion of war. The occasion of war, and war itself (wherein envious men, who are lovers of themselves more than lovers of God, lust, kill, and desire to have men's lives or estates) ariseth from lust. All bloody principles and practices, as to our own particulars, we utterly deny; with all outward wars and strife, and fightings with outward weapons, for any end, or under any pretence whatsoever; this is our testimony to the whole world.

"And whereas it is objected:

"But although you now say 'that you cannot fight, nor take up arms at all, yet if the Spirit move you, then you will change your principle, and you will sell your coat, and buy a sword, and fight for the kingdom of Christ.'

"To this we answer, Christ said to Peter, 'Put up thy sword in his place'; though he had said before, he that had no sword might sell his coat and buy one (to the fulfilling of the law and the Scripture), yet after, when he had bid him put it up, he said, 'he that taketh the sword, shall perish with the sword.' And further, Christ said to Peter, 'Thinkest thou, that I cannot now pray to my Father, and he shall presently give me more than twelve legions of angels?' And this might satisfy Peter, Luke xxii. 36, after he had put up his sword, when he said to him, 'He that took it, should perish by it'; which satisfieth us, Matt. xxvi. 51–53. And in the Revelation, it is said, 'He that kills with the sword, shall perish with the sword; and here is the faith and the patience of the saints.' And so Christ's kingdom is not of this world, therefore do not his servants fight, as he told Pilate, the magistrate, who crucified him. And did they not look upon Christ as a raiser of sedition? And did not he pray, 'Forgive them'? But thus it is that we are numbered amongst transgressors, and fighters, that the Scriptures might be fulfilled.

"That the Spirit of Christ, by which we are guided, is not changeable, so as once to command us from a thing as evil, and again to move unto it; and we certainly know, and testify to the world, that the Spirit of Christ, which leads us into all truth, will never move us to fight and war against any man with outward weapons, neither for the kingdom of Christ, nor for the kingdoms of this world.

"First, because the kingdom of Christ God will exalt, according to this promise, and cause it to grow and flourish in righteousness; 'not by might, nor by power (of outward sword), but by my Spirit, saith the Lord,' Zech. iv. 6. So those that use any weapon to fight for Christ, or for the establishing of his kingdom or government,—their spirit, principle, and practice we deny.

"Secondly, we do earnestly desire and wait, that, by the Word of God's power, and its effectual operation in the hearts of men, the kingdoms of this world may become the kingdoms of the Lord, and of his Christ; that he may rule and reign in men by his Spirit and truth; that thereby all people, out of every profession, may be brought into love and unity with God, and one with another; and that they may all come to witness the prophet's words, who said, 'Nation shall not lift up sword against nation, neither shall they learn war anymore,' Isa. ii. 4; Mic. iv. 3.

"So we, whom the Lord hath called into the obedience of his truth, have denied wars and fightings, and cannot more learn them. This is a certain testimony unto all the world, of the truth of our hearts in this particular, that as God persuadeth every man's heart to believe, so they may receive it. For we have not, as some others, gone about with cunningly devised fables, nor have we ever denied in practice what we have professed in principle; but in sincerity and truth, and by the word of God, have we laboured to manifest unto all men, that both we and our ways might be witnessed in the hearts of all. And whereas all manner of evil hath been falsely spoken of us, we hereby speak the plain truth of our hearts, to take away the occasion of that offence; that so being innocent, we may not suffer for other men's offences, nor be made a prey of by the wills of men for that of which we were never guilty; but in the uprightness of our hearts we may, under the power ordained of God for the punishment of evildoers, and for the praise of them that do well, live a peaceable and godly life, in all godliness and honesty. For although we have always suffered, and do now more abundantly suffer, yet we know that it is for righteousness' sake; 'for our rejoicing is this, the testimony of our consciences, that in simplicity and godly sincerity, not with fleshly wisdom, but by the grace of God, we have had our conversation in the world,' 2 Cor. i. 12, which for us is a witness for the convincing of our enemies. For this we can say to all the world, we have wronged no man, we have used no force nor violence against any man; we have been found in no plots, nor guilty of sedition. When we have been wronged, we have not sought to revenge ourselves; we have not made resistance against authority; but wherein we could not obey for conscience' sake, we have suffered the most of any people in the nation. We have been counted as sheep for the slaughter, imprisoned, haled out of synagogues, cast into dungeons and noisome vaults, where many have died in bonds, shut up from our friends, denied needful sustenance for many days together, with other the like cruelties. And the cause of all these sufferings is not for any evil, but for things relating to the worship of our God, and in obedience to his requirings. For which cause we shall freely give up our bodies a sacrifice, rather than disobey the Lord; for we know, as the Lord hath kept us innocent, so he will plead our cause, when there is none in the earth to plead it. So we, in obedience unto his truth, do not love our lives unto death, that we may do his will, and wrong no man in our generation, but seek the good and peace of all men. He who hath commanded us that we shall not swear at all, Matt. v. 34, hath also commanded us that we shall not kill, Matt. v. 21; so that we can neither kill men, nor swear for or against them. This is both our principle and practice, and has been from the beginning; so that if we suffer, as suspected to take up arms, or make war against any, it is without any ground from us; for it neither is, nor ever was in our hearts, since we owned the truth of God; neither shall we ever do it, because it is contrary to the Spirit of Christ, his doctrine, and the practices of his apostles; even contrary to him, for whom we suffer all things, and endure all things.

"And whereas men come against us with clubs, staves, drawn swords, pistols cocked, and beat, cut, and abuse us, yet we never resisted them; but to them our hair, backs, and cheeks, have been ready. It is not an honour to manhood or nobility to run upon harmless people, who lift not up a hand against them, with arms and weapons.

"Therefore consider these things, ye men of understanding; for plotters, raisers of insurrections, tumultuous ones, and fighters, running with swords, clubs, staves, and pistols, one against another; these, we say, are of the world, and have their foundation from this unrighteous world, from the foundation of which the Lamb hath been slain; which Lamb hath redeemed us from this unrighteous world, and we are not of it, but are heirs of a world of which there is no end, and of a kingdom where no corruptible thing enters. Our weapons are spiritual, and not carnal, yet mighty through God, to the pulling down of the strongholds of sin and Satan, who is the author of wars, fighting, murder, and plots. Our swords are broken into plough-shares, and spears into pruning-hooks, as prophesied of in Micah iv. Therefore we cannot learn war anymore, neither rise up against nation or kingdom with outward weapons, though you have numbered us amongst the transgressors and plotters. The Lord knows our innocency herein, and will plead our cause with all people upon earth, at the day of their judgment, when all men shall have a reward according to their works.

"Therefore in love we warn you for your souls' good, not to wrong the innocent, nor the babes of Christ, which he hath in his hand, which he cares for as the apple of his eye; neither seek to destroy the heritage of God, nor turn your swords backward upon such as the law was not made for, i.e., the righteous; but for sinners and transgressors, to keep them down. For those are not peacemakers, nor lovers of enemies, neither can they overcome evil with good, who wrong them that are friends to you and all men, and wish your good, and the good of all people on the earth. If you oppress us, as they did the children of

Israel in Egypt, and if you oppress us as they did when Christ was born, and as they did the Christians in the primitive times; we can say, 'The Lord forgive you'; and leave the Lord to deal with you, and not revenge ourselves. If you say, as the council said to Peter and John, 'speak no more in that name'; and if you serve us, as they served the three children spoken of in Daniel, God is the same that ever he was, that lives forever and ever, who hath the innocent in his arms.

"O, Friends! Offend not the Lord and his little ones, neither afflict his people; but consider and be moderate. Do not run on hastily, but consider mercy, justice, and judgment; that is the way for you to prosper, and obtain favour of the Lord. Our meetings were stopped and broken up in the days of Oliver, under pretence of plotting against him; in the days of the Committee of Safety we were looked upon as plotters to bring in King Charles; and now our peaceable meetings are termed seditious. O! That men should lose their reason, and go contrary to their own conscience; knowing that we have suffered all things, and have been accounted plotters from the beginning, though we have declared against them both by word of mouth and printing, and are clear from any such thing! We have suffered all along, because we would not take up carnal weapons to fight, and are thus made a prey, because we are the innocent lambs of Christ, and cannot avenge ourselves! These things are left on your hearts to consider; but we are out of all those things, in the patience of the saints; and we know, as Christ said, 'He that takes the sword, shall perish with the sword'; Matt. xxvi. 52; Rev. xiii. 10.

"This is given forth from the people called Quakers, to satisfy the king and his council, and all those that have any jealousy concerning us, that all occasion of suspicion may be taken away, and our innocency cleared.

"Postscript—Though we are numbered amongst transgressors, and have been given up to rude, merciless men, by whom our meetings are broken up, in which we edified one another in our holy faith, and prayed together to the Lord that lives forever, yet his is our pleader in this day. The Lord saith, 'They that feared his name spoke often together' (as in Malachi); which were as his jewels. For this cause, and no evil-doing, are we cast into holes, dungeons, houses of correction, prisons (neither old nor young being spared, men nor women), and made a prey of in the sight of all nations, under the pretence of being seditious, etc., so that all rude people run upon us to take possession. For which we say, 'The Lord forgive them that have thus done to us'; who doth, and will enable us to suffer; and never shall we lift up hand against any that thus use us; but desire the Lord may have mercy upon them, that they may consider what they have done. For how is it possible for them to requite us for the wrong they have done to us? Who to all nations have sounded us abroad as seditious, who never found plotters against any, since we knew the life and power of Jesus Christ manifested in us, who hath redeemed us from the world, all works of darkness, and plotters therein, by which we know the election, before the world began. So we say, the Lord have mercy upon our enemies and forgive them, for what they have done unto us!

"O! Do as you would be done by; do unto all men as you would have them do unto you; for this is the law and the prophets.

"All plots, insurrections, and riotous meetings we deny, knowing them to be of the devil, the murderer; which we in Christ, who was before they were, triumph over. And all wars and fightings with carnal weapons we deny, who have the sword of the Spirit; and all that wrong us, we leave to the Lord. This is to clear our innocency from the aspersion cast upon us, that we are seditious or plotters."

From Barnet-Hills we came to Swannington in Leicestershire, where William Smith and some other Friends came to me; but they went away towards night, leaving me at a Friend's house in Swannington. At night, as I was sitting in the hall, speaking to a widow woman and her daughter, there came one called Lord Beaumont with a company of soldiers, who, slapping their swords on the door, rushed into the house with swords and pistols in their hands, crying, "Put out the candles, and make fast the doors." Then they seized upon the Friends in the house, and asked, "if there were no more about the house?" The Friends told them, there was one man more in the hall. There being some Friends out of Derbyshire, one of them was named Thomas Fauks; and this Lord Beaumont, after he had asked all their names, bid his man set down that man's name Thomas Fox; but the Friend said, his name was not Fox, but Fauks. In the meantime some of the soldiers came, and brought me out of the hall to him. He asked me my name; I told him, my name was George Fox, and that I was well known by that name. "Ay," said he, "you are known all the world over." I said, "I was known for no hurt, but for good." Then he put his hands into my pockets to search them, and pulled out my comb-case, and afterwards commanded one of his officers to search further for letters, as he pretended. I told him, I was no letter carrier, and asked him, why he came amongst a peaceable people with swords and pistols, without a constable, contrary to the king's proclamation, and to the late act?

For he could not say, there was a meeting, I being only talking with a poor widow woman and her daughter. By reasoning thus with him, he came somewhat down; yet sending for the constables, he gave them charge of us, and to bring us before him next morning. Accordingly the constables set a watch of the town's-people upon us that night, and had us next morning to his house, about a mile from Swannington. When we came before him, he told us "we met contrary to the act." I desired him to show us the act. "Why," says he, "you have it in your pocket." I told him, he did not find us in a meeting. Then he asked us, "whether we would take the oaths of allegiance and supremacy?" I told him, I never took any oath in my life, nor engagement, nor covenant. Yet still he would force the oath upon us. I desired him to show us the oath, that we might see whether we were the persons it was to be tendered to, and whether it was not for the discovery of Popish recusants. At length he brought a little book; but we called for the statute-book. He would not show us that, but caused a mittimus to be made, which mentioned, "that we were to have had a meeting." With this he delivered us to the constables to convey us to Leicester jail. But when they had brought us back to Swannington, being harvest time, it was hard to get anybody to go with us; for the people were loath to go with their neighbours to prison, especially in such a busy time. They would have given us our mittimus, to carry it ourselves to the jail; for it had been usual for constables to give Friends their own mittimuses (for they durst trust Friends), and they have gone themselves with them to the jailer. But we told them, though our Friends had sometimes done so, yet we would not take this mittimus, but some of them should go with us to the jail. At last they hired a poor labouring man to go with us, who was loath to go, though hired. So we rode to Leicester, being five in number; some carried their Bibles open in their hands, declaring the truth to the people, as we rode, in the fields and through the towns, and telling them, "we were prisoners of the Lord Jesus Christ, going to suffer bonds for his name and truth's sake." One woman Friend carried her wheel on her lap to spin on in prison; and the people were mightily affected. At Leicester we went to an inn. The master of the house seemed troubled that we should go to the prison; and being himself in commission, he sent for lawyers in the town to advise with, and would have taken up the mittimus, and kept us in his own house, and not have let us go into the jail. But I told Friends, it would be a great charge to lie at an inn; and many Friends and people would be coming to visit us, and it might be hard for him to bear our having meetings in his house; besides, we had many Friends in the prison already, and we had rather be with them. So we let the man know, that we were sensible of his kindness, and to prison we went; the poor man that brought us thither, delivering both the mittimus and us to the jailer. This jailer had been a very wicked, cruel man. Six or seven Friends being in prison before we came, he had taken some occasion to quarrel with them, and thrust them into the dungeon amongst the felons, where there was hardly room for them to lie down. We stayed all that day in the prison yard, and desired the jailer to let us have some straw. He surily answered, "you do not look like men that would lie on straw." After a while William Smith, a Friend, came to me, and he being acquainted in the house, I asked him, "what rooms there were in it, and what rooms Friends had usually been put into, before they were put into the dungeon?" I asked him also, Whether the jailer or his wife was master? He said, the wife was master; and that though she was lame, and sat mostly in her chair, being only able to go on crutches, yet she would beat her husband when he came within her reach, if he did not do as she would have him. I considered, probably many Friends might come to visit us, and that, if we had a room to ourselves, it would be better for them to speak to me, and me to them, as there should be occasion. Wherefore I desired William Smith to go speak with the woman, and acquaint her, if she would let us have a room, suffer our Friends to come out of the dungeon, and leave it to us, to give her what we would, it might be better for her. He went, and after some reasoning with her, she consented; and we were had into a room. Then we were told, that the jailer would not suffer us to have any drink out of the town into the prison, but that what beer we drank, we must take of him. I told them, I would remedy that, for we would get a pail of water and a little wormwood once a day, and that might serve us; so we should have none of his beer, and the water he could not deny us.

Before we came, when the few Friends that were prisoners there, met together on First-days, if any of them was moved to pray to the Lord, the jailer would come up with his quarter-staff in his hand, and his mastiff dog at his heels, and pluck them down by the hair of the head, and strike them with his staff; but when he struck Friends, the mastiff dog, instead of falling upon them, would take the staff out of his hand. When the First-day came, I spoke to one of my fellow-prisoners, to carry a stool and set it in the yard, and give notice to the debtors and felons, that there would be a meeting in the yard, and they that would hear the word of the Lord declared might come thither. So the debtors and prisoners gathered in the yard, and we went down, and had a very precious meeting, the jailer not meddling. Thus every First-day we had a meeting as long as we stayed in prison; and several came in out of the town and country. Many were convinced, and some received the Lord's truth there, who have stood faithful witnesses for it ever since.

When the sessions came, we were brought before the justices, with many more Friends, sent to prison whilst we were there, to the number of about twenty. Being brought into the court, the jailer put us into the place where the thieves were put, and then some of the justices began to tender the oaths of allegiance and supremacy to us. I told them, I never took any oath in my life, and they knew we could not swear, because Christ and his apostle forbade it; therefore they put it but as a snare to us. We told them, if they could prove, that after Christ and the apostle had forbid swearing, they did ever command Christians to swear, then we would take these oaths; otherwise we were resolved to obey Christ's command and the apostle's exhortation. They said, "we must take the oath, that we might manifest our allegiance to the king." I told them, I had been formerly sent up a prisoner by Colonel Hacker, from that town to London, under pretence that I held meetings to plot to bring in King Charles. I also desired them to read our mittimus, which set forth the cause of our commitment to be, that "we were to have a meeting"; and I said, Lord Beaumont could not by that act send us to jail, unless we had been taken at a meeting, and found to be such persons as the act speaks of; therefore we desired they would read the mittimus, and see how wrongfully we were imprisoned. They would not take notice of the mittimus, but called a jury, and indicted us for refusing to take the oaths of allegiance and supremacy. When the jury was sworn and instructed, as they were going out, one that had been an alderman of the city, spoke to them, and bid them, "have a good conscience"; and one of the jury, being a peevish man, told the justices, there was one affronted the jury; whereupon they called him up, and tendered him the oath also, and he took it.

While we were standing where the thieves used to stand, a cutpurse had his hand in several Friends' pockets. Friends declared it to the justices and showed them the man. They called him up before them, and upon examination he could not deny it; yet they set him at liberty.

It was not long before the jury returned, and brought us in guilty; and then, after some words, the justices whispered together, and bid the jailer take us down to prison again; but the Lord's power was over them and his everlasting truth, which we declared boldly amongst them. There being a great concourse of people, most of them followed us; so that the cryer and bailiffs were fain to call the people back again to the court. We declared the truth as we went down the streets all along, till we came to the jail, the streets being full of people. When we were in our chamber again, after some time the jailer came to us, and desired all to go forth that were not prisoners. When they were gone, he said, "Gentlemen, it is the court's pleasure, that ye should all be set at liberty, except those that are in for tithes; and you know, there are fees due to me; but I shall leave it to you to give me what you will."

CHAPTER XV

1663–66

Having passed through Norfolk, Suffolk, Essex, and Hertfordshire, we came to London again; where I stayed a while, visiting Friends in their meetings, which were very large, and the Lord's power was over all. After some time I left the city again, and travelled into Kent, having Thomas Briggs with me. We went to Ashford, where we had a quiet, and a very blessed meeting; and on First-day we had a very good and peaceable one at Cranbrook. Then we went to Tenterden, and had one there, to which many Friends came from several parts, and many other people came in, and were reached by the truth. When the meeting was over, I walked with Thomas Briggs into a field, while our horses were got ready; and turning my head, I espied a captain coming, and great company of soldiers with lighted matches and muskets. Some of them came to us, and said, "we must go to their captain." When they had brought us before him, he asked, "where is George Fox? Which is he?" I said, "I am the man." Then he came to me and was somewhat struck, and said, "I will secure you among the soldiers." So he called for them to take me. He took Thomas Briggs, and the man of the house, with many more; but the power of the Lord was mightily over them all. Then he came to me again, and said, "I must go along with him to the town"; and he carried himself pretty civilly, bidding the soldiers bring the rest after. As we walked, I asked him, "why they did thus"; for I had not seen so much to do a great while, and I bid him be civil to his peaceable neighbours. When we were come to the town, they had us to an inn that was the jailer's house; and after a while the mayor of the town, and this captain, and the lieutenant, who were justices, came together and examined me, "why I came thither to make a disturbance?" I told them, I did not come to make a disturbance, neither had I made any since I came. They said, "there was a law against the Quakers' meetings, made only against them." I told them, I knew no such law. Then they brought forth the act that was made against Quakers and others; I told them, that was against such as were a terror to the king's subjects, and were enemies, and held principles dangerous to the government, and therefore that was not against us, for we held truth; and our principles were not dangerous to the government, and our meetings were peaceable, as they knew, who knew their neighbours were a peaceable people. They told me, "I was an enemy to the king." I answered, we loved all people and were enemies to none; that I, for my own part, had been cast into Derby dungeon, about the time of Worcester fight, because I would not take up arms against him, and that I was afterwards brought by Colonel Hacker to London, as a plotter to bring in King Charles, and was kept prisoner there till set at liberty by Oliver. They asked me, "whether I was imprisoned in the time of the insurrection?" I said, yes; I had been imprisoned then, and since that also, and had been set at liberty by the king's own command. I opened the act to them, and showed them the king's late declaration; gave them the examples of other justices, and told them also what the House of Lords had said of it. I spoke also to them concerning their own conditions, exhorting them to live in the fear of God, to be tender towards their neighbours that feared Him, and to mind God's wisdom, by which all things were made and created, that they might come to receive it, be ordered by it, and by it order all things to God's glory. They demanded bond of us for our appearance at the sessions; but we, pleading our innocency, refused to give bond. Then they would have us promise to come no more there; but we kept clear of that also. When they saw they could not bring us to their terms, they told us, "we should see they were civil to us, for it was the mayor's pleasure we should all be set at liberty." I told them their civility was noble, and so we parted.

I was kept till the assize; and Judge Turner and Judge Twisden coming that circuit, I was brought before Judge Twisden on the 14th day of the month called March, in the year 1663. When I was set to the bar, I said, "Peace be amongst you all." The judge looked upon me, and said, "What! Do you come into the court with your hat on?" Upon which, the jailer taking it off, I said, "The hat is not the honour that comes from God." Then said the judge to me, "Will you take the oath of allegiance, George Fox?" I said, "I never took any oath in my life, nor any covenant or engagement." "Well," said he, "will you swear or not?" I answered, "I am a Christian, and Christ commands me 'not to swear,' and so does the apostle James, and whether I should obey God or man, do thou judge." "I ask you again," said he, "whether you will swear or not?" I answered again, "I am neither Turk, Jew, nor heathen, but a Christian, and should show forth Christianity." And I asked him, "if he did not know that Christians in the primitive times, under the ten persecutions, and some also of the martyrs in Queen Mary's days, refused swearing, because Christ and the apostle had forbidden it?" I told him also, "they had had experience enough, how many men had first sworn for the king and then against him. But as for me, I had never taken an oath in my life; and my allegiance did not lie in swearing, but in truth and faithfulness; for I honour all men, much more the king. But Christ, who is the great Prophet, and King of kings, who is the Saviour of the world, and the great Judge of all the earth, saith, 'I must not swear.' Now, whether must I obey Christ or thee? For it is in tenderness of conscience, and in obedience to the commands of Christ that I do not swear; and we have the word of a king for tender consciences." Then I asked the judge, "if he owned the king?" "Yes," said he, "I do own the king." "Why then," said I, "dost thou not observe his declaration from Breda, and his promises made since he came into England, 'that no man should be called in question for matters of religion, so long as he lived peaceably?' If thou ownest the king," said I, "why dost thou call me into question, and put me upon taking an oath, which is a matter of religion, seeing neither thou nor any else can charge me with unpeaceable living?" Upon this he was moved, and looking angrily at me, said, "Sirrah, will you swear?" I told him, "I was none of his sirrahs, I was a Christian; and for him, an old man and a judge, to sit there and give nicknames to prisoners, it did not become either his gray hairs or his office." "Well," said he, "I am a Christian too." "Then do Christian works," said I. "Sirrah!" said he, "thou thinkest to frighten me with thy words." Then catching himself, and looking aside, he said, "Hark! I am using the word (sirrah) again"; and so checked himself. I said, "I spoke to thee in love; for that language did not become thee, a judge. Thou oughtest to instruct a prisoner in the law, if he were ignorant and out of the way." "And I speak in love to thee too," said he. "But," said I, "love gives no nicknames." Then he roused himself up, and said, "I will not be afraid of thee, George Fox; thou speakest so loud, thy voice drowns mine and the court's; I must call for three or four criers to drown thy voice: thou hast good lungs." "I am a prisoner here," said I, "for the Lord Jesus Christ's sake; for his sake do I suffer, for him do I stand this day; and if my voice were five times louder, I should lift it up, and sound it for Christ's sake, for whose cause I stand this day before your judgment seat, in obedience to Christ, who commands not to swear; before whose judgment seat you must all be brought and must give an account." "Well," said the judge, "George Fox, say, whether thou wilt take the oath, yea or nay?" I replied, "I say, as I said before, whether ought I to obey God or man, judge thou? If I could take any oath at all, I should take this; for I do not deny some oaths only, or on some occasions, but all oaths, according to Christ's doctrine, who hath commanded his followers not to swear at all. Now if thou or any of you, or your ministers or priests, here, will prove that ever Christ or his apostles, after they had forbid all swearing, commanded Christians to swear, then I will swear." I saw several priests there, but not one of them offered to speak. "Then," said the judge, "I am a servant to the king, and the king sent me not to dispute with you, but to put the laws in execution; therefore tender him the oath of allegiance." "If thou love the king," said I, "why dost thou break his word, and not keep his declarations and speeches, wherein he promised liberty to tender consciences? I am a man of a tender conscience, and, in obedience to Christ's command, I cannot swear." "Then you will not swear," said the judge; "take him away, jailer." I said, "It is for Christ's sake that I cannot swear, and for obedience to his command I suffer, and so the Lord forgive you all." So the jailer took me away; but I felt the mighty power of the Lord was over them all.

Now Justice Fleming being one of the fiercest and most violent justices in persecuting Friends, and sending his honest neighbours to prison for religion's sake, and many Friends being at this time in Lancaster jail committed by him, and some have died in prison, we that were then prisoners had it upon us to write to him, as follows:

"O Justice Fleming!

"Mercy, compassion, love, and kindness adorn and grace men and magistrates. O! Dost thou not hear the cry of the widows, and the cry of the fatherless, who were made so through persecution! Were they not driven, like sheep, from constable to constable, as though they had been the greatest transgressors or malefactors in the land? Which grieved and tendered the hearts of many sober people, to see how their innocent neighbours and countrymen, who were of a peaceable carriage, and honest in their lives and conversations amongst men, were used and served! One more is dead whom thou sent to prison, having left five children, both fatherless and motherless. How canst thou do otherwise than take care of these fatherless infants, and also of the other's wife and family? Is it not thy place? Consider Job (Ch. xxix). He was a father to the poor, he delivered the poor that cried, and the fatherless that had none to help. He broke the jaws of the wicked, and plucked the spoil out of his teeth. But oh! Measure thy life, and his, and take heed of the day of God's eternal judgment, which will come, and the sentence and decree from Christ, when every man must give an account, and receive a reward according to

his deeds. Then it will be said, 'O, where are the months that are
past!' Again, Justice Fleming, consider, when John Stubbs was
brought before thee, having a wife and four small children, and little to
live on, but what they honestly got by their own diligence, as soon as
he appeared thou criedst out, 'Put the oath to that man.' And when he
confessed that he was but a poor man, thou hadst no regard; but cast
away pity, not hearing what he would say. And now he is kept in
prison, because he could not swear, and break the command of Christ
and the apostle; it is to be hoped thou wilt take care for his family,
that his children do not starve; and see that they do not want bread.
Can this be allegiance to the king, to do that which Christ and his
apostle say is evil, and brings into condemnation? Would not you have
cast Christ and the apostle into prison, who commanded 'not to swear,'
if they had been in your days?

"Consider also thy poor neighbour, William Wilson, who was
known to all the parish and neighbours to be an industrious man, and
careful to maintain his wife and children; yet had little, but what he
got with his hands in diligence and travels to supply himself. How
should his wife maintain her children, when thou hast cast her husband into prison, and thereby made him incapable of working for
them? Therefore it may be expected, thou wilt have a care of his wife
and children, and see they do not want; for how should they live, having no other way to be sustained, but by the little that he got? Surely
the noise of this is in the very markets, the death of thy two neighbours; and the cry of the widows and fatherless is heard. All those fatherless and widows are made so for righteousness' sake. For might
not John Stubbs and William Wilson have had their liberty still, if
they would have sworn, though they had been such as go after mountebanks and stage-plays, or run a hunting? O! Consider, for the Lord's
mind is otherwise; he is tender. And the king hath declared his mind
to be, that there should be no cruelty inflicted upon his peaceable subjects. Besides, several poor, honest people were fined, who had need to
have something given them; and it had been more honourable to have
given them something, than to fine them and send them to prison;
some of whom live upon the charity of other people. What honour or
grace can it be to thee, to cast thy poor neighbours into prison who
are peaceable, seeing thou knowest these people cannot do that which
thou requirest of them, if it were to save their lives, or all that they
have? Because in tenderness they cannot take any oath, thou makest
that a snare to them. What, thinkest thou, do the people say concerning this? 'We know,' say they, 'the Quakers' principle, that keep to yea
and nay; but we see others swear and forswear.' For many of you have

sworn first one way and then another. So we leave it to the Spirit of God in thy conscience, Justice Fleming, who wast so eager for the taking of George Fox, and so offended with them that had not taken him, and now hast fallen upon thy poor neighbours. But, oh! Where is thy pity for their poor, fatherless children, and motherless infants? O, take heed of Herod's hard-heartedness, and casting away all pity! Esau did so, not Jacob.

"Here is also Thomas Walters, of Bolton, cast into prison, and the oath imposed on him through thee; and for denying to swear at all, in obedience to Christ's command, he is continued in prison; having five small children, and his wife near confinement. Surely thou shouldst take care for them also, and see that his wife and small children do not want; who are as fatherless, and she as a widow, through thee. Dost thou not hear in thy ears the cry of the fatherless, and the cry of the widows, and the blood of the innocent speak, who through thee have been persecuted to prison, and are now dead? O! Heavy sentence at the day of judgment! How wilt thou answer, when thou and thy works come to be judged, when thou shalt be brought before the judgment seat of the Almighty, who in thy prosperity hast made widows and fatherless for righteousness' sake, and for tenderness of conscience towards God? The Lord knows and sees it! O man! Consider in thy lifetime, how thou hast stained thyself with the blood of the innocent! When thou hadst power, and might have done good amongst thy peaceable neighbours, and would not, but used thy power not to a good intent, but contrary to the Lord's mind and to the king's. The king's favour, his mercy, and clemency to sober people, and to tender consciences, have been manifested by declarations and proclamations, which thou hast abused and slighted by persecuting his peaceable subjects. For at London, and in other parts, the Quakers' meetings are peaceable; and if thou look but as far as Yorkshire, where the plot hath been, Friends' innocency hath cleared itself in the hearts of sober justices; and for you here to fall upon your peaceable neighbours and people, and to be rigorous and violent against them that are tender, godly, and righteous, it is no honour to you. How many drunkards and swearers, fighters, and such as are subject to vice, have you caused to be brought before your courts? It were more honourable for you to look after such; for the law was not made for the righteous, but for sinners and transgressors. Therefore, consider, and be humbled for these things; for the Lord may do to thee as thou hast done to others; and thou dost not know how soon there may be a cry in thy own family, as the cry is amongst thy neighbours, of the fatherless and widows that are made so through thee. But the Quakers can and do say, 'the Lord forgive thee, and lay not these things to thy charge, if it be his will.'"

CHAPTER XVI

1666–69

As I was in bed at Bristol, the word of the Lord came to me, that I must go back to London. Next morning Alexander Parker and several others came to me: I asked them, "what they felt?" They in like manner asked me, "what was upon me?" I told them, "I felt I must return to London." They said, "the same was upon them." So we gave up to return to London; for whatever way the Lord moved and led us, thither we went in his power. Leaving Bristol, we passed into Wiltshire, and established the men's monthly meetings in the Lord's power there; and visited Friends till we came to London.

After we had visited Friends in the city, I was moved to exhort them to bring all their marriages to the men's and women's meetings, that they might lay them before the faithful; that care might be taken to prevent those disorders that had been committed by some. For many had married contrary to their relations' minds; and some young, raw people that came amongst us, had mixed with the world. Widows had married without making provision for their children by their former husbands, before their second marriage. Yet I had given forth a paper concerning marriages about the year 1653, when truth was but little spread over the nation; advising Friends who might be concerned in that case, "that they might lay it before the faithful in time, before anything was concluded, and afterwards publish it in the end of a meeting, or in a market, as they were moved thereto. And when all things were found clear, they being free from all others and their relations satisfied, they might appoint a meeting on purpose for the taking of each other, in the presence of at least twelve faithful witnesses." Yet these directions not being observed, and truth being now more spread over the nation, it was therefore ordered, by the same power and Spirit of God, "that marriages should be laid before the men's monthly and quarterly meetings, or as the meetings were then established; that Friends might see that the relations of those that proceeded to marriage, were satisfied; that the parties were clear from all others; and that widows had made provision for their first husband's children, before they married again; and what else was needful to be inquired into; that all things might be kept clean and pure, and be done in righteousness to the glory of God." Afterwards it was ordered, in the wisdom of God, "that if either of the parties, that intended to marry, came out of another nation, county, or monthly meeting, they should bring a certificate from the monthly meeting to which they belonged; for the satisfaction of the monthly meeting before which they came to lay their intentions of marriage."

These things, with many other services for God, being set in order, and settled in the churches in the city, I passed out of London, in the leadings of the Lord's power, into Hertfordshire. After I had visited Friends, and the men's monthly meetings were settled there, I had a great meeting at Baldock, of many sorts of people. Then returning towards London by Waltham, I advised the setting up of a school there for teaching boys; and also a girls' school at Shacklewell for instructing them in whatsoever things were civil and useful.

CHAPTER XVII

1669–71

After this meeting in Gloucestershire was over, we travelled till we came to Bristol; where I met with Margaret Fell, who was come to visit her daughter Yeomans. I had seen from the Lord a considerable time before, that I should take Margaret Fell to be my wife. And when I first mentioned it to her, she felt the answer of Life from God thereunto. But though the Lord had opened this thing to me, yet I had not received a command from the Lord for the accomplishing of it then. Wherefore I let the thing rest, and went on in the work and service of the Lord as before, according as he led me; travelling up and down in this nation, and through Ireland. But now being at Bristol, and finding Margaret Fell there, it opened in me from the Lord, that the thing should be accomplished. After we had discoursed the matter together, I told her, "if she also was satisfied with the accomplishing of it now, she should first send for her children"; which she did. When the rest of her daughters were come, I asked both them and her sons-in-law, "if they had anything against it, or for it"; and they all severally expressed their satisfaction therein. Then I asked Margaret, "if she had fulfilled and performed her husband's will to her children." She replied, "the children knew that." Whereupon I asked them, "whether, if their mother married, they should not lose by it?" And I asked Margaret, "whether she had done anything in lieu of it, which might answer it to the children?" The children said, "she had answered it to them, and desired me to speak no more of it." I told them, "I was plain, and would have all things done plainly; for I sought not any outward advantage to myself." So after I had thus acquainted the children with it, our intention of marriage was laid before Friends, both privately and publicly, to their full satisfaction, many of whom gave testimony thereunto that it was of God. Afterwards, a meeting being appointed for the accomplishing thereof, in the meeting-house at Broad-Mead in Bristol, we took each other, the Lord joining us together in the honourable marriage, in the everlasting covenant and immortal Seed of life. In the sense whereof, living and weighty testimonies were borne thereunto by Friends, in the movings of the heavenly power which united us together. Then was a certificate, relating both the proceedings and the marriage, openly read, and signed by the relations, and by most of the ancient Friends of that city, besides many others from divers parts of the nation.

We stayed about a week in Bristol, and then went together to Oldstone; where taking leave of each other in the Lord, we parted, betaking ourselves to our several services, Margaret returning homewards to the north, and I passing on in the work of the Lord, as before. I travelled through Wiltshire, Berkshire, Oxfordshire, and Buckinghamshire, and so to London, visiting Friends, in all which countries I had many large and precious meetings.

Being in London, it came upon me to write to Friends throughout the nation, about "putting out poor children to trades." Wherefore I sent the following epistle to the quarterly meetings of Friends in all counties:

"My dear Friends:

"Let every quarterly meeting make inquiry through all the monthly and other meetings, to know all Friends that are widows, or others, that have children fit to put out to apprenticeships; so that once a quarter you may set forth an apprentice from your quarterly meeting; and so you may set forth four in a year in each county, or more, if there be occasion. This apprentice, when out of his time, may help his father or mother, and support the family that is decayed; and in so doing, all may come to live comfortably. This being done in your quarterly meetings, ye will have knowledge through the county in the monthly and particular meetings, of masters fit for them, and of such trades as their parents or you desire, or the children are most inclinable to. Thus being placed out with Friends, they may be trained up in truth; and by this means in the wisdom of God, you may preserve Friends' children in the truth, and enable them to be a strength and help to their families, and nursers and preservers of their relations in their ancient days. Thus also things being ordered in the wisdom of God, you will take off a continual maintenance, and free yourselves from much cumber. For in the country, ye know, ye may set forth an apprentice for a little to several trades, as bricklayers, masons, carpenters, wheelwrights, ploughwrights, tailors, tanners, curriers, blacksmiths, shoemakers, nailers, butchers, weavers of linen and woollen, stuffs and serges, etc. And you may do well to have a stock in your quarterly meetings for that purpose. All that is given by any Friends at their decease (except it be given to some particular use, person, or meeting), may be brought to the public stock for that purpose. This will be a way for the preserving of many that are poor among you, and it will be a way of making up poor families. In several counties it is practiced already. Some quarterly meetings set forth two apprentices; and sometimes the children of others that are laid on the parish. You may bind them for fewer or more years, according to which ye may come to help the children of poor Friends, that they may come to support their families, and preserve them in the fear of God. So no more, but my love in the everlasting Seed, by which ye will have wisdom to order all things to the glory of God.

G.F.

London, 1st of 11th Month, 1669."

I stayed not long in London; but having visited Friends, and finding things there quiet and well, the Lord's power being over all, I passed into Essex, and Hertfordshire, where I had many precious meetings. Intending to go as far as Leicestershire, I wrote a letter to my wife, before I left London, to acquaint her therewith, that if she found it convenient to her she might meet me there. From Hertfordshire I turned into Cambridgeshire, thence into Huntingdonshire, and so into Leicestershire; where, instead of meeting with my wife, I heard that she was haled out of her house to Lancaster prison again, by an order obtained from the king and council, to fetch her back to prison upon the old premunire; though she had been discharged from that imprisonment by their order the year before. Wherefore, having visited Friends as far as Leicestershire, I returned by Derbyshire into Warwickshire, and so to London, having had many large and blessed meetings in the several counties I passed through, and been sweetly refreshed amongst Friends in my travels.

As soon as I reached London, I hastened Mary Lower and Sarah Fell (two of my wife's daughters) to the king, to acquaint him how their mother was dealt with, and see if they could obtain a full discharge for her, that she might enjoy her estate and liberty without molestation. This was somewhat difficult, but by diligent attendance they at length obtained it; the king given command to Sir John Otway, to signify his pleasure therein by letter to the sheriff, and others concerned therein in the country. Which letter Sarah Fell going down with her brother and sister Rous, carried with her to Lancaster; and by them I wrote to my wife, as follows:

"My dear heart in the truth and life, that changeth not:

"It was upon me that Mary Lower and Sarah should go to the king concerning thy imprisonment, and to Kirby, that the power of the Lord might appear over them all in thy deliverance. They went, and then they thought to come down; but it was upon me to stay them a little longer, that they might follow the business till it was effected; which it now is, and is here sent. The late declaration of mine hath been very serviceable, people being generally satisfied with it. So no more, but my love in the holy Seed.

G.F."

The declaration here mentioned was a printed sheet, written upon occasion of a new persecution stirred up. For by the time I was returned out of Leicestershire to London, a fresh storm was risen, occasioned (it was thought) by that tumultuous meeting in a steeplehouse in Wiltshire or Gloucestershire, mentioned a little before; from which, it was said, some members of parliament took advantage to get an act passed against seditious conventicles; which soon after came forth and was turned against us, who of all people were free from sedition and tumult. Whereupon I wrote a declaration, showing from the preamble and terms of the act, that we were not such a people, nor our meeting such as were described in that act. I wrote also another short paper on the occasion of that act against meetings, opening our case to the magistrates, as follows:

"O Friends, consider this act, which limits us to five. Is this doing as ye would be done by? Would ye be so served yourselves? We own Christ Jesus as well as you, his coming, death, and resurrection; and if we be contrary minded to you in some things, is not this the apostle's exhortation, 'to wait till God hath revealed it'? Doth not he say, 'what is not of faith, is sin'? Seeing we have not faith in things, which ye would have us to do, would it not be sin in us, if we should act contrary to our faith? Why should any man have power over another man's faith, seeing Christ is the author of it? When the apostles preached in the name of Jesus, and great multitudes heard them, and the rulers forbade them to speak any more in that name, did not they bid them judge whether it were better to obey God or man? Would not this act have taken hold of the twelve apostles and seventy disciples; for they met often together? If there had been a law made then, that not above five should have met with Christ, would not that have been a hindering of him from meeting with his disciples? Do ye think that He, who is the wisdom of God, or his disciples, would have obeyed it? If such a law had been made in the apostles' days, that not above five might meet together, who had been different minded from either the Jews or the Gentiles, do ye think the churches of Christ at Corinth, Philippi, Ephesus, Thessalonica, or the rest of the gathered churches, would have obeyed it? O therefore consider! For we are Christians, and partake of the nature and life of Christ. Strive not to limit the Holy One; for God's power cannot be limited, and is not to be quenched. Do unto all men as ye would have them do unto you; for that is the law and the prophets.

"This is from those who wish you all well, and desire your everlasting good and prosperity, called Quakers; who seek the peace and good of all people, though they afflict us, and cause us to suffer.

G.F."

As I had endeavoured to soften the magistrates, and to take off the sharpness of their edge in the execution of the act, so it was upon me to write a few lines to Friends "to strengthen and encourage them to stand fast in their testimony, and bear, with Christian patience and content, the suffering that was coming upon them." This I did in the following epistle:

"My dear Friends, Keep in the faith of God above all outward things, and in his power, that hath given you dominion over all. The same power of God is still with you to deliver you as formerly; for God and his power is the same; his Seed is over all, and before all; and will be, when that which makes to suffer, is gone. Be of good faith in that which changeth not; for whatsoever any do against the truth, it will come upon themselves, and fall as a millstone on their heads. If the Lord suffer you to be tried, let all be given up; and look at the Lord and his power, which is over the whole world, and will remain when the world is gone. In the Lord's power and truth rejoice over that which makes to suffer, in the Seed, which was before it was; for the life, truth, and power of God is over all. All keep in that; and if ye suffer in that, it is to the Lord.

"Friends, the Lord hath blessed you in outward things; and now the Lord may try you, whether your minds be in outward things, or with the Lord that gave you them? Therefore keep in the Seed by which all outward things were made, and which is over them all. What! Shall not I pray, and speak to God, with my face towards heavenly Jerusalem, according to my wonted time? Let not anyone's Delilah shave his head, lest he lose his strength; neither rest in its lap, lest the Philistines be upon you. For your rest is in Christ Jesus; therefore rest not in anything else.

G.F.

London, 12th of 2nd Month, 1670."

Next day, finding my service for the Lord finished there, we passed toward Rochester. On the way, as I was walking down a hill, a great weight and oppression fell upon my spirit; I got on my horse again, but the weight remained so that I was hardly able to ride. At length we came to Rochester, but I was much spent, being so extremely laden and burdened with the world's spirits, that my life was oppressed under them. I got with difficulty to Gravesend, and lay at an inn there; but could hardly either eat or sleep. The next day John Rous and Alexander Parker went for London; and John Stubbs being come to me, we went over the ferry into Essex. We came to Hornchurch, where was a meeting on First-day. After it I rode with great uneasiness to Stratford, to a Friend's house, whose name was Williams, and who had formerly been a captain. Here I lay exceedingly weak, and at last lost both hearing and sight. Several Friends came to me from London: and I told them that "I should be as a sign to such as would not see, and such as would not hear the truth." In this condition I continued some time. Several came about me; and though I could not see their persons, I felt and discerned their spirits, who were honest hearted, and who were not. Divers Friends who practice physic, came to see me, and would have given me medicines, but I was not to meddle with any; for I was sensible I had a travail to go through; and therefore desired none but solid, weighty Friends might be about me. Under great sufferings and travails, sorrows and oppressions, I lay for several weeks, whereby I was brought so low and weak in body, that few thought I could live. Some that were with me went away, saying "they would not see me die"; and it was reported both in London and in the country, that I was deceased; but I felt the Lord's power inwardly supporting me. When they that about me had given me up to die, I spoke to them to get a coach to carry me to Gerrard Roberts's, about twelve miles off; for I found it was my place to go thither. I had now recovered a little glimmering sight, so that I could discern the people and fields as I went, and that was all. When I came to Gerrard's, he was very weak; and I was moved to speak to him, and encourage him. After I had stayed about three weeks there, it was with me to go to Enfield. Friends were afraid of my removing; but I told them I might safely go. When I had taken my leave of Gerrard, and was come to Enfield, I went first to visit Amor Stoddart, who lay very weak, and almost speechless. I was moved to tell him, "he had been faithful as a man, and faithful to God; and that the immortal Seed of life was his crown." Many more words I was moved to speak to him, though I was then so weak, I was hardly able to stand; and within a few days after, Amor died. I went to the widow Dry's at Enfield, in which I lay all that winter, warring in spirit with the evil spirits of the world, that warred against truth and Friends. For there were great persecutions at this time; some meeting houses were pulled down, and many were broken up by soldiers. Sometimes a troop of horse, or a company of foot came; and some broke their swords, carbines, muskets, and pikes, with beating Friends; and many they wounded, so that their blood lay in the streets. Amongst others that were active in this cruel persecution at London, my old adversary Colonel Kirby was one; who, with a company of foot, went to break up several meetings; and he would often inquire for me at the meetings he broke up. One time as he went over the water to Horsleydown, there happening some scuffle between some of his soldiers and some of the watermen, he bid his men "fire at them." They did so, and killed some.

I was under great sufferings at this time, beyond what I have words to declare. For I was brought into the deep, and saw all the religions of the world, and people that lived in them, and the priests that held them up, who were as a company of men-eaters, eating up the people like bread, and gnawing the flesh from off their bones. But as for true religion and worship, and ministers of God, alack! I saw there were none amongst those of the world that pretended to it. For they that pretended to be the church, were but a company of men-eaters, men of cruel visages, and of long teeth; and, though they had cried against the men-eaters in America, I saw they were in the same nature. And as the great professing Jews did "eat up God's people like bread," and the false prophets and priests then preached peace to people, so long as they "put into their mouths and fed them"; but if they fed them not, they prepared war against them, "they ate their flesh off their bones, and chopped them for the caldron"; so these that profess themselves Christians now (both priests and professors), and are not in the same power and Spirit that Christ and the holy prophets and apostles were in, are in the same nature that the old professing Jews were in, and are men-eaters as well as they. These stirred up persecution and set the wicked informers to work; so that a Friend could hardly speak a few words in a private family, before they sat down to eat meat, but some were ready to inform against them. A particular instance of which I have heard as follows:

At Droitwich John Cartwright came to a Friend's house, and

being moved of the Lord to speak a few words before he sat down to supper, there came an informer, and stood hearkening under the window. When he had heard the Friend speak, hoping to get some gain to himself, he went and informed, and got a warrant to distrain his goods, under pretence that there was a meeting at his house; whereas there were none in the house at that time, but the Friend, the man of the house, his wife, and their maid-servant. But this evil-minded man, as he came back with his warrant in the night, fell off his horse, and broke his neck. So there was a wretched end of a wicked informer, who hoped to enrich himself by spoiling Friends; but the Lord prevented him, and cut him off in his wickedness.

Now, though it was a cruel, bloody, persecuting time, yet the Lord's power went over all, and his everlasting Seed prevailed; and Friends were made to stand firm and faithful in the Lord's power. Some sober people of other professions would say, "if Friends did not stand, the nation would run into debauchery."

Though by reason of my weakness, I could not travel amongst Friends as I used to do, yet in the motion of life, I sent the following lines as an encouraging testimony to them:

"My Dear Friends:

"The Seed is above all. In it walk; in which ye all have life. Be not amazed at the weather; for always the just suffered by the unjust, but the just had the dominion. All along ye may see, by faith the mountains were subdued; and the rage of the wicked, and his fiery darts, were quenched. Though the waves and storms are high, yet your faith will keep you so as to swim above them; for they are but for a time, and the truth is without time. Therefore keep on the mountain of holiness, ye who are led to it by the light, where nothing shall hurt. Do not think that anything will outlast the truth, which standeth sure; and is over that which is out of the truth; for the good will overcome the evil; the light, darkness; the life, death; virtue, vice; and righteousness, unrighteousness. The false prophet cannot overcome the true; but the true prophet, Christ, will overcome all the false. So be faithful, and live in that which doth not think the time long.

                                                                G.F."

After some time it pleased the Lord to allay the heat of this violent persecution; and I felt in spirit an overcoming of the spirits of those men-eaters, that had stirred it up, and carried it on to that height of cruelty, though I was outwardly very weak. And I plainly felt, and those Friends that were with me, and that came to visit me, took notice, that as the persecution ceased, I came from under the travails and sufferings, that had lain with such weight upon me; so that towards the spring I began to recover, and to walk up and down, beyond the expectation of many, who did not think I could ever have gone abroad again.

Whilst I was under this spiritual suffering, the state of the New Jerusalem, which comes down out of heaven, was opened to me; which some carnal-minded people had looked upon to be like an outward city dropped out of the element. I saw the beauty and glory of it, the length, the breadth, and the height thereof, all in complete proportion. I saw, that all who are within the light of Christ, and in his faith, which he is the author of; and in the Spirit, the Holy Ghost, which Christ and the holy prophets and apostles were in; and within the grace, and truth, and power of God, which are the walls of the city; such are within the city, are members of it, and have right to eat of the tree of life, which yields her fruit every month, and whose leaves are for the healing of the nations. But they that are out of the grace, truth, light, Spirit, and power of God; they who resist the Holy Ghost, quench, vex, and grieve the Spirit of God; who hate the light, turn the grace of God into wantonness, and do despite to the Spirit of Grace; they who have erred from the faith, and made shipwreck of it and of a good conscience, who abuse the power of God, and despise prophesying, revelation, and inspiration; these are the dogs and unbelievers that are without the city. These make up the great city Babylon, confusion, and her cage, the power of darkness; and the evil spirit of error surrounds and covers them over. In this great city Babylon are the false prophets, in the false power and false spirit; the beast, in the dragon's power, and the whore that is gone a whoring from the Spirit of God, and from Christ her husband. But the Lord's power is over all this power of darkness, false prophets, and their worshippers, who are for the lake which burns with fire. Many things more did I see concerning the heavenly city, the New Jerusalem, which are hard to be uttered, and would be hard to be received. But, in short, this holy city is within the light, and all that are within the light, are within the city; the gates thereof stand open all the day (for there is no night there), that all may come in. Christ's blood being shed for every man, he tasted death for every man, and enlighteneth every man that cometh into the world; and his grace that brings salvation having appeared to all men, there is no place or language where his voice may not be heard. The Christians in the primitive times were called by Christ, "a city set upon a hill"; they were also called "the light of the world," and "the salt of the earth"; but when Christians lost the light, and salt, and power of God, then they came to be trodden under foot, like unsavoury salt. Even as the Jews, who while they kept the law of God, were preserved above all nations; but when they turned their backs on God and his law, they were trodden under foot of other nations. Adam and Eve, while they obeyed God, were kept in his image and in the paradise of God, in dominion over all the works of his hands; but when they disobeyed God, they lost his image, the righteousness and the holiness in which they were made; they lost their dominion, were driven out of paradise; and so fell under the dark power of Satan, and came under the chains of darkness. But the promise of God was, "that the Seed of the woman, Christ Jesus, should bruise the serpent's head," should break his power and authority, which had led into captivity, and had held man therein. So Christ, who is the first and the last, sets man free, and is the resurrection of the just and unjust, the judge of the quick and dead; and they that are in him are invested with everlasting rest and peace, out of all the labours, and travails, and miseries of Adam in the fall. So he is sufficient and of ability to restore man into the state he was in before he fell; and not into that state only, but into that also that never fell, even to himself.

I had also in this time a great exercise and travail of spirit upon me, concerning the powers and rules of these nations, from the sense I had of the many tender visitations and faithful warnings, that had been given them, and of their great abuse thereof, who had refused to hear, and rejected the counsel of the Lord. And though I knew Friends would be clear of their blood, yet I could not but mourn over them, and gave forth these few lines following concerning them:

"We have given them a visitation, have faithfully warned them, have declared to them our innocency and uprightness, and that we never did any hurt to the king, nor to any of his people. We have nothing in our hearts but love and good will to him and his people, and desire their eternal welfare. But if they will not hear, the day of judgment and of sorrow, of torment, misery, and sudden destruction, will come from the Lord upon them, that have been the cause of the sufferings of many thousands of simple, innocent, harmless people that have done them no hurt, nor have had any ill-will towards him or them; but have desired their eternal good for the eternal truth's sake. Destruction will come upon them that turn the sword backward. Therefore do not blind your eyes, the Lord will bring swift destruction and misery upon you; surely he will do it, and will relieve his innocent people, who have groaned for your deliverance out of wickedness. Blessed be the Lord God, that he hath a people in this nation, that seek the good of all men upon the face of the earth; for we have the mind of the Lord Jesus Christ, that desires not the death of a sinner, but the salvation and good of all. Blessed be the name of the Lord our God forever.

G.F."

CHAPTER XVIII

1671–72

I mentioned before, that, upon the notice I received of my wife's being imprisoned again, I sent two of her daughters to the king, and they procured his order to the sheriff of Lancashire, for her discharge. But though I expected she would be set at liberty thereby, this violent storm of persecution coming suddenly on, the persecutors there found means to hold her still in prison. But now the persecution a little ceasing, I was moved to speak to Martha Fisher and another woman Friend, to go to the king about her liberty. They went in faith, and in the Lord's power, who gave them favour with the king, so that he granted a discharge under the broad-seal, to clear both her and her estate, after she had been ten years a prisoner, and premunired; the like whereof was scarcely to be heard of in England. I sent down the discharge forthwith by a Friend; by

whom also I wrote to her, informing her how to get it delivered to
the justices, and acquainting her that it was upon me from the Lord
to go beyond the seas to visit America; and therefore desired her to
hasten to London, as soon as she could conveniently, after she had
obtained her liberty, because the ship was then fitting for the voyage. In the meantime I got to Kingston, and stayed at John Rous's
till my wife came up, and then I began to prepare for the voyage.
But the Yearly Meeting being near at hand, I stayed till that was
over. Many Friends came up to it from all parts of the nation, and a
very large and precious meeting it was; for the Lord's power was
over all, and his glorious everlasting-renowned Seed of life was exalted above all.

After this meeting was over, and I had finished my services for
the Lord in England, the ship and the Friends that intended to go
with me being ready, I went to Gravesend on the 12th of 6th
month, my wife and several Friends accompanying me to the
Downs. We went from Wapping in a barge to the ship, which lay a
little below Gravesend, and there we found the Friends that were
bound for voyage with me, who had gone down to the ship the
night before. Their names were Thomas Briggs, William Edmundson, John Rous, John Stubbs, Solomon Eccles, James Lancaster,
John Cartwright, Robert Widders, George Pattison, John Hull, Elizabeth Hooton, and Elizabeth Miers. The vessel was a yacht, called
the *Industry;* the captain's name was Thomas Forster, and the number of passengers about fifty. I lay that night on board, but most of
the Friends at Gravesend. Early next morning the passengers, and
those Friends that intended to accompany us to the Downs, being
come on board, we took our leave in great tenderness of those that
came with us to Gravesend only, and set sail about six in the morning for the Downs. Having a fair wind, we outsailed all the ships
that were outward bound, and got thither by evening. Some of us
went ashore that night, and lodged at Deal; where, we understood,
an officer had orders from the governor to take our names in writing; which he did next morning, though we told him they had been
taken at Gravesend. In the afternoon, the wind serving, I took leave
of my wife and other Friends, and went on board. Before we could
sail, there being two of the king's frigates riding in the Downs, the
captain of one of them sent his pressmaster on board us, who took
three of our seamen. This would certainly have delayed, if not

wholly prevented, our voyage, had not the captain of the other frigate, being informed of the leakiness of our vessel, and the length of
our voyage, in compassion and much civility, spared us two of his
own men. Before this was over, a custom-house officer came on
board to peruse packets and get fees; so that we were kept from
sailing till about sunset; during which delay a very considerable
number of merchantmen, outward-bound, were got several leagues
before us. Being clear, we set sail in the evening, and next morning
overtook part of that fleet about the height of Dover. We soon
reached the rest, and in a little time left them all behind; for our
yacht was counted a very swift sailer. But she was very leaky, so
that the seamen and some of the passengers did, for the most part,
pump day and night. One day they observed, that in two hours
time she sucked in sixteen inches of water in the well.

When we had been about three weeks at sea, one afternoon we
spied a vessel about four leagues astern of us. Our master said it
was a Sallee man-of-war, that seemed to give us chase. Our master
said, "Come, let us go to supper, and when it grows dark we shall
lose him." This he spoke to please and pacify the passengers, some
of whom began to be very apprehensive of the danger. But Friends
were well satisfied in themselves, having faith in God, and no fear
upon their spirits. When the sun was gone down, I saw the ship out
of my cabin making towards us. When it grew dark, we altered our
course to miss her; but she altered also, and gained upon us. At
night the master and others came into my cabin, and asked me,
"what they should do?" I told them, "I was no mariner," and I
asked them, "what they thought was best to do?" They said,
"There were but two ways, either to outrun him, or tack about, and
hold the same course we were going before." I told them, "if he
were a thief, they might be sure he would tack about too; and as
for outrunning him, it was to no purpose to talk of that, for they
saw he sailed faster than we." They asked me again, "what they
should do? for," they said, "if the mariners had taken Paul's counsel, they had not come to the damage they did." I answered, "it was
trial of faith, and therefore the Lord was to be waited on for counsel." So retiring in spirit, the Lord showed me, "that his life and
power was placed between us and the ship that pursued us." I told
this to the master and the rest, and that the best way was to tack
about and steer our right course. I desired them also to put out all

their candles, but the one they steered by, and to speak to all the passengers to be still and quiet. About eleven at night the watch called and said, "they were just upon us." That disquieted some of the passengers; whereupon I sat up in my cabin, and looking through the porthole, the moon being not quite down, I saw them very near us. I was getting up to go out of the cabin; but remembering the word of the Lord, "that his life and power was placed between us and them," I lay down again. The master and some of the seamen came again, and asked me, "if they might not steer such a point?" I told them, "they might do as they would." By this time the moon was quite down, a fresh gale arose, and the Lord hid us from them; and we sailed briskly on and saw them no more. The next day, being the first day of the week, we had a public meeting in the ship, as we usually had on that day throughout the voyage, and the Lord's presence was greatly among us. And I desired the people "to mind the mercies of the Lord, who had delivered them; for they might have been all in the Turks' hands by that time, had not the Lord's hand saved them." About a week after, the master and some of the seamen endeavoured to persuade the passengers, that it was not a Turkish pirate that chased us, but a merchantman going to the Canaries. When I heard of it, I asked them, "Why then did they speak so to me? Why did they trouble the passengers? And why did they tack about from him and alter their course?" I told them "they should take heed of slighting the mercies of God."

Afterwards, while we were at Barbadoes, there came in a merchant from Sallee, and told the people, "that one of the Sallee men-of-war saw a monstrous yacht at sea, the greatest that ever he saw, and had her in chase, and was just upon her, but that there was a spirit in her that he could not take." This confirmed us in the belief that it was a Sallee-man we saw make after us, and that it was the Lord that delivered us out of his hands.

I was not seasick during the voyage, as many of the Friends and other passengers were; but the many hurts and bruises I had formerly received, and the infirmities I had contracted in England by extreme cold and hardships, that I had undergone in many long and sore imprisonments, returned upon me at sea; so that I was very ill in my stomach, and full of violent pains in my bones and limbs. This was after I had been at sea about a month; for about three weeks after I came first to sea, I perspired abundantly, chiefly my head, and my body broke out in pimples, and my legs and feet swelled extremely, so that my stockings and slippers could not be drawn on without difficulty and great pain. Suddenly the sweating ceased, so that when I came into the hot climate, where others perspired most freely, I could not perspire at all; but my flesh was hot, dry, and burning; and that which before broke out in pimples, struck in again to my stomach and heart, so that I was very ill, and weak beyond expression. Thus I continued during the rest of the voyage, which was about a month; for we were above seven weeks at sea.

On the third of the eighth month, early in the morning, we discovered the island of Barbadoes, but it was between nine and ten at night ere we came to anchor in Carlisle Bay. We got on shore as soon as we could, and I, with some others, walked to a Friend's house, a merchant, whose name was Richard Forstall, above a quarter of a mile from the bridge. But being very ill and weak, I was so tired with that little walk, that I was in a manner spent by the time I got thither. There I abode very ill for several days, and though they several times gave me things to make me perspire, they could not effect it. But what they gave me did rather parch and dry up my body, and made me probably worse than otherwise I might have been. Thus I continued about three weeks after I landed, having much pain in my bones, joints, and whole body, so that I could hardly get any rest; yet I was pretty cheerful, and my spirit kept above it all. Neither did my illness take me off from the service of truth, but both while I was at sea, and after I came to Barbadoes, before I was able to travel about, I gave forth several papers (having a Friend to write for me), some of which I sent by the first conveyance for England to be printed.

After I had rested three or four days at Richard Forstall's, where many Friends came to visit me, John Rous having borrowed a coach of Colonel Chamberlain, came to fetch me to his father, Thomas Rous's house. But it was late ere we could get thither, and little or no rest could I take that night. A few days after, Colonel Chamberlain, who had so kindly lent his coach, paid me a visit, and was very courteous towards me.

Soon after I came into the island, I was informed of a remarkable passage, wherein the justice of God did eminently appear; it was thus: There was a young man of Barbadoes, whose name was John Drakes (a person of some note in the world's account, but a common swearer and wicked man), who, when in London, had a mind to marry a Friend's daughter, left by her mother very young, and with a considerable portion, to the care and government of several Friends, whereof I was one. He made application to me, that he might have my consent to marry this young maid. I told him, "I was one of her overseers appointed by her mother, who was a widow, to take care of her; that if her mother had intended her for a match to any man of another profession, she would have disposed of her accordingly; but she committed her to us, that she might be trained up in the fear of the Lord, and therefore I should betray the trust reposed in me, if I should consent that he who was out of the fear of God, should marry her; which I would not do." When he saw that he could not obtain his desire, he returned to Barbadoes with great offence of mind against me, but without just cause. Afterwards, when he heard I was coming to Barbadoes, he swore desperately, and threatened, that "if he could possibly procure it, he would have me burned to death when I came there." Which a Friend hearing, asked him "what I had done to him, that he was so violent against me?" He would not answer, but said again, "I'll have him burned." Whereupon the Friend replied, "Do not march on too furiously, lest thou come too soon to thy journey's end." About ten days after, he was struck with a violent burning fever, of which he died; and by which his body was so scorched, that the people said, "it was as black as a coal." Three days before I landed, his body was laid in the dust. This was taken notice of as a sad example.

While I continued so weak, that I could not go abroad to meetings, the other Friends that came over with me, bestirred themselves in the Lord's work. The day but one after we landed, they had a great meeting at the bridge, and after that several others in different parts of the island; which alarmed the people of all sorts, so that many came to our meetings, and some of the chief rank. For they had got my name, understanding I was come upon the island, and expected to see me at those meetings, not knowing that I was unable to go abroad. And indeed, my weakness continued the longer on me, by reason that my spirit was much pressed down at first with the filth and dirt and unrighteousness of the people, which lay as a heavy weight and load upon me. But after I had been above a month upon the island, my spirit became somewhat easier, and I began to recover in some measure my health and strength, and to get abroad among Friends. In the meantime, having opportunity to send to England, I wrote to Friends there, to let them know how it was with me, as follows:

"Dear Friends:

"I have been very weak these seven weeks past, and not able to write myself. My desire is to you and for you all, that ye may live in the fear of God, and in love one unto another, and be subject one to another in the fear of God. I have been weaker in my body than ever I was in my life that I remember, yea, my pains have been such as I cannot express; yet my heart and spirit is strong. I have hardly perspired these seven weeks past, though I am come into a very hot climate, where hardly any but are well nigh continually perspiring; but as for me, my old bruises, colds, numbness, and pains, struck inwardly, even to my very heart. So that I have taken little rest, and the chief things that were comfortable to my stomach, were a little water and powdered ginger; but now I begin to drink a little beer as well as water, and sometimes a little wine and water mixed. Great pains and travails I have felt, and in measure am under; but it is well, my life is over all. This island was to me as all on a fire ere I came to it, but now it is somewhat quenched and abated. I came in weakness amongst those that are strong, and have so continued; but now I am got a little cheery, and over it. Many Friends, and some considerable persons of the world have been with me. I tired out my body much when amongst you in England; it is the Lord's power that helps me; therefore I desire you all to prize the power of the Lord and his truth. I was but weak in body when I left you, after I had been in my great travail amongst you; but after that, it struck all back again into my body, which was not well settled after so sore travails in England. Then I was so tired at sea, that I could not rest, and have had little or no stomach a long time. Since I came into this island, my life hath been very much burdened; but I hope, if the Lord give me strength to manage his work, I shall work thoroughly, and bring things that have been out of course, into better order. So, dear Friends, live all in the peaceable truth, and in the love of it, serving the Lord in newness of life; for glorious things and precious truths have been manifested among you plentifully, and to you the riches of the kingdom have been handed. I have been almost a month in this island, but have not been able to go abroad or ride out; only very lately I rode out twice, a quarter of a mile at a time, which wearied me much. My love in the truth is to you all.

G.F."

Because I was not well able to travel, the Friends of the island concluded to have their men's and women's meeting for the service of the church at Thomas Rous's, where I lay; by which means I was present at each of their meetings, and had very good service for the Lord in both. For they had need of information in many things, divers disorders having crept in for want of care and watchfulness. I exhorted them, more especially at the men's meeting, "to be watchful and careful with respect to marriages, to prevent Friends marrying in near kindreds, and also to prevent over hasty proceedings towards second marriages, after the death of a former husband or wife; advising that a decent regard might be had in such cases to the memory of the deceased husband or wife. As to Friends' children marrying too young, as at thirteen or fourteen years of age, I showed them the unfitness thereof, and the inconveniences and hurts that attend such childish marriages. I admonished them to purge the floor thoroughly, to sweep their houses very clean, that nothing might remain that would defile, and to take care that nothing be spoken, out of their meetings, to the blemishing or defaming one of another. Concerning the registering of marriages, births, and burials, I advised them to keep exact records of each in distinct books for that only use; and also to record in a book for that purpose, the condemnations of such as went out from truth into disorderly practices, and the repentance and restoration of such of them as returned again. I recommended to their care the providing of convenient burying places for Friends, which in some parts were yet wanting. Some directions also I gave them concerning wills, and the ordering of legacies left by Friends for public uses, and other things relating to the affairs of the church. Then as to their blacks or negroes, I desired them to endeavour to train them up in the fear of God, those that were bought, and those born in their families, that all might come to the knowledge of the Lord; that so, with Joshua, every master of a family might say, 'As for me and my house, we will serve the Lord.' I desired them also that they would cause their overseers to deal mildly and gently with their negroes, and not use cruelty towards them, as the manner of some hath been and is; and that after certain years of servitude, they would make them free." Many sweet and precious things were opened in these meetings by the Spirit, and in the power of the Lord, to the edifying, confirming, and building up of Friends, both in the faith and holy order of the gospel.

I set sail from Barbadoes to Jamaica on the 8th of the 11th month, 1671; Robert Widders, William Edmundson, Solomon Eccles, and Elizabeth Hooton, going with me. Thomas Briggs and John Stubbs remained in Barbadoes; with whom were John Rous and William Bailey.

CHAPTER XIX

1672–73

We went on board on the 8th of 1st Month, 1671–72; and having contrary winds, were a full week sailing forwards and backwards, before we could get out of sight of Jamaica. A difficult voyage this proved, and dangerous, especially in passing through the Gulf of Florida, where we met with many trials by winds and storms. But the great God, who is Lord of the sea and land, and who rideth upon the wings of the wind, did by his power preserve us through many and great dangers, when by extreme stress of weather our vessel was many times likely to be upset, and much of her tackling broken. And indeed we were sensible that the Lord was a God at hand, and that his ear was open to the supplications of his people. For when the winds were so strong and boisterous, and the storms and tempests so great, that the sailors knew not what to do, but let the ship go which way she would; then did we pray unto the Lord, who graciously heard us, calmed the winds and the seas, gave us seasonable weather, and made us to rejoice in his salvation; blessed and praised be the holy name of the Lord, whose power hath dominion over all, whom the winds and the seas obey.

We were between six and seven weeks in this passage from Jamaica to Maryland. Some days before we came to land, after we had entered the bay of Patuxent River, a great storm arose, which cast a boat upon us for shelter, in which were several people of account in the world. We took them in; but the boat was lost, with five hundred pounds' worth of goods in it, as they said. They continued on board us several days, not having any means to get off; and we had a very good meeting with them in the ship. But provision grew short, for they brought none in with them; and ours, by reason of the length of our voyage, were well nigh spent when they came to us; so that with their living with us too, we had now little or none left. Whereupon George Pattison took a boat, and ventured his life to get to shore; the hazard was so great, that all but Friends concluded he would be cast away. Yet it pleased the Lord to bring him safe to land; and in a short time after, the Friends of the place came to fetch us to land also, in a seasonable time, for our provisions were quite spent.

We partook also of another great deliverance in this voyage, through the good providence of the Lord, which we came to understand afterwards. For when we were determined to come from Jamaica, we had our choice of two vessels, that were both bound for the same coast. One of these was a frigate, the other a yacht. The master of the frigate, we thought, asked unreasonably for our passage; which made us agree with the master of the yacht, who offered to carry us ten shillings a piece cheaper than the other. We went on board the yacht, and the frigate came out together with us, intending to be consorts during the voyage; and for several days we sailed together; but what with calms and contrary winds, we were in a while separated. After that, the frigate, losing her way, fell among the Spaniards; by whom she was taken and plundered, and the master and mate made prisoners; afterwards, being retaken by the English, she was sent home to her owners in Virginia. Which when we came to understand, we saw and admired the providence of God, who preserved us out of our enemies' hands; and he that was covetous fell among the covetous.

While we were at Shrewsbury an accident befell, which, for the time, was a great exercise to us. John Jay, a Friend of Barbadoes, who came with us from Rhode Island, and intended to accompany us through the woods to Maryland, being to try a horse, got upon his back; and the horse fell a-running, and cast him down upon his head, and broke his neck, as the people said. They that were near him took him up as dead, carried him a good way, and laid him on a tree. I got to him as soon as I could; and feeling him, concluded he was dead. As I stood by him, pitying him and his family, I took hold of his hair, and his head turned any way, his neck was so limber. Whereupon I took his head in both my hands, and setting my knee against the tree, I raised his head, and perceived there was nothing out or broken that way. Then I put one hand under his chin, and the other behind his head, and raised his head two or three times with all my strength, and brought it in. I soon perceived his neck began to grow stiff again, and then he began to rattle in the throat, and quickly after to breathe. The people were amazed; but I bid them have a good heart, be of good faith, and carry him into the house. They did so, and set him by the fire. I bid them get him something warm to drink, and put him to bed. After he had been in the house a while he began to speak; but did not know where he had been. The next day we passed away (and he with us, pretty well) about sixteen miles to a meeting at Middletown, through woods and bogs, and over a river; where we swam our horses, and got over ourselves upon a hollow tree. Many hundred miles did he travel with us after this.

Not far from hence [Carolina on the Macocomocock River] we had a meeting among the people, and they were taken with the truth: blessed be the Lord! Then passing down the river Maratick in a canoe, we went down the bay Connie-Oak, and came to a captain's house, who was very loving, and lent us his boat, for we were much wet in the canoe, the water splashing in upon us. With this boat we went to the governor's house; but the water in some places was so shallow that the boat being laden, could not swim; so that we were fain to put off our shoes and stockings, and wade through the water some distance. The governor, with his wife, received us lovingly; but a doctor there would needs dispute with us. And truly his opposing us was of good service, giving occasion for the opening of many things to the people, concerning the light and Spirit of God, which he denied to be in everyone; and affirmed that it was not in the Indians. Whereupon I called an Indian to us, and asked him, "Whether or not, when he lied, or did wrong to anyone, there was not something in him that reproved him for it?" he said, "There was such a thing in him, that did so reprove him; and he was ashamed when he had done wrong, or spoken wrong." So we shamed the doctor before the governor and the people; insomuch that the poor man ran out so far, that at length he would not own the Scriptures. We tarried at the governor's that night; and next morning he very courteously walked with us himself about two miles through the woods, to a place whither he had sent our boat about to meet us. Taking leave of him, we entered our boat, and went that day about thirty miles to Joseph Scott's, one of the representatives of the country. There we had a sound, precious meeting; the people were tender, and much desired after meetings. Wherefore at a house about four miles further, we had another meeting, to which the governor's secretary came, who was chief secretary of the province, and had been formerly convinced.

I went from this place among the Indians, and spoke unto them by an interpreter; showing them, "that God made all things in six days, and made but one woman for one man; and that God drowned the old world, because of their wickedness. Afterwards I spoke to them concerning Christ, showing them, that he died for all men, for their sins, as well as for others; and had enlightened them as well as others; and that if they did that which was evil, he would burn them, but if they did well, they should not be burned." There was among them their young king; and others of their chief men, who seemed to receive kindly what I said to them.

After this meeting [the general meeting for the province of Maryland] we took our leave of Friends, parting in great tenderness, in the sense of the heavenly life and virtuous power of the Lord, that was livingly felt amongst us; and went by water to the place where we were to take shipping, many Friends accompanying us thither and tarrying with us that night. Next day, the 21st of the 3rd month, 1673, we set sail for England; the same day Richard Covell came on board our ship, having had his own taken from him by the Dutch. We had foul weather and contrary winds, which caused us to cast anchor often, so that we were till the 31st ere we could get past the capes of Virginia and come out into the main sea. But after this we made good speed, and on the 28th of the 4th month cast anchor at King's Road, which is the harbour for Bristol.

We had on our passage very high winds and tempestuous weather, which made the sea exceedingly rough, the waves rising like mountains; so that the masters and sailors wondered at it, and said they never saw the like before. But though the wind was strong, it set for the most part with us, so that we sailed before it; and the great God who commands the winds, who is Lord of heaven, of earth, and the seas, and whose wonders are seen in the deep, steered our course and preserved us from many imminent dangers. The same good hand of Providence that went with us, and carried us safely over, watched over us in our return, and brought us safely back again; thanksgiving and praises be to his holy name forever! Many sweet and precious meetings we had on board the ship during this voyage (commonly two a week), where the blessed presence of the Lord did greatly refresh us, and often break in upon and tender the company.

CHAPTER XX

1673–75

Many deep and precious things were opened in those meetings by the Eternal Spirit, which searcheth and revealeth the deep things of God. After I had finished my service for the Lord in that city Bristol, I departed thence into Gloucestershire, where we had many large and precious meetings; and the Lord's everlasting power flowed over all. From Gloucestershire I passed into Wiltshire, where also we had many blessed meetings. At Slattenford, in Wiltshire, we had a very good meeting, though we met there with much opposition from some who had set themselves against Women's Meetings; which I was moved of the Lord to recommend to Friends, for the benefit and advantage of the church of Christ. "That faithful women, who were called to the belief of the truth, be made partakers of the same precious faith, and heirs of the same everlasting gospel of life and salvation that men are, might in like manner come into the possession and practice of the gospel order, and therein be meet-helps unto the men in the restoration, in the service of truth, in the affairs of the church, as they are outwardly in civil, or temporal things. That so all the family of God, women as well as men, might know, possess, perform, and discharge their offices and services in the house of God, whereby the poor might be better taken care of, the younger instructed, informed, and taught in the way of God; the loose and disorderly reproved and admonished in the fear of the Lord; the clearness of persons proposing marriage more closely and strictly inquired into in the wisdom of God; and all the members of the spiritual body, the church, might watch over and be helpful to each other in love." But after these opposers had run into much contention and wrangling, the power of the Lord struck down one of the chief of them, so that his spirit sunk, and he came to be sensible of the evil he had done in opposing God's heavenly power, and confessed his error before Friends; and afterwards gave forth a paper of condemnation, wherein he declared, "that he did wilfully oppose (although I often warned him to take heed), until the fire of the Lord did burn within him; and he saw the angel of the Lord with his sword drawn in his hand, ready to cut him off," etc.

Notwithstanding the opposition at the meeting at Slattenford, yet a very good and serviceable one it was; for occasion was thereby administered to answer their objections and cavils, and to open the services of women in and for the church. At this the women's meetings, for that county, were established in the blessed power of God.

CHAPTER XXI

1677

That day and the next I stayed at Amsterdam, visiting Friends, and assisting them in some business concerning their meetings. Three Baptists came to discourse with me, to whom I opened things to their satisfaction, and they parted from me in kindness. I wrote a letter also to the Princess Elizabeth, which Isabel Yeomans delivered to her, when George Keith's wife and she went to visit her:

"Princess Elizabeth:

"I have heard of thy tenderness towards the Lord and his holy truth, by some Friends that have visited thee, and also by some of thy letters, which I have seen: it is indeed a great thing for a person of thy quality to have such a tender mind after the Lord and his precious truth; seeing so many are swallowed up with voluptuousness, and the pleasures of this world; yet all make an outward profession of God and Christ one way or other, but without any deep, inward sense and feeling of him. For it is not many mighty, nor wise of the world, that can become fools for Christ's sake, or can become low in the humility of Christ Jesus from their mighty state, through which they might receive a mightier estate, and a mightier kingdom through the inward Holy Spirit—the divine light and power of God; and a mightier wisdom which is from above, pure and peaceable. This wisdom is above that which is below; that is earthly, sensual, and devilish, by which men destroy one another, yea, about their religions, ways, worships, and churches; but this they have not from God nor Christ. The wisdom which is from above, by which all things were made and created, which the holy fear of God in the heart is the beginning of, keeps the heart clean: and by this wisdom are all God's children to be ordered, and with it to order all things to God's glory. This is the wisdom that is justified of her children. In this fear of God and this wisdom, my desire is, that thou mayest be preserved to God's glory. For the Lord is come to teach his people himself, and to set up his ensign, that the nations may flow unto it. There hath been an apostasy since the apostles' days, from the divine light of Christ, which should have given them 'the light of the knowledge of the glory of God, in the face of Christ Jesus'; and from the Holy Spirit, which would have led them into all truth; and therefore have people set up so many leaders without them, to give them knowledge; and also from the holy and precious faith, which Jesus Christ is the author and finisher of; which purifies the heart, and gives victory over that which separates from God; through which faith they have access to God, and in which they please God; the mystery of which is held in a pure conscience. And also from the gospel which was preached in the apostles' days (which gospel is the power of God), which brings life and immortality to light in man and woman, by which people should have seen over the devil that has darkened mortality. For the eyes of people have been after men, and not after the Lord, who writes his law in the hearts, and puts it into the minds, of all the children of the new covenant of light, life, and grace, through which they all come to know the Lord, from the least to the greatest; so that the knowledge of the Lord may cover the earth, as the waters do the sea. This work of the Lord is beginning again, as it was in the apostles' days; people shall come to receive an unction in them again from the Holy One, by which they shall know all things, and shall not need any man to teach them, but as the anointing doth teach them; and also to know, what the righteousness of faith speaks, the Word nigh in the heart and mouth, to obey it and to do it. This was the Word of faith the apostles preached; which is now received and preached again, and which it is the duty of all true Christians to receive. So now people are coming out of the apostasy to the light of Christ and his Spirit, and to receive faith from him, and not from men; to receive the gospel from him, their unction from him, the Word; and as they receive him, they declare him freely, as his command was to his disciples, and is still to the learners and receivers of him. For the Lord God, in his Son Jesus Christ, is come to teach his people, and to bring them from all the world's ways to Christ, the way, the truth, and the life, who is the way to the Father; and from all the world's teachers and speakers, to him the Speaker and Teacher, as Heb. i. 1; and from all the world's worshippers, to worship God in the Spirit and in the truth, which worship Christ set up above sixteen hundred years ago, when he put down the Jews' worship at the temple at Jerusalem, and the worship at the mountain where Jacob's well was; to bring people from all the world's religions, which they have made since the apostles' days, to the religion that was set up by Christ and his apostles, which is pure and undefiled before God, and keeps from the spots of the world; to bring them out of all the world's churches and fellowships, made and set up since the apostles' days, to the church that is in God, the Father of our Lord Jesus Christ; Thess. i. 1, and to bring to the unity and fellowship in the Holy Spirit, that doth mortify, circumcise, and baptize, to plunge down sin and corruption, that has got up in man and woman by transgression. In this Holy Spirit there is a holy fellowship and unity: yea, it is the bond of the Prince of princes, and King of kings, and Lord of lords' peace; which heavenly peace all true Christians are to maintain with spiritual weapons, not with carnal.

"And now, my friend, the holy men of God wrote the Scriptures as they were moved by the Holy Ghost; and all Christendom are on heaps about those Scriptures, because they are not led by the same Holy Ghost as those were that gave forth the Scriptures; which Holy Ghost they must come to in themselves, and be led by, if they come into all the truth of them, and to have the comfort of God, of Christ, and of them. For none can call Jesus Lord, but by the Holy Ghost; and all that call Christ Lord without the Holy Ghost, take his name in vain. Likewise all that name his name are to depart from iniquity; then they name his name with reverence, in truth and righteousness. O therefore, feel the grace and truth in thy heart, that is come by Jesus Christ, that will teach thee how to live, and what to deny. It will establish thy heart, season thy words, and bring thy salvation; it will be a teacher unto thee at all times. By it thou mayest receive Christ from whom it comes; and as many as receive him, to them he gives power, not only to stand against sin and evil, but to become the sons of God; if sons, then heirs of a life, a world, and kingdom, without end, and of the eternal riches and treasures thereof. So in haste, with my love in the Lord Jesus Christ, who tasted death for every man, and bruises the serpent's head, who is between man and God, that through Christ man may come to God again, and praise him through Jesus Christ, the Amen; who is the spiritual and heavenly rock and foundation for all God's people to build upon, to the praise and glory of God, who is over all, blessed forevermore.

G.F.

"Amsterdam, the 7th of the 6th Month, 1677.

"Postscript.—The bearer hereof is a daughter-in-law of mine, that comes with Gertrude Dirick Nieson and George Keith's wife, to visit thee.

G.F."

The Princess Elizabeth's Answer

"Dear Friend:

"I cannot but have a tender love to those that love the Lord Jesus Christ, and to whom it is given, not only to believe in him, but also to suffer him; therefore your letter and your friends' visit have been both very welcome to me. I shall follow their and your counsel as far as God will afford me light and unction; remaining still your loving friend,

Elizabeth."

CHAPTER XXII

1687–90

Postscript of Thomas Ellwood

Thus, reader, thou hast had some account of the life and travels, labours, sufferings, and manifold trials and exercises of this holy man of God, from his youth to almost the time of his death, of which himself kept a journal; out of which the foregoing sheets were transcribed. It remains that an account be added of the time, place, and manner of his death and burial, which were thus:

The day after he had written the foregoing epistle to Friends in Ireland [not included in the condensed text], he went to the meeting at Gracechurch Street, which was large, being the First-day of the week; and the Lord enabled him to preach the truth fully and effectually, opening many deep and weighty things with great power and clearness. After which having prayed, and the meeting being ended, he went to Henry Goldney's, in White-Hart-Court, near the meeting house; and some Friends going with him there, he told them "he thought he felt the cold strike to his heart, as he came out of the meeting"; "yet," he added, "I am glad I was here: now I am clear, I am fully clear." As soon as the Friends withdrew, he lay down upon a bed (as he sometimes used to do, through weariness after meeting), but soon rose again; and in a little time lay down again, complaining still of cold. And his strength sensibly decaying, he was soon obliged to go into bed; where he lay in much contentment and peace, and very sensible to the last. And as, in the whole course of his life, his spirit, in the universal love of God, was bent upon the exalting of truth and righteousness, and the making known the way thereof to the nations and people afar off; so now, in the time of his outward weakness, his mind was intent upon, and (as it were) wholly taken up with that; and some particular Friends he sent for, to whom he expressed his mind and desire for the spreading of Friends' books, and truth thereby in the world. Divers Friends came to visit him in his illness; to some of whom he said, "All is well; the Seed of God reigns over all, and over death itself. And though," said he, "I am weak in body, yet the power of God is over all, and the Seed reigns over all disorderly spirits." Thus lying in a heavenly frame of mind, his spirit wholly exercised towards the Lord, he grew weaker and weaker in his natural strength; and on the third day of the week, between the hours of nine and ten in the evening, he quietly departed this life in peace, and sweetly fell asleep in the Lord, whose blessed truth he had livingly and powerfully preached in the meeting but two days before. Thus ended he his day in his faithful testimony, in perfect love and unity with his brethren, and in peace and goodwill to all men, on the 13th of the 11th Month, 1690, being in the 67th year of his age.

After the death of George Fox, an epistle was found written with his own hand, and left sealed up, with this superscription; "Not to be opened before the time"; that is, not till after his decease. When it was opened, it was found to be addressed to "Friends, and to all the Children of God, in all places in the world." It was afterwards printed, and is inserted in the Appendix to this Journal.

On the day appointed for the interment of George Fox, a very great concourse of Friends, and others, assembled at the meeting house in White-Hart-Court, near Gracechurch Street, about the middle of the day, to attend his body to the grave. The meeting held about two hours with great and heavenly solemnity, manifestly attended with the Lord's blessed presence and glorious power; in which divers living testimonies were given, from a lively remembrance and sense of the blessed ministry of this dear and ancient servant of the Lord, his early entering into the Lord's work at the breaking forth of this gospel day, his innocent life, long and great travels, and unwearied labours of love in the everlasting gospel, for the turning and gathering of many thousands from darkness to the light of Christ Jesus, the foundation of true faith; the manifold sufferings, afflictions, and oppositions, which he met withal for his faithful testimony, both from his open adversaries, and from false brethren; and his preservations, deliverances, and dominion in, out of, and over them all, by the power of God; to whom the glory and honour always was by him, and is, and always ought to be by all, ascribed.

After the meeting was ended, his body was borne by Friends, and accompanied by very great numbers, to Friends' burying ground, near Bunhill Fields; where, after a solemn waiting upon the Lord, and several living testimonies borne, recommending the company to the guidance and protection of the Divine Spirit and power, by which this holy man of God had been raised up, furnished, supported, and preserved, to the end of his day, his body was committed to the earth; but his memorial shall remain, and be everlastingly blessed among the righteous.

TESTIMONY OF MARGARET FOX,

concerning her late husband

GEORGE FOX:

with a brief account of some of his travels, sufferings, and hardships endured for the truth's sake

It having pleased Almighty God to take away my dear husband out of this evil, troublesome world, who was not a man thereof, being chosen out of it; who had his life and being in another region, and whose testimony was against the world, that the deeds thereof were evil, and therefore the world hated him: so I am now to give in my account and testimony for him, whom the Lord hath taken unto his blessed kingdom and glory. And it is before me from the Lord, and in my view, to give a relation, and leave upon record the dealings of the Lord with us from the beginning.

He was the instrument in the hand of the Lord in this present age, which he made use of to send forth into the world, to preach the everlasting gospel, which had been hid from many ages and generations; the Lord revealed it unto him, and made him open that new and living way, that leads to life eternal, when he was but a youth, and a stripling. And when he declared it in his own country of Leicestershire, and in Derbyshire, Nottinghamshire, and Warwickshire, his declaration being against the hireling priests and their practices, it raised a great fury and opposition amongst the priests and people against him; yet there were always some that owned him in several places; but very few that stood firm to him when persecution came on him. He and one other were put in prison at Derby, but the other declined, and left him in prison there, where he continued almost a whole year; and when he was released out of prison, he went on his testimony abroad, and was put in prison again at Nottingham; and there he continued a while, and after was released again.

He then travelled on into Yorkshire, and passed up and down

that great county, and several received him, as William Dewsbury, Richard Farnsworth, Thomas Aldam, and others, who all came to be faithful ministers of the Spirit for the Lord. He continued in that country, and travelled through Holderness and the Wolds, and abundance were convinced: and several were brought to prison at York for their testimony to the truth, both men and women: so that we heard of such a people that were risen, and we did very much inquire after them. And after a while he travelled up farther towards the Dales in Yorkshire, as Wensleydale, and Sedbergh; and amongst the hills, dales, and mountains he came on, and convinced many of the eternal Truth.

In the year 1652 it pleased the Lord to draw him towards us; so he came on from Sedbergh, and so to Westmorland, as Firbank Chapel, where John Blakelin came with him; and so on to Preston, Grayrigg, Kendal, Underbarrow, Poolbank, Cartmell, and Stavely; and so on to Swarthmore, my dwelling house, whither he brought the blessed tidings of the everlasting gospel, which I, and many hundreds in these parts, have cause to praise the Lord for. My then husband, Thomas Fell, was not at home at that time, but gone to the Welsh circuit, being one of the judges of assize; and our house being a place open to entertain ministers and religious people at, one of George Fox's friends brought him hither, where he stayed all night. The next day being a lecture, or a fast day, he went to Ulverstone steeplehouse, but came not in till people were gathered; I and my children had been a long time there before. And when they were singing before the sermon, he came in; and when they had done singing, he stood up upon a seat or form, and desired that he might have liberty to speak; and he that was in the pulpit said he might. And the first words that he spoke were as followeth: "He is not a Jew that is one outward; neither is that circumcision which is outward: but he is a Jew that is one inward; neither is that circumcision which is of the heart." And so he went on, and said, how that Christ was the Light of the world, and lighteth every man that cometh into the world; and that by this Light they might be gathered to God, etc. I stood up in my pew and wondered at his doctrine; for I had never heard such before. And then he went on, and opened the Scriptures, and said, "the Scriptures were the prophets' words, and Christ's and the apostles' words, and what, as they spoke, they enjoyed and possessed, and had it from the Lord": and said, "then what had any to do with the Scriptures, but as they came to the Spirit that gave them forth. You will say, Christ saith this, and the apostles say this; but what canst thou say? Art thou a child of Light, and hast thou walked in the Light, and what thou speakest, is it inwardly from God?" etc. This opened me so, that it cut me to the heart; and then I saw clearly we were all wrong. So I sat down in my pew again, and cried bitterly: and I cried in my spirit to the Lord, "We are all thieves; we are all thieves; we have taken the Scriptures in words, and know nothing of them in ourselves." So that served me, that I cannot well tell what he spoke afterwards; but he went on in declaring against the false prophets, and priests, and deceivers of the people. And there was one John Sawrey, a justice of peace, and a professor, that bid the churchwarden take him away; and he laid his hands on him several times, and took them off again, and let him alone; and then after a while he gave over, and came to our house again that night. And he spoke in the family amongst the servants, and they were all generally convinced; as William Caton, Thomas Salthouse, Mary Askew, Anne Clayton, and several other servants. And I was struck into such a sadness, I knew not what to do, my husband being from home. I saw it was the truth, and I could not deny it; and I did as the apostle saith, "I received the truth in the love of it": and it was opened to me so clear, that I had never a tittle in my heart against it; but I desired the Lord that I might be kept in it; and then I desired no greater portion.

Then he went on to Dalton, Aldingham, Dendrum, and Ramside chapels and steeplehouses, and several places up and down, and the people followed him mightily; and abundance were convinced, and saw that what he spoke was truth; but the priests were all in a rage. About two weeks after, James Naylor and Richard Farnsworth followed him, and inquired him out, till they came to Swarthmore, and there stayed a while with me at our house, and did me much good, for I was under great heaviness and judgment. But the power of the Lord entered upon me within about two weeks that he came; and about three weeks' end my husband came home; and many were in a mighty rage. And a deal of the captains and great ones of the country went to meet my then husband as he was coming home, and informed him "that a great disaster was befallen amongst his family, and that they were witches; and that they had taken us out of our religion; and that he might either set them away, or all the country would be undone." But no weapon formed against the Lord shall prosper, as you may see hereafter.

So my husband came home greatly offended: and any may think what a condition I was like to be in, that either I must displease my husband, or offend God; for he was very much troubled with us all in the house and family, they had so prepossessed him against us. But James Naylor and Richard Farnsworth were both then at our house, and I desired them to come and speak to him, and so they did, very moderately and wisely; but he was at first displeased with them, till they told him they came in love and goodwill to his house. And after that he had heard them speak a while, he was better satisfied; and they offered as if they would go away; but I desired them to stay, and not to go away yet, for George Fox will come this evening. And I would have had my husband to have heard them all, and satisfied himself farther about them; because they had so prepossessed him against them of such dangerous, fearful things, in his coming first home. And then was he pretty moderate and quiet; and his dinner being ready, he went to it; and I went in, and sat me down by him. And whilst I was sitting, the power of the Lord seized upon me; and he was struck with amazement, and knew not what to think; but was quiet and still. And the children were all quiet and still, and grown sober, and could not play on their music that they were learning: and all these things made him quiet and still.

At night George Fox came: and after supper my husband was sitting in the parlour, and I asked him, if George Fox might come in; and he said, Yes. So George came in without any compliment, and walked into the room, and began to speak presently; and the family, and James Naylor, and Richard Farnsworth came all in: and he spoke very excellently as ever I heard him, and opened Christ's and the apostles' practices, which they were in, in their day. And he opened the night of apostasy since the apostles' days, and laid open the priests and their practices in the apostasy; that if all in England had been there, I thought they could not have denied the truth of those things. And so my husband came to see clearly the truth of what he spoke, and was very quiet of Ulverstone, and got my husband into the garden, and spoke much to him there; but my husband had seen so much the night before, that the priest got little entrance upon him. And when the priest Lampitt was come into the house, George spoke sharply to him, and asked him "when God spoke to him, and called him to go and preach to the people?" but after a while the priest went away: this was on a sixth day of the week, about the fifth month, 1652. And at our house divers Friends were speaking one to another, how there were several convinced hereaways; and we could not tell where to get a meeting: my husband also being present, he overheard, and said of his own accord, "You may meet here, if you will": and that was the first meeting we had that he offered of his own accord. And then notice was given that day and the next to Friends, and there was a good large meeting the first day, which was the first meeting that was at Swarthmore; and so continued there a meeting from 1652 till 1690. And my husband went that day to the steeplehouse, and none with him but his clerk and his groom that rode with him; and the priest and people were all fearfully troubled: but praised be the Lord, they never got their wills upon us to this day.

After a few weeks George went to Ulverstone steeplehouse again, and the said Justice Sawrey, with others, set the rude rabble upon him; and they beat him so that he fell down as in a swoon, and was sore bruised and blackened in his body, and on his head and arms. Then my husband was not at home; but when he came home he was displeased that they should do so; and spoke to Justice Sawrey, and said it was against law to make riots. And after that he was sore beat and stoned at Walney, till he fell down; and also at Dalton was he sore beat and abused; so that he had very hard usage in divers places in those parts. And then when a meeting was settled there, he went again into Westmorland, and settled meetings there; and there was a great convincement, and abundance of brave ministers came out thereaways, as John Camm, John Audland, Francis Howgill, Edward Burrough, Miles Halhead, and John Blakelin, with divers others. He also went over the sands to Lancaster, and Yealand, and Kellet, where Robert Widders, Richard Hubberthorn, and John Lawson, with many others, were convinced. And about that time he was in those parts, many priests and professors rose up, and falsely accused him of blasphemy, and did endeavour to take away his life; and got people to swear at a sessions at Lancaster that he had spoken blasphemy. But my then husband and Colonel West, having had some sight and knowledge of the truth, withstood the two persecuting justices, John Sawrey and Thompson, and brought him off, and cleared him; for indeed he was innocent. And after the sessions there was a great meeting in the town of Lancaster; and many of the town's-people came in, and many were convinced. And thus he was up and down about Lancaster, Yealand, Westmorland, and some parts of Yorkshire, and our parts above one year; in which time there were above twenty-four ministers brought forth, that were ready to go with their testimony of the Eternal truth unto the world; and soon after Francis Howgill and John Camm went to speak to Oliver Cromwell.

In the year 1653, George's drawings were into Cumberland, by Millom, Lamplugh, Embleton, and Brigham, Pardshaw, and Cockermouth, where at or near Embleton he had a dispute with some priests, as Larkham and Benson; but chiefly with John Wilkinson, a preacher at Embleton and Brigham, who was afterwards convinced, and owned the Truth, and was a serviceable minister both in England, Ireland, and Scotland. Then he went to Coldbeck and several places, till he came to Carlisle, and went to their steeplehouse; there they beat and abused him, and had him before the magistrates, who examined him, and put him in prison in the common jail among the thieves. At the assizes was one Anthony Pearson, who had been a justice of peace, and was convinced at Appleby (when he was upon the bench) by James Naylor and Francis Howgill, who were then prisoners there, and brought before him; so Anthony Pearson spoke to the justices at Carlisle, he being acquainted with them, having married his wife out of Cumberland; and after a while they released him. Afterwards he went into several parts of Cumberland, and many were convinced, and owned the Truth; and he gathered and settled meetings there amongst them, and up and down in several parts in the North.

In the year 1654, he went southward to his own country of Leicestershire, visiting Friends. And then Colonel Hacker sent him to Oliver Cromwell; and after having been kept prisoner a while, he was brought before Oliver, and released. He then stayed a while, visiting Friends in London, and the meetings therein; and so passed westward to Bristol, and visited Friends there. He afterwards went into Cornwall, where they put him in prison at Launceston, and one Edward Pyot with him, where he had a bad, long imprisonment. When he was released, he passed into many parts in that county of Cornwall, and settled meetings there. Then he travelled through many counties, visiting Friends and settling meetings all along; and so came into the North, and to Swarthmore, and to Cumberland.

And so for Scotland he passed in the year 1657, and there went with him Robert Widders, James Lancaster, John Grave, and others. He travelled through many places in that nation, as Douglas, Heads, Hamilton, Glasgow, and to Edinburgh, where they took him, and carried him before General Monk and the council, and examined him, and asked him his business into that nation; who answered, he came to visit the seed of God. And after they had threatened him, and charged him to depart their nation of Scotland, they let him go. Then he went to Linlithgow, and Stirling, and Johnstone, and many places, visiting the people; and several were convinced. And after he had stayed a pretty while, and settled some meetings, he returned into Northumberland, and into the bishopric of Durham, visiting Friends and settling meetings as he went; and then returned back again to Swarthmore, and stayed amongst Friends a while, and so returned south again. In 1658, Judge Fell died.

In 1660 he came out of the South into the North, and had a great general meeting about Balby in Yorkshire; and so came on, visiting Friends in many places, till he came to Swarthmore again. And King Charles then being come in, the justices sent out warrants, and took him at Swarthmore, charging him in their warrants, that he drew away the king's liege people, to the endangering and embruing the nation in blood; and sent him prisoner to Lancaster castle. And I have a great family, and he being taken in my house, I was moved of the Lord to go to the king at Whitehall; and took with me a declaration, and an information of our principles, and a long time, and much ado I had, to get to him. But at last, when I got to him, I told him if he was guilty of those things, I was guilty, for he was taken in my house; and I gave him the paper of our principles, and desired that he would set him at liberty, as he had promised that none should suffer for tender consciences; and we were of tender consciences, and desired nothing but the liberty of our consciences. Then with much ado, after he had been kept prisoner near half a year at Lancaster, we got a habeas corpus, and removed him to the king's bench, where he was released. And then would I gladly have come home to my great family, but was bound in my spirit, and could not have freedom to get away for a whole year. The king had promised me several times that we should have our liberty, but then the Monarchy-men rose; and then came the great and general imprisonment of Friends the nation through; and so could I not have freedom nor liberty to come home, till we had got a general proclamation for all our Friends' liberty. Then I had freedom and peace to come home.

In 1663 he came North again, and to Swarthmore. Then they sent out warrants, and took him again; and had him to Holcrof before the justices, who tendered him the oath of allegiance, and sent him prisoner to Lancaster castle. And about a month after, the justices sent for me also out of my house, and tendered me the oath, and sent me prisoner to Lancaster. And the next assizes they again tendered the oath of allegiance and supremacy to us both, and premunired me; but they had missed the date, and other things in the indictment, and so it was quashed; but they tendered him the oath again, and kept him prisoner a year and a half at Lancaster castle. And then they sent him to Scarbro' castle in Yorkshire, where they kept him prisoner close under the soldiers much of a year and a half, so that a Friend could scarcely have spoken to him; yet after that, it pleased the Lord that he was released; but I continued in prison, and a prisoner four years at that time; and an order was procured from the council, whereby I was set at liberty. And in that time I went down into Cornwall with my son and daughter Lower, and came back by London to the Yearly Meeting; and there I met with him again; and then he told me the time was drawing on towards our marriage, but he might first go into Ireland. And a little before this time was he prisoner in his own country at Leicester for a while, and then released. So into Ireland he went, and I went into Kent and Sussex, and came back to London again; and afterwards I went to the West, towards Bristol, in 1669, and there I stayed till he came over from Ireland, which was eleven years after my former husband's decease. In Ireland he had a great service for the Lord and his eternal truth, amongst Friends and many people there, but escaped many dangers, and times of being taken prisoner, they having laid in wait aforehand for him in many places. And then he being returned, at Bristol he declared his intentions of marriage; and there also was our marriage solemnized. Within ten days after

I came homewards, but my husband stayed up and down in the countries amongst Friends, visiting them.

Soon after I came home, there came another order from the council to cast me into prison again; and the sheriff of Lancashire sent his bailiff, and pulled me out of my own house, and had me prisoner to Lancaster castle (upon the old premunire), where I continued a whole year, and most part of that time was I sick and weakly; my husband also was weak and sickly at that time. After a while he recovered, and went about to get me out of prison, and a discharge at last was got under the great seal; and so I was set at liberty. Then I went to go up to London again, for my husband was intending for America. He was full two years away, before he came back again into England; and having arrived at Bristol, he came thence to London, intending to come to the middle of the nation with me; but when we came into some parts of Worcestershire, they got there information of him; and one Justice Parker, by his warrant, sent him and my son Lower to Worcester jail. The justices there tendered him the oath, and premunired him, but released my son Lower, who stayed with him most of the time he was prisoner there.

After some time he fell sick, in a long, lingering sickness, and many times was very ill; so they writ to me from London, that if I would see him alive, I might go to him; which accordingly I did. After I had tarried seventeen weeks with him at Worcester, and no discharge likely to be obtained for him, I went up to London, and wrote to the king an account of his long imprisonment, and how he was taken in his travel homewards, and that he was weak and sick, and not likely to live if they kept him long there. I went with it to Whitehall myself, where I met with the king and gave him the paper; and he said, I must go to the chancellor, he could do nothing in it. Then I wrote also to the lord chancellor, and went to his house, gave him my paper, and spoke to him, that the king had left it wholly to him; and if he did not take pity and release him out of that prison, I feared he would end his days there. The Lord Chancellor Finch was a very tender man, and spoke to the judge, who gave out an habeas corpus presently. When we got it we sent it down to Worcester, and they would not part with him at first, but said he was premunired, and was not to go out on that manner. Then we were forced to go to Judge North, and to the attorney-general, and we got another order, and sent down from them; and with much ado, and great labour and industry of William Mead and other friends, we got him up to London, where he appeared in Westminster Hall at the king's bench, before Judge Hale, who was a very honest, tender man; and he knew they had imprisoned him but in envy. So that which they had against him was read, and our counsel pleaded that he was taken up in his travel and journey. And there was but a little said till he was acquitted. This was the last prison that he was in, being freed by the court of king's bench.

When he was at liberty he recovered again; and then I was very desirous to go home with him, which we did. This was the first time that he came to Swarthmore after we were married; and he stayed here much of two years, and then went to London again to the Yearly Meeting; and after a while went into Holland, and some parts of Germany, where he stayed a pretty while, and then returned to London again at the next Yearly Meeting. And after he had stayed a while in and about London, he came into the North to Swarthmore again, and stayed that time near two years; and then he grew weakly, being troubled with pains and aches, having had many sore and long travels, beatings, and hard imprisonments. But after some time he rode to York, and so passed on through Nottinghamshire and several counties, visiting Friends, till he came to London to the Yearly Meeting, and stayed there, and thereaways, till he finished his course, and laid down his head in peace.

And though the Lord had provided an outward habitation for him, yet he was not willing to stay at it, because it was so remote and far from London, where his service most lay. And my concern for God, and his holy eternal truth, was then in the North, where God had placed and sent me, and likewise for the ordering and governing of my children and family; so that we were very willing both of us, to live apart for some years upon God's account, and his truth's service, and to deny ourselves of that comfort which we might have had in being together, for the sake and service of the Lord and his truth. And if any took occasion, or judged hard of us because of that, the Lord will judge them; for we were innocent. And for my own part, I was willing to take many long journeys, for taking away all occasion of evil thoughts; and tho' I lived two hundred miles from London, yet have I been nine times there, upon the Lord and his truth's account; and of all the times that I was at London, this last time was most comfortable, that the Lord was pleased to give me strength and ability to travel that great journey, being seventy-six years of age, to see my dear husband, who was better in his health and strength than many times I had seen him before. I look upon it, that the Lord's special hand was in it, that I should go then, for he lived but about half a year after I left him; which makes me admire the wisdom and goodness of God, in ordering my journey at that time.

And now he hath finished his course, and his testimony, and is entered into his eternal rest and felicity. I trust in the same powerful God, that his holy arm and power will carry me through, whatever he hath yet for me to do; and that he will be my strength and support, and the bearer up of my head unto the end, and in the end. For I know his faithfulness and goodness, and I have experience of his love; to whom be glory and powerful dominion forever. Amen.

M.F.

THOMAS ELLWOOD'S ACCOUNT OF THAT EMINENT AND HONOURABLE SERVANT OF THE LORD, GEORGE FOX

(It was Thomas Ellwood who first transcribed this Journal for the press.)

This holy man was raised up by God in an extraordinary manner, for an extraordinary work, even to awaken the sleeping world, by proclaiming the mighty day of the Lord to the nations, and publishing again the everlasting gospel to the inhabitants of the earth, after the long and dismal night of apostasy and darkness. For this work the Lord began to prepare him by many and various trials and exercises from his very childhood; and having fitted and furnished him for it, he called him into it very young, and made him instrumental, by the effectual working of the Holy Ghost, through his ministry, to call many others into the same work, and to turn many thousands from darkness to the light of Christ, and from the power of Satan unto God.

I knew him not till the year 1660; from that time to the time of his death I knew him well, conversed with him often, observed him much, loved him dearly, and honoured him truly; and upon good experience can say, he was indeed a heavenly-minded man, zealous for the name of the Lord, and preferred the honour of God before all things. He was valiant for the truth, bold in asserting it, patient in suffering for it, unwearied in labouring in it, steady in his testimony to it; immovable as a rock. Deep he was in divine knowledge, clear in opening heavenly mysteries, plain and powerful in preaching, fervent in prayer. He was richly endued with heavenly wisdom, quick in discerning, sound in judgment, able and ready in giving, discreet in keeping counsel; a lover of righteousness, an encourager of virtue, justice, temperance, meekness, purity, chastity, modesty, humility, charity, and self-denial in all, both by word and example. Graceful he was in countenance, manly in personage, grave in gesture, courteous in conversation, weighty in communication, instructive in discourse, free from affectation in speech or carriage; a severe reprover of hard and obstinate sinners; a mild and gentle admonisher of such as were tender, and sensible of their failings; not apt to resent personal wrongs; easy to forgive injuries; but zealously earnest, where the honour of God, the prosperity of truth, the peace of the church, were concerned; very tender, compassionate, and pitiful he was to all that were under any sort of affliction; full of brotherly love, full of fatherly care; for, indeed, the care of the churches of Christ was daily upon him, the prosperity and peace whereof he studiously sought. Beloved he was of God; beloved of God's people; and (which was not the least part of his honour) the common butt of all apostates' envy; whose good, notwithstanding, he earnestly sought.

He lived to see the desire of his soul, the spreading of that blessed principle of divine light, through many of the European nations, and not a few of the American islands and provinces, and the gathering many thousands into an establishment therein; which the Lord vouchsafed him the honour to be the first effectual publisher of, in this latter age of the world. And having fought a good fight, finished his course, and kept the faith, his righteous soul, freed from the earthly tabernacle, in which he had led an exemplary life of holiness, was translated into those heavenly mansions, where Christ our Lord went to prepare a place for his; there to possess that glorious crown of righteousness, which is laid up for, and shall be given by the Lord the righteous judge to all them that love his appearance.

Ages to come and people yet unborn shall call him blessed, and bless the Lord for raising him up. And blessed shall we also be, if we so walk, as we had him for an example; for whom this Testimony lives in my heart, "He lived and died the SERVANT of the Lord."

T.E.

THE JOURNAL OF
JOHN WOOLMAN

Abridged from THE JOURNAL OF JOHN WOOLMAN
(John G. Whittier Edition)

EDITOR'S INTRODUCTION TO
THE *JOURNAL* OF JOHN WOOLMAN

The *Journal* of John Woolman, an American saint of the colonial era, has a message that is unusually relevant to the present day. Confronted with numerous severe crises—world hunger, energy shortage, poverty, oppression—many Americans are searching for alternative life-styles, life-styles that are less wasteful and more sensitive to the needs of all persons everywhere. Two centuries and more before such crises became evident to others, John Woolman perceived the seed that would produce them. Sensitive and conscientious person that he was, he opted for a life-style and calling that could prevent undue waste and oppression. The *Journal*, first published two years after he died in 1772, was one of the vehicles for communication of his message, which he embodied in his life and activities.

THE *JOURNAL*

The *Journal* is not a diary such as that kept by David Brainerd. Nor was it composed only for private edification. Like the *Journal* of George Fox, it was written with the deliberate design of informing and influencing perceptions and behavior. Woolman first began composing it in 1756, the same year in which he gave up his burgeoning merchandising business lest he become too entangled in the affairs of daily life to follow God's "openings." In Woolman's own words, "I have often felt the motion of love to leave some hints in writing of my experience of the goodness of God, and now, in the thirty-sixth year of my age, I begin this work." Thenceforward he added to it periodically at the ends of his journeys on behalf of slaves or Indians, which usually occurred annually. At his death he left three different manuscripts, which he had pored over in order to prepare the fittest copy possible.

The reader of the *Journal* will not find a biography of Woolman, even if there are biographical bits and pieces in it. Woolman deliberately and carefully selected items for inclusion, so that, as Edwin

H. Cady has remarked, we may see "a man who so heroically sought the will of God and the spirit of Christ that he achieved the image of Christ and became a hero of humility."[1] This does not mean he distorted the facts. Actually his journeys, extensive as they seem from reading the *Journal,* consumed an average of about a month out of each year. Woolman spent the rest of his time as tailor, fruit grower, notary, husband, and father, matters that are interesting but repetitious. In what he recorded, he was getting down to cases regarding his major "exercise."

Some may find the *Journal* slow and a bit tedious to read. Woolman wrote in the subdued, unornate, direct style characteristic of Quakers. The official editors made the style still more prosaic in a few places. But it is a mistake to become preoccupied with style in this case. It is the message, a message wrapped up in human life and activity, that will excite and inspire us. In Woolman himself we may see warmth, vibrancy, sensitivity, the love of Christ responding to situations in which our human lot is cast. In simple yet profound ways he admonishes and instructs us about the life of the saint in the midst of time.

The John Greenleaf Whittier edition of the *Journal,* published in 1871, has been used in this volume. This edition was based on an 1840 edition of the first edition, which was edited by others after Woolman's death. Since 1922, three critical editions based on Woolman's original manuscription have been published. While late editions have made numerous changes and some additions in the text, they have not substantially altered the content of the work.[2]

JOHN WOOLMAN

John Woolman was born in Northampton, Burlington County, West Jersey (now New Jersey) on October 19, 1720. He was the fourth of six children of Samuel and Elizabeth Woolman. The Woolmans were industrious and pious Quakers of modest means who saw to it that their children were properly educated both academically and spiritually. John records that his parents frequently directed the children to read aloud from the Bible or religious books on Sunday after meetings. They also practiced a firm but positive discipline. Once, John notes, at age twelve, when he sassed his mother during his father's absence, his father simply noted the fact that he had misbehaved and advised him "to be more careful in future." But the boy did not forget. He never remembered another time when he "spoke unhandsomely to either of my parents, however foolish in some other things."

Woolman's religious sensitivities awakened early in this setting. By age seven, he recorded, he "began to be acquainted with the operations of Divine love." Several experiences sensitized and conscientized him in an unusual way for the ministry he later performed. One was reading Revelation 22, which drew his mind "to seek after that pure habitation . . . God had prepared for His servants." Another was an early perception that people in his age seemed to live with "less steadiness and firmness" than those described in the Scriptures. A third was a dream at age nine involving a sun worm, whose meaning is unclear to us today. A fourth was an act of cruelty on his part, which taught him the price of cruelty: one day he threw stones and killed a mother robin and, then, reflecting on the fate of the young, he had to kill them also.

According to his own account, Woolman shared the vanities of adolescence but managed to avoid "profane language or scandalous conduct." Sometimes his vital early piety welled up to make him remorseful for his "backsliding." Nonetheless, at one period, he claims to have veered toward the chasm of "youthful disobedience." He associated with frivolous companions. He ceased to read Scriptures and meditate on heavenly things. However, a serious illness brought him up short. Though fearing to approach God, he humbled himself and, as he described the experience, "At length that word which is as a fire and a hammer broke and dissolved my rebellious heart." The result was "inward relief" and a vow that, health restored, he would "walk humbly before him."

Woolman's struggle did not end here, however. For a period of two years, ages sixteen to eighteen, he wrestled with the problem all youth face: how to make the faith of their fathers and mothers their own. He found himself pulled now to one side and now to another by the company he kept: his young friends, on one side, and the circle of pious adults his parents associated with, on the other. Eventually his persistence in attending meetings, reading the Scrip-

tures and other good books, and meditation won out, evoking from
him that confession that guided him throughout his life:

> that true religion consisted in an inward life, wherein the heart doth
> love and reverence God the Creator, and learns to exercise true justice
> and goodness, not only toward all men, but also toward the brute
> creatures; that, as the mind was moved on an inward principle to love
> God as an invisible, incomprehensible Being, so, by the same principle,
> it was moved to love Him in all His manifestations in the visible
> world; that, as by His breath the flame of life was kindled in all ani-
> mal sensible creatures, to say we love God as unseen, and at the same
> time exercise cruelty toward the least creature moving by His life, or
> by life derived from Him, was a contradiction in itself.

Woolman soon got a chance to test the insight he had pieced together in his adolescent years. At age twenty-one he was hired by
an unnamed Quaker merchant and baker (perhaps John Ogburn,
who later sold Woolman some property, including a small shop) to
"tend shop and keep books" in Mount Holly, a small town near the
family homestead. As usual, he took the employment with seriousness of purpose, concerned that he not let his new resolution
slip. The business prospered, and Woolman held firmly to his devout life-style. He grew in favor and stature both with his fellow
Quakers and with his employer. In his first two years at Mount
Holly he began to manifest already some signs of the prophetic disposition that issued as his lifetime labors on behalf of the
oppressed. In this instance the "exercise" had to do with confront-
ing the owner of a disorderly public house.

At the outset, however, Woolman failed to meet his own high
standards. He wrote a bill of sale for a black woman slave owned
by his master, salving his conscience momentarily with the knowledge that an elderly Quaker bought her. Even then, the transaction
"so afflicted" his conscience that he told both his employer and the
buyer that slave keeping was "inconsistent with the Christian religion." Later, his pangs of conscience grew. When another Quaker
asked him to write such a bill of sale for a recently purchased slave,
he refused, gently explaining, in what became a trademark approach for him, that he "was not easy to write it." It was clear that
he would never write another such document.

Woolman's mission in life fixed itself more and more vividly in
his mind. Having served his employer for several years, he decided
that it was time to make a break. Ever mindful of the way merchan-

dising encumbers one and consumes time and energy, he chose to learn the tailor's trade, which he learned from another employee. Subsequently, he resisted the pull of prosperity toward expansion into other areas. His rationale for this is perhaps the most fundamental insight of Woolman's entire career. It intrudes into every activity and every writing. And if Woolman made any contribution as a theorist, it lies in the area of his tenacious grasp of the insight that many social evils are rooted in the love of wealth and power rather than persons.

In retrospect Woolman believed "the power of truth" had "weaned" him "from the desire of outward greatness" and taught him contentment "with real conveniences, that were not costly." As yet unmarried, he needed little income. Consequently, he did not yield to attractive business opportunities which would be accompanied by "more outward care and cumber than was required." He saw too that success in business did not satisfy one's craving; it merely whetted the appetite for more wealth. For John Woolman, the saint, the real concern of life was "so to pass my time that nothing might hinder me from the most steady attention to the voice of the true Shepherd."

This crucial decision freed John Woolman to pursue a ministry, which he had shown to be his calling in 1742 by speaking in meetings, devoting about one month each year to travel. At first these journeys, begun in 1746, were aimed at the strengthening of Quakers throughout the colonies, witnessing "for the cause of truth among a backsliding people." On the very first one, however, Woolman and his traveling companion, Isaac Andrews, came face to face with the evils of slavery. Subsequently other impressions about human suffering awakened. Since the *Journal* is not really a logbook of Woolman's travels, a discussion of the insights of this "quiet revolutionary" will help us more to appreciate Woolman than a chronological treatment.

Many modern crusaders for social change would have difficulty understanding Woolman's approach and manner. He was far removed from those of our day who must have immediate change even if it necessitates violence. His tone was never strident. And he always tried to deal fairly with another person's point of view and take into account the total situation. Undergirding his patience was a profound belief in Providence: as the Apostle Paul states, "in all things God is working together for good for those who love him"

(Rom. 8:28), a verse Woolman often alluded to in his writings. He never presumed that the whole burden of change rested on his shoulders, or even those of his contemporaries. He simply threw his straws into the wind and let God carry them where he would. This may be illustrated in the many issues to which he sought to awaken concern in others.

The issue that occupied Woolman persistently throughout his life was that of *slavery*. In retrospect, it is difficult to believe that such an institution ever existed in America, more difficult to conceive its extent. Blacks were purchased in Africa and herded aboard slave ships like cattle. On these vessels they were loaded in tiers, forced to lie down chained together in a space approximately eighteen by sixteen inches by five feet six inches. Often diseases broke out, wiping out an entire boatload. Sometimes a ship sank to the bottom in heavy seas, taking all lives. When the ships reached the American shores, slaves were sold like cattle, often without regard for families. Their lot under white owners varied. Many experienced good treatment, and slaveholders often cited humane care as a reason for continuing the custom. However, the lot of many others was dreadful. Deprivation of freedom, as Woolman saw so clearly, is itself inhumane. But many cruelties and abuses were added to loss of liberty, to make the institution all the more reprehensible. Black women were bred like cattle, raped by their owners, and subjected to many other abuses. Runaways suffered the cruelest forms of punishment. It is not surprising that the conscience of a sensitive soul like Woolman should be pricked. What is more surprising is the tenacity with which some defended the institution.

Woolman, however, did not denounce every slaveowner he met. He acknowledged the fact that some treated their slaves well. It eased his conscience to see that a few masters "bore a good share of the burden, and lived frugally, so that their servants were well provided for, and their labour moderate. . . ." The conviction grew, however, as he traveled, that the institution could not be squared with Christian perceptions but, rather, appeared as "a dark gloominess hanging over the land."

After his return from Carolina in 1746 Woolman composed his first treatise "On Keeping Negroes." As was typical of his concern to be sure he was acting according to truth, he showed it first to his dying father and obtained his approval and encouragement to publish. In 1762 he supplemented and strengthened his arguments in a second manuscript on the same subject. Woolman saw the solution to the slavery problem in Matthew 6:33 ("Seek first the Kingdom of God . . .") and in Matthew 25:40 ("Forasmuch as ye did it to the least of these my brethren, ye did it unto me"). Whites would go on buying and selling slaves so long as they did not learn that, for a happy life, human beings have few needs. It is uncontrolled desire for comforts and conveniences far beyond what is needful which is the underlying cause of abuse of others' freedom. If we will seek first his Kingdom, then we will see that all are brothers—black and white. We will be concerned for the comfort and well-being of all.

With great deftness Woolman replied to each of the scriptural arguments advanced in support of slaveholding. He also undercut the contention that the custom was really an act of charity by questioning whether any slaveowner acted out of such an unsullied motive. But he returned ever again to the actual motive: "Many are desirous of purchasing and keeping slaves that they may live in some measure conformable to those customs of the times which have in them a tincture of luxury; for when we in the least degree depart from that use of the creatures which the Creator of all things intended for them, there luxury begins."[3] In response to those who wanted to relieve their consciences he cited descriptions of the barbarites that attended the slave trade. What has happened is that error has gotten established by general opinion. The only solution is to hear again the God of love and parent of mankind speak to us about proper human relationships.

Woolman's approach to social change is most instructive. He made the most of opportunities that came to him to witness about the evils of slavery. When Quakers asked him to write wills, as they often did, he did so exactingly. But if the will involved slaves, he carefully explained his scruples about this matter, so that, on more than one occasion, he became responsible for a voluntary emancipation.

Recognized as a "minister" by his fellow Quakers, he aimed his message first at his own. As a very young man in Mount Holly, he had learned a painful lesson about speaking before he had an "opening." Ever after, he was careful to wait for "the spring of Divine love." In this way he placed the burden of his heart weightily upon the hearts of the people whom he sought to awaken to social injustice. As a result, he early gained the support of the Quaker meetings in his fight against slavery. In 1758, the Philadelphia Yearly Meeting adopted a formal minute urging Quakers to free their slaves, arranging for visitation of slaveholders, and decreeing that Quakers who bought or sold slaves would be excluded. In 1754 the Overseers of the Press in Philadelphia authorized publication of his treatise "On Keeping Negroes."

But John Woolman, like his mentor, George Fox, was not chiefly a man of words but a man of action. He bore in his person and in his deeds the message that smoldered inside. When he received hospitality in Quaker homes where he ate, drank, and lodged free of cost with people "who lived in ease on the hard labour of their slaves," it made him uneasy. Little by little, he hit on a plan both to deal with his conscience and to leave an unmistakable message. As he departed, explaining his qualms, he would press a sum of money upon the master with instructions to give it to the most deserving of the slaves. Some, of course, resisted and possibly were offended. But the gentle saint had a way of disarming them and, no doubt, setting them to thinking at the same time.

Ever sensitive to ways in which his own life-style might add fuel to the flames, in 1761 he became convinced that he should not wear clothes with dye in them, for dye for men's suits came from indigo, a product of slave labor. However, true to his perceptions, Woolman did not immediately throw aside his fashionable clothes and begin wearing undyed ones. He wore the old ones out, lest he waste any of the divine bounty. When he could no longer wear the old, he made new, unbleached muslin suits. For those who did not know him, he became the object of ridicule, insults, and scorn. On his visit to England, according to secondary reports, English Friends, accustomed to better dress, gave him a cool reception as he presented his certificate from Friends in America, and one person even suggested that, since he had concluded his business, he might return home. In his gentle way he sat quietly as the sting of this rebuff subsided. Then he rose quietly to state that he had a task to perform in England and to request employment in his trade as he traveled to discharge it. After another season of silent waiting, he lay before them the burden of his heart. This time, the

Quaker who had suggested that he leave begged Woolman's pardon and declared his unity with him. Subsequently he labored with full Quaker support in England.

Woolman also stopped retailing rum, sugar, and molasses, which were produced by slave labor in the West Indies. Gradually he gave up personal use of sugar so as to avoid support of the system. In a treatise he prepared in 1769 he explained that, while he did not censure others in their customs, he believed God "hath heard the groans of this oppressed people, and that He is preparing some to have a tender feeling of their condition," so that he personally had to act as he did. He worried that, if too many stopped using such products immediately, the people of the West Indies would suffer excessively. But the few who acted as he did left a witness. To identify more fully with slaves, in 1766 he began walking rather than riding during his journeys.

Woolman would have understood perfectly the ambivalence we sometimes find ourselves in regarding proper Christian behavior, even though he thought such ambiguities would be lessened if we adopted a simpler life-style. A decision he made, along with others, to sell a nine-year-old orphaned slave boy, James, into slavery until age thirty haunted him for many years after. He undoubtedly did so with sufficient concern for the child's future, even though by this time, 1754, his mind was clear on the wrongness of the practice. His *Journal* entry for June 11, 1769, however, shows how Woolman sought to rectify his error, a fact that again instructs us:

> With abasement of heart I may now say that sometimes as I have sat in a meeting with my heart exercised towards that awful Being who respecteth not persons nor colours, and have thought upon this lad, I have felt that all was not clear in my mind respecting him; and as I have attended to this exercise and fervently sought the Lord, it hath appeared to me that I should make some restitution; but in what way I saw not till lately, when being under some concern that I might be resigned to go on a visit to some part of the West Indies, and under close engagement of spirit seeking to the Lord for counsel herein, the aforesaid transaction came heavily upon me, and my mind for a time was covered with darkness and sorrow. Under this sore affliction my heart was softened to receive instruction, and I now first perceived that as I had been one of the two executors who had sold this lad for nine years longer than it is common for our own children

to serve, so I should now offer part of my substance to redeem the last half of the nine years; but as the time was not yet come, I executed a bond, binding myself and my executors to pay to the man to whom he was sold what to candid men might appear equitable for the last four and a half years of his time, in case the said youth should be living, and in a condition likely to provide comfortably for himself.

Today many will be surprised that Woolman kept on with his campaign when visible results were often negligible. The secret of that, of course, lay in his deep conviction, his confidence in divine Providence, and his life of prayer. He was confident that God was in some way using what he was doing. Thanks in great part to his efforts, after 1787 no American Quaker owned a slave. Such success is remarkable, considering the reverse impact a more aggressive effort by Benjamin Lay had had. Lay even got himself expelled from the Society at the Yearly Meeting in 1730 for expressing essentially the same views as Woolman. Woolman undoubtedly realized that he could not effect his purposes by taking the same, aggressive route.[4]

A second matter that aroused Woolman's human and Christian sensibilities was exploitation of the Indians. In this, as in the matter of slavery, Woolman located the mounting tensions between Indians and white colonists in economic factors. Concern about this had grown for a long time in his mind, when, on meeting some Delawares in Philadelphia in August of 1761, he found himself drawn, despite the dangers, to make a visit to Wyaloosing, an Indian town two hundred miles from Philadelphia. The journey finally got underway in May of 1763, as soon as the right arrangements for travel could be made. It lasted five weeks.

Woolman's interest in the Indians was not evangelistic. Actually he took great pains not to interfere with a Moravian mission effort among them. He perceived in the Indians themselves a measure of acquaintance with "that Divine power which subjects the rough and froward will of the creature," and the Indians evidently sensed the same in him.

Woolman's dangerous excursion was prompted by reports of increased hostilities. He went as a peace messenger. Before he departed for Wyaloosing, in fact, concerned friends dispatched a messenger to warn him not to go, in view of a massacre of English settlers near Pittsburgh. He knew the terror in which many settlers lived. Later, he heard an acquaintance describe the horrible tortures the latter had witnessed. But Woolman was possessed of immense courage and prompted by a powerful sense of mission. When he arrived at an Indian settlement at Wyoming, an Indian grasped his tomahawk in his hand as he drew near his hut. But Woolman disarmed him by "speaking to him in a friendly way," assuming that the Indian meant no harm but simply wanted to be ready in case he encountered violence.

John Woolman did not blame the Indians for their reactions, however much he rued murders and tortures and feared for his own life. He saw some just causes for the Indian wrath. One was the way they had been taken advantage of by the white settlers, handing over their ancestral land "for a small consideration." Another was the fact that traders took advantage of them by exchanging rum for furs rather than clothing or other necessities. Accessory to this was the plight of poor folks who lived on the frontier caught in a web woven by the wealthy, who charged them high rents, so that they either took land away from the Indians or sold them rum. A third cause was the fact that English settlers and hunters depleted the game Indians depended on for food.

A third matter that aroused Woolman's attention, closely related to the two preceding ones, was exploitation of the poor by the wealthy. In an age when the industrial revolution was just getting underway, the full effects of this exploitation were barely visible in the colonies. But Woolman got a stark look when he went to England in 1772, and the problem occupied his mind frequently in his travels throughout that country. He foresaw distress in burgeoning industrial towns and cities, "where dirtiness under foot and the scent arising from that filth . . . more or less infects the air of all thickly settled towns. . . ." He prayed that the inhabitants "might come into cleanness . . . about their houses and garments." Perhaps, he mused, God would open the way for some now in cities to live the country life, where the Spirit was less restricted.

Woolman peered beneath the surface for a solution to such exploitation. His moving "Plea for the Poor," composed about 1763 or 1764, following his Indian mission but not published until about 1793, actually addressed itself to the sources of slavery, exploitation of Indians, wars, cruelty to animals, and other human ills arising from selfishness and covetousness. He summed up his solution to exploitation with the following words:

> Our gracious Creator cares and provides for all his creatures. His tender mercies are over all his works; and so far as his love influences our minds, so far we become interested in his workmanship and feel a desire to take hold of every opportunity to lessen the distresses of the afflicted and increase the happiness of the creation. *Here we have a prospect of one common interest from which our own is inseparable—that to turn all the treasures we possess into the channel of universal love becomes the business of our lives.* Men of large estates whose hearts are thus enlarged are like fathers to the poor, and in looking over their brethren in distressed circumstances and considering their own more easy condition, find a field for humble meditation and feel the strength of those obligations they are under to be kind and tender-hearted toward them.
>
> Poor men eased of their burdens and released from too close an application to business are at liberty to hire others to their assistance, to provide well for their animals, and find time to perform those visits amongst their acquaintances which belongs to a well-guided social life.
>
> When these reflect on the opportunity those had to oppress them, and consider the goodness of their conduct, they behold it lovely and consistent with brotherhood; and as the man whose mind is conformed to universal love hath his trust settled in God and finds a firm foundation to stand on in any changes or revolutions that happen amongst men, so also the goodness of his conduct tends to spread a kind, benevolent disposition in the world.[5]

In a word, the solution lies in application of the golden rule (Matt. 7:12) to social life.

This same perspective sensitized Woolman in a fourth area, mistreatment of horses and postboys in the stagecoach traffic in England. On his journey to England in 1772 he noticed that horses were driven at breakneck speeds in order to make time. Sometimes a stage would cover a hundred miles in twenty-four hours. Such bruising treatment of horses frequently resulted in their death or blindness. At the same time, young postboys had to ride outside the coach, often all night long through the winter, causing great suffering. Sometimes they froze to death.

Woolman had already warned Quakers about these things at the General Meeting at Philadelphia and the Yearly Meeting in London, advising them not to send mail by post. Now, confronted directly with the evidence, he pointed squarely at the cause: "So great is the hurry in the spirit of this world, that in aiming to do business quickly and to gain wealth, the creation at this day doth loudly groan." Then, as was typical of him by this time, he responded by refusing to ride the coaches or send mail by them. He walked wherever he went.

A fifth matter came to Woolman's attention on board ship en route to England; namely, the awful lot of young sailors. Woolman traveled in steerage, despite efforts of his friends to change his mind. His objection to the cabin was not financial; he could have afforded it, and others volunteered to pay for his passage. The problem, as he saw it, was that cabin-class travel offered what he considered "superfluities," about which he had scruples. Sailing in steerage gave him a firsthand experience of a sailor's lot. He spent hours talking to young sailors and gained their confidence and admiration. But the dangers and corruptions they faced evoked "an inward exercise of soul." These youth worked long hours in all sorts of weather, received poor rations, and were driven to drink. Typically, again, Woolman traced their plight to the covetousness of shipowners. His heart was bursting to see the conversion of the latter.

O that all may learn of Christ, who was meek and lowly of heart. Then in faithfully following Him He will teach us to be content with food and raiment without respect to the customs or honours of this world. Men thus redeemed will feel a tender concern for their fellow-creatures, and a desire that those in the lowest stations may be assisted and encouraged, and where owners of ships attain to the perfect law of liberty and are doers of the Word, these will be blessed in their deeds.

The rest of Woolman's story may be told quickly. In 1749 he married Sarah Ellis, whom he described as "a well inclined damsel." He seldom mentions her in the *Journal* or other writings, perhaps to avoid embarrassing her in any way, but they had a fully happy marriage. Several passages in the *Journal* indicate that Woolman did not make his decisions concerning travel unilaterally and without regard for his wife's feelings. When he received news about the massacre at Pittsburgh as he was getting ready to set out on his Indian mission in 1763, for example, he did not tell Sarah

until he had "turned to the Lord for his heavenly instruction."
When he related the report to her, she became deeply distressed.
And when he, after a few more hours of agonizing, announced his
decision to go anyway, "she bore it with a good degree of resignation." Woolman reveals the tenderness of both persons when he
adds, "In this conflict of spirit there were great searchings of heart
and strong cries to the Lord, that no motion might be in the least
degree attended to but that of the pure spirit of truth." One can
imagine what agony attended his decision to make the fateful trip
to England in 1772. But Sarah, like her husband, would not allow
her personal concern to interfere. Reciprocally, he saw to it that all
his affairs were in order, knowing that he might well never return.[6]

As he labored under heavy concern for slaves, Woolman turned
his attention increasingly to areas beyond the colonies, where factors
underlying slavery had their source. About 1769, while suffering illness, he began to feel "exercised for my fellow-creatures in
the West Indies." A year or so later, he presented his concern
to the Monthly Meeting, then to the Quarterly and the General Spring meetings, all three of which issued certificates for him
to go. The way he wrestled with this decision is instructive of the
profound concern he had to act in accordance with divine leading,
not by his own choice. His decision reached a crisis when he went
about choosing a ship in which to sail to Barbadoes. Even the vessel
had to be right, partly on account of Woolman's scruples regarding
trade with the West Indies and partly on account of his desire that
the Spirit fully guide his effort. His serious consideration led him to
the conviction that he should return home for a while. Shortly afterward, he came down with pleurisy. In a near scrape with death
he experienced a horrible nightmare involving the hanging of an
old black man to feed his flesh to a macabre creature, part fox and
part cat. It symbolized the slave trade in all its horrors.

Woolman's long and near fatal bout with pleurisy precluded further consideration of a trip to the West Indies. Indeed, he made no
journeys for the next year or so. When he had recovered
sufficiently, he went about his usual tasks as husband, father, and
provider. In 1771 his daughter Mary, born in 1750, married Samuel
Comfort. He also composed two treatises: *Considerations on the
True Harmony of Mankind*, published in 1770, and *Conversations
on the True Harmony of Mankind*, written in 1770 but not pub-

lished until 1837. In both of these he urged the following of Christ in loving all the creatures, the theme of his life. If we truly followed Christ, we would not wish a life-style that placed burdens upon others. Rather, we would be content with meeting needs. The harmony of society is broken by self-centered pursuit of wealth and power. It is restored by following the golden rule. In sum, he argued,

> Christ being the Light dwells always in the Light, and if our walking be thus, and in every affair and concern we faithfully follow this divine Leader, he preserves from giving just cause for any to quarrel with us. And where this foundation is laid, and mutually kept to by families conversant with each other, the way is open for those comforts in Society which Our Heavenly Father intends as a part of our hapiness [sic] in this world, and then we may experience the goodness and pleasantness of dwelling together in Unity. But where ways of living take place which tend to oppression, and in the pursuit of wealth, people do that to others which they know would not be acceptable to themselves, either in exercising an absolute power over them, or otherwise laying on them unequitable burdens; here a fear lest that measure should be meted to them which they have measured to others, incites a care to support that by craft and cunning devices which stands not on the firm foundation of Righteousness. Thus the harmony of society is broken; and from hence commotions and wars do frequently arise in the world.[7]

These writings reveal the expansion of John Woolman's sense of mission. He felt drawn increasingly to leave a witness in the centers of trade and commerce from whence exploitation arose. For the world of John Woolman this meant England. En route and in England he bore the same magnificent testimony he bore elsewhere—a testimony about loving neighbors as we love ourselves. The message burned and glowed within him. It illumined all whose lives Woolman touched. Before he died, at York, England, on October 7, 1772, of smallpox contracted somewhere along the way, he composed five small essays. Their titles are revealing of his heart's deepest concerns: "On Loving Our Neighbors as Ourselves," "On the Slave Trade," "On Trading in Superfluities," "On a Sailor's Life," and "On Silent Worship." His last words during his illness bear the same message. Unable to speak during the last week, on the last day he wrote, "I believe my being here is the wisdom of Christ; I know not as to life or death."

E. Glenn Hinson

NOTES

1. E. H. Cady, *John Woolman: The Mind of the Quaker Saint* (New York: Washington Square Press, 1966), p. 132.

2. For a discussion of the textual history see Phillips P. Moulton (ed.), *The Journal and Major Essays of John Woolman*, in "A Library of Protestant Thought" (New York: Oxford University Press, 1971), pp. 273–82.

3. "On Keeping Negroes," Part II; *The Journal and Major Essays of John Woolman*, ed. Phillips P. Moulton (New York: Oxford University Press, 1971), p. 226.

4. See Cady, op. cit., pp. 70–75.

5. "A Plea for the Poor," Ch. 3; Moulton, p. 241; my italics.

6. Janet Whitney, *John Woolman, American Quaker* (Boston: Little, Brown, 1942), pp. 379–80, has given a touching reconstruction of these last preparations.

7. "Considerations on the True Harmony of Mankind," Ch. I; in *The Journal and Essays of John Woolman*, ed. Amelia Mott Gummere (Philadephia: Friends' Book Store, 1922), p. 444.

THE JOURNAL OF
JOHN WOOLMAN

CHAPTER I

1720–42

His Birth and Parentage.—Some Account of the Operations of Divine Grace on his Mind in his Youth.—His first Appearance in the Ministry.—And his Considerations, while young, on the Keeping of Slaves.

I have often felt the motion of love to leave some hints in writing of my experience of the goodness of God, and now, in the thirty-sixth year of my age, I begin this work.

I was born in Northampton, in Burlington County, West Jersey, in the year 1720. Before I was seven years old I began to be acquainted with the operations of Divine love. Through the care of my parents, I was taught to read nearly as soon as I was capable of it; and as I went from school one day, I remember that while my companions were playing by the way, I went forward out of sight, and sitting down, I read the twenty-second chapter of Revelation: "He showed me a pure river of water of life, clear as crystal, proceeding out of the throne of God and of the Lamb," &c. In reading it, my mind was drawn to seek after that pure habitation which I then believed God had prepared for His servants. The place where I sat, and the sweetness that attended my mind, remain fresh in my memory. This, and the like gracious visitations, had such an effect upon me that when boys used ill language it troubled me; and, through the continued mercies of God, I was preserved from that evil.

The pious instructions of my parents were often fresh in my mind, when I happened to be among wicked children, and were of use to me. Having a large family of children, they used frequently, on First-days, after meeting, to set us one after another to read the Holy Scriptures, or some religious books, the rest sitting by without much conversation; I have since often thought it was a good practice. From what I had read and heard, I believed there had been, in past ages, people who walked in uprightness before God in a degree exceeding any that I knew or heard of now living: and the apprehension of there being less steadiness and firmness amongst people in the present age often troubled me while I was a child.

I may here mention a remarkable circumstance that occurred in my childhood. On going to a neighbour's house, I saw on the way a robin sitting on her nest, and as I came near she went off; but having young ones, she flew about, and with many cries expressed her concern for them. I stood and threw stones at her, and one striking her she fell down dead. At first I was pleased with the exploit, but after a few minutes was seized with horror, at having, in a sportive way, killed an innocent creature while she was careful for her young. I beheld her lying dead, and thought those young ones, for which she was so careful, must now perish for want of their dam to nourish them. After some painful considerations on the subject, I climbed up the tree, took all the young birds, and killed them, supposing that better than to leave them to pine away and die miserably. In this case I believed that Scripture proverb was fulfilled, "The tender mercies of the wicked are cruel." I then went on my errand, and for some hours could think of little else but the cruelties I had committed, and was much troubled. Thus He whose tender mercies are over all His works hath placed a principle in the human mind, which incites to exercise goodness towards every living creature; and this being singly attended to, people become tender-hearted and sympathising; but when frequently and totally rejected, the mind becomes shut up in a contrary disposition.

About the twelfth year of my age, my father being abroad, my mother reproved me for some misconduct, to which I made an undutiful reply. The next First-day, as I was with my father returning from meeting, he told me that he understood I had behaved amiss to my mother, and advised me to be more careful in future. I knew myself blamable, and in shame and confusion remained silent. Being thus awakened to a sense of my wickedness, I felt remorse in my mind, and on getting home I retired and prayed to the Lord to forgive me, and I do not remember that I ever afterwards spoke unhandsomely to either of my parents, however foolish in some other things.

Having attained the age of sixteen years, I began to love wanton company; and though I was preserved from profane language or scandalous conduct, yet I perceived a plant in me which produced much wild grapes; my merciful Father did not, however, forsake me utterly, but at times, through His grace, I was brought seriously to consider my ways, and the sight of my backslidings affected me with sorrow, yet for want of rightly attending to the reproofs of instruction, vanity was added to vanity, and repentance to repentance. Upon the whole, my mind became more and more alienated from the truth, and I hastened toward destruction. While I meditate on the gulf towards which I travelled, and reflect on my youthful disobedience, for these things I weep, mine eye runneth down with water.

Advancing in age, the number of my acquaintance increased, and thereby my way grew more difficult. Though I had found comfort in reading the Holy Scriptures and thinking on heavenly things, I was now estranged therefrom. I knew I was going from the flock of Christ and had no resolution to return, hence serious reflections were uneasy to me, and youthful vanities and diversions were my greatest pleasure. In this road I found many like myself, and we associated in that which is adverse to true friendship.

In this swift race it pleased God to visit me with sickness, so that I doubted of recovery; then did darkness, horror, and amazement with full force seize me, even when my pain and distress of body were very great. I thought it would have been better for me never to have had being, than to see the day which I now saw. I was filled with confusion, and in great affliction, both of mind and body, I lay and bewailed myself. I had not confidence to lift up my cries to God, whom I had thus offended; but in a deep sense of my great folly I was humbled before Him. At length that word which is as a fire and a hammer broke and dissolved my rebellious heart; my cries were put up in contrition; and in the multitude of His mercies I found inward relief, and a close engagement that if He was pleased to restore my health I might walk humbly before Him.

After my recovery this exercise remained with me a considerable time, but by degrees giving way to youthful vanities, and associating with wanton young people, I lost ground. The Lord had been very gracious, and spoke peace to me in the time of my distress, and I now most ungratefully turned again to folly; at times I felt sharp reproof, but I did not get low enough to cry for help. I was not so hardy as to commit things scandalous, but to exceed in vanity and to promote mirth was my chief study. Still I retained a love and esteem for pious people, and their company brought an awe upon me. My dear parents several times admonished me in the fear of the Lord, and their admonition entered into my heart and had a good effect for a season; but not getting deep enough to pray rightly, the tempter, when he came, found entrance. Once having spent a part of the day in wantonness, when I went to bed at night there lay in a window near my bed a Bible, which I opened, and first cast my eye on the text, "We lie down in our shame, and our confusion covereth us." This I knew to be my case, and meeting with so unexpected a reproof I was somewhat affected with it, and went to bed under remorse of conscience, which I soon cast off again.

Thus time passed on; my heart was replenished with mirth and wantonness, while pleasing scenes of vanity were presented to my imagination, till I attained the age of eighteen years, near which time I felt the judgments of God in my soul, like a consuming fire, and looking over my past life the prospect was moving. I was often sad, and longed to be delivered from those vanities; then again my heart was strongly inclined to them, and there was in me a sore conflict. At times I turned to folly, and then again sorrow and confusion took hold of me. In a while I resolved totally to leave off some of my vanities, but there was a secret reserve in my heart of the more refined part of them, and I was not low enough to find true peace. Thus for some months I had great troubles; my will was unsubjected, which rendered my labours fruitless. At length, through the merciful continuance of heavenly visitation, I was made to bow down in spirit before the Lord. One evening I had spent some time in reading a pious author, and walking out alone, I humbly prayed to the Lord for His help, that I might be delivered from all those vanities which so ensnared me. Thus being brought low, He helped me, and as I learned to bear the cross I felt refreshment to come from His presence, but not keeping in that strength which gave victory I lost ground again, the sense of which greatly affected me. I sought deserts and lonely places, and there with tears did confess my sins to God and humbly craved His help. And I may say with reverence, He was near to me in my troubles, and in those times of humiliation opened my ear to discipline. I was now led to look seriously at the means by which I was drawn from the pure truth, and learned that if I would live such a life as the faithful servants of God lived, I must not go into company as heretofore in my own will, but all the cravings of sense must be governed by a Divine principle. In times of sorrow and abasement these instructions were sealed upon me, and I felt the power of Christ prevail over selfish desires, so that I was preserved in a good degree of steadiness, and being young, and believing at that time that a single life was best for me, I was strengthened to keep from such company as had often been a snare to me.

I kept steadily to meetings; spent First-day afternoons chiefly in reading the Scriptures and other good books, and was early convinced in my mind that true religion consisted in an inward life, wherein the heart doth love and reverence God the Creator, and learns to exercise true justice and goodness, not only toward all men, but also toward the brute creatures; that, as the mind was removed by an inward principle to love God as an invisible, incomprehensible Being, so, by the same principle, it was moved to love Him in all His manifestations in the visible world; that, as by His breath the flame of life was kindled in all animal sensible creatures, to say we love God as unseen, and at the same time exercise cruelty toward the least creature moving by His life, or by life derived from Him, was a contradiction in itself. I found no narrowness respecting sects and opinions, but believed that sincere, upright-hearted people, in every society, who truly love God, were accepted of Him.

As I lived under the cross, and simply followed the opening of truth, my mind, from day to day, was more enlightened, my former acquaintances were left to judge of me as they would, for I found it safest for me to live in private, and keep these things sealed up in my own breast. While I silently ponder on that change wrought in me, I find no language equal to convey to another a clear idea of it. I looked upon the works of God in this visible creation, and an awfulness covered me. My heart was tender and often contrite, and universal love to my fellow-creatures increased in me. This will be understood by such as have trodden in the same path. Some glances of real beauty may be seen in their faces who dwell in true meekness. There is a harmony in the sound of that voice to which Divine love gives utterance, and some appearance of right order in their temper and conduct whose passions are regulated; yet these do not fully show forth that inward life to those who have not felt it; this white stone and new name is only known rightly by such as receive it.

Now, though I had been thus strengthened to bear the cross, I still found myself in great danger, having many weaknesses attending me, and strong temptations to wrestle with; in the feeling whereof I frequently withdrew into private places, and often with tears besought the Lord to help me, and His gracious ear was open to my cry.

All this time I lived with my parents, and wrought on the plantation; and having had schooling pretty well for a planter, I used to improve myself in winter evenings, and other leisure times. Being now in the twenty-first year of my age, with my father's consent I engaged with a man, in much business as a shop-keeper and baker, to tend shop and keep books. At home I had lived retired; and now having a prospect of being much in the way of company, I felt frequent and fervent cries in my heart to God, the Father of Mercies, that He would preserve me from all taint and corruption; that, in this more public employment, I might serve Him, my gracious Redeemer, in that humility and self-denial which I had in a small degree exercised in a more private life.

The man who employed me furnished a shop in Mount Holly, about five miles from my father's house, and six from his own, and there I lived alone and tended his shop. Shortly after my settlement here I was visited by several young people, my former acquaintances, who supposed that vanities would be as agreeable to me now as ever. At these times I cried to the Lord in secret for wisdom and strength; for I felt myself encompassed with difficulties, and had fresh occasion to bewail the follies of times past, in contracting a familiarity with libertine people; and as I had now left my father's house outwardly, I found my Heavenly Father to be merciful to me beyond what I can express.

By day I was much amongst people, and had many trials to go through; but in the evenings I was mostly alone, and I may with thankfulness acknowledge, that in those times the spirit of supplication was often poured upon me; under which I was frequently exercised, and felt my strength renewed.

After a while my former acquaintances gave over expecting me as one of their company, and I began to be known to some whose conversation was helpful to me. And now, as I had experienced the love of God, through Jesus Christ, to redeem me from many pollutions, and to be a succour to me through a sea of conflicts, with which no person was fully acquainted, and as my heart was often enlarged in this heavenly principle, I felt a tender compassion for the youth who remained entangled in snares like those which had entangled me. This love and tenderness increased, and my mind was strongly engaged for the good of my fellow-creatures. I went to meetings in an awful frame of mind, and endeavoured to be inwardly acquainted with the language of the true Shepherd. One day, being under a strong exercise of spirit, I stood up and said some words in a meeting; but not keeping close to the Divine opening, I said more than was required of me. Being soon sensible of my error, I was afflicted in mind some weeks, without any light or comfort, even to the degree that I could not take satisfaction in anything. I remembered God, and was troubled, and in the depth of my distress He had pity upon me, and sent the Comforter. I then felt forgiveness for my offence; my mind became calm and quiet, and I was truly thankful to my gracious Redeemer for His mercies. About six weeks after this, feeling the spring of Divine love opened, and a concern to speak, I said a few words in a meeting, in which I found peace. Being thus humbled and disciplined under the cross, my understanding became more strengthened to distinguish the pure Spirit which inwardly moves upon the heart, and which taught me to wait in silence sometimes many weeks together, until I felt that rise which prepares the creature to stand like a trumpet, through which the Lord speaks to His flock.

From an inward purifying, and steadfast abiding under it springs a lively operative desire for the good of others. All the faithful are not called to the public ministry; but whoever are, are called to minister of that which they have tasted and handled spiritually. The outward modes of worship are various; but whenever any are true ministers of Jesus Christ, it is from the operation of His Spirit upon their hearts, first purifying them, and thus giving them a just sense of the conditions of others. This truth was early fixed on my mind, and I was taught to watch the pure opening, and to take heed lest, while I was standing to speak, my own will should get uppermost, and cause me to utter words from worldly wisdom, and depart from the channel of the true gospel ministry.

In the management of my outward affairs, I may say with thankfulness, I found truth to be my support; and I was respected in my master's family, who came to live in Mount Holly within two years after my going there.

In a few months after I came here, my master bought several Scotchmen servants, from on board a vessel, and brought them to Mount Holly to sell, one of whom was taken sick and died. In the latter part of the sickness, being delirious, he used to curse and swear most sorrowfully; and the next night after his burial I was left to sleep alone in the chamber where he died. I perceived in me a timorousness; I knew, however, I had not injured the man, but assisted in taking care of him according to my capacity. I was not free to ask any one on that occasion to sleep with me. Nature was feeble; but every trial was a fresh incitement to give myself up wholly to the service of God, for I found no helper like Him in times of trouble.

About the twenty-third year of my age, I had many fresh and heavenly openings, in respect to the care and providence of the Almighty over His creatures in general, and over man as the most noble amongst those which are visible. And being clearly convinced in my judgment that to place my whole trust in God was best for me, I felt renewed engagements that in all things I might act on an inward principle of virtue, and pursue worldly business no further than as truth opened my way.

About the time called Christmas I observed many people, both in town and from the country, resorting to public-houses, and spending their time in drinking and vain sports, tending to corrupt one another; on which account I was much troubled. At one house in particular there was much disorder; and I believed it was a duty incumbent on me to speak to the master of that house. I considered I was young, and that several elderly Friends in town had opportunity to see these things; but though I would gladly have been excused, yet I could not feel my mind clear.

The exercise was heavy; and as I was reading what the Almighty said to Ezekiel, respecting his duty as a watchman, the matter was set home more clearly. With prayers and tears I besought the Lord for His assistance, and He, in loving-kindness, gave me a resigned heart. At a suitable opportunity I went to the public-house; and seeing the man amongst much company, I called him aside, and in the fear and dread of the Almighty expressed to him what rested on my mind. He took it kindly, and afterwards showed more regard to me than before. In a few years afterwards he died, middle-aged; and I often thought that had I neglected my duty in that case it would have given me great trouble; and I was humbly thankful to my gracious Father, who had supported me herein.

My employer, having a negro woman,* sold her, and desired me to write a bill of sale, the man being waiting who bought her. The thing was sudden; and though I felt uneasy at the thoughts of writing an instrument of slavery for one of my fellow-creatures, yet I remembered that I was hired by the year, that it was my master who directed me to do it, and that it was an elderly man, a member of our Society, who bought her; so through weakness I gave way, and wrote it; but at the executing of it I was so afflicted in my

* The number of slaves in New Jersey at the commencement of Woolman's labours for emancipation was undoubtedly large. As late as 1800 there were 12,442. Perth Amboy was a place of deposit for the newly imported Africans, and long barracks were erected for their accommodation. In 1734, when Woolman was a lad of fourteen, an insurrection took place, which had for its object the massacre of the masters, and an alliance with the Indians and French. Some years later a Negro convicted of crime was burned alive at Perth Amboy. An immense number of Negroes, gathered from all the neighbouring townships, were compelled to be witnesses of the slow torment of the victim.

mind, that I said before my master and the Friend that I believed slave-keeping to be a practice inconsistent with the Christian religion. This, in some degree, abated my uneasiness; yet as often as I reflected seriously upon it I thought I should have been clearer if I had desired to be excused from it, as a thing against my conscience; for such it was. Some time after this a young man of our Society spoke to me to write a conveyance of a slave to him, he having lately taken a negro into his house. I told him I was not easy to write it; for though many of our meeting and in other places kept slaves, I still believed the practice was not right, and desired to be excused from the writing. I spoke to him in good-will; and he told me that keeping slaves was not altogether agreeable to his mind; but that the slave being a gift made to his wife he had accepted her.

CHAPTER II

1743–48

His first Journey, on a Religious Visit, in East Jersey.— Thoughts on Merchandising, and Learning a Trade.— Second Journey into Pennsylvania, Maryland, Virginia, and North Carolina.—Third Journey through part of West and East Jersey.—Fourth Journey through New York and Long Island, to New England. —And his fifth Journey to the Eastern Shore of Maryland, and the Lower Counties on Delaware.

My esteemed friend Abraham Farrington being about to make a visit to Friends on the eastern side of this province, and having no companion, he proposed to me to go with him; and after a conference with some elderly Friends I agreed to go. We set out on the 5th of Ninth Month, 1743; had an evening meeting at a tavern in Brunswick, a town in which none of our Society dwelt; the room was full, and the people quiet. Thence to Amboy, and had an evening meeting in the court-house, to which came many people, amongst whom were several members of Assembly, they being in town on the public affairs of the province. In both these meetings my ancient companion was engaged to preach largely in the love of the gospel. Thence we went to Woodbridge, Rahway, and Plainfield, and had six or seven meetings in places where Friends' meetings are not usually held, chiefly attended by Presbyterians, and my beloved companion was frequently strengthened to publish the word of life amongst them. As for me, I was often silent through the meetings, and when I spake, it was with much care, that I might speak only what truth opened. My mind was often tender, and I learned some profitable lessons. We were out about two weeks.

Near this time, being on some outward business in which several families were concerned, and which was attended with difficulties, some things relating thereto not being clearly stated, nor rightly understood by all, there arose some heat in the minds of the parties, and one valuable Friend got off his watch. I had a great regard for him and felt a strong inclination, after matters were settled, to speak to him concerning his conduct in that case; but being a youth, and he far advanced in age and experience, my way appeared difficult; after some days' deliberation, and inward seeking to the Lord for assistance, I was made subject, so that I expressed what lay upon me in a way which became my youth and his years; and though it was a hard task to me it was well taken, and I believe was useful to us both.

Having now been several years with my employer, and he doing less in merchandise than heretofore, I was thoughtful about some other way of business, perceiving merchandise to be attended with much cumber in the way of trading in these parts.

My mind, through the power of truth, was in a good degree weaned from the desire of outward greatness, and I was learning to be content with real conveniences, that were not costly, so that a way of life free from much entanglement appeared best for me, though the income might be small. I had several offers of business that appeared profitable, but I did not see my way clearly to accept of them, believing they would be attended with more outward care and cumber than was required of me to engage in. I saw that an humble man, with the blessing of the Lord, might live on a little, and that where the heart was set on greatness, success in business did not satisfy the craving; but that commonly with an increase of wealth the desire of wealth increased. There was a care on my mind so to pass my time that nothing might hinder me from the most steady attention to the voice of the true Shepherd.

My employer, though now a retailer of goods, was by trade a tailor, and kept a servant man at that business; and I began to think about learning the trade, expecting that if I should settle I might by this trade and a little retailing of goods get a living in a plain way, without the load of great business. I mentioned it to my employer, and we soon agreed on terms, and when I had leisure from the affairs of merchandise I worked with this man. I believed the hand of Providence pointed out this business for me, and I was taught to be content with it, though I felt at times a disposition that would have sought for something greater; but through the revelation of Jesus Christ I had seen the happiness of humility, and there was an earnest desire in me to enter deeply into it; at times this desire arose to a degree of fervent supplication, wherein my soul was so environed with heavenly light and consolation that things were made easy to me which had been otherwise.

After some time my employer's wife died; she was a virtuous woman, and generally beloved of her neighbours. Soon after this he left shop-keeping, and we parted. I then wrought at my trade as a tailor; carefully attended meetings for worship and discipline; and found an enlargement of gospel love in my mind, and therein a concern to visit Friends in some of the back settlements of Pennsylvania and Virginia. Being thoughtful about a companion, I expressed it to my beloved friend, Isaac Andrews, who told me that he had drawings to the same places, and also to go through Maryland, Virginia, and Carolina. After a considerable time, and several conferences with him, I felt easy to accompany him throughout, if way opened for it. I opened the case in our Monthly Meeting, and Friends expressing their unity therewith, we obtained certificates to travel as companions,—he from Haddonfield, and I from Burlington.

We left our province on the 12th of Third Month, 1746, and had several meetings in the upper part of Chester County, and near Lancaster; in some of which the love of Christ prevailed, uniting us together in His service. We then crossed the river Susquehanna, and had several meetings in a new settlement, called the Red Lands.

It is the poorer sort of people that commonly begin to improve remote deserts; with a small stock they have houses to build, lands to clear and fence, corn to raise, clothes to provide, and children to educate, so that Friends who visit such may well sympathize with them in their hardships in the wilderness; and though the best entertainment that they can give may seem coarse to some who are used to cities or old settled places, it becomes the disciples of Christ to be therewith content. Our hearts were sometimes enlarged in the love of our Heavenly Father amongst these people, and the sweet influence of His spirit supported us through some difficulties: to Him be the praise.

We passed on to Manoquacy, Fairfax, Hopewell, and Shanando, and had meetings, some of which were comfortable and edifying. From Shanando, we set off in the afternoon for the old settlements of Friends in Virginia; the first night we, with our guide, lodged in the woods, our horses feeding near us; but he being poorly provided with a horse, and we young, and having good horses, were free the next day to part with him. In two days after we reached our friend John Cheagle's, in Virginia. We took the meetings in our way through Virginia; were in some degree baptized into a feeling sense of the conditions of the people, and our exercise in general was more painful in these old settlements than it had been amongst the back inhabitants; yet through the goodness of our Heavenly Father the well of living waters was at times opened to our encouragement, and the refreshment of the sincere-hearted. We went on to Perquimans, in North Carolina; had several large meetings, and found some openness in those parts, and a hopeful appearance amongst the young people. Afterwards we turned again to Virginia, and attended most of the meetings which we had not been at before, labouring amongst Friends in the love of Jesus Christ, as ability was given; thence went to the mountains, up James River to a new settlement, and had several meetings amongst the people, some of whom had lately joined in membership with our Society. In our journeyings to and fro, we found some honest-hearted Friends, who appeared to be concerned for the cause of truth among a backsliding people.

From Virginia, we crossed over the river Potomac, at Hoe's Ferry, and made a general visit to the meetings of Friends on the Western shore of Maryland, and were at their Quarterly Meeting.

We had some hard labours amongst them, endeavouring to discharge our duty honestly as way opened, in the love of truth. Thence, taking sundry meetings on our way, we passed towards home, which, through the favour of Divine Providence, we reached the 16th of Sixth Month, 1746; and I may say, that through the assistance of the Holy Spirit, which mortifies selfish desires, my companion and I travelled in harmony, and parted in the nearness of true brotherly love.

Two things were remarkable to me in this journey; first, in regard to my entertainment. When I ate, drank, and lodged free-cost with people who lived in ease on the hard labour of their slaves I felt uneasy; and as my mind was inward to the Lord, I found this uneasiness return upon me, at times, through the whole visit. Where the masters bore a good share of the burden, and lived frugally, so that their servants were well provided for, and their labour moderate, I felt more easy; but where they lived in a costly way, and laid heavy burdens on their slaves, my exercise was often great, and I frequently had conversation with them in private concerning it. Secondly, this trade of importing slaves from their native country being much encouraged amongst them, and the white people and their children so generally living without much labour, was frequently the subject of my serious thoughts. I saw in these southern provinces so many vices and corruptions, increased by this trade and this way of life, that it appeared to me as a dark gloominess hanging over the land; and though now many willingly run into it, yet in future the consequence will be grievous to posterity. I express it as it hath appeared to me, not once, nor twice, but as a matter fixed on my mind.

Soon after my return home I felt an increasing concern for Friends on our sea-coast; and on the 8th of Eighth Month, 1746, I left home with the unity of Friends, and in company with my beloved friend and neighbour Peter Andrews, brother to my companion before-mentioned, and visited them in their meetings generally about Salem, Cape May, Great and Little Egg Harbour; we had meetings also at Barnagat, Manahockin, and Mane Squan, and so to the Yearly Meeting at Shrewsbury. Through the goodness of the Lord way was opened, and the strength of Divine love was sometimes felt in our assemblies, to the comfort and help of those who were rightly concerned before Him. We were out twenty-two days, and rode, by computation, three hundred and forty miles. At Shrews-bury Yearly Meeting we met with our dear friends Michael Light-foot and Abraham Farrington, who had good service there.

The winter following died my eldest sister, Elizabeth Woolman, of the small-pox, aged thirty-one years.

Of late I found drawings in my mind to visit Friends in New England, and having an opportunity of joining in company with my beloved friend Peter Andrews, we obtained certificates from our Monthly Meeting, and set forward on the 16th of Third Month, 1747. We reached the Yearly Meeting at Long Island, at which were our friends, Samuel Nottingham from England, John Griffith, Jane Hoskins, and Elizabeth Hudson from Pennsylvania, and Jacob Andrews from Chesterfield, several of whom were favoured in their public exercise; and, through the goodness of the Lord, we had some edifying meetings. After this my companion and I visited Friends on Long Island; and through the mercies of God we were helped in the work.

Besides going to the settled meetings of Friends, we were at a general meeting at Setawket, chiefly made up of other societies; we had also a meeting at Oyster Bay in a dwelling-house, at which were many people. At the former there was not much said by way of testimony, but it was, I believe, a good meeting; at the latter, through the springing up of living waters, it was a day to be thank-fully remembered. Having visited the island, we went over to the main, taking meetings in our way, to Oblong, Nine-partners, and New Milford. In these back-settlements we met with several people who, through the immediate workings of the Spirit of Christ on their minds, were drawn from the vanities of the world to an in-ward acquaintance with Him. They were educated in the way of the Presbyterians. A considerable number of the youth, members of that society, used often to spend their time together in merriment, but some of the principal young men of the company, being visited by the powerful workings of the Spirit of Christ, and thereby led humbly to take up His cross, could no longer join in those vanities. As these stood steadfast to that inward convincement, they were made a blessing to some of their former companions; so that through the power of truth several were brought into a close exer-cise concerning the eternal well-being of their souls. These young people continued for a time to frequent their public worship; and, besides that, had meetings of their own, which meetings were awhile allowed by their preacher, who sometimes met with them: but in time their judgment in matters of religion disagreeing with some of the articles of the Presbyterians their meetings were disapproved by that society; and such of them as stood firm to their duty, as it was inwardly manifested, had many difficulties to go through. In a while their meetings were dropped; some of them returned to the Presbyterians, and others joined to our religious society.

I had conversation with some of the latter to my help and edification, and believe several of them are acquainted with the nature of that worship which is performed in spirit and in truth. Amos Powel, a Friend from Long Island, accompanied me through Connecticut, which is chiefly inhabited by Presbyterians, who were generally civil to us. After three days' riding, we came amongst Friends in the colony of Rhode Island, and visited them in and about Newport, Dartmouth, and generally in those parts; we then went to Boston, and proceeded eastward as far as Dover. Not far from thence we met our friend Thomas Gawthrop, from England, who was then on a visit to these provinces. From Newport we sailed to Nantucket; were there nearly a week; and from thence came over to Dartmouth. Having finished our visit in these parts, we crossed the Sound from New London to Long Island, and taking some meetings on the island proceeded towards home, which we reached the 13th of Seventh Month, 1747, having rode about fifteen hundred miles, and sailed about one hundred and fifty.

In this journey, I may say in general, we were sometimes in much weakness, and laboured under discouragements, and at other times, through the renewed manifestations of Divine love, we had seasons of refreshment wherein the power of truth prevailed. We were taught by renewed experience to labour for an inward stillness; at no time to seek for words, but to live in the spirit of truth, and utter that to the people which truth opened in us. My beloved companion and I belonged both to one meeting, came forth in the ministry near the same time, and were inwardly united in the work. He was about thirteen years older than I, bore the heaviest burden, and was an instrument of the greatest use.

Finding a concern to visit Friends in the lower counties of Delaware, and on the eastern shore of Maryland, and having an opportunity to join with my well-beloved ancient friend, John Sykes, we obtained certificates, and set off the 7th of Eighth Month, 1748, were at the meetings of Friends in the lower counties, attended the Yearly Meeting at Little Creek, and made a visit to most of the meetings on the eastern shore, and so home by the way of Nottingham. We were abroad about six weeks, and rode, by computation, about five hundred and fifty miles.

Our exercise at times was heavy, but through the goodness of the Lord we were often refreshed, and I may say by experience "He is a stronghold in the day of trouble." Though our Society in these parts appeared to me to be in a declining condition, yet I believe the Lord hath a people amongst them who labour to serve Him uprightly, but they have many difficulties to encounter.

CHAPTER III

1749–56

His Marriage.—The Death of his Father.—His Journeys into the upper part of New Jersey, and afterwards into Pennsylvania.—Considerations on keeping Slaves, and Visits to the Families of Friends at several times and places.—An Epistle from the General Meeting.—His journey to Long Island.—Considerations on Trading and on the use of Spirituous Liquors and Costly Apparel.—Letter to a Friend.

About this time, believing it good for me to settle, and thinking seriously about a companion, my heart was turned to the Lord with desires that He would give me wisdom to proceed therein agreeably to His will, and He was pleased to give me a well-inclined damsel, Sarah Ellis, to whom I was married the 18th of Eighth Month, 1749.

In the fall of the year 1750 died my father, Samuel Woolman, of a fever, aged about sixty years. In his lifetime he manifested much care for us his children, that in our youth we might learn to fear the Lord; and often endeavoured to imprint in our minds the true principles of virtue, and particularly to cherish in us a spirit of tenderness, not only towards poor people, but also towards all creatures of which we had the command.

After my return from Carolina in 1746, I made some observations on keeping slaves, which some time before his decease I showed to him; he perused the manuscript, proposed a few alterations, and appeared well satisfied that I found a concern on that account. In his last sickness, as I was watching with him one night, he being so far spent that there was no expectation of his recovery, though he had the perfect use of his understanding, he asked me concerning the manuscript, and whether I expected soon to proceed to take the advice of Friends in publishing it? After some further conversation thereon, he said, "I have all along been deeply affected with the oppression of the poor negroes; and now, at last, my concern for them is as great as ever."

By his direction I had written his will in a time of health, and that night he desired me to read it to him, which I did; and he said it was agreeable to his mind. He then made mention of his end, which he believed was near; and signified that though he was sensible of many imperfections in the course of his life, yet his experience of the power of truth, and of the love and goodness of God from time to time, even till now, was such that he had no doubt that on leaving this life he should enter into one more happy.

The next day his sister Elizabeth came to see him, and told them of the decease of their sister Anne, who died a few days before; he then said, "I reckon sister Anne was free to leave this world." Elizabeth said she was. He then said, "I also am free to leave it"; and being in great weakness of body said, "I hope I shall shortly go to rest." He continued in a weighty frame of mind, and was sensible till near the last.

Second of Ninth Month, 1751.—Feeling drawings in my mind to visit Friends at the Great Meadows, in the upper part of West Jersey, with the unity of our Monthly Meeting, I went there, and had some searching laborious exercise amongst Friends in those parts, and found inward peace therein.

Ninth Month, 1753.—In company with my well-esteemed friend, John Sykes, and with the unity of Friends, I travelled about two weeks, visiting Friends in Buck's County. We laboured in the love of the gospel, according to the measure received; and through the mercies of Him who is strength to the poor who trust in Him, we found satisfaction in our visit. In the next winter, way opening to visit Friends' families within the compass of our Monthly Meeting, partly by the labours of two Friends from Pennsylvania, I joined in some part of the work, having had a desire some time that it might go forward amongst us.

About this time, a person at some distance lying sick, his brother came to me to write his will. I knew he had slaves, and, asking his brother, was told he intended to leave them as slaves to his children. As writing is a profitable employ, and as offending sober people was disagreeable to my inclination, I was straitened in my mind; but as I looked to the Lord, he inclined my heart to His testimony. I told the man that I believed the practice of continuing slavery to this people was not right, and that I had a scruple in my mind against doing writings of that kind; that though many in our Society kept them as slaves, still I was not easy to be concerned in it, and desired to be excused from going to write the Will. I spake to him in the fear of the Lord, and he made no reply to what I said, but went away; he also had some concerns in the practice, and I thought he was displeased with me. In this case I had fresh confirmation that acting contrary to present outward interest, from a motive of Divine Love and in regard to truth and righteousness, and thereby incurring the resentments of people, opens the way to a treasure better than silver, and to a friendship exceeding the friendship of men.

The manuscript before mentioned having laid by me several years, the publication of it rested weightily upon me, and this year I offered it to the revisal of my friends, who, having examined and made some small alterations in it, directed a number of copies thereof to be published and dispersed amongst members of our Society.*

In the year 1754 I found my mind drawn to join in a visit to Friends' families belonging to Chesterfield Monthly Meeting, and having the approbation of our own, I went to their Monthly Meeting in order to confer with Friends, and see if way opened for it. I had conference with some of their members, the proposal having

* This pamphlet bears the imprint of Benjamin Franklin, 1754.

been opened before in their meeting, and one Friend agreed to join with me as a companion for a beginning; but when meeting was ended, I felt great distress of mind, and doubted what way to take, or whether to go home and wait for greater clearness. I kept my distress secret, and going with a Friend to his house, my desires were to the great Shepherd for His heavenly instruction. In the morning I felt easy to proceed on the visit, though very low in my mind. As mine eye was turned to the Lord, waiting in families in deep reverence before Him, He was pleased graciously to afford help, so that we had many comfortable opportunities, and it appeared as a fresh visitation to some young people. I spent several weeks this winter in the service, part of which time was employed near home. And again in the following winter I was several weeks in the same service; some part of the time at Shrewsbury, in company with my beloved friend, John Sykes; and I have cause humbly to acknowledge that through the goodness of the Lord our hearts were at times enlarged in His love, and strength was given to go through the trials which, in the course of our visit, attended us.

From a disagreement between the powers of England and France, it was now a time of trouble on this continent, and an epistle to Friends went forth from our general spring meeting, which I thought good to give a place in this Journal.

An Epistle from our general Spring Meeting of ministers and elders for Pennsylvania and New Jersey, held at Philadelphia, from the 29th of the Third Month to the 1st of the Fourth Month inclusive, 1755.

TO FRIENDS ON THE CONTINENT OF AMERICA:—

DEAR FRIENDS,—In an humble sense of Divine goodness, and the gracious continuation of God's love to His people, we tenderly salute you, and are at this time herein engaged in mind, that all of us who profess the truth, as held forth and published by our worthy predecessors in this latter age of the world, may keep near to that Life which is the Light of men, and be strengthened to hold fast the profession of our faith without wavering, that our trust may not be in man, but in the Lord alone, who ruleth in the army of heaven and in the kingdoms of men, before whom the earth is "as the dust of the balance, and her inhabitants as grasshoppers." (Isa. xl. 12, 22.)

Being convinced that the gracious design of the Almighty in

sending His Son into the world was to repair the breach made by disobedience, to finish sin and transgression, that His kingdom might come, and His will be done on earth as it is in heaven, we have found it to be our duty to cease from those national contests which are productive of misery and bloodshed, and submit our cause to Him, the Most High, whose tender love to His children exceeds the most warm affections of natural parents, and who hath promised to His seed throughout the earth, as to one individual, "I will never leave thee, nor forsake thee." (Heb. xiii. 5.) And we, through the gracious dealings of the Lord our God, have had experience of that work which is carried on, "not by earthly might, nor by power, but by my Spirit, saith the Lord of Hosts." (Zech. iv. 6.) By which operation that spiritual kingdom is set up, which is to subdue and break in pieces all kingdoms that oppose it, and shall stand for ever. In a deep sense thereof, and of the safety, stability, and peace that are in it, we are desirous that all who profess the truth may be inwardly acquainted with it, and thereby be qualified to conduct ourselves in all parts of our life as becomes our peaceable profession; and we trust as there is a faithful continuance to depend wholly upon the Almighty arm, from one generation to another, the peaceable kingdom will gradually be extended "from sea to sea, and from the river to the ends of the earth" (Zech. ix. 10), to the completion of those prophecies already begun, that "nation shall not lift up a sword against nation, nor learn war any more." (Isa. ii. 4. Micah iv. 3.)

And, dearly beloved friends, seeing that we have these promises, and believe that God is beginning to fulfil them, let us constantly endeavour to have our minds sufficiently disentangled from the surfeiting cares of this life, and redeemed from the love of the world, that no earthly possessions nor enjoyments may bias our judgments, or turn us from that resignation and entire trust in God to which His blessing is most surely annexed; then may we say, "Our redeemer is mighty, he will plead our cause for us." (Jer. i. 34.) And if, for the further promoting of His most gracious purposes in the earth, He should give us to taste of that bitter cup of which His faithful ones have often partaken, O that we might be rightly prepared to receive it!

And now, dear friends, with respect to the commotions and stirrings of the powers of the earth at this time near us, we are desirous that none of us may be moved thereat, but repose ourselves in the munition of that rock which all these shakings shall not move, even in the knowledge and feeling of the eternal power of God, keeping us subjectly given up to His heavenly will, and feeling it daily to mortify that which remains in any of us which is of this world: for the worldly part in any is the changeable part, and that is up and down, full and empty, joyful and sorrowful, as things go well or ill in this world. For as the truth is but one, and many are made partakers of its spirit, so the world is but one, and many are made partakers of the spirit of it; and so many as do partake of it, so many will be straitened and perplexed with it. But they who are single to the truth, waiting daily to feel the life and virtue of it in their hearts, shall rejoice in the midst of adversity, and have to experience with the prophet, that "although the fig-tree shall not blossom, neither shall fruit be in the vines; the labour of the olive shall fail, and the fields shall yield no meat; the flock shall be cut off from the fold, and there shall be no herd in the stalls; yet will they rejoice in the Lord, and joy in the God of their salvation." (Hab. iii. 17, 18.)

If, contrary to this, we profess the truth, and, not living under the power and influence of it, are producing fruits disagreeable to the purity thereof, and trust to the strength of man to support ourselves, our confidence therein will be vain. For he who removed the hedge from his vineyard, and gave it to be trodden under foot by reason of the wild grapes it produced (Isa. v. 6), remains unchangeable; and if, for the chastisement of wickedness and the further promoting of His own glory, He doth arise, even to shake terribly the earth, who then may oppose Him, and prosper?

We remain, in the love of the gospel, your friends and brethren.

(Signed by fourteen Friends.)

Scrupling to do writings relative to keeping slaves has been a means of sundry small trials to me, in which I have so evidently felt my own will set aside, that I think it good to mention a few of them. Tradesmen and retailers of goods, who depend on their business for a living, are naturally inclined to keep the good-will of their customers; nor is it a pleasant thing for young men to be under any necessity to question the judgment or honesty of elderly men, and more especially of such as have a fair reputation. Deep-rooted customs, though wrong, are not easily altered; but it is the duty of all to be firm in that which they certainly know is right for them. A charitable, benevolent man, well acquainted with a negro, may, I believe, under some circumstances, keep him in his family as a servant, on no other motives than the negro's good; but man, as man, knows not what shall be after him, nor hath he any assurance that his children will attain to that perfection in wisdom and goodness necessary rightly to exercise such power; hence it is clear to me, that I ought not to be the scribe where Wills are drawn in which some children are made as masters over others during life.

About this time an ancient man of good esteem in the neighbourhood came to my house to get his Will written. He had young negroes, and I asked him privately how he purposed to dispose of them. He told me; I then said, "I cannot write thy Will without breaking my own peace," and respectfully gave him my reasons for it. He signified that he had a choice that I should have written it, but as I could not, consistently with my conscience, he did not desire it, and so he got it written by some other person. A few years after, there being great alterations in his family, he came again to get me to write his Will. His negroes were yet young, and his son, to whom he intended to give them, was, since he first spoke to me, from a libertine become a sober young man, and he supposed that I would have been free on that account to write it. We had much friendly talk on the subject, and then deferred it. A few days after he came again and directed their freedom, and I then wrote his Will.

Near the time that the last-mentioned Friend first spoke to me, a neighbour received a bad bruise in his body and sent for me to bleed him, which having done, he desired me to write his Will. I took notes, and amongst other things he told me to which of his children he gave his young negro. I considered the pain and distress he was in, and knew not how it would end, so I wrote his Will, save only that part concerning his slave, and carrying it to his bedside read it to him. I then told him in a friendly way that I could not write any instruments by which my fellow-creatures were made slaves, without bringing trouble on my own mind. I let him know that I charged nothing for what I had done, and desired to be excused from doing the other part in the way he proposed. We then had a serious conference on the subject; at length, he agreeing to set her free, I finished his Will.

Having found drawings in my mind to visit Friends on Long Island, after obtaining a certificate from our Monthly Meeting, I set off 12th of Fifth Month, 1756. When I reached the island, I lodged the first night at the house of my dear friend, Richard Hallett. The next day being the first of the week, I was at the meeting in New Town, in which we experienced the renewed manifestations of the love of Jesus Christ to the comfort of the honest-hearted. I went that night to Flushing, and the next day I and my beloved friend, Matthew Franklin, crossed the ferry at White Stone; were at three meetings on the main, and then returned to the island, where I spent the remainder of the week in visiting meetings. The Lord, I believe, hath a people in those parts who are honestly inclined to serve Him; but many, I fear, are too much clogged with the things of this life, and do not come forward bearing the cross in such faithfulness as He calls for.

My mind was deeply engaged in this visit, both in public and private, and at several places where I was, on observing that they had slaves, I found myself under a necessity, in a friendly way, to labour with them on that subject; expressing, as way opened, the inconsistency of that practice with the purity of the Christian religion, and the ill effects of it manifested amongst us.

The latter end of the week their Yearly Meeting began; at which were our friends, John Scarborough, Jane Hoskins, and Susannah Brown, from Pennsylvania. The public meetings were large, and measurably favoured with Divine goodness. The exercise of my mind at this meeting was chiefly on account of those who were considered as the foremost rank in the Society; and in a meeting of ministers and elders way opened for me to express in some measure what lay upon me; and when Friends were met for transacting the affairs of the church, having sat awhile silent, I felt a weight on my mind, and stood up; and through the gracious regard of our Heavenly Father strength was given fully to clear myself of a burden which for some days had been increasing upon me.

Through the humbling dispensations of Divine Providence, men are sometimes fitted for His service. The messages of the prophet Jeremiah were so disagreeable to the people, and so adverse to the spirit they lived in, that he became the object of their reproach, and

in the weakness of nature he thought of desisting from his prophetic office; but, saith he, "His word was in my heart as a burning
fire shut up in my bones; and I was weary with forbearing, and
could not stay." I saw at this time that if I was honest in declaring
that which truth opened in me, I could not please all men; and I
laboured to be content in the way of my duty, however disagreeable to my own inclination. After this I went homeward, taking
Woodbridge and Plainfield in my way, in both which meetings the
pure influence of Divine Love was manifested, in an humbling
sense whereof I went home. I had been out about twenty-four days,
and rode about three hundred and sixteen miles.

While I was out on this journey my heart was much affected with
a sense of the state of the churches in our southern provinces; and
believing the Lord was calling me to some further labour amongst
them, I was bowed in reverence before Him, with fervent desires
that I might find strength to resign myself to His heavenly will.

Until this year, 1756, I continued to retail goods, besides following my trade as a tailor; about which time I grew uneasy on account of my business growing too cumbersome. I had begun with
selling trimming for garments, and from thence proceeded to sell
cloths and linens; and at length, having got a considerable shop of
goods, my trade increased every year, and the way to large business
appeared open, but I felt a stop in my mind.

Through the mercies of the Almighty, I had, in a good degree,
learned to be content with a plain way of living. I had but a small
family; and, on serious consideration, believed truth did not require
me to engage much in cumbering affairs. It had been my general
practice to buy and sell things really useful. Things that served
chiefly to please the vain mind in people, I was not easy to trade in;
seldom did it; and whenever I did, I found it weaken me as a
Christian.

The increase of business became my burden; for though my natural inclination was toward merchandise, yet I believed truth required me to live more free from outward cumbers; and there was
now a strife in my mind between the two. In this exercise my
prayers were put up to the Lord, who graciously heard me, and
gave me a heart resigned to His holy will. Then I lessened my outward business, and, as I had opportunity, told my customers of my
intentions, that they might consider what shop to turn to; and in a

while I wholly laid down merchandise, and followed my trade as a tailor by myself, having no apprentice. I also had a nursery of apple-trees, in which I employed some of my time in hoeing, grafting, trimming, and inoculating.† In merchandise it is the custom where I lived to sell chiefly on credit, and poor people often get in debt; when payment is expected, not having wherewith to pay, their creditors often sue for it at law. Having frequently observed occurrences of this kind, I found it good for me to advise poor people to take such goods as were most useful, and not costly.

In the time of trading I had an opportunity of seeing that the too liberal use of spirituous liquors and the custom of wearing too costly apparel led some people into great inconveniences; and that these two things appear to be often connected with each other. By not attending to that use of things which is consistent with universal righteousness, there is an increase of labour which extends beyond what our Heavenly Father intends for us. And by great labour, and often by much sweating, there is even among such as are not drunkards a craving for liquors to revive the spirits; that partly by the luxurious drinking of some, and partly by the drinking of others (led to it through immoderate labour), very great quantities of rum are every year consumed in our colonies; the greater part of which we should have no need of, did we steadily attend to pure wisdom.

When men take pleasure in feeling their minds elevated with strong drink, and so indulge their appetite as to disorder their understandings, neglect their duty as members of a family or civil society, and cast off all regard to religion, their case is much to be pit-

† He seems to have regarded agriculture as the business most conducive to moral and physical health. He thought, "If the leadings of the Spirit were more attended to, more people would be engaged in the sweet employment of husbandry, where labour is agreeable and healthful." He does not condemn the honest acquisition of wealth in other business free from oppression; even "merchandising," he thought, *might* be carried on innocently and in pure reason. Christ does not forbid the laying up of a needful support for family and friends; the command is, "Lay not up for YOURSELVES treasures on earth." From his little farm on the Rancocas he looked out with a mingled feeling of wonder and sorrow upon the hurry and unrest of the world; and especially was he pained to see luxury and extravagance overgrowing the early plainness and simplicity of his own religious society. He regarded the merely rich man with unfeigned pity. With nothing of his scorn, he had all of Thoreau's commiseration, for people who went about bowed down with the weight of broad acres and great houses on their backs.

ied. And where those whose lives are for the most part regular, and whose examples have a strong influence on the minds of others, adhere to some customs which powerfully draw to the use of more strong liquor than pure wisdom allows, it hinders the spreading of the spirit of meekness, and strengthens the hands of the more excessive drinkers. This is a case to be lamented.

Every degree of luxury hath some connection with evil; and if those who profess to be disciples of Christ, and are looked upon as leaders of the people, have that mind in them which was also in Christ, and so stand separate from every wrong way, it is a means of help to the weaker. As I have sometimes been much spent in the heat and have taken spirits to revive me, I have found by experience, that in such circumstances the mind is not so calm, nor so fitly disposed for Divine meditation, as when all such extremes are avoided. I have felt an increasing care to attend to that Holy Spirit which sets right bounds to our desires, and leads those who faithfully follow it to apply all the gifts of Divine Providence to the purposes for which they were intended. Did those who have the care of great estates attend with singleness of heart to this heavenly Instructor, which so opens and enlarges the mind as to cause men to love their neighbours as themselves, they would have wisdom given them to manage their concerns, without employing some people in providing the luxuries of life, or others in labouring too hard; but for want of steadily regarding this principle of Divine love, a selfish spirit takes place in the minds of people, which is attended with darkness and manifold confusions in the world.

Though trading in things useful is an honest employ, yet through the great number of superfluities which are bought and sold, and through the corruption of the times, they who apply to merchandise for a living have great need to be well experienced in that precept which the Prophet Jeremiah laid down for his scribe: "Seekest thou great things for thyself? seek them not."

In the winter this year I was engaged with Friends in visiting families, and through the goodness of the Lord we oftentimes experienced His heart-tendering presence amongst us.

A Copy of a Letter written to a Friend.

"In this, thy late affliction, I have found a deep fellow-feeling with thee, and have had a secret hope throughout that it might please the Father of Mercies to raise thee up and sanctify thy troubles to thee; that thou being more fully acquainted with that way which the world esteems foolish, mayst feel the clothing of Divine fortitude, and be strengthened to resist that spirit which leads from the simplicity of the everlasting truth.

"We may see ourselves crippled and halting, and from a strong bias to things pleasant and easy, find an impossibility to advance forward; but things impossible with men are possible with God; and our wills being made subject to His, all temptations are surmountable.

"This work of subjecting the will is compared to the mineral in the furnace, which, through fervent heat, is reduced from its first principle: 'He refines them as silver is refined; he shall sit as a refiner and purifier of silver.' By these comparisons we are instructed in the necessity of the melting operation of the hand of God upon us, to prepare our hearts truly to adore Him, and manifest that adoration by inwardly turning away from that spirit, in all its workings, which is not of Him. To forward this work the all-wise God is sometimes pleased, through outward distress, to bring us near the gates of death; that life being painful and afflicting, and the prospect of eternity opened before us, all earthly bonds may be loosened, and the mind prepared for that deep and sacred instruction which otherwise would not be received. If kind parents love their children and delight in their happiness, then He who is perfect goodness in sending abroad mortal contagions doth assuredly direct their use. Are the righteous removed by it? their change is happy. Are the wicked taken away in their wickedness? the Almighty is clear. Do we pass through with anguish and great bitterness, and yet recover? He intends that we should be purged from dross, and our ear opened to discipline.

"And now, as thou art again restored, after thy sore affliction and doubts of recovery, forget not Him who hath helped thee, but in humble gratitude hold fast His instructions, and thereby shun those by-paths which lead from the firm foundation. I am sensible of that variety of company to which one in thy business must be exposed; I have painfully felt the force of conversation proceeding from men deeply rooted in an earthly mind, and can sympathize with others in such conflicts, because much weakness still attends me.

"I find that to be a fool as to worldly wisdom, and to commit my cause to God, not fearing to offend men, who take offence at the simplicity of truth, is the only way to remain unmoved at the sentiments of others.

"The fear of man brings a snare. By halting in our duty, and giving back in the time of trial, our hands grow weaker, our spirits get mingled with the people, our ears grow dull as to hearing the language of the true Shepherd, so that when we look at the way of the righteous, it seems as though it was not for us to follow them.

"A love clothes my mind while I write, which is superior to all expression; and I find my heart open to encourage to a holy emulation, to advance forward in Christian firmness. Deep humility is a strong bulwark, and as we enter into it we find safety and true exaltation. The foolishness of God is wiser than man, and the weakness of God is stronger than man. Being unclothed of our own wisdom, and knowing the abasement of the creature, we find that power to arise which gives health and vigour to us."

CHAPTER IV

1757–58

Visit to the Families of Friends at Burlington.—Journey to Pennsylvania, Maryland, Virginia, and North Carolina.—Considerations on the State of Friends there, and the exercise he was under in Traveling among those so generally concerned in keeping Slaves, with some Observations on this Subject.—Epistle to Friends at New Garden and Crane Creek.— Thoughts on the Neglect of a Religious care in the Education of the Negroes.

Thirteenth of Fifth Month, 1757.—Being in good health, and abroad with Friends visiting families, I lodged at a Friend's house in Burlington. Going to bed about the time usual with me, I awoke in the night, and my meditations, as I lay, were on the goodness and mercy of the Lord, in a sense whereof my heart was contrited. After this I went to sleep again; in a short time I awoke; it was yet dark, and no appearance of day or moonshine, and as I opened mine eyes I saw a light in my chamber, at the apparent distance of five feet, about nine inches in diameter, of a clear, easy brightness, and near its centre the most radiant. As I lay still looking upon it without any surprise, words were spoken to my inward ear, which filled my whole inward man. They were not the effect of thought, nor any conclusion in relation to the appearance, but as the language of the Holy One spoken in my mind. The words were, CERTAIN EVIDENCE OF DIVINE TRUTH. They were again repeated exactly in the same manner, and then the light disappeared.

Feeling the exercise in relation to a visit to the Southern Provinces to increase upon me, I acquainted our Monthly Meeting therewith, and obtained their certificate. Expecting to go alone, one of my brothers who lived in Philadelphia, having some business in North Carolina, proposed going with me part of the way; but as he had a view of some outward affairs, to accept of him as a companion was some difficulty with me, whereupon I had conversation with him at sundry times. At length feeling easy in my mind, I had conversation with several elderly Friends of Philadelphia on the subject, and he obtaining a certificate suitable to the occasion, we set off in the Fifth Month, 1757. Coming to Nottingham week-day meeting, we lodged at John Churchman's, where I met with our friend, Benjamin Buffington, from New England, who was returning from a visit to the Southern Provinces. Thence we crossed the river Susquehanna, and lodged at William Cox's in Maryland.

Soon after I entered this province a deep and painful exercise came upon me, which I often had some feeling of, since my mind was drawn toward these parts, and with which I had acquainted my brother before we agreed to join as companions. As the people in this and the Southern Provinces live much on the labour of slaves, many of whom are used hardly, my concern was that I might attend with singleness of heart to the voice of the true Shepherd, and be so supported as to remain unmoved at the faces of men.

As it is common for Friends on such a visit to have entertainment free of cost, a difficulty arose in my mind with respect to saving my money by kindness received from what appeared to me to be the gain of oppression. Receiving a gift, considered as a gift, brings the receiver under obligations to the benefactor, and has a natural tendency to draw the obliged into a party with the giver. To prevent difficulties of this kind, and to preserve the minds of judges from any bias, was that Divine prohibition: "Thou shalt not receive any gift; for a gift blindeth the wise, and perverteth the words of the righteous." (Exod. xxiii. 8.) As the disciples were sent forth without any provision for their journey, and our Lord said the workman is worthy of his meat, their labour in the gospel was considered as a reward for their entertainment, and therefore not received as a gift; yet, in regard to my present journey, I could not see my way clear in that respect. The difference appeared thus: the entertainment the disciples met with was from them whose hearts God had opened to receive them, from a love to them and the truth they published; but we, considered as members of the same religious society, look upon it as a piece of civility to receive each other in such visits; and such reception, at times, is partly in regard to reputation, and not from an inward unity of heart and spirit. Conduct is more convincing than language, and where people, by their actions, manifest that the slave-trade is not so disagreeable to their principles but that it may be encouraged, there is not a sound uniting with some Friends who visit them.

The prospect of so weighty a work, and of being so distinguished from many whom I esteemed before myself, brought me very low, and such were the conflicts of my soul that I had a near sympathy with the Prophet, in the time of his weakness, when he said: "If thou deal thus with me, kill me, I pray thee, if I have found favour in thy sight." (Num. xi. 15.) But I soon saw that this proceeded from the want of a full resignation to the Divine will. Many were the afflictions which attended me, and in great abasement, with many tears, my cries were to the Almighty for His gracious and Fatherly assistance, and after a time of deep trial I was favoured to understand the state mentioned by the Psalmist more clearly than ever I have done before; to wit: "My soul is even as a weaned child." (Psalm cxxxi. 2.) Being thus helped to sink down into resignation, I felt a deliverance from that tempest in which I had been sorely exercised, and in calmness of mind went forward, trusting that the Lord Jesus Christ, as I faithfully attended to Him, would be a counsellor to me in all difficulties, and that by His strength I should be enabled even to leave money with the members of society where I had entertainment, when I found that omitting it would obstruct that work to which I believed He had called me. As I copy this after my return, I may here add, that oftentimes I did so under a sense of duty. The way in which I did it was thus: when I expected soon to leave a Friend's house where I had entertainment, if I believed that I should not keep clear from the gain of oppression without leaving money, I spoke to one of the heads of the family privately, and desired them to accept of those pieces of silver, and give them to such of their negroes as they believed would make the best use of them; and at other times I gave them to the negroes myself, as the way looked clearest to me. Before I came out, I had provided a large number of small pieces for this purpose and thus offering them to some who appeared to be wealthy people was a trial both to me and them. But the fear of the Lord so covered me at times that my way was made easier than I expected; and few, if any, manifested any resentment at the offer, and most of them, after some conversation accepted of them.

Ninth of Fifth Month.—A Friend at whose house we breakfasted setting us a little on our way, I had conversation with him, in the fear of the Lord, concerning his slaves, in which my heart was tender; I used much plainness of speech with him, and he appeared to take it kindly. We pursued our journey without appointing meetings, being pressed in my mind to be at the Yearly Meeting in Virginia. In my travelling on the road, I often felt a cry rise from the centre of my mind, thus: "O Lord, I am a stranger on the earth, hide not thy face from me." On the 11th, we crossed the rivers Patowmack and Rapahannock, and lodged at Port Royal. On the way we had the company of a colonel of the militia, who appeared to be a thoughtful man. I took occasion to remark on the difference in general betwixt a people used to labour moderately for their living, training up their children in frugality and business, and those who live on the labour of slaves; the former, in my view, being the most happy life. He concurred in the remark, and mentioned the trouble arising from the untoward, slothful disposition of the negroes, adding that one of our labourers would do as much in a day as two of their slaves. I replied that free men, whose minds were properly on their business, found a satisfaction in improving, cultivating, and providing for their families; but negroes, labouring to support others who claim them as their property, and expecting nothing but slavery during life, had not the like inducement to be industrious.

After some further conversation, I said that men having power too often misapplied it; that though we made slaves of the negroes, and the Turks made slaves of the Christians, I believed that liberty was the natural right of all men equally. This he did not deny, but said the lives of the negroes were so wretched in their own country that many of them lived better here than there. I replied, "There is great odds in regard to us on what principle we act"; and so the conversation on that subject ended. I may here add that another person, some time afterwards, mentioned the wretchedness of the negroes, occasioned by their intestine wars, as an argument in favour of our fetching them away for slaves. To which I replied, if compassion for the Africans, on account of their domestic troubles, was the real motive of our purchasing them, that spirit of tenderness being attended to, would incite us to use them kindly, that, as strangers brought out of affliction, their lives might be happy among us. And as they are human creatures, whose souls are as precious as ours, and who may receive the same help and comfort from the Holy Scriptures as we do, we could not omit suitable endeavours to instruct them therein; but that while we manifest by our conduct that our views in purchasing them are to advance ourselves, and while our buying captives taken in war animates those parties to push on the war, and increase desolation amongst them, to say they live unhappily in Africa is far from being an argument in our favour. I further said, the present circumstances of these provinces to me appear difficult; the slaves look like a burdensome stone to such as burden themselves with them; and that if the white people retain a resolution to prefer their outward prospects of gain to all other considerations, and do not act conscientiously toward them as fellow-creatures, I believe that burden will grow heavier and heavier, until times change in a way disagreeable to us. The person appeared very serious, and owned that in considering their condition and the manner of their treatment in these provinces he had sometimes thought it might be just in the Almighty to so order it.

Having travelled through Maryland, we came amongst Friends at Cedar Creek in Virginia, on the 12th; and the next day rode, in company with several of them, a day's journey to Camp Creek. As I was riding along in the morning, my mind was deeply affected in a sense I had of the need of Divine aid to support me in the various difficulties which attended me, and in uncommon distress of mind I cried in secret to the Most High, "O Lord, be merciful, I beseech Thee, to Thy poor afflicted creature!" After some time, I felt inward relief, and soon after a Friend in company began to talk in support of the slave-trade, and said the negroes were understood to be the offspring of Cain, their blackness being the mark which God set upon him after he murdered Abel, his brother; that it was the design of Providence they should be slaves, as a condition proper to the race of so wicked a man as Cain was. Then another spake in support of what had been said. To all which I replied in substance as follows: that Noah and his family were all who survived the flood, according to Scripture; and as Noah was of Seth's race, the family of Cain was wholly destroyed. One of them said that after the flood Ham went to the land of Nod and took a wife; that Nod was a land far distant, inhabited by Cain's race, and that the flood did not reach it; and as Ham was sentenced to be a servant of servants to his brethren, these two families, being thus joined, were undoubtedly fit only for slaves. I replied, the flood was a judgment upon the world for their abominations, and it was granted that Cain's stock was the most wicked, and therefore unreasonable to suppose that they were spared. As to Ham's going to the land of Nod for a wife, no time being fixed, Nod might be inhabited by some of Noah's family before Ham married a second time; moreover the text saith "That all flesh died that moved upon the earth." (Gen. vii. 21.) I further reminded them how the prophets repeatedly declare "that the son shall not suffer for the iniquity of the father, but every one be answerable for his own sins." I was troubled to perceive the darkness of their imaginations, and in some pressure of spirit said, "The love of ease and gain are the motives in general for keeping slaves, and men are wont to take hold of weak arguments to support a cause which is unreasonable. I have no interest on either side, save only the interest which I desire to have in the truth. I believe liberty is their right, and as I see they are not only deprived of it, but treated in other respects with inhumanity in many places, I believe He who is a refuge for the oppressed will, in His own time, plead their cause, and happy will it be for such as walk in uprightness before Him." And thus our conversation ended.

Fourteenth of Fifth Month.—I was this day at Camp Creek Monthly Meeting, and then rode to the mountains up James River, and had a meeting at a Friend's house, in both which I felt sorrow of heart, and my tears were poured out before the Lord, who was pleased to afford a degree of strength by which way was opened to clear my mind amongst Friends in those places. From thence I went to Fork Creek, and so to Cedar Creek again, at which place I now had a meeting. Here I found a tender seed, and as I was preserved in the ministry to keep low with the truth, the same truth in their hearts answered it, that it was a time of mutual refreshment from the presence of the Lord. I lodged at James Standley's, father of William Standley, one of the young men who suffered imprisonment at Winchester last summer on account of their testimony against fighting, and I had some satisfactory conversation with him concerning it. Hence I went to the Swamp Meeting, and to Wayanoke Meeting, and then crossed James River, and lodged near Burleigh. From the time of my entering Maryland I have been much under sorrow, which of late so increased upon me that my mind was almost overwhelmed, and I may say with the Psalmist, "In my distress I called upon the Lord, and cried to my God," who, in infinite goodness, looked upon my affliction, and in my private retirement sent the Comforter for my relief, for which I humbly bless His holy name.

The sense I had of the state of the churches brought a weight of distress upon me. The gold to me appeared dim, and the fine gold changed, and though this is the case too generally, yet the sense of it in these parts hath in a particular manner borne heavy upon me. It appeared to me that through the prevailing of the spirit of this world the minds of many were brought to an inward desolation, and instead of the spirit of meekness, gentleness, and heavenly wisdom, which are the necessary companions of the true sheep of Christ, a spirit of fierceness and the love of dominion too generally prevailed. From small beginnings in error great buildings by degrees are raised, and from one age to another are more and more strengthened by the general concurrence of the people; and as men obtain reputation by their profession of the truth, their virtues are mentioned as arguments in favour of general error; and those of less note, to justify themselves say, such and such good men did the like. By what other steps could the people of Judah arise to that height in wickedness as to give just ground for the Prophet Isaiah to declare, in the name of the Lord, "that none calleth for justice, nor any pleadeth for truth" (Isa. lix. 4), or for the almighty to call upon the great city of Jerusalem just before the Babylonish captivity, "If ye can find a man, if there be any who executeth judgment, that seeketh the truth, and I will pardon it"? (Jer. v. 1.)

The prospect of a way being open to the same degeneracy, in some parts of this newly settled land of America, in respect to our conduct towards the negroes, hath deeply bowed my mind in this journey, and though briefly to relate how these people are treated is no agreeable work, yet, after often reading over the notes I made as I travelled, I find my mind engaged to preserve them. Many of the white people in those provinces take little or no care of negro marriages; and when negroes marry after their own way, some make so little account of those marriages, that with views of outward interest they often part men from their wives by selling them far asunder, which is common when estates are sold by executors at vendue. Many whose labour is heavy being followed in their business in the field by a man with a whip, hired for that purpose, have in common little else allowed but one peck of Indian corn and some salt, for one week, with a few potatoes; the potatoes they commonly raise by their labour on the first day of the week. The correction ensuing on their disobedience to overseers, or slothfulness in business, is often very severe, and sometimes desperate.

Men and women have many times scarcely clothes sufficient to hide their nakedness, and boys and girls ten and twelve years old are often quite naked amongst their master's children. Some of our Society, and some of the society called New-lights, use some endeavours to instruct those they have in reading; but in common this is not only neglected, but disapproved. These are the people by whose labour the other inhabitants are in a great measure supported, and many of them in the luxuries of life. These are the people who have made no agreement to serve us, and who have not forfeited their liberty that we know of. These are the souls for whom Christ died, and for our conduct towards them we must answer before Him who is no respecter of persons. They who know the only true God, and Jesus Christ whom He hath sent, and are thus acquainted with the merciful, benevolent, gospel spirit, will therein perceive that the indignation of God is kindled against oppression and cruelty, and in beholding the great distress of so numerous a people will find cause for mourning.

From my lodgings I went to Burleigh Meeting, where I felt my mind drawn in quiet, resigned state. After long silence I felt an engagement to stand up, and through the powerful operation of Divine love we were favoured with an edifying meeting. The next meeting we had was at Blackwater, and from thence went to the Yearly Meeting at the Western Branch. When business began, some queries were introduced by some of their members for consideration, and, if approved, they were to be answered hereafter by their respective Monthly Meetings. They were the Pennsylvania queries, which had been examined by a committee of Virginia Yearly Meeting appointed the last year, who made some alterations in them, one of which alterations was made in favour of a custom which troubled me. The query was, "Are there any concerned in the importation of negroes, or in buying them after imported?" which was thus altered, "Are there any concerned in the importation of negroes, or buying them to trade in?" As one query admitted with unanimity was, "Are any concerned in buying or vending goods unlawfully imported, or prize goods?" I found my mind engaged to say that as we profess the truth, and were there assembled to support the testimony of it, it was necessary for us to dwell deep and act in that wisdom which is pure, or otherwise we could not prosper. I then mentioned their alteration, and referring to the last-mentioned query, added, that as purchasing any merchandise taken by the sword was always allowed to be inconsistent with our principles, so negroes being captives of war, or taken by stealth, it was inconsistent with our testimony to buy them; and their being our fellow-creatures, and sold as slaves, added greatly to the iniquity. Friends appeared attentive to what was said; some expressed a care and concern about their negroes; none made any objection, by way of reply to what I said, but the query was admitted as they had altered it.

As some of their members have heretofore traded in negroes, as in other merchandise, this query being admitted will be one step further than they have hitherto gone, and I did not see it my duty to press for an alteration, but felt easy to leave it all to Him who alone is able to turn the hearts of the mighty, and make way for the spreading of truth on the earth, by means agreeable to His infinite wisdom. In regard to those they already had, I felt my mind engaged to labour with them, and said that as we believe the Scriptures were given forth by holy men, as they were moved by the Holy Ghost, and many of us know by experience that they are often helpful and comfortable, and believe ourselves bound to duty to teach our children to read them; I believed that if we were divested of all selfish views, the same good Spirit that gave them forth would engage us to teach the negroes to read, that they might have the benefit of them. Some present manifested a concern to take more care in the education of their negroes.

Twenty-ninth of Fifth Month.—At the house where I lodged was a meeting of ministers and elders. I found an engagement to speak freely and plainly to them concerning their slaves; mentioning how they as the first rank in the society, whose conduct in that case was much noticed by others, were under the stronger obligations to look carefully to themselves—expressing how needful it was for them in that situation to be thoroughly divested of all selfish views; that, living in the pure truth, and acting conscientiously towards those people in their education and otherwise, they might be instrumental in helping forward a work so exceedingly necessary, and so much neglected amongst them. At the twelfth hour the meeting for worship began, which was a solid meeting.

The next day, about the tenth hour, Friends met to finish their business, and then the meeting for worship ensued, which to me was a laborious time; but through the goodness of the Lord, truth, I believed, gained some ground, and it was a strengthening opportunity to the honest-hearted.

About this time I wrote an epistle to Friends in the back settlements of North Carolina, as follows:—

TO FRIENDS AT THEIR MONTHLY MEETING AT NEW GARDEN AND CANE CREEK, IN NORTH CAROLINA:—

DEAR FRIENDS,—It having pleased the Lord to draw me forth on a visit to some parts of Virginia and Carolina, you have often been in my mind; and though my way is not clear to come in person to visit you, yet I feel it in my heart to communicate a few things, as they arise in the love of truth. First, my dear friends, dwell in humility; and take heed that no views of outward gain get too deep hold of you, that so your eyes being single to the Lord, you may be preserved in the way of safety. Where people let loose their minds after the love of outward things, and are more engaged in pursuing the profits and seeking the friendships of this world than to be inwardly acquainted with the way of true peace, they walk in a vain shadow, while the true comfort of life is wanting. Their examples are often hurtful to others; and their treasures thus collected do many times prove dangerous snares to their children.

But where people are sincerely devoted to follow Christ, and dwell under the influence of His Holy Spirit, their stability and firmness, through a Divine blessing, is at times like dew on the tender plants round about them, and the weightiness of their spirits secretly works on the minds of others. In this condition, through the spreading influence of Divine love, they feel a care over the flock, and way is opened for maintaining good order in the Society. And though we may meet with opposition from another spirit, yet, as there is a dwelling in meekness, feeling our spirits subject, and moving only in the gentle, peaceable wisdom, the inward reward of quietness will be greater than all our difficulties. Where the pure life is kept to, and meetings of discipline are held in the authority of it, we find by experience that they are comfortable, and tend to the health of the body.

While I write, the youth come fresh in my way. Dear young people, choose God for your portion; love His truth, and be not ashamed of it; choose for your company such as serve Him in uprightness; and shun as most dangerous the conversation of those whose lives are of an ill savour; for by frequenting such company some hopeful young people have come to great loss, and been drawn from less evils to greater, to their utter ruin. In the bloom of youth no ornament is so lovely as that of virtue, nor any enjoyments equal to those which we partake of in fully resigning ourselves to the Divine will. These enjoyments add sweetness to all other comforts, and give true satisfaction in company and conversation, where people are mutually acquainted with it; and as your minds are thus seasoned with the truth, you will find strength to abide steadfast to the testimony of it, and be prepared for services in the church.

And now, dear friends and brethren, as you are improving a wilderness, and may be numbered amongst the first planters in one part of a province, I beseech you, in the love of Jesus Christ, wisely to consider the force of your examples, and think how much your successors may be thereby affected. It is a help in a country, yea, and a great favour and blessing, when customs first settled are agreeable to sound wisdom; but when they are otherwise the effect of them is grievous; and children feel themselves encompassed with difficulties prepared for them by their predecessors.

As moderate care and exercise, under the direction of true wisdom, are useful both to mind and body, so by these means in general the real wants of life are easily supplied, our gracious Father having so proportioned one to the other that keeping in the medium we may pass on quietly. Where slaves are purchased to do our labour numerous difficulties attend it. To rational creatures bondage is uneasy, and frequently occasions sourness and discontent in them; which affects the family and such as claim the mastery over them. Thus people and their children are many times encompassed with vexations, which arise from their applying to wrong methods to get a living.

I have been informed that there is a large number of Friends in your parts who have no slaves; and in tender and most affectionate love I beseech you to keep clear from purchasing any. Look, my dear friends, to Divine Providence, and follow in simplicity that exercise of body, that plainness and frugality, which true wisdom leads to; so may you be preserved from those dangers which attend such as are aiming at outward ease and greatness.

Treasures, though small, attained on a true principle of virtue, are sweet; and while we walk in the light of the Lord there is true comfort and satisfaction in the possession; neither the murmurs of an oppressed people, nor a throbbing uneasy conscience, nor anxious thoughts about the events of things, hinder the enjoyment of them.

When we look towards the end of life, and think on the division of our substance among our successors, if we know that it was collected in the fear of the Lord, in honesty, in equity, and in uprightness of heart before Him, we may consider it as His gift to us, and, with a single eye to His blessing, bestow it on those we leave behind us. Such is the happiness of the plain ways of true virtue. "The work of righteousness shall be peace; and the effect of righteousness, quietness and assurance forever." (Isa. xxxii. 17.)

Dwell here, my dear friends; then in remote and solitary deserts you may find true peace and satisfaction. If the Lord be our God, in truth and reality, there is safety for us; for He is a stronghold in the day of trouble, and knoweth them that trust in Him.

ISLE OF WIGHT COUNTY, in Virginia, 20th of the 5th Month, 1757.

From the Yearly Meeting in Virginia I went to Carolina, and on the 1st of Sixth Month was at Wells Monthly Meeting, where the spring of the gospel ministry was opened, and the love of Jesus Christ experienced among us; to His name be the praise.

Here my brother joined with some Friends from New Garden who were going homeward; and I went next to Simons Creek Monthly Meeting, where I was silent during the meeting for worship. When business came on, my mind was exercised concerning the poor slaves, but I did not feel my way clear to speak. In this condition I was bowed in spirit before the Lord, and with tears and inward supplication besought Him so to open my understanding that I might know His will concerning me; and, at length, my mind was settled in silence. Near the end of their business a member of their meeting expressed a concern that had some time lain upon him, on account of Friends so much neglecting their duty in the education of their slaves, and proposed having meetings sometimes appointed for them on a week-day, to be attended only by some Friends to be named in their Monthly Meetings. Many present appeared to unite with the proposal. One said he had often wondered that they, being our fellow-creatures, and capable of religious understanding, had been so exceedingly neglected; another expressed the like concern, and appeared zealous that in future it might be more closely considered. At length a minute was made, and the further consideration of it referred to their next Monthly Meeting. The Friend who made this proposal hath negroes; he told me that he was at New Garden, about two hundred and fifty miles from home, and came back alone; that in this solitary journey this exercise, in regard to the education of their negroes, was from time to time renewed in his mind. A Friend of some note in Virginia, who hath slaves, told me that he being far from home on a lonesome journey had many serious thoughts about them: and his mind was so impressed therewith that he believed he saw a time coming when Divine Providence would alter the circumstances of these people, respecting their condition as slaves.

From hence I went to a meeting at Newbegun Creek, and sat a

considerable time in much weakness; then I felt truth open the way to speak a little in much plainness and simplicity, till at length, through the increase of Divine love amongst us, we had a seasoning opportunity. This was also the case at the head of Little River, where we had a crowded meeting on the first-day. I went thence to the Old Neck, where I was led into a careful searching out of the secret workings of the mystery of iniquity, which, under the cover of religion, exalts itself against that pure spirit which leads in the way of meekness and self-denial. Pineywoods was the last meeting I was at in Carolina; it was large, and my heart being deeply engaged, I was drawn forth into a fervent labour amongst them.

When I was at Newbegun Creek a Friend was there who laboured for his living, having no negroes, and who had been a minister many years. He came to me the next day, and as we rode together he signified that he wanted to talk with me concerning a difficulty he had been under, which he related nearly as follows. That as moneys had of late years been raised by a tax to carry on the wars, he had a scruple in his mind in regard to paying it, and chose rather to suffer distraint of his goods; but as he was the only person who refused it in those parts, and knew not that any one else was in the like circumstances, he signified that it had been a heavy trial to him, especially as some of his brethren had been uneasy with his conduct in that case. He added, that from a sympathy he felt with me yesterday in meeting, he found freedom thus to open the matter in the way of querying concerning Friends in our parts; I told him the state of Friends amongst us as well as I was able, and also that I had for some time been under the like scruple. I believed him to be one who was concerned to walk uprightly before the Lord, and esteemed it my duty to preserve this note concerning him, Samuel Newby.

From hence I went back into Virginia, and had a meeting near James Cowpland's; it was a time of inward suffering, but through the goodness of the Lord I was made content; at another meeting, through the renewings of pure love, we had a very comfortable season.

Travelling up and down of late, I have had renewed evidences that to be faithful to the Lord, and content with His will concerning me, is a most necessary and useful lesson for me to be learning; looking less at the effects of my labour than in the pure motion and reality of the concern, as it arises from heavenly love. In the Lord Jehovah is everlasting strength; and as the mind, by humble resignation, is united to Him, and we utter words from an inward knowledge that they arise from the heavenly spring, though our way may be difficult, and it may require close attention to keep in it, and though the manner in which we may be led may tend to our own abasement; yet, if we continue in patience and meekness, heavenly peace will be the reward of our labours.

I attended Curles Meeting, which, though small, was reviving to the honest-hearted. Afterwards I went to Black Creek and Caroline Meetings, from whence, accompanied by William Standley before mentioned, I rode to Goose Creek, being much through the woods, and about one hundred miles. We lodged the first night at a public-house; the second in the woods; and the next day we reached a Friend's house at Goose Creek. In the woods we were under some disadvantage, having no fire-works nor bells for our horses, but we stopped a little before night and let them feed on the wild grass, which was plentiful, in the meantime cutting with our knives a store against night. We then secured our horses, and gathering some bushes under an oak we lay down; but the mosquitoes being numerous and the ground damp I slept but little. Thus lying in the wilderness, and looking at the stars, I was led to contemplate on the condition of our first parents when they were sent forth from the garden; how the Almighty, though they had been disobedient, continued to be a father to them, and showed them what tended to their felicity as intelligent creatures, and was acceptable to Him. To provide things relative to our outward living, in the way of true wisdom, is good, and the gift of improving in things useful is a good gift, and comes from the Father of Lights. Many have had this gift; and from age to age there have been improvements of this kind made in the world. But some, not keeping to the pure gift, have in the creaturely cunning and self-exaltation sought out many inventions. As the first motive to these inventions of men, and distinct from that uprightness in which man was created, was evil, so the effects have been and are evil. It is, therefore, as necessary for us at this day constantly to attend on the heavenly gift, to be qualified to use rightly the good things in this life amidst great improvements, as it was for our first parents when they were without any improvements, without any friend or father but God only.

I was at a meeting at Goose Creek, and next at a Monthly Meeting at Fairfax, where, through the gracious dealing of the Almighty with us, His power prevailed over many hearts. From thence I went to Monoquacy and Pipe Creek in Maryland; at both places I had cause humbly to adore Him who had supported me through many exercises, and by whose help I was enabled to reach the true witness in the hearts of others. There were some hopeful young people in those parts. I had meetings afterwards at John Everit's in Monalen, and at Huntingdon, and I was made humbly thankful to the Lord, who opened my heart amongst the people in these new settlements, so that it was a time of encouragement to the honest-minded.

At Monalen a Friend gave me some account of a religious society among the Dutch, called Mennonists, and amongst other things related a passage in substance as follows: One of the Mennonists having acquaintance with a man of another society at a considerable distance, and being with his wagon on business near the house of his said acquaintance, and night coming on, he had thoughts of putting up with him, but passing by his fields, and observing the distressed appearance of his slaves, he kindled a fire in the woods hard by, and lay there that night. His said acquaintance hearing where he lodged, and afterwards meeting the Mennonist, told him of it, adding he should have been heartily welcome at his house, and from their acquaintance in former time wondered at his conduct in that case. The Mennonist replied, "Ever since I lodged by thy field I have wanted an opportunity to speak with thee. I had intended to come to thy house for entertainment, but seeing thy slaves at their work, and observing the manner of their dress, I had no liking to come to partake with thee." He then admonished him to use them with more humanity, and added, "As I lay by the fire that night, I thought that as I was a man of substance thou wouldst have received me freely; but if I had been as poor as one of thy slaves, and had no power to help myself, I should have received from thy hand no kinder usage than they."

In this journey I was out about two months, and travelled about eleven hundred and fifty miles. I returned home under an humbling sense of the gracious dealings of the Lord with me, in preserving me through many trials and afflictions.

CHAPTER V

1757–58

Considerations on the Payment of a Tax laid for Carrying on the War against the Indians.—Meetings of the Committee of the Yearly Meeting at Philadelphia.—Some Notes on Thomas a Kempis and John Huss.—The present Circumstances of Friends in Pennsylvania and New Jersey very Different from those of our Predecessors.—The Drafting of the Militia in New Jersey to serve in the Army, with some Observations on the State of the Members of our Society at that time.—Visit to Friends in Pennsylvania, accompanied by Benjamin Jones.—Proceedings at the Monthly, Quarterly, and Yearly Meetings in Philadelphia, respecting those who keep Slaves.

A few years past, money being made current in our province for carrying on wars, and to be called in again by taxes laid on the inhabitants, my mind was often affected with the thoughts of paying such taxes; and I believe it right for me to preserve a memorandum concerning it. I was told that Friends in England frequently paid taxes, when the money was applied to such purposes. I had conversation with several noted Friends on the subject, who all favoured the payment of such taxes; some of them I preferred before myself, and this made me easier for a time; yet there was in the depth of my mind a scruple which I never could get over; and at certain times I was greatly distressed on that account.

I believed that there were some upright-hearted men who paid such taxes, yet could not see that their example was a sufficient reason for me to do so, while I believe that the Spirit of truth required of me, as an individual, to suffer patiently the distress of goods, rather than pay actively.

To refuse the active payment of a tax which our Society generally paid was exceedingly disagreeable; but to do a thing contrary
to my conscience appeared yet more dreadful. When this exercise
came upon me, I knew of none under the like difficulty; and in my
distress I besought the Lord to enable me to give up all, that so I
might follow Him wheresoever He was pleased to lead me. Under
this exercise I went to our Yearly Meeting at Philadelphia in the
year 1755; at which a committee was appointed of some from each
Quarterly Meeting, to correspond with the meeting for sufferings in
London; and another to visit our Monthly and Quarterly Meetings.
After their appointment, before the last adjournment of the meeting, it was agreed that these two committees should meet together
in Friends' school-house in the city, to consider some things in
which the cause of truth was concerned. They accordingly had a
weighty conference in the fear of the Lord; at which time I perceived there were many Friends under a scruple like that before
mentioned.*

As scrupling to pay a tax on account of the application hath seldom been heard of heretofore, even amongst men of integrity, who
have steadily borne their testimony against outward wars in their
time, I may therefore note some things which have occurred to my
mind, as I have been inwardly exercised on that account. From the
steady opposition which faithful Friends in early times made to
wrong things then approved, they were hated and persecuted by
men living in the spirit of this world, and, suffering with firmness,
they were made a blessing to the church, and the work prospered.
It equally concerns men in every age to take heed to their own
spirits: and in comparing their situation with ours, to me it appears
that there was less danger of their being infected with the spirit of
this world, in paying such taxes, than is the case with us now. They
had little or no share in civil government, and many of them declared that they were, through the power of God separated from
the spirit in which wars were, and being afflicted by the rulers on
account of their testimony, there was less likelihood of their uniting
in spirit with them in things inconsistent with the purity of truth.
We, from the first settlement of this land, have known little or no

* Christians refused to pay taxes to support heathen temples. See Cave's
Primitive Christianity, Part III, p. 327.

troubles of that sort. The profession of our predecessors was for a time accounted reproachful, but at length their uprightness being understood by the rulers, and their innocent sufferings moving them, our way of worship was tolerated, and many of our members in these colonies became active in civil government. Being thus tried with favour and prosperity, this world appeared inviting; our minds have been turned to the improvement of our country, to merchandise and the sciences, amongst which are many things useful, if followed in pure wisdom; but in our present condition I believe it will not be denied that a carnal mind is gaining upon us. Some of our members, who are officers in civil government, are, in one case or other, called upon in their respective stations to assist in things relative to the wars; but being in doubt whether to act or to crave to be excused from their office, if they see their brethren united in the payment of a tax to carry on the said wars, may think their case not much different, and so might quench the tender movings of the Holy Spirit in their minds. Thus, by small degrees, we might approach so near to fighting that the distinction would be little else than the name of a peaceable people.

It requires great self-denial and resignation of ourselves to God, to attain that state wherein we can freely cease from fighting when wrongfully invaded, if, by our fighting, there were a probability of overcoming the invaders. Whoever rightly attains to it does in some degree feel that spirit in which our Redeemer gave His life for us; and through Divine goodness many of our predecessors, and many now living, have learned this blessed lesson; but many others, having their religion chiefly by education, and not being enough acquainted with that cross which crucifies to the world, do manifest a temper distinguishable from that of an entire trust in God. In calmly considering these things, it hath not appeared strange to me that an exercise hath now fallen upon some, which, with respect to the outward means, is different from what was known to many of those who went before us.

Some time after the Yearly Meeting, the said committees met at Philadelphia, and, by adjournments, continued sitting several days. The calamities of war were now increasing; the frontier inhabitants of Pennsylvania were frequently surprised; some were slain, and many taken captive by the Indians; and while these committees sat, the corpse of one so slain was brought in a wagon, and taken through the streets of the city in his bloody garments, to alarm the people and rouse them to war.

Friends thus met were not all of one mind in relation to the tax, which, to those who scrupled it, made the way more difficult. To refuse an active payment at such a time might be construed into an act of disloyalty, and appeared likely to displease the rulers, not only here but in England; still there was a scruple so fixed on the minds of many Friends that nothing moved it. It was a conference the most weighty that ever I was at, and the hearts of many were bowed in reverence before the Most High. Some Friends of the said committees who appeared easy to pay the tax, after several adjournments, withdrew; others of them continued till the last. At length an epistle of tender love and caution to Friends in Pennsylvania was drawn up, and being read several times and corrected, was signed by such as were free to sign it, and afterward sent to the Monthly and Quarterly Meetings.

Ninth of Eighth Month, 1757.—Orders came at night to the military officers in our county (Burlington), directing them to draft the militia, and prepare a number of men to go off as soldiers, to the relief of the English at Fort William Henry, in New York government; a few days after which, there was a general review of the militia at Mount Holly, and a number of men were chosen and sent off under some officers. Shortly after, there came orders to draft three times as many, who were to hold themselves in readiness to march when fresh orders came. On the 17th there was a meeting of the military officers at Mount Holly, who agreed on draft; orders were sent to the men so chosen to meet their respective captains at set times and places, those in our township to meet at Mount Holly, amongst whom were a considerable number of our Society. My mind being affected herewith, I had fresh opportunity to see and consider the advantage of living in the real substance of religion, where practice doth harmonize with principle. Amongst the officers are men of understanding, who have some regard to sincerity where they see it; and when such in the execution of their office have men to deal with whom they believe to be upright-hearted, it is a painful task to put them to trouble on account of scruples of conscience, and they will be likely to avoid it as much and as easily as may be. But where men profess to be so meek and heavenly-minded, and to have their trust so firmly settled in God that they cannot join in wars, and yet by their spirit and conduct in common life manifest a contrary disposition, their difficulties are great at such a time.

When officers who are anxiously endeavouring to get troops to answer the demands of their superiors, see men who are insincere pretend scruples of conscience in hopes of being excused from a dangerous employment, it is likely they will be roughly handled. In this time of commotion some of our young men left these parts and tarried abroad till it was over; some came, and proposed to go as soldiers; others appeared to have a real tender scruple in their minds against joining in wars, and were much humbled under the apprehension of a trial so near. I had conversation with several of them to my satisfaction. When the captain came to town, some of the last-mentioned went and told him in substance as follows: That they could not bear arms for conscience' sake; nor could they hire any to go in their places, being resigned as to the event. At length the captain acquainted them all that they might return home for the present, but he required them to provide themselves as soldiers, and be in readiness to march when called upon. This was such a time as I had not seen before; and yet I may say, with thankfulness to the Lord, that I believed the trial was intended for our good; and I was favoured with resignation to Him. The French army having taken the fort they were besieging, destroyed it and went away; the company of men who were first drafted, after some days' march, had orders to return home, and those on the second draft were no more called upon on that occasion.

Fourth of Fourth Month, 1758.—Orders came to some officers in Mount Holly to prepare quarters for a short time for about one hundred soldiers. An officer and two other men, all inhabitants of our town, came to my house. The officer told me that he came to desire me to provide lodging and entertainment for two soldiers, and that six shillings a week per man would be allowed as pay for it. The case being new and unexpected I made no answer suddenly, but sat a time silent, my mind being inward. I was fully convinced that the proceedings in wars are inconsistent with the purity of the Christian religion; and to be hired to entertain men, who were then under pay as soldiers, was a difficulty with me. I expected they had legal authority for what they did; and after a short time I said to the officer, if the men are sent here for entertainment I believe I shall not refuse to admit them into my house, but the nature of the case is such that I expect I cannot keep them on hire; one of the men intimated that he thought I might do it consistently with my religious principles. To which I made no reply, believing silence at that time best for me. Though they spake of two, there came only one, who tarried at my house about two weeks, and behaved himself civilly. When the officer came to pay me, I told him I could not take pay, having admitted him into my house in a passive obedience to authority. I was on horseback when he spake to me, and as I turned from him, he said he was obliged to me, to which I said nothing; but, thinking on the expression, I grew uneasy; and afterwards, being near where he lived, I went and told him on what grounds I refused taking pay for keeping the soldier.

I have been informed that Thomas a Kempis lived and died in the profession of the Roman Catholic religion; and, in reading his writings, I have believed him to be a man of true Christian spirit, as fully so as many who died martyrs because they could not join with some superstitions in that church. All true Christians are of the same spirit, but their gifts are diverse, Jesus Christ appointing to each one his peculiar office, agreeably to His infinite wisdom.

John Huss contended against the errors which had crept into the church, in opposition to the Council of Constance, which the historian reports to have consisted of some thousand persons. He modestly vindicated the cause which he believed was right; and though his language and conduct towards his judges appear to have been respectful, yet he never could be moved from the principles settled in his mind. To use his own words: "This I most humbly require and desire of you all, even for His sake who is the God of us all, that I be not compelled to the thing which my conscience doth repugn or strive against." And again, in his answer to the Emperor: "I refuse nothing, most noble Emperor, whatsoever the council shall decree or determine upon me, only this one thing I except, that I do not offend God and my conscience."† At length, rather than act contrary to that which he believed the Lord required of him, he chose to suffer death by fire. Thomas a Kempis, without disputing against the articles then generally agreed to, appears to have laboured, by pious example as well as by preaching

† Fox's *Acts and Monuments*, p. 233.

and writing, to promote virtue and the inward spiritual religion; and I believe they were both sincere-hearted followers of Christ. True charity is an excellent virtue; and sincerely to labour for their good, whose belief in all points doth not agree with ours, is a happy state.

Near the beginning of the year 1758, I went one evening, in company with a Friend, to visit a sick person; and before our return we were told of a woman living near, who had for several days been disconsolate, occasioned by a dream, wherein death, and the judgments of the Almighty after death, were represented to her mind in a moving manner. Her sadness on that account being worn off, the Friend with whom I was in company went to see her, and had some religious conversation with her and her husband. With this visit they were somewhat affected, and the man, with many tears, expressed his satisfaction. In a short time after the poor man, being on the river in a storm of wind, was with one more drowned.

Eighth Month, 1758.—Having had drawings in my mind to be at the Quarterly Meeting at Chester County, and at some meetings in the county of Philadelphia, I went first to said Quarterly Meeting, which was large. Several weighty matters came under consideration and debate, and the Lord was pleased to qualify some of His servants with strength and firmness to bear the burden of the day. Though I said but little, my mind was deeply exercised; and, under a sense of God's love, in the anointing and fitting of some young men for His work, I was comforted, and my heart was tendered before Him. From hence I went to the Youth's Meeting at Darby, where my beloved friend and brother Benjamin Jones met me by an appointment before I left home, to join in the visit. We were at Radnor, Merion, Richland, North Wales, Plymouth, and Abington meetings, and had cause to bow in reverence before the Lord, our gracious God, by whose help way was opened for us from day to day. I was out about two weeks, and rode about two hundred miles.

The Monthly Meeting of Philadelphia having been under a concern on account of some Friends who this summer (1758) had bought negro slaves, proposed to their Quarterly Meeting to have the minute reconsidered in the Yearly Meeting, which was made last on that subject, and the said Quarterly Meeting appointed a committee to consider it, and to report to their next. This committee having met once and adjourned, and I, going to Philadelphia to meet a committee of the Yearly Meeting, was in town the evening on which the Quarterly Meeting's committee met the second time, and finding an inclination to set with them, I, with some others was admitted, and Friends had a weighty conference on the subject. Soon after their next Quarterly Meeting I heard that the case was coming to our Yearly Meeting. This brought a weighty exercise upon me, and under a sense of my own infirmities, and the great danger I felt of turning aside from perfect purity, my mind was often drawn to retire alone, and put up my prayers to the Lord that He would be graciously pleased to strengthen me; that setting aside all views of self-interest and the friendship of this world, I might stand fully resigned to His holy will.

In this Yearly Meeting several weighty matters were considered, and toward the last that in relation to dealing with persons who purchase slaves. During the several sittings of the said meeting, my mind was frequently covered with inward prayer, and I could say with David, "that tears were my meat day and night." The case of slave-keeping lay heavy upon me, nor did I find any engagement to speak directly to any other matter before the meeting. Now when this case was opened several faithful Friends spake weightily thereto, with which I was comforted; and feeling a concern to cast in my mite, I said in substance as follows:—

"In the difficulties attending us in this life, nothing is more precious than the mind of truth inwardly manifested; and it is my earnest desire that in this weighty matter we may be so truly humbled, as to be favoured with a clear understanding of the mind of truth, and follow it; this would be of more advantage to the Society than any medium not in the clearness of Divine wisdom. The case is difficult to some who have slaves, but if such set aside all self-interest, and come to be weaned from the desire of getting estates, or even from holding them together, when truth requires the contrary, I believe way will so open that they will know how to steer through those difficulties."

Many Friends appeared to be deeply bowed under the weight of the work, and manifested much firmness in their love to the cause of truth and universal righteousness on the earth. And though none did openly justify the practice of slave-keeping in general, yet some appeared concerned lest the meeting should go into such measures as might give uneasiness to many brethren, alleging that if Friends patiently continued under the exercise, the Lord in His time might open a way for the deliverance of these people. Finding an engagement to speak, I said, "My mind is often led to consider the purity of the Divine Being, and the justice of His judgments; and herein my soul is covered with awfulness. I cannot omit to hint of some cases where people have not been treated with the purity of justice, and the event hath been lamentable. Many slaves on this continent are oppressed, and their cries have reached the ears of the Most High. Such are the purity and certainty of His judgments, that He cannot be partial in our favour. In infinite love and goodness He hath opened our understanding from one time to another concerning our duty towards this people, and it is not a time for delay. Should we now be sensible of what He requires of us, and through a respect to the private interest of some persons, or through a regard to some friendships which do not stand on an immutable foundation, neglect to do our duty in firmness and constancy, still waiting for some extraordinary means to bring about their deliverance, God may by terrible things in righteousness answer us in this matter."

Many faithful brethren laboured with great firmness, and the love of truth in a good degree prevailed. Several who had negroes expressed their desire that a rule might be made to deal with such Friends as offenders who bought slaves in future. To this it was answered that the root of this evil would never be effectually struck at, until a thorough search was made into the circumstances of such Friends as kept negroes, with respect to the righteousness of their motives in keeping them, that impartial justice might be administered throughout. Several Friends expressed their desire that a visit might be made to such Friends as kept slaves, and many others said that they believed liberty was the negro's right; to which, at length, no opposition was publicly made. A minute was made more full on that subject than any heretofore; and the names of several Friends entered who were free to join in a visit to such as kept slaves.

CHAPTER VI

1758–59

*Visit to the Quarterly Meetings in Chester County.—
Joins Daniel Stanton and John Scarborough in a Visit
to such as kept Slaves there.—Some Observations on
the Conduct which those should maintain who speak
in Meetings for Discipline.—More Visits to such as
kept Slaves, and to Friends near Salem.—Account of
the Yearly Meeting in the Year 1759, and of the increasing concern in Divers Provinces to Labour
against Buying and Keeping Slaves.—The Yearly
Meeting Epistle.—Thoughts on the Smallpox spreading, and on Inoculation.*

Eleventh of Eleventh Month, 1758.—This day I set out for Concord; the Quarterly Meeting heretofore held there was now, by
reason of a great increase of members, divided into two by the
agreement of Friends at our last Yearly Meeting. Here I met with
our beloved friends Samuel Spavold and Mary Kirby from England, and with Joseph White from Buck's County; the latter had
taken leave of his family in order to go on a religious visit to
Friends in England, and, through Divine goodness, we were favoured with a strengthening opportunity together.

After this meeting I joined with my friends, Daniel Stanton and
John Scarborough, in visiting Friends who had slaves. At night we
had a family meeting at William Trimble's, many young people
being there; and it was a precious, reviving opportunity. Next
morning we had a comfortable sitting with a sick neighbour, and
thence to the burial of the corpse of a Friend at Uwchland Meeting, at which were many people, and it was a time of Divine
favour, after which we visited some who had slaves. In the evening
we had a family meeting at a Friend's house, where the channel of
the gospel love was opened, and my mind was comforted after a

hard day's labour. The next day we were at Goshen Monthly Meeting, and on the 18th attended the Quarterly Meeting at London Grove, it being first held at that place. Here we met again with all the before-mentioned Friends, and had some edifying meetings. Near the conclusion of the meeting for business, Friends were incited to constancy in supporting the testimony of truth, and reminded of the necessity which the disciples of Christ are under to attend principally to His business as He is pleased to open it to us, and to be particularly careful to have our minds redeemed from the love of wealth, and our outward affairs in as little room as may be, that no temporal concerns may entangle our affections, or hinder us from diligently following the dictates of truth in labouring to promote the pure spirit of meekness and heavenly-mindedness amongst the children of men in these days of calamity and distress, wherein God is visiting our land with His just judgments.

Each of these Quarterly Meetings was large and sat nearly eight hours. I had occasion to consider that it is a weighty thing to speak much in large meetings for business, for except our minds are rightly prepared, and we clearly understand the case we speak to, instead of forwarding, we hinder business, and make more labour for those on whom the burden of the work is laid. If selfish views or a partial spirit have any room in our minds, we are unfit for the Lord's work; if we have a clear prospect of the business, and proper weight on our minds to speak, we should avoid useless apologies and repetitions. Where people are gathered from far, and adjourning a meeting of business is attended with great difficulty, it behoves all to be cautious how they detain a meeting, especially when they have sat six or seven hours, and have a great distance to ride home. After this meeting I rode home.

In the beginning of the twelfth month I joined in company with my friends John Sykes and Daniel Stanton, in visiting such as had slaves. Some whose hearts were rightly exercised about them appeared to be glad of our visit, but in some places our way was more difficult. I often saw the necessity of keeping down to that root from whence our concern proceeded, and have cause, in reverent thankfulness, humbly to bow down before the Lord, who was near to me, and preserved my mind in calmness under some sharp conflicts, and begat a spirit of sympathy and tenderness in me towards some who were grievously entangled by the spirit of this world.

First Month, 1759.—Having found my mind drawn to visit some of the more active members in our Society at Philadelphia, who had slaves, I met my friend John Churchman there by agreement, and we continued about a week in the city. We visited some that were sick, and some widows and their families, and the other part of our time was mostly employed in visiting such as had slaves. It was a time of deep exercise, but looking often to the Lord for His assistance, He in unspeakable kindness favoured us with the influence of that Spirit which crucifies to the greatness and splendour of this world, and enabling us to go through some heavy labours, in which we found peace.

Twenty-fourth of Third Month, 1759.—After attending our general Spring Meeting at Philadelphia I again joined with John Churchman on a visit to some who had slaves in Philadelphia, and with thankfulness to our Heavenly Father I may say that Divine love and a true sympathising tenderness of heart prevailed at times in this service.

Having at times perceived a shyness in some Friends of considerable note towards me, I found an engagement in gospel love to pay a visit to one of them; and as I dwelt under the exercise, I felt a resignedness in my mind to go and tell him privately that I had a desire to have an opportunity with him alone; to this proposal he readily agreed, and then, in the fear of the Lord, things relating to that shyness were searched to the bottom, and we had a large conference, which, I believe was of use to both of us, and I am thankful that way was opened for it.

Fourteenth of Sixth Month.—Having felt drawings in my mind to visit Friends about Salem, and having the approbation of our Monthly Meeting, I attended their Quarterly Meeting, and was out seven days, and attended seven meetings; in some of them I was chiefly silent; in others, through the baptizing power of truth, my heart was enlarged in heavenly love, and I found a near fellowship with the brethren and sisters, in the manifold trials attending their Christian progress through this world.

Seventh-Month.—I have found an increasing concern on my mind to visit some active members in our Society who have slaves, and having no opportunity of the company of such as were named in the minutes of the Yearly Meeting, I went alone to their houses, and, in the fear of the Lord, acquainted them with the exercise I was under; and thus, sometimes by a few words, I found myself discharged from a heavy burden. After this, our friend John Churchman coming into our province with a view to be at some meetings, and to join again in the visit to those who had slaves, I bore him company in the said visit to some active members, and found inward satisfaction.

At our Yearly Meeting this year, we had some weighty seasons, in which the power of truth was largely extended, to the strengthening of the honest-minded. As the epistles which were to be sent to the Yearly Meetings on this continent were read, I observed that in most of them, both this year and the last, it was recommended to Friends to labour against buying and keeping slaves, and in some of them the subject was closely treated upon. As this practice hath long been a heavy exercise to me, and I have often waded through mortifying labours on that account, and at times in some meetings have been almost alone therein, I was humbly bowed in thankfulness in observing the increasing concern in our religious society, and seeing how the Lord was raising up and qualifying servants for His work, not only in this respect, but for promoting the cause of truth in general.

This meeting continued near a week. For several days, in the fore part of it, my mind was drawn into a deep inward stillness, and being at times covered with the spirit of supplication, my heart was secretly poured out before the Lord. Near the conclusion of the meeting for business, way opened in the pure flowings of Divine love for me to express what lay upon me, which, as it then arose in my mind, was first to show how deep answers to deep in the hearts of the sincere and upright; though, in their different growths, they may not all have attained to the same clearness in some points relating to our testimony. And I was then led to mention the integrity and constancy of many martyrs who gave their lives for the testimony of Jesus, and yet, in some points, they held doctrines distinguishable from some which we hold, that, in all ages, where people were faithful to the light and understanding which the Most High afforded them, they found acceptance with Him, and though there may be different ways of thinking amongst us in some particulars, yet, if we mutually keep to that spirit and power which crucifies to the world, which teaches us to be content with things really needful, and to avoid all superfluities, and give up our hearts to fear and serve the Lord, true unity may still be preserved amongst us; that if those who were at times under suffering on account of some scruples of conscience, kept low and humble, and in their conduct in life manifested a spirit of true charity, it would be more likely to reach the witness in others, and be of more service in the church, than if their suffering were attended with a contrary spirit and conduct. In this exercise I was drawn into a sympathizing tenderness with the sheep of Christ, however distinguished one from another in this world, and the like disposition appeared to spread over others in the meeting. Great is the goodness of the Lord towards his poor creatures.

An epistle went forth from this Yearly Meeting which I think good to give a place in this Journal. It is as follows.—

From the Yearly Meeting held at Philadelphia, for Pennsylvania and New Jersey, from the twenty-second day of the Ninth Month to the twenty-eighth of the same, inclusive, 1759.

TO THE QUARTERLY AND MONTHLY MEETINGS OF FRIENDS BELONGING TO THE SAID YEARLY MEETING.

DEARLY BELOVED FRIENDS AND BRETHREN,—In an awful sense of the wisdom and goodness of the Lord our God, whose tender mercies have been continued to us in this land, we affectionately salute you, with sincere and fervent desires that we may reverently regard the dispensations of His providence, and improve under them.

The empires and kingdoms of the earth are subject to His almighty power. He is the God of the spirits of all flesh, and deals with His people agreeably to that wisdom, the depth whereof is to us unsearchable. We in these provinces may say, He hath, as a gracious and tender parent, dealt bountifully with us, even from the days of our fathers. It was He who strengthened them to labour through the difficulties attending the improvement of a wilderness, and made way for them in the hearts of the natives, so that by them they were comforted in times of want and distress. It was by the gracious influences of His Holy Spirit that they were disposed to work righteousness, and walk uprightly towards each other, and towards the natives; in life and conversation to manifest the excellency of the principles and doctrines of the Christian religion, whereby they retain their esteem and friendship. Whilst they were labouring for the necessaries of life, many of them were fervently engaged to promote piety and virtue in the earth, and to educate their children in the fear of the Lord.

If we carefully consider the peaceable measures pursued in the first settlement of the land, and that freedom from the desolations of wars which for a long time we enjoyed, we shall find ourselves under strong obligations to the Almighty, who, when the earth is so generally polluted with wickedness, gives us a being in a part so signally favoured with tranquility and plenty, and in which the glad tidings of the gospel of Christ are so freely published that we may justly say with the psalmist, "What shall we render unto the Lord for all his benefits?"

Our own real good, and the good of our posterity, in some measure depend on the part we act, and it nearly concerns us to try our foundations impartially. Such are the different rewards of the just and unjust in a future state, that to attend diligently to the dictates of the spirit of Christ, to devote ourselves to His service, and to engage fervently in His cause, during our short stay in this world, is a choice well becoming a free, intelligent creature. We shall thus clearly see and consider that the dealings of God with mankind, in a national capacity, as recorded in Holy Writ, do sufficiently evidence the truth of that saying, "It is righteousness which exalteth a nation"; and though He doth not at all times suddenly execute His judgments on a sinful people in this life, yet we see in many instances that when "men follow lying vanities they forsake their own mercies"; and as a proud, selfish spirit prevails and spreads among a people, so partial judgment, oppression, discord, envy and confusions increase, and provinces and kingdoms are made to drink the cup of adversity as a reward of their own doing. Thus the inspired prophet, reasoning with the degenerated Jews, saith, "Thine own wickedness shall correct thee, and thy backsliding shall reprove thee; know, therefore, that it is an evil thing and bitter that thou hast forsaken the Lord thy God, and that my fear is not in thee, saith the Lord God of Hosts." (Jeremiah ii. 19.)

The God of our fathers, who hath bestowed on us many benefits, furnished a table for us in the wilderness, and made the deserts and solitary places to rejoice. He doth now mercifully call upon us to serve Him more faithfully. We may truly say with the Prophet, "It is His voice which crieth to the city, and men of wisdom see His name. They regard the rod, and Him who hath appointed it." People who look chiefly at things outward too little consider the original cause of the present troubles; but they who fear the Lord, and think often upon His name, see and feel that a wrong spirit is spreading amongst the inhabitants of our country; that the hearts of many are waxed fat, and their ears dull of hearing; that the Most High, in His visitations to us, instead of calling, lifteth up His voice and crieth: He crieth to our country, and His voice waxeth louder and louder. In former wars between the English and other nations, since the settlement of our provinces, the calamities attending them have fallen chiefly on other places, but now of late they have reached to our borders; many of our fellow-subjects have suffered on and near our frontiers, some have been slain in battle, some killed in their houses, and some in their fields, some wounded and left in great misery, and others separated from their wives and little children, who have been carried captives among the Indians. We have seen men and women who have been witnesses of these scenes of sorrow, and, being reduced to want, have come to our houses asking relief. It is not long since many young men in one of these provinces were drafted, in order to be taken as soldiers; some were at that time in great distress, and had occasion to consider that their lives had been too little conformable to the purity and spirituality of that religion which we profess, and found themselves too little acquainted with that inward humility, in which true fortitude to endure hardness for the truth's sake is experienced. Many parents were concerned for their children, and in that time of trial were led to consider that their care to get outward treasure for them had been greater than their care for their settlement in that religion which crucifieth to the world, and enableth to bear a clear testimony to the peaceable government of the Messiah. These troubles are removed, and for a time we are released from them.

Let us not forget that "The Most High hath his way in the deep, in clouds, and in thick darkness"; that it is His voice which crieth to the city and to the country, and O that these loud and awakening cries may have a proper effect upon us, that heavier chastisement may not become necessary! For though things, as to the outward, may for a short time afford a pleasing prospect, yet, while a selfish spirit, that is not subject to the cross of Christ, continueth to spread and prevail, there can be no long continuance in outward peace and tranquility. If we desire an inheritance incorruptible, and to be at rest in that state of peace and happiness which ever continues; if we desire in this life to dwell under the favour and protection of that Almighty Being whose habitation is in holiness, whose ways are all equal, and whose anger is now kindled because of our back-slidings,—let us then awfully regard these beginnings of His sore judgments, and with abasement and humiliation turn to Him whom we have offended.

Contending with one equal in strength is an uneasy exercise; but if the Lord is become our enemy, if we persist in contending with Him who is omnipotent, our overthrow will be unavoidable.

Do we feel an affectionate regard to posterity? and are we employed to promote their happiness? Do our minds, in things outward, look beyond our own dissolution? and are we contriving for the prosperity of our children after us? Let us then, like wise builders, lay the foundation deep, and by our constant uniform regard to an inward piety and virtue let them see that we really value it. Let us labour in the fear of the Lord, that their innocent minds, while young and tender, may be preserved from corruptions; that as they advance in age they may rightly understand their true interest, may consider the uncertainty of temporal things, and, above all, have their hope and confidence firmly settled in the blessing of that Almighty Being who inhabits eternity and preserves and supports the world.

In all our cares about worldly treasures, let us steadily bear in mind that riches possessed by children who do not truly serve God are likely to prove snares that may more grievously entangle them in that spirit of selfishness and exaltation which stands in opposition to real peace and happiness and renders those who submit to the influence of it enemies to the cross of Christ.

To keep a watchful eye towards real objects of charity, to visit the poor in their lonesome dwelling-places, to comfort those who, through the dispensations of Divine Providence, are in strait and painful circumstances in this life, and steadily to endeavour to honour God with our substance, from a real sense of the love of Christ influencing our minds, is more likely to bring a blessing to our children, and will afford more satisfaction to a Christian favoured with

plenty, than an earnest desire to collect much wealth to leave behind us, for "here we have no continuing city"; may we therefore
diligently "seek one that is to come, whose builder and maker is
God."

"Finally, brethren, whatsoever things are true, whatsoever things
are just, whatsoever things are pure, whatsoever things are lovely,
whatsoever things are of good report, if there be any virtue, if there
be any praise, think on these things, and do them, and the God of
peace shall be with you."

(Signed by appointment, and on behalf of said meeting.)

Twenty-eighth of Eleventh Month.—This day I attended the
Quarterly Meeting in Bucks County. In the meeting of ministers
and elders my heart was enlarged in the love of Jesus Christ, and
the favour of the Most High was extended to us in that and the ensuing meeting.

I had conversation at my lodging with my beloved friend Samuel
Eastburn, who expressed a concern to join in a visit to some
Friends in that county who had negroes, and as I had felt a drawing in my mind to the said work, I came home and put things in
order. On the 11th of Twelfth Month I went over the river, and on
the next day was at Buckingham Meeting, where, through the de-
scendings of heavenly dew, my mind was comforted and drawn
into a near unity with the flock of Jesus Christ.

Entering upon this business appeared weighty, and before I left
home my mind was often sad, under which exercise I felt at times
the Holy Spirit which helps our infirmities, and through which my
prayers were at times put up to God in private that He would be
pleased to purge me from all selfishness, that I might be
strengthened to discharge my duty faithfully, how hard soever to
the natural part. We proceeded on the visit in a weighty frame of
spirit, and went to the houses of the most active members who had
negroes throughout the county. Through the goodness of the Lord
my mind was preserved in resignation in times of trial, and though
the work was hard to nature, yet through the strength of that love
which is stronger than death, tenderness of heart was often felt
amongst us in our visits, and we parted from several families with
greater satisfaction than we expected.

We visited Joseph White's family, he being in England; we had
also a family sitting at the house of an elder who bore us company,

and were at Makefield on the first day; at all which times my heart was truly thankful to the Lord who was graciously pleased to renew His loving-kindness to us, His poor servants, uniting us together in His work.

In the winter of this year, the small-pox being in our town, and many being inoculated, of whom a few died, some things were opened in my mind which I wrote as follows:—

The more fully our lives are conformable to the will of God, the better it is for us; I have looked on the small-pox as a messenger from the Almighty, to be an assistant in the cause of virtue, and to incite us to consider whether we employ our time only in such things as are consistent with perfect wisdom and goodness. Building houses suitable to dwell in, for ourselves and our creatures; preparing clothing suitable for the climate and season, and food convenient, are all duties incumbent on us. And under these general heads are many branches of business in which we may venture health and life, as necessity may require.

This disease being in a house, and my business calling me to go near it, incites me to consider whether this is a real indispensable duty; whether it is not in conformity to some custom which would be better laid aside, or, whether it does not proceed from too eager a pursuit after some outward treasure. If the business before me springs not from a clear understanding and a regard to that use of things which perfect wisdom approves, to be brought to a sense of it and stopped in my pursuit is a kindness; for when I proceed to business without some evidence of duty, I have found by experience that it tends to weakness.

If I am so situated that there appears no probability of missing the infection, it tends to make me think whether my manner of life in things outward has nothing in it which may unfit my body to receive this messenger in a way the most favourable to me. Do I use food and drink in no other sort and in no other degree than was designed by Him who gave these creatures for our sustenance? Do I never abuse my body by inordinate labour, striving to accomplish some end which I have unwisely proposed? Do I use action enough in some useful employ, or do I sit too much idle while some persons who labour to support me have too great a share of it? If in any of these things I am deficient, to be incited to consider it is a favour to me. Employment is necessary in social life, and this infection, which often proves mortal, incites me to think whether these social acts of mine are real duties. If I go on a visit to the widows and fatherless, do I go purely on a principle of charity, free from any selfish views? If I go to a religious meeting, it puts me on thinking whether I go in sincerity and in a clear sense of duty, or whether it is not partly in conformity to custom, or partly from a sensible delight which my animal spirits feel in the company of other people, and whether to support my reputation as a religious man has no share in it.

Do affairs relating to civil society call me near this infection? If I go, it is at the hazard of my health and life, and it becomes me to think seriously whether love to truth and righteousness is the motive of my attending; whether the manner of proceeding is altogether equitable, or whether aught of narrowness, party interest, respect to outward dignities, names, or distinctions among men, do not stain the beauty of those assemblies, and render it doubtful; in point of duty whether a disciple of Christ ought to attend as a member united to the body or not. Whenever there are blemishes which for a series of time remain such, that which is a means of stirring us up to look attentively on these blemishes, and to labour according to our capacities, to have health and soundness restored in our country, we may justly account a kindness from our gracious Father, who appointed that means.

The care of a wise and good man for his only son is inferior to the regard of the great Parent of the universe for His creatures. He hath the command of all the powers and operations in nature, and "doth not afflict willingly, nor grieve the children of men." Chastisement is intended for instruction, and instruction being received by gentle chastisement, greater calamities are prevented. By an earthquake, hundreds of houses are sometimes shaken down in a few minutes, multitudes of people perish suddenly, and many more, being crushed and bruised in the ruins of the buildings, pine away and die in great misery.

By the breaking in of enraged merciless armies, flourishing countries have been laid waste, great numbers of people have perished in a short time, and many more have been pressed with poverty and grief. By the pestilence, people have died so fast in a city, that, through fear, grief, and confusion, those in health have found great difficulty in burying the dead, even without coffins. By famine, great numbers of people in some places have been brought to the utmost distress, and have pined away for want of the necessaries of life. Thus, when the kind invitations and gentle chastisements of a gracious God have not been attended to, his sore judgments have at times been poured out upon people.

While some rules approved in civil society and conformable to human policy, so called, are distinguishable from the purity of truth and righteousness,—while many professing the truth are declining from that ardent love and heavenly-mindedness which was amongst the primitive followers of Jesus Christ, it is time for us to attend diligently to the intent of every chastisement, and to consider the most deep and inward design of them.

The Most High doth not often speak with an outward voice to our outward ears, but if we humbly meditate on His perfections, consider that He is perfect wisdom and goodness, and that to afflict His creatures to no purpose would be utterly averse to His nature, we shall hear and understand His language both in His gentle and more heavy chastisements, and shall take heed that we do not, in the wisdom of this world, endeavour to escape His hand by means too powerful for us.

Had He endowed men with understanding to prevent this disease (the small-pox) by means which had never proved hurtful nor mortal, such a discovery might be considered as the period of chastisement by this distemper, where that knowledge extended.* But as life and health are His gifts, and are not to be disposed of in our own wills, to take upon us by inoculation when in health a disorder of which some die, requires great clearness of knowledge that it is our duty to do so.

* Whatever may be thought of these scruples of John Woolman in regard to inoculation, his objections can scarcely be considered valid against vaccination, which, since his time, has so greatly mitigated the disease. He almost seems to have anticipated some such preventive.

CHAPTER VII

1760

Visit, in Company with Samuel Eastburn, to Long Island, Rhode Island, Boston, etc.—Remarks on the Slave-Trade at Newport; also on Lotteries.—Some Observations on the Island of Nantucket.

Fourth Month, 1760.—Having for some time past felt a sympathy in my mind with Friends eastward, I opened my concern in our Monthly Meeting, and, obtaining a certificate, set forward on the 17th of this month, in company with my beloved friend Samuel Eastburn. We had meetings at Woodbridge, Rahway, and Plainfield, and were at their Monthly Meeting of ministers and elders in Rahway. We laboured under some discouragement, but through the invisible power of truth our visit was made reviving to the lowly-minded, with whom I felt a near unity of spirit, being much reduced in my mind. We passed on and visited most of the meetings on Long Island. It was my concern from day to day to say neither more nor less than what the Spirit of truth opened in me, being jealous over myself lest I should say anything to make my testimony look agreeable to that mind in people which is not in pure obedience to the cross of Christ.

The spring of the ministry was often low, and through the subjecting power of truth we were kept low with it; from place to place they whose hearts were truly concerned for the cause of Christ appeared to be comforted in our labours, and though it was in general a time of abasement of the creature, yet through His goodness who is a helper of the poor we had some truly edifying seasons both in meetings and in families where we tarried; sometimes we found strength to labour earnestly with the unfaithful, especially with those whose station in families or in the Society was such that their example had a powerful tendency to open the way for others to go aside from the purity and soundness of the blessed truth.

At Jericho, on Long Island, I wrote home as follows:—

24th of the Fourth Month, 1760.

DEARLY BELOVED WIFE!

We are favoured with health; have been at sundry meetings in East Jersey and on this island. My mind hath been much in an inward, watchful frame since I left thee, greatly desiring that our proceedings may be singly in the will of our Heavenly Father.

As the present appearance of things is not joyous, I have been much shut up from outward cheerfulness, remembering that promise, "Then shalt thou delight thyself in the Lord"; as this from day to day has been revived in my memory, I have considered that His internal presence in our minds is a delight of all others the most pure, and that the honest-hearted not only delight in this, but in the effect of it upon them. He regards the helpless and distressed, and reveals His love to His children under affliction, who delight in beholding His benevolence, and in feeling Divine charity moving in them. Of this I may speak a little, for though since I left you I have often an engaging love and affection towards thee and my daughter, and friends about home, and going out at this time, when sickness is so great amongst you, is a trial upon me; yet I often remember there are many widows and fatherless, many who have poor tutors, many who have evil examples before them, and many whose minds are in captivity; for whose sake my heart is at times moved with compassion, so that I feel my mind resigned to leave you for a season, to exercise that gift which the Lord hath bestowed on me, which though small compared with some, yet in this I rejoice, that I feel love unfeigned towards my fellow-creatures. I recommend you to the Almighty, who I trust, cares for you; and under a sense of His heavenly love remain,

Thy loving husband, J.W.

We crossed from the east end of Long Island to New London, about thirty miles, in a large open boat; while we were out, the wind rising high, the waves several times beat over us, so that to me it appeared dangerous, but my mind was at the time turned to Him who made and governs the deep, and my life was resigned to

Him; as He was mercifully pleased to preserve us I had fresh occasion to consider every day as a day lent to me, and felt a renewed engagement to devote my time, and all I had, to Him who gave it.

We had five meetings in Narraganset, and went thence to Newport on Rhode Island. Our gracious Father preserved us in an humble dependence on Him through deep exercises that were mortifying to the creaturely will. In several families in the country where we lodged, I felt an engagement on my mind to have a conference with them in private, concerning their slaves; and through Divine aid I was favoured to give up thereto. Though in this concern I differ from many whose service in travelling is, I believe, greater than mine, yet I do not think hardly of them for omitting it; I do not repine at having so unpleasant a task assigned me, but look with awfulness to Him who appoints to His servants their respective employments, and is good to all who serve Him sincerely.

We got to Newport in the evening, and on the next day visited two sick persons, with whom we had comfortable sittings, and in the afternoon attended the burial of a Friend. The next day we were at meetings at Newport, in the forenoon and afternoon; the spring of the ministry was opened, and strength was given to declare the Word of Life to the people.

The day following we went on our journey, but the great number of slaves in these parts, and the continuance of that trade from thence to Guinea, made a deep impression on me, and my cries were often put up to the Heavenly Father in secret, that He would enable me to discharge my duty faithfully in such way as He might be pleased to point out to me.

We took Swansea, Freetown, and Taunton in our way to Boston, where also we had a meeting; our exercise was deep, and the love of truth prevailed, for which I bless the Lord. We went eastward about eighty miles beyond Boston, taking meetings, and were in a good degree preserved in an humble dependence on that arm which drew us out; and though we had some hard labour with the disobedient, by laying things home and close to such as were stout against the truth, yet through the goodness of God we had at times to partake of heavenly comfort with those who were meek, and were often favoured to part with Friends in the nearness of true gospel fellowship. We returned to Boston and had another comfortable opportunity with Friends there, and thence rode back a day's journey eastward of Boston. Our guide being a heavy man, and the weather hot, my companion and I expressed our freedom to go on without him, to which he consented, and we respectfully took our leave of him; this we did as believing the journey would have been hard to him and his horse.

In visiting the meetings in those parts we were measurably baptized into a feeling of the state of the Society, and in bowedness of spirit went to the Yearly Meeting at Newport, where we met with John Storer from England, Elizabeth Shipley, Ann Gaunt, Hannah Foster, and Mercy Redman, from our parts, all ministers of the gospel, of whose company I was glad. Understanding that a large number of slaves had been imported from Africa into that town, and were then on sale by a member of our Society, my appetite failed, and I grew outwardly weak, and had a feeling of the condition of Habakkuk, as thus expressed, "When I heard, my belly trembled, my lips quivered, I trembled in myself, that I might rest in the day of trouble." I had many cogitations, and was sorely distressed. I was desirous that Friends might petition the Legislature to use their endeavours to discourage the future importation of slaves, for I saw that this trade was a great evil, and tended to multiply troubles, and to bring distresses on the people for whose welfare my heart was deeply concerned. But I perceived several difficulties in regard to petitioning, and such was the exercise of my mind that I thought of endeavouring to get an opportunity to speak a few words in the House of Assembly, then sitting in town.

This exercise came upon me in the afternoon on the second day of the Yearly Meeting, and on going to bed I got no sleep till my mind was wholly resigned thereto. In the morning I inquired of a Friend how long the Assembly was likely to continue sitting, who told me it was expected to be prorogued that day or the next. As I was desirous to attend the business of the meeting, and perceived the Assembly was likely to separate before the business was over, after considerable exercise, humbly seeking to the Lord for instruction, my mind settled to attend on the business of the meeting, on the last day of which I had prepared a short essay of a petition to be presented to the Legislature, if way opened. And being informed that there were some appointed by that Yearly Meeting to speak with those in authority on cases relating to the Society, I opened my mind to several of them, and showed them the essay I had made, and afterwards I opened the case in the meeting for business, in substance as follows:—

I have been under a concern for some time on account of the great number of slaves which are imported into this colony. I am aware that it is a tender point to speak to, but apprehend I am not clear in the sight of Heaven without doing so. I have prepared an essay of a petition to be presented to the Legislature, if way open; and what I have to propose to this meeting is that some Friends may be named to withdraw and look over it, and report whether they believe it suitable to be read in the meeting. If they should think well of reading it, it will remain for the meeting to consider whether to take any further notice of it, as a meeting, or not. After a short conference some Friends went out, and, looking over it, expressed their willingness to have it read, which being done, many expressed their unity with the proposal, and some signified that to have the subjects of the petition enlarged upon, and signed out of meeting by such as were free, would be more suitable than to do it there. Though I expected at first that if it was done it would be in that way, yet such was the exercise of my mind that to move it in the hearing of Friends when assembled appeared to me as a duty, for my heart yearned towards the inhabitants of these parts, believing that by this trade there had been an increase of inquietude amongst them, and way had been made for the spreading of a spirit opposite to that meekness and humility which is a sure resting-place for the soul; and that the continuance of this trade would not only render their healing more difficult, but would increase their malady.

Having proceeded thus far, I felt easy to leave the essay amongst Friends, for them to proceed in it as they believed best. And now an exercise revived in my mind in relation to lotteries, which were common in those parts. I had mentioned the subject in a former sitting of this meeting, when arguments were used in favour of Friends being held excused who were only concerned in such lotteries as were agreeable to law. And now, on moving it again, it was opposed as before; but the hearts of some solid Friends appeared to be united to discourage the practice amongst their members, and the matter was zealously handled by some on both sides. In this debate it appeared very clear to me that the spirit of lotteries was a spirit of selfishness, which tended to confuse and darken the understanding, and that pleading for it in our meetings, which were set apart for the Lord's work, was not right. In the heat of zeal, I made reply to what an ancient Friend said, and when I sat down I saw that my words were not enough seasoned with charity. After this I spoke no more on the subject. At length a minute was made, a copy of which was to be sent to their several Quarterly Meetings, inciting Friends to labour to discourage the practice amongst all professing with us.

Some time after this minute was made I remained uneasy with the manner of my speaking to the ancient Friend, and could not see my way clear to conceal my uneasiness, though I was concerned that I might say nothing to weaken the cause in which I had laboured. After some close exercise and hearty repentance for not having attended closely to the safe guide, I stood up, and reciting the passage, acquainted Friends that though I durst not go from what I had said as to the matter, yet I was uneasy with the manner of my speaking, believing milder language would have been better. As this was uttered in some degree of creaturely abasement after a warm debate, it appeared to have a good savour amongst us.

The Yearly Meeting being now over, there yet remained on my mind a secret though heavy exercise, in regard to some leading active members about Newport, who were in the practice of keeping slaves. This I mentioned to two ancient Friends who came out of the country, and proposed to them, if way opened, to have some conversation with those members. One of them and I, having consulted one of the most noted elders who had slaves, he, in a respectful manner, encouraged me to proceed to clear myself of what lay upon me. Near the beginning of the Yearly Meeting, I had had a private conference with this said elder and his wife, concerning their slaves, so that the way seemed clear to me to advise with him about the manner of proceeding. I told him I was free to have a conference with them all together in a private house; or if he thought they would take it unkind to be asked to come together, and to be spoken with in the hearing of one another, I was free to spend some time amongst them, and to visit them all in their own houses. He expressed his liking to the first proposal, not doubting their willingness to come together; and as I proposed a visit to only ministers, elders, and overseers, he named some others whom he desired might also be present. A careful messenger being wanted to acquaint them in a proper manner, he offered to go to all their houses, to open the matter to them,—and did so. About the eighth hour the next morning we met in the meeting-house chamber, the last-mentioned country Friend, my companion, and John Storer being with us. After a short time of retirement, I acquainted them with the steps I had taken in procuring that meeting, and opened the concern I was under, and we then proceeded to a free conference upon the subject. My exercise was heavy, and I was deeply bowed in spirit before the Lord, who was pleased to favour with the seasoning virtue of truth, which wrought a tenderness amongst us; and the subject was mutually handled in a calm and peaceable spirit. At length, feeling my mind released from the burden which I had been under, I took my leave of them in a good degree of satisfaction; and by the tenderness they manifested in regard to the practice, and the concern several of them expressed in relation to the manner of disposing of their negroes after their decease, I believed that a good exercise was spreading amongst them; and I am humbly thankful to God, who supported my mind and preserved me in a good degree of resignation through these trials.

Thou who sometimes travellest in the work of the ministry, and art made very welcome by thy friends, seest many tokens of their satisfaction in having thee for their guest. It is good for thee to dwell deep, that thou mayest feel and understand the spirits of people. If we believe truth points towards a conference on some subjects in a private way, it is needful for us to take heed that their kindness, their freedom, and affability do not hinder us from the Lord's work. I have experienced that, in the midst of kindness and smooth conduct, to speak close and home to them who entertain us, on points that relate to outward interest, is hard labour. Sometimes, when I have felt truth lead towards it, I have found myself disqualified by a superficial friendship; and as the sense thereof hath abased me, and my cries have been to the Lord, so I have been humbled and made content to appear weak, or as a fool for His sake; and thus a door hath been opened to enter upon it. To attempt to do the Lord's work in our own way, and to speak of that which is the burden of the Word, in a way easy to the natural part, doth not reach the bottom of the disorder. To see the failings of our friends, and think hard of them, without opening that which we ought to open, and still carry a face of friendship, tends to undermine the foundation of true unity. The office of a minister of Christ is weighty. And they who now go forth as watchmen have need to be steadily on their guard against the snares of prosperity and an outside friendship.

After the Yearly Meeting we were at meetings at Newton, Cushnet, Long Plain, Rochester, and Dartmouth. From thence we sailed for Nantucket, in company with Ann Gaunt, Mercy Redman, and several other Friends. The wind being slack we only reached Tarpawling Cove the first day; where, going on shore, we found room in a public-house, and beds for a few of us,—the rest slept on the floor. We went on board again about break of day, and though the wind was small, we were favoured to come within about four miles of Nantucket; and then about ten of us got into our boat and rowed to the harbour before dark; a large boat went off and brought in the rest of the passengers about midnight. The next day but one was their Yearly Meeting, which held four days, the last of which was their Monthly Meeting for business. We had a laborious time amongst them; our minds were closely exercised, and I believe it was a time of great searching of heart. The longer I was on the island the more I became sensible that there was a considerable number of valuable Friends there, though an evil spirit, tending to strife, had been at work amongst them. I was cautious of making any visits except as my mind was particularly drawn to them; and in that way we had some sittings in Friends' houses, where the heavenly wing was at times spread over us, to our mutual comfort. My beloved companion had very acceptable service on this island.

When meeting was over we all agreed to sail the next day if the weather was suitable and we were well; and being called up the latter part of the night, about fifty of us went on board a vessel; but, the wind changing, the seamen thought best to stay in the harbour till it altered, so we returned on shore. Feeling clear as to any further visits, I spent my time in my chamber, chiefly alone; and after some hours, my heart being filled with the spirit of supplication, my prayers and tears were poured out before my Heavenly Father for His help and instruction in the manifold difficulties which attended me in life. While I was waiting upon the Lord, there came a messenger from the women Friends who lodged at another house, desiring to confer with us about appointing a meeting, which to me appeared weighty, as we had been at so many before; but after a short conference, and advising with some elderly Friends, a meeting was appointed, in which the Friend who first moved it, and who had been much shut up before, was largely opened in the love of the gospel. The next morning about break of day going again on board the vessel, we reached Falmouth on the Main before night, where our horses being brought, we proceeded towards Sandwich Quarterly Meeting.

Being two days in going to Nantucket, and having been there once before, I observed many shoals in their bay, which make sailing more dangerous, especially in stormy nights; also, that a great shoal, which encloses their harbour, prevents the entrance of sloops except when the tide is up. Waiting without for the rising of the tide is sometimes hazardous in storms, and by waiting within they sometimes miss a fair wind. I took notice that there was on that small island a great number of inhabitants, and the soil not very fertile, the timber being so gone that for vessels, fences, and firewood, they depend chiefly on buying from the Main, for the cost whereof, with most of their other expenses, they depend principally upon the whale fishery. I considered that as towns grew larger, and lands near navigable waters were more cleared, it would require more labour to get timber and wood. I understood that the whales, being much hunted and sometimes wounded and not killed, grow more shy and difficult to come at. I considered that the formation of the earth, the seas, the islands, bays, and rivers, the motions of the winds, and great waters, which cause bars and shoals in particular places, were all the works of Him who is perfect wisdom and goodness; and as people attend to His heavenly instruction, and put their trust in Him, He provides for them in all parts where He gives them a being; and as in this visit to these people I felt a strong desire for their firm establishment on the sure foundation, besides what was said more publicly, I was concerned to speak with the women Friends in their Monthly Meeting of business, many being present, and in the fresh spring of pure love to open before them the advantage, both inwardly and outwardly, of attending singly to the pure guidance of the Holy Spirit, and therein to educate their children in true humility and the disuse of all superfluities. I reminded them of the difficulties their husbands and sons were frequently exposed to at sea, and that the more plain and simple their way of living was the less need there would be of running great hazards to support them. I also encouraged the young women to continue their neat, decent way of attending themselves on the affairs of the house; showing, as the way opened, that where people were truly humble, used themselves to business, and were content with a plain way of life, they had more true peace and calmness of mind than they who, aspiring to greatness and outward show, have grasped hard for an income to support themselves therein. And as I observed they had few or no slaves, I had to encourage them to be content without them, making mention of the numerous troubles and vexations which frequently attended the minds of people who depend on slaves to do their labour.

We attended the Quarterly Meeting at Sandwich, in company with Ann Gaunt and Mercy Redman, which was preceded by a Monthly Meeting, and in the whole held three days. We were in various ways exercised amongst them, in gospel love, according to the several gifts bestowed on us, and were at times overshadowed with the virtue of truth, to the comfort of the sincere and stirring up of the negligent. Here we parted with Ann and Mercy, and went to Rhode Island, taking one meeting in our way, which was a satisfactory time. Reaching Newport the evening before their Quarterly Meeting, we attended it, and after that had a meeting with our young people, separated from those of other societies. We went through much labour in this town; and now, in taking leave of it, though I felt close inward exercise to the last, I found inward peace, and was in some degree comforted in a belief that a good number remain in that place who retain a sense of truth, and that there are some young people attentive to the voice of the Heavenly Shepherd. The last meeting, in which Friends from the several parts of the quarter came together, was a select meeting, and through the renewed manifestation of the Father's love the hearts of the sincere were united together.

The poverty of spirit and inward weakness, with which I was much tried the fore part of this journey, has of late appeared to me a dispensation of kindness. Appointing meetings never appeared more weighty to me, and I was led into a deep search, whether in all things my mind was resigned to the will of God; often querying with myself what should be the cause of such inward poverty, and greatly desiring that no secret reserve in my heart might hinder my access to the Divine fountain. In these humbling times I was made watchful, and excited to attend to the secret movings of the heavenly principle in my mind, which prepared the way to some duties, that, in more easy and prosperous times as to the outward, I believe I should have been in danger of omitting.

From Newport we went to Greenwich, Shanticut, and Warwick, and were helped to labour amongst Friends in the love of our gracious Redeemer. Afterwards, accompanied by our friend John Casey from Newport, we rode through Connecticut to Oblong, visited the meetings in those parts, and thence proceeded to the Quarterly Meeting at Ryewoods. Through the gracious extendings of Divine help, we had some seasoning opportunities in those places. We also visited Friends at New York and Flushing and thence to Rahway. Here our roads parting, I took leave of my beloved companion and true yokemate Samuel Eastburn, and reached home the 10th of Eighth Month, where I found my family well. For the favours and protection of the Lord, both inward and outward, extended to me in this journey, my heart is humbled in grateful acknowledgments, and I find renewed desires to dwell and walk in resignedness before Him.

CHAPTER VIII

1761–62

Visits Pennsylvania, Shrewsbury, and Squan.—Publishes the Second Part of his Considerations on keeping Negroes.—The Grounds of his appearing in some Respects singular in his Dress.—Visit to the Families of Friends of Ancocas and Mount Holly Meetings.—Visits to the Indians at Wehaloosing on the River Susquehanna.

Having felt my mind drawn towards a visit to a few meetings in Pennsylvania, I was very desirous to be rightly instructed as to the time of setting off. On the 10th of Fifth Month, 1761, being the first day of the week, I went to Haddonfield Meeting, concluding to seek for heavenly instruction, and come home, or go on, as I might then believe best for me, and there through the springing up of pure love I felt encouragement, and so crossed the river. In this visit I was at two Quarterly and three Monthly Meetings, and in the love of truth I felt my way open to labour with some noted Friends who kept negroes. As I was favoured to keep to the root, and endeavour to discharge what I believe was required of me, I found inward peace therein, from time to time, and thankfulness of heart to the Lord, who was graciously pleased to be a guide to me.

Eighth Month, 1761.—Having felt drawings in my mind to visit Friends in and about Shrewsbury, I went there, and was at their Monthly Meeting, and their first-day meeting; I had also a meeting at Squan, and another at Squanquam, and, as way opened, had conversation with some noted Friends concerning their slaves. I returned home in a thankful sense of the goodness of the Lord.

From the concern I felt growing in me for some years, I wrote part the second of a work entitled "Considerations on keeping Negroes," which was printed this year, 1762. When the overseers of the press had done with it, they offered to get a number printed, to be paid for out of the Yearly Meeting's stock, to be given away; but I being most easy to publish it at my own expense, and offering my reasons, they appeared satisfied.

This stock is the contribution of the members of our religious society in general, among whom are some who keep negroes, and, being inclined to continue them in slavery, are not likely to be satisfied with such books being spread among a people, especially at their own expense, many of whose slaves are taught to read, and such, receiving them as a gift, often conceal them. But as they who make a purchase generally buy that which they have a mind for, I believed it best to sell them, expecting by that means they would more generally be read with attention. Advertisements were signed by order of the overseers of the press, and directed to be read in the Monthly Meetings of business within our own Yearly Meeting, informing where the books were, and that the price was no more than the cost of printing and binding them. Many were taken off in our parts; some I sent to Virginia, some to New York, some to my acquaintance at Newport, and some I kept, intending to give part of them away, where there appeared a prospect of service.

In my youth I was used to hard labour, and though I was middling healthy, yet my nature was not fitted to endure so much as many others. Being often weary, I was prepared to sympathize with those whose circumstances in life, as free men, required constant labour to answer the demands of their creditors, as well as with others under oppression. In the uneasiness of body which I have many times felt by too much labour, not as a forced but a voluntary oppression, I have often been excited to think on the original cause of that oppression which is imposed on many in the world. The latter part of the time wherein I laboured on our plantation, my heart, through the fresh visitations of heavenly love, being often tender, and my leisure time being frequently spent in reading the life and doctrines of our blessed Redeemer, the account of the sufferings of martyrs, and the history of the first rise of our Society, a belief was gradually settled in my mind, that if such as had great estates generally lived in that humility and plainness which belong to a Christian life, and laid much easier rents and interests on their land and moneys, and thus led the way to a right use of things, so great a number of people might be employed in things useful, that labour both for men and other creatures would need to be no more than an agreeable employ, and divers branches of business, which serve chiefly to please the natural inclinations of our minds, and which at present seem necessary to circulate that wealth which some gather, might, in this way of pure wisdom, be discontinued. As I have thus considered these things, a query at times hath arisen: Do I, in all my proceedings, keep to that use of things which is agreeable to universal righteousness? And then there hath some degree of sadness at times come over me, because I accustomed myself to some things which have occasioned more labour than I believe Divine wisdom intended for us.

From my early acquaintance with truth I have often felt an inward distress, occasioned by the striving of a spirit in me against the operation of the heavenly principle; and in this state I have been affected with a sense of my own wretchedness, and in a mourning condition have felt earnest longings for that Divine help which brings the soul into true liberty. Sometimes on retiring into private places, the spirit of supplication hath been given me, and under a heavenly covering I have asked my gracious Father to give me a heart in all things resigned to the direction of His wisdom; in uttering language like this, the thought of my wearing hats and garments dyed with a dye hurtful to them, has made lasting impression on me.

In visiting people of note in the Society who had slaves, and labouring with them in brotherly love on that account, I have seen, and the sight has affected me, that a conformity to some customs distinguishable from pure wisdom has entangled many, and that the desire of gain to support these customs has greatly opposed the work of truth. Sometimes when the prospect of the work before me has been such that in bowedness of spirit I have been drawn into retired places, and have besought the Lord with tears, that He would take me wholly under His direction, and shew me the way in which I ought to walk, it hath revived with strength of conviction that if I would be His faithful servant I must in all things attend to His wisdom, and be teachable, and so cease from all customs contrary thereto, however used among religious people.

As He is the perfection of power, of wisdom, and of goodness, so I believe He hath provided that so much labour shall be necessary for men's support in this world as would, being rightly divided, be a suitable employment of their time; and that we cannot go into superfluities, or grasp after wealth in a way contrary to His wisdom, without having connection with some degree of oppression, and with that spirit which leads to self-exaltation and strife, and which frequently brings calamities on countries by parties contending about their claims.

Being thus fully convinced, and feeling an increasing desire to live in the spirit of peace, I have often been sorrowfully affected with thinking on the unquiet spirit in which wars are generally carried on and with the miseries of many of my fellow-creatures engaged therein; some suddenly destroyed; some wounded, and after much pain remaining cripples; some deprived of all their outward substance and reduced to want; and some carried into captivity. Thinking often on these things, the use of hats and garments dyed with a dye hurtful to them, and wearing more clothes in summer than are useful, grew more uneasy to me, believing them to be customs which have not their foundation in pure wisdom. The apprehension of being singular from my beloved friends was a strait upon me, and thus I continued in the use of some things contrary to my judgment.

On the 31st of Fifth Month, 1761, I was taken ill of a fever, and after it had continued near a week I was in great distress of body. One day there was a cry raised in me that I might understand the cause of my affliction, and improve under it, and my conformity to some customs which I believed were not right, was brought to my remembrance. In the continuance of this exercise I felt all the powers in me yield themselves up into the hands of Him who gave me being, and was made thankful that He had taken hold of me by His chastisements. Feeling the necessity of further purifying, there was now no desire in me for health until the design of my correction was answered. Thus I lay in abasement and brokenness of spirit, and as I felt a sinking down into a calm resignation, so I felt, as in an instant, an inward healing in my nature, and from that time forward I grew better.

Though my mind was thus settled in relation to hurtful dyes, I felt easy to wear my garments heretofore made, and continued to do so about nine months. Then I thought of getting a hat the natural colour of the fur, but the apprehension of being looked upon as one affecting singularity felt uneasy to me. Here I had occasion to consider that things, though small in themselves, being clearly enjoined by Divine authority, become great things to us; and I trusted that the Lord would support me in the trials that might attend singularity, so long as singularity was only for His sake. On this account I was under close exercise of mind in the time of our General Spring Meeting, 1762, greatly desiring to be rightly directed; when, being deeply bowed in spirit before the Lord, I was made willing to submit to what I apprehended was required of me, and when I returned home got a hat of the natural colour of the fur.

In attending meetings this singularity was a trial to me, and more especially at this time, as white hats were used by some who were fond of following the changeable modes of dress, and as some Friends who knew not from what motives I wore it grew shy at me, I felt my way for a time shut up in the exercise of the ministry. In this condition, my mind being turned toward my Heavenly Father with fervent cries that I might be preserved to walk before Him in the meekness of wisdom, my heart was often tender in meetings, and I felt an inward consolation which to me was very precious under these difficulties.

I had several dyed garments fit for use which I believed it best to wear till I had occasion for new ones. Some Friends were apprehensive that my wearing such a hat savoured of an affected singularity; those who spoke with me in a friendly way I generally informed, in a few words, that I believed my wearing it was not in my own will. I had at times been sensible that a superficial friendship had been dangerous to me; and many Friends being now uneasy with me, I had an inclination to acquaint some with the manner of my being led into these things; yet upon a deeper thought I was for a time most easy to omit it, believing the present dispensation was profitable, and trusting that if I kept my place the Lord in His own time would open the hearts of Friends towards me. I have since had cause to admire His goodness and loving-kindness in leading about and instructing me, and in opening and enlarging my heart in some of our meetings.

In the Eleventh Month this year, feeling an engagement of mind to visit some families in Mansfield, I joined my beloved friend Benjamin Jones, and we spent a few days together in that service. In the Second Month, 1763, I joined, in company with Elizabeth Smith and Mary Noble, in a visit to the families of Friends at Ancocas. In both these visits, through the baptizing power of truth, the sincere labourers were often comforted, and the hearts of Friends opened to receive us. In the Fourth Month following, I accompanied some Friends in a visit to the families of Friends in Mount Holly; during this visit my mind was often drawn into an inward awfulness, wherein strong desires were raised for the everlasting welfare of my fellow-creatures, and through the kindness of our Heavenly Father our hearts were at times enlarged, and Friends were invited, in the flowings of Divine love, to attend to that which would settle them on the sure foundation.

Having for many years felt love in my heart towards the natives of this land who dwell far back in the wilderness, whose ancestors were formerly the owners and possessors of the land where we dwell, and who for a small consideration assigned their inheritance to us, and being at Philadelphia in the 8th Month, 1761, on a visit to some Friends who had slaves, I fell in company with some of those natives who lived on the east branch of the river Susquehanna, at an Indian town called Wehaloosing, two hundred miles from Philadelphia. In conversation with them by an interpreter, as also by observations on their countenances and conduct, I believed some of them were measurably acquainted with that Divine power which subjects the rough and froward will of the creature. At times I felt inward drawings towards a visit to that place, which I mentioned to none except my dear wife until it came to some ripeness. In the winter of 1762 I laid my prospects before my friends at our Monthly and Quarterly, and afterwards at our General Spring Meeting; and having the unity of Friends, and being thoughtful about an Indian pilot, there came a man and three women from a little beyond that town to Philadelphia on business. Being informed thereof by letter, I met them in town in the 5th Month, 1763; and after some conversation, finding they were sober people, I, with the concurrence of Friends in that place, agreed to join them as companions in their return, and we appointed to meet at Samuel Foulk's, at Richland, in Bucks County, on the 7th of Sixth Month. Now, as this visit felt weighty, and was performed at a time when travelling appeared perilous, so the dispensations of Divine Providence in preparing my mind for it have been memorable, and I believe it good for me to give some account thereof.

After I had given up to go, the thoughts of the journey were often attended with unusual sadness; at which times my heart was frequently turned to the Lord with inward breathings for His heavenly support, that I might not fail to follow Him wheresoever He might lead me. Being at our youth's meeting at Chesterfield, about a week before the time I expected to set off, I was there led to speak on that prayer of our Redeemer to the Father: "I pray not that thou shouldest take them out of the world, but that thou shouldest keep them from the evil." And in attending to the pure openings of truth, I had to mention what He elsewhere said to His Father: "I know that thou hearest me at all times"; so, as some of His followers kept their places, and as His prayer was granted, it followed necessarily that they were kept from evil; and as some of those met with great hardships and afflictions in this world, and at last suffered death by cruel men, so it appears that whatsoever befalls men while they live in pure obedience to God certainly works for their good, and may not be considered an evil as it relates to them. As I spake on this subject my heart was much tendered, and great awfulness came over me. On the first day of the week, being at our own afternoon meeting, and my heart being enlarged in love, I was led to speak on the care and protection of the Lord over His people, and to make mention of that passage where a band of Syrians, who were endeavouring to take captive the prophet, were disappointed; and how the Psalmist said, "The angel of the Lord encampeth round about them that fear him." Thus, in true love and tenderness, I parted from Friends, expecting the next morning to proceed on my journey. Being weary I went early to bed. After I had been asleep a short time I was awoke by a man calling at my door, and inviting me to meet some Friends at a public-house in our town, who came from Philadelphia so late that Friends were generally gone to bed. These Friends informed me that an express had arrived the last morning from Pittsburgh, and brought news that the Indians had taken a fort from the English westward, and had slain and scalped some English people near the said Pittsburgh, and in divers places. Some elderly Friends in Philadelphia, knowing the time of my intending to set off, had conferred together, and thought good to inform me of these things before I left home, that I might consider them and proceed as I believed best. Going to bed again, I told not my wife till morning. My heart was turned to the Lord for His heavenly instruction; and it was an humbling time to me. When I told my dear wife, she appeared to be deeply concerned about it; but in a few hours' time my mind became settled in a belief that it was my duty to proceed on my journey, and she bore it with a good degree of resignation. In this conflict of spirit there were great searchings of heart and strong cries to the Lord, that no motion might in the least degree be attended to but that of the pure spirit of truth.

The subjects before mentioned, on which I had so lately spoken in public, were now fresh before me, and I was brought inwardly to commit myself to the Lord, to be disposed of as He saw best. I took leave of my family and neighbours in much bowedness of spirit, and went to our Monthly Meeting at Burlington. After taking leave of Friends there, I crossed the river, accompanied by my friends Israel and John Pemberton; and parting the next morning with Israel, John bore me company to Samuel Foulk's, where I met the before-mentioned Indians; and we were glad to see each other. Here my friend Benjamin Parvin met me, and proposed joining me as a companion,—we had before exchanged some letters on the subject, and now I had a sharp trial on his account; for, as the journey appeared perilous, I thought if he went chiefly to bear me company, and we should be taken captive, my having been the means of drawing him into these difficulties would add to my own afflictions; so I told him my mind freely, and let him know that I was resigned to go alone; but after all, if he really believed it to be his duty to go on, I believed his company would be very comfortable to me. It was, indeed, a time of deep exercise, and Benjamin appeared to be so fastened to the visit that he could not be easy to leave me; so we went on, accompanied by our friends John Pemberton and William Lightfoot of Pikeland. We lodged at Bethlehem, and there parting with John, William and we went forward on the 9th of the Sixth Month, and got lodging on the floor of a house, about five miles from Fort Allen. There we parted with William, and at this place we met with an Indian trader lately come from Wyoming. In conversation with him, I perceived that many white people often sell rum to the Indians, which I believe is a great evil. In the first place, they are thereby deprived of the use of reason and, their spirits being violently agitated, quarrels often arise which end in mischief, and the bitterness and resentment occasioned hereby are frequently of long continuance. Again, their skins and furs, gotten through much fatigue and hard travels in hunting, with which they intended to buy clothing, they often sell at a low rate for more rum, when they became intoxicated; and afterward, when they suffer for want of the necessaries of life, are angry with those who, for the sake of gain, took advantage of their weakness. Their chiefs have often complained of this in their treaties with the English. Where cunning people pass counterfeits and impose on others that which is good for nothing, it is considered as wickedness; but for the sake of gain to sell that which we know does people harm, and which often works their ruin, manifests a hardened and corrupt heart, and is an evil which demands the care of all true lovers of virtue to suppress. While my mind this evening was thus employed, I also remembered that the people on the frontiers, among whom this evil is too common, are often poor; and that they venture to the outside of a colony in order to live more independently of the wealthy, who often set high rents on their land. I was renewedly confirmed in a belief, that if all our inhabitants lived according to sound wisdom, labouring to promote universal love and righteousness, and ceased from every inordinate desire after wealth, and from all customs which are tinctured with luxury, the way would be easy for our inhabitants, though they might be much more numerous than at present, to live comfortably on honest employments, without the temptation they are so often under of being drawn into schemes to make settlements on lands which have not been purchased of the Indians, or of applying to that wicked practice of selling rum to them.

Tenth of Sixth Month.—We set out early this morning and crossed the western branch of Delaware, called the Great Lehie, near Fort Allen. The water being high, we went over in a canoe. There we met an Indian, had friendly conversation with him, and gave him some biscuit; and he, having killed a deer, gave some of it to the Indians with us. After travelling some miles, we met several Indian men and women with a cow and horse, and some household goods, who were lately come from their dwelling at Wyoming, and were going to settle at another place. We made them some small presents, and, as some of them understood English, I told them my motive for coming into their country, with which they appeared satisfied. One of our guides talking awhile with an ancient woman concerning us, the poor old woman came to my companion and me, and took her leave of us with an appearance of sincere affection. We pitched our tent near the banks of the same river, having laboured hard in crossing some of those mountains called the Blue Ridge. The roughness of the stones and the cavities between them, with the steepness of the hills, made it appear dangerous. But we were preserved in safety, through the kindness of Him whose works in these mountainous deserts appeared awful, and towards whom my heart was turned during this day's travel.

Near our tent, on the sides of large trees peeled for that purpose, were various representations of men going to and returning from the wars, and of some being killed in battle. This was a path heretofore used by warriors, and as I walked about viewing those Indian histories, which were painted mostly in red or black, and thinking on the innumerable afflictions which the proud, fierce spirit produceth in the world, also on the toils and fatigues of warriors in travelling over mountains and deserts; on their miseries and distresses when far from home and wounded by their enemies; of their bruises and great weariness in chasing one another over the rocks and mountains; of the restless, unquiet state of mind of those who live in this spirit, and of the hatred which mutually grows up in the minds of their children,—the desire to cherish the spirit of love and peace among these people arose very fresh in me. This was the first night that we lodged in the woods, and being wet with travelling in the rain, as were also our blankets, the ground, our tent, and the bushes under which we purposed to lay, all looked discouraging; but I believed that it was the Lord who had thus far brought me forward, and that He would dispose of me as He saw good, and so I felt easy. We kindled a fire, with our tent open to it, then laid some bushes next the ground, and put our blankets upon them for our bed, and, lying down, got some sleep. In the morning, feeling a little unwell, I went into the river; the water was cold, but soon after I felt fresh and well. About eight o'clock we set forward and crossed a high mountain supposed to be upward of four miles over, the north side being the steepest. About noon we were overtaken by one of the Moravian brethren going to Wehaloosing, and an Indian man with him who could talk English; and we being together while our horses ate grass had some friendly conversation; but they, travelling faster than we, soon left us. This Moravian, I understood, had this spring spent some time at Wehaloosing, and was invited by some of the Indians to come again.

Twelfth of Sixth Month being the first of the week and a rainy day, we continued in our tent, and I was led to think on the nature of the exercise which hath attended me. Love was the first motion, and thence a concern arose to spend some time with the Indians, that I might feel and understand their life and the spirit they live in, if haply I might receive some instruction from them, or they might be in any degree helped forward by my following the leadings of truth among them; and as it pleased the Lord to make way for my going at a time when the troubles of war were increasing, and when, by reason of much wet weather, travelling was more difficult than usual at that season, I looked upon it as a more favourable opportunity to season my mind, and to bring me into a nearer sympathy with them. As mine eye was to the great Father of Mercies, humbly desiring to learn His will concerning me, I was made quiet and content.

Our guide's horse strayed, though hoppled, in the night, and after searching some time for him his footsteps were discovered in the path going back, whereupon my kind companion went off in the rain, and after about seven hours returned with him. Here we lodged again, tying up our horses before we went to bed, and loosing them to feed about break of day.

Thirteenth of Sixth Month.—The sun appearing, we set forward, and as I rode over the barren hills my meditations were on the alterations in the circumstances of the natives of this land since the coming in of the English. The lands near the sea are conveniently situated for fishing; the lands near the rivers, where the tides flow, and some above, are in many places fertile, and not mountainous, while the changing of the tides makes passing up and down easy with any kind of traffic. The natives have in some places, for trifling considerations, sold their inheritance so favourably situated, and in other places have been driven back by superior force; their way of clothing themselves is also altered from what it was, and they being far removed from us have to pass over mountains, swamps, and barren deserts, so that travelling is very troublesome in bringing their skins and furs to trade with us. By the extension of English settlements, and partly by the increase of English hunters, the wild beasts on which the natives chiefly depend for subsistence are not so plentiful as they were, and people too often, for the sake of gain, induce them to waste their skins and furs in purchasing a liquor which tends to the ruin of them and their families.

My own will and desires were now very much broken, and my heart was with much earnestness turned to the Lord, to whom alone I looked for help in the dangers before me. I had a prospect of the English along the coast for upwards of nine hundred miles, where I travelled, and their favourable situation and the difficulties attending the natives as well as the negroes in many places were open before me. A weighty and heavenly care came over my mind, and love filled my heart towards all mankind, in which I felt a strong engagement that we might be obedient to the Lord while in tender mercy He is yet calling to us, and that we might so attend to pure universal righteousness as to give no just cause of offence to the Gentiles, who do not profess Christianity, whether they be the blacks from Africa, or the native inhabitants of this continent. Here I was led into a close and laborious inquiry whether I, as an individual, kept clear from all things which tended to stir up or were connected with wars, either in this land or in Africa; my heart was deeply concerned that in future I might in all things keep steadily to the pure truth, and live and walk in the plainness and simplicity of a sincere follower of Christ. In this lonely journey I did greatly bewail the spreading of a wrong spirit, believing that the prosperous, convenient situation of the English would require a constant attention in us to Divine love and wisdom, in order to their being guided and supported in a way answerable to the will of that good, gracious, and Almighty Being, who hath an equal regard to all mankind. And here luxury and covetousness, with the numerous oppressions and other evils attending them, appeared very afflicting to me, and I felt in that which is immutable that the seeds of great calamity and desolation are sown and growing fast on this continent. Nor have I words sufficient to set forth the longing I then felt, that we who are placed along the coast, and have tasted the love and goodness of God, might arise in the strength thereof, and, like faithful messengers, labour to check the growth of these seeds, that they may not ripen to the ruin of our posterity.

On reaching the Indian settlement at Wyoming, we were told that an Indian runner had been at that place a day or two before us, and brought news of the Indians having taken an English fort westward, and destroyed the people, and that they were endeavouring to take another; also, that another Indian runner came there about the middle of the previous night from a town about ten miles from Wehaloosing, and brought the news that some Indian warriors from distant parts came to that town with two English scalps, and told the people that it was war with the English.

Our guides took us to the house of a very ancient man. Soon after we had put in our baggage there came a man from another Indian house some distance off. Perceiving there was a man near the door I went out; the man had a tomahawk wrapped under his matchcoat out of sight. As I approached him he took it in his hand; I went forward, and, speaking to him in a friendly way, perceived he understood some English. My companion joining me, we had some talk with him concerning the nature of our visit in these parts; he then went into the house with us, and, talking with our guides, soon appeared friendly, sat down and smoked his pipe. Though taking his hatchet in his hand at the instant I drew near to him had a disagreeable appearance, I believe he had no other intent than to be in readiness in case any violence were offered to him.

On hearing the news brought by these Indian runners, and being told by the Indians where we lodged, that the Indians about Wyoming expected in a few days to move to some larger towns, I thought, to all outward appearance, it would be dangerous travelling at this time. After a hard day's journey I was brought into a painful exercise at night, in which I had to trace back and view the steps I had taken from my first moving in the visit; and though I had to bewail some weakness which at times had attended me, yet I could not find that I had ever given way to wilful disobedience. Believing I had, under a sense of duty, come thus far, I was now earnest in spirit, beseeching the Lord to show me what I ought to do. In this great distress I grew jealous of myself, lest the desire of reputation as a man firmly settled to persevere through dangers, or the fear of disgrace from my returning without performing the visit, might have some place in me. Full of these thoughts, I lay great part of the night, while my beloved companion slept by me, till the Lord, my gracious Father, who saw the conflicts of my soul, was pleased to give quietness. Then I was again strengthened to commit my life, and all things relating thereto, into His heavenly hands, and got a little sleep towards day.

Fourteenth of Sixth Month.—We sought out and visited all the Indians hereabouts that we could meet with, in number about twenty. They were chiefly in one place, about a mile from where we lodged. I expressed to them the care I had on my mind for their good, and told them that true love had made me willing thus to leave my family to come and see the Indians and speak with them in their houses. Some of them appeared kind and friendly. After taking leave of them, we went up the river Susquehanna about three miles, to the house of an Indian called Jacob January. He had killed his hog, and the women were making store of bread and preparing to move up the river. Here our pilots had left their canoe when they came down in the spring, and lying dry it had become leaky. This detained us some hours, so that we had a good deal of friendly conversation with the family; and, eating dinner with them, we made them some small presents. Then putting our baggage into the canoe, some of them pushed slowly up the stream, and the rest of us rode our horses. We swam them over a creek called Lahawahamunk, and pitched our tent above it in the evening. In a sense of God's goodness in helping me in my distress, sustaining me under trials, and inclining my heart to trust in Him, I lay down in an humble, bowed frame of mind, and had a comfortable night's lodging.

Fifteenth of Sixth Month.—We proceeded forward till the afternoon, when, a storm appearing, we met our canoe at an appointed place and stayed all night, the rain continuing so heavy that it beat through our tent and wet both us and our baggage. The next day we found abundance of trees blown down by the storm yesterday, and had occasion reverently to consider the kind dealings of the Lord, who provided a safe place for us in a valley while this storm continued. We were much hindered by the trees which had fallen across our path, and in some swamps our way was so stopped that we got through with extreme difficulty. I had this day often to consider myself as a sojourner in this world. A belief in the all-sufficiency of God to support His people in their pilgrimage felt comfortable to me, and I was industriously employed to get to a state of perfect resignation.

We seldom saw our canoe but at appointed places, by reason of the path going off from the river. This afternoon Job Chilaway, an Indian from Wehaloosing, who talks good English and is acquainted with several people in and about Philadelphia, met our people on the river. Understanding where we expected to lodge, he pushed back about six miles, and came to us after night; and in a while our own canoe arrived, it being hard work pushing up the stream. Job told us that an Indian came in haste to their town yesterday and told them that three warriors from a distance lodged in a town above Wehaloosing a few nights past, and that these three men were going against the English at Juniata. Job was going down the river to the province-store at Shamokin. Though I was so far favoured with health as to continue travelling, yet, through the various difficulties in our journey, and the different way of living from which I had been used to, I grew sick. The news of these warriors being on their march so near us, and not knowing whether we might not fall in with them, was a fresh trial of my faith; and though through the strength of Divine love, I had several times been enabled to commit myself to the Divine disposal, I still found the want of a renewal of my strength, that I might be able to persevere therein; and my cries for help were put up to the Lord, who, in great mercy, gave me a resigned heart, in which I found quietness.

Parting from Job Chilaway on the 17th, we went on and reached Wehaloosing about the middle of the afternoon. The first Indian that we saw was a woman of modest countenance, with a Bible, who spake first to our guide, and then with an harmonious voice expressed her gladness at seeing us, having before heard of our coming. By the direction of our guide we sat down on a log while he went to the town to tell the people we were come. My companion and I, sitting thus together in a deep inward stillness, the poor woman came and sat near us; and, great awfulness coming over us, we rejoiced in a sense of God's love manifested to our poor souls. After a while we heard a conch-shell blow several times, and then came John Curtis and another Indian man, who kindly invited us into a house near the town, where we found about sixty people sitting in silence. After sitting with them a short time I stood up, and in some tenderness of spirit acquainted them, in a few short sentences, with the nature of my visit, and that a concern for their good had made me willing to come thus far to see them; which, some of them understanding, interpreted to the others, and there appeared gladness among them. I then showed them my certificate, which was explained to them; and the Moravian who overtook us on the way, being now here, bade me welcome. But the Indians knowing that this Moravian and I were of different religious societies, and as some of their people had encouraged him to come and stay awhile with them, they were, I believe, concerned that there might be no jarring or discord in their meetings; and having, I suppose, conferred together, they acquainted me that the people, at my request, would at any time come together and hold meetings. They also told me that they expected the Moravian would speak in their settled meetings, which are commonly held in the morning and near evening. So finding liberty in my heart to speak to the Moravian, I told him of the care I felt on my mind for the good of these people, and my belief that no ill effects would follow if I sometimes spake in their meetings when love engaged me thereto, without calling them together at times when they did not meet of course. He expressed his good-will towards my speaking at any time all that I found in my heart to say.

On the evening of the 18th I was at their meeting, where pure gospel love was felt, to the tendering of some of our hearts. The interpreters endeavoured to acquaint the people with what I said, in short sentences, but found some difficulty, as none of them were quite perfect in the English and Delaware tongues, so they helped one another, and we laboured along, Divine love attending. Afterwards, feeling my mind covered with the spirit of prayer, I told the interpreters that I found it in my heart to pray to God, and believed, if I prayed aright, He would hear me; and I expressed my willingness for them to omit interpreting; so our meeting ended with a degree of Divine love. Before the people went out, I observed Papunehang (the man who had been zealous in labouring for a reformation in that town, being then very tender) speaking to one of the interpreters, and I was afterwards told that he said in substance as follows: "I love to feel where words come from."

Nineteenth of Sixth Month and first of the week.—This morning the Indian who came with the Moravian, being also a member of that society, prayed in the meeting, and then the Moravian spake a short time to the people. In the afternoon, my heart being filled with a heavenly care for their good, I spake to them awhile by interpreters; but none of them being perfect in the work, and I feeling the current of love run strong, told the interpreters that I believed some of the people would understand me, and so I proceeded without them; and I believe the Holy Ghost wrought on some hearts to edification where all the words were not understood. I looked upon it as a time of Divine favour, and my heart was tendered and truly thankful before the Lord. After I sat down, one of the interpreters seemed spirited to give the Indians the substance of what I said.

Before our first meeting this morning, I was led to meditate on the manifold difficulties of these Indians who, by the permission of the Six Nations, dwell in these parts. A near sympathy with them was raised in me, and, my heart being enlarged in the love of Christ, I thought that the affectionate care of a good man for his only brother in affliction does not exceed what I then felt for that people. I came to this place through much trouble; and though through the mercies of God I believed that if I died in the journey it would be well with me, yet the thoughts of falling into the hands of Indian warriors were, in times of weakness, afflicting to me; and being of a tender constitution of body, the thoughts of captivity among them were also grievous; supposing that as they were strong and hardy they might demand service of me beyond what I could well bear. But the Lord alone was my keeper, and I believed that if I went into captivity it would be for some good end. Thus, from time to time, my mind was centred in resignation, in which I always found quietness. And this day, though I had the same dangerous wilderness between me and home, I was inwardly joyful that the Lord had strengthened me to come on this visit, and had manifested a fatherly care over me in my poor lowly condition, when, in mine own eyes, I appeared inferior to many among the Indians.

When the last-mentioned meeting was ended, it being night, Papunehang went to bed; and hearing him speak with an harmonious voice, I suppose for a minute or two, I asked the interpreter, who told me that he was expressing his thankfulness to God for the favours he had received that day, and prayed that He would continue to favour him with the same, which he had experienced in that meeting. Though Papunehang had before agreed to receive the Moravian and join with them, he still appeared kind and loving to us.

I was at two meetings on the 20th, and silent in them. The following morning, in meeting, my heart was enlarged in pure love among them, and in short plain sentences I expressed several things that rested upon me, which one of the interpreters gave the people pretty readily. The meeting ended in supplication, and I had cause humbly to acknowledge the loving kindness of the Lord towards us; and then I believed that a door remained open for the faithful disciples of Jesus Christ to labour among these people. And now, feeling my mind at liberty to return, I took my leave of them in general at the conclusion of what I said in meeting, and we then prepared to go homeward. But some of their most active men told us that when we were ready to move, the people would choose to come and shake hands with us. Those who usually came to meeting did so; and from a secret draught in my mind I went among some who did not usually go to meeting, and took my leave of them also. The Moravian and his Indian interpreter appeared respectful to us at parting. This town, Wehaloosing, stands on the bank of the Susquehanna, and consists, I believe, of about forty houses, mostly compact together, some about thirty feet long and eighteen wide—some bigger, some less. They are built mostly of split plank, one end being set in the ground, and the other pinned to a plate on which rafters are laid, and then covered with bark. I understand a great flood last winter overflowed the greater part of the ground where the town stands, and some were now about moving their houses to higher ground.

We expected only two Indians to be of our company, but when we were ready to go, we found many of them were going to Bethlehem with skins and furs, and chose to go in company with us. So they loaded two canoes in which they desired us to go, telling us that the waters were so raised with the rains that the horses should be taken by such as were better acquainted with the fording-places. We, therefore, with several Indians, went in the canoes, and others went on horses, there being seven besides ours. We met with the horsemen once on the way by appointment, and at night we lodged a little below a branch called Tankhannah, and some of the young men, going out a little before dusk with their guns, brought in a deer.

Through diligence we reached Wyoming before night, the 22nd, and understood that the Indians were mostly gone from this place. We went up a small creek into the woods with our canoes, and, pitching our tent, carried out our baggage, and before dark our horses came to us. Next morning, the horses being loaded and our baggage prepared, we set forward, being in all fourteen, and with diligent travelling were favoured to get near half-way to Fort Allen. The land on this road from Wyoming to our frontier being mostly poor, and good grass being scarce, the Indians chose a piece of low ground to lodge on, as the best for grazing. I had sweat much in travelling, and, being weary, slept soundly. In the night I perceived that I had taken cold, of which I was favoured soon to get better.

Twenty-fourth of Sixth Month.—This day we passed Fort Allen and lodged near it in the woods. We forded the westerly branch of the Delaware three times, which was a shorter way than going over the top of the Blue Mountains called the Second Ridge. In the second time of fording where the river cuts through the mountain, the waters being rapid and pretty deep, my companion's mare, being a tall, tractable animal, was sundry times driven back through the river, being laden with the burdens of some small horses which were thought unable to come through with their loads. The troubles westward, and the difficulty for Indians to pass through our frontier, I apprehended, were the reasons why so many came, expecting that our being in company would prevent the outside inhabitants being surprised. We reached Bethlehem on the 25th, taking care to keep foremost, and to acquaint people on and near the road who these Indians were. This we found very needful, for the frontier inhabitants were often alarmed at the report of the English being killed by Indians westward. Among our company were some whom I did not remember to have seen at meeting, and some of these at first were very reserved; but we being several days together, and behaving in a friendly manner towards them, and making them suitable return for the services they did us, they became more free and sociable.

Twenty-sixth of Sixth Month.—Having carefully endeavoured to settle all affairs with the Indians relative to our journey, we took leave of them, and I thought they generally parted from us affectionately. We went forward to Richland and had a very comfortable meeting among our friends, it being the first day of the week. Here I parted with my kind friend and companion Benjamin Parvin, and, accompanied by my friend Samuel Foulk, we rode to John Cadwallader's, from whence I reached home the next day, and found my family tolerably well. They and my friends appeared glad to see me return from a journey which they apprehended would be dangerous; but my mind, while I was out, had been so employed in striving for perfect resignation, and had so often been confirmed in a belief, that, whatever the Lord might be pleased to allot for me, it would work for good, that I was careful lest I should admit any degree of selfishness in being glad overmuch, and laboured to improve by those trials in such a manner as my gracious Father and Protector designed. Between the English settlements and Wehaloosing we had only a narrow path, which in many places is much grown up with bushes, and interrupted by abundance of trees lying across it. These, together with the mountain swamps and rough stones, make it a difficult road to travel, and the more so because rattlesnakes abound here, of which we killed four. People who have never been in such places have but an imperfect idea of them; and I was not only taught patience, but also made thankful to God, who thus led about and instructed me, that I might have a quick and lively feeling of the afflictions of my fellow-creatures, whose situation in life is difficult.

CHAPTER IX

1763-69

Religious Conversation with a Company met to see the Tricks of a Juggler.—Account of John Smith's Advice and of the Proceedings of a Committee at the Yearly Meeting in 1764.—Contemplations on the Nature of True Wisdom.—Visit to the Families of Friends at Mount Holly, Mansfield, and Burlington, and to the Meetings on the Sea Coast from Cape May towards Squan.—Some Account of Joseph Nichols and his Followers.—On the different State of the First Settlers in Pennsylvania who depended on their own Labour, compared with those of the Southern Provinces who kept Negroes.—Visit to the Northern Parts of New Jersey and the Western Parts of Maryland and Pennsylvania; also to the Families of Friends at Mount Holly and several parts of Maryland.—Further Considerations on keeping Slaves, and his Concern for having been a Party to the Sale of One.—Thoughts on Friends exercising Offices in Civil Government.

The latter part of the summer, 1763, there came a man to Mount Holly who had previously published a printed advertisement that at a certain public-house he would show many wonderful operations, which were therein enumerated. At the appointed time he did, by sleight of hand, perform sundry things which appeared strange to the spectators. Understanding that the show was to be repeated the next night, and that the people were to meet about sunset, I felt an exercise on that account. So I went to the public-house in the evening, and told the man of the house that I had an inclination to spend a part of the evening there; with which he signified that he was content. Then, sitting down by the door, I spoke to the people in the fear of the Lord, as they came together, concerning this show, and laboured to convince them that their thus assembling to see these sleight-of-hand tricks, and bestowing their money to support men who, in that capacity, were of no use to the world, was contrary to the nature of the Christian religion. One of the company endeavoured to show by arguments the reasonableness of their proceedings herein; but after considering some texts of Scripture and calmly debating the matter he gave up the point. After spending about an hour among them, and feeling my mind easy, I departed.

Twenty-fifth of Ninth Month, 1764.—At our Yearly Meeting at Philadelphia this day, John Smith, of Marlborough, aged upwards of eighty years, a faithful minister, though not eloquent, stood up in our meeting of ministers and elders, and, appearing to be under a great exercise of spirit, informed Friends in substance as follows: "That he had been a member of our Society upwards of sixty years, and he well remembered that, in those early times, Friends were a plain, lowly-minded people, and that there was much tenderness and contrition in their meetings. That, at twenty years from that time, the Society increasing in wealth and in some degree conforming to the fashions of the world, true humility was less apparent, and their meetings in general were not so lively and edifying. That at the end of forty years many of them were grown very rich, and many of the Society made a specious appearance in the world; that wearing fine costly garments, and using silver and other watches, became customary with them, their sons, and their daughters. These marks of outward wealth and greatness appeared on some in our meetings of ministers and elders; and, as such things became more prevalent, so the powerful overshadowings of the Holy Ghost were less manifest in the Society. That there had been a continued increase of such ways of life, even until the present time; and that the weakness which hath now overspread the Society and the barrenness manifested among us is matter of much sorrow." He then mentioned the uncertainty of his attending these meetings in future, expecting his dissolution was near; and, having tenderly expressed his concern for us, signified that he had seen in the true light that the Lord would bring back His people from these things, into which they were thus degenerated, but that His faithful servants must go through great and heavy exercise.

Twentieth of Ninth Month.—The committee appointed by the Yearly Meeting to visit the Quarterly and Monthly Meetings gave an account in writing of their proceedings in that service. They signified that in the course of the visit they had been apprehensive that some persons holding offices in government inconsistent with our principles, and others who kept slaves, remaining active members in our meetings for discipline, had been one means of weakness prevailing in some places. After this report was read, an exercise revived in my mind which had attended me for several years, and inward cries to the Lord were raised in me that the fear of man might not prevent me from doing what He required of me, and, standing up, I spoke in substance as follows: "I have felt a tenderness in my mind towards persons in two circumstances mentioned in that report; namely, towards such active members as keep slaves and such as hold offices in civil government; and I have desired that Friends, in all their conduct, may be kindly affectioned one towards another. Many Friends who keep slaves are under some exercise on that account; and at times think about trying them with freedom, but find many things in their way. The way of living and the annual expenses of some of them, are such that it seems impracticable for them to set their slaves free without changing their own way of life. It has been my lot to be often abroad; and I have observed in some places, at Quarterly and Yearly Meetings, and at some houses where travelling Friends and their horses are often entertained, that the yearly expense of individuals therein is very considerable. And Friends in some places crowding much on persons in these circumstances for entertainment, hath rested as a burden on my mind for some years past. I now express it in the fear of the Lord, greatly desiring that Friends here present may duly consider it."

In the fall of this year, having hired a man to work, I perceived in conversation with him that he had been a soldier in the late war on this continent; and he informed me in the evening, in a narrative of his captivity among the Indians, that he saw two of his fellow-captives tortured to death in a very cruel manner. This relation affected me with sadness, under which I went to bed; and the next morning, soon after I awoke, a fresh and living sense of Divine love overspread my mind, in which I had a renewed prospect of the nature of that wisdom from above which leads to a right use of all gifts, both spiritual and temporal, and gives content therein. Under a feeling thereof, I wrote as follows:—

"Hath He who gave me a being attended with many wants unknown to brute creatures given me a capacity superior to theirs, and shown me that a moderate application to business is suitable to my present condition; and that this, attended with His blessing, may supply all my outward wants while they remain within the bounds He hath fixed, and while no imaginary wants proceeding from an evil spirit have any place in me? Attend, then, O my soul! to this pure wisdom as thy sure conductor through the manifold dangers of this world.

"Doth pride lead to vanity? Doth vanity form imaginary wants? Do these wants prompt men to exert their power in requiring more from others than they would be willing to perform themselves, were the same required of them? Do those proceedings beget hard thoughts? Do hard thoughts, when ripe, become malice? Does malice, when ripe, become revengeful, and in the end inflict terrible pains on our fellow-creatures and spread desolations in the world?

"Do mankind, walking in uprightness, delight in each other's happiness? And do those who are capable of this attainment, by giving way to an evil spirit, employ their skill and strength to afflict and destroy one another? Remember then, O my soul, the quietude of those in whom Christ governs, and in all thy proceedings feel after it.

"Doth He condescend to bless thee with His presence? To move and influence thee to action? To dwell and to walk in thee? Remember then thy station as a being sacred to God. Accept of the strength freely offered to thee, and take heed that no weakness in conforming to unwise, expensive, and hard-hearted customs, gendering to discord and strife, be given way to. Doth He claim my body as His temple, and graciously require that I may be sacred to Him? O that I may prize this favour, and that my whole life may be conformable to this character! Remember, O my soul! that the Prince of Peace is thy Lord; that He communicates His unmixed wisdom to His family, that they, living in perfect simplicity, may give no just cause of offence to any creature, but that they may walk as He walked!"

Having felt an openness in my heart towards visiting families in our own meeting, and especially in the town of Mount Holly, the place of my abode, I mentioned it at our Monthly Meeting in the fore part of the winter of 1764, which being agreed to, and several Friends of our meeting being united in the exercise, we proceeded therein; and through Divine favour we were helped in the work, so that it appeared to me as a fresh reviving of godly care among Friends. The latter part of the same winter I joined my friend William Jones in a visit to Friends' families in Mansfield, in which labour I had cause to admire the goodness of the Lord toward us.

My mind being drawn towards Friends along the sea-coast from Cape May to near Squan, and also to visit some people in these parts, among whom there is no settled worship, I joined with my beloved friend Benjamin Jones in a visit to them, having Friends' unity therein. We set off the 24th of Tenth Month, 1765, and had a prosperous and very satisfactory journey, feeling at times, through the goodness of the Heavenly Shepherd, the gospel to flow freely towards a poor people scattered in these places. Soon after our return I joined my friends John Sleeper and Elizabeth Smith in a visit to Friends' families at Burlington, there being at this time about fifty families of our Society in that city; and we had cause humbly to adore our Heavenly Father, who baptized us into a feeling of the state of the people, and strengthened us to labour in true gospel love among them.

Having had a concern at times for several years to pay a religious visit to Friends on the eastern shore of Maryland, and to travel on foot among them, that by so travelling I might have a more lively feeling of the condition of the oppressed slaves, set an example of lowliness before the eyes of their masters, and be more out of the way of temptation to unprofitable converse; and the time drawing near in which I believed it my duty to lay my concern before our Monthly Meeting, I perceived, in conversation with my beloved friend John Sleeper, that he also was under a similar concern to travel on foot in the form of a servant among them, as he expressed it. This he told me before he knew aught of my exercise. Being thus drawn the same way, we laid our exercise and the nature of it before Friends; and, obtaining certificates, we set off the 6th of Fifth Month, 1766, and were at meetings with Friends at Wilmington, Duck Creek, Little Creek, and Motherkill. My heart was often tendered under the Divine influence, and enlarged in love towards the people among whom we travelled.

From Motherkill we crossed the country about thirty-five miles to Tuckahoe, in Maryland, and had a meeting there, and also at Marshy Creek. At the last three meetings there were a considerable number of the followers of one Joseph Nichols, a preacher, who, I understand, is not in outward fellowship with any religious society, but professeth nearly the same principles as those of our Society, and often travels up and down, appointing meetings which many people attend. I heard of some who had been irreligious people that were now his followers, and were become sober, well-behaved men and women. Some irregularities, I hear, have been among the people at several of his meetings; but from what I have perceived I believe the man and some of his followers are honestly disposed, but that skilful fathers are wanting among them.

We then went to Choptank and Third Haven, and thence to Queen Anne's. The weather for some days past having been hot and dry, and we having travelled pretty steadily and having had hard labour in meetings, I grew weakly, at which I was for a time discouraged; but looking over our journey and considering how the Lord had supported our minds and bodies, so that we had gone forward much faster than I expected before we came out, I saw that I had been in danger of too strongly desiring to get quickly through the journey, and that the bodily weakness now attending me was a kindness; and then, in contrition of spirit, I became very thankful to my gracious Father for this manifestation of His love, and in humble submission to His will my trust in Him was renewed.

In this part of our journey I had many thoughts on the different circumstances of Friends who inhabit Pennsylvania and Jersey from those who dwell in Maryland, Virginia, and Carolina. Pennsylvania and New Jersey were settled by Friends who were convinced of our principles in England in times of suffering; these, coming over, bought lands of the natives, and applied to husbandry in a peaceable way, and many of their children were taught to labour for their living. Few of these, I believe, settled in any of the southern provinces; but by the faithful labours of travelling Friends in early times there was considerable convincement among the inhabitants of these parts. I also remembered having read of the warlike disposition of many of the first settlers in those provinces, and of their numerous engagements with the natives in which much blood was shed even in the infancy of the colonies. Some of the people inhabiting those places, being grounded in customs contrary to the pure truth, were affected with the powerful preaching of the Word of Life and joined in fellowship with our Society, and in so doing they had a great work to go through. In the history of the reformation from Popery it is observable that the progress was gradual from age to age. The uprightness of the first reformers in attending to the light and understanding given to them opened the way for sincere-hearted people to proceed further afterwards; and thus each one truly fearing God and labouring in the works of righteousness appointed for him in his day findeth acceptance with Him. Through the darkness of the times and the corruption of manners and customs, some upright men may have had little more for their day's work than to attend to the righteous principle in their minds as it related to their own conduct in life without pointing out to others the whole extent of that into which the same principle would lead succeeding ages. Thus, for instance, among an imperious, warlike people, supported by oppressed slaves, some of these masters, I suppose, are awakened to feel and to see their error, and through sincere repentance cease from oppression and become like fathers to their servants, showing by their example a pattern of humility in living, and moderation in governing, for the instruction and admonition of their oppressing neighbours; these, without carrying the reformation further, have, I believe, found acceptance with the Lord. Such was the beginning; and those who succeeded them, and who faithfully attended to the nature and spirit of the reformation, have seen the necessity of proceeding forward, and have not only to instruct others by their own example in governing well, but have also to use means to prevent their successors from having so much power to oppress others.

Here I was renewedly confirmed in my mind that the Lord (whose tender mercies are over all His works, and whose ear is open to the cries and groans of the oppressed) is graciously moving in the hearts of people to draw them off from the desire of wealth and to bring them into such an humble, lowly way of living, that they may see their way clearly to repair to the standard of true righteousness, and may not only break the yoke of oppression, but may know Him to be their strength and support in times of outward affliction.

We crossed Chester River, had a meeting there, and also at Cecil and Sassafras. My bodily weakness, joined with a heavy exercise of mind, was to me an humbling dispensation, and I had a very lively feeling of the state of the oppressed; yet I often thought that what I suffered was little compared with the sufferings of the blessed Jesus and many of His faithful followers; and I may say with thankfulness that I was made content. From Sassafras we went pretty directly home, where we found our families well. For several weeks after our return I had often to look over our journey; and though to me it appeared as a small service, and that some faithful messengers will yet have more bitter cups to drink in those southern provinces for Christ's sake than we have had, yet I found peace in that I had been helped to walk in sincerity according to the understanding and strength given to me.

Thirteenth of Eleventh Month.—With the unity of Friends at our Monthly Meeting, and in company with my beloved friend Benjamin Jones, I set out on a visit to Friends in the upper part of this province, having had drawings of love in my heart that way for a considerable time. We travelled as far as Hardwick, and I had inward peace in my labours of love among them. Through the humbling dispensations of Divine Providence my mind hath been further brought into a feeling of the difficulties of Friends and their servants southwestward; and being often engaged in spirit on their account I believed it my duty to walk into some parts of the western shore of Maryland on a religious visit. Having obtained a certificate from Friends of our Monthly Meeting, I took leave of my family under the heart-tendering operation of truth, and on the 20th of Fourth Month, 1767, rode to the ferry opposite to Philadelphia, and thence walked to William Horne's, at Derby, the same evening. Next day I pursued my journey alone and reached Concord Week-Day Meeting.

Discouragements and a weight of distress had at times attended me in this lonesome walk, but through these afflictions I was mercifully preserved. Sitting down with Friends, my mind was turned towards the Lord to wait for His holy leadings; and in infinite love He was pleased to soften my heart into humble contrition, and renewedly to strengthen me to go forward, so that to me it was a time of heavenly refreshment in a silent meeting. The next day I came to New Garden Week-Day Meeting, in which I sat in bowedness of spirit, and being baptized into a feeling of the state of some present, the Lord gave us a heart-tendering season; to His name be the praise. Passing on, I was at Little Britain on first-day; in the afternoon several Friends came to the house where I lodged and we had a little afternoon meeting, and through the humbling power of truth I had to admire the loving-kindness of the Lord manifested to us.

Twenty-sixth of Fourth Month.—I crossed the Susquehanna, and coming among people in outward ease and greatness, supported chiefly on the labour of slaves, my heart was much affected, and in awful retiredness my mind was gathered inward to the Lord, humbly desiring that in true resignation I might receive instruction from Him respecting my duty among this people. Though travelling on foot was wearisome to my body, yet it was agreeable to the state of my mind. Being weakly, I was covered with sorrow and heaviness on account of the prevailing spirit of this world by which customs grievous and oppressive are introduced on the one hand, and pride and wantonness on the other.

In this lonely walk and state of abasement and humiliation, the condition of the church in these parts was opened before me, and I may truly say with the Prophet, "I was bowed down with the hearing of it; I was dismayed at the seeing of it." Under this exercise I attended the Quarterly Meeting at Gunpowder, and in bowedness of spirit I had to express with much plainness my feelings respecting Friends living in fulness on the labours of the poor oppressed negroes; and that promise of the Most High was now revived, "I will gather all nations and tongues, and they shall come and see my glory." Here the sufferings of Christ and His tasting death for every man, and the travels, sufferings, and martyrdom of the Apostles and primitive Christians in labouring for the conversion of the Gentiles, were livingly revived in me, and according to the measure of strength afforded I laboured in some tenderness of spirit, being deeply affected among them. The difference between the present treatment which these Gentiles, the negroes, receive at our hands, and the labours of the primitive Christians for the conversion of the Gentiles, were pressed home, and the power of truth came over us, under a feeling of which my mind was united to a tender-hearted people in these parts. The meeting concluded in a sense of God's goodness towards His humble, dependent children.

The next day was a general meeting for worship, much crowded, in which I was deeply engaged in inward cries to the Lord for help, that I might stand wholly resigned, and move only as He might be pleased to lead me. I was mercifully helped to labour honestly and fervently among them, in which I found inward peace, and the sincere were comforted. From this place I turned towards Pipe Creek and the Red Lands, and had several meetings among Friends in those parts. My heart was often tenderly affected under a sense of the Lord's goodness in sanctifying my troubles and exercises, turning them to my comfort, and I believe to the benefit of many others, for I may say with thankfulness that in this visit it appeared like a tendering visitation in most places.

I passed on to the Western Quarterly Meeting in Pennsylvania. During the several days of this meeting I was mercifully preserved in an inward feeling after the mind of truth, and my public labours tended to my humiliation, with which I was content. After the Quarterly Meeting for worship ended, I felt drawings to go to the women's meeting for business, which was very full; here the humility of Jesus Christ as a pattern for us to walk by was livingly opened before me, and in treating on it my heart was enlarged, and it was a baptizing time. I was afterwards at meetings at Concord, Middletown, Providence, and Haddonfield, whence I returned home and found my family well. A sense of the Lord's merciful preservation in this my journey excites reverent thankfulness to Him.

Second of Ninth Month, 1767.—With the unity of Friends, I set off on a visit to Friends in the upper parts of Berks and Philadelphia counties; was at eleven meetings in about two weeks, and have renewed cause to bow in reverence before the Lord, who, by the powerful extendings of His humbling goodness, opened my way among Friends, and I trust made the meetings profitable to us. The following winter I joined some Friends in a family visit to some part of our meeting, in which exercise the pure influence of Divine love made our visits reviving.

Fifth of Fifth Month, 1768.—I left home under the humbling hand of the Lord, with a certificate to visit some meetings in Maryland, and to proceed without a horse seemed clearest to me. I was at the Quarterly Meetings at Philadelphia and Concord, whence I proceeded to Chester River, and, crossing the bay, was at the Yearly Meeting at West River; I then returned to Chester River, and, taking a few meetings in my way, proceeded home. It was a journey of much inward waiting, and as my eye was to the Lord, way was several times opened to my humbling admiration when things appeared very difficult. On my return I felt a very comfortable relief of mind, having through Divine help laboured in much plainness, both with Friends selected and in the more public meetings, so that I trust the pure witness in many minds was reached.

Eleventh of Sixth Month, 1769.—There have been sundry cases of late years within the limits of our Monthly Meeting, respecting the exercising of pure righteousness towards the negroes, in which I have lived under a labour of heart that equity might be steadily preserved. On this account I have had some close exercises among Friends, in which, I may thankfully say, I find peace. And as my meditations have been on universal love, my own conduct in time past became of late very grievous to me. As persons setting negroes free in our province are bound by law to maintain them in case they have need of relief, some in the time of my youth who scrupled to keep slaves for term of life were wont to detain their young negroes in their service without wages till they were thirty years of age. With this custom I so far agreed that being joined with another Friend in executing the will of a deceased Friend, I once sold a negro lad till he might attain the age of thirty years, and applied the money to the use of the estate.

With abasement of heart I may now say that sometimes as I have sat in a meeting with my heart exercised towards that awful Being who respecteth not persons nor colours, and have thought upon this lad, I have felt that all was not clear in my mind respecting him; and as I have attended to this exercise and fervently sought the Lord, it hath appeared to me that I should make some restitution; but in what way I saw not till lately, when being under some concern that I might be resigned to go on a visit to some part of the West Indies, and under close engagement of spirit seeking to the Lord for counsel herein, the aforesaid transaction came heavily upon me, and my mind for a time was covered with darkness and sorrow. Under this sore affliction my heart was softened to receive instruction, and I now first perceived that as I had been one of the two executors who had sold this lad for nine years longer than it is common for our own children to serve, so I should now offer part of my substance to redeem the last half of the nine years; but as the time was not yet come, I executed a bond, binding myself and my executors to pay to the man to whom he was sold what to candid men might appear equitable for the last four and a half years of his time, in case the said youth should be living, and in a condition likely to provide comfortably for himself.

Ninth of Tenth Month.—My heart hath often been deeply afflicted under a feeling that the standard of pure righteousness is not lifted up to the people by us, as a Society, in that clearness which it might have been, had we been as faithful as we ought to be to the teachings of Christ. And as my mind hath been inward to the Lord, the purity of Christ's government hath been made clear to my understanding, and I have believed, in the opening of universal love, that where a people who are convinced of the truth of the inward teachings of Christ are active in putting laws in execution which are not consistent with pure wisdom, it hath a necessary tendency to bring dimness over their minds. My heart having been thus exercised for several years with a tender sympathy towards my fellow-members, I have within a few months past expressed my concern on this subject in several meetings for discipline.

CHAPTER X

1769–70

Bodily Indisposition.—Exercise of his Mind for the Good of the People in the West Indies.—Communicates to Friends his concern to visit some of those Islands.—Preparations to Embark.—Considerations on the Trade to the West Indies.—Release from his Concern and return Home.—Religious Engagements.—Sickness, and Exercise of his Mind therein.

Twelfth of Third Month, 1769.—Having for some years past dieted myself on account of illness and weakness of body, and not having ability to travel by land as heretofore, I was at times favoured to look with awfulness towards the Lord, before whom are all my ways, who alone hath the power of life and death, and to feel thankfulness raised in me for this His fatherly chastisement, believing that if I was truly humbled under it, all would work for good. While under this bodily weakness, my mind was at times exercised for my fellow-creatures in the West Indies, and I grew jealous over myself lest the disagreeableness of the prospect should hinder me from obediently attending thereto; for, though I knew not that the Lord required me to go there, yet I believed that resignation was now called for in that respect. Feeling a danger of not being wholly devoted to Him, I was frequently engaged to watch unto prayer that I might be preserved; and upwards of a year having passed, as I one day walked in a solitary wood, my mind being covered with awfulness, cries were raised in me to my merciful Father, that He would graciously keep me in faithfulness; and it then settled on my mind, as a duty, to open my condition to Friends at our Monthly Meeting, which I did soon after, as follows:—

"An exercise hath attended me for some time past, and of late hath been more weighty upon me, which is, that I believe it is required of me to be resigned to go on a visit to some parts of the West Indies." In the Quarterly and General Spring meetings I found no clearness to express anything further, than that I believed resignation herein was required of me. Having obtained certificates from all the said meetings, I felt like a sojourner at my outward habitation, and kept free from worldly encumbrances, and I was often bowed in spirit before the Lord, with inward breathings to Him that I might be rightly directed. I may here note that the circumstance before related of my having, when young, joined with another executor in selling a negro lad till he might attain the age of thirty years, was now the cause of much sorrow to me; and, after having settled matters relating to this youth, I provided a sea-store and bed, and things for the voyage. Hearing of a vessel likely to sail from Philadelphia for Barbadoes, I spake with one of the owners at Burlington, and soon after went to Philadelphia on purpose to speak to him again. He told me there was a Friend in town who was part owner of the said vessel. I felt no inclination to speak with the latter, but returned home. Awhile after I took leave of my family, and, going to Philadelphia, had some weighty conversation with the first-mentioned owner, and showed him a writing, as follows:—

"On the 25th of Eleventh Month, 1769, as an exercise with respect to a visit to Barbadoes hath been weighty on my mind, I may express some of the trials which have attended me, under which I have at times rejoiced that I have felt my own self-will subjected.

"Some years ago I retailed rum, sugar, and molasses, the fruits of the labour of slaves, but had not then much concern about them save only that the rum might be used in moderation; nor was this concern so weightily attended to as I now believe it ought to have been. Having of late years been further informed respecting the oppressions too generally exercised in these islands, and thinking often on the dangers there are in connections of interest and fellowship with the works of darkness (Eph. v. 11), I have felt an increasing concern to be wholly given up to the leadings of the Holy Spirit, and it hath seemed right that my small gain from this branch of trade should be applied in promoting righteousness on the earth. This was the first motion towards a visit to Barbadoes. I believed also that part of my outward substance should be applied in paying my passage, if I went, and providing things in a lowly way for my subsistence; but when the time drew near in which I believed it required of me to be in readiness, a difficulty arose which hath been a continual trial for some months past, under which I have, with abasement of mind from day to day, sought the Lord for instruction, having often had a feeling of the condition of one formerly, who bewailed himself because the Lord hid His face from him. During these exercises my heart hath often been contrite, and I have had a tender feeling of the temptations of my fellow-creatures, labouring under expensive customs not agreeable to the simplicity that 'there is in Christ' (2 Cor. xi. 3), and sometimes in the renewings of gospel love I have been helped to minister to others.

"That which hath so closely engaged my mind, in seeking to the Lord for instruction, is, whether, after the full information I have had of the oppression which the slaves lie under who raised the West India produce, which I have gained by reading a caution and warning to Great Britain and her colonies, written by Anthony Benezet, it is right for me to take passage in a vessel employed in the West India trade.

"To trade freely with oppressors without labouring to dissuade them from such unkind treatment, and to seek for gain by such traffic, tends, I believe, to make them more easy respecting their conduct than they would be, if the cause of universal righteousness was humbly and firmly attended to by those in general with whom they have commerce; and that complaint of the Lord by His prophet, "They have strengthened the hands of the wicked," hath very often revived in my mind. I may here add some circumstances which occurred to me before I had any prospect of a visit there. David longed for some water in a well beyond an army of Philistines who were at war with Israel, and some of his men, to please him, ventured their lives in passing through this army, and brought that water.

"It doth not appear that the Israelites were then scarce of water, but rather that David gave way to delicacy of taste; and having reflected on the danger to which these men had been exposed, he considered this water as their blood, and his heart smote him that he could not drink it, but he poured it out to the Lord. The oppression of the slaves which I have seen in several journeys southward on this continent, and the report of their treatment in the West Indies, have deeply affected me, and a care to live in the spirit of peace and minister no just cause of offence to my fellow-creatures, having from time to time livingly revived in my mind, I have for some years past declined to gratify my palate with those sugars.

"I do not censure my brethren in these things, but I believe the Father of Mercies, to whom all mankind by creation are equally related, hath heard the groans of this oppressed people, and that He is preparing some to have a tender feeling of their condition. Trading in, or the frequent use of any produce known to be raised by the labour of those who are under such lamentable oppression, hath appeared to be a subject which may hereafter require the more serious consideration of the humble followers of Christ, the Prince of Peace.

"After long and mournful exercise I am now free to mention how things have opened in my mind, with desires that if it may please the Lord further to open His will to any of His children in this matter, they may faithfully follow Him in such further manifestation.

"The number of those who decline the use of West India produce, on account of the hard usage of the slaves who raise it, appears small, even among people truly pious; and the labours in Christian love on that subject of those who do, are not very extensive. Were the trade from this continent to the West Indies to be stopped at once, I believe many there would suffer for want of bread. Did we on this continent and the inhabitants of the West Indies generally dwell in pure righteousness, I believe a small trade between us might be right. Under these considerations, when the thoughts of wholly declining the use of trading-vessels and of trying to hire a vessel to go under ballast have arisen in my mind, I have believed that the labours in gospel love hitherto bestowed in the cause of universal righteousness have not reached that height. If the trade to the West Indies were no more than was consistent with pure wisdom, I believe the passage-money would for good reasons be higher than it is now; and therefore, under deep exercise of mind, I have believed that I should not take advantage of this great trade and small passage-money, but, as a testimony in favour of less trading, should pay more than is common for others to pay if I go at this time."

The first-mentioned owner, having read the paper, went with me to the other owner, who also read under which I felt myself bowed in reverence before the Most High. At length one of them asked me if I would go and see the vessel. But not having clearness in my mind to go, I went to my lodging and retired in private under great exercise of mind; and my tears were poured out before the Lord with inward cries that He would graciously help me under these trials. I believe my mind was resigned, but I did not feel clearness to proceed; and my own weakness and the necessity of Divine instruction were impressed upon me.

I was for a time as one who knew not what to do, and was tossed as in a tempest; under which affliction the doctrine of Christ, "Take no thought for the morrow," arose livingly before me, and I was favoured to get into a good degree of stillness. Having been near two days in town, I believed my obedience to my Heavenly Father consisted in returning homeward; I therefore went over among Friends on the Jersey shore and tarried till the morning on which the vessel was appointed to sail. As I lay in bed the latter part of that night my mind was comforted, and I felt what I esteemed a fresh confirmation that it was the Lord's will that I should pass through some further exercises near home; so I went thither, and still felt like a sojourner with my family. In the fresh spring of pure love, I had some labours in a private way among Friends on a subject relating to truth's testimony, under which I had frequently been exercised in heart for some years. I remember, as I walked on the road under this exercise, that passage in Ezekiel came fresh upon me, "Whithersoever their faces were turned thither they went." And I was graciously helped to discharge my duty in the fear and dread of the Almighty.

In the course of a few weeks it pleased the Lord to visit me with a pleurisy; and after I had lain a few days and felt the disorder very grievous, I was thoughtful how it might end. I had of late, through various exercises, been much weaned from the pleasant things of this life; and I now thought if it were the Lord's will to put an end to my labours and graciously to receive me into the arms of His mercy, death would be acceptable to me; but if it were His will further to refine me under affliction, and to make me in any degree useful in His church, I desired not to die. I may with thankfulness say that in this case I felt resignedness wrought in me and had no inclination to send for a doctor, believing, if it were the Lord's will through outward means to raise me up, some sympathizing Friends would be sent to minister to me; which accordingly was the case. But though I was carefully attended, yet the disorder was at times so heavy that I had no expectation of recovery. One night in particular my bodily distress was great; my feet grew cold, and the cold increased up my legs towards my body; at that time I had no inclination to ask my nurse to apply anything warm to my feet, expecting my end was near. After I had lain near ten hours in this condition, I closed my eyes, thinking whether I might now be delivered out of the body; but in these awful moments my mind was livingly opened to behold the church; and strong engagements were begotten in me for the everlasting well-being of my fellow-creatures. I felt in the spring of pure love that I might remain some time longer in the body, to fill up according to my measure that which remains of the afflictions of Christ, and to labour for the good of the church; after which I requested my nurse to apply warmth to my feet, and I revived. The next night, feeling a weighty exercise of spirit and having a solid Friend sitting up with me, I requested him to write what I said, which he did as follows:—

Fourth-day of the First Month, 1770, about five in the morning— "I have seen in the Light of the Lord that the day is approaching when the man that is most wise in human policy shall be the greatest fool; and the arm that is mighty to support injustice shall be broken to pieces; the enemies of righteousness shall make a terrible rattle, and shall mightily torment one another; for He that is omnipotent is rising up to judgment, and will plead the cause of the oppressed; and He commanded me to open the vision."*

Near a week after this, feeling my mind livingly opened, I sent for a neighbour, who, at my request, wrote as follows:—

"The place of prayer is a precious habitation; for I now saw that the prayers of the saints were precious incense; and a trumpet was given to me that I might sound forth this language; that the children might hear it and be invited together to this precious habitation, where the prayers of the saints, as sweet incense, arise before the throne of God and the Lamb. I saw this habitation to be safe,— to be inwardly quiet when there were great stirrings and commotions in the world.

"Prayer, at this day, in pure resignation, is a precious place: the trumpet is sounded; the call goes forth to the church that she gather to the place of pure inward prayer; and her habitation is safe."

CHAPTER XI

1772

Embarks at Chester, with Samuel Emlen, in a Ship bound for London.—Exercise of Mind respecting the Hardships of the Sailors.—Considerations on the Dangers of training Youth to a Seafaring Life.—Thoughts during a Storm at Sea.—Arrival in London.

Having been some time under a religious concern to prepare for crossing the seas, in order to visit Friends in the northern parts of England, and more particularly in Yorkshire, after consideration I

---

* The reader, who may be disposed to regard this as the language of distempered imagination, may perhaps find a truer explanation of it in the late civil conflict by which "the arm mighty to support injustice" has been "broken in pieces," and in which it may be said the Lord did "rise up to judgment and plead the cause of the oppressed."

thought it expedient to inform Friends of it at our Monthly Meeting at Burlington, who, having unity with me therein, gave me a certificate. I afterwards communicated the same to our Quarterly Meeting, and they likewise certified their concurrence. Some time after, at the General Spring Meeting of ministers and elders, I thought it my duty to acquaint them with the religious exercise which attended my mind; and they likewise signified their unity therewith by a certificate, dated the 24th of Third Month, 1772, directed to Friends in Great Britain.

In the Fourth Month following, I thought the time was come for me to make some inquiry for a suitable conveyance; and as my concern was principally towards the northern parts of England, it seemed most proper to go in a vessel bound to Liverpool or Whitehaven. While I was at Philadelphia deliberating on this subject I was informed that my beloved friend, Samuel Emlen, junior, intended to go to London, and had taken a passage for himself in the cabin of the ship called the *Mary and Elizabeth,* of which James Sparks was master, and John Head, of the city of Philadelphia, one of the owners; and feeling a draught in my mind towards the steerage of the same ship, I went first and opened to Samuel the feeling I had concerning it.

My beloved friend wept when I spake to him, and appeared glad that I had thoughts of going in the vessel with him, though my prospect was toward the steerage; and he offering to go with me, we went on board, first into the cabin—a commodious room—and then into the steerage, where we sat down on a chest, the sailors being busy about us. The owner of the ship also came and sat down with us. My mind was turned toward Christ, the heavenly Counsellor, and feeling at this time my own will subjected, my heart was contrite before Him. A motion was made by the owner to go and sit in the cabin, as a place more retired; but I felt easy to leave the ship, and, making no agreement as to a passage in her, told the owner if I took a passage in the ship I believed it would be in the steerage; but did not say much as to my exercise in that case.

After I went to my lodgings, and the case was a little known in town, a Friend laid before me the great inconvenience attending a passage in the steerage, which for a time appeared very discouraging to me.

I soon after went to bed, and my mind was under a deep exercise before the Lord, whose helping hand was manifested to me as I slept that night, and His love strengthened my heart. In the morning I went with two Friends on board the vessel again, and after a short time spent therein, I went with Samuel Emlen to the house of the owner, to whom, in the hearing of Samuel only, I opened my exercise in relation to a scruple I felt with regard to a passage in the cabin, in substance as follows:—

"That on the outside of that part of the ship where the cabin was, I observed sundry sorts of carved work and imagery; that in the cabin I observed some superfluity of workmanship of several sorts; and that according to the ways of men's reckoning, the sum of money to be paid for a passage in that apartment has some relation to the expense of furnishing it to please the minds of such as give way to a conformity to this world; and that in this, as in other cases, the moneys received from the passengers are calculated to defray the cost of these superfluities, as well as the other expenses of their passage. I therefore felt a scruple with regard to paying my money to be applied to such purposes."

As my mind was now opened, I told the owner that I had, at several times, in my travels, seen great oppressions on this continent, at which my heart had been much affected and brought into a feeling of the state of the sufferers; and having many times been engaged in the fear and love of God, to labour with those under whom the oppressed have been borne down and afflicted, I have often perceived that with a view to get riches and to provide estates for children, that they may live conformably to the customs and honours of this world, many are entangled in the spirit of oppression, and the exercise of my soul has been such, that I could not find peace in joining in anything which I saw was against that wisdom which is pure.

After this I agreed for a passage in the steerage; and hearing that Joseph White had desired to see me, I went to his house, and next day home, where I tarried two nights. Early the next morning, I parted with my family under a sense of the humbling hand of God upon me, and, going to Philadelphia, had an opportunity with several of my beloved friends, who appeared to be concerned for me on account of the unpleasant situation of that part of the vessel in which I was likely to lodge. In these opportunities my mind, through the mercies of the Lord, was kept low in an inward waiting for His help; and Friends having expressed their desire that I might have a more convenient place than the steerage, did not urge it, but appeared disposed to leave me to the Lord.

Having stayed two nights at Philadelphia, I went the next day to Derby Monthly Meeting, where, through the strength of Divine love, my heart was enlarged towards the youth there present, under which I was helped to labour in some tenderness of spirit. I lodged at William Horn's and afterwards went to Chester, where I met with Samuel Emlen, and we went on board 1st of Fifth Month, 1772. As I sat alone on the deck, I felt a satisfactory evidence that my proceedings were not in my own will, but under the power of the cross of Christ.

Seventh of Fifth Month.—We have had rough weather mostly since I came on board, and the passengers, James Reynolds, John Till Adams, Sarah Logan with her hired maid, and John Bispham, all sea-sick at times; from which sickness through the tender mercies of my Heavenly Father, I have been preserved, my afflictions now being of another kind. There appeared an openness in the minds of the master of the ship and in the cabin passengers towards me. We are often together on the deck, and sometimes in the cabin. My mind, through the merciful help of the Lord, hath been preserved in a good degree watchful and quiet, for which I have great cause to be thankful.

As my lodging in the steerage, now near a week, hath afforded me sundry opportunities of seeing, hearing and feeling with respect to the life and spirit of many poor sailors, an exercise of soul hath attended me in regard to placing out children and youth where they may be likely to be exampled and instructed in the pure fear of the Lord.

Being much among the seamen I have, from a motion of love, taken sundry opportunities with one of them at a time, and have in free conversation laboured to turn their minds towards the fear of the Lord. This day we had a meeting in the cabin, where my heart was contrite under a feeling of Divine love.

I believe a communication with different parts of the world by sea is at times consistent with the will of our Heavenly Father, and to educate some youth in the practice of sailing, I believe may be right; but how lamentable is the present corruption of the world! How impure are the channels through which trade is conducted!

How great is the danger to which poor lads are exposed when placed on shipboard to learn the art of sailing! Five lads training up for the seas were on board this ship. Two of them were brought up in our Society, and the other, by name James Naylor, is a member, to whose father James Naylor, mentioned in Sewel's history, appears to have been uncle. I often feel a tenderness of heart towards these poor lads, and at times look at them as though they were my children according to the flesh.

O that all may take heed and beware of covetousness! O that all may learn of Christ, who was meek and lowly of heart. Then in faithfully following Him He will teach us to be content with food and raiment without respect to the customs or honours of this world. Men thus redeemed will feel a tender concern for their fellow-creatures, and a desire that those in the lowest stations may be assisted and encouraged, and where owners of ships attain to the perfect law of liberty and are doers of the Word, these will be blessed in their deeds.

A ship at sea commonly sails all night, and the seamen take their watches four hours at a time. Rising to work in the night, it is not commonly pleasant in any case, but in dark rainy nights it is very disagreeable, even though each man were furnished with all conveniences. If, after having been on deck several hours in the night, they come down into the steerage soaking wet, and are so closely stowed that proper convenience for change of garments is not easily come at, but for want of proper room their wet garments are thrown in heaps, and sometimes, through much crowding, are trodden under foot in going to their lodgings and getting out of them—it is difficult at times for each to find his own. Here are trials for the poor sailors.

Now, as I have been with them in my lodge, my heart hath often yearned for them, and tender desires have been raised in me that all owners and masters of vessels may dwell in the love of God and therein act uprightly, and by seeking less for gain and looking carefully to their ways they may earnestly labour to remove all cause of provocation from the poor seamen, so that they may neither fret nor use excess of strong drink; for, indeed, the poor creatures, in the wet and cold, seem to apply at times to strong drink to supply the want of other convenience. Great reformation is wanting in the world, and the necessity of it among those who do business on great waters hath at this time been abundantly opened before me.

Eighth of Fifth Month.—This morning the clouds gathered, the wind blew strong from the south-east, and before noon so increased that sailing appeared dangerous. The seamen then bound up some of their sails and took down others, and the storm increasing, they put the dead-lights, so called, into the cabin windows and lighted a lamp as at night. The wind now blew vehemently, and the sea wrought to that degree that an awful seriousness prevailed in the cabin, in which I spent, I believe, about seventeen hours, for the cabin passengers had given me frequent invitations, and I thought the poor wet toiling seamen had need of all the room in the crowded steerage. They now ceased from sailing and put the vessel in the posture called lying to.

My mind during this tempest, through the gracious assistance of the Lord, was preserved in a good degree of resignation; and at times I expressed a few words in His love to my shipmates in regard to the all-sufficiency of Him who formed the great deep, and whose care is so extensive that a sparrow falls not without His notice; and thus in a tender frame of mind I spoke to them of the necessity of our yielding in true obedience to the instructions of our Heavenly Father, who sometimes through adversities intendeth our refinement.

About eleven at night I went out on the deck. The sea wrought exceedingly, and the high foaming waves round about had in some sort the appearance of fire, but did not give much if any light. The sailor at the helm said he lately saw a corposant at the head of the mast. I observed that the master of the ship ordered the carpenter to keep on the deck; and, though he said little, I apprehended his care was that the carpenter with his axe might be in readiness in case of any extremity. Soon after this the vehemency of the wind abated, and before morning they again put the ship under sail.

Tenth of Fifth Month.—It being the first day of the week and fine weather, we had a meeting in the cabin, at which most of the seamen were present; this meeting was to me a strengthening time. 13th.—As I continue to lodge in the steerage, I feel an openness this morning to express something further of the state of my mind in respect to poor lads bound apprentice to learn the art of sailing. As I believe sailing is of use in the world, a labour of soul attends me that the pure counsel of truth may be humbly waited for in this case by all concerned in the business of the seas. A pious father whose mind is exercised for the everlasting welfare of his child, may not with a peaceable mind place him out to an employment among a people whose common course of life is manifestly corrupt and profane. Great is the present defect among seafaring men in regard to virtue and piety; and, by reason of an abundant traffic, and many ships being used for war, so many people are employed on the sea that the subject of placing lads to this employment appears very weighty.

When I remember the saying of the Most High through His prophet, "This people have I formed for myself; they shall show forth my praise," and think of placing children among such to learn the practice of sailing, the consistency of it with a pious education seems to me like that mentioned by the prophet, "There is no answer from God."

Profane examples are very corrupting and very forcible. And as my mind day after day and night after night hath been affected with a sympathizing tenderness towards poor children who are put to the employment of sailors, I have sometimes had weighty conversation with the sailors in the steerage, who were mostly respectful to me, and became more so the longer I was with them. They mostly appeared to take kindly what I said to them; but their minds were so deeply impressed with the almost universal depravity among sailors that the poor creatures in their answers to me have revived in my remembrance that of the degenerate Jews a little before the captivity, as repeated by Jeremiah the prophet, "There is no hope."

Now under this exercise a sense of the desire of outward gain prevailing among us felt grievous; and a strong call to the professed followers of Christ was raised in me that all may take heed lest, through loving this present world, they be found in a continued neglect of duty with respect to a faithful labour for reformation.

To silence every motion proceeding from the love of money and humbly to wait upon God to know His will concerning us have appeared necessary. He alone is able to strengthen us to dig deep, to remove all which lies between us and the safe foundation, and so to direct us in our outward employments that pure universal love may shine forth in our proceedings. Desires arising from the spirit of truth are pure desires; and when a mind divinely opened towards a

young generation is made sensible of corrupting examples powerfully working and extensively spreading among them, how moving
is the prospect! In a world of dangers and difficulties like a deso-
late, thorny wilderness, how precious, how comfortable, how safe,
are the leadings of Christ the good Shepherd, who said, "I know
my sheep, and am known of mine!"

Sixteenth of Fifth Month.—Wind for several days past often high,
what the sailors call squally, with a rough sea and frequent rains.
This last night has been a very trying one to the poor seamen, the
water the most part of the night running over the main-deck, and
sometimes breaking waves came on the quarter-deck. The latter
part of the night, as I lay in bed, my mind was humbled under the
power of Divine love; and resignedness to the great Creator of the
earth and the seas was renewedly wrought in me, and His fatherly
care over His children felt precious to my soul. I was now desirous
to embrace every opportunity of being inwardly acquainted with
the hardships and difficulties of my fellow-creatures, and to labour
in His love for the spreading of pure righteousness on the earth.
Opportunities were frequent of hearing conversation among the
sailors respecting the voyages to Africa and the manner of bringing
the deeply oppressed slaves into our islands. They are frequently
brought on board the vessels in chains and fetters, with hearts
loaded with grief under the apprehension of miserable slavery; so
that my mind was frequently engaged to meditate on these things.

Seventeenth of Fifth Month and first of the week.—We had a
meeting in the cabin, to which the seamen generally came. My
spirit was contrite before the Lord, whose love at this time affected
my heart. In the afternoon I felt a tender sympathy of soul with my
poor wife and family left behind, in which state my heart was enlarged in desires that they may walk in that humble obedience
wherein the everlasting Father may be their guide and support
through all their difficulties in this world; and a sense of that
gracious assistance, through which my mind hath been strengthened
to take up the cross and leave them to travel in the love of truth,
hath begotten thankfulness in my heart to our great Helper.

Twenty-fourth of Fifth Month.—A clear, pleasant morning. As I
sat on deck I felt a reviving in my nature, which had been weakened through much rainy weather and high winds and being shut
up in a close, unhealthy air. Several nights of late I have felt my

breathing difficult; and a little after the rising of the second watch, which is about midnight, I have got up and stood near an hour with my face near the hatchway, to get the fresh air at the small vacancy under the hatch door, which is commonly shut down, partly to keep out rain and sometimes to keep the breaking waves from dashing into the steerage. I may with thankfulness to the Father of Mercies acknowledge that in my present weak state my mind hath been supported to bear this affliction with patience; and I have looked at the present dispensation as a kindness from the great Father of mankind, who, in this my floating pilgrimage, is in some degree bringing me to feel what many thousands of my fellow-creatures often suffer in a greater degree.

My appetite failing, the trial hath been the heavier; and I have felt tender breathings in my soul after God, the fountain of comfort, whose inward help hath supplied at times the want of outward convenience; and strong desires have attended me that His family, who are acquainted with the movings of His Holy Spirit, may be so redeemed from the love of money and from that spirit in which men seek honour one of another, that in all business, by sea or land, they may constantly keep in view the coming of His kingdom on earth as it is in Heaven, and, by faithfully following this safe guide, may show forth examples tending to lead out of that under which the creation groans. This day we had a meeting in the cabin, in which I was favoured in some degree to experience the fulfilling of that saying of the prophet, "The Lord hath been a strength to the poor, a strength to the needy in their distress"; for which my heart is bowed in thankfulness before Him.

Twenty-eighth of Fifth Month.—Wet weather of late, and small winds, inclining to calms. Our seamen cast a lead, I suppose about one hundred fathoms, but found no bottom. Foggy weather this morning. Through the kindness of the great Preserver of men my mind remains quiet; and a degree of exercise from day to day attends me, that the pure peaceable government of Christ may spread and prevail among mankind.

The leading of a young generation in that pure way in which the wisdom of this world hath no place, where parents and tutors, humbly waiting for the heavenly Counsellor, may example them in the truth as it is in Jesus, hath for several days been the exercise of my mind. Oh, how safe, how quiet, is that state where the soul stands in pure obedience to the voice of Christ, and a watchful care is maintained not to follow the voice of the stranger! Here Christ is felt to be our Shepherd, and under His leading, people are brought to a stability; and where He doth not lead forward, we are bound in the bonds of pure love to stand still and wait upon Him.

In the love of money and in the wisdom of this world, business is proposed, then the urgency of affairs pushes forward, and the mind cannot in this state discern the good and perfect will of God concerning us. The love of God is manifested in graciously calling us to come out of that which stands in confusion; but if we bow not in the name of Jesus, if we give not up those prospects of gain which in the wisdom of this world are open before us, but say in our hearts, "I must needs go on, and in going on I hope to keep as near the purity of truth as the business before me will admit of," the mind remains entangled and the shining of the light of life into the soul is obstructed.

Surely the Lord calls to mourning and deep humiliation, that in His fear we may be instructed and led safely through the great difficulties and perplexities in this present age. In an entire subjection of our wills the Lord graciously opens a way for His people, where all their wants are bounded by His wisdom; and here we experience the substance of what Moses the prophet figured out in the water of separation as a purification from sin.

Esau is mentioned as a child red all over like a hairy garment. In Esau is represented the natural will of man. In preparing the water of separation a red heifer without blemish, on which there had been no yoke, was to be slain and her blood sprinkled by the priest seven times towards the tabernacle of the congregation; then her skin, her flesh, and all pertaining to her, was to be burnt without the camp, and of her ashes the water was prepared. Thus, the crucifying of the old man, or natural will, is represented; and hence comes a separation from that carnal mind which is death. "He who toucheth the dead body of a man and purifieth not himself with the water of separation, defileth the tabernacle of the Lord; he is unclean." (Num. xix. 13.)

If any through the love of gain engage in business wherein they dwell as among the tombs and touch the bodies of those who are dead should, through the infinite love of God, feel the power of the cross of Christ to crucify them to the world, and therein learn humbly to follow the Divine Leader, here is the judgment of this world, here the prince of this world is cast out. The water of separation is felt; and though we have been among the slain, and through the desire of gain have touched the dead body of a man, yet in the purifying love of Christ we are washed in the water of separation; we are brought off from that business, from that gain, and from that fellowship which is not agreeable to His holy will. I have felt a renewed confirmation in the time of this voyage, that the Lord, in His infinite love, is calling to His visited children so to give up all outward possessions and means of getting treasures, that His Holy Spirit may have free course in their hearts and direct them in all their proceedings. To feel the substance pointed at in this figure, man must know death as to his own will.

"No man can see God and live." This was spoken by the Almighty to Moses the prophet and opened by our blessed Redeemer. As death comes on our own wills, and a new life is formed in us, the heart is purified and prepared to understand clearly, "Blessed are the pure in heart, for they shall see God." In purity of heart the mind is divinely opened to behold the nature of universal righteousness, or the righteousness of the kingdom of God. "No man hath seen the Father save he that is of God, he hath seen the Father."

The natural mind is active about the things of this life, and in this natural activity business is proposed and a will is formed in us to go forward in it. And so long as this natural will remains unsubjected, so long there remains an obstruction to the clearness of Divine light operating in us; but when we love God with all our heart and with all our strength, in this love we love our neighbour as ourselves; and a tenderness of heart is felt towards all people for whom Christ died, even those who, as to outward circumstances, may be to us as the Jews were to the Samaritans. "Who is my neighbour?" See this question answered by our Saviour. (Luke x. 30.) In this love we can say that Jesus is the Lord; and in this reformation in our souls, manifested in a full reformation of our lives, wherein all things are new, and all things are of God (2 Cor. v. 18), the desire of gain is subjected.

When employment is honestly followed in the light of truth, and people become diligent in business "fervent in spirit, serving the Lord" (Rom. xii, 11), the meaning of the name is opened to us:

"This is the name by which He shall be called, THE LORD OUR RIGHTEOUSNESS." (Jer. xxiii. 6.) O, how precious is this name! it is like ointment poured out. The chaste virgins are in love with the Redeemer; and for promoting His peaceable kingdom in the world are content to endure hardness like good soldiers; and are so separated in spirit from the desire of riches, that in their employments they become extensively careful to give no offence, either to Jew or Heathen, or to the church of Christ.

Thirty-first of Fifth Month and first of the week.—We had a meeting in the cabin, with nearly all the ship's company the whole being near thirty. In this meeting the Lord in mercy favoured us with the extending of His love.

Second of Sixth Month.—Last evening the seamen found bottom at about seventy fathoms. This morning, a fair wind and pleasant. I sat on deck; my heart was overcome with the love of Christ, and melted into contrition before Him. In this state the prospect of that work to which I found my mind drawn when in my native land being, in some degree, opened before me, I felt like a little child; and my cries were put up to my Heavenly Father for preservation, that in an humble dependence on Him, my soul might be strengthened in His love and kept inwardly waiting for His counsel. This afternoon we saw that part of England called the Lizard.

Some fowls yet remained of those the passengers took for their sea-store. I believe about fourteen perished in the storms at sea, by the waves breaking over the quarter-deck, and a considerable number with sickness at different times. I observed the cocks crew as we came down the Delaware, and while we were near the land, but afterwards I think I did not hear one of them crow till we came near the English coast, when they again crowed a few times. In observing their dull appearance at sea, and the pining sickness of some of them, I often remembered the Fountain of goodness, who gave being to all creatures, and whose love extends to caring for the sparrows. I believe where the love of God is verily perfected, and the true spirit of government watchfully attended to, a tenderness towards all creatures made subject to us will be experienced, and a care felt in us that we do not lessen that sweetness of life in the animal creation which the great Creator intends for them under our government.

Fourth of Sixth Month.—Wet weather, high winds, and so dark

that we could see but a little way. I perceived our seamen were apprehensive of the danger of missing the channel, which I understood was narrow. In a while it grew lighter, and they saw the land and knew where we were. Thus the Father of Mercies was pleased to try us with the sight of dangers, and then graciously, from time to time, deliver us from them; thus sparing our lives, that in humility and reverence we might walk before Him and put our trust in Him. About noon a pilot came off from Dover, where my beloved friend Samuel Emlen went on shore and thence to London, about seventy-two miles by land; but I felt easy in staying in the ship.

Seventh of Sixth Month and first of the week.—A clear morning: we lay at anchor for the tide, and had a parting meeting with the ship's company, in which my heart was enlarged in a fervent concern for them, that they may come to experience salvation through Christ. Had a head-wind up the Thames; lay sometimes at anchor; saw many ships passing, and some at anchor near; and I had large opportunity of feeling the spirit in which the poor bewildered sailors too generally live. That lamentable degeneracy which so much prevails in the people employed on the sea, so affected my heart that I cannot easily convey the feeling I had to another.

The present state of the seafaring life in general appears so opposite to that of a pious education, so full of corruption and extreme alienation from God, so full of the most dangerous examples to young people that in looking towards a young generation I feel a care for them, that they may have an education different from the present one of lads at sea, and that all of us who are acquainted with the pure gospel spirit may lay this case to heart, may remember the lamentable corruptions which attend the conveyance of merchandise across the seas, and so abide in the love of Christ that, being delivered from the entangling expenses of a curious, delicate, and luxurious life, we may learn contentment with a little, and promote the seafaring life no further than that spirit which leads into all truth attends us in our proceedings.

CHAPTER XII

1772

Attends the Yearly Meeting in London.—Then proceeds towards Yorkshire.—Visits Quarterly and other Meetings in the Counties of Hertford, Warwick, Oxford, Nottingham, York, and Westmoreland.—Returns to Yorkshire.—Instructive Observations and Letters.— Hears of the Decease of William Hunt.—Some Account of him.—The Author's Last Illness and Death at York.

On the 8th of Sixth Month, 1772, we landed at London, and I went straightway to the Yearly Meeting of ministers and elders, which had been gathered, I suppose, about half an hour.*

* There is a story told of his first appearance in England which I have from my friend William J. Alinson, editor of the *Friends' Review,* and which he assures me is well authenticated. The vessel reached London on the morning of the fifth day of the week, and John Woolman, knowing that the meeting was then in session, lost no time in reaching it. Coming in late and unannounced, his peculiar dress and manner excited attention and apprehension that he was an itinerant enthusiast. He presented his certificate from Friends in America, but the dissatisfaction still remained, and someone remarked that perhaps the stranger Friend might feel that his dedication of himself to this apprehended service was accepted, without further labour, and that he might now feel free to return to his home. John Woolman sat silent for a space, seeking the unerring counsel of Divine wisdom. He was profoundly affected by the unfavourable reception he met with, and his tears flowed freely. In the love of Christ and his fellow men he had, at a painful sacrifice, taken his life in his hands, and left behind the peace and endearments of home. That love still flowed out toward the people of England; must it henceforth be pent up in his own heart? He rose at last, and stated that he could not feel himself released from his prospect of labour in England. Yet he could not travel in the ministry without the unity of Friends; and while that was withheld he could not feel easy to be of any cost to them. He could not go back as had been suggested; but he was acquainted with a mechanical trade, and while the impediment to his services continued, he hoped

In this meeting my mind was humbly contrite. In the afternoon the meeting for business was opened, which by adjournments held near a week. In these meetings I often felt a living concern for the establishment of Friends in the pure life of truth. My heart was enlarged in the meetings of ministers, that for business, and in several meetings for public worship, and I felt my mind united in true love to the faithful labourers now gathered at this Yearly Meeting. On the 15th I went to a Quarterly Meeting at Hertford.

First of Seventh Month.—I have been at Quarterly Meetings at Sherrington, Northampton, Banbury, and Shipton, and have had sundry meetings between. My mind hath been bowed under a sense of Divine goodness manifested among us; my heart hath been often enlarged in true love, both among ministers and elders and in public meetings, and through the Lord's goodness I believe it hath been a fresh visitation to many, in particular to the youth.

Seventeenth.—I was this day at Birmingham; I have been at meetings at Coventry, Warwick, in Oxfordshire, and sundry other places, and have felt the humbling hand of the Lord upon me; but through His tender mercies I find peace in the labours I have gone through.

Twenty-sixth.—I have continued traveling northward, visiting meetings. Was this day at Nottingham; the forenoon meeting was especially, through Divine love, a heart-tendering season. Next day

Friends would be kindly willing to employ him in such business as he was capable of, that he might not be chargeable to any.

A deep silence prevailed over the assembly, many of whom were touched by the wise simplicity of the stranger's words and manner. After a season of waiting, John Woolman felt that words were given him to utter as a minister of Christ. The spirit of his Master bore witness to them in the hearts of his hearers. When he closed, the Friend who had advised against his further service rose up and humbly confessed his error, and avowed his full unity with the stranger. All doubt was removed; there was a general expression of unity and sympathy, and John Woolman, owned by his brethren, passed on to his work.

There is no portrait of John Woolman; and had photography been known in his day it is not at all probable that the sun artist would have been permitted to delineate his features. That, while eschewing all superfluity and expensive luxury, he was scrupulously neat in his dress and person may be inferred from his general character and from the fact that one of his serious objections to dyed clothing was that it served to conceal uncleanness, and was, therefore, detrimental to real purity. It is, however, quite probable that his outer man, on the occasion referred to, was suggestive of a hasty toilet in the crowded steerage.

I had a meeting in a Friend's family, which, through the strengthening arm of the Lord, was a time to be thankfully remembered.

Second of Eighth Month and first of the week.—I was this day at Sheffield, a large inland town. I was at sundry meetings last week, and feel inward thankfulness for that Divine support which hath been graciously extended to me. On the 9th I was at Rushworth. I have lately passed through some painful labour, but have been comforted under a sense of that Divine visitation which I feel extended towards many young people.

Sixteenth of Eighth Month and the first of the week, I was at Settle. It hath of late been a time of inward poverty, under which my mind hath been preserved in a watchful, tender state, feeling for the mind of the Holy Leader, and I find peace in the labours I have passed through.

On inquiry at many places I find the price of rye about five shillings; wheat, eight shillings per bushel; oatmeal, twelve shillings for a hundred and twenty pounds; mutton from threepence to fivepence per pound; bacon from sevenpence to ninepence; cheese, from fourpence to sixpence; butter, from eightpence to tenpence; house-rent for a poor man from twenty-five shillings to forty shillings per year, to be paid weekly; wood for fire very scarce and dear; coal in some places two shillings and sixpence per hundredweight; but near the pits not a quarter so much. O, may the wealthy consider the poor!

The wages of labouring men in several counties towards London at tenpence per day in common business, the employer finds small beer and the labourer finds his own food; but in harvest and hay time wages are about one shilling per day, and the labourer hath all his diet. In some parts of the north of England poor labouring men have their food where they work, and appear in common to do rather better than nearer London. Industrious women who spin in the factories get some fourpence, some fivepence, and so on to six, seven, eight, nine, or tenpence per day, and find their own house-room and diet. Great numbers of poor people live chiefly on bread and water in the southern parts of England, as well as in the northern parts; and there are many poor children not even taught to read. May those who have abundance lay these things to heart!

Stage-coaches frequently go upwards of one hundred miles in

twenty-four hours; and I have heard Friends say in several places that it is common for horses to be killed with hard driving, and that many others are driven till they grow blind. Post-boys pursue their business, each one to his stage, all night through the winter. Some boys who ride long stages suffer greatly in winter nights, and at several places I have heard of their being frozen to death. So great is the hurry in the spirit of this world, that in aiming to do business quickly and to gain wealth, the creation at this day doth loudly groan.

As my journey hath been without a horse, I have had several offers of being assisted on my way in these stage-coaches, but have not been in them; nor have I had freedom to send letters by these posts in the present way of their riding, the stages being so fixed, and one boy dependent on another as to time, and going at great speed, that in long cold winter nights the poor boys suffer much. I heard in America of the way of these posts, and cautioned Friends in the General Meeting of ministers and elders at Philadelphia, and in the Yearly Meeting of ministers and elders in London, not to send letters to me on any common occasion by post. And though on this account I may be likely not to hear so often from my family left behind, yet for righteousness' sake I am, through Divine favour, made content.

I have felt great distress of mind since I came on this island, on account of the members of our Society being mixed with the world in various sorts of traffic, carried on in impure channels. Great is the trade to Africa for slaves; and for the loading of these ships a great number of people are employed in their factories, among whom are many of our Society. Friends in early times refused on a religious principle to make or trade in superfluities, of which we have many testimonies on record; but for want of faithfulness, some, whose examples were of note in our Society, gave way, from which others took more liberty. Members of our Society worked in superfluities, and bought and sold them, and thus dimness of sight came over many; at length Friends got into the use of some superfluities in dress and in the furniture of their houses, which hath spread from less to more, till superfluity of some kinds is common among us.

In this declining state many look at the example of others, and too much neglect the pure feeling of truth. Of late years a deep exercise hath attended my mind, that Friends may dig deep, may carefully cast forth the loose matter and get down to the rock, the sure foundation, and there hearken to that Divine voice which gives a clear and certain sound; and I have felt in that which doth not deceive, that if Friends who have known the truth, keep in that tenderness of heart where all views of outward gain are given up, and their trust is only in the Lord, He will graciously lead some to be patterns of deep self-denial in things relating to trade and handicraft labour; and others who have plenty of the treasures of this world will be examples of a plain frugal life, and pay wages to such as they may hire more liberally than is now customary in some places.

Twenty-third of Eighth Month.—I was this day at Preston Patrick, and had a comfortable meeting. I have several times been entertained at the houses of Friends who had sundry things about them that had the appearance of outward greatness, and as I have kept inward, way hath opened for conversation with such in private, in which Divine goodness hath favoured us together with heart-tendering times.

Twenty-sixth of Eighth Month.—Being now at George Crosfield's, in the county of Westmoreland, I feel a concern to commit to writing the following uncommon circumstance:

In a time of sickness, a little more than two years and a half ago, I was brought so near the gates of death that I forgot my name. Being then desirous to know who I was, I saw a mass of matter of a dull gloomy colour between the south and the east, and was informed that this mass was human beings in as great misery as they could be and live, and that I was mixed with them, and that henceforth I might not consider myself as a distinct or separate being. In this state I remained several hours. I then heard a soft melodious voice, more pure and harmonious than any I had heard with my ears before; I believed it was the voice of an angel who spake to the other angels; the words were, "John Woolman is dead." I soon remembered that I was once John Woolman, and being assured that I was alive in the body, I greatly wondered what that heavenly voice could mean. I believed beyond doubting that it was the voice of an holy angel, but as yet it was a mystery to me.

I was then carried in spirit to the mines where poor oppressed people were digging rich treasures for those called Christians, and heard them blaspheme the name of Christ, at which I was grieved, for His name to me was precious. I was then informed that these heathens were told that those who oppressed them were the followers of Christ, and they said among themselves, "If Christ directed them to use us in this sort, then Christ is a cruel tyrant."

All this time the song of the angel remained a mystery; and in the morning, my dear wife and some others coming to my bedside, I asked them if they knew who I was, and they telling me I was John Woolman, thought I was light-headed, for I told them not what the angel said, nor was I disposed to talk much to any one, but was very desirous to get so deep that I might understand this mystery.

My tongue was often so dry that I could not speak till I had moved it about and gathered some moisture, and as I lay still for a time I at length felt a Divine power prepare my mouth that I could speak, and I then said, "I am crucified with Christ, nevertheless I live; yet not I, but Christ liveth in me. And the life which I now live in the flesh I live by the faith of the Son of God, who loved me and gave himself for me." Then the mystery was opened and I perceived there was joy in heaven over a sinner who had repented, and that the language "John Woolman is dead" meant no more than the death of my own will.

My natural understanding now returned as before, and I saw that people setting off their tables with silver vessels at entertainments was often stained with worldly glory, and that in the present state of things I should take heed how I fed myself out of such vessels. Going to our Monthly Meeting soon after my recovery, I dined at a Friend's house where drink was brought in silver vessels, and not in any other. Wanting something to drink, I told him my case with weeping, and he ordered some drink for me in another vessel. I afterwards went through the same exercise in several Friends' houses in America, as well as in England, and I have cause to acknowledge with humble reverence the loving-kindness of my Heavenly Father, who hath preserved me in such a tender frame of mind, that none, I believe, have ever been offended at what I have said on that subject.

After this sickness I spake not in public meetings for worship for nearly one year, but my mind was very often in company with the oppressed slaves as I sat in meetings; and though under this dispensation I was shut up from speaking, yet the spring of the gospel ministry was many times lovingly opened in me, and the Divine gift operated by abundance of weeping, in feeling the oppression of this people. It being so long since I passed through this dispensation, and the matter remaining fresh and lively in my mind, I believe it safest for me to commit to writing.

Thirtieth of Eighth Month.—This morning I wrote a letter in substance as follows:—

BELOVED FRIEND,—My mind is often affected as I pass along under a sense of the state of many poor people who sit under that sort of ministry which requires much outward labour to support it; and the loving-kindness of our Heavenly Father in opening a pure gospel ministry in this nation hath often raised thankfulness in my heart to Him. I often remember the conflicts of the faithful under persecution, and now look at the free exercise of the pure gift uninterrupted by outward laws, as a trust committed to us, which requires our deepest gratitude and most careful attention. I feel a tender concern that the work of reformation so prosperously carried on in this land within a few ages past may go forward and spread among the nations, and may not go backward through dust gathering on our garments, who have been called to a work so great and so precious.

Last evening during thy absence I had a little opportunity with some of thy family, in which I rejoiced, and feeling a sweetness on my mind towards thee, I now endeavour to open a little of the feeling I had there.

I have heard that you in these parts have at certain seasons Meetings of Conference in relation to Friends living up to our principles, in which several meetings unite in one. With this I feel unity, having in some measure felt truth lead that way among Friends in America, and I have found, my dear friend, that in these labours all superfluities in our own living are against us. I feel that pure love towards thee in which there is freedom.

I look at that precious gift bestowed on thee with awfulness before Him who gave it, and feel a desire that we may be so separated to the gospel of Christ, that those things which proceed from the spirit of this world may have no place among us.

Thy friend, JOHN WOOLMAN.

I rested a few days in body and mind with our friend, Jane Crosfield, who was once in America. On the sixth day of the week I was at Kendal, in Westmoreland, and at Greyrig Meeting the 30th day of the month, and first of the week. I have known poverty of late, and have been graciously supported to keep in the patience, and am thankful under a sense of the goodness of the Lord towards those who are of a contrite spirit.

Sixth of Ninth Month and first of the week.—I was this day at Counterside, a large meeting-house, and very full. Through the opening of pure love, it was a strengthening time to me, and I believe to many more.

Thirteenth of Ninth Month.—This day I was at Leyburn, a small meeting; but, the towns-people coming in, the house was crowded. It was a time of heavy labour, and I believe was a profitable meeting. At this place I heard that my kinsman, William Hunt, from North Carolina, who was on a religious visit to Friends in England, departed this life on the 9th of this month, of the small-pox at Newcastle. He appeared in the ministry when a youth, and his labours therein were of good savour. He travelled much in that work in America. I once heard him say in public testimony, that his concern in that visit was to be devoted to the service of Christ so fully that he might not spend one minute in pleasing himself, which words, joined with his example, was a means of stirring up the pure mind in me.

Having of late often travelled in wet weather through narrow streets in towns and villages, where dirtiness under foot and the scent arising from that filth which more or less infects the air of all thickly settled towns were disagreeable; and, being but weakly, I have felt distress both in body and mind with that which is impure. In these journeys I have been where much cloth hath been dyed, and have, at sundry times, walked over ground where much of their dye-stuffs has drained away. This hath produced a longing in my mind that people might come into cleanness of spirit, cleanness of person, and cleanness about their houses and garments.

Some of the great carry delicacy to a great height themselves, and yet real cleanliness is not generally promoted. Dyes being invented partly to please the eye and partly to hide dirt, I have felt in this weak state, when travelling in dirtiness, and affected with unwholesome scents, a strong desire that the nature of dyeing cloth to hide dirt may be more fully considered.

Washing our garments to keep them sweet is cleanly, but it is the opposite to real cleanliness to hide dirt in them. Through giving way to hiding dirt in our garments a spirit which would conceal that which is disagreeable is strengthened. Real cleanliness becometh a holy people; but hiding that which is not clean by colouring our garments seems contrary to the sweetness of sincerity. Through some sorts of dyes cloth is rendered less useful. And if the value of dyestuffs, and expense of dyeing, and the damage done to cloth, were all added together, and that cost applied to keeping all sweet and clean, how much more would real cleanliness prevail.

On this visit to England I have felt some instructions sealed on my mind, which I am concerned to leave in writing for the use of such as are called to the station of a minister of Christ.

Christ being the Prince of Peace, and we being no more than ministers, it is necessary for us not only to feel a concern in our first going forth, but to experience the renewing thereof in the appointment of meetings. I felt a concern in America to prepare for this voyage, and being through the mercy of God brought safe hither, my heart was like a vessel that wanted vent. For several weeks after my arrival, when my mouth was opened in meetings, it was like the raising of a gate in a water-course when a weight of water lay upon it. In these labours there was a fresh visitation to many, especially to the youth; but sometimes I felt poor and empty, and yet there appeared a necessity to appoint meetings. In this I was exercised to abide in the pure life of truth, and in all my labours to watch diligently against the motions of self in my own mind.

I have frequently found a necessity to stand up when the spring of the ministry was low, and to speak from the necessity in that which subjecteth the will of the creature; and herein I was united with the suffering seed, and found inward sweetness in these mortifying labours. As I have been preserved in a watchful attention to the divine Leader, under these dispensations, enlargement at times hath followed, and the power of truth hath risen higher in some meetings than I ever knew it before through me. Thus I have been more and more instructed as to the necessity of depending, not upon a concern which I felt in America to come on a visit to England, but upon the daily instructions of Christ, the Prince of Peace.

Of late I have sometimes felt a stop in the appointment of meetings, not wholly, but in part; and I do not feel liberty to appoint them so quickly, one after another, as I have done heretofore. The work of the ministry being a work of Divine love, I feel that the openings thereof are to be waited for in all our appointments. O, how deep is Divine wisdom! Christ puts forth His ministers and goeth before them; and O, how great is the danger of departing from the pure feeling of that which leadeth safely? Christ knoweth the state of the people, and in the pure feeling of the gospel ministry their states are opened to His servants. Christ knoweth when the fruit-bearing branches themselves have need of purging. O that these lessons may be remembered by me! and that all who appoint meetings may proceed in the pure feeling of duty!

I have sometimes felt a necessity to stand up, but that spirit which is of the world hath so much prevailed in many, and the pure life of truth hath been so pressed down, that I have gone forward, not as one travelling in a road cast up and well prepared, but as a man walking through a miry place in which are stones here and there safe to step on, but so situated that, one step being taken, time is necessary to see where to step next. Now I find that in a state of pure obedience the mind learns contentment in appearing weak and foolish to that wisdom which is of the world; and in these lowly labours, they who stand in a low place and are rightly exercised under the cross will find nourishment. The gift is pure; and while the eye is single in attending thereto the understanding is preserved clear; self is kept out. We rejoice in filling up that which remains of the afflictions of Christ for His body's sake, which is the church.

The natural man loveth eloquence, and many love to hear eloquent orations, and if there be not a careful attention to the gift, men who have once laboured in the pure gospel ministry, growing weary of suffering, and ashamed of appearing weak, may kindle a fire, compass themselves about with sparks, and walk in the light, not of Christ, who is under suffering, but of that fire which they in departing from the gift have kindled, in order that those hearers who have left the meek, suffering state for worldly wisdom may be warmed with this fire and speak highly of their labours. That which is of God gathers to God, and that which is of the world is owned by the world.

In this journey a labour hath attended my mind, that the ministers among us may be preserved in the meek, feeling life of truth, where we may have no desire but to follow Christ and to be with Him, that when He is under suffering, we may suffer with Him, and never desire to rise up in dominion, but as He, by the virtue of His own spirit, may raise us.

A REPORT ON WOOLMAN'S DEATH

A few days after writing these considerations, our dear friend in the course of his religious visits came to the city of York,† and attended most of the sittings of the Quarterly Meeting there; but before it was over he was taken ill of the small-pox. Our friend Thomas Priestman, and others who attended him, preserved the following minutes of his expressions in the time of his sickness.

First-day the 27th of the Ninth Month, 1772—His disorder appeared to be the small-pox. Being asked to have a doctor's advice, he signified he had not freedom or liberty in his mind so to do,

† During the four months of his labours in England he visited the Quarterly and subordinate meetings of Friends in seven counties, and found time to write essays upon "Loving our Neighbours," "A Sailor's Life," and "Silent Worship." His mind seems to have been greatly exercised by a sense of the intimate connection of luxury and oppression; the burden of the labouring poor rested heavily upon him. In his lonely wanderings on foot through the rural districts (for he did not feel free to use the post on account of the hard treatment of the horses), or in his temporary sojourn in crowded manufacturing towns, the eager competitions and earnest pursuit of gain of one class, and the poverty and physical and moral degradation of another, so oppressed him that his health suffered and his strength failed. It is observable that, in his frequent mention throughout his Journal of inward trials and afflictions, he nowhere betrays any personal solicitude, and merely selfish anxiety, for his own soul. His singular conscientious scruples, his close self-questionings, are prompted by a tender concern for universal well-being; an earnest desire that no act or omission of his own should add to the evil and misery under which the creation groans. He offered no prayers for special personal favours. He was, to use his own words, mixed with his fellow-creatures in their misery, and could not consider himself a distinct and separate being. He left all that concerns self to the will of his Father in Heaven, trusting to find a place among the "many mansions," but never asking to see the title-deeds of his inheritance. His last public labour was a testimony in the York Meeting in behalf of the poor and enslaved. His last prayer on his death-bed was a commendation of his "fellow creatures separated from the Divine harmony" to the Omnipotent Power whom he had learned to call his Father.

standing wholly resigned to His will who gave him life, and whose power he had witnessed to raise and heal him in sickness before, when he seemed nigh unto death; and if he was to wind up now, he was perfectly resigned, having no will either to live or die, and did not choose any should be sent for to him; but a young man, an apothecary, coming of his own accord the next day and desiring to do something for him, he said he found a freedom to confer with him and the other Friends about him, and if anything should be proposed as to medicine that did not come through defiled channels or oppressive hands, he should be willing to consider and take it, so far as he found freedom.

Second day.—He said he felt the disorder to affect his head so that he could think little and but as a child, and desired, if his understanding should be more affected, to have nothing given him that those about him knew he had a testimony against.

Third day.—He uttered the following prayer: "O Lord, my God! the amazing horrors of darkness were gathered around me and covered me all over, and I saw no way to go forth. I felt the depth and extent of the misery of my fellow-creatures separated from the Divine harmony, and it was heavier than I could bear, and I was crushed down under it. I lifted up my hand, I stretched out my arm, but there was none to help me; I looked round about and was amazed. In the depths of misery, O Lord! I remembered that Thou art omnipotent; that I had called Thee Father; and I felt that I loved Thee, and I was made quiet in my will, and I waited for deliverance from Thee. Thou hadst pity upon me when no man could help me. I saw that meekness under suffering was showed to us in the most affecting example of Thy Son, and Thou taught me to follow Him, and I said, 'Thy will, O Father, be done!' "

Fourth day morning.—Being asked how he felt himself he meekly answered, "I don't know that I have slept this night; I feel the disorder making its progress, but my mind is mercifully preserved in stillness and peace." Some time after, he said he was sensible that the pains of death must be hard to bear, and if he escaped them now he must some time pass through them, and he did not know that he could be better prepared, but had no will in it. He said he had settled his outward affairs to his mind, had taken leave of his wife and family as never to return, leaving them to the Divine protection, adding, "Though I feel them near to me at this time, yet I have freely given them up, having a hope that they will be provided for." And a little after said, "This trial is made easier than I could have thought, my will being wholly taken away; if I was anxious for the event it would have been harder; but I am not, and my mind enjoys a perfect calm."

In the night, a young woman having given him something to drink, he said, "My child, thou seemest very kind to me, a poor creature; the Lord will reward thee for it." Awhile after he cried out with great earnestness of spirit. "O my Father! my Father! how comfortable art Thou to my soul in this trying season!" Being asked if he could take a little nourishment, after some pause he replied, "My child, I cannot tell what to say to it; I seem nearly arrived where my soul shall have rest from all its troubles." After giving in something to be inserted in his journal, he said, "I believe the Lord will now excuse me from exercises of this kind; and I see no work but one, which is to be the last wrought by me in this world; the messenger will come and will release me from all these troubles, but it must be in the Lord's time, which I am waiting for." He said he had laboured to do whatever was required according to the ability received, in the remembrance of which he had peace; and though the disorder was strong at times, and would like a whirlwind come over his mind, yet it had hitherto been kept steady and centred in everlasting love; adding, "And if that be mercifully continued, I ask and desire no more." Another time he said he had long had a view of visiting this nation, and, some time before he came, had a dream, in which he saw himself in the northern parts of it, and that the spring of the Gospel was opened in him much as it was in the beginning of Friends such as George Fox and William Dewsbury, and he saw the different states of the people as clear as he had ever seen flowers in a garden; but in his going along he was suddenly stopped, though he could not see for what end; but, looking towards home, fell into a flood of tears, which waked him.

At another time he said, "My draught seemed strongest towards the north, and I mentioned in my own Monthly Meeting, that attending the Quarterly Meeting at York, and being there, looked like home to me."

Fifth-day Night.—Having repeatedly consented to take medicine, but without effect, the Friend then waiting on him said through distress, "What shall I do now?" He answered with great composure, "Rejoice evermore, and in everything give thanks," but added a little after, "This is sometimes hard to come at."

On sixth-day morning he broke forth early in supplication on this wise, "O Lord, it was Thy power that enabled me to forsake sin in my youth, and I have felt Thy bruises for disobedience; but as I bowed under them Thou healedst me, continuing a father and a friend; I feel Thy power now, and I beg that in the approaching trying moment Thou wilt keep my heart steadfast unto Thee." On his giving directions to a Friend concerning some little things, she said, "I will take care, but hope thou wilt live to order them thyself." He replied, "My hope is in Christ; and though I may seem a little better, a change in the disorder may soon happen, and my little strength be dissolved, and if it so happen I shall be gathered to my everlasting rest." On her saying she did not doubt that, but could not help mourning to see so many faithful servants removed at so low a time, he said, "All good cometh from the Lord, whose power is the same, and He can work as He sees best." The same day he had directions given about wrapping his corpse; perceiving a Friend to weep, he said, "I would rather thou wouldst guard against weeping for me, my sister; I sorrow not, though I have had some painful conflicts, but now they seem over, and matters well settled; and I look at the face of my dear Redeemer, for sweet is His voice, and His countenance is comely."

First-day, 4th of Tenth Month.—Being very weak and in general difficult to be understood, he uttered a few words in commemoration of the Lord's goodness, and added, "How tenderly have I been waited on in this time of affliction, in which I may say in Job's words, Tedious days and 'wearisome nights are appointed to me'; and how many are spending their time and money in vanity and superfluities, while thousands and tens of thousands want the necessaries of life, who might be relieved by them, and their distress at such a time as this in some degree softened by the administering of suitable things."

Second-day morning.—The apothecary, who appeared very anxious to assist him, being present, he queried about the probability of such a load of matter being thrown off his weak body; and the apothecary making some remarks implying he thought it might, he spoke with an audible voice on this wise: "My dependence is on the Lord Jesus, who I trust will forgive my sins, which is all I hope for; and if it be His will to raise up this body again, I am content; and if to die, I am resigned; but if thou canst not be easy without trying to assist nature, I submit." After this his throat was so much affected that it was very difficult for him to speak so as to be understood, and he frequently wrote when he wanted anything. About the second hour on fourth-day morning he asked for pen and ink, and at several times, with much difficulty, wrote thus: "I believe my being here is in the wisdom of Christ; I know not as to life or death."

About a quarter before six the same morning he seemed to fall into an easy sleep, which continued about half an hour, when, seeming to awake, he breathed a few times with more difficulty, and expired without sigh, groan, or struggle.

THE DIARY OF
DAVID BRAINERD

as edited by
Jonathan Edwards

EDITOR'S INTRODUCTION TO
THE *DIARY* OF DAVID BRAINERD

The *Diary* of David Brainerd, missionary to the Indians in Pennsylvania, New Jersey, and Delaware between 1742 and 1747, is one of the choice fruits of Puritan piety produced by the so-called Great Awakening. In content it is an example of Puritan introspection regarding "the work of grace on the soul," and Richard Baxter would have been proud of the thorough and vivid way his progeny scrutinized his inward disposition. At the same time there is a singularity about Brainerd's *Diary*, one that goes beyond the earlier Puritan tradition. Its distinctive character is related to the Awakening itself, with its emphasis upon "religious affections." In some respects, the experience of "New Light" Christians in the Awakening appears in a magnified way under the Brainerd magnifying glass. Other "born again" Christians would see their experience handled in an enlarged and vivid way, as if Brainerd had spoken out of their own hearts.

The appeal of the *Diary* is, of course, a result of several factors. Since the initial publication of Brainerd's reports on his work among the Indians, later called *The Journal*, this work has excited interest in missions and inspired many imitators. Brainerd was a heroic figure, recklessly throwing away his life, mindless of suffering or death, in order that he might bring the gospel to the "lost heathen." The Scottish Society for Propagating Christian Knowledge understandably exploited the Brainerd image to stimulate further interest in their missionary endeavors.

But the *Diary* has a much deeper source of appeal in the experience of Brainerd himself. Today, to be sure, we may find the way Brainerd so often wallowed in guilt and self-pity excessive, even "sick." In Brainerd's case the sense of guilt exceeded the normal Puritan theological twist; it was embedded deeply in the experience of religious fervor, which got out of hand and led to his dismissal from Yale College. It was also inseparably annexed to his physical illness, which took his life at age twenty-nine. Having said all that, we must go on to remark that the religious experiences recorded in the *Diary* have a ring of authenticity. They reflect "the struggle of a soul" truly to serve God, to give the full measure of devotion, nothing held back. They give us an *inner* reading, as it were, on the life of a saint. That, in the end, is the reason the *Diary* has gained classic status.

THE *DIARY*

As it has come down to us, the *Diary* is essentially the work of Jonathan Edwards (1703–58), Brainerd's mentor and the theologian of the Great Awakening par excellence. Brainerd died in Edwards' home, cared for in his last days by the latter's daughter, Jerusha, who died at age eighteen, less than a year after Brainerd himself. Brainerd left his papers in Edwards' hands to dispose of "as he thought would be most for God's glory, and the interest of Religion."[1] It was Edwards who condensed and made selections from the much larger original. This fact, of course, will warn us to read critically and not to assume that we are hearing Brainerd pure and unalloyed. The fact is, Edwards found in Brainerd's experience with the Indians support for his controversial proposals concerning church discipline which led to his expulsion from his parish, Northampton, Massachusetts, in 1750. Edwards, William A. Clebsch has pointed out,[2] "seemed to be demanding perfect saintliness made visible in deed as well as word." Brainerd supplied him with a perfect example. Thence, by way of comments, summaries, and especially his long "Reflections on the Preceding Memoirs," Edwards "wove Brainerd's diaries into a classic case study illustrating the criteria of holiness that Edwards had adumbrated in his seminal work on religious affections."[3]

Although the *Diary* of Brainerd contains daily entries, it is not like those which most of us have tried to keep as children. Brainerd makes factual entries here and there. For the most part, however, he was reporting on his spiritual temperament and feelings. He measured his devotion by how fully his spirit inclined toward God, by the "warmth" and "sweetness" of his experience, by the purging of egocentric motives. Early on, immediately after his dismissal from Yale, his melancholia seems to have had the upper hand much of the time. He could not hurl himself down far enough into the depths. Later, we can see a lifting of spirits as his work among the

Indians prospered. Throughout, however, there is ample evidence of a longing for death that goes beyond what was typical of Puritans. At times Brainerd may have approached suicide, but his religious commitment held him back, and it channeled his longing into religious service.

The religious experiences recorded in the *Diary* sometimes seem somewhat stereotyped, shaped in a Puritan mold, especially as fashioned by Jonathan Edwards' famous work on *Religious Affections*. In evaluating the authenticity of Indian conversions, for instance, Brainerd looked first for complete renunciation of human ability to save oneself or to contribute anything toward that end. Like Edwards, he was suspicious of "religious affections," that is, emotional manifestations. Salvation, he judged, requires unrestrained acknowledgment of God's complete sovereignty and human unworthiness and depravity. Insofar as we can determine whether we are among the "elect," its effects will manifest themselves in transformed life-style. In his assessment of the remarkable Indian response at Crossweeksung, Brainerd typically cited examples of radical conversions. Three times (August 8, 1745; February 1, 1746; May 9, 1746) he reported on the conversion of a conjurer, murderer, and general hell raiser who had given up all hope of his own salvation but continued still attending meetings, praying in secret, and undergoing visible reformation. After a public "experience," in which "he seemed to have a lively soul-refreshing view of the excellency of Christ and the way of salvation by him; which melted him into tears, and filled him with admiration, comfort, satisfaction and praise to God," Brainerd reported that "he has appeared to be a humble, devout and affectionate Christian; serious and exemplary in his conversation and behavior, frequently complaining of his barrenness, his want of spiritual warmth, life and activity, and yet frequently favoured with quickening and refreshing influences." From these evidences, Brainerd concluded that "so far as I am capable of judging, he bears the marks of one 'created anew in Christ Jesus to good works.' "

Brainerd also expected similar tokens of reform within the small company of Indians who gathered at Crossweeksung and later moved to Cranberry. In April 1746, after touring the settlement just before they moved, he commented, "Never did I see such an appearance of Christian love among any people in all my life. . . . I think there could be no greater tokens of mutual affection among the people of God, in the early days of Christianity, than what now appeared here."

The current *Diary* is based upon a composite of two writings: (1) the two-part *Journal* of Brainerd recording his work among the Indians between June 19, 1745, and June 19, 1746, published by the Scottish S.P.C.K. while Brainerd was still alive; and (2) *An Account of the Life of the late Rev. David Brainerd; Missionary to the Indians,* a biography by Edwards composed largely of extracts from the Brainerd *Diary* but omitting the year covered by the *Journal,* published in 1749. I have made an effort in this condensation to conserve the flavor of Brainerd's experience while eliminating some of the repetition of the original. Two chapters (IX and X) could easily be deleted, for they contained some general remarks by Brainerd on missionary methods in winning the Indians. I omitted also comments by Edwards that were superfluous; for example, his "Reflections on the Preceding Memoirs." The substance of the *Diary* has not been materially altered.

DAVID BRAINERD

Brainerd's own experience fitted into the same mold as that of his converts, but there is in it also an extraordinary mystical element which is reminiscent of the experience of saints in other ages: Bernard of Clairvaux, Francis of Assisi, John of the Cross.

Born April 20, 1718, at Haddam, Connecticut, Brainerd was the son of Hezekiah Brainerd, member of the His Majesty's Council for the colony, and Dorothy Hobart, daughter of the Reverend Jeremiah Hobart, minister of the (Congregational) church at Topsfield, then at Hempstead on Long Island, and finally at Haddam, where he died at age eighty-five. His paternal grandfather, Daniel Brainerd, was a justice of the peace and a deacon in the church at Haddam. His maternal grandfather was the Reverend Peter Hobart, a minister in the Anglican church at Hingham, England, who had to flee on account of his Puritan views, and settled in Hingham, Massachusetts.

The third son in a family of five sons and four daughters, David Brainerd experienced tragedy early. At age thirteen, his mother died, leaving him an orphan and responsibility for his younger brothers. It is not difficult to detect why, as he noted in his *Diary*, he was "somewhat sober, and inclined to be melancholy" from his youth.

His early religious experience is marked throughout by signs of the Great Awakening. The Awakening began about 1726 in New Jersey around the evangelistic activities of Dutch Reformed minister Theodore Freylinghuysen, at about the same time Brainerd professed his first "conviction" of sin. It gained further momentum through the activities of William Tennent, with whom the young Brainerd had close association in his missionary work at Crossweeksung and to whom he looked for guidance and encouragement. Tennent and his son, Gilbert, subsequently founded Log Cabin College, later to become Princeton University, as a prop for the evangelical revival. The wave of revival spread elsewhere, cresting in New England between 1735 and 1742. Its most eminent leader was none other than Jonathan Edwards, the author-editor of the Brainerd *Memoirs*. The flame of revival ignited in Edwards' Northampton parish in 1735. It burned brilliantly for a few years, spreading to Connecticut, where it touched the life of Brainerd and his family during his adolescent years. It reached Yale in February 1741, during Brainerd's second year.

As Brainerd himself evaluated his religious pilgrimage, there were two "conversions." The first was more or less perfunctory, the second profound, agonizing, and genuine.

The first began with his "conviction of sin" at age seven or eight, perhaps at the time of his father's death, the date of which he failed to record. At any rate, even Brainerd recognized in it a rather morbid character. "Then I became concerned for my soul, and terrified at the thoughts of death," he said, "and was driven to the performance of religious duties: but it appeared a melancholy business, that destroyed my eagerness for play." The "conviction," as one would expect, proved "short-lived." Though the youth continued to pray and to perform other religious duties, he did not quicken his commitment again until about age thirteen. At this time, the winter of 1732, he was "roused out of this carnal security." Although not certain what first prompted this renewed interest in religion, he recalled being "much excited by the prevalence of a mortal sickness in Haddam." His mother's death, in March

1732, made him very melancholy and doubtless added to his religious concern, if it did not inaugurate it. He depicted his new situation in terms of fervor in prayer, delight in reading, zeal in performing religious duties, being "dead to the world," and preoccupation with "soul's concerns."

This spiritual fervor dampened somewhat after his mother's death, but it did not die altogether. Moving to East Haddam in April 1733, he continued to engage in "secret prayer" and was "not much addicted to the company and amusements of the young." When he did gather with the latter, he felt guilty, to the point of fearing to pray. About the time of his nineteenth birthday he moved to Durham to work on his farm. There he began to long for a liberal education and, in the next year, to apply himself to study and religious duties. At that time he firmly dedicated himself to God, being watchful of his behavior and intensely sober because he "designed" to devote himself to the ministry.

In April 1738 he returned to Haddam to live and study with a Mr. Fiske, pastor of the church there. He adopted a "wholly regular" life-style, "full of religion, such as it was"; read the Bible through more than twice in less than a year; spent much time in prayer "and other secret duties"; paid strict attention to sermons and tried to retain their content; met on Sunday evenings with other young persons for private religious exercises; and thought much of joining the Church. After Fiske's death he continued his studies with his own brother Nehemiah, minister at Eastbury, Connecticut.

In the winter and spring of 1738–39, however, Brainerd's concern about the reality of his conversion grew, fanned by the Awakening going on around him. In retrospect, he looked back on his renewed commitment as evidence of externalism and self-righteousness. "In short," he wrote, "I had a very good outside, and rested entirely on my duties, though I was not sensible of it." His search reached crisis proportions about February 1739, when he found himself in "a most horrible frame of contesting with the Almighty." In his mind he challenged the Puritan doctrinal pillars of inherited sin, faith alone, and divine sovereignty and wished "there were some other God that could control him." He was driven to see that he had "to relinquish all self-confidence, all hopes of ever helping myself by any means whatsoever."

The "conversion" which Brainerd seemed to have longed and struggled for so intensely came at last on July 12, 1739. What he later emphasized in his description was awareness of divine sovereignty and majesty over against his own unworthiness—the watchword of Calvinist theology. At the same time, however, we cannot help but see in it resemblances to Isaiah's call (Isa. 6:1–10) and the ecstatic experiences of the Apostle Paul (2 Cor. 12:1–10; Acts 9:3–9) or other mystics through the ages. His account deserves to be singled out by quotation:

> . . . as I was walking in a dark thick grove, unspeakable glory seemed to open to the view and apprehension of my soul. . . . My soul rejoiced with joy unspeakable, to see such a God, such a glorious divine Being; and I was inwardly pleased and satisfied that he should be God over all for ever and ever. My soul was so captivated and delighted with the excellency, loveliness, greatness, and other perfections of God, that I was even swallowed up in him; at least to the degree, that I had not thought (as I remember) at first, about my own salvation, and scarce reflected that there was such a creature as myself.
>
> Thus God, I trust, brought me to a hearty disposition to exalt him, and set him on the throne, and principally and ultimately to aim at his honour and glory, as King of the universe. I continued in this state of inward joy, peace, and astonishment, till near dark, without any sensible abatement; and then began to think and examine what I had seen; and felt sweetly composed in my mind all the evening following. I felt myself in a new world, and every thing about me appeared with a different aspect from what it was wont to do.

Brainerd's fear, guilt, anger, despair, and other undesirable affections had been overpowered by a more powerful opposite affection.[4] He would have ups and downs still, but he never doubted the reality of the Almighty thereafter.

In September 1739 Brainerd entered Yale, fearful lest he suffer a religious lapse. At one juncture he noted that his ambition in his studies "greatly wronged the activity and vigour of my spiritual life," but this was counterbalanced by a number of divine "visits." His description of these experiences is strongly reminiscent of Bernard of Clairvaux's confession that "the Word has visited me, and has even done so very often." He and Brainerd share a romantic vocabulary depicting the mystical encounters: "sweetness," "joy," "refreshment."

In August 1740 Brainerd began to experience evidences of the tuberculosis that eventually claimed his life. His brother Nehemiah preceded him in death with the same affliction, in November 1742. Returning for his second year at Yale, he "felt the power of religion almost daily, for the space of six weeks," but, in late January 1741, "grew more cold and dull" as a result of his studiousness. About the end of February, however, "a great and general Awakening spread itself over the college. . . ." Along with others, Brainerd got carried away in his enthusiasm and committed the deed that led to expulsion and loaded him with an almost unbearable sense of guilt and remorse. The incident became a watershed for the brief remainder of his life.

From the vantage point of two and a half centuries, the incident itself would seem trivial, but we cannot measure the sensitivities of an earlier day by our own. During the fervent days of the revival at Yale, a Fellow of the College, Mr. Whittelsey, prayed with a group of the students including Brainerd. The prayer evidently lacked the fervor the students thought suitable. After Mr. Whittelsey left, another student asked Brainerd what he thought of him. Brainerd replied, "He has no more grace than this chair." A freshman student, overhearing the remark, casually reported it to a woman in New Haven. She related this to the rector. He summoned the freshman and compelled him to tell who had said this. The rector demanded that Brainerd make a public confession and humble himself before the whole college. To this was added the charge that he was accused by someone of saying "that he wondered [the rector] did not expect to drop down dead for fining the scholars who followed Mr. Tennent to Milford, though there was *no proof* of it. . . ." When Brainerd refused to do as required, he was expelled.

How deeply the whole affair affected Brainerd is shown by several things. One, Brainerd left instructions that this part of his *Diary* be destroyed, and he added little to it for some time. Two, he made numerous efforts to effect reconciliation. In June and July 1743 he rode the sixty miles from Kaunaumeek to New Haven, each time suffering the painful opening of the old wound in vain. In September he sent a long letter of apology to the rector and trustees. The Governors of the College agreed to readmit him but not to give him his degree until he put in another twelve months of residence. Since he would not agree in view of his contract with the

S.P.C.K., he forfeited his opportunity. Third, he plunged deeper and deeper into depression until his appointment to the Indian mission directed his melancholy personality in other channels. Indeed, his attraction to the latter may have been prompted in part by the prospects it offered to atone for his indiscretion. In April 1742 he noted in his *Diary* that "if God should so order it," he was willing "to suffer banishment from [his] native land, among the Heathen," to "do something for their salvation, in distresses and deaths of any kind." Throughout his preparation for this ministry, however, he felt unworthy in the extreme. Preaching before the Correspondents of the Society that appointed him, in November 1742, he expressed grief for the congregation "that they should sit there to hear such a dead dog as I preach." His psychological suffering, combined with physical, caused him frequently to long for death. If typical of Puritans in this, Brainerd certainly outstripped most others. Even after his attention was diverted to his first mission, at Kaunaumeek, he "was grieved at the very thoughts of a fiery, angry, and intemperate zeal in religion; [and] mourned over past follies in this regard. . . ."

All of us have to go on living, however, failures, indiscretions, sins, and trials notwithstanding, and Brainerd got beyond his crisis by finding an external compensation for his inward grief. In this instance the introspective style he had inherited from his Puritan forebears, scrutinizing every wart on his soul in the way it did, probably heightened his guilt and delayed his recovery of self-esteem. Nevertheless, modern psychiatry would suggest that it might also have resulted in more permanent healing, especially if Brainerd's health had allowed. More important still, the whole purgative experience, hellish as it was, furnished him with sensibilities and skills for ministry that he would not have developed in a more pedestrian pilgrimage. Experiences that try our souls also enlarge our souls. In Brainerd's case his exaggerated awareness of his human deficiencies and defects caused him to drill a deeper well to find sources that would suffice. On June 15, 1742, shortly before his licensing for ministry by the Danbury Association (July 29), he wrote, "I never seemed to be so unhinged from myself, and to be so wholly devoted to God. My heart was swallowed up in God most of the day. In the evening I had such a view of the soul being as it were enlarged, to contain more holiness, that it seemed ready to separate from my body."

Most persons would have used deteriorating health such as Brainerd's as an excuse to escape an arduous mission like his; *he* was driven to it, almost as if by a death wish. Travel alone entailed indescribable hardships. For a person suffering from advanced tuberculosis, as Brainerd was, it was all the more taxing to ride horseback over rough terrain in subfreezing temperatures, sleep exposed to the elements, ford swollen streams and rivers, and subsist on whatever food was at hand, for days on end. Even when settled with the Indian people among whom he ministered, he suffered inconveniences and privations persons of lesser dedication could scarcely have borne. At Kaunaumeek he resided first in a cramped room with a Scottish family, then in a wigwam, before moving into his own cabin. His graphic description of life in a wigwam shows the price he paid for his effort.

My circumstances are such, that I have no comfort of any kind, but what I have in God. I live in the most lonesome wilderness; have but one single person to converse with that can speak English. Most of the talk I hear, is either Highland Scotch, or Indian. I have no fellow-christian to whom I may unbosom myself, or lay open my spiritual sorrows; with whom I may take sweet counsel in conversation about heavenly things, and join in social prayer. I live poorly with regard to the comforts of life: most of my diet consists of boiled corn, hasty-pudding, &c. I lodge on a bundle of straw, my labour is hard and extremely difficult, and I have little appearance of success, to comfort me. The Indians have no land to live on, but what the Dutch people lay claim to; and these threaten to drive them off. They have no regard to the souls of the poor Indians; and by what I can learn, they hate me because I come to preach to them. But that which makes all my difficulties grievous to be borne, is, that God hides his face from me.

The physical rigors of the work, as we may see here, were only a fraction of his difficulties. Many of the Indian tribes harbored an intense hostility to Christianity, as John Woolman also discovered. They had suffered too much exploitation and too many deceptions to trust those who supposedly represented Christian faith. Their suspicions were aroused all the more by the efforts of missionaries such as Brainerd to win them to a particular cultural expression of

Christianity and not merely to awaken them to the inner light, as the Quakers sought.[5] Brainerd longed for his converts to gather and establish a Christian commonwealth like that in New England, and, in a limited way, saw his dream realized at Cranberry.

Even where the Indians were more receptive, as at Kaunaumeek and Crossweeksung, the task of evangelizing them presented immense problems. First Brainerd had to learn the language. By instruction of the S.P.C.K., he rode twenty miles from Kaunaumeek to Stockbridge through the winter of 1743–44, beginning November 29, to study under the experienced missionary John Sergeant. Before that, he had relied wholly on interpreters; afterward, he enjoyed a bit more freedom, but still used an interpreter at Crossweeksung, the interpreter becoming his first convert. Alongside the linguistic problem loomed a much larger one, namely, the translation of the Christian message, born in a totally different cultural environment, into ideas and images the Indian people could understand, and then inculcating these so that the message would affect their lives.

To accomplish all of this, Brainerd worked tirelessly, often long into the night, an effort his frail constitution could scarcely afford, to render prayers, Scriptures, sermons, and catechetical items into the Indian language. At Kaunaumeek his exertions obtained no tangible results. The same proved true of his labors among the Six Nations on the Forks of Delaware, where he labored for a time after his ordination to the gospel ministry (June 12, 1744) at Newark, and along the Susquehanna, to which he made recurrent trips until the last few months of his life. Occasionally he witnessed persons "much affected" by his preaching, as he did in the case of an aged Indian on the Forks of Delaware in December 1744. Generally speaking, however, his efforts turned out to be little more than a trial run for his astonishingly fruitful ministry at Crossweeksung, which began June 19, 1745, and continued until March 20, 1747, when grit alone no longer sufficed to propel him.

Brainerd's work at Crossweeksung undoubtedly benefited from spin-off of the Great Awakening. As a matter of fact, William Tennent, minister in the nearby town of Freehold, had already preached to the Indians before Brainerd arrived. With this *praeparatio evangelica*, therefore, the Brainerd revival soon took wing. Just over a month after he arrived, Brainerd baptized his interpreter, Moses Finda Fautaury, about fifty years of age, and his wife. Five days later, he baptized their children. Soon attendance at the almost daily meetings mounted, from about forty in July to nearly eighty on November 3. By November 4 Brainerd had baptized forty-seven persons—twenty-three adults and twenty-four children. The harvest continued right up to the end of his ministry there.

Always cautious about the authenticity of "conversions," Brainerd saw many reassuring indications. Returning from a fruitless trip along the Susquehanna on October 5, 1745, he exulted: "O what a difference is there between these, and the Indians with whom I had lately treated upon the Susquehannah! To be with those seemed to be like being banished from God and all his people; to be with these, like being admitted into his family, and to the enjoyment of his divine presence!" He noted with satisfaction later that the impressions of the sermons upon his hearers "appeared solid, rational, and deep; . . . and far from being the effects of any sudden fright or groundless perturbation of mind." When he began catechizing according to the Assembly's Shorter Catechism, in December, moreover, he was pleasantly surprised to find that the Indians' doctrinal knowledge exceeded his own expectations. In visiting his folk on New Year's Day, 1746, he discovered "scarcely one but what was under some serious impressions respecting their spiritual concerns." His converts even journeyed with him to the Forks of Delaware in February to assist with the evangelizing of Indians there. Although he seems to have gotten a more favorable reception, the results still proved disappointing, and he was not optimistic about the permanence of his effect there. He held out greater hopes for Indians who came from elsewhere to live at Crossweeksung and later at Cranberry. His hope rested in a "peaceable settlement of the Indians together in a body."

An unkind twist in Brainerd's success was a rumor that arose in February 1746, among white settlers, that he had been sent by Roman Catholics to foment an insurrection among the Indians against the English. While he was at Kaunaumeek, in October 1743, he had learned of a rupture between England and France and been warned of the danger of an Indian uprising. Ten years later the worst fears materialized, costing hundreds of lives. Now some demanded that Brainerd be seized and punished. He remained anxious about the matter for a long time, insisting that he worked without regard to denomination and was certainly not a Roman Catholic.

Meantime the valiant witness's time was ticking away fast. More than a year before his halting of his ministry he observed, on January 13, 1746, that his health was "so much impaired" and his "spirits so wasted" by his labors and solitary life. Whereas before he had noted occasional improvement of health, thereafter the entries were altogether bleak. In June he complained again of "vapoury disorders" and "dejection of spirits." On Sunday, June 29, he doubted whether he could continue his round of duties but noted with relief that "God amazingly renewed and lengthened out my strength." During his final, exhausting trip to the Susquehanna, in August and September, he made note of rapid deterioration of his health. On August 20, after suffering from cold sweat the night before and coughing blood in the morning, he entertained "a secret hope that I might speedily get a dismission from earth, and all its toils and sorrows." On September 3 he was too weak to do anything at all and barely managed to drag himself back to Cranberry by September 20.

Thereafter his health was such that he made fewer and fewer entries in his *Diary*. On November 3 he began a journey to New England, but illness forced him to stop in Elizabeth Town, New Jersey. This time he did not recover sufficiently to try again until April 21, 1747. His health improved enough in mid-March to attend a public worship service and, on March 18–20, to say farewell to his beloved people at Cranberry. He rode at a leisurely pace to East-Haddam, arriving in early May.

In his *Diary* entry for May 17 he recorded that he "began to long to die." Jonathan Edwards recalled Brainerd's recurrent petition in prayer "that we might not outlive our usefulness." Astonishingly, he recovered enough to make one last journey from the Edwards' home in Northampton to Boston and back, June 9 to July 25. He spent his last days visiting with his brothers John and Israel and "correcting" his private early writings. He died October 9, 1747, his wish to give the last measure of devotion finally fulfilled.

E. Glenn Hinson

NOTES

1. Advertisement, *Memoirs of the Rev. David Brainerd; Missionary to the Indians,* eds. Jonathan Edwards and Sereno Edwards Dwight (New Haven: S. Converse, 1822), p. 7.

2. *American Religious Thought: A History* (Chicago: University of Chicago Press, 1973), p. 37.

3. Ibid., p. 38.

4. See the analysis of William James in *The Varieties of Religious Experience* (New York: Collier Books, 1961), pp. 177–78, 206.

5. See Brainerd's critique of the Quaker approach, which caused him great difficulty in winning Indians to the Calvinist perspective.

THE DIARY OF
DAVID BRAINERD

———◆———

CHAPTER I

*From his birth, to the time when he began to study for
the Ministry.*

David Brainerd was born April 20, 1718, at Haddam, in Connecticut.
His father was Hezekiah Brainerd, Esq.; one of his Majesty's council
for that colony; who was the son of Daniel Brainerd, Esq.; a justice of
the peace, and a deacon of the Church of Christ in Haddam. His
mother was Dorothy Hobart, daughter of the Rev. Jeremiah Hobart;
who preached a while at Topsfield, then removed to Hempstead on
Long-Island, and afterwards—by reason of numbers turning Quakers,
and many others being so irreligious that they would do nothing towards the support of the gospel—settled in the work of the ministry at
Haddam; where he died, in the 85th year of his age. He went to public worship in the forenoon, and died in his chair between meetings.
This Rev. gentleman was a son of the Rev. Peter Hobart; who was,
first, minister of the gospel at Hingham, in the county of Norfolk, in
England; and, owning to the persecution of the Puritans, removed
with his family to New-England, and was settled in the ministry at

Hingham, in Massachusetts. He had five sons, Joshua, Jeremiah, Gershom, Japheth, and Nehemiah. Joshua was minister at Southold, on Long-Island. Jeremiah was David Brainerd's grandfather. Gershom was minister of Groton, in Connecticut. Japheth was a physician; he went as surgeon of a ship to England, before the time of taking his second degree at college, and designed to go from thence to the East Indies; but never was heard of more. Nehemiah was fellow of Harvard college, and afterwards minister at Newton in Massachusetts.—The mother of Dorothy Hobart, was a daughter of the Rev. Samuel Whiting, minister of the gospel, first at Boston, in Lincolnshire, and afterwards at Lynn in Massachusetts, New England. He had three sons, who were ministers of the gospel.

David Brainerd was the third son of his parents. They had five sons and four daughters. Their eldest son is Hezekiah Brainerd, Esq.; a justice of the peace, and for several years past, a representative of the town of Haddam, in the general assembly of Connecticut; the second was the Rev. Nehemiah Brainerd, a worthy minister at Eastbury in Connecticut, who died of a consumption, Nov. 10, 1742; the fourth is Mr. John Brainerd, who succeeds his brother David, as missionary to the Indians, and pastor of the same church of Christian Indians in New-Jersey; and the fifth was Israel, lately student at Yale-College, in New-Haven, who died since his brother David.—Mrs. Dorothy Brainerd having lived about five years a widow, died when her son, of whose life I am about to give an account, was about fourteen years of age: so that in his youth he was left both fatherless and motherless. What account he has given of himself, and his own life, may be seen in what follows.

I was from my youth somewhat sober, and inclined to melancholy; but do not remember any thing of conviction of sin, worthy of remark, till I was, I believe, about seven or eight years of age. Then I became concerned for my soul, and terrified at the thoughts of death; and was driven to the performance of religious duties: but it appeared a melancholy business, that destroyed my eagerness for play. And though, alas! this religious concern was but short-lived, I sometimes attended secret prayer; and thus lived at "ease in Zion, without God in the world," and without much concern, as I remember, till I was above thirteen years of age. In the winter of 1732, I was roused out of this carnal security, by I scarce know what means at first; but was much excited by the prevalence of a mortal sickness in Haddam. I was frequent, constant, and somewhat fervent in prayer; and took delight in reading, especially Mr. Haneway's *Token for Children*. I felt sometimes much melted in the duties of religion, took great delight in the performance of them, and sometimes hoped that I was converted, or at least in a good and hopeful way for heaven and happiness; not knowing what conversion was. The Spirit of God at this time proceeded far with me. I was remarkably dead to the world; my thoughts were almost wholly employed about my soul's concerns; and I may indeed say, "Almost I was persuaded to be a Christian." I was also exceedingly distressed and melancholy at the death of my mother, in March, 1732. But afterwards my religious concern began to decline, and by degrees I fell back into a considerable degree of security, though I still attended secret prayer.

About the 15th of April, 1733, I removed from my father's house to East-Haddam, where I spent four years; but still "without God in the world," though, for the most part, I went a round of secret duty. I was not much addicted to the company and amusements of the young; but this I know, that when I did go into such company, I never returned with so good a conscience as when I went. It always added new guilt, made me afraid to come to the throne of grace, and spoiled those good frames with which I was wont sometimes to please myself. But, alas! all my good frames were but self-righteousness, not founded on a desire for the glory of God.

About the latter end of April, 1737, being full nineteen years of age, I removed to Durham, to work on my farm, and so continued about one year; frequently longing, from mere natural principles, after a liberal education. When about twenty years of age, I applied myself to study; and was now engaged more than ever in the duties of religion. I became very strict, and watchful over my thoughts, words, and actions; concluded that I must be sober indeed, because I designed to devote myself to the ministry; and imagined that I did dedicate myself to the Lord.

Sometimes in April, 1738, I went to Mr. Fiske's, and lived with him during his life. I remember he advised me wholly to abandon young company, and associate myself with grave elderly people: which counsel I followed. My manner of life was now wholly regular, and full of religion, such as it was; for I read my Bible more than twice through in less than a year, spent much time every day in prayer and other secret duties, gave great attention to the word preached, and endeavoured to my utmost to retain it. So much concerned was I about religion, that I agreed with some young persons to meet privately on Sabbath evenings for religious exercises, and thought myself sincere in these duties; and after our meeting was ended, I used to repeat the discourse of the day to myself; recollecting what I could, though sometimes very late at night. I used occasionally on Monday mornings to recollect the same sermons; experienced a considerable degree of enjoyment in prayer, and had many thoughts of joining the church. In short, I had a very good outside, and rested entirely on my duties, though I was not sensible of it.

After Mr. Fiske's death, I proceeded in my studies with my brother; was still very constant in religious duties, often wondered at the levity of professors, and lamented their carelessness in religious matters.—Thus I proceeded a considerable length on a self-righteous foundation; and should have been entirely lost and undone, had not the mere mercy of God prevented.

Sometime in the beginning of winter, 1728, it pleased God, one Sabbath morning, as I was walking out for prayer, to give me on a sudden such a sense of my danger, and the wrath of God, that I stood amazed, and my former good frames presently vanished. From the view which I had of my sin and vileness, I was much distressed all that day, fearing that the vengeance of God would soon overtake me. I was much dejected; kept much alone; and sometimes envied the birds and beasts their happiness, because they were not exposed to eternal misery, as I evidently saw that I was. Thus I lived from day to day, being frequently in great distress: sometimes there appeared mountains before me to obstruct my hopes of mercy; and the work of conversion appeared so great, that I thought I should never be the subject of it. I used, however, to pray and cry to God, and perform other duties with great earnestness; and thus hoped by some means to make the case better.

Hundreds of times, I renounced all pretences of any worth in my duties, as I thought, even while performing them, and often confessed to God that I deserved nothing, for the very best of them, but eternal condemnation; yet still I had a secret hope of recommending myself to God by my religious duties. When I prayed affectionately, and my heart seemed in some measure to melt, I hoped that God would be thereby moved to pity me. My prayers then looked with some appearance of goodness in them, and I seemed to mourn for sin. Then I could in some measure venture on the mercy of God in Christ, as I thought; though the preponderating thought, the foundation of my hope was some imagination of goodness in my meltings of heart, the warmth of my affections, and my extraordinary enlargements in prayer. Though at times the gate appeared so very strait, that it looked next to impossible to enter; yet, at other times, I flattered myself that it was not so very difficult, and hoped I should by diligence and watchfulness soon gain the point. Sometimes after enlargement in duty and considerable affection, I hoped I had made a good step towards heaven; and imagined that God was affected as I was, and would hear such sincere cries, as I called them. And so sometimes, when I withdrew for secret prayer in great distress, I returned comfortable; and thus healed myself with my *duties*.

In February 1739, I set apart a day for secret fasting and prayer, and spent the day in almost incessant cries to God for mercy, that he would open my eyes to see the evil of sin, and the way of life by Jesus Christ. God was pleased that day to make considerable discoveries of my heart to me. Still I trusted in all the duties I performed, though there was no manner of goodness in them; there being in them no respect to the glory of God, nor any such principle in my heart. Yet God was pleased to make my endeavours, that day, a means to shew me my *helplessness* in some measure.

Sometimes I was greatly encouraged, and imagined that God loved me, and was pleased with me,—and thought I should soon be fully reconciled to God. But the whole was founded on mere presumption, arising from enlargement in duty, or warmth of affections, or some good resolutions, or the like. And when, at times, great distress began to arise, on a sight of my vileness, and inability to deliver myself from a sovereign God, I used to put off the discovery, as what I could not bear. Once, I remember, a terrible pang of distress seized me; and the thought of renouncing myself, and standing naked before God, stripped of all goodness, was so dreadful to me, that I was ready to say to it, as Felix to Paul, "Go thy way for this time." Thus, though I daily longed for greater conviction of sin; supposing that I must see more of my dreadful state in order to a remedy; yet, when the discoveries of my vile, wicked heart, were made to me, the sight was so dreadful, and shewed me so plainly my exposedness to damnation, that I could not endure it. I constantly strove after whatever qualifications I imagined others obtained before the reception of Christ, in order to recommend me to his favour. Sometimes I felt the power of a hard heart, and supposed it must be softened before Christ would accept of me; and when I felt any meltings of heart, I hoped now the work was almost done. Hence, when my distress still remained, I was wont to murmur at God's dealings with me; and thought, when others felt their hearts softened, God shewed them mercy; but my distress remained still.

At times I grew remiss and sluggish without any great convictions of sin, for a considerable time together; but after such a season, convictions seized me more violently. One night I remember in particular, when I was walking solitarily abroad, I had opened to me such a view of my sin, that I feared the ground would cleave asunder under my feet, and become my grave; and would send my soul quick into hell, before I could get home. Though I was forced to go to bed, lest my distress should be discovered by others, which I much feared; yet I scarcely durst sleep at all, for I thought it would be a great wonder if I should be out of hell in the morning. And though my distress was sometimes thus great, yet I greatly dreaded the loss of convictions, and returning back to a state of carnal security, and to my former insensibility of impending wrath; which made me exceedingly exact in my behaviour, lest I should stifle the motions of God's Holy Spirit. When at any time I took a view of my convictions, and thought the degree of them to be considerable, I was wont to trust in them; but this confidence, and the hopes of soon making some notable advances towards deliverance, would ease my mind, and I soon became more senseless and remiss. —Again, when I discerned my convictions to grow languid, and thought them about to leave me; this immediately alarmed and distressed me.—Sometimes I expected to take a large step, and get very far towards conversion, by some particular opportunity or means I had in view.

The many disappointments, great distresses and perplexity which I experienced, put me into a most horrible frame of contesting with the Almighty; with an inward vehemence and virulence finding fault with his ways of dealing with mankind. I found great fault with the imputation of Adam's sin to his posterity: and my wicked heart often wished for some other way of salvation, than by Jesus Christ. Being like the troubled sea, my thoughts confused, I used to contrive to escape the wrath of God by some other means. I had strange projects, full of Atheism, contriving to disappoint God's designs and decrees concerning me, or to escape his notice, and hide myself from him. But when, upon reflection, I saw these projects were vain, and would not serve me, and that I could contrive nothing for my own relief; this would throw my mind into the most horrid frame, to wish there was no God, or to wish there were some other God that could control him. These thoughts and desires were the secret inclinations of my heart, frequently acting before I was aware; but, alas! they were mine, although I was frightened when I came to reflect on them. When I considered, it distressed me to think, that my heart was so full of enmity against God; and it made me tremble, lest his vengeance should suddenly fall upon me. I used before to imagine, that my heart was not so bad as the scriptures and some other books represented it. Sometimes I used to take much pains to work it up into a good frame, a humble submissive disposition; and hoped there was then some goodness in me. But, on a sudden, the thoughts of the strictness of the law, or the sovereignty of God, would so irritate the corruption of my heart, that I had so watched over, and hoped I had brought to a good frame, that it would break over all bounds, and burst forth on all sides, like floods of waters when they break down their dam.

Being sensible of the necessity of deep humiliation in order to a saving interest in Christ, I used to set myself to produce in my own heart the convictions requisite in such a humiliation; as, a conviction that God would be just, if he cast me off for ever; that if ever God should bestow mercy on me, it would be mere grace, though I should be in distress many years first, and be never so much engaged in duty; and that God was not in the least obliged to pity me the more for all past duties, cries, and tears. I strove to my utmost to bring myself to a firm belief of these things and a hearty assent to them; and hoped that now I was brought off from myself, truly humbled, and that I bowed to the divine sovereignty. I was wont to tell God in my prayers, that now I had those very dispositions of soul which he required, and on which he shewed mercy to others, and thereupon to beg and plead for mercy to me. But when I found no relief, and was still oppressed with guilt, and fears of wrath, my soul was in a tumult, and my heart rose against God, as dealing hardly with me. Yet then my conscience flew in my face, putting me in mind of my late confession to God of his justice in my condemnation. This, giving me a sight of the badness of my heart, threw me again into distress; and I wished that I had watched my heart more narrowly, to keep it from breaking out against God's dealings with me. I even wished that I had not pleaded for mercy on account of my humiliation; because thereby I had lost all my seeming goodness.—Thus, scores of times, I vainly imagined myself humbled and prepared for saving mercy. While I was in this distressed, bewildered, and tumultuous state of mind, the corruption of my heart was especially irritated with the following things.

1. The strictness of the divine Law. For I found it was impossible for me, after my utmost pains, to answer its demands. I often made new resolutions, and as often broke them. I imputed the whole to carelessness, and the want of being more watchful, and used to call myself a fool for my negligence. But when, upon a stronger resolution, and greater endeavours, and close application to fasting and prayer, I found all attempts fail; then I quarrelled with the law of God, as unreasonably rigid. I thought, if it extended only to my outward actions and behaviours, that I could bear with it; but I found that it condemned me for my evil thoughts, and sins of my heart, which I could not possibly prevent. I was extremely loath to own my utter helplessness in this matter: but after repeated disappointments, thought that, rather than perish, I could do a little more still; especially if such and such circumstances might but attend my endeavours and strivings. I hoped, that I should strive more earnestly than ever, if the matter came to extremity, though I never could find the time to do my utmost, in the manner I intended. This hope of future more favourable circumstances, and of doing something great hereafter, kept me from utter despair in myself, and from seeing myself falling into the hands of a sovereign God, and dependent on nothing but free and boundless grace.

2. That faith alone was the condition of salvation; that God would not come down to lower terms; and that he would not promise life and salvation upon my sincere and hearty prayers and endeavours. That word, Mark xvi. 16, "He that believeth not, shall be damned," cut off all hope there.—I found that faith was the sover-

eign gift of God; that I could not get it as of myself; and could not oblige God to bestow it upon me, by any of my performances. (Eph. ii. 1,8.) "This," I was ready to say, "is a hard saying, who can hear it?" I could not bear, that all I had done should stand for mere nothing; as I had been very conscientious in duty, had been exceeding religious a great while, and had, as I thought, done much more than many others who had obtained mercy. I confessed indeed the vileness of my duties; but then, what made them at that time seem vile, was my wandering thoughts in them; not because I was all over defiled like a devil, and the principle corrupt from whence they flowed, so that I could not possibly do any thing that was good. Hence I called what I did by the name of honest faithful endeavours; and could not bear it, that God had made no promises of salvation to them.

3. That I could not find out what faith was; or what it was to believe and come to Christ. I read the calls of Christ to the weary and heavy laden; but could find no way that he directed them to come in. I thought I would gladly come, if I knew how; though the path of duty were never so difficult. I read Stoddard's *Guide to Christ* (which I trust was, in the hand of God, the happy means of my conversion), and my heart rose against the author; for though he told me my very heart all along under convictions, and seemed to be very beneficial to me in his directions; yet here he failed; he did not tell me any thing I could do that would bring me to Christ, but left me as it were with a great gulf between, without any direction to get through. For I was not yet effectually and experimentally taught, that there could be no way prescribed, whereby a natural man could, of his own strength, obtain that which is supernatural, and which the highest angel cannot give.

4. The sovereignty of God. I could not bear, that it should be wholly at God's pleasure, to save or damn me, just as he would. That passage, Rom. ix. 11–23, was a constant vexation to me, especially verse 21. Reading or meditating on this, always destroyed my seeming good frames; for when I thought I was almost humbled, and almost resigned, this passage would make my enmity against the sovereignty of God appear. When I came to reflect on the inward enmity and blasphemy, which arose on this occasion, I was the more afraid of God, and driven further from any hopes of reconciliation with him. It gave me a dreadful view of myself; I

dreaded more than ever to see myself in God's hands, at his sovereign disposal; and it made me more opposite than ever to submit to his sovereignty; for I thought God designed my damnation.

All this time the Spirit of God was powerfully at work with me; and I was inwardly pressed to relinquish all self-confidence, all hopes of ever helping myself by any means whatsoever. The conviction of my lost estate was sometimes so clear and manifest before my eyes, that it was as if it had been declared to me in so many words, "It is done, it is done, it is for ever impossible to deliver yourself." For about three or four days my soul was thus greatly distressed. At some turns, for a few moments, I seemed to myself lost and undone; but then would shrink back immediately from the sight, because I dared not venture myself into the hands of God, as wholly helpless, and at the disposal of his sovereign pleasure. I dared not see that important truth concerning myself, that I was dead in trespasses and sins. But when I had, as it were, thrust away these views of myself at any time, I felt distressed to have the same discoveries of myself again; for I greatly feared being given over of God to final stupidity. When I thought of putting it off to a more convenient season, the conviction was so close and powerful, with regard to the present time, that it was the best, and probably the only time, that I dared not put it off.

It was the sight of truth concerning myself, truth respecting my state, as a creature fallen and alienated from God, and that consequently could make no demands on God for mercy, but must subscribe to the absolute sovereignty of the divine Being; the sight of the truth, I say, my soul shrank away from, and trembled to think of beholding. Thus, he that doth neither cares to come to it, because it will reprove his deeds, and shew him his just deserts, John iii. 20. Sometimes before, I had taken much pains, as I thought, to submit to the sovereignty of God; yet I mistook the thing,—and did not once imagine, that seeing and being made experimentally sensible of this truth, which my soul now so much dreaded and trembled at, was the frame of soul which I had so earnestly desired. I had ever hoped, that when I had attained to that humiliation, which I supposed necessary to precede faith, then it would not be fair for God to cast me off; but now I saw it was so far from any goodness in me, to own myself spiritually dead, and destitute of all goodness, that, on the contrary, my mouth would be for ever stopped by it; and it looked as dreadful to me, to see myself, and the relation I stood in to God—I a sinner and criminal, and he a great judge and Sovereign—as it would be to a poor trembling creature, to venture off some high precipice. Hence I put it off for a minute or two, and tried for better circumstances to do it in; either I must read a passage or two, or pray first, or something of the like nature; or else put off my submission to God's sovereignty with an objection, that I did not know how to submit. But the truth was, I could see no safety in owning myself in the hands of a sovereign God, and could lay no claim to any thing better than damnation.*

After a considerable time spent in similar exercises and distresses, one morning, while I was walking in a solitary place, as usual, I at once saw that all my contrivances and projects to effect or procure deliverance and salvation for myself, were utterly in vain; I was brought quite to a stand, as finding myself totally lost. I had thought many times before, that the difficulties in my way were very great; but now I saw, in another and very different light, that it was for ever impossible for me to do any thing towards helping or delivering myself. I then thought of blaming myself, that I had not done more, and been more engaged, while I had opportunity—for it seemed now as if the season of doing was for ever over and gone—but I instantly saw, that, let me have done what I would, it would no more have tended to my helping myself, than what I had done; that I had made all the pleas I ever could have made to all eternity; and that all my pleas were vain. The tumult that had been before in my mind, was now quieted; and I was somewhat eased of that distress which I felt while struggling against a sight of myself, and of the divine sovereignty. I had the greatest certainty, that my state was for ever miserable, for all that I could do; and wondered that I had never been sensible of it before.

While I remained in this state, my notions respecting my duties were quite different from what I had ever entertained in times past. Before this, the more I did in duty, the more hard I thought it would be for God to cast me off; though at the same time I confessed, and thought I saw, that there was no goodness or merit in my duties; but now, the more I did in prayer or any other duty,

* Insertion of Edwards deleted.

the more I saw that I was indebted to God for allowing me to ask for mercy; for I saw that self-interest had led me to pray, and that I had never once prayed from any respect to the glory of God. Now I saw that there was no necessary connection between my prayers and the bestowment of divine mercy; that they laid not the least obligation upon God to bestow his grace upon me; and that there was no more virtue or goodness in them, than there would be in my paddling with my hand in the water (which was the comparison I had then in my mind); and this because they were not performed from any love or regard to God. I saw that I had been heaping up my devotions before God, fasting, praying, &c. pretending, and indeed really thinking sometimes, that I was aiming at the glory of God; whereas I never once truly intended it, but only my own happiness. I saw that as I had never done anything for God, I had no claim on any thing from him, but perdition, on account of my hypocrisy and mockery. Oh, how different did my duties now appear from what they used to do! I used to charge them with sin and imperfection; but this was only on account of the wanderings and vain thoughts attending them, and not because I had no regard to God in them; for this I thought I had. But when I saw evidently that I had regard to nothing but self-interest; then they appeared a vile mockery of God, self-worship, and a continual course of lies.—I saw that something worse had attended my duties than barely a few wanderings; for the whole was nothing but self-worship, and an horrid abuse of God.

I continued, as I remember, in this state of mind, from Friday morning till the Sabbath evening following (July 12, 1739), when I was walking again in the same solitary place, where I was brought to see myself lost and helpless, as before mentioned. Here, in a mournful melancholy state, I was attempting to pray; but found no heart to engage in that or any other duty; my former concern, exercise, and religious affections were now gone. I thought that the Spirit of God had quite left me; but still was not distressed; yet disconsolate, as if there was nothing in heaven or earth could make me happy. Having been thus endeavouring to pray—though, as I thought, very stupid and senseless—for near half an hour; then, as I was walking in a dark thick grove, unspeakable glory seemed to open to the view and apprehension of my soul. I do not mean any external brightness, for I saw no such thing; nor do I intend any imagination of a body of light, some where in the third heavens, or any thing of that nature; but it was a new inward apprehension or view that I had of God, such as I never had before, nor any thing which had the least resemblance of it. I stood still; wondered; and admired! I knew that I never had seen before any thing comparable to it for excellency and beauty; it was widely different from all the conceptions that ever I had of God, or things divine. I had no particular apprehension of any one person in the Trinity, either the Father, the Son, or the Holy Ghost; but it appeared to be Divine glory. My soul rejoiced with joy unspeakable, to see such a God, such a glorious divine Being; and I was inwardly pleased and satisfied that he should be God over all for ever and ever. My soul was so captivated and delighted with the excellency, loveliness, greatness, and other perfections of God, that I was even swallowed up in him; at least to that degree, that I had no thought (as I remember) at first, about my own salvation, and scarce reflected that there was such a creature as myself.

Thus God, I trust, brought me to a hearty disposition to exalt him, and set him on the throne, and principally and ultimately to aim at his honour and glory, as King of the universe. I continued in this state of inward joy, peace, and astonishment, till near dark, without any sensible abatement; and then began to think and examine what I had seen; and felt sweetly composed in my mind all the evening following. I felt myself in a new world, and every thing about me appeared with a different aspect from what it was wont to do. At this time, the way of salvation opened to me with such infinite wisdom, suitableness, and excellency, that I wondered I should ever think of any other way of salvation; was amazed that I had not dropped my own contrivances, and complied with this lovely, blessed, and excellent way before. If I could have been saved by my own duties, or any other way that I had formerly contrived, my whole soul would now have refused it. I wondered that all the world did not see and comply with this way of salvation, entirely by the righteousness of Christ.

The sweet relish of what I then felt, continued with me for several days, almost constantly, in a greater or less degree.—I could not but sweetly rejoice in God, lying down and rising up. The next Lord's day I felt something of the same kind, though not so powerful as before. But not long after I was again involved in thick darkness, and under great distress; yet not of the same kind with my distress under convictions. I was guilty, afraid, and ashamed to come before God; was exceedingly pressed with a sense of guilt: but it was not long before I felt, I trust, true repentance and joy in God.—About the latter end of August, I again fell under great darkness; it seemed as if the presence of God was clean gone for ever; though I was not so much distressed about my spiritual state, as I was at my being shut out from God's presence, as I then sensibly was. But it pleased the Lord to return graciously to me not long after.†

In the beginning of September I went to Yale College, and entered there; but with some degree of reluctancy, fearing lest I should not be able to lead a life of strict religion, in the midst of so many temptations.—After this, in the vacancy, before I went to tarry at college, it pleased God to visit my soul with clearer manifestations of himself and his grace. I was spending some time in prayer and self-examination, when the Lord, by his grace, so shined into my heart, that I enjoyed full assurance of his favour, for that time; and my soul was unspeakably refreshed with divine and heavenly enjoyments. At this time especially, as well as some others, sundry passages of God's word opened to my soul with divine clearness, power, and sweetness, so as to appear exceeding precious, and with clear and certain evidence of its being the word of God. I enjoyed considerable sweetness in religion all the winter following.

In Jan. 1740, the measles spread much in college; and I, having taken the distemper, went home to Haddam. But some days before I was taken sick, I seemed to be greatly deserted, and my soul mourned the absence of the Comforter exceedingly. It seemed to me, that all comfort was forever gone.—I prayed and cried to God for help, yet found no present comfort or relief. But through divine goodness, a night or two before I was taken ill, while I was walking alone in a very retired place, and engaged in meditation and prayer, I enjoyed a sweet refreshing visit, as I trust, from above; so that my soul was raised far above the fears of death. Indeed, I rather longed for death, than feared it. Oh, how much more

† Insertion of Edwards deleted.

refreshing this one season was, than all the pleasures and delights that earth can afford! After a day or two I was taken with the measles, and was very ill indeed, so that I almost despaired of life; but had no distressing fears of death at all. Through divine goodness, I soon recovered; yet, owing to hard study, and to my being much exposed on account of my freshmanship, as I had but little time for spiritual duties, my soul often mourned for want of more time and opportunity to be alone with God. In the spring and summer following, I had better advantages for retirement, and enjoyed more comfort in religion. My ambition in my studies greatly wronged the activity and vigour of my spiritual life; yet, usually, "in the multitude of my thoughts within me, God's comforts principally delighted my soul." These were my greatest consolations day by day.

One day, I think it was in June, 1740, I walked to a considerable distance from college, in the fields alone, at noon, and in prayer found such unspeakable sweetness and delight in God, that I thought, if I must continue still in this evil world, I wanted always to be there, to behold God's glory. My soul dearly loved all mankind, and longed exceedingly that they should enjoy what I enjoyed. It seemed to be a little resemblance of heaven. On Lord's day, July 6, being sacrament-day, I found some divine life and spiritual refreshment in that holy ordinance. When I came from the Lord's table, I wondered how my fellow-students could live as I was sensible most did.—Next Lord's day, July 13, I had some special sweetness in religion.—Again, Lord's day, July 20, my soul was in a sweet and precious frame.

Some time in August following, I became so weakly and disordered, by too close application to my studies, that I was advised by my tutor to go home, and disengage my mind from study as much as I could; for I was grown so weak, that I began to spit blood. I took his advice, and endeavoured to lay aside my studies. But being brought very low, I looked death in the face more steadfastly; and the Lord was pleased to give me renewedly a sweet sense and relish of divine things; and particularly October 13, I found divine help and consolation in the precious duties of secret prayer and self-examination, and my soul took delight in the blessed God:—so likewise on the 17th of October.

Oct. 18. In my morning devotions, my soul was exceedingly

melted, and bitterly mourned over my great sinfulness and vileness. I never before had felt so pungent and deep a sense of the odious nature of sin, as at this time. My soul was then unusually carried forth in love to God, and had a lively sense of God's love to me. And this love and hope, at that time, cast out fear. Both morning and evening I spent some time in self-examination, to find the truth of grace, as also my fitness to approach God at his table the next day; and through infinite grace, found the Holy Spirit influencing my soul with love to God, as a witness within myself.

Lord's day, Oct. 19. In the morning I felt my soul hungering and thirsting after righteousness. In the forenoon, while I was looking on the sacramental elements, and thinking that Jesus Christ would soon be "set forth crucified before me," my soul was filled with light and love, so that I was almost in an ecstacy; my body was so weak, I could scarcely stand. I felt at the same time an exceeding tenderness and most fervent love towards all mankind; so that my soul and all the powers of it seemed, as it were, to melt into softness and sweetness. But during the communion, there was some abatement of this life and fervour. This love and joy cast out fear; and my soul longed for perfect grace and glory. This frame continued till the evening, when my soul was sweetly spiritual in secret duties.

Oct. 20. I again found the assistance of the Holy Spirit in secret duties, both morning and evening, and life and comfort in religion through the whole day.—Oct. 21. I had likewise experience of the goodness of God in "shedding abroad his love in my heart," and giving me delight and consolation in religious duties; and all the remaining part of the week my soul seemed to be taken up with divine things. I now so longed after God, and to be freed from sin, that, when I felt myself recovering, and thought I must return to college again, which had proved so hurtful to my spiritual interest the year past, I could not but be grieved, and thought I had much rather have died; for it distressed me to think of getting away from God. But before I went, I enjoyed several other sweet and precious seasons of communion with God (particularly Oct. 30, and Nov. 4), wherein my soul enjoyed unspeakable comfort.

I returned to college about Nov. 6, and, through the goodness of God, felt the power of religion almost daily, for the space of six weeks.—Nov. 28. In my evening devotion, I enjoyed precious discoveries of God, and was unspeakably refreshed with that passage, Heb. xii. 22–24. My soul longed to wing away to the paradise of God; I longed to be conformed to God in all things.—A day or two after, I enjoyed much of the light of God's countenance, most of the day; and my soul rested in God.

Dec. 9. I was in a comfortable frame of soul most of the day; but especially in evening devotions, when God was pleased wonderfully to assist and strengthen me; so that I thought nothing should ever move me from the love of God in Christ Jesus my Lord.—Oh! one hour with God infinitely exceeds all the pleasures and delights of this lower world.

Towards the latter end of January, 1741, I grew more cold and dull in religion, by means of my old temptation, viz. ambition in my studies.—But through divine goodness, a great and general Awakening spread itself over the college, about the latter end of February, in which I was much quickened, and more abundantly engaged in religion.‡

CHAPTER II

From about the time when he began the study of Theology, to his Licensure.

In the Spring of 1742, Brainerd went to live with the Rev. Mr. Mills of Ripton, to pursue his studies with him, for the work of the ministry. Here he spent the greater part of the time until the Association licensed him to preach; but frequently rode to visit the neighbouring ministers, particularly Mr. Cooke of Stratford, Mr. Graham of Southbury, and Mr. Bellamy of Bethlehem. While with Mr. Mills, he began the third book of his diary in which the account he wrote of himself, is as follows:

April 1, 1742. I seem to be declining, with respect to my life and warmth in divine things; and have had not so free access to God in prayer, as usual of late. Oh that God would humble me deeply in

‡ A note by Edwards describes Brainerd's expulsion from Yale as a result of an excess of zeal in criticizing a professor for lack of piety.

the dust before him! I deserve hell every day, for not loving my Lord more, who has, I trust, loved me, and given himself for me; and every time I am enabled to exercise any grace renewedly, I am renewedly indebted to the God of all grace for special assistance. Where then is boasting? Surely it is excluded, when we think how we are dependent on God for the existence and every act of grace. O if ever I get to heaven, it will be because God pleases and nothing else; for I never did any thing of myself, but get away from God! My soul will be astonished at the unsearchable riches of divine grace, when I arrive at the mansions, which the blessed Saviour is gone before to prepare.

April 2. In the afternoon, I felt in secret prayer, much resigned, calm and serene. What are all the storms of this lower world, if Jesus by his spirit does but come walking on the seas!—Sometime past, I had much pleasure in the prospect of the Heathen being brought home to Christ, and desired that the Lord would employ me in that work: but now my soul more frequently desires to die, to be with Christ. Oh that my soul were wrapt up in divine love, and my longing desires after God increased! In the evening, was refreshed in prayer, with the hopes of the advancement of Christ's kingdom in the world.

April 3. Was very much amiss this morning, and had a bad night. I thought, if God would take me to himself now, my soul would exceedingly rejoice. Oh that I may be always humble and resigned to God, and that he would cause my soul to be more fixed on himself, that I may be more fitted both for doing and suffering.

Lord's day, April 4. My heart was wandering and lifeless. In the evening God gave me faith in prayer, made my soul melt in some measure, and gave me to taste a divine sweetness. O my blessed God! Let me climb up near to him, and love, and long, and plead, and wrestle, and stretch after him, and for deliverance from the body of sin and death.—Alas! my soul mourned to think I should ever lose sight of its beloved again. "O come, Lord Jesus, Amen."

On the evening of the next day, he complains, that he seemed to be void of all relish of divine things, felt much of the prevalence of corruption, and saw in himself a disposition to all manner of sin; which brought a very great gloom on his mind, and cast him down into the depths of melancholy; so that he speaks of himself as amazed, having no comfort, but filled with horror, seeing no comfort in heaven or earth.

April 6. I walked out this morning to the same place where I was last night, and felt as I did then; but was somewhat relieved by reading some passages in my diary, and seemed to feel as if I might pray to the great God again with freedom; but was suddenly struck with a damp, from the sense I had of my own vileness.—Then I cried to God to cleanse me from my exceeding filthiness, to give me repentance and pardon. I then began to find it sweet to pray; and could think of undergoing the greatest sufferings, in the cause of Christ, with pleasure; and found myself willing, if God should so order it, to suffer banishment from my native land, among the Heathen, that I might do something for their salvation, in distresses and deaths of any kind.—Then God gave me to wrestle earnestly for others, for the kingdom of Christ in the world, and for dear Christian friends.—I felt weaned from the world, and from my own reputation amongst men, willing to be despised, and to be a gazing stock for the world to behold.—It is impossible for me to express how I then felt: I had not much joy, but some sense of the majesty of God, which made me as it were tremble. I saw myself mean and vile, which made me more willing that God should do what he would with me; it was all infinitely reasonable.

April 7. I had not so much fervency, but felt somewhat as I did yesterday morning, in prayer.—At noon I spent some time in secret, with some fervency, but scarce any sweetness; and felt very dull in the evening.

April 8. Had raised hopes to-day respecting the Heathen. Oh that God would bring in great numbers of them to Jesus Christ! I cannot but hope that I shall see that glorious day.—Every thing in this world seems exceeding vile and little to me: I look so on myself.—I had some little dawn of comfort to-day in prayer; but especially to-night, I think I had some faith and power of intercession with God. I was enabled to plead with God for the growth of grace in myself; and many of the dear children of God then lay with weight upon my soul. Blessed be the Lord! It is good to wrestle for divine blessings.

April 9. Most of my time in morning devotion was spent without sensible sweetness; yet I had one delightful prospect of arriving at the heavenly world. I am more amazed than ever at such thoughts; for I see myself infinitely vile and unworthy. I feel very heartless and dull; and though I long for the presence of God, and seem constantly to reach towards God in desires; yet I cannot feel that divine and heavenly sweetness that I used to enjoy.—No poor creature stands in need of divine grace more than I, and none abuse it more than I have done, and still do.

April 10. Spent much time in secret prayer this morning, not without some comfort in divine things, and hope I had some faith in exercise; but am so low, and feel so little of the sensible presence of God, that I hardly know what to call faith, and am made to possess the sins of my youth, and the dreadful sin of my nature. I am all sin; I cannot think nor act, but every motion is sin. I feel some faint hopes, that God will, of his infinite mercy, return again with showers of converting grace to poor gospel-abusing sinners; and my hopes of being employed in the cause of God, which of late have been almost extinct, seem now a little revived. Oh that all my late distresses and awful apprehensions, might prove but Christ's school, to make me fit for greater service, by teaching me the great lesson of humility!

Lord's Day, April 11. In the morning, I felt but little life, except that my heart was somewhat drawn out in thankfulness to God, for his amazing grace and condescension to me, in past influences and assistances of his spirit. Afterwards, I had some sweetness in the thoughts of arriving at the heavenly world. O for the happy day! After public worship, God gave me special assistance in prayer; I wrestled with my dear Lord, with much sweetness; and intercession was made a delightful employment to me. In the evening, as I was viewing the light in the north, I was delighted in contemplation on the glorious morning of the Resurrection.

April 12. This morning the Lord was pleased to lift up the light of his countenance upon me in secret prayer, and made the season very precious to my soul. Though I have been so depressed of late, respecting my hopes of future serviceableness in the cause of God; yet now I had much encouragement respecting that matter. I was especially assisted to intercede and plead for poor souls, and for the enlargement of Christ's kingdom in the world, and for special grace for myself, to fit me for special services. I felt exceedingly calm, and quite resigned to God, respecting my future employment, when and where he pleased. My faith lifted me above the world, and removed all those mountains over which of late I could not look. I wanted not the favour of man to lean upon; for I knew that Christ's favour was infinitely better, and that it was no matter when nor where, nor how Christ should send me, nor what trials he should still exercise me with, if I might be prepared for his work and will. I now found revived in my mind, the wonderful discovery of infinite wisdom in all the dispensations of God towards me, which I had, a little before I met with my great trial at college; every thing appeared full of divine wisdom.

April 13. I saw myself to be very mean and vile; and wondered at those who showed me respect. Afterward I was somewhat comforted in secret retirement, and assisted to wrestle with God, with some power, spirituality, and sweetness. Blessed be the Lord, he is never unmindful of me, but always sends me needed supplies; and, from time to time, when I am like one dead, he raises me to life. Oh that I may never distrust Infinite goodness!

April 14. My soul longed for communion with Christ, and for the mortification of indwelling corruption, especially spiritual pride. O, there is a sweet day coming, wherein the weary will be at rest! My soul has enjoyed much sweetness this day, in the hopes of its speedy arrival.

April 15. My desires apparently centered in God; and I found a sensible attraction of soul after him sundry times today. I know that I long for God, and a conformity to his will, in inward purity and holiness, ten thousand times more than for any thing here below.

April 16 and 17. I seldom prayed without some sensible joy in the Lord. Sometimes I longed much to be dissolved and to be with Christ. Oh that God would enable me to grow in grace every day! Alas! my barrenness is such, that God might well say, "Cut it down." I am afraid of a dead heart on the Sabbath now begun. Oh that God would quicken me by his grace!

Lord's day, April 18. I retired early this morning into the woods for prayer; had the assistance of God's Spirit, and faith in exercise; and was enabled to plead with fervency for the advancement of Christ's kingdom in the world, and to intercede for dear, absent friends. At noon, God enabled me to wrestle with him, and to feel, as I trust, the power of divine love, in prayer. At night, I saw myself infinitely indebted to God, and had a view of my failures in duty. It seemed to me, that I had done, as it were, nothing for God, and that I never had lived to him but a few hours of my life.

April 19. I set apart this day for fasting and prayer to God for his grace; especially to prepare me for the work of the ministry; to give me divine aid and direction, in my preparations for that great work; and in his own time to send me into his harvest. Accordingly, in the morning, I endeavoured to plead for the divine presence for the day, and not without some life. In the forenoon, I felt the power of intercession for precious, immortal souls; for the advancement of the kingdom of my dear Lord and Saviour in the world; and withal, a most sweet resignation, and even consolation and joy, in the thoughts of suffering hardships, distresses, and even death itself, in the promotion of it; and had peculiar enlargement in pleading for the enlightening and conversion of the poor Heathen. In the afternoon, God was with me of a truth. O, it was blessed company indeed! God enabled me so to agonize in prayer, that I was quite wet with perspiration, though in the shade, and the cool wind. My soul was drawn out very much from the world, for multitudes of souls. I think I had more enlargement for sinners, than for the children of God; though I felt as if I could spend my life in cries for both. I enjoyed great sweetness in communion with my dear Saviour. I think I never in my life felt such an entire weanedness from this world, and so much resigned to God in every thing. Oh that I may always live to and upon my blessed God! Amen, Amen.

April 20. This day, I am twenty-four years of age. O how much mercy have I received the year past! How often has God caused his goodness to pass before me! And how poorly have I answered the vows I made this time twelve-month, to be wholly the Lord's, to be forever devoted in his service! The Lord help me to live more to his glory for the time to come. This has been a sweet, a happy day to me; blessed be God. I think my soul was never so drawn out in intercession for others, as it has been this night. Had a most fervent wrestle with the Lord to-night for my enemies; and I hardly ever so longed to live to God, and to be altogether devoted to him; I wanted to wear out my life in his service, and for his glory.

April 21. Felt much calmness and resignation; and God again enabled me to wrestle for numbers of souls, and had much fervency in the sweet duty of intercession. I enjoyed of late more sweetness in intercession for others, than in any other part of prayer. My blessed Lord really let me come near to him and plead with him.

The frame of mind, and exercises of soul, which he expresses the three days next following, are much of the same kind, with those expressed the two day's past.

Lord's day, April 25. This morning, I spent about two hours in secret duties, and was enabled, more than ordinarily, to agonize for immortal souls; though it was early in the morning, and the sun scarcely shined at all, yet my body was quite wet with sweat. I felt much pressed now, as frequently of late, to plead for the meekness and calmness of the Lamb of God in my soul; and through divine goodness, felt much of it this morning. O it is a sweet disposition, heartily to forgive all injuries done us; to wish our greatest enemies as well, as we do our own souls! Blessed Jesus, may I daily be more and more conformed to thee! At night, I was exceedingly melted with divine love, and had some feeling sense of the blessedness of the upper world. Those words hung upon me, with much divine sweetness, Psalm lxxxiv. 7. "They go from strength to strength, every one of them in Zion appeareth before God." O the near access that God sometimes gives us in our addresses to him! This may well be termed appearing before God: it is so indeed, in the true spiritual sense, and in the sweetest sense. I think that I have not had such power of intercession these many months, both for God's children, and for dead sinners, as I have had this evening. I wished and longed for the coming of my dear Lord: I longed to join the angelic hosts in praises, wholly free from imperfection. O, the blessed moment hastens! All I want is to be more holy, more like my dear Lord. Oh for sanctification! My very soul pants for the complete restoration of the blessed image of my Saviour; that I may be fit for the blessed enjoyments and employments of the heavenly world.

> Farewell, vain world; my soul can bid Adieu:
> Your Saviour taught me to abandon you.
> Your charms may gratify a sensual mind;
> But cannot please a soul for God design'd.
> Forbear t'entice, cease then my soul to call:
> 'Tis fix'd through grace; my God shall be my all.
> While he thus lets me heavenly glories view,
> Your beauties fade, my heart's no room for you.

The Lord refreshed my soul with many sweet passages of his word. O the New Jerusalem! my soul longed for it. O the song of

Moses and the Lamb! And that blessed song, that no man can learn, but they who are redeemed from the earth! and the glorious white robes, that were given to the souls under the altar!

> Lord, I'm a stranger here alone;
> Earth no true comforts can afford:
> Yet, absent from my dearest one,
> My soul delights to cry 'My Lord!'
> Jesus, my Lord, my only love,
> Possess my soul, nor thence depart:
> Grant me kind visits, heavenly dove;
> My God shall then have all my heart.

April 26. Continued in a sweet frame of mind; but in the afternoon, felt somewhat of spiritual pride stirring. God was pleased to make it a humbling season at first; though afterwards he gave me sweetness. O my soul exceedingly longs for that blessed state of perfect deliverance from all sin! At night, God enabled me to give my soul up to him, to cast myself upon him, to be ordered and disposed of according to his sovereign pleasure; and I enjoyed great peace and consolation in so doing. My soul took sweet delight in God; my thoughts freely and sweetly centered in him. O that I could spend every moment of my life to his glory!

April 27. I retired pretty early for secret devotions; and in prayer, God was pleased to pour such ineffable comforts into my soul, that I could do nothing for some time but say over and over, 'O my sweet Saviour! O my sweet Saviour! whom have I in Heaven but thee? and there is none upon earth that I desire beside thee.' If I had had a thousand lives, my soul would gladly have laid them all down at once, to have been with Christ. My soul never enjoyed so much of heaven before; it was the most refined and most spiritual season of communion with God, I ever yet felt. I never felt so great a degree of resignation in my life. In the afternoon, I withdrew, to meet with my God, but found myself much declined, and God made it a humbling season to my soul. I mourned over the body of death that is in me. It grieved me exceedingly, that I could not pray to and praise God with my heart full of divine heavenly love. Oh that my soul might never offer any dead, cold services to my God! In the evening had not so much divine love, as in the morning; but had a sweet season of fervent intercession.

April 28. I withdrew to my usual place of retirement, in great peace and tranquility, spent about two hours in secret duties, and felt much as I did yesterday morning, only weaker, and more overcome. I seemed to depend wholly on my dear Lord; wholly weaned from all other dependences. I knew not what to say to my God, but only lean on his bosom, as it were, and breathe out my desires after a perfect conformity to him in all things. Thirsting desires, and insatiable longings, possessed my soul after perfect holiness. God was so precious to my soul, that the world, with all its enjoyments, was infinitely vile. I had no more value for the favour of men, than for pebbles. The Lord was my all, and that he over-ruled all, greatly delighted me. I think that my faith and dependence on God, scarce ever rose so high. I saw him such a Fountain of goodness, that it seemed impossible I should distrust him again, or be any way anxious about any thing that should happen to me. I now enjoyed great sweetness in praying for absent friends, and for the enlargement of Christ's kingdom in the world. Much of the power of these divine enjoyments remained with me through the day. In the evening, my heart seemed to melt, and I trust was really humbled for indwelling corruption, and I mourned like a dove. I felt that all my unhappiness arose from my being a sinner. With resignation, I could bid welcome to all other trials; but sin hung heavy upon me; for God discovered to me the corruption of my heart. I went to bed with a heavy heart, because I was a sinner; though I did not in the least doubt of God's love. O that God would purge away my dross, and take away my tin, and make me ten times refined!

April 29. I was kept off at a distance from God;—but had some enlargement in intercession for precious souls.

April 30. I was somewhat dejected in spirit: nothing grieves me so much, as that I cannot live constantly to God's glory. I could bear any desertion or spiritual conflicts, if I could but have my heart all the while burning within me with love to God and desires of his glory. But this is impossible; for when I feel these, I cannot be dejected in my soul, but only rejoice in my Saviour, who has delivered me from the reigning power, and will shortly deliver me from the indwelling of sin.

May 1. I was enabled to cry to God with fervency for ministerial qualifications, that he would appear for the advancement of his own kingdom, and that he would bring in the Heathen. Had much assistance in my studies. This has been a profitable week to me; I have enjoyed many communications of the blessed Spirit in my soul.

Lord's day, May 2. God was pleased this morning to give me such a sight of myself, as made me appear very vile in my own eyes. I felt corruption stirring in my heart, which I could by no means suppress; felt more and more deserted; was exceeding weak, and almost sick with my inward trials.

May 3. Had a sense of vile ingratitude. In the morning I withdrew to my usual place of retirement, and mourned for my abuse of my dear Lord; spent the day in fasting and prayer. God gave me much power of wrestling for his cause and kingdom; and it was a happy day to my soul. God was with me all the day; and I was more above the world, than ever in my life.

Through the remaining part of this week, he complains almost every day of desertion, inward trials and conflicts, attended with dejection of spirit; yet speaks of times of relief and sweetness, and daily refreshing visits of the divine Spirit, affording special assistance and comfort, and enabling him, at times, to enjoy much fervency and enlargement in religious duties.

Lord's day, May 9. I think I never felt so much of the cursed pride of my heart, as well as the stubbornness of my will before. O dreadful! what a vile wretch I am! I could submit to be nothing, and to lie down in the dust. Oh that God would humble me in the dust! I felt myself such a sinner, all day, that I had scarce any comfort. Oh when shall I be delivered from the body of this death! I greatly feared, lest through stupidity and carelessness I should lose the benefit of these trials. Oh that they might be sanctified to my soul! Nothing seemed to touch me but only this, that I was a sinner. —Had fervency and refreshment in social prayer in the evening.

May 10. I rode to New-Haven; saw some christian friends there; and had comfort in joining in prayer with them, and hearing of the goodness of God to them, since I last saw them.

May 11. I rode from New-Haven to Wethersfield; was very dull most of the day; had little spirituality in this journey, though I often longed to be alone with God; was much perplexed with vile thoughts; was sometimes afraid of every thing: but God was my Helper. Catched a little time for retirement in the evening, to my comfort and rejoicing. Alas! I cannot live in the midst of a tumult. I long to enjoy God alone.

May 12. I had a distressing view of the pride, enmity and vileness of my heart. Afterwards had sweet refreshment in conversing and worshipping God, with christian friends.

May 13. Saw so much of the wickedness of my heart, that I longed to get away from myself. I never before thought that there was so much spiritual pride in my soul. I felt almost pressed to death with my own vileness. O what a body of death is there in me! Lord, deliver my soul! I could not find any convenient place for retirement, and was greatly exercised. Rode to Hartford in the afternoon: had some refreshment and comfort in religious exercises with christian friends; but longed for more retirement. O the closest walk with God is the sweetest heaven that can be enjoyed on earth!

May 14. I waited on a council of ministers convened at Hartford, and spread before them the treatment I had met with from the rector and tutors of Yale College; who thought it adviseable to intercede for me with the rector and trustees, and to intreat them to restore me to my former privileges in college. After this, spent some time in religious exercises with christian friends.

May 15. I rode from Hartford to Hebron; was somewhat dejected on the road; appeared exceeding vile in my own eyes, saw much pride and stubbornness in my heart. Indeed I never saw such a week as this before; for I have been almost ready to die with the view of the wickedness of my heart. I could not have thought I had such a body of death in me. Oh that God would deliver my soul!

The three next days (which he spent at Hebron, Lebanon, and Norwich) he complains still of dulness and desertion, and expresses a sense of his vileness, and longing to hide himself in some cave or den of the earth: but yet speaks of some intervals of comfort and soul-refreshment each day.

May 19. (At Millington) I was so amazingly deserted this morning, that I seemed to feel a sort of horror in my soul. Alas! when God withdraws, what is there that can afford any comfort to the soul!

Through the eight days next following, he expresses more calmness and comfort, and considerable life, fervency, and sweetness in religion.

May 28. (At New-Haven) I think I scarce ever felt so calm in my life; I rejoiced in resignation, and giving myself up to God, to be wholly and entirely devoted to him for ever.

On the three following days, there was, by the account he gives, a continuance of the same excellent frame of mind, last expressed: but it seems not to be altogether to so great a degree.

June 1. Had much of the presence of God in family prayer, and had some comfort in secret. I was greatly refreshed from the word of God this morning, which appeared exceedingly sweet to me: some things which appeared mysterious, were opened to me. Oh that the kingdom of the dear Saviour might come with power, and the healing waters of the sanctuary spread far and wide for the healing of the nations!—Came to Ripton; but was very weak. However, being visited by a number of young people in the evening, I prayed with them.

The remaining part of this week, he speaks of being much diverted and hindered in the business of religion, by great weakness of body, and necessary affairs, to which he had to attend; and complains of having but little power in religion; but observes, that God hereby shewed him, that he was like a helpless infant cast out in the open field.

Lord's day, June 6. I feel much deserted: but all this teaches me my nothingness and vileness more than ever.

June 7. Felt still powerless in secret prayer. Afterwards I prayed and conversed with some little life. God feeds me with crumbs: blessed be his name for any thing. I felt a great desire that all God's people might know how mean and little and vile I am; that they might see I am nothing, that so they may pray for me aright, and not have the least dependence upon me.

June 8. I enjoyed one sweet and precious season this day: I never felt it so sweet to be nothing, and less than nothing, and to be accounted nothing.

The three next days he complains of desertion, and want of fervency in religion; but yet his diary shews that every day his heart was engaged in religion, as his great, and, as it were, only business.

June 12. Spent much time in prayer this morning, and enjoyed much sweetness:—Felt insatiable longings after God much of the day. I wondered how poor souls do to live, that have no God. The world, with all its enjoyments, quite vanished. I see myself very helpless: but I have a blessed God to go to. I longed exceedingly to be dissolved, and to be with Christ, to behold his glory. O my weak, weary soul longs to arrive at my Father's house!

Lord's day, June 13. Felt somewhat calm and resigned in the public worship: at the sacrament saw myself very vile and worthless. Oh that I may always lie low in the dust. My soul seemed steadily to go forth after God, in longing desires to live upon him.

June 14. Felt somewhat of the sweetness of communion with God, and the constraining force of his love; how admirably it captivates the soul, and makes all the desires and affections to centre in God!—I set apart this day for secret fasting and prayer, to intreat God to direct and bless me with regard to the great work which I have in view, of preaching the gospel—and that the Lord would return to me, and shew me the light of his countenance. Had little life and power in the forenoon: near the middle of the afternoon, God enabled me to wrestle ardently in intercession for my absent friends: but just at night, the Lord visited me marvelously in prayer. I think my soul never was in such an agony before. I felt no restraint; for the treasures of divine grace were opened to me. I wrestled for absent friends, for the ingathering of souls, for multitudes of poor souls, and for many that I thought were the children of God, personally, in many distant places. I was in such an agony, from sun half an hour high, till near dark, that I was all over wet with sweat: but yet it seemed to me that I had wasted away the day, and had done nothing. O my dear Saviour did sweat blood for poor souls! I longed for more compassion towards them. Felt still in a sweet frame, under a sense of divine love and grace; and went to bed in such a frame, with my heart set on God.

June 15. Had the most ardent longings after God, which I ever felt in my life. At noon, in my secret retirement, I could do nothing but tell my dear Lord, in a sweet calm, that he knew I desired nothing but himself, nothing but holiness; that he had given me these desires, and he only could give me the thing desired. I never seemed to be so unhinged from myself, and to be so wholly devoted to God. My heart was swallowed up in God most of the day. In the evening I had such a view of the soul being as it were enlarged, to contain more holiness, that it seemed ready to separate from my body. I then wrestled in an agony for divine blessings; had my heart drawn out in prayer for some christian friends, beyond what I ever had before. I feel differently now from what I ever did under any enjoyments before; more engaged to live to God for ever, and less pleased with my own frames. I am not satisfied with my frames, nor feel at all more easy after such strugglings than before; for it seems far too little, if I could always be so. O how short do I fall of my duty in my sweetest moments!

In his diary for the two next days, he expresses somewhat of the same frame, but in a far less degree.

June 18. Considering my great unfitness for the work of the ministry, my present deadness, and total inability to do any thing for the glory of God that way, feeling myself very helpless, and at a great loss what the Lord would have me to do; I set apart this day for prayer to God, and spent most of the day in that duty, but amazingly deserted most of the day. Yet I found God graciously near, once in particular; while I was pleading for more compassion for immortal souls, my heart seemed to be opened at once, and I was enabled to cry with great ardency, for a few minutes. O I was distressed to think, that I should offer such dead cold services to the living God! My soul seemed to breathe after holiness, a life of constant devotedness to God. But I am almost lost sometimes in the pursuit of this blessedness, and ready to sink, because I continually fall short, and miss of my desire. Oh that the Lord would help me to hold out, yet a little while, until the happy hour of deliverance comes!

June 19. Felt much disordered; my spirits were very low: but yet enjoyed some freedom and sweetness in the duties of religion. Blessed be God.

Lord's day, June 20. Spent much time alone. My soul earnestly wished to be holy, and reached after God; but seemed not to obtain my desire. I hungered and thirsted; but was not refreshed and satisfied. My soul rested on God, as my only portion. Oh that I could grow in grace more abundantly every day!

The next day he speaks of his having assistance in his studies, and power, fervency, and comfort in prayer.

June 22. In the morning spent about two hours in prayer and meditation, with considerable delight. Towards night felt my soul go out in earnest desires after God, in secret retirement. In the evening, was sweetly composed and resigned to God's will; was enabled to leave myself and all my concerns with him, and to have my whole dependence upon him. My secret retirement was very refreshing to my soul; it appeared such a happiness to have God for my portion, that I had rather be any other creature in this lower creation, than not come to the enjoyment of God. I had rather be a beast, than a man, without God, if I were to live here to eternity. Lord, endear thyself more to me!

In his diary for the next seven days, he expresses a variety of exercises of mind. He speaks of great longings after God and holiness, and earnest desires for the conversion of others; of fervency in prayer, power to wrestle with God, composure, comfort, and sweetness, from time to time; but expresses a sense of the abomination of his heart, and bitterly complains of his barrenness, and the body of death; and says, "he saw clearly that whatever he enjoyed, better than hell, was of free grace." He complains of falling much below the character of a child of God; and is sometimes very disconsolate and dejected.

June 30. Spent this day alone in the woods, in fasting and prayer; underwent the most dreadful conflicts in my soul, which I ever felt, in some respects. I saw myself so vile, that I was ready to say, "I shall now perish by the hand of Saul." I thought that I had no power to stand for the cause of God, but was almost "afraid of the shaking of a leaf." Spent almost the whole day in prayer, incessantly. I could not bear to think of christians shewing me any respect. I almost despaired of doing any service in the world: I could not feel any hope or comfort respecting the heathen, which used to afford me some refreshment in the darkest hours of this nature. I spent the day in bitterness of soul. Near night I felt a little better; and afterwards enjoyed some sweetness in secret prayer.

July 1. Had some enjoyment in prayer this morning; and far more than usual in secret prayer to-night, and desired nothing so ardently as that God should do with me just as he pleased.

July 2. Felt composed in secret prayer in the morning.—My desires ascended to God this day, as I was travelling: and was comfortable in the evening. Blessed be God for all my consolations.

July 3. My heart seemed again to sink. The disgrace I was laid under at College, seemed to damp me; as it opens the mouths of opposers. I had no refuge but in God. Blessed be his name, that I may go to him at all times, and find him a present help.

Lord's day, July 4. Had considerable assistance. In the evening I withdrew, and enjoyed a happy season in secret prayer. God was pleased to give me the exercise of faith, and thereby brought the invisible and eternal world near to my soul; which appeared sweetly to me. I hoped, that my weary pilgrimage in the world would be short; and that it would not be long before I was brought to my heavenly home and Father's house. I was resigned to God's will, to tarry his time, to do his work, and suffer his pleasure. I felt thankfulness to God for all my pressing desertions of late; for I am persuaded that they have been made a means of making me more humble, and much more resigned. I felt pleased to be little, to be nothing, and to lie in the dust. I enjoyed life and consolation in pleading for the dear children of God, and the kingdom of Christ in the world: and my soul earnestly breathed after holiness, and the enjoyment of God. O come, Lord Jesus, come quickly.

By his diary for the remaining days of this week, it appears that he enjoyed considerable composure and tranquillity, and had sweetness and fervency of spirit in prayer, from day to day.

Lord's day, July 11. Was deserted, and exceedingly dejected in the morning. In the afternoon, had some life and assistance, and felt resigned. I saw myself to be exceeding vile.

On the two next days he expresses inward comfort, resignation, and strength in God.

July 14. Felt a degree of humble resigned sweetness: spent a considerable time in secret, giving myself up wholly to the Lord. Heard Mr. Bellamy preach towards night; felt very sweetly part of the time: longed for nearer access to God.

The four next days, he expresses considerable comfort and fervency of spirit, in Christian conversation and religious exercises.

July 19. My desires seem especially to be after weanedness from the world, perfect deadness to it, and that I may be crucified to all its allurements. My soul desires to feel itself more of a pilgrim and stranger here below; that nothing may divert me from pressing through the lonely desert, till I arrive at my Father's house.

July 20. It was sweet to give away myself to God, to be disposed of at his pleasure. I had some feeling sense of the sweetness of being a pilgrim on earth.

The next day, he expresses himself as determined to be wholly devoted to God; and it appears by his diary, that he spent the whole day in a most diligent exercise of religion, and with great comfort.

July 22. Journeying from Southbury to Ripton, I called at a house by the way, where being very kindly entertained and refreshed, I was filled with amazement and shame, that God should stir up the hearts of any to shew so much kindness to such a dead dog as I; was made sensible, in some measure, how exceeding vile it is not to be wholly devoted to God. I wondered that God would suffer any of his creatures to feed and sustain me from time to time.

In his diary for the six next days, are expressed various exercises and experiences, such as, sweet composure and fervency of spirit in meditation and prayer, weanedness from the world, being sensibly a pilgrim and stranger on the earth, engagedness of mind to spend every moment of time for God, &c.

July 29. I was examined by the Association met at Danbury, as to my learning, and also my experience in religion, and received a licence from them to preach the gospel of Christ. Afterwards felt much devoted to God; joined in prayer with one of the ministers, my peculiar friend, in a convenient place; and went to bed resolving to live devoted to God all my days.

CHAPTER III

From his Licensure, till his Examination and Commission as a Missionary.*

Aug. 12 [1742.] This morning and last night I was exercised with sore inward trials: I had no power to pray: but seemed shut out from God. I had in a great measure lost my hopes of God's sending

* Several entries deleted from this chapter as indicated.

me among the Heathen afar off, and of seeing them flock home to Christ. I saw so much of my vileness, that I wondered that God would let me live, and that people did not stone me; much more that they would ever hear me preach! It seemed as though I never could nor should preach any more; yet about nine or ten o'clock, the people came over, and I was forced to preach. And blessed be God, he gave me his presence and Spirit in prayer and preaching: so that I was much assisted, and spake with power from Job xiv. 14. Some Indians cried out in great distress, and all appeared greatly concerned. After we had prayed and exhorted them to seek the Lord with constancy, and hired an English woman to keep a kind of school among them, we came away about one o'clock, and came to Judea, about fifteen or sixteen miles. There God was pleased to visit my soul with much comfort. Blessed be the Lord for all things I meet with.

Aug. 20. I appeared so vile to myself, that I hardly dared to think of being seen, especially on account of spiritual pride. However, to-night I enjoyed a sweet hour alone with God (at Ripton): I was lifted above the frowns and flatteries of this lower world, had a sweet relish of heavenly joys, and my soul did, as it were, get into the eternal world, and really taste of heaven. I had a sweet season of intercession for dear friends in Christ; and God helped me to cry fervently for Zion. Blessed be God for this season.

Sept. 8. Felt very sweetly, when I first rose in the morning. In family prayer, had some enlargement, but not much spirituality, till eternity came up before me, and looked near; I found some sweetness in the thoughts of bidding a dying farewell to this tiresome world. Though sometime ago I reckoned upon seeing my dear friends at commencement; yet being now denied the opportunity, for fear of imprisonment, I felt totally resigned, and as contented to spend this day alone in the woods, as I could have done, if I had been allowed to go to town. Felt exceedingly weaned from the world to-day. In the afternoon, I discoursed on divine things, with a dear christian friend, whereby we were both refreshed. Then I prayed, with a sweet sense of the blessedness of communion with God: I think I scarce ever enjoyed more of God in any one prayer. O it was a blessed season indeed to my soul! I know not that ever I saw so much of my own nothingness, in my life; never wondered so, that God allowed me to preach his word. This has been a sweet and comfortable day to my soul. Blessed be God. Prayed again with my dear friend, with something of the divine presence. I long to be wholly conformed to God, and transformed into his image.

Sept. 10. Longed with intense desire after God; my whole soul seemed impatient to be conformed to him, and to become "holy, as he is holy." In the afternoon, prayed with a dear friend privately, and had the presence of God with us; our souls united together to reach after a blessed immortality, to be unclothed of the body of sin and death, and to enter the blessed world, where no unclean thing enters. O, with what intense desire did our souls long for that blessed day, that we might be freed from sin, and for ever live to and in our God! In the evening, took leave of that house; but first kneeled down and prayed; the Lord was of a truth in the midst of us; it was a sweet parting season; felt in myself much sweetness and affection in the things of God. Blessed be God for every such divine gale of his Spirit, to speed me on in my way to the new Jerusalem! Felt some sweetness afterwards, and spent the evening in conversation with friends, and prayed with some life, and retired to rest very late.

Lord's day, Oct. 17. Had a considerable sense of my helplessness and inability; saw that I must be dependent on God for all I want; and especially when I went to the place of public worship. I found I could not speak a word for God, without his special help and assistance. I went into the assembly trembling, as I frequently do, under a sense of my insufficiency to do any thing in the cause of God, as I ought to do. But it pleased God to afford me much assistance, and there seemed to be a considerable effect on the hearers. In the evening, I felt a disposition to praise God, for his goodness to me, that he had enabled me in some measure to be faithful; and my soul rejoiced to think, that I had thus performed the work of one day more, and was one day nearer my eternal, and I trust my heavenly home. Oh that I may be "faithful to the death, fulfilling as an hireling my day," till the shades of the evening of life shall free my soul from the toils of the day! This evening, in secret prayer, I felt exceedingly solemn, and such longing desires after deliverance from sin, and after conformity to God, as melted my heart. O I longed to be "delivered from this body of death"! I felt inward, pleasing pain, that I could not be conformed to God entirely, fully, and forever. I scarce ever preach without being first visited with inward conflicts, and sore trials. Blessed be the Lord for these trials and distresses, as they are blessed for my humbling.

Oct. 21. Had a very deep sense of the vanity of the world, most of the day; had little more regard to it, than if I had been to go into eternity the next hour. Through divine goodness, I felt very serious and solemn. O, I love to live on the brink of eternity, in my views and meditations! This gives me a sweet, awful, and reverential sense and apprehension of God and divine things, when I see myself as it were, standing before the judgment seat of Christ.

Oct. 22. Uncommonly weaned from the world to-day: my soul delighted to be a stranger and pilgrim on the earth; I felt a disposition in me never to have any thing to do with this world. The character given of some of the ancient people of God, in Heb. xi. 13, was very pleasing to me, "They confessed that they were pilgrims and strangers on the earth," by their daily practice; and Oh that I could always do so! Spent some considerable time in a pleasant grove, in prayer and meditation. Oh it is sweet, to be thus weaned from friends, and from myself, and dead to the present world, that so I may live wholly to and upon the blessed God! Saw myself little, low, and vile in myself. In the afternoon, preached at Bethlehem, from Deut. viii. 2. God helped me to speak to the hearts of dear christians. Blessed be the Lord for this season: I trust they and I shall rejoice on this account, to all eternity. Dear Mr. Bellamy came in, while I was making the first prayer (being returned home from a journey); and after meeting, we walked away together, and spent the evening in sweetly conversing on divine things, and praying together, with sweet and tender love to each other, and retired to rest with our hearts in a serious spiritual frame.

Oct. 26. At West Suffield. Underwent the most dreadful distresses, under a sense of my own unworthiness. It seemed to me, that I deserved rather to be driven out of the place, than to have any body treat me with any kindness, or come to hear me preach. And verily my spirits were so depressed at this time (as at many others), that it was impossible I should treat immortal souls with faithfulness. I could not deal closely and faithfully with them, I felt so infinitely vile in myself. O what dust and ashes I am, to think of preaching the gospel to others! Indeed, I never can be faithful for one moment, but shall certainly "daub with untempered mortar," if God do not grant me special help. In the evening, I went to the meeting-house, and it looked to me near as easy for one to rise out of the grave and preach, as for me. However, God afforded me some life and power, both in prayer and sermon; and was pleased to lift me up, and shew me that he could enable me to preach. O the wonderful goodness of God to so vile a sinner! Returned to my quarters; and enjoyed some sweetness in prayer alone, and mourned that I could not live more to God.

Oct. 27. I spent the forenoon in prayer and meditation; was not a little concerned about preaching in the afternoon; felt exceedingly without strength, and very helpless indeed; and went into the meeting-house, ashamed to see any come to hear such an unspeakably worthless wretch. However, God enabled me to speak with clearness, power, and pungency. But there was some noise and tumult in the assembly, that I did not well like; and I endeavoured to bear public testimony against it with moderation and mildness, through the current of my discourse. In the evening, was enabled to be in some measure thankful, and devoted to God.

CHAPTER IV

From the time of his Examination and Commission as a Missionary, to his entrance on his Mission among the Indians at Kaunaumeek. *

Dec. 11 [1742]. Conversed with a dear friend, to whom I had thought of giving a liberal education, and being at the whole charge of it, that he might be fitted for the gospel ministry. I

* Several entries deleted from this chapter as indicated.

acquainted him with my thoughts in that matter, and so left him to consider of it, till I should see him again. Then I rode to Bethlehem, came to Mr. Bellamy's lodgings, and spent the evening with him in sweet conversation and prayer. We recommended the concern of sending my friend to college to the God of all grace. Blessed be the Lord for this evening's opportunity together.

Lord's day, Dec. 12. I felt, in the morning, as if I had little or no power either to pray or preach; and felt a distressing need of divine help. I went to meeting trembling; but it pleased God to assist me in prayer and sermon. I think my soul scarce ever penetrated so far into the immaterial world, in any one prayer that I ever made, nor were my devotions ever so free from gross conceptions and imaginations framed from beholding material objects. I preached with some sweetness, from Matt. vi. 33. "But seek ye first the kingdom of God," &c.; and in the afternoon, from Rom. xv. 30. "And now I beseech you, brethren," &c. There was much affection in the assembly. This has been a sweet Sabbath to me; and blessed be God, I have reason to think that my religion is become more spiritual, by means of my late inward conflicts. Amen. May I always be willing that God should use his own methods with me!

Dec. 15. Enjoyed something of God to-day, both in secret and in social prayer; but was sensible of much barrenness and defect in duty, as well as my inability to help myself for the time to come, or to perform the work and business I have to do. Afterwards, felt much of the sweetness of religion, and the tenderness of the gospel-temper. I found a dear love to all mankind, and was much afraid lest some motion of anger or resentment should, some time or other, creep into my heart. Had some comforting, soul-refreshing discourse with dear friends, just as we took our leave of each other; and supposed it might be likely we should not meet again till we came to the eternal world. I doubt not, through grace, but that some of us shall have a happy meeting there, and bless God for this season, as well as many others. Amen.

Jan. 14, 1743. My spiritual conflicts to-day were unspeakably dreadful, heavier than the mountains and over-flowing floods. I seemed inclosed, as it were, in hell itself: I was deprived of all sense of God, even of the being of a God; and that was my misery.

I had no awful apprehensions of God as angry. This was distress, the nearest akin to the damned's torments, that I ever endured: their torment, I am sure, will consist much in a privation of God, and consequently of all good. This taught me the absolute dependence of a creature upon God the Creator, for every crumb of happiness it enjoys. Oh, I feel that, if there is no God, though I might live for ever here, and enjoy not only this, but all other worlds, I should be ten thousand times more miserable than a reptile. My soul was in such anguish I could not eat; but felt as I suppose a poor wretch would that is just going to the place of execution. I was almost swallowed up with anguish, when I saw people gathering together, to hear me preach. However, I went in that distress to the house of God, and found not much relief in the first prayer: it seemed as if God would let loose the people upon me to destroy me; nor were the thoughts of death distressing to me, like my own vileness. But afterwards in my discourse from Deut. viii. 2, God was pleased to give me some freedom and enlargement, some power and spirituality; and I spent the evening somewhat comfortably.

Lord's day, Jan. 23. I scarce ever felt myself so unfit to exist as now: saw I was not worthy of a place among the Indians, where I am going, if God permit: thought I should be ashamed to look them in the face, and much more to have any respect shewn me there. Indeed I felt myself banished from the earth, as if all places were too good for such a wretch. I thought I should be ashamed to go among the very savages of Africa; I appeared to myself a creature fit for nothing, neither heaven nor earth.—None know, but those who feel it, what the soul endures that is sensibly shut out from the presence of God: alas! it is more bitter than death.

Feb. 17. In the morning, found myself comfortable, and rested on God in some measure.—Preached this day at a little village belonging to East Hampton; and God was pleased to give me his gracious presence and assistance, so that I spake with freedom, boldness, and some power. In the evening, spent some time with a dear christian friend; and felt serious, as on the brink of eternity. My soul enjoyed sweetness in lively apprehensions of standing before the glorious God: prayed with my dear friend with sweetness, and discoursed with the utmost solemnity. And truly it was a little emblem of heaven itself.—I find my soul is more refined and weaned from a dependence on my frames and spiritual feelings.

Feb. 18. Felt somewhat sweetly most of the day, and found access to the throne of grace. Blessed be the Lord for any intervals of heavenly delight and composure, while I am engaged in the field of battle. Oh, that I might be serious, solemn, and always vigilant, while in an evil world! Had some opportunity alone to-day, and found some freedom in study. O, I long to live to God!

Feb. 19. Was exceeding infirm to-day, greatly troubled with pain in my head and dizziness, scarce able to sit up. However, enjoyed something of God in prayer, and performed some necessary studies. I exceedingly long to die; and yet, through divine goodness, have felt very willing to live, for two or three days past.

Lord's day, Feb. 20. I was perplexed on account of my carelessness; thought I could not be suitably concerned about the important work of the day, and so was restless with my easiness. Was exceeding infirm again today; but the Lord strengthened me, both in the outward and inward man, so that I preached with some life and spirituality, especially in the afternoon, wherein I was enabled to speak closely against selfish religion, that loves Christ for his benefits, but not for himself.

Lord's day, March 13. At noon, I thought it impossible for me to preach, by reason of bodily weakness, and inward deadness. In the first prayer, I was so weak that I could hardly stand; but in the sermon, God strengthened me, so that I spake near an hour and a half with sweet freedom, clearness, and some tender power, from Gen. v. 24. "And Enoch walked with God." I was sweetly assisted to insist on a close walk with God, and to leave this as my parting advice to God's people here, that they should walk with God. May the God of all grace succeed my poor labours in this place!

CHAPTER V

From the Commencement of his Labours at Kaunau-
*meek, to his Ordination.**

April 1, 1743. I rode to Kaunaumeek, near twenty miles from
Stockbridge, where the Indians live with whom I am concerned,
and there lodged on a little heap of straw. I was greatly exercised
with inward trials and distresses all day; and in the evening, my
heart was sunk, and I seemed to have no God to go to. Oh that God
would help me!

The next five days, he was for the most part in a dejected, depressed
state of mind, and sometimes extremely so. He speaks of God's "waves
and billows rolling over his soul"; and of his being ready sometimes
to say, "Surely his mercy is clean gone forever, and he will be favoura-
ble no more"; and says the anguish he endured, was nameless and
inconceivable; but at the same time speaks thus concerning his dis-
tresses, "What God designs by all my distresses, I know not; but this
I know, I deserve them all, and thousands more." He gives an account
of the Indians kindly receiving, and being seriously attentive to his
instructions.

April 7. Appeared to myself exceedingly ignorant, weak, helpless,
unworthy, and altogether unequal to my work. It seemed to me,
that I should never do any service, or have any success among the
Indians. My soul was weary of my life; I longed for death, beyond
measure. When I thought of any godly soul departed; my soul was
ready to envy him his privilege, thinking, "O when will my turn
come! must it be years first!" But I know these ardent desires, at
this and other times, rose partly for want of resignation to God under
all miseries; and so were but impatience. Towards night, I had the
exercise of faith in prayer, and some assistance in writing. Oh that
God would keep me near him!

April 8. Was exceedingly pressed under a sense of my pride,

* Several entries deleted from this chapter as indicated.

selfishness, bitterness, and party spirit, in times past, while I attempted to promote the cause of God. Its vile nature and dreadful consequences appeared in such odious colours to me, that my very heart was pained. I saw how poor souls stumbled over it into everlasting destruction, that I was constrained to make that prayer in the bitterness of my soul, "O Lord, deliver me from blood-guiltiness." I saw my desert of hell on this account. My soul was full of inward anguish and shame before God, that I had spent so much time in conversation tending only to promote a party spirit. I saw that I had not suitably prized mortification, self-denial, resignation under all adversities, meekness, love, candour, and holiness of heart and life: and this day was almost wholly spent in such bitter, and soul-afflicting reflections on my past frames and conduct. Of late, I have thought much of having the kingdom of Christ advanced in the world; but now I saw I had enough to do within myself. The Lord be merciful to me a sinner, and wash my soul!

April 9. Remained much in the same state as yesterday; excepting that the sense of my vileness was not so quick and acute.

Lord's day, April 10. Rose early in the morning, and walked out and spent a considerable time in the woods, in prayer and meditation. Preached to the Indians, both forenoon and afternoon. They behaved soberly in general: two or three in particular appeared under some religious concern; with whom I discoursed privately; and one told me, "that her heart had ended, ever since she had heard me preach first."

April 16. Still in the depths of distress. In the afternoon, preached to my people; but was more discouraged with them than before; feared that nothing would ever be done for them to any happy effect. I retired, and poured out my soul to God for mercy; but without any sensible relief. Soon after came an Irishman and a Dutchman, with a design, as they said, to hear me preach the next day; but none can tell how I felt, to hear their profane talk. O I longed that some dear christian knew my distress. I got into a kind of hovel, and there groaned out my complaint to God; and withal felt more sensible gratitude and thankfulness to God, that he had made me to differ from these men, as I knew through grace he had.

Lord's day, April 17. In the morning, was again distressed as soon as I awaked, hearing much talk about the world, and the things of it. I perceived that the men were in some measure afraid of me; and I discoursed about sanctifying the Sabbath, if possible to solemnize their minds; but when they were at a little distance, they again talked freely about secular affairs. O I thought what a hell it would be, to live with such men to eternity! The Lord gave me some assistance in preaching, all day, and some resignation, and a small degree of comfort in prayer, at night.

Kaunaumeek, April 30, 1743

DEAR BROTHER,

I should tell you, "I long to see you," but my own experience has taught me, that there is no happiness, and plenary satisfaction to be enjoyed in earthly friends, though ever so near and dear, or in any other enjoyment, that is not God himself. Therefore, if the God of all grace be pleased graciously to afford us each his presence and grace, that we may perform the work, and endure the trials he calls us to, in a most distressing tiresome wilderness, till we arrive at our journey's end: the local distance, at which we are held from each other at present is a matter of no great moment or importance to either of us. But alas! the presence of God is what I want. I live in the most lonely melancholy desert, about eighteen miles from Albany; for it was not thought best that I should go to Delaware River, as I believe I hinted to you in a letter from New-York. I board with a poor Scotchman: his wife can talk scarce any English. My diet consists mostly of hasty-pudding, boiled corn, and bread baked in the ashes, and sometimes a little meat and butter. My lodging is a little heap of straw, laid upon some boards, a little way from the ground; for it is a log room, without any floor, that I lodge in. My work is exceedingly hard and difficult: I travel on foot a mile and a half, the worst of ways, almost daily, and back again; for I live so far from my Indians. I have not seen an English person this month. These, and many other circumstances, equally uncomfortable, attend me; and yet my spiritual conflicts and distresses, so far exceed all these, that I scarce think of them, or hardly observe that I am not entertained in the most sumptuous manner. The Lord grant that I may learn to "endure hardness, as a good soldier of Jesus Christ!" As to my success here, I cannot say much as yet. The

Indians seem generally kind, and well disposed towards me, are mostly very attentive to my instructions, and seem willing to be taught further. Two or three, I hope, are under some convictions; but there seems to be little of the special workings of the divine Spirit among them yet; which gives me many a heart-sinking hour. Sometimes I hope that God has abundant blessings in store for them and me; but at other times I am so overwhelmed with distress, that I cannot see how his dealings with me are consistent with covenant love and faithfulness: and I say, "Surely his tender mercies are clean gone forever." But however, I see that I needed all this chastisement already: "It is good for me," that I have endured these trials, and have hitherto little or no apparent success. Do not be discouraged by my distresses. I was under great distress, at Mr. Pomroy's, when I saw you last; but "God has been with me of a truth," since that: he helped me sometimes sweetly at Long-Island, and elsewhere. But let us always remember, that we must through much tribulation, enter into God's eternal kingdom of rest and peace. The righteous are scarcely saved: it is an infinite wonder that we have well grounded hopes of being saved at all. For my part, I feel the most vile of any creature living; and I am sure sometimes, there is not such another existing on this side hell. Now all you can do for me, is, to pray incessantly, that God would make me humble, holy, resigned, and heavenly minded, by all my trials. "Be strong in the Lord, and in the power of his might." Let us run, wrestle, and fight, that we may win the prize, and obtain that complete happiness, to be "holy, as God is holy." So wishing, and praying that you may advance in learning and grace, and be fit for special service for God, I remain your affectionate brother,

DAVID BRAINERD.

May 18. My circumstances are such, that I have no comfort of any kind, but what I have in God. I live in the most lonesome wilderness; have but one single person to converse with that can speak English. Most of the talk I hear, is either Highland Scotch, or Indian. I have no fellow-christian to whom I may unbosom myself, or lay open my spiritual sorrows; with whom I may take sweet counsel in conversation about heavenly things, and join in social prayer. I live poorly with regard to the comforts of life: most of my diet consists of boiled corn, hasty-pudding, &c. I lodge on a bundle of straw, my labour is hard and extremely difficult, and I have little appearance of success, to comfort me. The Indians have no land to live on, but what the Dutch people lay claim to; and these threaten to drive them off. They have no regard to the souls of the poor Indians; and by what I can learn, they hate me because I come to preach to them. But that which makes all my difficulties grievous to be borne, is, that God hides his face from me.

July 2. [Edward's note] My soul is, and has for a long time been in a piteous condition, wading through a series of sorrows, of various kinds. I have been so crushed down sometimes with a sense of my meanness and infinite unworthiness, that I have been ashamed that any, even the meanest of my fellow-creatures, should so much as spend a thought about me; and have wished sometimes, while travelling among the thick brakes, to drop, as one of them, into everlasting oblivion. In this case, sometimes, I have almost resolved never again to see any of my acquaintance: and really thought, I could not do it and hold up my face; and have longed for the remotest region, for a retreat from all my friends, that I might not be seen or heard of any more. Sometimes the consideration of my ignorance has been a means of my great distress and anxiety. And especially my soul has been in anguish with fear, shame, and guilt, that ever I had preached, or had any thought that way.—Sometimes my soul has been in distress on feeling some particular corruptions rise and swell like a mighty torrent, with present violence; having, at the same time, ten thousand former sins and follies presented to view, in all their blackness and aggravations.—And these, while destitute of most of the conveniences of life, and I may say, of all the pleasures of it; without a friend to communicate any of my sorrows to, and sometimes without any place of retirement, where I may unburden my soul before God, which has greatly contributed to my distress.—Of late, more especially, my great difficulty has been a sort of carelessness, a kind of regardless temper of mind, whence I have been disposed to indolence and trifling: and this temper of mind has constantly been attended with guilt and shame; so that sometimes I have been in a kind of horror, to find myself so unlike the blessed God. I have thought I grew worse under all my trials; and nothing has cut and wounded my soul more than this. O, if I am one of God's chosen, as I trust through infinite grace I am, I find of a truth, that the righteous are scarcely saved.

It is apparent, that one main occasion of that distressing gloominess of mind which he was so much exercised with at Kaunaumeek, was reflection on his past errors and misguided zeal at college, in the beginning of the late religious commotions. And therefore he repeated his endeavours this year for reconciliation with the governors of the college, whom he had at that time offended. Although he had been at New-Haven, in June, this year, and attempted a reconciliation, as mentioned already; yet, in the beginning of July, he made another journey thither, and renewed his attempt, but still in vain.

Although he was much dejected, most of the time of which I am now speaking; yet he had many intermissions of his melancholy, and some seasons of comfort, sweet tranquillity and resignation of mind, and frequent special assistance in public services, as appear in his diary. The manner of his relief from his sorrow, once in particular, is worthy to be mentioned in his own words.

Aug. 4. Was enabled to pray much, through the whole day; and through divine goodness found some intenseness of soul in the duty, as I used to do, and some ability to persevere in my supplications. I had some apprehensions of divine things, which afforded me courage and resolution. It is good, I find, to persevere in attempts to pray, if I cannot pray with perseverance, i.e. continue long in my addresses to the divine Being. I have generally found, that the more I do in secret prayer, the more I have delighted to do, and have enjoyed more of a spirit of prayer: and frequently have found the contrary, when with journeying or otherwise I have been much deprived of retirement. A seasonable, steady performance of SECRET DUTIES IN THEIR PROPER HOURS, and a CAREFUL IMPROVEMENT OF ALL TIME, filling up every hour with some profitable labour, either of heart, head, or hands, are excellent means of spiritual peace and boldness before God.—Christ, indeed, is our peace, and by him we have boldness of access to God; but a good conscience, void of offence, is an excellent preparation for an approach into the divine presence. There is a difference between self-confidence or a self-righteous pleasing of ourselves—as with our own duties, attainments, and spiritual enjoyments—of which good men are sometimes guilty, and that holy confidence arising from the testimony of a good conscience, which good Hezekiah had, when he says, "Remember, O Lord, I beseech thee, how I have walked before thee in truth, and with a perfect heart." Then, says the holy psalmist, shall I not be ashamed when I have respect to all thy commandments. Filling up our time with and for God, is the way to rise up and lie down in peace.

Sept. 13. Rode to New-Haven. Was sometimes dejected; not in the sweetest frame. Lodged at ****. Had some profitable christian conversation. I find, though my inward trials were great, and a life of solitude gives them greater advantage to settle, and penetrate to the very inmost recesses of the soul; yet it is better to be alone, than incumbered with noise and tumult. I find it very difficult maintaining any sense of divine things, while removing from place to place, diverted with new objects, and filled with care and business. A settled steady business is best adapted to a life of strict religion.

Sept. 14. This day I ought to have taken my degree; but God sees fit to deny it me. And though I was greatly afraid of being overwhelmed with perplexity and confusion, when I should see my class-mates take theirs; yet, at the very time, God enabled me with calmness and resignation to say, "the will of the Lord be done." Indeed, through divine goodness, I have scarcely felt my mind so calm, sedate, and comfortable for some time. I have long feared this season, and expected my humility, meekness, patience and resignation would be much tried; but found much more pleasure and divine comfort, than I expected. Felt spiritually serious, tender and affectionate in private prayer with a dear christian friend to-day.

Sept. 15. Had some satisfaction in hearing the ministers discourse. It is always a comfort to me, to hear religious and spiritual conversation. Oh that ministers and people were more spiritual and devoted to God!—Towards night, with the advice of christian friends, I offered the following reflections in writing, to the rector and trustees of the college—which are for substance the same that I had freely offered to the rector before, and intreated him to accept —that if possible I might cut off all occasion of offence, from those who seek occasion. What I offered, is as follows:

Whereas I have said before several persons, concerning Mr. Whittelsey, one of the tutors of Yale College, that I did not believe he had any more grace than the chair I then leaned upon; I humbly confess, that herein I have sinned against God, and acted contrary to the rules of his word, and have injured Mr. Whittelsey. I had no right to make thus free with his character; and had no just reason to say as I did concerning him. My fault herein was the more aggravated, in that I said this concerning one who was so much my superiour, and one whom I was obliged to treat with special respect and honour, by reason of the relation I stood in to him in the college. Such a manner of behaviour, I confess did not become a christian; it was taking too much upon me, and did not savour of that humble respect, which I ought to have expressed towards Mr. Whittelsey. I have long since been convinced of the falseness of those apprehensions, by which I then justified such a conduct. I have often reflected on this act with grief; I hope, on account of the sin of it: and am willing to lie low, and be abased before God and man for it. I humbly ask the forgiveness of the governors of the college, and of the whole society; but of Mr. Whittelsey in particular. And whereas I have been accused by one person of saying concerning the reverend rector of Yale College, that I wondered he did not expect to drop down dead for fining the scholars that followed Mr. Tennent to Milford; I seriously profess, that I do not remember my saying any thing to this purpose. But if I did, which I am not certain I did not, I utterly condemn it, and detest all such kind of behaviour; and especially in an under-graduate towards the rector. And I now appear to judge and condemn myself for going once to the separate meeting in New-Haven, a little before I was expelled, though the rector had refused to give me leave. For this I humbly ask the rector's forgiveness. And whether the governors of the college shall ever see cause to remove the academical censure I lie under, or no, or to admit me to the privileges I desire; yet I am willing to appear, if they think fit, openly to own, and to humble myself for those things I have herein confessed.—

God has made me willing to do any thing, that I can do, consistent with truth, for the sake of peace, and that I might not be a stumbling block to others. For this reason I can cheerfully forego, and give up what I verily believe, after the most mature and impartial search is my right, in some instances. God has given me the disposition, that, if a man has done me an hundred injuries, and I (though ever so much provoked to it) have done him only one, I feel disposed, and heartily willing humbly to confess my fault to him, and on my knees to ask forgiveness of him; though at the same time he should justify himself in all the injuries he has done me, and should only make use of my humble confession to blacken my character the more, and represent me as the only person guilty; yea, though he should as it were insult me, and say, "he knew all this before, and that I was making work for repentance." Though what I said concerning Mr. Whittelsey was only spoken in private, to a friend or two; and being partly overheard, was related to the rector, and by him extorted from my friends; yet, seeing it was divulged and made public, I was willing to confess my fault therein publicly. But I trust God will plead my cause.

I was witness to the very christian spirit which Brainerd shewed at that time; being then at New-Haven, and one whom he thought fit to consult on that occasion. This was my first opportunity of a personal acquaintance with him. There truly appeared in him a great degree of calmness and humility; without the least appearance of rising of spirit for any ill treatment which he supposed he had suffered or the least backwardness to abase himself before them who, as he thought, had wronged him. What he did was without any objection or appearance of reluctance, even in private to his friends, to whom he freely opened himself. Earnest application was made on his behalf to the authority of the college, that he might have his degree then given him; and particularly by the Rev. Mr. Burr of Newark, one of the correspondents of the honourable society in Scotland; he being sent from New-Jersey to New-Haven, by the rest of the commissioners, for that end; and many arguments were used, but without success. Indeed, the Governors of the College were so far satisfied with the reflections which Brainerd had made on himself, that they appeared willing to admit him again into college; but not to give him his degree, till he should have remained there at least twelve-months, which being contrary to what the Correspondents, to whom he was now engaged, had declared to be their mind, he did not consent to it. He desired his degree, as he thought it would tend to his being more extensively useful; but still when he was denied it, he manifested no disappointment or resentment. The next day he went to Derby; then to Southbury, where he spent the Sabbath: and speaks of some spiritual comfort; but complains much of unfixedness, and wanderings of mind in religion.

Oct. 4. This day rode home to my own house and people. The poor Indians appeared very glad of my return. Found my house and all things in safety. I presently fell on my knees, and blessed

God for my safe return, after a long and tedious journey, and a season of sickness in several places where I had been, and after I had been ill myself. God has renewed his kindness to me, in preserving me one journey more. I have taken many considerable journeys since this time last year, and yet God has never suffered one of my bones to be broken, or any distressing calamity to befall me, excepting the ill turn I had in my last journey. I have been often exposed to cold and hunger in the wilderness, where the comforts to life were not to be had; have frequently been lost in the woods; and sometimes obliged to ride much of the night; and once lay out in the woods all night; yet, blessed be God, he has preserved me!

Nov. 3. Spent this day in secret fasting and prayer, from morning till night. Early in the morning, I had some small degree of assistance in prayer. Afterwards, read the story of Elijah the prophet, 1 Kings xvii. xviii. and xix. chapters, and also 2 Kings, ii. and iv. chapters. My soul was much moved, observing the faith, zeal, and power of that holy man; how he wrestled with God in prayer, &c. My soul then cried with Elisha, "Where is the Lord God of Elijah!" O I longed for more faith! My soul breathed after God, and pleaded with him, that a "double portion of that spirit," which was given to Elijah, might "rest on me." And that which was divinely refreshing and strengthening to my soul, was, I saw that God is the same that he was in the days of Elijah.—Was enabled to wrestle with God by prayer, in a more affectionate, fervent, humble, intense, and importunate manner, than I have for many months past. Nothing seemed too hard for God to perform; nothing too great for me to hope for from him. I had for many months entirely lost all hopes of being made instrumental of doing any special service for God in the world; it has appeared entirely impossible, that one so vile should be thus employed for God. But at this time God was pleased to revive this hope. Afterwards read from the iii. chapter of Exodus to the xx. and saw more of the glory and majesty of God discovered in those chapters, than ever I had seen before; frequently in the mean time falling on my knees, and crying to God for the faith of Moses, and for a manifestation of the divine glory.— Especially the iii. and iv. and part of the xiv. and xv. chapters were unspeakably sweet to my soul: my soul blessed God, that he had shewn himself so gracious to his servants of old. The xv. chapter seemed to be the very language which my soul uttered to God in the season of my first spiritual comfort, when I had just got through the Red Sea, by a way that I had no expectation of. O how my soul then rejoiced in God! And now those things came fresh and lively to my mind; now my soul blessed God afresh that he had opened that unthought-of way to deliver me from the fear of the Egyptians, when I almost despaired of life.—Afterwards read the story of Abraham's pilgrimage in the land of Canaan. My soul was melted, in observing his faith, how he leaned on God; how he communed with God; and what a stranger he was here in the world. After that, read the story of Joseph's sufferings, and God's goodness to him: blessed God for these examples of faith and patience. My soul was ardent in prayer, was enabled to wrestle ardently for myself, for christian friends, and for the church of God. And felt more desire to see the power of God in the conversion of souls, than I have done for a long season. Blessed be God for this season of fasting and prayer!—May his goodness always abide with me, and draw my soul to him!

Nov. 29. Began to study the Indian tongue, with Mr. Sergeant at Stockbridge. Was perplexed for want of more retirement. I love to live alone in my own little cottage, where I can spend much time in prayer, &c.

Nov. 30. Pursued my study of Indian: but was very weak and disordered in body, and was troubled in mind at the barrenness of the day, that I had done so little for God. I had some enlargement in prayer at night. O a barn, or stable, hedge, or any other place, is truly desirable, if God is there! Sometimes, of late, my hopes of Zion's prosperity are more raised, than they were in the summer. My soul seems to confide in God that he will yet "shew forth his salvation" to his people, and make Zion "the joy of the whole earth." O how excellent is the loving-kindness of the Lord. My soul sometimes inwardly exults at the lively thoughts of what God has already done for his church, and what "mine eyes have seen of the salvation of God." It is sweet, to hear nothing but spiritual discourse from God's children; and sinners "enquiring the way to Zion," saying, "What shall we do?" &c. Oh that I may see more of this blessed work!

Dec. 27. Had a small degree of warmth in secret prayer, in the evening; but alas! had but little spiritual life, and consequently but little comfort. Oh, the pressure of a body of death!

This day he wrote to his brother John, at Yale College, the following letter.

Kaunaumeek, Dec. 27, 1743.

DEAR BROTHER,

I long to see you, and to know how you fare in your journey through a world of inexpressible sorrow; where we are compassed about with "vanity, confusion, and vexation of spirit." I am more weary of life, I think, than ever I was. The whole world appears to me like a huge vacuum, a vast empty space, whence nothing desirable, or at least satisfactory, can possibly be derived; and I long daily to die more and more to it, even though I obtain not that comfort from spiritual things which I earnestly desire. Worldly pleasures, such as flow from greatness, riches, honors, and sensual gratifications, are infinitely worse than none. May the Lord deliver us more and more from these vanities. I have spent most of the fall and winter hitherto in a very weak state of body; and sometimes under pressing inward trials and spiritual conflicts; but "having obtained help from God, I continue to this day"; and am now somewhat better in health, than I was sometime ago. I find nothing more conducive to a life of Christianity, than a diligent, industrious, and faithful improvement of precious time. Let us then faithfully perform that business, which is allotted to us by divine Providence, to the utmost of our bodily strength, and mental vigour. Why should we sink, and grow discouraged, with any particular trials and perplexities, which we are called to encounter in the world? Death and Eternity are just before us; a few tossing billows more will waft us into the world of spirits, and we hope, through infinite grace, into endless pleasures, and uninterrupted rest and peace. Let us then "run, with patience, the race set before us," Heb. xii. 1, 2. And, Oh, that we could depend more upon the living God, and less upon our own wisdom and strength!—Dear brother, may the God of all grace comfort your heart, and succeed your studies, and make you an instrument of good to his people in your day. This is the constant prayer of

Your affectionate brother,
DAVID BRAINERD.

Lord's day, Jan. 1, 1744. In the morning, had some small degree of assistance in prayer. Saw myself so vile and unworthy, that I could not look my people in the face, when I came to preach. O my meanness, folly, ignorance, and inward pollution!—In the evening, had a little assistance in prayer, so that the duty was delightful, rather than burdensome. Reflected on the goodness of God to me in the past year, &c. Of a truth God has been kind and gracious to me, though he has caused me to pass through many sorrows; he has provided for me bountifully, so that I have been enabled, in about fifteen months past, to bestow to charitable uses about an hundred pounds New-England money, that I can now remember. Blessed be the Lord, that has so far used me as his steward, to distribute a portion of his goods. May I always remember, that all I have comes from God. Blessed be the Lord, that has carried me through all the toils, fatigues, and hardships of the year past, as well as the spiritual sorrows and conflicts that have attended it. O that I could begin this year with God, and spend the whole of it to his glory, either in life or death!

Jan. 2. Had some affecting sense of my own impotency and spiritual weakness.—It is nothing but the power of God that keeps me from all manner of wickedness. I see I am nothing, and can do nothing without help from above. Oh, for divine grace! In the evening had some ardour of soul in prayer, and longing desires to have God for my guide and safeguard at all times.

The following Letter to his brother Israel, at Haddam, was written this day.

Kaunaumeek, Jan. 2, 1744.

MY DEAR BROTHER,

There is but one thing that deserves our highest care and most ardent desires; and that is, that we may answer the great end for which we were made, viz. to glorify that God, who has given us our being and all our comforts, and do all the good we possibly can to our fellow-men, while we live in the world. Verily life is not worth the having, if it be not improved for this noble end and purpose. Yet, alas, how little is this thought of among mankind! Most men seem to live to themselves without much regard to the glory of God, or the good of their fellow creatures. They earnestly desire, and eagerly pursue after the riches, the honours, and the pleasures of life, as if they really supposed, that wealth or greatness, or merriment, could make their immortal souls happy. But alas! what false and delusive dreams are these! And how miserable will those erelong be who are not awaked out of them, to see, that all their happiness consists in living to God, and becoming "holy, as he is holy"! Oh, may you never fall into the tempers and vanities, the sensuality and folly of the present world! You are by divine Providence, left as it were alone in a wide world, to act for yourself: be sure then to remember, that it is a world of temptation. You have no earthly parents to be the means of forming your youth to piety and virtue, by their pious examples, and seasonable counsels; let this then excite you with greater diligence and fervency to look up to the Father of mercies for grace and assistance against all the vanities of the world. If you would glorify God, or answer his just expectations from you, and make your own soul happy in this and the coming world, observe these few directions; though not from a father, yet from a brother who is touched with a tender concern for your present and future happiness.

First; Resolve upon, and daily endeavour to practise a life of seriousness and strict sobriety. The wise man will tell you the great advantage of such a life, Eccl. vii. 3. Think of the life of Christ; and when you can find that he was pleased with jesting and vain merriment, then you may indulge it in yourself.

Again; be careful to make a good improvement of precious time. When you cease from labour, fill up your time in reading, meditation, and prayer; and while your hands are labouring, let your heart be employed, as much as possible, in divine thoughts.

Further; Take heed that you faithfully perform the business which you have to do in the world, from a regard to the commands of God; and not from an ambitious desire of being esteemed better than others. We should always look upon ourselves as God's servants, placed in God's world, to do his work; and accordingly labour faithfully for him; not with a design to grow rich and great, but to glorify God, and to do all the good we possibly can.

Again; Never expect any satisfaction or happiness from the world. If you hope for happiness in the world, hope for it from God, and not from the world. Do not think you shall be more happy if you live to such or such a state of life, if you live to be yourself, to be settled in the world, or if you should gain an estate in it: but look upon it that you shall then be happy, when you can be constantly employed for God, and not for yourself; and desire to live in this world, not to do and suffer what God allots to you. When you can be of the spirit and temper of angels, who are willing to come down into this lower world, to perform what God commands them, though their desires are heavenly, and not in the least set on earthly things, then you will be of that temper which you ought to have, Col. iii. 2.

Once more; Never think that you can live to God by your own power or strength; but always look to, and rely on him for assistance, yea for all strength and grace. There is no greater truth than this, that "we can do nothing of ourselves" (John xv. 5 and 2 Cor. iii. 5); yet nothing but our own experience can effectually teach it us. Indeed, we are a long time in learning, that all our strength and salvation, is in God. This is a life which I think no unconverted man can possibly live; and yet it is a life which every godly soul is pressing after, in some good measure. Let it then be your great concern, thus to devote yourself and your all to God.

I long to see you, that I may say much more to you than I now can, for your benefit and welfare; but I desire to commit you to, and leave you with, the Father of mercies, and God of all grace; praying that you may be directed safely through an evil world, to God's heavenly kingdom.

I am your affectionate loving brother,
DAVID BRAINERD.

Jan. 3. Was employed much of the day in writing; and spent some time in other necessary employment. But my time passes away so swiftly, that I am astonished when I reflect on it, and see how little I do. My state of solitude does not make the hours hang heavy upon my hands. O what reason of thankfulness have I on account of this retirement! I find, that I do not, and it seems I cannot lead a christian life, when I am abroad, and cannot spend time in devotion, christian conversation, and serious meditation, as I should do. Those weeks that I am obliged now to be from home, in order to learn the Indian tongue, are mostly spent in perplexity and barrenness, without much sweet relish of divine things; and I feel myself a stranger at the throne of grace, for want of more frequent and continued retirement. When I return home, and give myself to meditation, prayer, and fasting, a new scene opens to my mind, and my soul longs for mortification, self-denial, humility, and divorcement from all the things of the world. This evening, my heart was somewhat warm and fervent in prayer and meditation, so that I was loth to indulge sleep. Continued in those duties till about midnight.

Jan. 24. Near noon rode over to Canaan. In the evening, I was unexpectedly visited by a considerable number of people, with whom I was enabled to converse profitably on divine things; took pains to describe the difference between a regular and irregular SELF-LOVE; the one consisting with a supreme love to God, but the other not; the former uniting God's glory, and the soul's happiness, that they become one common interest, but the latter, disjoining and separating God's glory and man's happiness, seeking the latter with a neglect of the former. Illustrated this by that genuine love that is founded between the sexes; which is diverse from that which is wrought up towards a person only by rational argument, or hope of self-interest. Love is a pleasing passion, it affords pleasure to the mind where it is; but yet, genuine love is not, nor can be placed on any object with that design of pleasure itself.

Feb. 7. Was much engaged in some sweet meditations on the powers and affections of the godly soul in the pursuit of their beloved object; wrote something of the native language of spiritual sensation, in its soft and tender whispers; declaring, that it now "feels and tastes, that the Lord is gracious; that he is the supreme good, the only soul-satisfying happiness; that he is a complete, sufficient, and almighty portion; saying,

"Whom have I in Heaven but thee? and there is none upon earth that I desire beside this blessed portion. O, I feel that it is heaven to please him, and to be just what he would have me to be! Oh that my soul were holy, as he is holy! Oh that it were pure, even as Christ is pure; and perfect as my Father in heaven is perfect! These I feel are the sweetest commands in God's book, comprising all others. And shall I break them! must I break them! am I under the necessity of it as long as I live in the world! O my soul, wo, wo is me, that I am a sinner, because I now necessarily grieve and offend this blessed God, who is infinite in goodness and grace! O methinks if he would punish me for my sins, it would not wound my heart so deep to offend him: but though I sin continually, yet he continually repeats his kindness to me! O methinks I could bear any sufferings; but how can I bear to grieve and dishonour this blessed God! How shall I yield ten thousand times more honour to him? What shall I do to glorify and worship this best of beings? Oh that I could consecrate myself, soul and body, to his service forever! Oh that I could give up myself to him, so as never more to attempt to be my own, or to have any will or affections that are not perfectly conformed to him! But, alas, alas! I find I cannot be thus entirely devoted to God; I cannot live, and not sin. O ye angels, do ye glorify him incessantly; and if possible, prostrate yourselves lower before the blessed King of heaven! I long to bear a part with you; and, if it were possible, to help you. O when we have done all that we can, to all eternity, we shall not be able to offer the ten thousandth part of the homage which the glorious God deserves!

Felt something spiritual, devout, resigned, and mortified to the world, much of the day; and especially towards and in the evening. Blessed be God, that he enables me to love him for himself.

Feb. 8. Was in a comfortable frame of soul, most of the day; though sensible of, and restless under, spiritual barrenness. I find that both mind and body are quickly tired with intenseness and fervour in the things of God. Oh that I could be as incessant as angels in devotion and spiritual fervour.

Feb. 9. Observed this day as a day of fasting and prayer, intreating of God to bestow upon me his blessing and grace; especially to enable me to live a life of mortification to the world, as well as of resignation and patience. Enjoyed some realizing sense of divine power and goodness in prayer, several times; and was enabled to roll the burden of myself, and friends, and Zion, upon the goodness and grace of God; but, in the general, was more dry and barren than I have usually been of late, upon such occasions.

Feb. 10. Was exceedingly oppressed, most of the day, with shame, grief, and fear, under a sense of my past folly, as well as present barrenness and coldness. When God sets before me my past misconduct, especially any instances of misguided zeal, it sinks my soul into shame and confusion, makes me afraid of a shaking leaf. My fear is such as the prophet Jeremy complains of, Jer. xx. 10. I have no confidence to hold up my face, even before my fellow worms; but only when my soul confides in God, and I find the sweet temper of Christ, the spirit of humility, solemnity and mortification, and resignation, alive in my soul. But, in the evening, was unexpectedly refreshed in pouring out my complaint to God; my shame and fear was turned into a sweet composure and acquiescence in God.

March 10. In the morning, felt exceeding dead to the world, and all its enjoyments. I thought I was ready and willing to give up life and all its comforts, as soon as called to it; and yet then had as much comfort of life as almost ever I had. Life itself now appeared but an empty bubble; the riches, honours, and common enjoyments of life appeared extremely tasteless. I longed to be perpetually and entirely crucified to all things here below, by the cross of Christ. My soul was sweetly resigned to God's disposal of me, in every regard; and I saw that nothing had happened but what was best for me. I confided in God, that he would never leave me, though I should "walk through the valley of the shadow of death." It was then my meat and drink to be holy, to live to the Lord, and die to the Lord. And I thought that I then enjoyed such a heaven, as far exceeded the most sublime conceptions of an unregenerate soul; and even unspeakably beyond what I myself could conceive of at another time. I did not wonder that Peter said, "Lord, it is good to be here," when thus refreshed with divine glories. My soul was full of love and tenderness in the duty of intercession; especially felt a most sweet affection to some precious godly ministers, of my acquaintance. Prayed earnestly for dear christians, and for those I have reason to fear are my enemies; and could not have spoken a word of bitterness, or entertained a bitter thought, against the vilest man living. Had a sense of my own great unworthiness. My soul seemed to breathe forth love and praise to God afresh, when I thought he would let his children love and receive me as one of their brethren and fellow citizens. When I thought of their treating me in that manner, I longed to lie at their feet; and could think of no way to express the sincerity and simplicity of my love and esteem of them, as being much better than myself. Towards night, was very sorrowful; seemed to myself the worst creature living; and could not pray, nor meditate, nor think of holding up my face before the world.—Was a little relieved in prayer, in the evening; but longed to get on my knees, and ask forgiveness of every body that ever had seen any thing amiss in my past conduct, especially in my religious zeal. Was afterwards much perplexed, so that I could not sleep quietly.

March 12. In the morning, was in a devout, tender, and loving frame of mind; and was enabled to cry to God, I hope, with a child-like spirit, with importunity, resignation, and composure of mind. My spirit was full of quietness, and love to mankind; and longed that peace should reign on the earth; was grieved at the very thoughts of a fiery, angry, and intemperate zeal in religion; mourned over past follies in that regard; and confided in God for strength and grace sufficient for my future work and trials. Spent the day mainly in labour, making preparation for my intended journey.

June 11. This day the Presbytery met together at Newark, in order to my ordination. Was very weak and disordered in body; yet endeavoured to repose my confidence in God. Spent most of the day alone; especially in the forenoon. At three in the afternoon preached my probation sermon, from Acts xxvi. 17, 18. Delivering thee from the people, and from the Gentiles, &c. being a text given me for that end. Felt not well either in body or mind; however, God carried me through comfortably. Afterwards, passed an examination before the Presbytery. Was much tired, and my mind burdened with the greatness of that charge I was in the most solemn manner about to take upon me: my mind was so pressed with the weight of the work incumbent upon me, that I could not sleep this night, though very weary and in great need of rest.

June 12. Was this morning further examined, respecting my experimental acquaintance with christianity. At ten o'clock my ordination was attended; the sermon preached by the Rev. Mr. Pemberton. At this time I was affected with a sense of the important trust committed to me; yet was composed, and solemn, without distraction; and I hope that then, as many times before, I gave myself up to God, to be for him, and not for another. Oh that I might always be engaged in the service of God, and duly remember the solemn charge I have received, in the presence of God, angels, and men. Amen. May I be assisted of God for this purpose.—Towards night, rode to Elizabeth-Town.

CHAPTER VI

*From his Ordination, to the commencement of his Labours at Crossweeksung.**

June 25 [1744.] Was somewhat better in health than of late; and was able to spend a considerable part of the day in prayer and close study. Had more freedom and fervency in prayer than usual of late; especially longed for the presence of God in my work, and that the poor Heathen might be converted. And in evening prayer my faith and hope in God were much raised. To an eye of reason every thing that respects the conversion of the Heathen is as dark as midnight; and yet I cannot but hope in God for the accomplishment of something glorious among them. My soul longed much for the advancement of the Redeemer's kingdom on earth. Was very fearful lest I should admit some vain thought, and so lose the sense I then had of divine things. Oh for an abiding heavenly temper!

June 26. In the morning, my desires seemed to rise, and ascend up freely to God. Was busy most of the day in translating prayers into the language of the Delaware Indians; met with great difficulty, because my interpreter was altogether unacquainted with

* Several entries deleted from this chapter as indicated.

the business. But though I was much discouraged with the extreme difficulty of that work, yet God supported me; and especially in the evening, gave me sweet refreshment. In prayer my soul was enlarged, and my faith drawn into sensible exercise; was enabled to cry to God for my poor Indians; and though the work of their conversion appeared impossible with man, yet with God I saw all things were possible. My faith was much strengthened, by observing the wonderful assistance God afforded his servants Nehemiah and Ezra, in reforming his people, and re-establishing his ancient church. I was much assisted in prayer for my dear christian friends, and for others whom I apprehended to be christless; but was more especially concerned for the poor Heathen, and those of my own charge: was enabled to be instant in prayer for them; and hoped that God would bow the heavens and come down for their salvation. It seemed to me, that there could be no impediment sufficient to obstruct that glorious work, seeing the living God, as I strongly hoped, was engaged for it. I continued in a solemn frame, lifting up my heart to God for assistance and grace, that I might be more mortified to this present world, that my whole soul might be taken up continually in concern for the advancement of Christ's kingdom. Earnestly desired that God would purge me more, that I might be a chosen vessel to bear his name among the Heathens. Continued in this frame till I fell asleep.

June 27. Felt something of the same solemn concern, and spirit of prayer, which I enjoyed last night, soon after I rose in the morning. In the afternoon, rode several miles to see if I could procure any lands for the poor Indians, that they might live together, and be under better advantages for instruction.—While I was riding, had a deep sense of the greatness and difficulty of my work; and my soul seemed to rely wholly upon God for success, in the diligent and faithful use of means. Saw, with the greatest certainty, that the arm of the Lord must be revealed, for the help of these poor Heathen, if ever they were delivered from the bondage of the powers of darkness. Spent most of the time, while riding, in lifting up my heart for grace and assistance.

June 28. Spent the morning in reading several parts of the holy scripture, and in fervent prayer for my Indians, that God would set up his kingdom among them, and bring them into his church. About nine, I withdrew to my usual place of retirement in the woods; and there again enjoyed some assistance in prayer. My great concern was for the conversion of the Heathen to God; and the Lord helped me to plead with him for it. Towards noon, rode up to the Indians, in order to preach to them; and while going, my heart went up to God in prayer for them; could freely tell God, he knew that the cause in which I was engaged was not mine; but that it was his own cause, and that it would be for his own glory to convert the poor Indians: and blessed be God, I felt no desire of their conversion, that I might receive honour from the world, as being the instrument of it. Had some freedom in speaking to the Indians.

Lord's day, July 1. In the morning, was perplexed with wandering vain thoughts; was much grieved, judged and condemned myself before God. O how miserable did I feel, because I could not live to God! At ten, rode away with a heavy heart, to preach to my Indians. Upon the road I attempted to lift up my heart to God; but was infested with an unsettled wandering frame of mind; and was exceeding restless and perplexed, and filled with shame and confusion before God. I seemed to myself to be "more brutish than any man"; and thought, none deserved to be "cast out of God's presence" so much as I. If I attempted to lift up my heart to God, as I frequently did by the way, on a sudden, before I was aware, my thoughts were wandering "to the ends of the earth"; and my soul was filled with surprise and anxiety, to find it thus. Thus also, after I came to the Indians, my mind was confused; and I felt nothing sensibly of that sweet reliance on God, with which my soul has been comforted in days past. Spent the forenoon in this posture of mind, and preached to the Indians without any heart. In the afternoon, I felt still barren, when I began to preach, and for about half an hour. I seemed to myself to know nothing, and to have nothing to say to the Indians; but soon after, I found in myself a spirit of love, and warmth, and power, to address the poor Indians; and God helped me to plead with them, to "turn from all the vanities of the Heathen, to the living God"; I am persuaded that the Lord touched their consciences; for I never saw such attention raised in them. When I came away from them, I spent the whole time while I was riding to my lodgings, three miles distance, in prayer and praise to God. After I had rode more than two miles, it came into my mind to dedicate myself to God again; which I did with great solemnity

and unspeakable satisfaction; especially gave up myself to him renewedly in the work of the ministry. This I did by divine grace, I
hope, without any exception or reserve; not in the least shrinking
back from any difficulties that might attend this great and blessed
work. I seemed to be most free, cheerful, and full in this dedication
of myself. My whole soul cried "Lord, to thee I dedicate myself! O
accept of me, and let me be thine for ever. Lord, I desire nothing
else; I desire nothing more. O come, come, Lord, accept a poor
worm. Whom have I in heaven but thee? and there is none upon
earth, that I desire beside thee." After this, was enabled to praise
God with my whole soul, that he had enabled me to devote and
consecrate all my powers to him in this solemn manner. My heart
rejoiced in my particular work as a missionary; rejoiced in my necessity of self-denial in many respects; and still continued to give
up myself to God, and implore mercy of him, praying incessantly,
every moment, with sweet fervency. My nature being very weak, of
late, and much spent, was now considerably overcome: my fingers
grew very feeble, and somewhat numb, so that I could scarcely
stretch them out straight; and when I lighted from my horse, could
hardly walk; my joints seemed all to be loosed. But I felt abundant
strength in the inner man. Preached to the white people: God
helped me much, especially in prayer. Sundry of my poor Indians
were so moved as to come to meeting also; and one appeared much
concerned.

July 6. Awoke this morning in the fear of God: soon called to
mind my sadness in the evening past; and spent my first waking
minutes in prayer for sanctification, that my soul may be washed
from its exceeding pollution and defilement. After I arose, I spent
some time in reading God's word, and in prayer. I cried to God
under a sense of my great indigence. I am, of late, most of all concerned for ministerial qualifications, and the conversion of the Heathen. Last year, I longed to be prepared for a world of glory, and
speedily to depart out of this world; but of late all my concern almost is for the conversion of the Heathen; and for that end I long
to live. But blessed be God, I have less desire to live for any of the
pleasures of the world, than I ever had. I long and love to be a pilgrim; and want grace to imitate the life, labours, and sufferings of
St. Paul among the Heathen. And when I long for holiness now, it

is not so much for myself as formerly; but rather that thereby I may become an "able minister of the New-Testament," especially to the Heathen. Spent about two hours this morning in reading and prayer by turns; and was in a watchful tender frame, afraid of every thing that might cool my affections, and draw away my heart from God. Was a little strengthened in my studies; but near night was very weak and weary.

Lord's day, July 8. Was ill last night, not able to rest quietly. Had some small degree of assistance in preaching to the Indians; and afterwards was enabled to preach to the white people with some power, especially in the close of my discourse, from Jer. iii. 23. Truly in vain is salvation hoped for from the hills, &c. The Lord also assisted me in some measure in the first prayer; blessed be his name. Near night, though very weary, was enabled to read God's word with some sweet relish of it, and to pray with affection, fervency, and I trust with faith: my soul was more sensibly dependent on God than usual. Was watchful, tender, and jealous of my own heart, lest I should admit carelessness and vain thoughts, and grieve the blessed Spirit, so that he should withdraw his sweet, kind, and tender influences. Longed to "depart, and be with Christ," more than at any time of late. My soul was exceedingly united to the saints of ancient times, as well as those now living; especially my soul melted for the society of Elijah and Elisha. Was enabled to cry to God with a child-like spirit, and to continue instant in prayer for some time. Was much enlarged in the sweet duty of intercession; was enabled to remember great numbers of dear friends, and precious souls, as well as Christ's ministers. Continued in this frame, afraid of every idle thought, till I dropped asleep.

July 21. This morning, I was greatly oppressed with guilt and shame, from a sense of inward vileness and pollution. About nine, withdrew to the woods for prayer; but had not much comfort; I appeared to myself the vilest, meanest creature upon earth, and could scarcely live with myself; so mean and vile I appeared, that I thought I should never be able to hold up my face in heaven, if God of his infinite grace should bring me thither. Towards night my burden respecting my work among the Indians began to increase much; and was aggravated much by hearing sundry things which looked very discouraging; in particular, that they intended to meet together the next day for an idolatrous feast and dance. Then I began to be in anguish: I thought that I must in conscience go and endeavour to break them up; yet knew not how to attempt such a thing. However, I withdrew for prayer, hoping for strength from above. In prayer I was exceedingly enlarged, and my soul was as much drawn out as I ever remember it to have been in my life. I was in such anguish, and pleaded with so much earnestness and importunity, that when I rose from my knees I felt extremely weak and overcome; I could scarcely walk straight; my joints were loosed; the sweat ran down my face and body; and nature seemed as if it would dissolve. So far as I could judge, I was wholly free from selfish ends in my fervent supplications for the poor Indians. I knew that they were met together to worship devils, and not God; and this made me cry earnestly, that God would now appear, and help me in my attempts to break up this idolatrous meeting. My soul pleaded long; and I thought that God would hear, and would go with me to vindicate his own cause: I seemed to confide in God for his presence and assistance. And thus I spent the evening, praying incessantly for divine assistance, and that I might not be self-dependent, but still have my whole dependence upon God. What I passed through was remarkable, and indeed inexpressible. All things here below vanished; and there appeared to be nothing of any considerable importance to me, but holiness of heart and life, and the conversion of the Heathen to God. All my cares, fears, and desires, which might be said to be of a worldly nature, disappeared; and were, in my esteem, of little more importance than a puff of wind. I exceedingly longed that God would get to himself a name among the Heathen; and I appealed to him with the greatest freedom, that he knew I "preferred him above my chief joy." Indeed, I had no notion of joy from this world; I cared not where or how I lived, or what hardships I went through, so that I could but gain souls to Christ. I continued in this frame all the evening and night. While I was asleep, I dreamed of these things; and when I waked (as I frequently did), the first thing I thought of was this great work of pleading for God against Satan.

Lord's day, July 22. When I waked, my soul was burdened with what seemed to be before me. I cried to God, before I could get out of my bed; and as soon as I was dressed, I withdrew into the woods, to pour out my burdened soul to God, especially for assistance in my great work; for I could scarcely think of any thing else. I enjoyed the same freedom and fervency as the last evening; and did with unspeakable freedom give up myself afresh to God, for life or death, for all hardships he should call me to among the Heathen; and felt as if nothing could discourage me from this blessed work. I had a strong hope that God would "bow the heavens and come down," and do some marvellous work among the Heathen. While I was riding to the Indians—three miles my heart was continually going up to God for his presence and assistance; and hoping, and almost expecting, that God would make this the day of his power and grace amongst the poor Indians. When I came to them, I found them engaged in their frolic; but through divine goodness I persuaded them to desist and attend to my preaching: yet still there appeared nothing of the special power of God among them. Preached again to them in the afternoon, and observed the Indians were more sober than before; but still saw nothing special among them. Hence Satan took occasion to tempt and buffet me with these cursed suggestions, There is no God, or if there be, he is not able to convert the Indians, before they have more knowledge, &c. I was very weak and weary, and my soul borne down with perplexity; but was mortified to all the world, and was determined still to wait upon God for the conversion of the Heathen, though the devil tempted me to the contrary.

July 23. Retained still a deep and pressing sense of what lay with so much weight upon me yesterday; but was more calm and quiet. Enjoyed freedom and composure, after the temptations of the last evening; had sweet resignation to the divine will; and desired nothing so much as the conversion of the Heathen to God, and that his kingdom might come in my own heart, and the hearts of others. Rode to a settlement of Irish people, about fifteen miles south-westward; spent my time in prayer and meditation by the way. Near night, preached from Matt. v. 3. Blessed are the poor in spirit, &c.—God was pleased to afford me some degree of freedom and fervency. Blessed be God for any measure of assistance.

July 24. Rode about seventeen miles westward, over a hideous mountain, to a number of Indians. Got together near thirty of them: preached to them in the evening, and lodged among them.—

Was weak, and felt in some degree disconsolate; yet could have no freedom in the thought of any other circumstances or business in life. All my desire was the conversion of the Heathen; and all my hope was in God. God does not suffer me to please or comfort myself with hopes of seeing friend, returning to my dear acquaintance, and enjoying worldly comforts.

On Tuesday of this week he wrote the following letter to an intimate and dear friend. It indicates affections in no ordinary degree chastened and spiritual.

                                    Forks of Delaware, July 31, 1744
—Certainly the greatest, the noblest pleasure of intelligent creatures must result from their acquaintance with the blessed God, and with their own rational and immortal souls. O, how divinely sweet and entertaining is it, to look into our own souls, when we can find all our powers and passions united and engaged in pursuit after God; our whole souls longing and passionately breathing after a conformity to him, and the full enjoyment of him! Verily no hours pass away with so much divine pleasure, as those which are spent in communing with God and our own hearts. O, how sweet is a spirit of devotion, a spirit of seriousness and divine solemnity, a spirit of gospel simplicity, love and tenderness! O, how desirable, and how profitable to the christian life, is a spirit of holy watchfulness, and godly jealousy over ourselves; when our souls are afraid of nothing so much as that we shall grieve and offend the blessed God, whom at such times we apprehend, or at least hope, to be a Father and Friend; whom we then love and long to please, rather than to be happy ourselves; or at least we delight to derive our happiness from pleasing and glorifying him! Surely this is a pious temper, worthy of the highest ambition and closest pursuit of intelligent creatures and holy christians. O, how vastly superior are the pleasure, peace, and satisfaction derived from these divine frames, to that which we, alas! sometimes pursue in things impertinent and trifling! Our own bitter experience teaches us, that "in the midst of such laughter the heart is sorrowful," and there is no true satisfaction but in God. But, alas! how shall we obtain and retain this sweet spirit of religion and devotion? Let us follow the apostle's direction, Phil. ii. 12, and labour upon the encouragement

which he there mentions, ver. 13, for it is God only can afford us this favour; and he will be sought to, and it is fit we should wait upon him for so rich a mercy. Oh, may the God of all grace afford us the grace and influences of his divine Spirit; and help us that we may from our hearts esteem it our greatest liberty and happiness, that "whether we live, we may live to the Lord, or whether we die, we may die to the Lord"; that in life and death, we may be his!

I am in a very poor state of health; I think, scarce ever poorer: but, through divine goodness, I am not discontented under my weakness, and confinement to this wilderness. I bless God for this retirement; I never was more thankful for any thing, than I have been of late for the necessity I am under of self-denial in many respects. I love to be a pilgrim and stranger in this wilderness; it seems most fit for such a poor, ignorant, worthless, despised creature as I. I would not change my present mission for any other business in the whole world. I may tell you freely, without vanity and ostentation, God has of late given me great freedom and fervency in prayer, when I have been so weak and feeble that my nature seemed as if it would speedily dissolve. I feel as if my all was lost, and I was undone for this world, if the poor Heathen may not be converted. I feel, in general, different from what I did, when I saw you last; at least more crucified to all the enjoyments of life. It would be very refreshing to me to see you here in this desert; especially in my weak disconsolate hours; but, I think, I could be content never to see you, or any of my friends again in this world, if God would bless my labours here to the conversion of the poor Indians.

I have much that I could willingly communicate to you, which I must omit till Providence gives us leave to see each other. In the mean time, I rest

> Your obliged friend and servant,
> DAVID BRAINERD.

Lord's day, Sept. 2. Was enabled to speak to my poor Indians with much concern and fervency; and I am persuaded, that God enabled me to exercise faith in him, while I was speaking to them. I perceived that some of them were afraid to hearken to and embrace Christianity, lest they should be enchanted and poisoned by some of the *powaws:* but I was enabled to plead with them not to fear these; and, confiding in God for safety and deliverance, I bid a challenge to all these powers of darkness, to do their worst on me first. I told my people that I was a Christian, and asked them why the powaws did not bewitch and poison me. I scarcely ever felt more sensible of my own unworthiness, than in this action. I saw that the honour of God was concerned in the affair; and desired to be preserved—not from selfish views, but—for a testimony of the divine power and goodness, and of the truth of Christianity, and that God might be glorified. Afterwards, I found my soul rejoice in God for his assisting grace.

Oct. 1. Was engaged this day in making preparations for my intended journey to the Susquehannah. Withdrew several times to the woods for secret duties, and endeavoured to plead for the divine presence to go with me to the poor Pagans, to whom I was going to preach the gospel. Towards night rode about four miles, and met brother Byram; who was come at my desire, to be my companion in travel to the Indians. I rejoiced to see him; and, I trust, God made his conversation profitable to me. I saw him, as I thought, more dead to the world, its anxious cares, and alluring objects, than I was: and this made me look within myself, and gave me a greater sense of my guilt, ingratitude, and misery.

Oct. 2. Set out on my journey, in company with dear brother Byram, and my interpreter, and two chief Indians from the Forks of Delaware. Travelled about twenty-five miles, and lodged in one of the last houses on our road; after which there was nothing but a hideous and howling wilderness.

Oct. 3. We went on our way into the wilderness, and found the most difficult and dangerous travelling, by far, that ever any of us had seen. We had scarce any thing else but lofty mountains, deep valleys, and hideous rocks, to make our way through. However, I felt some sweetness in divine things, part of the day, and had my mind intensely engaged in meditation on a divine subject. Near night, my beast on which I rode, hung one of her legs in the rocks, and fell down under me; but through divine goodness, I was not hurt. However, she broke her leg; and being in such a hideous place, and near thirty miles from any house, I saw nothing that could be done to preserve her life, and so was obliged to kill her, and to prosecute my journey on foot. This accident made me admire the divine goodness to me, that my bones were not broken, and the multitude of them filled with strong pain. Just at dark, we kindled a fire, cut up a few bushes, and made a shelter over our heads, to save us from the frost, which was very hard that night; and committing ourselves to God by prayer, we lay down on the ground, and slept quietly.

The next day, they went forward on their journey, and at night took up their lodgings in the woods in like manner.

Oct. 5. We reached the Susquehannah river, at a place called Opeholhaupung, and found there twelve Indian houses. After I had saluted the king in a friendly manner, I told him my business, and that my desire was to teach them Christianity. After some consultation, the Indians gathered, and I preached to them. And when I had done, I asked if they would hear me again. They replied, that they would consider of it; and soon after sent me word, that they would immediately attend, if I would preach: which I did, with freedom, both times. When I asked them again, whether they would hear me further, they replied, they would the next day. I was exceeding sensible of the impossibility of doing any thing for the poor Heathen without special assistance from above; and my soul seemed to rest on God, and leave it to him to do as he pleased in that which I saw was his own cause. Indeed, through divine goodness, I had felt somewhat of this frame most of the time while I was travelling thither; and in some measure before I set out.

Oct. 6. Rose early and besought the Lord for help in my great work. Near noon, preached again to the Indians; and in the afternoon, visited them from house to house, and invited them to come and hear me again the next day, and put off their hunting design, which they were just entering upon, till Monday. "This night," I trust, "the Lord stood by me," to encourage and strengthen my soul: I spent more than an hour in secret retirement; was enabled to "pour out my heart before God," for the increase of grace in my soul, for ministerial endowments, for success among the poor Indians, for God's ministers and people, for distant dear friends, &c. Blessed be God!

The next day, he complains of great want of fixedness and intenseness in religion, so that he could not keep any spiritual thought one minute without distraction; which occasioned anguish of spirit. He felt amazingly guilty, and extremely miserable; and cries out, "O, my soul, what death it is, to have the affections unable to centre in God, by reason of darkness, and consequent roving after that satisfaction elsewhere, that is only to be found here!" However, he preached twice to the Indians with considerable freedom and power; but was afterwards damped by the objections they made against Christianity. In the evening, in a sense of his great defects in preaching, he "intreated God not to impute to him blood-guiltiness," but yet was at the same time enabled to rejoice in God.

Oct. 8. Visited the Indians with a design to take my leave of them, supposing they would this morning go out to hunting early; but beyond my expectation and hope, they desired to hear me preach again. I gladly complied with their request, and afterwards endeavoured to answer their objections against Christianity. Then they went away; and we spent the rest of the afternoon in reading and prayer, intending to go home-ward very early the next day. My soul was in some measure refreshed in secret prayer and meditation. Blessed be the Lord for all his goodness.

Oct. 9. We rose about four in the morning, and commending ourselves to God by prayer, and asking his special protection, we set out on our journey homewards about five, and travelled with great steadiness till past six at night; and then made us a fire, and a shelter of barks, and so rested. I had some clear and comfortable thoughts on a divine subject, by the way, towards night.—In the night, the wolves howled around us; but God preserved us.

TO THE REV. EBENEZER PEMBERTON

Forks of Delaware, Nov. 5, 1744.

REV. SIR,

Since you are pleased to require of me some brief and general account of my conduct in the affair of my mission among the Indians; the pains and endeavours I have used to propagate Christian knowledge among them; the difficulties I have met with in pursuance of that great work; and the hopeful and encouraging appearances I have observed in any of them; I shall now endeavour to answer your demands, by giving a brief but faithful account of the most material things relating to that important affair, with which I have been and am still concerned. This I shall do with more freedom and cheerfulness, both because I apprehend it will be a likely means to give pious persons, who are concerned for the kingdom of Christ, some just apprehension of the many and great difficulties that attend the propagation of it among the poor Pagans; and consequently, it is hoped, will engage their more frequent and fervent prayers to God, that those may be succeeded, who are employed in this arduous work. Besides, I persuade myself, that the tidings of the gospel spreading among the poor Heathen, will be, to those who are waiting for the accomplishment of the "glorious things spoken of the city of our God," as "good news from a far country"; and that these will be so far from "despising the day of small things," that, on the contrary, the least dawn of encouragement and hope, in this important affair, will rather inspire their pious breasts with more generous and warm desires, that "the kingdoms of this world, may speedily become the kingdoms of our Lord, and of his Christ."—I shall therefore immediately proceed to the business before me, and briefly touch upon the most important matters that have concerned my mission, from the beginning to this present time.

On March 15, 1743, I waited on the Correspondents for the Indian mission at New York; and the week following, attended their meeting at Woodbridge, in New Jersey, and was speedily dismissed by them with orders to attempt the instruction of a number of Indians in a place some miles distant from the city of Albany. And on the first day of April following, I arrived among the Indians, at a place called by them Kaunaumeek, in the county of Albany, nearly twenty miles distant from the city eastward.

The place, as to its situation, was sufficiently lonesome and unpleasant, being encompassed with mountains and woods; twenty miles distant from any English inhabitants; six or seven from any Dutch; and more than two from a family that came, some time since, from the Highlands of Scotland, and had then lived, as I remember, about two years in this wilderness. In this family I lodged about the space of three months, the master of it being the only person with whom I could readily converse in those parts, except my interpreter; others understanding very little English.

After I had spent about three months in this situation, I found my distance from the Indians a very great disadvantage to my work among them, and very burdensome to myself; as I was obliged to travel forward and backward almost daily on foot, having no pasture in which I could keep my horse for that purpose. And after all my pains, could not be with the Indians in the evening and morning, which were usually the best hours to find them at home, and when they could best attend my instructions.—I therefore resolved to remove, and live with or near the Indians, that I might watch the opportunities, when they were generally at home, and take the advantage of such seasons for their instructions.

Accordingly I removed soon after; and, for some time, lived with them in one of their *wigwams;* and, not long after, built me a small house, where I spent the remainder of that year entirely alone; my interpreter, who was an Indian, choosing rather to live in a wigwam among his own countrymen.—This way of living I found attended with many difficulties, and uncomfortable circumstances, in a place where I could get none of the necessaries and common comforts of life (no, not so much as a morsel of bread), but what I brought from places fifteen and twenty miles distant, and oftentimes was obliged, for some time together, to content myself without, for want of an opportunity to procure the things I needed.

But although the difficulties of this solitary way of living are not the least, or most inconsiderable (and doubtless are, in fact, many more and greater to those who experience, than they can readily appear to those who only view them at a distance), yet I can truly say that the burden I felt respecting my great work among the poor Indians, the fear and concern that continually hung upon my spirit, lest they should be prejudiced against Christianity, and their minds imbittered against me, and my labours among them by means of the insinuations of some who, although they are called christians, seem to have no concern for Christ's kingdom, but had rather (as their conduct plainly discovers) that the Indians should remain Heathens, that they may with the more ease cheat, and so enrich themselves by them—were much more pressing to me, than all the difficulties that attended the circumstances of my living.

As to the state or temper of mind in which I found these Indians, at my first coming among them, I may justly say, it was much more desirable and encouraging, than what appears among those who are altogether uncultivated. Their Heathenish jealousies and suspicion, and their prejudices against Christianity, were in a great measure removed by the long-continued labours of the Reverend Mr. Sergeant among a number of the same tribe, in a place little more than twenty miles distant. Hence, these were, in some good degree, prepared to entertain the truths of Christianity, instead of objecting against them, and appearing almost entirely untractable, as is common with them at first, and as, perhaps, these appeared a few years ago. Some of them, at least, appeared very well disposed towards religion, and seemed much pleased with my coming among them.

In my labours with them, in order to "turn them from darkness to light," I studied what was most plain and easy, and best suited to their capacities; and endeavoured to set before them from time to time, as they were able to receive them, the most important and necessary truths of Christianity; such as most immediately concerned their speedy conversion to God, and such as I judged had the greatest tendency, as means to effect that glorious change in them. But especially I made it the scope and drift of all my labours, to lead them into a thorough acquaintance with these two things—First, The sinfulness and misery of the estate they were naturally in; the evil of their hearts, the pollution of their natures; the heavy guilt they were under, and their exposedness to everlasting punishment; as also their utter inability to save themselves, either from their sins, or from those miseries which are the just punishment of them; and their unworthiness of any mercy at the hand of God, on account of any thing they themselves could do to procure his favour, and consequently their extreme need of Christ to save them.—And, secondly, I frequently endeavoured to open to them the fulness, all-sufficiency, and freeness of that redemption, which the Son of God has wrought out by his obedience and sufferings, for perishing sinners: how this provision he had made, was suited to all their wants; and how he called and invited them to accept of everlasting life freely, notwithstanding all their sinfulness, inability, unworthiness, &c.

After I had been with the Indians several months, I composed sundry forms of prayer, adapted to their circumstances and capacities; which, with the help of my interpreter, I translated into the Indian language, and soon learned to pronounce their words, so as to pray with them in their own tongue. I also translated sundry psalms into their language, and soon after we were able to sing in the worship of God.

When my people had gained some acquaintance with many of the truths of Christianity, so that they were capable of receiving and understanding many others, which at first could not be taught them, by reason of their ignorance of those that were necessary to be previously known, and upon which others depended; I then gave them an historical account of God's dealings with his ancient professing people the Jews; some of the rites and ceremonies they were obliged to observe, as their sacrifices, &c.; and what these were designed to represent to them: as also some of the surprising miracles God wrought for their salvation, while they trusted in him, and sore punishments he sometimes brought upon them, when they forsook and sinned against him. Afterwards I proceeded to give them a relation of the birth, life, miracles, sufferings, death, and resurrection of Christ; as well as his ascension, and the wonderful effusion of the holy Spirit consequent thereupon.

And having thus endeavoured to prepare the way by such a general account of things, I next proceeded to read and expound to them the gospel of St. Matthew (at least the substance of it) in course, wherein they had a more distinct and particular view of what they had before some general notion.—These expositions I attended almost every evening, when there was any considerable number of them at home; except when I was obliged to be absent myself, in order to learn the Indian language with the Rev. Mr. Sergeant.—Besides these means of instruction, there was likewise an English school constantly kept by my interpreter among the Indians; which I used frequently to visit, in order to give the children and young people some proper instructions, and serious exhortations suited to their age.

The degree of knowledge to which some of them attained was considerable. Many of the truths of Christianity seemed fixed in their minds, especially in some instances, so that they would speak to me of them, and ask such questions about them, as were necessary to render them more plain and clear to their understandings.— The children, also, and young people, who attended the school, made considerable proficiency (at least some of them) in their learning; so that had they understood the English language well, they would have been able to read somewhat readily in a psalter.

But that which was most of all desirable, and gave me the greatest encouragement amidst many difficulties and disconsolate hours, was, that the truths of God's word seemed, at times, to be attended with some power upon the hearts and consciences of the Indians. And especially this appeared evident in a few instances, who were awakened to some sense of their miserable estate by nature, and appeared solicitous for deliverance from it. Several of them came, of their own accord, to discourse with me about their souls' concerns; and some, with tears, inquired "what they should do to be saved?" and whether the God that Christians served, would be merciful to those that had been frequently drunk, &c.

And although I cannot say that I have satisfactory evidences of their being "renewed in the spirit of their mind," and savingly converted to God; yet the Spirit of God did, I apprehend, in such a manner attend the means of grace, and so operate upon their minds thereby, as might justly afford matter of encouragement to hope, that God designed good to them, and that he was preparing his way into their souls.

There likewise appeared a reformation in the lives and manners of the Indians.—Their idolatrous sacrifices (of which there was but one or two, that I know of, after my coming among them) were wholly laid aside. And their Heathenish custom of dancing, hallooing, &c. they seemed in a considerable measure to have abandoned. And I could not but hope, that they were reformed in some measure from the sin of drunkenness. They likewise manifested a regard for the Lord's day, and not only behaved soberly themselves, but took care also to keep their children in order.

Yet, after all, I must confess, that as there were many hopeful appearances among them, so there were some things more discouraging. And while I rejoiced to observe any seriousness and concern among them about the affairs of their souls, still I was not without continual fear and concern, lest such encouraging appearances might prove "like a morning cloud, that passeth away."

When I had spent near a year with the Indians, I informed them that I expected to leave them in the spring then approaching, and to be sent to another tribe of Indians, at a great distance from them. On hearing this, they appeared very sorrowful, and some of them endeavoured to persuade me to continue with them; urging that they had now heard so much about their souls' concerns, that they could never more be willing to live as they had done, without a minister, and further instructions in the way to heaven, &c. Whereupon I told them, they ought to be willing that others also should hear about their souls' concerns, seeing those needed it as much as themselves. Yet further to dissuade me from going, they added, that those Indians, to whom I had thoughts of going (as they had heard) were not willing to become Christians as they were, and therefore urged me to tarry with them. I then told them, that they might receive further instruction without me; but the Indians, to whom I expected to be sent, could not, there being no minister near to teach them. And hereupon I advised them, in case I should leave them, and be sent elsewhere, to remove to Stockbridge, where they might be supplied with land, and conveniences of living, and be under the ministry of the Rev. Mr. Sergeant: with which advice and proposal, they seemed disposed to comply.

On April 6, 1744, I was ordered and directed by the correspondents for the Indian mission, to take leave of the people, with whom I had then spent a full year, and to go, as soon as conveniently I could, to a tribe of Indians on Delaware river in Pennsylvania.

These orders I soon attended, and on April 29th took leave of my people, who were mostly removed to Stockbridge under the care of the Rev. Mr. Sergeant. I then set out on my journey toward Delaware: and on May 10th, met with a number of Indians in a place called Miunissinks, about a hundred and forty miles from Kaunaumeek (the place where I spent the last year), and directly in my way to Delaware river. With these Indians I spent some time, and first addressed their king in a friendly manner; and after some discourse, and attempts to contract a friendship with him, I told him I had a desire (for his benefit and happiness) to instruct them in Christianity. At which he laughed, turned his back upon me, and went away. I then addressed another principal man in the same manner, who said he was willing to hear me. After some time, I followed the king into his house, and renewed my discourse to him: but he declined talking, and left the affair to another, who appeared to be a rational man. He began, and talked very warmly near a quarter of an hour together: he required why I desired the Indians to become Christians, seeing the Christians were so much worse than the Indians in their present state. The Christians, he said, would lie, steal, and drink, worse than the Indians. It was they first taught the Indians to be drunk: and they stole from one another, to that degree, that their rulers were obliged to hang them for it, and that was not sufficient to deter others from the like practice. But the Indians, he added, were none of them ever hanged for stealing, and yet they did not steal half so much; and he supposed that if the Indians should become Christians, they would then be as bad as these. And hereupon he said, they would live as their fathers lived, and go where their fathers were when they died. I then freely owned, lamented, and joined with him in condemning the ill conduct of some who are called Christians: told him, these were not Christians in heart; that I hated such wicked practices, and did not desire the Indians to become such as these.—And when he appeared calmer, I asked him if he was willing that I should come and see them again? He replied, he should be willing to see me again, as a friend, if I would not desire them to become Christians.— I then bid them farewell, and prosecuted my journey toward Delaware. And May 13th, I arrived at a place called by the Indians Sakhauwotung, within the Forks of Delaware in Pennsylvania.

Here also, when I came to the Indians, I saluted their king, and others, in a manner I thought most engaging. And soon after informed the king of my desire to instruct them in the Christian religion. After he had consulted a few minutes with two or three old men, he told me he was willing to hear. I then preached to those few that were present; who appeared very attentive and well disposed. And the king in particular seemed both to wonder, and at the same time to be well pleased with what I taught them, respecting the divine Being, &c. And since that time he has ever shewn himself friendly to me, giving me free liberty to preach in his house, whenever I think fit.—Here therefore I have spent the greater part of the summer past, preaching usually in the king's house.

The number of Indians in this place is but small; most of those that formerly belonged here, are dispersed, and removed to places farther back in the country. There are not more than ten houses hereabouts, that continue to be inhabited; and some of these are several miles distant from others, which makes it difficult for the Indians to meet together so frequently as could be desired.

When I first began to preach here, the number of my hearers was very small; often not exeeding twenty or twenty-five persons: But towards the latter part of the summer, their number increased, so that I have frequently had forty persons, or more, at once; and oftentimes most belonging to those parts, came together to hear me preach.

The effects which the truths of God's word have had upon some of the Indians in this place, are somewhat encouraging. Sundry of them are brought to renounce idolatry, and to decline partaking of those feasts which they used to offer in sacrifice to certain supposed unknown powers. And some few among them have, for a considerable time, manifested a serious concern for their souls' eternal welfare, and still continue to "inquire the way to Zion," with such diligence, affection, and becoming solicitude, as gives me reason to hope that "God who, I trust, has begun this work in them," will carry it on, until it shall issue in their saving conversion to himself. These not only detest their old idolatrous notions, but strive also to bring their friends off from them. And as they are seeking salvation for their own souls, so they seem desirous, and some of them take pains, that others might be excited to do the like.

In July last I heard of a number of Indians residing at a place called Kauksesauchung, more than thirty miles westward from the place where I usually preach. I visited them, found about thirty persons, and proposed my desire of preaching to them; they readily complied, and I preached to them only twice, they being just then removing from this place where they only lived for the present, to Susquehannah river, where they belonged.

While I was preaching, they appeared sober, and attentive; and were somewhat surprised, having never before heard of these things. There were two or three who suspected that I had some ill design upon them; and urged, that the white people had abused them, and taken their lands from them, and therefore they had no reason to think that they were now concerned for their happiness; but, on the contrary, that they designed to make them slaves, or get them on board their vessels, and make them fight with the people over the water (as they expressed it), meaning the French and Spaniards. However, the most of them appeared very friendly, and told me, they were going directly home to Susquehannah, and desired I would make them a visit there, and manifested a considerable desire of further instruction.—This invitation gave me some encouragement in my great work; and made me hope, that God designed to "open an effectual door to me" for spreading the gospel among the poor Heathen farther westward.

In the beginning of October last, with the advice and direction of the correspondents for the Indian mission, I undertook a journey to Susquehannah. And after three days tedious travel, two of them through a wilderness almost unpassable, by reason of mountains and rocks, and two nights lodging in the open wilderness, I came to an Indian settlement on the side of Susquehannah river, called Opeholhaupung; where were twelve Indian houses, and (as nigh as I could learn) about seventy souls, old and young, belonging to them.

Here also, soon after my arrival, I visited the king, addressing him with expressions of kindness; and after a few words of friendship, informed him of my desire to teach them the knowledge of Christianity. He hesitated not long before he told me, that he was willing to hear. I then preached; and continued there several days, preaching every day, as long as the Indians were at home. And they, in order to hear me, deferred the design of their general hunting (which they were just then entering upon) for the space of three or four days.

The men, I think universally (except one) attended my preaching. Only the women, supposing the affair we were upon was of a public nature, belonging only to the men, and not what every individual person should concern himself with, could not readily be persuaded to come and hear: but, after much pains used with them for that purpose, some few ventured to come, and stand at a distance.

When I had preached to the Indians several times, some of them very frankly proposed what they had to object against Christianity; and so gave me a fair opportunity for using my best endeavours to remove from their minds those scruples and jealousies they laboured under: and when I had endeavoured to answer their objections, some appeared much satisfied. I then asked the king, if he was willing I should visit and preach to them again, if I should live to the next spring? He replied, he should be heartily willing for his own part, and added, he wished the young people would learn, &c. I then put the same question to the rest; some answered they would be very glad, and none manifested any dislike to it.

There were sundry other things in their behaviour, which appeared with a comfortable and encouraging aspect; that, upon the whole, I could not but rejoice I had taken that journey among them, although it was attended with many difficulties and hardships. The method I used with them, and the instructions I gave them, I am persuaded were means, in some measure, to remove their heathenish jealousies and prejudices against Christianity: and I could not but hope, that God of all grace was preparing their minds to receive "the truth as it is in Jesus." If this may be the happy consequence, I shall not only rejoice in my past labours and fatigues; but shall, I trust also "be willing to spend and be spent," if I may thereby be instrumental "to turn them from darkness to light, and from the power of Satan to God."

Thus, Sir, I have given you a faithful account of what has been most considerable respecting my mission among the Indians; in which I have studied all convenient brevity. I shall only now take leave to add a word or two respecting the difficulties that attend the Christianizing of these poor Pagans.

In the first place, their minds are filled with prejudices against Christianity, on account of the vicious lives and unchristian behaviour of some that are called Christians. These not only set before them the worst examples, but some of them take pains, expressly in words, to dissuade them from becoming Christians; foreseeing, that if these should be converted to God, "the hope of their unlawful gain," would thereby be lost.

Again, these poor Heathens are extremely attached to the customs, traditions, and fabulous notions of their fathers. And this one seems to be the foundation of all their other notions, viz. that "it was not the same God made them, who made the white people," but another, who commanded them to live by hunting, &c. and not to conform to the customs of the white people.—Hence, when they are desired to become Christians, they frequently reply, that "they will live as their fathers lived, and go to their fathers when they die." And if the miracles of Christ and his apostles be mentioned, to prove the truth of Christianity, they also mention sundry miracles, which their fathers have told them were anciently wrought among the Indians, and which Satan makes them believe were so.—They are much attached to idolatry; frequently making feasts, which they eat in honour to some unknown beings, who, they suppose, speak to them in dreams; promising them success in hunting, and other affairs, in case they will sacrifice to them. They oftentimes also offer their sacrifices to the spirits of the dead; who, they suppose, stand in need of favours from the living, and yet are in such a state as that they can well reward all the offices of kindness that are shewn them. And they impute all their calamities to the neglect of these sacrifices.

Furthermore, they are much awed by those among themselves, who are called powwows, who are supposed to have a power of enchanting, or poisoning them to death, or at least in a very distressing manner. And they apprehend it would be their sad fate to be thus enchanted in case they should become Christians.

Lastly, the manner of their living is likewise a great disadvantage to the design of their being Christianized. They are almost continually roving from place to place; and it is but rare, that an opportunity can be had with some of them for their instruction. There is scarce any time of the year, wherein the men can be found generally at home, except about six weeks before, and in the season of planting their corn, and about two months in the latter part of the summer, from the time they begin to roast their corn, until it is fit to gather in.

As to the hardships that necessarily attend a mission among them, the fatigues of frequent journeying in the wilderness, the unpleasantness of a mean and hard way of living, and the great difficulty of addressing "a people of a strange language," these I shall, at present, pass over in silence; designing what I have already said of difficulties attending this work, not for the discouragement of any, but rather for the incitement of all who "love the appearing of the kingdom of Christ," to frequent the throne of grace with earnest supplications, that the Heathen, who were anciently promised to Christ "for his inheritance," may now actually and speedily be brought into his kingdom of grace, and made heirs of immortal glory.

> I am, Sir.
> Your obedient, humble servant,
> DAVID BRAINERD.

Dec. 6. Having now a happy opportunity of being retired in a house of my own, which I have lately procured and moved into;

considering that it is now a long time since I have been able, either on account of bodily weakness, or for want of retirement, or some other difficulty to spend any time in secret fasting and prayer; considering also the greatness of my work, the extreme difficulties that attend it, and that my poor Indians are now worshiping devils, notwithstanding all the pains I have taken with them, which almost overwhelms my spirit; moreover, considering my extreme barrenness, spiritual deadness and dejection, of late; as also the power of some particular corruptions; I set apart this day for secret prayer and fasting, to implore the blessing of God on myself, on my poor people, on my friends, and on the church of God. At first, I felt a great backwardness to the duties of the day, on account of the seeming impossibility of performing them; but the Lord helped me to break through this difficulty. God was pleased by the use of means, to give me some clear conviction of my sinfulness, and a discovery of the plague of my own heart, more affecting than what I have of late had. And especially I saw my sinfulness in this, that when God had withdrawn himself, then, instead of living and dying in pursuit of him, I have been disposed to one of these two things; either, first, to yield an unbecoming respect to some earthly objects, as if happiness were derived from them; or, secondly, to be secretly froward and impatient, and unsuitably desirous of death, so that I have sometimes thought I could not bear to think that my life must be lengthened out. That which often drove me to this impatient desire of death, was a despair of doing any good in life; and I chose death rather than a life spent for nothing. But now God made me sensible of my sin in these things, and enabled me to cry to him for forgiveness. Yet this was not all which I wanted, for my soul appeared exceedingly polluted, my heart seemed like a nest of vipers, or a cage of unclean and hateful birds; and therefore I wanted to be purified "by the blood of sprinkling, that cleanseth from all sin." This, I hope, I was enabled to pray for in faith. I enjoyed much more intenseness, fervency, and spirituality, than I expected; God was better to me than my fears. Towards night, I felt my soul rejoice, that God is unchangeably happy and glorious; and that he will be glorified, whatever becomes of his creatures. I was enabled to persevere in prayer, until sometime in the evening: at which time I saw so much need of divine help, in every respect, that I knew not how to leave off, and had forgot that I needed food. This evening, I was much assisted in meditating on Is. lii. 3. For thus saith the Lord, ye have sold yourselves for nought, &c. Blessed be the Lord for any help in the past day.

Dec. 18. Went to the Indians, and discoursed to them near an hour, without any power to come close to their hearts. But at last I felt some fervency, and God helped me to speak with warmth. My interpreter also was amazingly assisted; and I doubt not but that "the Spirit of God was upon him"; though I had no reason to think he had any true and saving grace, but was only under conviction of his lost state; and presently upon this most of the grown persons were much affected, and the tears ran down their cheeks. One old man, I suppose an hundred years old, was so much affected, that he wept, and seemed convinced of the importance of what I taught them. I staid with them a considerable time, exhorting and directing them; and came away, lifting up my heart to God in prayer and praise, and encouraged and exhorted my interpreter to "strive to enter in at the strait gate." Came home, and spent most of the evening in prayer and thanksgiving; and found myself much enlarged and quickened. Was greatly concerned, that the Lord's work which seemed to be begun, might be carried on with power, to the conversion of poor souls, and the glory of divine grace.

Jan. 14 [1745.] Spent this day under a great degree of bodily weakness and disorder; had very little freedom, either in my studies or devotions; and in the evening, I was much dejected and melancholy. It pains and distresses me, that I live so much of my time for nothing. I long to do much in a little time, and if it might be the Lord's will to finish my work speedily in this tiresome world. I am sure, I do not desire to live for any thing in this world; and through grace I am not afraid to look the king of terrors in the face: I know that I shall be afraid if God leaves me; and therefore I think it always my duty to provide for that solemn hour. But for a very considerable time past, my soul has rejoiced to think of death in its nearest approaches, and even when I have been very weak, and seemed nearest eternity. "Not unto me, not unto me, but to God be the glory." I feel that which convinces me, that if God do not enable me to maintain a holy dependence upon him, death will easily be a terror to me; but at present, I must say, "I long to depart, and to be with Christ," which is the best of all. When I am in a sweet resigned frame of soul, I am willing to tarry a while in a world of sorrow. I am willing to be from home as long as God sees fit it should be so; but when I want the influence of this temper, I am then apt to be impatient to be gone.—O, when will the day appear, that I shall be perfect in holiness, and in the enjoyment of God!

Lord's day, Jan. 27. Had the greatest degree of inward anguish, which I almost ever endured. I was perfectly overwhelmed, and so confused, that after I began to discourse to the Indians, before I could finish a sentence, sometimes I forgot entirely what I was aiming at; or if, with much difficulty, I had recollected what I had before designed, still it appeared strange, and like something I had long forgotten, and had now but an imperfect remembrance of. I know it was a degree of distraction, occasioned by vapoury disorders, melancholy, spiritual desertion, and some other things that particularly pressed upon me this morning, with an uncommon weight, the principal of which respected my Indians. This distressing gloom never went off the whole day; but was so far removed, that I was enabled to speak with some freedom and concern to the Indians, at two of their settlements; and I think, there was some appearance of the presence of God with us, some seriousness and seeming concern among the Indians, at least a few of them. In the evening, this gloom continued still, till family prayer, about nine o'clock, and almost through this, until I came near the close, when I was praying, as I usually do, for the illumination and conversion of my poor people; and then the cloud was scattered, so that I enjoyed sweetness and freedom, and conceived hopes, that God designed mercy for some of them. The same I enjoyed afterwards in secret prayer; in which precious duty I had for a considerable time sweetness and freedom, and, I hope, faith, in praying for myself, my poor Indians, and dear friends and acquaintance in New-England, and elsewhere, and for the dear interests of Zion in general. Bless the Lord, O my soul, and forget not all his benefits.

In the three next days, he was the subject of much dejection: but the three remaining days of the week seem to have been spent with much composure and comfort. On the next Sabbath, he preached at Greenwich in New Jersey. In the evening, he rode eight miles to visit a sick man at the point of death, and found him speechless and senseless.

Feb. 11. About break of day, the sick man died. I was affected at the sight; spent the morning with the mourners; and, after prayer again from Ps. lxxxix. 15. Blessed is the people that know, &c. The Lord gave me assistance; I felt a sweet love to souls, and to the kingdom of Christ; and longed that poor sinners might know the joyful sound. Several persons were much affected. After meeting, I was enabled to discourse, with freedom and concern, to some persons, who applied to me under spiritual trouble. Left the place, sweetly composed, and rode home to my house about eight miles distant. Discoursed to friends, and inculcated divine truths upon some. In the evening was in the most solemn frame which I almost ever remember to have experienced. I know not that ever death appeared more real to me, or that ever I saw myself in the condition of a dead corpse, laid out, and dressed for a lodging in the silent grave, so evidently as at this time. And yet I felt exceedingly tranquil; my mind was composed and calm, and death appeared without a sting. I think, I never felt such an universal mortification to all created objects as now. O, how great and solemn a thing it appeared to die! O, how it lays the greatest honour in the dust! And O, how vain and trifling did the riches, honours, and pleasures of the world appear! I could not, I dare not, so much as think of any of them; for death, death, solemn (though not frightful) death appeared at the door. O, I could see myself dead, and laid out, and inclosed in my coffin, and put down into the cold grave, with the greatest solemnity, but without terror! I spent most of the evening in conversing with a dear christian friend; and blessed be God, it was a comfortable evening to us both.—What are friends? What are comforts? What are sorrows? What are distresses?—"The time is short. It remains, that they which weep, be as though they wept not; and they which rejoice, as though they rejoiced not; for the fashion of this world passeth away. Oh come, Lord Jesus, come quickly. Amen."—Blessed be God for the comforts of the past day.

CHAPTER VII

*From the commencement of his residence at Cross-
weeksung, to the close of the first part of his Journal.*

*We are now come to that part of BRAINERD'S life, when he had the
greatest success in his labours for the good of souls, and in his particular business as a Missionary to the Indians. Long had he agonized in
prayer, and travailed in birth for their conversion. Often had he cherished the hope of witnessing that desirable event; only to find that
hope yield to fear, and end in disappointment. But after a patient
continuance in prayer, in labour, and in suffering, as it were through
a long night, at length he is permitted to behold the dawning of the
day. "Weeping continues for a night; but joy comes in the morning."
He went forth weeping, bearing precious seed; and now he comes rejoicing, bringing his sheaves with him. The desired event is brought to
pass at last; but at a time, in a place, and upon subjects, which scarcely
ever entered into his heart.*

*An account of this was originally published in his JOURNAL; con-
sisting of extracts from his Diary during one year of his residence at
Crossweeksung. Those extracts are now incorporated with the rest of
his Diary for the same period in regular chronological order.**

June 19. I had spent most of my time, for more than a year past,
among the Indians at the Forks of Delaware in Pennsylvania. During that time I made two journeys to the Susquehannah to treat
with the Indians on that river respecting Christianity; and, not having had any considerable appearance of special success in either of
those places, my spirits were depressed, and I was not a little discouraged. Hearing that there were a number of Indians at a place
called Crossweeksung, in New-Jersey, nearly eighty miles south-
east from the Forks of Delaware, I determined to make them a visit,
and see what might be done towards christianizing them; and accordingly arrived among them on Wednesday, June 19, 1745.

* The PREFACE by correspondents of the society which supported Brainerd's
work has been omitted. The remainder of the JOURNAL has been preserved
complete.

I found very few persons at the place which I visited, and perceived that the Indians in these parts were very much scattered. There were not more than two or three families in a place; and these small settlements, six, ten, fifteen, twenty, and thirty miles, and some more from that place. However, I preached to those few I found; who appeared well disposed, serious and attentive, and not inclined to cavil and object, as the Indians had done elsewhere. When I had concluded my discourse, I informed them; there being none but a few women and children; that I would willingly visit them again the next day. Whereupon they readily set out and travelled ten or fifteen miles, in order to give notice to some of their friends at that distance. These women, like the women of Samaria, seemed desirous that others should see the man, who had told them what they had done in their past lives, and the misery that attended their idolatrous ways. At night was worn out, and scarcely able to walk, or sit up. O! how tiresome is earth; how dull the body!

June 20. Visited and preached to the Indians again as I proposed numbers were gathered at the invitations of their friends, who had heard me the day before. These also appeared as attentive, orderly and well disposed as the others: and none made any objections, as Indians in other places have usually done. Towards night preached to the Indians again, and had more hearers than before. In the evening enjoyed some peace and serenity of mind, and comfort and composure in prayer, alone; and was enabled to lift up my head with some degree of joy, under an apprehension that my redemption draws nigh. O! blessed be God that there remains a rest to his poor weary people!

June 21. Rode to Freehold to see Mr. William Tennent, and spent the day comfortably with him. My sinking spirits were a little raised and encouraged; and I felt my soul breathing after God, in the midst of christian conversation; and in the evening was refreshed in secret prayer; saw myself a poor worthless creature, without wisdom to direct or strength to help myself.—O blessed be God, who lays me under a happy, a blessed necessity of living upon himself!

June 22. About noon rode to the Indians again, and next night preached to them. Found my body much strengthened, and was enabled to speak with abundant plainness and warmth. Their number, which at first consisted of seven or eight persons, was now increased to nearly thirty. There was not only a solemn attention among them, but some considerable impression, it was apparent, was made upon their minds by divine truth. Some began to feel their misery, and perishing state, and appeared concerned for a deliverance from it. The power of God evidently attended the word; so that several persons were brought under a great concern for their souls, and made to shed many tears, and to wish for Christ to save them. My soul was much refreshed and quickened in my work: and I could not but spend much time with them in order to open both their misery and their remedy. This was indeed a sweet afternoon to me. While riding, before I came to the Indians, my spirits were refreshed, and my soul enabled to cry to God almost incessantly, for many miles together. In the evening, also, I found that the consolations of God were not small. I was then willing to live, and in some respects desirous of it, that I might do something for the dear kingdom of Christ; and yet death appeared pleasant; so that I was in some measure in a strait between two; having a desire to depart. I am often weary of this world, and want to leave it on that account; but it is desirable to be drawn, rather than driven out of it.

Lord's day, June 23. Preached to the Indians, and spent the day with them. Their number still increased; and all with one consent, seemed to rejoice in my coming among them. Not a word of opposition was heard from any of them against christianity, although in times past they had been as much opposed to any thing of that nature, as any Indians whatsoever. Some of them, not many months before, were enraged with my interpreter, because he attempted to teach them something of christianity.

June 24. Preached to the Indians at their desire, and upon their own motion. To see poor Pagans desirous of hearing the gospel of Christ, animated me to discourse to them; although I was now very weakly, and my spirits much exhausted. They attended with the greatest seriousness and diligence; and some concern for their souls' salvation was apparent among them.

June 27. Visited and preached to the Indians again. Their number now amounted to about forty persons. Their solemnity and attention still continued, and a considerable concern for their souls, became apparent among numbers of them. My soul rejoiced to find, that God enabled me to be faithful, and that he was pleased to awaken these poor Indians by my means. O how heart-reviving and soul-refreshing it is to me, to see the fruit of my labours!

June 28. The Indians being now gathered, a considerable number of them, from their several and distant habitations requested me to preach twice a day to them; being desirous to hear as much as they possibly could while I was with them. I cheerfully complied with their request, and could not but admire the goodness of God, who I was persuaded, had inclined them thus to inquire after the way of salvation.

In the evening, my soul was revived, and my heart lifted up to God in prayer for my poor Indians, myself, and friends, and the dear church of God. O how refreshing, how sweet was this! Bless the Lord O my soul, and forget not his goodness and tender mercy!

June 29. Preached twice to the Indians; and could not but wonder at their seriousness, and the strictness of their attention. Saw, as I thought, the hand of God very evidently, and in a manner somewhat remarkable, making provision for their subsistence together, in order to their being instructed in divine things. For this day, and the day before, with only walking a little way from the place of our daily meeting, they killed three deer, which were a seasonable supply for their wants, and without which, they could not have subsisted together in order to attend the means of grace. Blessed be God who has inclined their hearts to hear. O how refreshing it is to me to see them attend, with such uncommon diligence and affection, with tears in their eyes and concern in their hearts! In the evening, could not lift up my heart to God in prayer, while riding to my lodging; and, blessed be his name, had assistance and freedom. O how much better than life is the presence of God!

Lord's day, June 30. Preached twice this day also. Observed yet more concern and affection among the poor Heathens than ever; so that they even constrained me to tarry yet longer with them, although my constitution was exceedingly worn out, and my health much impaired by my late fatigues and labours; and especially by my late journey to Susquehannah in May last, in which I lodged on the ground for several weeks together.

July 1. Preached again twice to a very serious and attentive assembly of Indians; they having now learned to attend the worship of God with christian decency in all respects. There were now between forty and fifty persons of them present, old and young. I spent a considerable time in discoursing with them in a more private way; inquiring of them what they remembered of the great truths which had been taught them from day to day; and may justly say, it was amazing to see how they had received and retained the instructions given to them, and what a measure of knowledge some of them had acquired in a few days.

July 2. Was obliged to leave these Indians at Crossweeksung, thinking it my duty as soon as my health would admit, again to visit those at the Forks of Delaware. When I came to take leave of them and to speak particularly to each of them, they all earnestly inquired when I would come again, and expressed a great desire of being further instructed. Of their own accord they agreed, that when I should come again, they would all meet and live together, during my continuance with them; and that they would use their utmost endeavours to gather all the other Indians in these parts who were yet more remote. When I parted from them, one told me, with many tears, "She wished God would change her heart"; another, that "she wanted to find Christ"; and an old man, who had been one of their chiefs, wept bitterly with concern for his soul. I then promised them to return as speedily as my health and business elsewhere would permit, and felt not a little concern at parting, lest the good impressions, then apparent upon numbers of them, might decline and wear off, when the means came to cease. Yet I could not but hope, that He, who I trusted, had begun a good work among them, and who, I knew, did not stand in need of means to carry it on, would maintain and promote it. At the same time, I must confess, that I had often seen encouraging appearances among the Indians elsewhere, prove wholly abortive, and it appeared that the favour would be too great, if God should now, after I had passed through so considerable a series of almost fruitless labours and fatigues, and after my rising hopes had been so often frustrated among these poor pagans, give me any special success in my labours with them, I could not believe, and scarcely dared to hope, that the event would be so happy; and scarcely ever found myself more suspended between hope and fear in any affair, or at any time, than in this.

This encouraging disposition, and readiness to receive instruction, now apparent among the Indians, seems to have been the happy effect of the conviction which one or two of them met with, sometimes since at the Forks of Delaware; who have since endeavoured to shew their friends the evil of idolatry. Though the other Indians seemed but little to regard, and rather to deride, them; yet this, perhaps, has put them into a thinking posture of mind, or at least, given them some thoughts about christianity, and excited in some of them a curiosity to hear; and so made way for the present encouraging attention. An apprehension that this might be the case, here, has given me encouragement that God may, in such a manner, bless the means which I have used with the Indians in other places; where, as yet, there is no appearance of it. If so, may his name have the glory of it: for I have learnt, by experience, that he only can open the ear, engage the attention, and incline the hearts of poor benighted, prejudiced pagans, to receive instruction.

Rode from the Indians to Brunswick, nearly forty miles, and lodged there. Felt my heart drawn after God in prayer, almost all the forenoon, especially in riding. In the evening, I could not help crying to God for those poor Indians; and, after I went to bed, my heart continued to go out to God for them till I dropped asleep. O, blessed be God, that I may pray!

He was now so fatigued by constant preaching to these Indians, yielding to their importunate desires, that he found it necessary to give himself some relaxation. He spent, therefore, about a week in New-Jersey, after he left the Indians; visiting several ministers, and performing some necessary business, before he went to the Forks of Delaware. Though he was weak in body, yet he seems to have been strong in spirit. On Friday, July 12, he arrived at his own house in the Forks of Delaware; continuing still free from melancholy; from day to day enjoying freedom, assistance, and refreshment in the inner man. But on Wednesday, the next week, he seems to have had some melancholy thoughts about his doing so little for God, being so much hindered by weakness of body.

Forks of Delaware, in Pennsylvania, July 1745.

Lord's day, July 14. Discoursed to the Indians twice. Several of them appeared concerned, and were, I have reason to think, in some measure convinced by the Divine Spirit, of their sin and misery; so that they wept much the whole time of divine service.

Afterwards, discoursed to a number of white people then present.

July 18. Preached to my people, who attended diligently beyond what had been common among these Indians: and some of them appeared concerned for their souls. Longed to spend the little inch of time I have in the world, more for God. Felt a spirit of seriousness, tenderness, sweetness and devotion; and wished to spend the whole night in prayer and communion with God.

July 19. In the evening, walked abroad for prayer and meditation, and enjoyed composure and freedom in these sweet exercises, especially in meditation on Rev. iii. 12: "Him that overcometh, will I make a pillar in the temple of my God." &c. This was then a delightful theme to me, and it refreshed my soul to dwell on it. O when shall I go no more out from the service and enjoyment of the dear Redeemer! Lord hasten the blessed day!

Lord's day, July 21. Preached to the Indians first, then to a number of white people present; and in the afternoon, to the Indians again. Divine truth seemed to make very considerable impressions upon several of them, and caused the tears to flow freely. Afterwards I baptized my interpreter, and his wife, who were the first whom I baptized among the Indians.

They are both persons of some experimental knowledge in religion; have both been awakened to a solemn concern for their souls; have to appearance, been brought to a sense of their misery, and undoneness in themselves; have both appeared to be comforted with divine consolations; and it is apparent that both have passed a great and I cannot but hope, a saving, change. It may perhaps be satisfactory and agreeable, that I should give some brief relation of this man's exercises and experience, since he has been with me; especially since he is employed as my interpreter to others. When I first employed him in this business, in the beginning of the summer of 1744, he was well fitted for his work, in regard to his acquaintance with the Indian and English languages, as well as with the manners of both nations; and in regard to his desire that the Indians should conform to the manners and customs of the English, and especially to their manner of living. But he seemed to have little or no impression of religion upon his mind, and in that respect was very unfit for his work; being incapable of understanding and communicating to others many things of importance, so that I laboured under great disadvantages in addressing the Indians, for want of his having an experimental, as well as more doctrinal, acquaintance with divine truths; and, at times, my spirits sunk, and were much discouraged under this difficulty; especially when I observed that divine truths made little or no impressions upon his mind for many weeks together. He indeed behaved soberly after I employed him; although before, he had been a hard drinker; and seemed honestly engaged, as far as was capable, in the performance of his work. Especially he appeared very desirous that the Indians should renounce their heathenish notions and practices, and conform to the customs of the christian world. But still he seemed to have no concern about his own soul, until he had been with me a considerable time.

Near the latter end of July, 1744, I preached to an assembly of white people, with more freedom and fervency than I could possibly address the Indians with, without their having first obtained a greater measure of doctrinal knowledge. At this time he was present, and was somewhat awakened to a concern for his soul; so that the next day he discoursed freely with me about his spiritual concerns, and gave me an opportunity to use further endeavours to fasten the impressions of his perishing state upon his mind. I could plainly perceive, for some time after this, that he addressed the Indians with more concern and fervency than he had formerly done.

But these impressions seemed quickly to decline; and he remained in a great measure careless and secure, until some time late in the autumn of the year following; when he fell into a weak and languishing state of body; and continued much disordered for several weeks together. At this season divine truth took hold of him, and made deep impressions upon his mind. He was brought under great concern for his soul; and his exercises were not now transient and unsteady, but constant and abiding, so that his mind was burdened from day to day; and it was now his great inquiry, "What he should do to be saved?" This spiritual trouble prevailed, until his sleep in a great measure departed from him, and he had little rest day or night; but walked about under great pressure of mind, for he was still able to walk, and appeared like another man to his neighbours, who could not but observe his behaviour with wonder. After he had been some time under this exercise, while he was striving to obtain mercy, he says there seemed to be an impassable mountain before him. He was pressing towards heaven, as he thought; but "his way was hedged up with thorns, so that he could not stir an inch further." He looked this way, and that way, but could find no way at all. He thought if he could but make his way through these thorns and briers, and climb up the first steep pitch of the mountain, that then there might be hope for him; but no way or means could he find to accomplish this. Here he laboured for a time, but all in vain. He saw it was impossible, he says, for him ever to help himself through this insupportable difficulty. "It signified just nothing at all for him to struggle and strive any more." Here, he says, he gave over striving, and felt that it was a gone case with him, as to his own power, and that all his attempts were, and for ever would be, vain and fruitless. Yet he was more calm and composed under this view of things, than he had been while striving to help himself.

While he was giving me this account of his exercises, I was not without fears that what he related was but the working of his own imagination, and not the effect of any divine illumination of mind. But, before I had time to discover my fears, he added, that at this time he felt himself in a miserable and perishing condition: that he saw plainly what he had been doing all his days; and that he had never done one good thing, as he expresses it. He knew he was not guilty of some wicked actions of which he knew some others guilty. He had not been accustomed to steal, quarrel, and murder; the latter of which vices are common among the Indians. He likewise knew that he had done many things that were right; he had been kind to his neighbours, &c. "But still his cry was, that he had never done one good thing." "I knew," said he, "that I had not been so bad as some others in some things; and that I had done many things which folks call good; but all this did me no good now. I saw that all was bad, and that I had never done one good thing"; meaning that he had never done any thing from a right principle, and with a right view, though he had done many things that were materially good and right. "And now I thought," said he, "that I must sink down to hell; that there was no hope for me, 'because I never could do any thing that was good': and if God let me alone ever so long, and I should try ever so much, still I should do nothing but what is bad."

This further account of his exercises satisfied me that it was not the mere working of his imagination; since he appeared so evidently to die to himself, and to be divorced from a dependence upon his own righteousness, and good deeds, to which mankind in a fallen state are so much attached; and upon which they are so ready to hope for salvation.

There was one thing more in his view of things at this time, which was very remarkable. He not only saw, he says, what a miserable state he himself was in, but he likewise saw that the world around him, in general, were in the same perishing circumstances, notwithstanding the profession which many of them made of christianity, and the hope which they entertained of obtaining everlasting happiness. This he saw clearly, as if he was now waked out of sleep, or had a cloud taken from his eyes. He saw that the life which he had lived was the way to eternal death, that he was now on the brink of endless misery; and when he looked around he saw multitudes of others, who had lived the same life with himself, persons who had no more goodness than he, and yet dreamed that they were safe enough, as he had formerly done. He was fully persuaded, by their conversation and behaviour, that they had never felt their sin and misery, as he now felt his.

After he had been for some time in this condition, sensible of the impossibility of helping himself by any thing which he could do, or of being delivered by any created arm; so that he had "given up all for lost," as to his own attempts, and was become more calm and composed; then, he says, it was borne in upon his mind, as if it had been audibly spoken to him, "There is hope, there is hope." Whereupon his soul seemed to rest, and he in some measure satisfied, though he had no considerable joy.

He cannot here remember distinctly any views he had of Christ, or give any clear account of his soul's acceptance of him, which makes his experience appear the more doubtful, and renders it less satisfactory to himself and others than it might be, if he could remember distinctly the apprehensions and actings of his mind at this season.—But these exercises of soul were attended and followed with a very great change in the man; so that it might justly be said he was become another man, if not a new man. His conversation and deportment were much altered; and even the careless world could not but wonder what had befallen him, to make so great a change in his temper, discourse, and behaviour. Especially there was a surprising alternation in his public performances. He now addressed the Indians with admirable fervency, and scarcely knew when to leave off. Sometimes, when I had concluded my discourse and was returning homeward, he would tarry behind to repeat and inculcate what had been spoken.

His change is abiding, and his life, so far as I know, unblemished to this day; though it is now more than six months since he experienced this change; in which space of time he has been as much exposed to strong drink as possible, in divers places where it has been moving as free as water; and yet has never, that I know of, discovered any hankering desire after it. He seems to have a very considerable experience of spiritual exercise, and discourses feelingly of the conflicts and consolations of a real christian. His heart echoes to the soul-humbling doctrines of grace, and he never appears better pleased than when he hears of the absolute sovereignty of God, and the salvation of sinners in a way of mere free grace. He has lately had also more satisfaction respecting his own state; and has been much enlightened and assisted in his work; so that he has been a great comfort to me.

After a strict observation of his serious and savoury conversation, his christian temper, and unblemished behaviour for such a length of time, as well as his experience, of which I have given an account; I think that I have reason to hope that he is "created anew in Christ Jesus to good works." His name is MOSES FINDA FAUTAURY. He is about fifty years of age, and is pretty well acquainted with the pagan notions and customs of his countrymen; and so is the better able now to expose them. He has, I am persuaded, already been, and I trust will yet be, a blessing to the other Indians.

July 23. Preached to the Indians, but had few hearers. Those who of late are constantly at home, seem, of late, to be under some impressions of a religious nature.

July 26. Preached to my people, and afterwards baptized my interpreter's children. In the evening, God was pleased to help me in prayer, beyond what I have experienced for some time. Especially, my soul was drawn out for the encouragement of Christ's kingdom, and for the conversion of my poor people; and my soul relied on God for the accomplishment of that great work. How sweet were the thoughts of death to me at this time! How I longed to be with Christ, to be employed in the glorious work of angels, and with an angel's vigour and delight! Yet how willing was I to stay awhile on earth, that I might do something, if the Lord pleased for his interest in the world. My soul, my very soul, longed for the ingathering of the poor Heathen; and I cried to God most willingly and heartily. I could not but cry. This was a sweet season; for I had some lively taste of Heaven, and a temper of mind suited in some measure to the employments and entertainments of it. My soul was grieved to leave the place; but my body was weak and worn out, and it was nearly nine o'clock. I longed that the remaining part of life might be filled up with more fervency and activity in the things of God. O the inward peace, composure, and god-like serenity of such a frame! Heaven must differ from this only in degree, not in kind. Lord! ever give me this bread of life.

Lord's day, July 28. Preached again, and found my people, at least some of them, more thoughtful than ever about their souls' concerns. I was told by some, that their seeing my interpreter and others baptized made them more concerned than any thing they had ever seen or heard before. There was indeed a considerable appearance of divine power among them while the ordinance was administered. May that divine influence spread and increase more abundantly!

In the evening my soul was melted, and my heart broken with a sense of past barrenness and deadness.—O how I then longed to live to God and bring forth much fruit to his glory!

July 29. Was much exercised with a sense of vileness, with guilt and shame before God.

Discoursed to a number of my people, and gave them some particular advice and direction; being now about to leave them for the present, in order to renew my visit to the Indians in New-Jersey. They were very attentive to my discourse, and earnestly desirous to know when I designed to return to them again.

On Wednesday, July 31, he set out on his return to Crossweeksung, and arrived there the next day. In his way thither, he had longing desires that he might come to the Indians there in the fulness of the blessing of the gospel of Christ, attended with a sense of his own weakness, dependence and worthlessness.

Crossweeksung, (New-Jersey) August, 1745

August 2. In the evening I retired, and my soul was drawn out in prayer to God; especially for my poor people, to whom I had sent word that they might gather together, that I might preach to them the next day. I was much enlarged in praying for their saving conversion; and scarcely ever found my desires of any thing of this nature so sensibly and clearly, to my own satisfaction, disinterested and free from selfish views. It seemed to me I had no care, or hardly any desire, to be the instrument of so glorious a work as I wished and prayed for among the Indians. If the blessed work might be accomplished to the honour of God, and the enlargement of the dear Redeemer's kingdom; this was all my desire and care; and for this mercy I hoped but with trembling; for I felt what Job expresses, chap. 9th, [verse] 16th, "If I had called, and he had answered me, yet would I not believe that he had hearkened unto my voice." My rising hopes, respecting the conversion of the Indians, have been so often dashed, that my spirit is as it were broken, and my courage wasted, and I hardly dare hope. I visited the Indians in these parts in June last, and tarried with them a considerable time, preaching almost daily: at which season God was pleased to pour upon them a spirit of awakening and concern for their souls, and surprisingly to engage their attention to divine truths. I now found them serious, and a number of them under deep concern for an interest in Christ.—Their convictions of their sinful and perishing state were, in my absence from them, much promoted by the labours and endeavours of REV. WILLIAM TENNENT; to whom I had advised them to apply for direction; and whose house they frequented much while I was gone. I preached to them this day with some view to Rev. xxii. 17. "And whosoever will, let him take of the water of life freely"; though I could not pretend to handle the subject methodically among them. The Lord, I am persuaded, enabled me, in a manner somewhat uncommon, to set before them the Lord Jesus Christ as a kind and compassionate Saviour, inviting distressed and perishing sinners to accept everlasting mercy. A surprising concern soon became apparent among them. There were about twenty adult persons together; many of the Indians at remote places not having as yet had time to come since my return hither; and not above two that I could see with dry eyes.

Some were much concerned, and discovered vehement longings of soul after Christ, to save them from the misery they felt and feared.

Lord's day, Aug. 4. Being invited by a neighbouring minister to assist in the administration of the Lord's supper, I complied with his request, and took the Indians along with me; not only those who were together the day before, but many more who were coming to hear me; so that there were nearly fifty in all, old and young. They attended the several discourses of the day; and some of them, who could understand English, were much affected; and all seemed to have their concern in some measure raised.

Now a change in their manners began to appear very visible. In the evening, when they came to sup together, they would not take a morsel until they had sent to me to come and supplicate a blessing on their food; at which time sundry of them wept; especially when I reminded them how they had in times past eat their feasts in honour to devils, and neglected to thank God for them.

August 5. After a sermon had been preached by another minister, I preached, and concluded the public work of the solemnity from John 7th, 37th. In the last day, &c.; and in my discourse addressed the Indians in particular, who sat in a part of the house by themselves; at which time one or two of them were struck with deep concern, as they afterwards told me, who had been little affected before; and others had their concern increased to a considerable degree. In the evening, the greater part of them being at the house where I lodged, I discoursed to them; and found them universally engaged about their souls' concerns; inquiring "what they should do to be saved." All their conversation among themselves turned upon religious matters, in which they were much assisted by my interpreter, who was with them day and night.

This day there was one woman, who had been much concerned for her soul ever since she first heard me preach, in June last, who obtained comfort, I trust, solid and well grounded. She seemed to be filled with love to Christ. At the same time she behaved humbly and tenderly, and appeared afraid of nothing so much as of offending and grieving him whom her soul loved.

Aug. 6. In the morning I discoursed to the Indians at the house where we lodged. Many of them were much affected, and appeared surprisingly tender; so that a few words about the concerns of their souls would cause the tears to flow freely, and produce many sobs and groans.—In the afternoon, they being returned to the place where I had usually preached among them, I again discoursed to them there. There were about fifty-five persons in all; about forty that were capable of attending Divine service with understanding. I insisted on 1 John, 4th, 10th. Herein is love, &c. They seemed eager of hearing; but there appeared nothing very remarkable, except their attention, till near the close of my discourse; and then Divine truths were attended with a surprising influence; and produced a great concern among them. There were scarcely three in forty who could refrain from tears and bitter cries. They all as one seemed in an agony of soul to obtain an interest in Christ; and the more I discoursed of the love and compassion of God in sending his Son to suffer for the sins of men; and the more I invited them to come and partake of his love; the more their distress was aggravated, because they felt themselves unable to come. It was surprising to see how their hearts seemed to be pierced with the tender and melting invitations of the gospel, when there was not a word of terror spoken to them.

There was this day two persons who obtained relief and comfort; which, when I came to discourse with them particularly, appeared solid, rational and scriptural. After I had inquired into the grounds of their comfort, and said many things which I thought proper to them; I asked them what they wanted that God should do farther for them? They replied, "they wanted Christ should wipe their hearts quite clean," &c. So surprising were now the doings of the Lord, that I can say no less of this day, and I need say no more of it, than that the arm of the Lord was powerfully and marvellously revealed in it.

Aug. 7. Preached to the Indians from Is. liii. 3–10. There was a remarkable influence attending the word, and great concern in the assembly; but scarcely equal to what appeared the day before; that is, not quite so universal. However, most were much affected, and many in great distress for their souls; and some few could neither go nor stand, but lay flat on the ground as if pierced at heart, crying incessantly for mercy. Several were newly awakened; and it is remarkable that, as fast as they came from remote places round about, the Spirit of God seemed to seize them with concern for their souls. After public service was concluded, I found two persons more who had newly met with comfort, of whom I had good hopes; and a third, of whom I could not but entertain some hopes, whose case did not appear so clear as the others; so that there were now six in all, who had got some relief from their spiritual distresses; and five, whose experience appeared very clear and satisfactory. It is worthy of remark, that those who obtained comfort first, were in general deeply affected with concern for their souls, when I preached to them in June last.

Aug. 8. In the afternoon I preached to the Indians, their number was now about sixty-five persons; men, women and children. I discoursed upon Luke xiv. 16–23, and was favoured with uncommon freedom in my discourse. There was much visible concern among them, while I was discoursing publicly; but afterwards, when I spoke to one and another more particularly, whom I perceived under much concern, the power of God seemed to descend upon the assembly "like a mighty rushing wind," and with an astonishing energy bore down all before it. I stood amazed at the influence, which seized the audience almost universally; and could compare it to nothing more aptly, than the irresistible force of a mighty torrent or swelling deluge, that with its insupportable weight and pressure bears down and sweeps before it whatever comes in its way. Almost all persons of all ages were bowed down with concern together, and scarcely one was able to withstand the shock of this surprising operation. Old men and women, who had been drunken wretches for many years, and some little children, not more than six or seven years of age, appeared in distress for their souls, as well as persons of middle age. It was apparent that these children, some of them at least, were not merely frightened with seeing the general concern; but were made sensible of their danger, the badness of their hearts, and their misery without Christ, as some of them expressed it. The most stubborn hearts were now obliged to bow. A principal man among the Indians, who before was most secure and self-righteous, and thought his state good, because he knew more than the generality of the Indians had formerly done; and who with a great degree of confidence the day before told me "he had been a Christian more than ten years"; was now brought under solemn concern for his soul, and wept bitterly. Another man advanced in years, who had been a murderer, a pawaw or conjurer, and a notorious drunkard, was likewise brought now to cry for mercy with many tears, and to complain much that he could be no more concerned when he saw his danger so very great.

They were almost universally praying and crying for mercy in every part of the house, and many out of doors; and numbers could neither go nor stand. Their concern was so great, each one for himself, that none seemed to take any notice of those about them, but each prayed freely for himself. I am led to think they were, to their own apprehensions, as much retired as if they had been individually by themselves, in the thickest desert; or I believe rather that they thought nothing about any thing but themselves, and their own state, and so were every one praying apart, although all together. It seemed to me that there was now an exact fulfilment of that prophecy, Zech. xii. 10, 11, 12; for there was now "a great mourning, like the mourning of Hadadrimmon";—and each seemed to "mourn apart." Methought this had a near resemblance to the day wherein I am persuaded the Lord did much to destroy the kingdom of darkness among this people.

This concern, in general, was most rational and just. Those who had been awakened any considerable time, complained especially of the badness of their hearts; and those who were newly awakened, of the badness of their lives and actions; and all were afraid of the anger of God, and of everlasting misery as the desert of their sins. Some of the white people, who came out of curiosity to hear what "that babbler would say" to the poor ignorant Indians, were much awakened; and some appeared to be wounded with a view of their perishing state. Those who had lately obtained relief, were filled with comfort at this season. They appeared calm and composed, and seemed to rejoice in Christ Jesus. Some of them took their distressed friends by the hand, telling them of the goodness of Christ, and the comfort that is to be enjoyed in him; and thence invited them to come and give up their hearts to him. I could observe some of them, in the most honest and unaffected manner, without any design of being taken notice of, lifting up their eyes to heaven, as if crying for mercy, while they saw the distress of the poor souls around them. There was one remarkable instance of awakening this day which I cannot fail to notice here. A young Indian woman, who, I believe, never knew before that she had a soul, nor ever thought of any such thing, hearing that there was something strange among the Indians, came, it seems to see what was the matter. In her way to the Indians she called at my lodgings; and when I told her that I designed presently to preach to the Indians, laughed, and seemed to mock; but went however to them. I had not proceeded far in my public discourse before she felt effectually that she had a soul; and, before I had concluded my discourse, was so convinced of her sin and misery, and so distressed with concern for her soul's salvation, that she seemed like one pierced through with a dart, and cried out incessantly. She could neither go nor stand, nor sit on her seat without being held up. After public service was over, she lay flat on the ground, praying earnestly, and would take no notice of, nor give any answer to, any who spoke to her. I hearkened to hear what she said, and perceived the burden of her prayer to be, *"Guttummauhalummeh wechaumeh kmeleh Nolah,"* i.e. "Have mercy on me, and help me to give you my heart." Thus she continued praying incessantly for many hours together. This was indeed a surprising day of God's power, and seemed enough to convince an Atheist of the truth, importance, and power of God's word.

Aug. 9. Spent almost the whole day with the Indians; the former part of it in discoursing to many of them privately, and especially to some who had lately received comfort, and endeavouring to inquire into the grounds of it, as well as to give them some proper instructions, cautions and directions.

In the afternoon discoursed to them publicly. There were now present about seventy persons, old and young. I opened and applied the parable of the sower, Matt. xiii. Was enabled to discourse with much plainness, and found afterwards that this discourse was very instructive to them. There were many tears among them, while I was discoursing publicly, but no considerable cry: yet some were much affected with a few words spoken from Matt. xi. 28. Come unto me all ye that labour, &c. with which I concluded my discourse. But, while I was discoursing near night to two or three of the awakened persons, a Divine influence seemed to attend what was spoken to them in a powerful manner; which caused the persons to cry out in anguish of soul, although I spoke not a word of terror; but on the contrary, set before them the fulness and all-sufficiency of Christ's merits, and his willingness to save all that come to him, and thereupon pressed them to come without delay. The cry of these was soon heard by others, who, though scattered before, immediately gathered round. I then proceeded in the same strain of gospel-invitation, till they were all melted into tears and cries, except two or three; and seemed in the greatest distress to find and secure an interest in the great Redeemer. Some, who had little more than a ruffle made in their passions the day before, seemed now to be deeply affected and wounded at heart; and the concern in general appeared nearly as prevalent as it was the day before. There was indeed a very great mourning among them, and yet every one seemed to mourn apart. For so great was their concern, that almost every one was praying and crying for himself, as if none had been near. "*Guttummauhalummeh; guttummauhalummeh*" i.e. "Have mercy upon me; have mercy upon me"; was the common cry. It was very affecting to see the poor Indians, who the other day were hollowing and yelling in their idolatrous feasts and drunken frolics, now crying to God with such importunity for an interest in his dear Son!—Found two or three persons who, I had reason to hope, had taken comfort upon good grounds since the evening before; and these with others who had obtained comfort, were together, and seemed to rejoice much that God was carrying on his work with such power upon others.

Aug. 10. Rode to the Indians, and began to discourse more privately to those who had obtained comfort and satisfaction; endeavouring to instruct, direct, caution, and comfort them. But others, being eager of hearing every word which related to spiritual concerns, soon came together one after another; and, when I had discoursed to the young converts more than half an hour, they seemed much melted with divine things, and earnestly desirous to be with Christ. I told them of the godly soul's perfect purity, and full enjoyment of Christ, immediately upon its separation from the body; and that it would be inconceivably more happy than they had ever been for any short space of time, when Christ seemed near to them in prayer or other duties. That I might make way for speaking of the resurrection of the body, and then of the complete blessedness of the man; I said, "But perhaps some of you will say, I love my body as well as my soul, and I cannot bear to think that my body shall lie dead, if my soul is happy." To which they all cheerfully replied, "Muttoh, Muttoh"; before I had opportunity to prosecute what I designed respecting the resurrection; i.e. "No, No." They did not regard their bodies, if their souls might be with Christ.—Then they appeared willing to be absent from the body, that they might be present with the Lord.

When I had spent some time with them, I turned to the other Indians, and spoke to them from Luke xix. 10. For the son of man is come to seek, &c. I had not discoursed long, before their concern rose to a great degree; and the house was filled with cries and groans. When I insisted on the compassion and care of the Lord Jesus Christ for those that were lost, who thought themselves undone, and could find no way of escape; this melted them down the more, and aggravated their desires, that they could not find and come to so kind a Saviour.

Sundry persons, who before had been slightly awakened, were now deeply wounded with a sense of their sin and misery. One man in particular, who was never before awakened, was now made to feel that "the word of the Lord was quick and powerful, and sharper than any two edged sword." He seemed to be pierced at heart with distress; and his concern appeared most rational and scriptural, for he said that "all the wickedness of his past life was brought fresh to his remembrance, and that he saw all the vile actions, he had done formerly, as if done but yesterday."

Found one who had newly received comfort, after pressing distress from day to day. Could not but rejoice, and admire the Divine goodness in what appeared this day. There seems to be some good done by every discourse; some newly awakened every day, and some comforted. It was refreshing to observe the conduct of those who obtained comfort; while others were distressed with fear and concern; that is lifting up their hearts to God for them.

Lord's day, Aug. 11. Discoursed in the forenoon from the parable of the prodigal son, Luke xv. Observed no such remarkable effect of the word upon the assembly as in days past. There were numbers of careless spectators of the white people, some Quakers and others. In the afternoon, I discoursed upon a part of St. Peter's sermon, Acts ii; and at the close of my discourse to the Indians, made an address to the white people; and divine truths seemed then to be attended with power, both to English and Indians. Several of the white heathen were awakened, and could not longer be idle spectators; but found they had souls to save or lose as well as the Indians; and a great concern spread through the whole assembly. So that this also appeared to be a day of God's power, especially towards the conclusion of it, although the influence attending the word seemed scarcely so powerful now as in days past.

The number of Indians, old and young, was now upwards of seventy; and one or two were newly awakened this day, who never had appeared to be moved with concern for their souls before. Those who had obtained relief and comfort, and had given hopeful evidences of having passed a saving change, appeared humble and devout, and behaved in an agreeable and Christian-like manner. I was refreshed to see the tenderness of conscience manifest in some of them; one instance of which I cannot but notice. Perceiving one of them very sorrowful in the morning, I inquired into the cause of her sorrow, and found the difficulty was, that she had been angry with her child the evening before, and was now exercised with fears lest her anger had been inordinate and sinful; which so grieved her, that she waked and began to sob before day light, and continued weeping for several hours together

Aug. 14. Spent the day with the Indians. There was one of them, who had some time since put away his wife, as is common amongst them, and taken another woman; and, being now brought under some serious impressions, was much concerned about that affair in particular, and seemed fully convinced of the wickedness of the practice, and earnestly desired to know what God would have him to do in his present circumstances. When the Law of God respecting marriage had been opened to them, and the cause of his leaving his wife inquired into; and when it appeared that she had given him no just occasion, by unchastity, to desert her, and that she was willing to forgive his past misconduct and to live peaceably with him for the future, and that she moreover insisted on it as her right to live with him; he was then told that it was his indispensable duty to renounce the woman whom he had last taken, and receive the other, who was his proper wife, and live peaceably with her during life. With this he readily and cheerfully complied; and thereupon publicly renounced the woman he had last taken, and publicly promised to live with and be kind to his wife during life; she also promising the same to him. Here appeared a clear demonstration of the power of God's word upon their hearts. I suppose a few weeks before, the whole world could not have persuaded this man to a compliance with Christian rules in this affair.

I was not without fears that this proceeding might be like putting "new wine into old bottles"; and that some might be prejudiced against Christianity, when they saw the demands made by it. But the man being much concerned about the matter, the determination of it could be deferred no longer; and it seemed to have a good rather than an ill effect among the Indians; who generally owned that the laws of Christ were good and right, respecting the affairs of marriage.—In the afternoon I preached to them from the apostle's discourse to Cornelius, Acts 10th, 34th, &c. There appeared some affectionate concern among them, though not equal to what appeared in several of the former days. They still attended and heard as for their lives, and the Lord's work seemed still to be promoted and propagated among them.

Aug. 15. Preached from Luke iv. 16–21. "And he came to Nazareth," &c. The word was attended with power upon the hearts of the hearers. There was much concern, many tears, and affecting cries among them; and some of a peculiar manner were deeply wounded and distressed for their souls. There were some newly awakened who came but this week, and convictions seemed to be promoted in others. Those who had received comfort, were likewise refreshed and strengthened; and the work of grace appeared to advance in all respects. The passions of the congregation in general were not so much moved, as in some days past; but their hearts seemed as solemnly and deeply affected with divine truths as ever, at least in many instances, although the concern did not seem so universal, and to reach every individual in such a manner as it appeared to do some days before.

Aug. 16. Spent a considerable time in conversing with sundry of the Indians. Found one who had got relief and comfort after pressing concern; and could not but hope, when I came to discourse particularly with her, that her comfort was of the right kind.—In the afternoon I preached to them from John vi. 26–34. Toward the close of my discourse, divine truths were attended with considerable power upon the audience; and more especially after public service was over, when I particularly addressed sundry distressed persons.

There was a great concern for their souls spread pretty generally among them; but especially there were two persons newly awakened to a sense of their sin and misery; one of whom was lately come, and the other had all along been very attentive and desirous of being awakened, but could never before have any lively view of her perishing state. Now her concern and spiritual distress was such, that I thought I had never seen any more pressing. Sundry old men were also in distress for their souls; so that they could not refrain from weeping and crying aloud; and their bitter groans were the most convincing as well as affecting evidence of the reality and depth of their inward anguish. God is powerfully at work among them. True and genuine convictions of sin are daily promoted in many instances; and some are newly awakened from time to time; although some few, who felt a commotion in their passions in the days past, seem now to discover that their hearts were never duly affected. I never saw the work of God appeared so independent of means as at this time. I discoursed to the people, and spake what I suppose had a proper tendency to promote convictions; but God's manner of working upon them seemed so entirely supernatural, and above means, that I could scarcely believe he used me as an instrument, or what I spake as means of carrying on his work. For it appeared, as I thought, to have no connexion with or dependence on means in any respect. Though I could not but continue to use the means, which I thought proper for the promotion of the work, yet God seemed, as I apprehended, to work entirely without them. I seemed to do nothing, and indeed to have nothing to do, but to "stand still, and see the salvation of God"; and found myself obliged and delighted to say, "Not unto us," not unto instruments and means, "but to thy name be glory." God appeared to work entirely alone, and I saw no room to attribute any part of this work to any created arm.

Aug. 17. Spent much time in private conferences with the Indians. Found one who had newly obtained relief and comfort, after a long season of spiritual trouble and distress;—he having been one of my hearers at the Forks of Delaware for more than a year, and now having followed me here under deep concern for his soul;—and had abundant reason to hope that his comfort was well grounded, and truly divine. Afterwards discoursed publicly from Acts viii. 29–39; and took occasion to treat concerning baptism, in order to their being instructed and prepared to partake of that ordinance. They were yet hungry and thirsty for the word of God, and appeared unwearied in their attendance upon it.

Lord's day, Aug. 18. Preached in the forenoon to an assembly of white people, made up of Presbyterians, Baptists, Quakers, &c. Afterwards preached to the Indians, from John vi. 35–40, He that eateth my flesh, &c. There was considerable concern visible among them, though not equal to what has frequently appeared of late.

Aug. 19. Preached from Isaiah 55th, 1st. Ho, every one that thirsteth. Divine truths were attended with power upon those who had received comfort, and others also. The former sweetly melted and refreshed with divine invitations; the latter much concerned for their souls, that they might obtain an interest in these glorious gospel provisions which were set before them. There were numbers of poor impotent souls that waited at the pool for healing; and the angel seemed, as at other times of late, to trouble the waters, so that there was yet a most desirable and comfortable prospect of the spiritual recovery of diseased perishing sinners. Near noon, I rode to Freehold, and preached to a considerable assembly, from Matt. 5th, 3rd. Blessed are the poor in spirit, &c. It pleased God to leave me to be very dry and barren; so that I do not remember to have been so straightened for a whole twelve-month past. God is just; and he has made me to acquiesce in his will in this respect. It is contrary to flesh and blood to be cut off from all freedom in a large auditory, where their expectations are much raised; but so it was with me; and God helped me to say amen to it. Good is the will of the Lord. In the evening I felt quiet and composed, and had freedom and comfort in secret prayer.

Aug. 20. Was composed and comfortable, still in a resigned frame. Travelled from Mr. Tennent's, in Freehold, to Elizabeth Town. Was refreshed to see friends and relate to them what God had done and was still doing among my poor people.

Aug. 21. Spent the forenoon in conversation with Mr. Dickinson, contriving something for the settlement of the Indians together in a body, that they might be under better advantages for instruction. In the afternoon spent some time agreeably with other friends; wrote to my brother at college; but was grieved that time slid away, while I did so little for God.

Aug. 23. In the morning was very weak, but favored with some freedom and sweetness in prayer, was comfortable and composed in mind. Afternoon rode to Crossweeksung to my poor people.

Spent some time with the Indians in private discourse; and, afterwards, preached to them from John vi. 44–50. No man can come to me except, &c. There was, as has been usual, a great attention and some affection among them. Several appeared deeply concerned for their souls, and could not but express their inward anguish by tears and cries. But the amazing divine influence, which has been so powerfully among them in general, seems at present in some degree abated; at least, in regard to its universality; though many who have obtained no special comfort still retain deep impressions of divine things.

Aug. 24. Spent the forenoon in discoursing to some of the Indians in order to their receiving the ordinance of baptism. When I had opened the nature of the ordinance, the obligations attending it, the duty of devoting ourselves to God in it, and the privilege of being in covenant with him; numbers of them seemed to be filled with love to God, delighted with the thoughts of giving themselves up to him in that solemn and public manner, and melted and refreshed with the hopes of enjoying the blessed Redeemer. Afterwards, I discoursed publicly from 1 Thess. iv. 13–17. But I would not have you be ignorant, &c. There was a solemn attention, and some visible concern and affection in the time of public service; which was afterwards increased by some further exhortations given to them to come to Christ, and give up their hearts to him, that they might be fitted to "ascend up and meet him in the air," when he shall "descend with a shout, and the voice of the archangel."

There were several Indians newly come, who thought their state good, and themselves happy, because they had sometimes lived with the white people under gospel light, had learned to read, were civil, &c., although they appeared utter strangers to their hearts, and altogether unacquainted with the power of religion, as well as with the doctrines of grace. With these I discoursed particularly after public worship; and was surprised to see their self-righteous dispositions, their strong attachment to the covenant of works for salvation, and the high value they put upon their supposed attainments. Yet after much discourse, one appeared in a measure convinced that "by the deeds of the law no flesh living can be justified"; and wept bitterly inquiring what he must do to be saved.

This was very comfortable to others, who had gained some experimental knowledge of their own hearts; for, before, they were grieved with the conversation and conduct of these new comers, who boasted of their knowledge, and thought well of themselves, but evidently discovered to those who had any experience of divine truths that they knew nothing of their own hearts.

Lord's day, Aug. 25. Preached in the forenoon from Luke xv. 37. A number of white people being present, I made an address to them at the close of my discourse to the Indians; but could not so much as keep them orderly; for scores of them kept walking and gazing about, and behaved more indecently than any Indians I have ever addressed. A view of their abusive conduct so sunk my spirits, that I could scarcely go on with my work.

In the afternoon discoursed from Rev. iii. 20; at which time they behaved seriously, though many others were vain. Afterwards baptized twenty-five persons of the Indians; fifteen adults and ten children. Most of the adults, I have comfortable reason to hope, are renewed persons; and there was not one of them but what I entertained some hopes of in that respect; though the case of two or three of them appeared more doubtful.

After the crowd of spectators was gone, I called the baptized persons together, and discoursed to them in particular; at the same time inviting others to attend. I reminded them of the solemn obligations they were now under to live to God; warned them of the evil and dreadful consequences of careless living, especially after their public profession of Christianity; gave them directions for future conduct; and encouraged them to watchfulness and devotion, by setting before them the comfort and happy conclusion of a religious life.

This was a desirable and sweet season indeed! Their hearts were engaged and cheerful in duty; and they rejoiced that they had, in a public and solemn manner, dedicated themselves to God. Love seemed to reign among them! They took each other by the hand with tenderness and affection, as if their hearts were knit together, while I was discoursing to them; and all their deportment towards each other was such, that a serious spectator might justly be excited to cry out with admiration, "behold how they love one another." Numbers of the other Indians, on seeing and hearing these things, were much affected, and wept bitterly; longing to be partakers of the same joy and comfort, which these discovered by their very countenances as well as conduct. I rode to my lodgings in the evening, blessing the Lord for his gracious visitation of the Indians, and the soul-refreshing things I had seen the day past among them; and praying that God would still carry on his divine work among them.

Aug. 26. Preached to my people from John vi. 51–55. After I had discoursed some time, I addressed them in particular, who entertained hopes that they were passed from death unto life. Opened to them the persevering nature of those consolations which Christ gives his people, and which I trusted he had bestowed upon some in that assembly; shewed them that such have already the beginnings of eternal life, and that their heaven shall speedily be completed.

I no longer begun to discourse in this strain, than the dear Christians in the congregation began to be melted with affection to, and desire of, the enjoyment of Christ, and of a state of perfect purity. They wept affectionately, yet joyfully; and their tears and sobs discovered brokenness of heart, and yet were attended with real comfort and sweetness. It was a tender, affectionate, humble and delightful meeting, and appeared to be the genuine effect of a spirit of adoption, and very far from that spirit of bondage under which they not long since laboured. The influence seemed to spread from these through the whole assembly; and there quickly appeared a wonderful concern among them. Many, who had not yet found Christ as an all-sufficient Saviour, were surprisingly engaged in seeking after him. It was indeed a lovely and very interesting assembly. Their number was now about ninety-five persons, old and young, and almost all affected with joy in Christ Jesus, or with the utmost concern to obtain an interest in him.

Being now convinced that it was my duty to take a journey far back to the Indians on the Susquehannah, it being now a proper season of the year to find them generally at home; after having spent some hours in public and private discourse with my people, I told them that I must now leave them for the present, and go to their brethren far remote, and preach to them; that I wanted the spirit of God should go with me, without whom nothing could be done to any good purpose among the Indians—as they themselves had opportunity to see and observe by the barrenness of our meetings at sometimes, when there was much pains taken to affect and awaken sinners, and yet to little or no purpose, and asked them if they could not be willing to spend the remainder of the day in prayer for me, that God would go with me, and succeed my endeavours for the conversion of these poor souls. They cheerfully complied with the motion, and soon after I left them, the sun being about an hour and an half high at night; they began and continued praying till break of day, or very near; never mistrusting as they tell me, till they went out and viewed the stars, and saw the morning star a considerable height, that it was later than bed time. Thus eager and unwearied were they in their devotions! A remarkable night it was; attended, as my interpreter tells me, with a powerful influence upon those who were yet under concern, as well as those who had received comfort. There were, I trust, this day, two distressed souls brought to the enjoyment of solid comfort in him whom the weary find rest. It was likewise remarkable, that this day an old Indian, who had all his days been an idolater, was brought to give up his rattles, which they use for music in their idolatrous feasts and dances, to the other Indians, who quickly destroyed them. This was done without any attempt of mine in the affair, I having said nothing to him about it, so that it seemed to be nothing but the power of God's word, without any particular application to this sin that produced this effect. Thus God has begun; thus he has hitherto surprisingly carried on a work of grace amongst these Indians. May the glory be ascribed to him who is the sole author of it.

I went from the Indians to my lodgings, rejoicing for the goodness of God to my poor people; and enjoyed freedom of soul in prayer, and other duties in the evening. Bless the Lord, O my soul!

The next day, he set out on a journey towards the Forks of Delaware, designed to go from thence to Susquehannah, before he returned to Crossweeksung. It was five days from his departure from Crossweeksung, before he reached the Forks; going round by the way of Philadelphia, and waiting on the Governor of Pennsylvania, to get a recommendation from him to the Chiefs of the Indians; which he obtained. He speaks of much comfort and spiritual refreshment, in this journey, and also, a sense of his exceeding unworthiness, thinking himself the meanest creature that ever lived.

Forks of Delaware, in Pennsylvania,
Sept. 1745.

Lord's day, Sept. 1. Preached to the Indians from Luke xi. 16–23. The word appeared to be attended with some power, and caused some tears in the assembly. Afterwards preached to a number of white people present, and observed many of them in tears; and some who had formerly been careless and unconcerned about religion, perhaps, as the Indians. Towards night, discoursed to the Indians again, and perceived a greater attention, and more visible concern among them, than has been usual in these parts. God gave me the spirit of prayer, and it was a blessed season in that respect. My soul cried to God for mercy, in an affectionate manner. In the evening, also, my soul rejoiced in God.

Sept. 3. Preached to the Indians from Isaiah liii. 3–6. He is despised and rejected of men, &c. The Divine presence seemed to be in the midst of the assembly, and a considerable concern spread among them. Sundry persons seemed to be awakened; among whom were two stupid creatures, whom I could scarce ever before keep awake while I was discoursing to them. I could not but rejoice at this appearance of things; although at the same time, I could not but fear, lest the concern which they at present manifested, might prove like a morning cloud, as something of that nature had formerly done in these parts.

Sept. 4. Rode 15 miles to an Irish settlement, and preached there from Luke xiv. 22. "And yet there is room." God was pleased to afford me some tenderness and enlargement in the first prayer, and much freedom as well as warmth in the sermon. There were many tears in the assembly; the people of God seemed to melt; and others to be in some measure awakened. Blessed be the Lord, who lets me see his work going on in one place and another!

Sept. 5. Discoursed to the Indians from the parable of the sower. Afterwards I conversed particularly with sundry persons; which occasioned them to weep, and even to cry out in an affecting manner, and seized others with surprise and concern. I doubt not but that a divine power accompanied what was then spoken. Several of these persons had been with me to Crossweeksung: and there had seen and some of them I trust, felt, the power of God's word, in an affecting and saving manner. I asked one of them, who had obtained comfort, and given hopeful evidences of being truly religious, "Why he now cried?" He replied, "When he thought how Christ was slain like a lamb, and spilt his blood for sinners, he could not help crying, when he was alone"; and thereupon burst into tears, and cried again. I then asked his wife who had likewise been abundantly comforted, why she cried? She answered, "that she was grieved that the Indians here would not come to Christ, as well as those at Crossweeksung." I asked her if she found a heart to pray for them; and whether Christ had seemed to be near her of late in prayer, as in times past; which is my usual method of expressing a sense of the divine presence. She replied "yes, he had been near to her, and at times when she had been praying alone, her heart loved to pray so, that she could not bear to leave the place, but wanted to stay and pray longer."

Sept. 6. Enjoyed some freedom and intenseness of mind, in prayer alone; and longed to have my soul more warmed with divine and heavenly things. Was somewhat melancholy towards night, and longed to die and quit a scene of sin and darkness, but was a little supported in prayer.

Sept. 7. Preached to the Indians from John vi. 35–39. There was not so much the appearance of concern among them as at several other times of late; yet they appeared serious and attentive.

Lord's day, Sept. 8. Discoursed to the Indians in the afternoon from Acts ii. 36–39. The word of God at this time seemed to fall with weight and influence upon them. There were but few present; but most that were, were in tears; and several cried out in distressing concern for their souls. There was one man considerably awakened, who never before discovered any concern for his soul. There appeared a remarkable work of the Divine Spirit among them generally, not unlike what has been of late at Crossweeksung. It seemed as if the divine influence had spread thence to this place; although something of it appeared here before in the awakening of my interpreter, his wife, and some few others. Several of the careless white people now present, were awakened, or at least startled, seeing the power of God so prevalent among the Indians. I then made a particular address to them, which seemed to make some impression upon them, and excite some affection in them.

There are sundry Indians in these parts, who have always refused to hear me preach, and have been enraged against those who have attended on my preaching. But of late they are more bitter than ever; scoffing at Christianity, and sometimes asking my hearers, "How often they have cried," and "Whether they have not now cried enough to do their turn," &c. So that they have already trial of cruel workings.

In the evening, God was pleased to assist me in prayer, and give me freedom at the throne of grace. I cried to God for the enlargement of his kingdom in the world, and in particular among my dear

people; and was enabled to pray for many dear ministers of my acquaintance, both in these parts, and in New-England, and also for
other dear friends in New-England. My soul was so engaged and
enlarged in the sweet exercise, that I spent an hour in it, and knew
not how to leave the mercy seat. O how I delighted to pray and cry
to God! I saw that God was both able and willing to do all that I
desired for myself, and his church in general. I was likewise much
enlarged, and assisted in family prayer. Afterwards when I was just
going to bed, God helped me to renew my petition, with ardour
and freedom. O it was to me a blessed evening of prayer! Bless the
Lord, O my soul.

Sept. 9. Left the Indians at the Forks of Delaware, and set out on
a journey towards Susquehannah river; directing my course towards the Indian town more than an hundred and twenty miles
westward from the Forks. Travelled about fifteen miles, and there
lodged.

Shaumoking, Sept. 1745.

Sept. 13. After having lodged out three nights, arrived at the Indian town I aimed at on the Susquehannah, called Shaumoking;
one of the places and the largest of them which I visited in May
last. I was kindly received, and entertained by the Indians; but had
little satisfaction by reason of the Heathenish dance and revel they
then held in the house where I was obliged to lodge; which I could
not suppress, though I often entreated them to desist, for the sake
of one of their own friends who was then sick in the house, and
whose disorder was much aggravated by the noise. Alas! how destitute of natural affection are these poor uncultivated Pagans! although they seem somewhat kind in their own way. Of a truth the
dark corners of the earth are full of the habitations of cruelty. This
town, as I observed in my Diary of May last, lies partly on the east
side of the river, partly on the west, and partly on a large island in
it; and contains upwards of fifty houses, and nearly three hundred
persons, though I never saw much more than half that number in it.
They are of three different tribes of Indians, speaking three languages wholly unintelligible to each other. About one half of its inhabitants are Delawares; the others being called Senakas and Tu-
telas. The Indians of this place, are accounted the most drunken,
mischievous, and ruffianlike fellows, of any in these parts; and
Satan seems to have his seat in this town in an eminent manner.

Sept. 14. Visited the Delaware King; who was supposed to be at the point of death when I was here in May last, but was now recovered; discoursed with him and others, respecting Christianity; spent the afternoon with them; and had more encouragement than I expected. The King appeared kindly disposed, and willing to be instructed. This gave me some encouragement, that God would open an effectual door for my preaching the gospel here, and set up his kingdom in this place. This was a support and refreshment to me in the wilderness, and rendered my solitary circumstances comfortable and pleasant. In the evening, my soul was enlarged, and sweetly engaged in prayer; especially that God would set up his kingdom in this place, where the devil now reigns in the most eminent manner. I was enabled to ask this for God, for his glory, and because I longed for the enlargement of his kingdom in the honour of his dear name. I could appeal to God with the greatest freedom, that it was his dear cause, and not my own, which engaged my heart. My soul cried, "Lord set up thy kingdom for thine own glory; glorify thyself, and I shall rejoice. Get honour to thy blessed name, and this is all I desire. Do with me just what thou wilt: Blessed be thy name forever that thou art God, and that thou wilt glorify thyself. O that the whole world would glorify thee! O let these poor people be brought to know thee, and love thee, for the glory of thy ever dear blessed name." I could not but hope that God would bring in these miserable, wicked Indians; though there appeared little human probability of it; for they were then dancing and revelling, as if possessed by the devil. But yet I hoped, though against hope, that God would be glorified, and that his name would be glorified by these poor Indians. I continued long in prayer and praise to God, and had great freedom, enlargement, and sweetness; remembering dear friends in New-England as well as the people of my charge. Was entirely free from that dejection of spirit, with which I am frequently exercised. Blessed be God!

Lord's day, Sept. 15. Visited the chief of the Delawares again, was kindly received by him, and discoursed to the Indians in the afternoon. Still entertained hopes that God would open their hearts to receive the gospel; though many of them in the place were so drunk from day to day that I could get no opportunity to speak to them. Towards night, discoursed with one who understood the languages of the Six Nations, as they are usually called; who discovered an inclination to hearken to Christianity, which gave me some hopes that the gospel might hereafter be sent to those nations far remote.

Sept. 16. Spent the forenoon with the Indians, endeavouring to instruct them from house to house, and to engage them, as far as I could, to be friendly to Christianity. Towards night, went to one part of the town, where they were sober, got together near fifty of them, and discoursed to them; having first obtained the king's cheerful consent. There was a surprising attention among them, and they manifested a considerable desire of being further instructed. There were also one or two who seemed to be touched with some concern for their souls, who appeared well pleased with some conversation in private after I had concluded my public discourse to them.

My spirits were much refreshed with this appearance of things, and I could not but return with my interpreter, having no other companion in this journey, to my poor hard lodgings, rejoicing in hopes that God designed to set up his kingdom here, where Satan now reigns in the most eminent manner; and found uncommon freedom in addressing the throne of grace for the accomplishment of so great and glorious a work.

Sept. 17. Spent the forenoon in visiting and discoursing to the Indians. About noon left Shaumoking (most of the Indians going out this day on their hunting design) and travelled down the river southwestward.

Sept. 19. Visited an Indian town, called Juncauta, situate on an island in the Susquehannah. Was much discouraged with the temper and behaviour of the Indians here; although they appeared friendly when I was with them the last spring, and then gave me encouragement to come and see them again. But they now seemed resolved to retain their pagan notions, and persist in their idolatrous practices.

Sept. 20. Visited the Indians again at Juncauta island, and found them almost universally very busy in making preparations for a great sacrifice and dance. Had no opportunity to get them together, in order to discourse with them about Christianity, by reason of their being so much engaged about their sacrifice. My spirits were much sunk with a prospect so very discouraging; and especially seeing I had now no interpreter but a pagan, who was as much attached to idolatry as any of them; my own interpreter having left me the day before, being obliged to attend upon some important business elsewhere, and knowing that he could neither speak nor understand the language of these Indians; so that I was under the greatest disadvantages imaginable. However, I attempted to discourse privately with some of them, but without any appearance of success: notwithstanding I still tarried with them.

In the evening they met together, nearly a hundred of them, and danced around a large fire, having prepared ten fat deer for the sacrifice. The fat of the inwards they burnt in the fire while they were dancing, and sometimes raised the flame to a prodigious height; at the same time yelling and shouting in such a manner, that they might easily have been heard two miles or more. They continued their sacred dance nearly all night, after which they ate the flesh of the sacrifice, and so retired each one to his own lodging.

Lord's day, Sept. 21. Spent the day with the Indians on the island. As soon as they were well up in the morning, I attempted to instruct them, and laboured for that purpose to get them together; but soon found they had something else to do, for near noon they gathered together all their powows, or conjurers, and set about half a dozen of them playing their juggling tricks, and acting their frantic distracted postures, in order to find out why they were then so sickly upon the island, numbers of them being at that time disordered with a fever and bloody flux. In this exercise they were engaged for several hours, making all the wild, ridiculous and distracted motions imaginable; sometimes singing; sometimes howling; sometimes extending their hands to the utmost stretch, and spreading all their fingers,—they seemed to push with them as if they designed to push something away, or at least keep it off at arm's end; sometimes stroking their faces with their hands, then spurting water as fine as mist; sometimes sitting flat on the earth, then bowing down their faces to the ground; then wringing their sides as if in pain and anguish, twisting their faces, turning up their eyes, grunting, puffing, &c.

Their monstrous actions tended to excite ideas of horror, and seemed to have something in them, as I thought, peculiarly suited to raise the devil, if he could be raised by any thing odd, ridiculous, and frightful. Some of them, I could observe, were much more fervent and devout in the business than others, and seemed to chant, peep, and mutter with a great degree of warmth and vigour, as if determined to awaken and engage the powers below. I sat at a small distance, not more than thirty feet from them, though undiscovered, with my bible in my hand, resolving, if possible, to spoil their sport, and prevent their receiving any answers from the infernal world, and there viewed the whole scene. They continued their hideous charms and incantations for more than three hours, until they had all wearied themselves out; although they had in that space of time taken several intervals of rest, and at length broke up, I apprehended, without receiving any answer at all.

After they had done powawing, I attempted to discourse with them about Christianity; but they soon scattered, and gave me no opportunity for any thing of that nature. A view of these things, while I was entirely alone in the wilderness, destitute of the society of any one who so much as "named the name of Christ," greatly sunk my spirits, and gave me the most gloomy turn of mind imaginable, almost stripped me of all resolution and hope respecting further attempts for propagating the gospel, and converting the Pagans, and rendered this the most burdensome and disagreeable Sabbath which I ever saw. But nothing, I can truly say, sunk and distressed me like the loss of my hope respecting their conversion. This concern appeared so great, and seemed to be so much my own, that I seemed to have nothing to do on earth, if this failed. A prospect of the greatest concern in the saving conversion of souls under gospel-light, would have done little or nothing towards compensating for the loss of my hope in this respect; and my spirits now were so damped and depressed, that I had no heart nor power to make any further attempts among them for that purpose, and could not possibly recover my hope, resolution, and courage, by the utmost of my endeavours.

The Indians of this island can many of them understand the English language considerably well; having formerly lived in some part of Maryland, among or near the white people; but are very drunken, vicious, and profane, although not so savage as those who have less acquaintance with the English. Their customs, in various respects, differ from those of the other Indians upon the river. They do not bury their dead in a common form, but let their flesh consume above ground, in close cribs made for that purpose. At the end of a year, or sometimes a longer space of time, they take the bones, when the flesh is all consumed, and wash and scrape them, and afterwards bury them with some ceremony. Their method of charming or conjuring over the sick, seems somewhat different from that of other Indians, though in substance the same. The whole of it among these and others, perhaps, is an intimation of what seems, by Naaman's expression, 2 Kings, 5th, 11th, to have been the custom of the ancient heathen. It seems chiefly to consist in their "stroking their hands over the diseased," repeatedly stroking them, "and calling upon their gods"; except the spurting of water like a mist, and some other frantic ceremonies common to the other conjurations which I have already mentioned.

When I was in this region in May last, I had an opportunity of learning many of the notions and customs of the Indians, as well as observing many of their practices. I then travelled more than an hundred and thirty miles upon the river, above the English settlements; and, in that journey, met with individuals of seven or eight distinct tribes, speaking as many different languages. But of all the sights I ever saw among them, or indeed any where else, none appeared so frightful or so near a kin to what is usually imagined of infernal powers, none ever excited such images of terror in my mind, as the appearance of one who was a devout and zealous Reformer, or rather, restorer of what he supposed was the ancient religion of the Indians. He made his appearance in his pontifical garb, which was a coat of bear skins, dressed with the hair on, and hanging down to his toes; a pair of bear skin stockings; and a great wooden face painted, the one half black, the other half tawny, about the colour of an Indian's skin, with an extravagant mouth, cut very much awry; the face fastened to a bear skin cap, which was drawn over his head. He advanced towards me with the instrument in his hand, which he used for music in his idolatrous worship; which was a dry tortoise shell with some corn in it, and the neck of it drawn on to a piece of wood, which made a very convenient handle. As he came forward, he beat his tune with the rattle, and danced with all his might, but did not suffer any part of his body, not so much as his fingers, to be seen. No one would have imagined from his appearance or actions, that he could have been a human creature, if they had not had some intimation of it otherwise. When he came near me, I could not but shrink away from him, although it was then noon day, and I knew who it was; his appearance and gestures were so prodigiously frightful. He had a house consecrated to religious uses, with divers images cut upon the several parts of it. I went in, and found the ground beat almost as hard as a rock, with their frequent dancing upon it. I discoursed with him about Christianity. Some of my discourse he seemed to like, but some of it he disliked extremely. He told me that God had taught him his religion, and that he never would turn from it; but wanted to find some who would join heartily with him in it; for the Indians, he said, were grown very degenerate and corrupt. He had thoughts, he said, of leaving all his friends, and travelling abroad, in order to find some who would join with him; for he believed that God had some good people some where, who felt as he did. He had not always, he said, felt as he now did; but had formerly been like the rest of the Indians, until about four or five years before that time. Then, he said, his heart was very much distressed, so that he could not live among the Indians, but got away into the woods, and lived alone for some months. At length, he says, God comforted his heart, and showed him what he should do; and since that time he had known God, and tried to serve him; and loved all men, be they who they would, so as he never did before. He treated me with uncommon courtesy, and seemed to be hearty in it. I was told by the Indians, that he opposed their drinking strong liquor with all his power; and that, if at any time he could not dissuade them from it by all he could say, he would leave them, and go crying into the woods. It was manifest that he had a set of religious notions which he had examined for himself, and not taken for granted, upon bare tradition; and he relished or disrelished whatever was spoken of a religious nature, as it either agreed or disagreed with his standard. While I was discoursing, he would sometimes say, "Now that I like; so God has taught me"; &c. and some of his sentiments seemed very just. Yet he utterly denied the existence of a devil, and declared there was no such creature known among the Indians of old times, whose religion he supposed he was attempting to revive. He likewise told me, that departed souls all went southward, and that the difference between the good and the bad, was this: that the former were admitted into a beautiful town with spiritual walls; and that the latter would for ever hover around these walls, in vain attempts to get in. He seemed to be sincere, honest, and conscientious in his own way, and according to his own religious notions; which was more than I ever saw in any other Pagan. I perceived that he was looked upon and derided among most of the Indians, as a precise zealot, who made a needless noise about religious matters; but I must say that there was something in his temper and disposition, which looked more like true religion, than any thing I ever observed amongst other heathens.

But alas! how deplorable is the state of the Indians upon this river! The brief representation which I have here given of their notions and manners, is sufficient to shew that they are "led captive by Satan at his will," in the most eminent manner; and methinks might likewise be sufficient to excite the compassion, and engage the prayers, of pious souls for these their fellow-men, who sit "in the regions of the shadow of death."

Sept. 22. Made some further attempts to instruct and Christianize the Indians on this Island, but all to no purpose. They live so near the white people that they are always in the way of strong liquor, as well as the ill examples of nominal christians; which renders it so unspeakably difficult to treat with them about Christianity.

BRAINERD left these Indians on the 23d of September, to return to the Forks of Delaware, in a very weak state of body, and under great dejection of mind, which continued the two first days of his journey.

Sept. 25. Rode still homeward. In the forenoon, enjoyed freedom and intenseness of mind in meditation on Job xlii. 5, 6, "I have heard of thee by the hearing of the ear, but now mine eye seeth thee; wherefore I abhor myself and repent in dust and ashes." The Lord gave me clearness to penetrate into the sweet truths contained in that text. It was a comfortable and sweet season to me.

Sept. 26. Was still much disordered in body, and able to ride but slowly. Continued my journey, however. Near night, arrived at the Irish settlement, about fifteen miles from mine own house. This day, while riding, I was much exercised with a sense of my barrenness; and verily thought there was no creature who had any true grace, but what was more spiritual and faithful. I could not think that any of God's children made so poor a hand of living to God.

Sept. 27. Spent a considerable time in the morning in prayer and praise to God. My mind was somewhat intense in the duty; and my heart, in some degree, warmed with a sense of divine things. My soul was melted to think that "God had accounted me faithful, putting me into the ministry." My soul was also, in some measure, enlarged in prayer for the dear people of my charge, as well as for other dear friends. Afternoon visited some christian friends, and spent the time I think profitably; my heart was warmed and more engaged in the things of God. In the evening I enjoyed enlargement, warmth and comfort in prayer: my soul relied on God for assistance and grace to enable me to do something in his cause: my heart was drawn out in thankfulness to God for what he had done for his own glory among my poor people of late. I felt encouraged to proceed in his work; being persuaded of his power, and hoping that his arm might be further revealed for the enlargement of his dear kingdom. My soul "rejoiced in hope of the glory of God," in hope of the advancement of his declarative glory in the world, as well as of enjoying him in a world of glory. O, blessed be God, the living God, for ever.

He continued in this comfortable sweet frame of mind the two next days. On the following day, he went to his own house in the Forks of Delaware, and continued still in the same frame. The next day, Tuesday, he visited his Indians.

Forks of Delaware, Oct. 1745.

Oct. 1. Discoursed to the Indians here, and spent some time in private conference with them about their souls' concerns, and afterwards invited them to accompany, or if not, to follow me to Crossweeksung as soon as they could conveniently; which invitation numbers of them cheerfully accepted.

Wednesday he spent principally in writing the meditations he had in his late journey to the Susquehannah. On Thursday he left the Forks of Delaware, and travelled towards Crossweeksung, where he arrived on Saturday, Oct. 5; and continued from day to day in a comfortable state of mind.

Crossweeksung, Oct. 1745.

Oct. 5. Preached to my people from John xiv. 1–6. The divine presence seemed to be in the assembly. Numbers were affected with divine truths, and it was a comfort to some in particular. O what a difference is there between these, and the Indians with whom I had lately treated upon the Susquehannah! To be with those seemed to be like being banished from God and all his people; to be with these, like being admitted into his family, and to the enjoyment of his divine presence! How great is the change lately made upon numbers of those Indians; who, not many months ago, were as thoughtless and averse to Christianity, as those upon the Susquehannah; and how astonishing is that Grace, which has made this change!

Lord's day, Oct. 6. Preached in the forenoon from John x. 7–11. There was a considerable melting among my people; the dear young christians were refreshed, comforted and strengthened; and one or two persons newly awakened.—In the afternoon I discoursed on the story of the Jailer, Acts xvi, and in the evening, expounded Acts xx. 1–12. There was at this time a very agreeable melting spread throughout the whole assembly. I think I scarce ever saw a more desirable affection in any number of people in my life. There was scarcely a dry eye to be seen among them; and yet nothing boisterous or unseemly, nothing that tended to disturb the public worship; but rather to encourage and excite a christian ardour and spirit of devotion.—Those, who I have reason to hope were seriously renewed, were first affected, and seemed to rejoice much, but with brokenness of spirit and godly fear. Their exercises were much the same with those mentioned in my journal of Aug. 26, evidently appearing to be the genuine effects of a spirit of adoption.

After public service was over, I withdrew, being much tired with the labours of the day; and the Indians continued praying among themselves for nearly two hours together; which continued exercises appeared to be attended with a blessed quickening influence from on high. I could not but earnestly wish that numbers of God's people had been present at this season to see and hear these things which I am sure must refresh the heart of every true lover of Zion's interest. To see those, who were very lately savage Pagans and idolaters, having no hope, and without God in the world, now filled with a sense of divine love and grace, and worshipping the Father in spirit and in truth, as numbers have appeared to do, was not a little affecting; and especially to see them appear so tender and humble, as well as lively, fervent, and devout in the divine service.

Oct. 7. Being called by the church and people of East-Hampton, on Long-Island, as a member of a council to assist and advise in affairs of difficulty in that church, I set out on my journey this morning before it was well light, and travelled to Elizabethtown, and there lodged. Enjoyed some comfort on the road in conversation with Mr. William Tennent, who was sent for on the same business.

BRAINERD prosecuted his journey with the other ministers who were sent for, and did not return till Oct. 24. While he was at East-Hampton, the importance of the business, on which the council were convened, lay with such weight on his mind, and he was so concerned for the interests of religion in that place, that he slept but little for several nights successively. In his way to and from East-Hampton, he had several seasons of sweet refreshment; wherein his soul was enlarged and comforted with divine consolations in secret retirement; and he had special assistance in public ministerial performances in the house of God; and yet at the same time a sense of extreme vileness and unprofitableness. From time to time he speaks of soul refreshments and comfort in conversation with the ministers who travelled with him, and seems to have little or nothing of melancholy until he came to the west end of Long-Island in his return. After that he was oppressed with dejection and gloominess of mind for several days together.

Crossweeksung, Oct. 1745.

Oct. 24. Discoursed from John iv. 13, 14. There was a great attention, a desirable affection, and an unaffected melting in the assembly. It is surprising to see how eager they are to hear the word of God. I have oftentimes thought that they would cheerfully and diligently attend divine worship twenty-four hours together, if they had an opportunity so to do.

Oct. 25. Discoursed to my people respecting the Resurrection, from Luke xx. 27–36. When I came to mention the blessedness which the godly shall enjoy at that season; their final freedom from death, sin and sorrow; their equality to the angels in their nearness to and enjoyment of Christ, some imperfect degree of which they are favored with in the present life, from whence springs their sweetest comfort; and their being the children of God, openly acknowledged by him as such:—I say, when I mentioned these things, numbers of them were much affected and melted with a view of this blessed state.

Oct. 26. Being called to assist in the administration of the Lord's supper in a neighbouring congregation, I invited my people to go with me. They in general embraced the opportunity cheerfully; and attended the several discourses of this solemnity with diligence and affection, most of them now understanding something of the English language.

Lord's day, Oct. 27. While I was preaching to a vast assembly of people abroad, who appeared generally easy and secure enough, there was one Indian woman, a stranger, who never heard me preach before, nor ever regarded any thing about religion, being now persuaded by some of her friends to come to meeting, though much against her will, was seized with distressing concern for her soul; and soon after expressed a great desire of going home, more than forty miles distant, to call her husband, that he also might be awakened to a concern for his soul. Some others of the Indians appeared to be affected with divine truths this day. The pious people of the English, numbers of whom I had opportunity to converse with, seemed refreshed with seeing the Indians worship God in that devout and solemn manner with the assembly of his people; and with those mentioned in Acts xi. 18, they could not but glorify God, saying, "Then hath God also to the Gentiles granted repentance unto life."

Preached again in the afternoon, to a great assembly; at which time some of my people appeared affected; and, when public worship was over, were inquisitive whether there would not be another sermon in the evening, or before the sacramental solemnity was concluded; being still desirous to hear God's word.

Oct. 28. Discoursed from Matt. xxii. 1–13. I was enabled to open the scriptures, and adapt my discourse and expression to the capacities of my people, I know not how, in a plain, easy, and familiar manner beyond all that I could have done by the utmost study: and this without any special difficulty; yea, with as much freedom as if I had been addressing a common audience, who had been instructed in the doctrines of Christianity all their days.—The word of God at this time seemed to fall upon the assembly with a divine power and influence, especially towards the close of my discourse: there was both a sweet melting and bitter mourning in the audience. The dear christians were refreshed and comforted, convictions revived in others, and several persons newly awakened who had never been with us before. So much of the divine presence appeared in the assembly, that it seemed "this was no other than the house of God and the gate of heaven." All, who had any savour and relish of divine things, were even constrained by the sweetness of that season to say, "Lord, it is good for us to be here": If ever there was among my people an appearance of the New Jerusalem "as a bride adorned for her husband," there was much of it at this time; and so agreeable was the entertainment, where such tokens of the divine presence were, that I could scarcely be willing in the evening to leave the place and repair to my lodgings. I was refreshed with a view of the continuance of this blessed work of grace among them, and with its influence upon strangers among the Indians, who had of late from time to time providentially come into this part of the country. Had an evening of sweet refreshing; my thoughts were raised to a blessed eternity; my soul was melted with desires of perfect holiness, and of perfectly glorifying God.

Oct. 29. About noon rode and viewed the Indian lands at Cranberry: was much dejected and greatly perplexed in mind: knew not how to see any body again, my soul was sunk within me. Oh that these trials might make me more humble and holy. Oh that God would keep me from giving way to sinful dejection, which may hinder my usefulness.

Oct. 30. My soul was refreshed with a view of the continuance of God's blessed work among the Indians.

Oct. 31. Spent most of the day in writing; enjoyed not much spiritual comfort; but was not so much sunk with melancholy as at other times.

Nov. 1. Discoursed from Luke xxiv. briefly explaining the whole chapter, and insisting especially upon some particular passages. The discourse was attended with some affectionate concern upon some of the hearers, though not equal to what has often appeared among them.

Nov. 2. Spent the day with the Indians; wrote some things of importance; and longed to do more for God than I did, or could do in this present feeble and imperfect state.

Lord's day, Nov. 3. Preached to my people from Luke xvi. 17. "And it is easier for heaven and earth," &c. more especially for the sake of several lately brought under deep concern for their souls. There was some apparent concern and affection in the assembly; though far less than has been usual of late.

Afterwards I baptized fourteen persons of the Indians: six adults and eight children. One of these was nearly fourscore years of age; and I have reason to hope that God has brought her savingly home to himself. Two of the others were men of fifty years old, who had been singular and remarkable among the Indians for their wickedness; one of them had been a murderer, and both notorious drunkards as well as excessively quarrelsome; but now I cannot but hope that both of them have become subjects of God's special grace, especially the worst of them. I deferred their baptism for many weeks after they had given evidence of having passed a great change, that I might have more opportunities to observe the fruits of the impressions which they had been under, and apprehended the way was now clear. There was not one of the adults whom I baptized, who had not given me comfortable grounds to hope that God had wrought a work of special grace in their hearts; although I could not have the same degree of satisfaction respecting one or two of them as the rest.

Nov. 4. Discoursed from John xi. briefly explaining most of the chapter. Divine truths made deep impressions upon many in the assembly. Numbers were affected with a view of the power of Christ manifested in his raising the dead; and especially when this instance of his power was improved to show his ability to raise dead souls, such as many of them felt themselves to be, to a spiritual life; as also to raise the dead at the last day, and dispense to them true rewards and punishments.

There [were] numbers of those who had come here lately from remote places, who were now brought under deep and pressing concern for their souls. One in particular, who not long since came half drunk, and railed on us, and attempted by all means to disturb us while engaged in divine worship, was now so concerned and distressed for her soul, that she seemed unable to get any ease without an interest in Christ. There were many tears and affectionate sobs and groans in the assembly in general; some weeping for themselves; others for their friends. Although persons are doubtless much more easily affected now than they were in the beginning of this religious concern, when tears and cries for their souls were things unheard of among them; yet I must say that their affection in general appeared genuine and unfeigned; and especially this appeared very conspicuous in those newly awakened. So that true and genuine convictions of sin seem still to be begun and promoted in many instances.

Baptized a child this day, and perceived numbers of the baptized persons affected with the administration of this ordinance, as being thereby reminded of their own solemn engagements.

I have now baptized in all forty-seven of the Indians; twenty-three adults, and twenty-four children; thirty-five of them belonged to this region, and the rest to the Forks of Delaware.—Through rich grace, none of them as yet have been left to disgrace their profession of Christianity by any scandalous or unbecoming behaviour.

I might now properly make many remarks on a work of grace so very remarkable as this has been in various respects; but shall confine myself to a few general hints only.

1. It is remarkable that God began to work among the Indians at a time when I had the least hope, and, to my apprehension the least rational prospect of seeing a work of grace propagated among them: my bodily strength being then much wasted by a late tedious journey to the Susquehannah, where I was necessarily exposed to hardships and fatigues among the Indians: my mind being also exceedingly depressed with a view of the unsuccessfulness of my labours. I had little reason so much as to hope that God had made me instrumental in the saving conversion of any of the Indians, except my interpreter and his wife. Hence I was ready to look upon myself as a burden to the honourable Society which employed and supported me in this business, and began to entertain serious thoughts of giving up my mission; and almost resolved I would do so at the conclusion of the present year, if I had then no better prospect of special success in my work than I had hitherto had. I cannot say that I entertained these thoughts because I was weary of the labours and fatigues which necessarily attended my present business, or because I had light and freedom in my own mind to turn any other way; but purely through dejection of spirit, pressing discouragement, and an apprehension of its being unjust to spend money consecrated to religious uses, only to civilize the Indians, and bring them to an external profession of Christianity. This was all which I could then see any prospect of effecting, while God seemed, as I thought, evidently to frown upon the design of their saving conversion, by withholding the convincing and renewing influences of his blessed Spirit from attending the means which I had hitherto used with them for that end.

In this frame of mind I first visited these Indians at Crossweeksung; apprehending that it was my indispensable duty, seeing

I had heard there was a number of these parts, to make some attempts for their conversion to God, though I cannot say, I had any hope of success, my spirits being now so extremely sunk. I do not know that my hopes respecting the conversion of the Indians were ever reduced to so low an ebb, since I had any special concern for them, at this time. Yet this was the very season in which God saw fit to begin this glorious work! Thus he "ordained strength out of weakness," by making bare his almighty arm at a time when all hopes and human probabilities most evidently appeared to fail. —Whence I learn, that it is good to follow the path of duty, though in the midst of darkness and discouragement.

2. It is remarkable how God providentially, and in a manner almost unaccountable, called these Indians together to be instructed in the great things that concerned their souls; and how he seized their minds with the most solemn and weighty concern for their eternal salvation, as fast as they came to the place where his word was preached. When I first came into these parts in June, I found not one man at the place I visited, but only four women and a few children; but before I had been here many days they gathered from all quarters, some from more than twenty miles distant; and when I made them a second visit in the beginning of August, some came more than forty miles to hear me. Many came without any intelligence of what was going on here, and consequently without any design of theirs, so much as to gratify their curiosity. Thus it seemed as if God had summoned them together from all quarters for nothing else but to deliver his message to them; and that he did this, with regard to some of them, without making use of any human means; although there was pains taken by some of them to give notice to others at remote places.

Nor is it less surprising that they were one after another affected with a solemn concern for their souls, almost as soon as they came upon the spot where divine truths were taught them. I could not but think often, that their coming to the place of our public worship, was like Saul and his messengers coming among the prophets; they no sooner came but they prophesied; and these were almost as soon affected with a sense of their sin and misery, and with an earnest concern for deliverance, as they made their appearance in our assembly. After this work of grace began with power among them, it was common for strangers of the Indians, before they had been with us one day, to be much awakened, deeply convinced of their sin and misery, and to enquire with great solicitude, "What they should do to be saved?"

3. It is likewise remarkable how God preserved these poor ignorant Indians from being prejudiced against me, and the truths I taught them, by those means that were used with them for that purpose by ungodly people. There were many attempts made by some ill-minded persons of the white people to prejudice them against, or fright them from, Christianity. They sometimes told them, that the Indians were well enough already;—that there was no need of all this noise about Christianity;—that if they were christians, they would be in no better, no safer, or happier state, than they were already in. Sometimes they told them, that I was a knave, a deceiver, and the like; that I daily taught them lies, and had no other design but to impose upon them, &c. When none of these, and such like suggestions, would avail to their purpose, they then tried another expedient, and told the Indians, "My design was to gather together as large a body of them as I possibly could, and then sell them to England for slaves"; than which nothing could be more likely to terrify the Indians, they being naturally of a jealous disposition, and the most averse to a state of servitude perhaps of any people living.

But all these wicked insinuations, through divine goodness overruling, constantly turned against the authors of them, and only served to engage the affections of the Indians more firmly to me; for they, being awakened to a solemn concern for their souls, could not but observe, that the persons who endeavoured to embitter their minds against me, were altogether unconcerned about their own souls, and not only so, but vicious and profane; and thence could not but argue, that if they had no concern for their own, it was not likely they should have for the souls of others.

It seems yet the more wonderful that the Indians were preserved from once hearkening to these suggestions, in as much as I was an utter stranger among them, and could give them no assurance of my sincere affection to, and concern for them, by any thing that was past,—while the persons who insinuated these things were their old acquaintance, who had frequent opportunities of gratifying their thirsty appetites with strong drink, and consequently, doubtless, had the greatest interest in their affections. But from this instance of their preservation from fatal prejudices, I have had occasion with admiration to say, "If God will work, who can hinder?"

4. Nor is it less wonderful how God was pleased to provide a remedy for my want of skill and freedom in the Indian language, by remarkably fitting my interpreter for, and assisting him in the performance of, his work. It might reasonably be supposed I must needs labour under a vast disadvantage in addressing the Indians by an interpreter; and that divine truths would undoubtedly lose much of the energy and pathos with which they might at first be delivered, by reason of their coming to the audience from a second hand. But although this has often, to my sorrow and discouragement, been the case in times past, when my interpreter had little or no sense of divine things; yet now it was quite otherwise. I cannot think my addresses to the Indians ordinarily, since the beginning of this season of grace, have lost any thing of the power or pungency with which they were made, unless it were sometimes for want of pertinent and pathetic terms and expressions in the Indian language; which difficulty could not have been much redressed by my personal acquaintance with their language. My interpreter had before gained some good degree of doctrinal knowledge, whereby he was rendered capable of understanding, and communicating, without mistakes, the intent and meaning of my discourses, and that without being confined strictly, and obliged to interpret verbatim. He had likewise, to appearance, an experimental acquaintance with divine things; and it pleased God at this season to inspire his mind with longing desires for the conversion of the Indians, and to give him admirable zeal and fervency in addressing them in order thereto. It is remarkable, that, when I was favoured with any special assistance in any work, and enabled to speak with more than common freedom, fervency, and power, under a lively and affecting sense of divine things, he was usually affected in the same manner almost instantly, and seemed at once quickened and enabled to speak in the same pathetic language, and under the same influence that I did. A surprising energy often accompanied the word at such seasons; so that the face of the whole assembly would be apparently changed almost in an instant, and tears and sobs became common among them.

He also appeared to have such a clear doctrinal view of God's usual methods of dealing with souls under a preparatory work of conviction and humiliation as he never had before; so that I could, with his help, discourse freely with the distressed persons about their internal exercises, their fears, discouragements, temptations, &c. He likewise took pains day and night to repeat and inculcate upon the minds of the Indians the truths which I taught them daily; and this he appeared to do, not from spiritual pride, and an affection of setting himself up as a public teacher, but from a spirit of faithfulness, and an honest concern for their souls.

His conversation among the Indians has likewise, so far as I know, been savoury, as becomes a christian, and a person employed in his work; and I may justly say, he has been a great comfort to me, and a great instrument of promoting this good work among the Indians; so that whatever be the state of his own soul, it is apparent God has remarkably fitted him for this work. Thus God has manifested that, without bestowing on me the gift of tongues, he could find a way wherein I might be as effectually enabled to convey the truths of his glorious gospel to the minds of these poor benighted Pagans.

5. It is further remarkable, that God has carried on his work here by such means, and in such a manner, as tended to obviate, and leave no room for, those prejudices and objections which have often been raised against such a work. When persons have been awakened to a solemn concern for their souls, by hearing the more awful truths of God's word, and the terrors of the divine law insisted upon, it has usually in such cases been objected by some, that such persons were only frighted with a fearful noise of hell and damnation; and that there was no evidence that their concern was the effect of a divine influence. But God has left no room for this objection in the present case; this work of grace having been begun and carried on, by almost one continued strain of gospel invitation to perishing sinners. This may reasonably be guessed, from a view of the passages of scripture I chiefly insisted upon in my discourses from time to time; which I have for that purpose inserted in my Diary.

Nor have I ever seen so general an awakening in any assembly in my life as appeared here while I was opening and insisting upon the parable of the great supper—Luke 14th. In which discourse, I was enabled to set before my hearers, the unsearchable riches of gospel grace. Not that I would be understood here, that I never instructed the Indians respecting their fallen state, and the sinfulness and misery of it: for this was what I at first, chiefly insisted upon them, and endeavoured to repeat and inculcate in almost every discourse, knowing that without this foundation, I should not build upon the sand, and that it would be in vain to invite them to Christ unless I could convince them of their need of him.—Mark ii. 17.

But still this great awakening, this surprising concern, was never excited by any harangues of terror, but always appeared most remarkable when I insisted upon the compassion of a dying Saviour, the plentiful provisions of the gospel, and the free offers of the divine grace, to needy, distressed sinners. Nor would I be understood to insinuate, that such a religious concern might justly be suspected as not being genuine, and from a divine influence, because produced from the preaching of terror: for this is perhaps, God's more usual way of awakening sinners, and appears entirely agreeable to scripture and sound reason. But what I meant here to observe is, that God saw fit to employ and bless milder means for the effectual awakening of these Indians, and thereby obviated the forementioned objection, which the world might otherwise have had a more plausible colour of making.

As there has been no room for any plausible objection against this work, with regard to the means; so neither with regard to the manner in which it has been carried on. It is true, persons' concern for their souls has been exceeding great; the convictions of their sin and misery have arisen to a high degree, and produced many tears, cries, and groans; but then they have not been attended with those disorders, either bodily or mental, which have sometimes prevailed among persons under religious impressions. There has here been no appearance of those convulsions, bodily agonies, frightful screamings, swoonings, and the like, which have been so much complained of in some places; although there have been some, who, with the jailer, have been made to tremble under a sense of their sin and misery; numbers who have been made to cry out from a distressing view of their perishing state;—and some, who have been, for a time, in a great measure, deprived of their bodily strength, yet without any such convulsive appearances.

Nor has there been any appearance of mental disorders here, such as visions, trances, imaginations of being under prophetic inspiration, and the like; or scarce any unbecoming disposition to appear remarkably affected either with concern or joy; though I must confess, I observed one or two persons, whose concern I thought, was in a considerable measure affected; and one whose joy appeared to be of the same kind. But these workings of spiritual pride, I endeavoured to crush in their first appearances, and have not since observed any affection, either of joy or sorrow, but what appeared genuine and unaffected. But,

6th and lastly, the effects of this work have likewise been very remarkable. I doubt not but that many of these people have gained more doctrinal knowledge of divine truths, since I first visited them in June last, than could have been instilled into their minds by the most diligent use of proper and instructive means for whole years together, without such a divine influence. Their Pagan notions and idolatrous practices, seem to be entirely abandoned in these parts. They are regulated, and appear regularly disposed in the affairs of marriage; an instance whereof I have given in my Journal of August 14. They seem generally divorced from drunkenness, their darling vice, the "sin that easily besets them"; so that I do not know of more than two or three who have been my steady hearers, that have drunk to excess since I first visited them; although before it was common for some or other of them to be drunk almost every day: and some of them seem now to fear this sin in particular, more than death itself. A principle of honesty and justice, appears in many of them; and they seem concerned to discharge their old debts, which they have neglected, and perhaps scarcely thought of for years past. Their manner of living, is much more decent and comfortable than formerly, having now the benefit of that money which they used to consume upon strong drink. Love seems to reign among them, especially those who have given evidences of having passed a saving change: and I never saw any appearance of bitterness or censoriousness in these, nor any disposition to "esteem themselves better than others," who had not received the like mercy.

As their sorrows under convictions have been great and pressing, so many of them have since appeared to "rejoice with joy unspeakable, and full of glory"; and yet I never saw any thing ecstatic or flighty in their joy. Their consolations do not incline them to lightness; but, on the contrary, are attended with solemnity, and oftentimes with tears, and an apparent brokenness of heart, as may be seen in several passages of my Diary. In this respect, some of them have been surprised at themselves, and have with concern observed to me, that "when their hearts have been glad," which is a phrase they commonly make use of to express joy, "they could not help crying for all."

And now, upon the whole, I think, I may justly say, that here are all the symptoms and evidences of a remarkable work of grace among these Indians, which can reasonably be desired or expected. May the great Author of this work maintain and promote the same here, and propagate it every where, till "the whole earth be filled with his glory"! Amen.

I have now rode more than three thousand miles, of which I have kept an exact account, since the beginning of March last, and almost the whole of it has been in my own proper business as a missionary, upon the design, either immediately, or more remotely, of propagating christian knowledge among the Indians. I have taken pains to look out for a colleague or companion, to travel with me; and have likewise used endeavours to procure something for his support, among religious persons in New-England, which cost me a journey of several hundred miles in length; but have not, as yet, found any person qualified and disposed for this good work, although I had some encouragement from ministers and others, that it was hoped a maintenance might be procured for one, when the man should be found.

I have likewise of late, represented to the gentlemen concerned with this mission, the necessity of having an English school speedily set up among these Indians, who are now willing to be at the pains of gathering together in a body, for this purpose. In order thereto, I have humbly proposed to them the collecting of money for the maintenance of a school-master, and the defraying of other necessary charges, in the promotion of this good work; which they are now attempting in the several congregations of christians to which they respectively belong.

The several companies of Indians to whom I have preached in the summer past, live at great distances from each other. It is more than seventy miles from Crossweeksung, in New-Jersey, to the Forks of Delaware in Pennsylvania; and thence to sundry of the Indian settlements which I visited on Susquehannah, is more than an hundred and twenty miles. So much of my time is necessarily consumed in journeying, that I can have but little for any of my necessary studies, and consequently for the study of the Indian languages in particular; and especially seeing I am obliged to discourse so frequently to the Indians at each of these places while I am with them, in order to redeem time to visit the rest. I am, at times, almost discouraged from attempting to gain any acquaintance with the Indian languages, they are so very numerous; some account of which I gave in my Diary of May last; and especially, seeing my other labours and fatigues engross almost the whole of my time, and bear exceedingly hard upon my constitution, so that my health is much impaired.—However, I have taken considerable pains to learn the Delaware language, and propose still to do so, so far as my other business and bodily health will admit. I have already made some proficiency in it, though I have laboured under many and great disadvantages in my attempts of that nature. It is but just to observe here, that all the pains I took to acquaint myself with the language of the Indians with whom I spent my first year, were of little or no service to me here among the Delawares; so that my work, when I came among these Indians, was all to begin anew.

As these poor ignorant Pagans stood in need of having "line upon line, and precept upon precept," in order to their being instructed and grounded in the principles of Christianity; so I preached "publicly, and taught from house to house," almost every day for whole weeks together, when I was with them. My public discourses did not then make up the one half of my work, while there were so many constantly coming to me with that important enquiry, "What must we do to be saved?" and opening to me the various exercises of their minds. Yet I can say to the praise of rich grace, that the apparent success, with which my labours were crowned, unspeakably more than compensated for the labour itself, and was likewise a great means of supporting and carrying me through the business and fatigues, which, it seems, my nature would have sunk under, without such an encouraging prospect. But although this success has afforded matter of support, comfort, and thankfulness; yet in this season I have found great need of assistance in my work, and have been much oppressed for want of one to bear a part of my labours and hardships. "May the Lord of the harvest send forth other labourers into this part of his harvest, that those who sit in darkness may see great light; and that the whole earth may be filled with the knowledge of himself! Amen."

CHAPTER VIII

From the close of the first part of his "JOURNAL," Nov. 5, 1745, to the 19th of June, 1746; when the second part of his Journal terminated. This, and the preceding chapter, occupy one year—the most interesting year of Brainerd's Life.

On Tuesday, Nov. 5, BRAINERD left the Indians, and spent the remaining part of the week in travelling to various parts of New-Jersey, in order to get a collection for the use of the Indians, and to obtain a schoolmaster to instruct them. In the meantime, he speaks of very sweet refreshment and entertainment with christian friends, and of being sweetly employed while riding, in meditation on divine subjects; his heart being enlarged, his mind clear, his spirit refreshed with divine truths, and his "heart burning within him while he went by the way, and the Lord opened to him the scriptures."

Lord's day, Nov. 10. [At Elizabeth Town.] Was comfortable in the morning both in body and mind: preached in the forenoon from 2 Cor. 5, 20. Now then we are ambassadors for Christ, &c. God was pleased to give me freedom and fervency in my discourse; and the presence of God seemed to be in the assembly; numbers were affected, and there were many tears among them. In the afternoon, preached from Luke xiv. 22. And yet there is room. Was favoured with divine assistance in the first prayer, and poured out my soul to God with a filial temper; the living God also assisted me in the sermon.

The next day he went to Newtown on Long Island, to a meeting of the Presbytery. He speaks of some sweet meditations which he had while there, on Christ's delivering up the kingdom to the Father; and of his soul being much refreshed and warmed with the consideration of that blissful day.

Nov. 15. Could not cross the ferry by reason of the violence of the wind; nor could I enjoy any place of retirement at the Ferry-house; so that I was in perplexity. Yet God gave me some satisfaction and sweetness in meditation, and in lifting up my heart to him in the midst of company. Although some were drinking and talking profanely, which was indeed a grief to me; yet my mind was calm and composed; and I could not but bless God, that I was not likely to spend an eternity in such company. In the evening I sat down and wrote with composure and freedom; and can say through pure grace it was a comfortable evening to my soul; an evening which I was enabled to spend in the service of God.

Nov. 16. Crossed the ferry about ten o'clock, and arrived at Elizabeth Town near night. Was in a calm, composed frame of mind, and felt an entire resignation, with respect to a loss I had lately sustained in having my horse stolen from me the last Wednesday night, at Newtown. Had some longings of soul for the dear people of Elizabeth Town, that God would pour out his Spirit upon them, and revive his work among them.

He spent the next four days at Elizabeth Town, for the most part in a free and comfortable state of mind; intensely engaged in the service of God, and enjoying at times the special assistance of his Spirit. On Thursday of this week he rode to Freehold, and spent the day under considerable dejection.

Nov. 22. Rode to Mr. Tennents, and from thence to Crossweeksung. Had but little freedom in meditation while riding; which was a grief and burden to my soul. Oh that I could fill up all my time, whether in the house or by the way, for God. I was enabled, I think, this day to give up my soul to God, and put over all his concerns into his hands; and found some real consolation in the thought of being entirely at the divine disposal, and having no will or interest of my own. I have received my all from God; Oh that I could return my all to God! Surely God is worthy of my highest affections and most devout adoration; he is infinitely worthy that I should make him my last end, and live for ever to him. Oh that I might never more, in any one instance, live to myself!

Lord's day, Nov. 24. Preached both parts of the day from the story of Zaccheus, Luke xix. 1–9. In the latter exercise, when I opened and insisted upon the salvation that comes to a sinner upon his becoming a son of Abraham or a true believer, the word seemed to be attended with divine power to the hearts of the hearers. Numbers were much affected with divine truths; former convictions were revived; one or two persons newly awakened; and a most affectionate engagement in divine service appeared among them universally. The impressions they were under appeared to be the genuine effect of God's word brought home to their hearts by the power and influence of the Divine Spirit.

Nov. 26. After having spent some time in private conferences with my people, I discoursed publicly among them from John v. 1–9. I was favored with some special freedom and fervency in my discourse, and a powerful energy accompanied divine truths. Many wept and sobbed affectionately, and scarcely any appeared unconcerned in the whole assembly. The influence which seized the audience, appeared gentle, and yet pungent and efficacious. It produced no boisterous commotions of the passions; but seemed deeply to affect the heart, and excite in the persons under convictions of their lost state, heavy groans and tears: and in others, who had obtained comfort, a sweet and humble melting. It seemed like the gentle but steady showers which effectually water the earth, without violently beating upon the surface. The persons lately awakened were some of them deeply distressed for their souls, and appeared earnestly solicitous to obtain an interest in Christ: and some of them, after public worship was over, in anguish of spirit, said "they knew not what to do, nor how to get their wicked hearts changed." &c.

Nov. 28. Discoursed to the Indians publicly, after having used some private endeavours to instruct and excite some of the duties of Christianity. Opened and made remarks upon the sacred story of our Lord's transfiguration, Luke ix. 28–36. Had a principal view in insisting upon this passage of scripture to the edification and consolation of God's people. Observed some, that I have reason to think are truly such, exceedingly affected with an account of the glory of Christ in his transfiguration, and filled with longing desires of being with him, that they might with open face behold his glory.

After public service was over, I asked one of them, who wept and sobbed most affectionately, What she now wanted? She replied, "Oh, to be with Christ. She did not know how to stay," &c. This was a blessed refreshing season to the religious people in general. The Lord Jesus Christ seemed to manifest his divine glory to them, as when transfigured before his disciples; and they were ready with the disciples universally to say, "Lord, it is good for us to be here."

The influence of God's word was not confined to those, who had given evidence of being truly gracious; though at this time I calculated my discourse for and directed it chiefly to such. But it appeared to be a season of divine power in the whole assembly; so that most were in some measure affected. One aged man, in particular, lately awakened, was now brought under a deep and pressing concern for his soul, was now earnestly inquisitive "how he might find Jesus Christ." God seems still to vouchsafe his divine presence, and the influence of his blessed Spirit to accompany his word, at least in some measure, in all our meetings for divine worship.

I enjoyed some divine comfort and fervency in the public exercise and afterwards. While riding to my lodgings, was favored with some sweet meditations on Luke ix. 31. "Who appeared in glory, and spake of his decease, which he should accomplish at Jerusalem." My thoughts ran with freedom; and I saw and felt what a glorious subject the death of Christ is for glorified souls to dwell upon in their conversation. O the death of Christ! how infinitely precious!

Nov. 30. Preached near night, after having spent some hours in private conference with some of my people about their souls' concerns. Explained and insisted upon the story of the rich man and Lazarus, Luke xvi. 19–26. The word made powerful impressions upon many in the assembly, especially while I discoursed of the blessedness of Lazarus in Abraham's bosom. This I could perceive affected them much more than what I spoke of the rich man's misery and torments; and thus it has been usually with them. They have almost always appeared much more affected with the comfortable than the dreadful truths of God's word. That which has distressed many of them under conviction is, that they found they wanted, and could not obtain, the happiness of the godly; at least, they have often appeared to be more affected with this than with the terrors of hell. But whatever be the means of their awakening, it is plain, numbers are made deeply sensible of their sin and misery, the wickedness and stubbornness of their own hearts, their utter inability to help themselves, or come to Christ for help, without divine assistance; and so are brought to see their perishing need of Christ to do all for them and to lie at the foot of sovereign mercy.

Lord's day, Dec. 1. Discoursed to my people in the forenoon from Luke xvi. 27–31. There appeared an unfeigned affection in divers persons, and some seemed deeply impressed with divine truths. In the afternoon, preached to a number of white people; at which time the Indians attended with diligence, and many of them were unable to understand a considerable part of the discourse. At night discoursed to my people again, and gave them particular cautions and directions relating to their conduct in divers respects, and pressed them to watchfulness in their deportment, seeing they were encompassed with those who waited for their halting, and who stood ready to draw them into temptations of every kind and then to expose religion by their missteps.

Dec. 2. Was much affected with grief that I had not lived more to God; and felt strong resolutions to double my diligence in my Master's service.

After this he went to a meeting of the Presbytery, at a place in N. Jersey, called Connecticut Farms; which occasioned his absence from his people the remainder of the week. He speaks of some seasons of sweetness and spiritual affection in his absence.

Lord's day, Dec. 8. Discoursed on the story of the blind man, John ix. There appeared no remarkable effect of the word upon the assembly at this time. The persons who have lately been much concerned for their souls, seemed now not so affected nor solicitous to obtain an interest in Christ as has been usual; although they attended divine service with seriousness and diligence. Such have been the doings of the Lord here in awakening sinners, and affecting the hearts of those who are brought to solid comfort with a fresh sense of divine things, from time to time, that it is now strange to see the assembly sit with dry eyes and without sobs and groans.

Dec. 9. Spent most of the day in procuring provisions in order to my setting up house-keeping among the Indians. Enjoyed little satisfaction through the day being very much out of my element.

Dec. 10. Was engaged in the same business as yesterday. Towards night got into my house.

Dec. 11. Spent the forenoon in necessary labours about my house. In the afternoon rode out upon business; and spent the evening with some satisfaction among friends in conversation on a serious and profitable subject.

Dec. 12. Preached from the parable of the Ten Virgins, Matt. xxv. The divine power seemed in some measure to attend this discourse; in which I was favoured with uncommon freedom and plainness of address, and enabled to open divine truths, and explain them to the capacities of my people in a manner beyond myself. There appeared in many persons an affectionate concern for their souls, although the concern in general seemed not so deep and pressing as it had formerly done. Yet it was refreshing to see many melted into tears and unaffected sobs; some with a sense of divine love, and some for the want of it.

Dec. 13. Spent the day mainly in labour about my house. In the evening, spent some time in writing; but was very weary and much outdone with the labour of the day.

Dec. 14. Rose early, and wrote by candle light some considerable time: spent most of the day in writing, but somewhat dejected. In the evening was exercised with pain in my head.

Dec. 15. Preached to the Indians from Luke xiii. 24–28. Divine truth fell with weight and power upon the audience and seemed to reach the hearts of many. Near night discoursed to them again from Matt. xxv. 31–46. At this season also the word appeared to be accompanied with a divine influence, and made powerful impressions upon the assembly in general, as well as upon numbers in a very special and particular manner. This was an amazing season of grace. "The word of the Lord," this day, "was quick and powerful, sharper than a two edged sword," and pierced the hearts of many. The assembly was greatly affected and deeply wrought upon; yet without so much apparent commotion of the passions as appeared in the beginning of this work of grace. The impressions made by the word of God upon the audience appeared solid, rational, and deep; worthy of the solemn truths by which they were produced; and far from being the effects of any sudden fright or groundless perturbation of mind. O, how did the hearts of the hearers seem to bow under the weight of divine truths; and how evident did it now appear, that they received and felt them, "not as the word of man, but as the word of God." None can form a just idea of the appearance of our assembly at this time but those who have seen a congregation solemnly awed, and deeply impressed by the special power and influence of divine truths delivered to them in the name of God.

Dec. 16. Discoursed to my people in the evening from Luke xi. 1–13. After having insisted some time upon the ninth verse, wherein there is a command and encouragement to ask for the divine favour, I called upon them to ask for a new heart with the utmost importunity; as the man mentioned in the parable, on which I was discoursing, pleaded for loaves of bread at midnight. There was much affection and concern in the assembly, and especially one woman appeared in great distress for her soul. She was brought to such an agony in seeking after Christ, that the sweat ran off her face for a considerable time together (although the evening was very cold); and her bitter cries were the most affecting indications of her heart.

The remainder of this day he spent chiefly in writing; some part of the time under a degree of melancholy; but some part of it with a sweet ardency in religion.

Dec. 21. My people having now attained to a considerable degree of knowledge in the principles of Christianity; I thought it proper to set up a catechetical lecture among them; and this evening attempted something in that form; proposing questions to them agreeably to the Assembly's Shorter Catechism, receiving their answers, and then explaining and insisting as appeared necessary and proper upon each question. After this I endeavoured to make some practical improvement of the whole. This was the method, I entered upon. They were able readily and rationally to answer many important questions which I proposed to them; so that, upon trial, I found their doctrinal knowledge to exceed my own expectations. In the improvement of my discourse, when I came to infer and open the blessedness of those, who have so great and glorious a God, as had before been spoken of, "for their everlasting friend and portion"; several were much affected, and especially when I exhorted, and endeavoured to persuade, them to be reconciled to God through his dear Son, and thus to secure an interest in his everlasting favour. So that they appeared not only enlightened and instructed, but affected and engaged in their soul's concern by this method of discoursing. After my labours with the Indians, I spent some time in writing some things divine and solemn; and was much wearied with the labours of the day, found that my spirits were extremely spent, and that I could do no more. I am conscious to myself, that my labours are as great and constant as my nature will admit; and ordinarily I go to the extent of my strength, so that I do all I can: but the misery is I do not labour with that heavenly temper, that single eye to the glory of God, that I long for.

Lord's day, Dec. 22. Discoursed upon the story of the young man in the Gospel, Matt. xix. 16–22. God made it a seasonable word, I am persuaded, to some souls. There were several of the Indians newly come here, who had frequently lived among Quakers; and being more civilized and conformed to English manners than the generality of the Indians, they had imbibed some of the Quakers' errors, especially this fundamental one, viz. That, if men will but live soberly and honestly according to the dictates of their own consciences, or the light within, there is then no danger or doubt of their salvation. These persons I found much worse to deal with than those who are wholly under Pagan darkness; who make no pretences to knowledge in Christianity at all, nor have any self-righteous foundation to stand upon. However, they all, except one, appeared now convinced that this sober honest life of itself was not sufficient to salvation; since Christ himself had declared it so in the case of the young man. They seemed in some measure concerned to obtain that change of heart, the necessity of which I had been labouring to shew them.

This was likewise a season of comfort to some souls, and in particular to one, the same mentioned in my journal of the 16th instant, who never before obtained any settled comfort, though I have abundant reason to think she had passed a saving change some days before. She now appeared in a heavenly frame of mind, composed, and delighted with the divine will. When I came to discourse particularly with her, and to enquire of her, how she obtained relief and deliverance from the spiritual distresses which she had lately suffered; she answered, in broken English, "Me try, me try save myself; last, my strength be all gone (meaning her ability to save herself); could not me stir bit further. Den last me forced let Jesus Christ alone send me hell, he if please." I said, "But, you was not willing to go to hell; was you?" She replied, "Could not me help it. My heart, he would wicked for all. Could not me make him good (meaning, she saw it was right she should go to hell, because her heart was wicked, and would be so after all she could do to mend it). I asked her, how she got out of this case. She answered still in the same broken language, "By by, my heart be glad desperately." I asked her, why her heart was glad? She replied, "Glad my heart, Jesus Christ do what he please with me. Den me tink, glad my heart Jesus Christ send me to hell. Did not me care where he put me; love him for all," &c. She could not readily be convinced, but that she was willing to go to hell if Christ was pleased to send her there, although the truth evidently was, that her will was so swallowed up in the divine will, that she could not frame any hell in her imagination which would be dreadful or undesirable, provided it was the will of God to send her to it. Towards night discoursed to them again in the catechetical method, which I entered upon the evening before. When I came to improve the truth, which I had explained to them, and to answer that question, "But how shall I know whether God has chosen me to everlasting life?" by pressing them to come and give up their hearts to Christ and thereby "to make their election sure," they then appeared much affected: and persons under concern were afresh engaged in seeking after an interest in him; while some others, who had obtained comfort before, were refreshed to find that love to God in themselves, which was an evidence of his electing love to them.

Dec. 23 and 24. Spent three days in writing with the utmost diligence. Felt in the main a sweet mortification to the world, and a desire to live and labour only for God; but wanted more warmth and spirituality, and a more sensible and affectionate regard for the glory of God.

Dec. 25. The Indians having been used, on Christmas day, to drink and revel among some of the white people in these parts; I thought it proper this day to call them together and discourse to them upon divine things; which I accordingly did from the parable of the barren fig tree, Luke xiii. 6–9. A divine influence, I am persuaded, accompanied the word at this season. The power of God appeared in the assembly, not by producing any remarkable crisis, but by rousing several stupid creatures who were scarcely ever moved with any concern before. The power attending divine truths seemed to have the influence of the earthquake rather than of the whirlwind upon them. Their passions were not so much alarmed as has been common here in times past, but their judgements appeared to be powerfully convinced by the masterly and conquering influence of divine truths. The impressions made upon the assembly in general, seemed not superficial, but deep, and heart affecting. O how ready did they now appear universally to embrace and comply with every thing which they heard, and were convinced was their duty. God was in the midst of us, of a truth, bowing and melting stubborn hearts! How many tears and sobs were then to be seen and heard among us! What liveliness and strict attention! What eagerness and intenseness of mind appeared in the whole assembly, in the time of divine service. They seemed to watch and wait for the droppings of God's word, as the thirsty earth, for the "former and latter rain."

Afterwards I discoursed to them on the duty of husbands and wives, from Eph. v. 22–23, and have reason to think this was a word in season. Spent some time further in the evening in inculcating the truths on which I had insisted in my former discourse, respecting the barren fig tree; and observed a powerful influence accompany what was spoken.

Dec. 26. This evening was visited by a person under great spiritual distress; the most remarkable instance of this kind I ever saw. She was, I believe, more than fourscore years old; and appeared to be much broken and very childish, through age; so that it seemed impossible for man to instil into her any notions of divine things; not so much as to give her any doctrinal instruction, because she seemed incapable of being taught. She was led by the hand into my house, and appeared in extreme anguish. I asked her, what ailed her? She answered, her heart was distressed, and she feared she should never find Christ. I asked her when she began to be concerned, with divers other questions relating to her distress. To all which she answered, for substance, to this effect: That she had never heard me preach many times, but never knew any thing about it, never felt it in her heart, till the last Sabbath, and then it came, she said, all one, as if a needle had been thrust into her heart; since which time, she had no rest day nor night. She added, that on the evening before Christmas, a number of Indians being together, at the house where she was, and discoursing about Christ, their talk pricked her heart so that she could not sit up, but fell down in her bed; at which time she went away, as she expressed it, and felt as if she dreamed, and yet is confident she did not dream. When she was thus gone, she saw two paths; one appeared very broad and crooked; and that turned to the left hand. The other appeared straight and very narrow; and that went up the hill to the right hand. She travelled, she said, for some time up the narrow right hand path, till at length something seemed to obstruct her journey. She sometimes called it darkness; and then described it otherwise, and seemed to compare it to a block or bar. She then remembered what she had heard me say about striving to enter in at the straight gate, although she took little notice of it, at the time when she heard me discourse upon the subject; and thought she would climb over this bar. But just as she was thinking of this, she came back again, as she termed it, meaning that she came to herself; whereupon her soul was extremely distressed, apprehending that she had now turned back, and forsaken Christ, and that there was therefore no hope of mercy for her.

As I was sensible that trances, and imaginary view of things are of dangerous tendency in religion, where sought after and depended upon; so I could not but be much concerned about this exercise, especially at first; apprehending this might be a design of Satan to bring a blemish upon the work of God here, by introducing visionary scenes, imaginary terrors, and all manner of mental disorders and delusions, in the room of genuine convictions of sin, and the enlightening influences of the blessed Spirit; and I was almost resolved to declare, that I looked upon this to be one of Satan's devices, and to caution my people against this and similar exercises of that nature. However, I determined first to enquire into her knowledge, to see whether she had any just views of things which might be the occasion of her present distressing concern, or whether it was a mere fright, arising only from imaginary terrors. I asked her divers questions respecting man's primitive, and more especially, his present state, and respecting her own heart; which she answered rationally, and to my surprise. I thought it next to impossible, if not altogether so, that a Pagan, who was become a child through age, should in that state gain so much knowledge by any mere human instruction, without being remarkably enlightened by a divine influence. I then proposed to her the provision made in the gospel for the salvation of sinners, and the ability and willingness of Christ "to save to the uttermost all, old as well as young, that come to him." To this she seemed to give a hearty assent; but instantly replied, "Ay, but I cannot come; my wicked heart will not come to Christ; I do not know how to come," &c. This she spoke in anguish of spirits, striking on her breast, with tears in her eyes, and with such earnestness in her looks, as was indeed piteous and affecting. She seems to be really convinced of her sin and misery, and her need of a change of heart. Her concern is abiding and constant, so that nothing appears why this exercise may not have a saving issue. Indeed there seems reason to hope such an issue, seeing she is so solicitous to obtain an interest in Christ; that her heart, as she expresses it, prays day and night.

How far God may make use of the imagination in awakening some persons under these, and similar circumstances, I cannot pretend to determine. Or, whether this exercise be from a divine influence, I shall leave others to judge. But this I must say, that its effects hitherto bespeak it to be such; nor can it, as I see, be accounted for in any rational way, but from the influence of some spirit either good or evil. The woman, I am sure, never heard divine things in the manner in which she now viewed them; and it would seem strange that she should get such a rational notion of them from the mere working of her own fancy, without some superior, or at least foreign, aid. Yet I must say, I have looked upon it as one of the glories of this work of grace among the Indians, and a special evidence of its being from a divine influence, that there has, till now, been no appearance of such things, no visionary notions, trances, and imaginations, intermixed with those rational convictions of sin, and solid consolations, of which numbers have been made the subjects. And might I have had my desire, there had been no appearance of any thing of this nature at all.

Dec. 27. Laboured in my studies to the utmost of my strength, and though I felt a steady disposition of mind to live to God, and a firm conviction that I had nothing in this world to live for, yet I did not find that sensible affection in the service of God which I wanted to have. My heart seemed barren, though my head and hands were full of labour.

Dec. 28. Discoursed to my people in the catechetical method on which I lately entered. In the improvement of my discourse, wherein I was comparing man's present with his primitive state, and shewing from what he had fallen, and the miseries in which he is now involved, and to which he is exposed in his natural estate; and pressing sinners to take a view of their deplorable circumstances without Christ, as also to strive that they might obtain an interest in him; the Lord, I trust, granted a remarkable influence of his blessed Spirit to accompany what was spoken; and a great concern appeared in the assembly. Many were melted into tears and sobs; and the impressions made upon them seemed deep and heart-affecting. In particular, there were two or three persons, who appeared to be brought to the last exercises of a preparatory work, and reduced almost to extremity; being in a great measure convinced of the impossibility of their helping themselves, or of mending their own hearts; and seemed to be upon the point of giving up all hope in themselves, and of venturing upon Christ, as poor, helpless, and undone. Yet they were in distress and anguish, because they saw no safety in so doing, unless they could do something towards saving themselves. One of these persons was the very aged woman above-mentioned, who now appeared "weary and heavy laden" with a sense of her sin and misery, and her perishing need of an interest in Christ.

This day BRAINERD wrote the following letter to his brother John at Yale College:—

Crossweeksung, N. Jersey, Dec. 28, 1745.

VERY DEAR BROTHER,

I am in one continued, perpetual, and uninterrupted hurry; and divine Providence throws so much upon me, that I do not see how it will ever be otherwise. May I obtain mercy of God to be faithful to the death! I cannot say that I am weary of my hurry. I only want strength and grace to do more for God than I have ever yet done.

My dear brother, the Lord of heaven, who has carried me through many trials, bless you for time and eternity, and fit you to do service for him in his Church below, and to enjoy his blissful presence in his Church triumphant!

My dear brother, the time is short. O let us fill it up for God; let us count the sufferings of this present time as nothing, if we can but run our race, and finish our course with joy. Oh let us strive to live for God! I bless the Lord, I have nothing to do with earth, but only to labour honestly in it for God, till I shall accomplish "as an hireling my day." I think I do not desire to live one minute for any thing which earth can afford. Oh that I could live for none but God, till my dying moment!

I am your affectionate brother,
DAVID BRAINERD.

Lord's day, Dec. 29. Preached from John iii. 1–5. A number of white people were present, as is usual upon the Sabbath. The discourse was accompanied with power, and seemed to have a silent, but deep and piercing influence upon the audience. Many wept and sobbed affectionately. There were some tears among the white people, as well as the Indians. Some could not refrain from crying out; though there were not many so exercised. But the impressions made upon their hearts appeared chiefly by the extraordinary earnestness of their attention, and their heavy sighs and tears.

After public worship was over, I went to my house, proposing to preach again after a short season of intermission. But they soon came in, one after another, with tears in their eyes, to know "What they should do to be saved." The divine spirit in such a manner set home upon their hearts what I spake to them, that the house was soon filled with cries and groans. They all flocked together upon this occasion; and those, whom I had reason to think in a christless state, were almost universally seized with concern for their souls. It was an amazing season of power among them; and seemed as if God had bowed the heavens and come down. So astonishingly prevalent was the operation upon old as well as young, that it seemed as if none would be left in a secure and natural state, but that God was now about to convert all the world. I was ready to think, then, that I should never again despair of the conversion of any man or woman living, be they who or what they would.

It is impossible to give a just and lively description of the appearance of things at this season; at least such as to convey a bright and adequate idea of the effects of this influence. A number might now be seen rejoicing, that God had not taken away the powerful influence of his blessed spirit from this place; refreshed to see so many striving to enter in at the straight gate; and animated with such concern for them, that they wanted to push them forward, as some of them expressed it. At the same time numbers both of men and women, old and young, might be seen in tears; and some in anguish of spirit appearing in their very countenances, like condemned malefactors bound towards the place of execution, with a heavy solicitude sitting in their faces; so that there seemed here, as I thought, a lively emblem of the solemn day of account: a mixture of heaven and hell; of joy and anguish inexpressible.

The concern and religious affection was such, that I could not pretend to have any formal religious exercise among them; but spent the time in discoursing to one and another, as I thought most proper and seasonable for each; and addressed them all together; and finally concluded with prayer. Such were their circumstances at this season, that I could scarcely have half an hour's rest from speaking, from about half an hour before twelve o'clock, at which time I began public worship, till after seven at night. There appeared to be four or five persons newly awakened this day, and the evening before; some of whom but very lately came among us.

Dec. 30. Was visited by four or five young persons, under concern for their souls; most of whom were lately awakened. They wept much while I discoursed with them; and endeavoured to press upon them the necessity of flying to Christ without delay for salvation.

Dec. 31. Spent some hours this day in visiting my people from house to house, and conversing with them about their spiritual concerns; endeavouring to press upon christless souls the necessity of renovation of heart; and scarce left a house without leaving some or other of its inhabitants in tears, appearing solicitously engaged to obtain an interest in Christ.

The Indians are now gathered together from all quarters to this place, and have built them little cottages, so that more than twenty families live within a quarter of a mile of me. A very convenient situation with regard both to public and private instruction.

Jan. 1, 1746. I am this day beginning a new year, and God has carried me through numerous trials and labours in the past. He has amazingly supported my feeble frame; for, having obtained help of God, I continue to this day. O that I might live nearer to God this year than I did the last! The business to which I have been called, and which I have been enabled to go through, I know, has been as great as nature could bear up under, and what would have sunk and overcome me quite, without special support. But alas, alas! though I have done the labours and endured the trials; with what spirit have I done the one, and endured the other? How cold has been the frame of my heart oftentimes! and how little have I sensibly eyed the glory of God in all my doings and sufferings! I have found that I could have no peace without filling up all my time with labour. Thus "necessity has been laid upon me"; yea, in that respect, I have loved to labour; but the misery is, I could not sensibly labour for God, as I would have done. May I for the future be enabled more sensibly to make the glory of God my all.

Spent considerable time in visiting my people again. Found scarcely one but what was under some serious impressions respecting their spiritual concerns.

Jan. 2. Visited some persons newly come among us, who had scarce ever heard any thing of Christianity before, except the empty name. Endeavoured to instruct them, particularly in the first principles of religion, in the most easy and familiar manner I could. There are strangers from remote parts, almost continually dropping in among us, so that I have occasion repeatedly to open and inculcate the first principles of Christianity.

Jan. 4. Prosecuted my catechetical method of instructing. Found my people able to answer questions with propriety, beyond what could have been expected from persons so lately brought out of Heathenish darkness. In the improvement of my discourse, there appeared some concern and affection in the assembly: and especially in those of whom I entertained hopes as being truly gracious, at least several of them were much affected and refreshed.

Lord's day, Jan. 5. Discoursed from Matt. xii. 10–13. There appeared not so much liveliness and affection in divine service as usual. The same truths which have often produced many tears and sobs in the assembly, seemed now to have no special influence upon any in it. Near night, I proposed to have proceeded in my usual method of catechising; but while we were engaged in the first prayer, the power of God seemed to descend upon the assembly in such a remarkable manner, and so many appeared under pressing concern for their souls that I thought it much more expedient to insist upon the plentiful provision made by divine grace for the redemption of perishing sinners, and to press them to a speedy acceptance of the great salvation, than to ask them questions about doctrinal points. What was most practical, seemed most seasonable to be insisted upon, while numbers appeared so extraordinarily solicitous to obtain an interest in the great Redeemer. Baptized two persons this day: one adult, the woman particularly mentioned in my Journal of Dec. 22, and one child.

This woman has discovered a very sweet and heavenly frame of mind from time to time, since her first reception of comfort. One morning in particular, she came to see me; discovering an unusual joy and satisfaction in her countenance; and when I inquired into the reason of it, she replied, "that God had made her feel that it was right for him to do what he pleased with all things; and that it would be right if he should cast her husband and son both into hell; and she saw it was so right for God to do what he pleased with them, that she could not but rejoice in God even if he should send them into hell"; though it was apparent she loved them dearly. She moreover enquired whether I was not sent to preach to the Indians by some good people a great way off. I replied, "Yes, by the good people in Scotland." She answered, "that her heart loved those good people so the evening before, that she could not help praying for them all night, her heart would go to God for them." Thus, the blessings of those ready to perish, is like to come upon those pious persons, who have communicated of their substance to the propagation of the gospel.

Jan. 6. Being very weak in body, I rode for my health. While riding, my thoughts were sweetly engaged for a time upon "the Stone cut out of the mountain without hands," which broke in pieces all before it, and waxed great and became a great mountain, and filled the whole earth: and I longed that Jesus should take to himself his great power, and reign to the ends of the earth. O how sweet were the moments, wherein I felt my soul warm with hopes of the enlargement of the Redeemer's Kingdom! I wanted nothing else, but that Christ should reign to the glory of his blessed name.

The next day he complains of want of fervency.

Jan. 8. In the evening, my heart was drawn out after God in secret; my soul was refreshed and quickened, and I trust faith was in exercise. I had great hopes of the ingathering of precious souls to Christ, not only among my own people, but others also. I was sweetly resigned and composed under my bodily weakness; and was willing to live or die, and desirous to labour for God to the utmost of my strength.

Jan. 9. Was still very weak, and exercised with vapoury disorders. In the evening, enjoyed some enlargement and spirituality in prayer. Oh that I could always spend my time profitably both in health and weakness.

Jan. 10. My soul was in a sweet, calm, and composed frame, and my heart filled with love to all the world; and christian simplicity and tenderness, seemed then to prevail and reign within me. Near night visited a serious Baptist minister, and had some agreeable conversation with him, and found that I could love Christ in his friends.

Jan. 11. Discoursed in a catechetical method, as usual, of late. Having opened our first parents' primitive apostasy from God, and our fall in him; I proceeded to apply my discourse by shewing the necessity we stood in of an Almighty Redeemer, and the absolute need every sinner has of an interest in his merits and mediation. There was some tenderness and affectionate concern apparent in the assembly.

Lord's day, Jan. 12. Preached from Isaiah lv. 6. The word of God seemed to fall upon the audience with a divine weight and influence, and evidently appeared to be "not the word of man." The blessed Spirit I am persuaded accompanied what was spoken, to the hearts of many; so that there was a powerful revival of conviction in numbers who were under spiritual exercise before.

Toward night, catechised in my usual method. Near the close of my discourse, there appeared a great concern, and much affection in the audience; which increased while I continued to invite them to come to an all-sufficient Redeemer, for eternal salvation. The spirit of God seems, from time to time to be striving with souls here. They are so frequently and repeatedly roused, that they seem unable at present, to lull themselves asleep.

Jan. 13. Was visited by several persons under deep concern for their souls; one of whom was newly awakened. It is a most agreeable work to treat with souls who are solicitously inquiring, "what they shall do to be saved." As we are never to be "weary in well doing," so the obligation seems to be peculiarly strong when the work is so very desirable. Yet I must say, my health is so much impaired, and my spirits so wasted with my labours and solitary manner of living; there being no human creature in the house with me; that their repeated and almost incessant applications to me for help and direction, are sometimes exceedingly burdensome; and so exhaust my spirits, that I become fit for nothing at all, entirely unable to prosecute my business, sometimes for days together. What contributes much towards this difficulty is, that I am obliged to spend much time in communicating a little matter to them: there being oftentimes many things to be premised before I can speak directly to what I principally aim at; which things would readily be taken for granted, where there was a competency of doctrinal knowledge.

Jan. 14. Spent some time in private conference with my people, and found some disposed to take comfort as I thought upon slight grounds. They are now generally awakened, and it is become so disgraceful, as well as terrifying to the conscience, to be destitute of religion, that they are in imminent danger of taking up with an appearance of grace, rather than to live under the fear and disgrace of an unregenerated state.

Jan. 15. My spirits were very low and flat, and I could not but think I was a burden to God's earth; and scarcely look any body in the face through shame and sense of barrenness. God pity a poor unprofitable creature.

The two next days he had some comfort and refreshment.

Jan. 18. Prosecuted my catechetical method of discoursing. There appeared a great solemnity, and some considerable affection in the assembly. This method of instruction I find very profitable. When I first entered upon it I was exercised with fears, lest my discourses would unavoidably be so doctrinal, that they would tend only to enlighten the head, but not to affect the heart. But the event proved quite otherwise; for these exercises have hitherto been remarkably blessed in the latter, as well as the former respects.

Lord's day, Jan. 19. Discoursed to my people from Isaiah lv. 7. Towards night catechised in my ordinary method; and this appeared to be a powerful season of grace among us. Numbers were much affected. Convictions were powerfully revived, and divers numbers of christians refreshed and strengthened; and one weary, heavy laden soul, I have abundant reason to hope, brought to true rest and solid comfort in Christ; who afterwards gave me such an account of God's dealing with his soul, as was abundantly satisfying, as well as refreshing to me.

He told me he had often heard me say that persons must see and feel themselves utterly helpless and undone—that they must be emptied of a dependence upon themselves and of all hope of saving themselves, in order to their coming to Christ for salvation. He had long been striving after this view of things; supposing that this would be an excellent frame of mind, to be thus emptied of a dependence upon his own goodness; that God would have respect to this frame, would then be well pleased with him, and bestow eternal life upon him. But when he came to feel himself in this helpless, undone condition, he found it quite contrary to all his thoughts and expectations; so that it was not the same frame, nor indeed any thing like the frame after which he had been seeking. Instead of its being a good frame of mind, he now found nothing but badness in himself, and saw it was forever impossible for him to make himself any better. He wondered, he said, that he had ever hoped to mend his own heart. He was amazed that he had never before seen, that it was utterly impossible for him by all his contrivances and endeavours, to do any thing in that way, since the matter now appeared to him in so clear a light. Instead of imagining, now that God would be pleased with him for the sake of this frame of mind, and this view of his undone estate, he saw clearly, and felt that it would be just with God to send him to eternal misery; and that there was no goodness in which he then felt; for he could not help seeing that he was naked, sinful, and miserable, and that there was nothing in such a sight to deserve God's love or pity.

He saw these things in a manner so clear and convincing, that it seemed to him he said, he could convince every body of their utter inability to help themselves, and their unworthiness of any help from God. In this frame of mind he came to public worship this evening; and while I was inviting sinners to come to Christ naked and empty, without any goodness of their own to recommend them to his acceptance, then he thought with himself that he had often tried to come and give up his heart to Christ, and he used to hope that some time or other he should be able to do so. But now he was convinced that he could not, and that it was utterly vain for him ever to try any more; and he could not, he said, find a heart to make any further attempt, because he saw it would signify nothing at all; nor did he now hope for a better opportunity or more ability hereafter, as he had formerly done, because he saw and was fully convinced that his own strength would forever fail.

While he was musing in this manner, he saw, he said, with his heart, which is a common phrase among them, something that was unspeakably good and lovely, and what he had never seen before; and "this stole away his heart whether he would or no." He did not, he said, know what it was that he saw. He did not say "this is Jesus Christ"; but it was such glory and beauty as he never saw before. He did not now give away his heart, as he had formerly intended and attempted to do; but it went away of itself after that glory which he then discovered. He used to make a bargain with Christ to give up his heart to him that he might have eternal life for it. But now he thought nothing about himself or what would become of him hereafter; but was pleased, and his mind wholly taken up with the unspeakable excellency of what he then beheld. After some time he was wonderfully pleased with the way of salvation by Christ; so that it seemed unspeakably better to be saved altogether by the mere free grace of God in Christ, than to have any hand in saving himself. The consequence of this exercise is, that he appears to retain a sense and relish of divine things, and to maintain a life of seriousness and true religion.

The next day BRAINERD set out on a journey to Elizabeth Town, to confer with the Correspondents at their meeting there; and enjoyed much spiritual refreshment from day to day, through this week. The things expressed in this space of time are such as these; serenity, composure, sweetness and tenderness of soul; thanksgiving to God for his success among the Indians; delight in prayer and praise; sweet and profitable meditations on various divine subjects; longing for more love, for more vigour to live to God, for a life more entirely devoted to him, that he might spend all his time profitably for God and his cause; conversing on spiritual subjects with affection; and lamentation for unprofitableness.

Lord's day, Jan. 26. [At Connecticut Farms.] Was calm and composed. Was made sensible of utter inability to preach without divine help; and was in some good measure willing to leave it with God, to give or withhold assistance, as he saw would be most for his own glory. Was favoured with a considerable degree of assistance in my public work. After public worship, I was in a sweet and solemn frame of mind, thankful to God that he had made me in some measure faithful in addressing precious souls, but grieved that I had been no more fervent in my work; and was tenderly affected towards all the world, longing that every sinner might be saved; and could not have entertained any bitterness towards the worst enemy living. In the evening, rode to Elizabeth Town; and while riding, was almost constantly engaged in lifting up my heart to God, lest I should lose that sweet, heavenly solemnity and composure of soul which I then enjoyed. Afterwards was pleased to think that God reigneth; and thought I could never be uneasy with any of his dispensations, but must be entirely satisfied, whatever trials he should cause me in his church to encounter. Never felt more sedateness, divine serenity and composure of mind; could freely have left the dearest earthly friend for the society of angels and spirits of just men made perfect: my affections soared aloft to the blessed Author of every dear enjoyment. I viewed the emptiness and unsatisfactory nature of the most desirable earthly objects, any further than God is seen in them, and longed for a life of spirituality and inward purity; without which I saw there could be no true pleasure.

Crossweeksung, Jan. 1746.

Jan. 28th. The Indians in these parts have, in times past, run themselves in debt, by their excessive drinking; and some have taken the advantage of them, and put them to trouble and charge, by arresting sundry of them; whereby it was supposed their hunting lands, in great part, were much endangered, and might speedily be taken from them. Being sensible that they could not subsist together in these parts, in order to their being a Christian congregation, if these lands should be taken, which was thought very likely; I thought it my duty to use my utmost endeavours to prevent so unhappy an event. Having acquainted the gentlemen concerned in this mission with the affair, according to the best information I could get of it, they thought it proper to expend the money, which they had been and still were collecting for the religious interest of the Indians, at least a part of it, for discharging their debts, and securing these lands, that there might be no entanglement of a christian congregation of Indians in these parts. Having received orders from them, I answered, in behalf of the Indians, eighty-two pounds, five shillings, N. Jersey currency, at eight shillings per ounce; and so prevented the danger of difficulty in this respect.

As God has wrought a wonderful work of grace among these Indians, and now inclines others from remote places to fall in among them almost continually; and as he has opened a door for the prevention of the difficulty now mentioned which seemed greatly to threaten their religious interests as well as worldly comforts; it is to be hoped that he designs to establish a church for himself among them, and hand down true religion to their posterity.

Jan. 30. Preached to the Indians from John iii. 16, 17. There was a solemn attention and some affection visible in the audience; especially several persons, who had long been concerned for their souls, seemed afresh excited and engaged in seeking after an interest in Christ. One, with much concern, afterwards told me "his heart was so pricked with my preaching he knew not where to turn or what to do."

Jan. 31. This day, the person whom I had made choice of and engaged for a school-master among the Indians, arrived among us, and was heartily welcomed by my people universally. Whereupon I distributed several dozen of primers among the children.

Feb. 1. My school-master entered upon his business among the Indians. He has generally about thirty children and young persons in his school in the day time, and about fifteen married people in the evening school. The number of the latter sort of persons being less than it would be if they could be more constantly at home, and could spare time from their necessary employments for an attendance upon these instructions.

Towards night enjoyed some of the clearest thoughts on a divine subject, viz. that treated of 1 Cor. xv. 13–16. But if there be no resurrection of the dead, &c., which I ever remember to have had upon any subject whatsoever; and spent two or three hours in writing them. I was refreshed with this intenseness; my mind was so engaged in these meditations I could scarcely turn it to any thing else, and indeed I could not be willing to part with so sweet an entertainment.

In the evening catechised in my usual method. Towards the close of my discourse, a surprising power seemed to attend the word, especially to some persons. One man considerably in years, who had been a remarkable drunkard, a conjurer and murderer, and was awakened some months before, was now brought to great extremity under his spiritual distress; so that he trembled for hours together, and apprehended himself just dropping into hell, without any power to rescue or relieve himself. Divers others appeared under great concern, as well as he, and solicitous to obtain a saving change.

Lord's day, Feb. 2. Preached from John v. 24, 25. There appeared as usual, some concern and affection in the assembly. Towards night proceeded in my usual method of catechising. Observed my people more ready in answering the questions proposed to them than ever before. It is apparent they advance daily in doctrinal knowledge. But what is still more desirable, the Spirit of God is yet operating among them; whereby experimental as well as speculative knowledge is propagated in their minds.

After public worship my bodily strength being much spent, my spirits sunk amazingly; and especially on hearing that I was generally taken to be a Roman Catholic, sent by the Papists to draw the Indians into an insurrection against the English; that some were in fear of me, and others were for having me taken up by authority and punished. Alas, what will not the devil do to bring a slur and disgrace on the work of God! O, how holy and circumspect had I need to be! Through divine goodness I have been enabled to mind my own business in these parts as well as elsewhere; and to let all men, and all denominations of men, alone, as to their party notions; and only preach the plain and necessary truths of Christianity, neither inviting to, nor excluding from, any meeting, any of any sort of persuasion whatsoever. Towards night, the Lord gave me freedom at the throne of grace in my first prayer before my catechetical lecture: and, in opening the 45th Psalm to my people, my soul confided in God; although the wicked world should slander and persecute me, or even condemn and execute me as a traitor to my king and country. Truly, "God is a present help in time of trouble." In the evening my soul was in some measure comforted, having some hope that one poor soul was brought home to God this day; though the case did by no means appear clear. Oh that I could fill up every moment of time, during my abode here below, in the service of my God and King.

Feb. 3. My spirits were still much sunk with what I heard the day before, of my being suspected to be engaged in the Pretender's interest. It grieved me, that after there had been so much evidence of a glorious work of grace among these poor Indians, as that the most carnal men could not but take notice of the great change made among them, so many poor souls should still suspect the whole to be only a Popish plot, and so cast an awful reproach on this blessed work of the divine Spirit, and at the same time wholly exclude themselves from receiving any benefit by this divine influence. This put me upon searching whether I had ever dropped any thing inadvertently, which might give occasion to any to suspect that I was stirring up the Indians against the English; and could think of nothing unless it was my attempting sometimes to vindicate the rights of the Indians, and complaining of the horrid practice of making the Indians drunk and then cheating them out of their lands and other property. Once I remembered I had done this with too much warmth of spirit, which much distressed me; thinking that it might possibly prejudice them against this work of grace to their everlasting destruction. God, I believe, did me good by this trial, which served to humble me, and shew me the necessity of watchfulness and of being wise as a serpent as well as harmless as a dove. This exercise led me to a throne of grace, and there I found some support: though I could not get the burden wholly removed. Was assisted in prayer, especially in the evening.

He remained still under a degree of anxiety about this affair, which continued to have the same effect upon him to cause him to reflect upon and humble himself, and frequent the throne of grace; but soon found himself much more relieved and supported. He was this week in an extremely weak state, and obliged, as he expresses it, "to consume considerable time in diversions for his health."

Feb. 5. Discoursed to a considerable number of the Indians in the evening; at which time numbers of them appeared much affected and melted with divine things.

Feb. 8. Spent a considerable part of the day in visiting my people from house to house, and conversing with them about their soul's concerns. Divers persons wept, while I discoursed to them, and appeared concerned for nothing so much as for an interest in the great Redeemer. In the evening catechised as usual. Divine truths made some impressions upon the audience; and were attended with an affectionate engagement of soul in some.

Lord's day, Feb. 9. Discoursed to my people from the story of the blind man. Mark x. 46–52. The word of God seemed weighty, and powerful upon the assembly at this time, and made considerable impressions upon many; several in particular, who have generally been remarkably stupid and careless under the means of grace, were now awakened, and wept affectionately. The most earnest attention, as well as tenderness and affection, appeared in the audience universally.

Baptized three persons; two adults, and one child. The adults, I have reason to hope, were both truly pious. There was considerable melting in the assembly, while I was discoursing particularly to the persons, and administering the ordinance. God has been pleased to own and bless the administration of this as well as of his other ordinances among the Indians. There are some here, who have been powerfully awakened at seeing others baptized; and some, who have obtained relief and comfort, just in the season when this ordinance has been administered.

Toward night catechised. God made this a powerful season to some. There were many affected. Former convictions appeared to be powerfully revived. There was likewise one, who had been a vile drunkard, remarkably awakened. He appeared to be in great anguish of soul, wept, and trembled, and continued to do so till near midnight. There was also a poor heavy-laden soul, who had been long under spiritual distress, as constant and pressing as I ever saw, who was now brought to a comfortable calm, and seemed to be bowed and reconciled to the divine sovereignty, and told me, she now felt and saw, that it was right for God to do with her as he pleased; and that her heart felt pleased and satisfied it should be so; although of late she had often found her heart rise and quarrel with God, because he would, if he pleased, send her to hell after all she had done, or could do to save herself. She added, that the heavy burden she had lain under was now removed; that she had tried to recover her concern and distress again, fearing that the spirit of God was departing from her, and would leave her wholly careless, but that she could not recover it; that she felt she never could do any thing to save herself, but must perish for ever if Christ did not do all for her; that she did not deserve he should help her; and that it would be right if he should leave her to perish. But Christ would save her though she could do nothing to save herself, &c. and here she seemed to rest.

The Monday after, he set out on a journey to the Forks of Delaware to visit the Indians there. He performed the journey under great weakness, and was sometimes exercised with much pain; but says nothing of his dejection and melancholy. He arrived at his own house, at the Forks, on Friday. During the week he appears from his Diary to have enjoyed a sweet composure of mind, thankfulness to God for his mercies to him and others, resignation to the divine will, and comfort in prayer and religious conversation. At the same time his heart was drawn out after God and affected with a sense of his own barrenness, as well as with the fulness and freeness of divine grace.

Forks of Delaware, February, 1746.

Lord's day, February 16. Knowing that numbers of the Indians in these parts were obstinately set against Christianity; and that some of them had refused to hear me preach in times past; I thought it might be proper and beneficial to the christian interest, here, to have a number of my religious people from Crossweeksung with me, to converse with them about religious matters; hoping it might be a means to convince them of the truth and importance of Christianity, to see and hear some of their own nation discoursing of divine things, and manifesting earnest desires that others might be brought out of heathenish darkness, as themselves were. For this purpose I selected half a dozen of the most serious and intelligent of those Indians, and having brought them to the Forks of Delaware, I this day met with them and the Indians of this place. Numbers of the latter probably could not have been prevailed upon to attend this meeting, had it not been for these religious Indians, who accompanied me hither, and preached to them. Some of those who had in times past been extremely averse to Christianity, now behaved soberly; and some others laughed and mocked. However, the word of God fell with such weight and power, that numbers seemed to be stunned, and expressed a willingness to hear me again of these matters.

Afterwards prayed with, and made an address to the white people present; and could not but observe some visible effects of the word, such as tears and sobs among them. After public worship, spent some time, and took pains to convince those that mocked, of the truth and importance of what I had been insisting upon; and so endeavoured to awaken their attention to divine truths. Had reason to think, from what I observed then and afterwards, that my endeavours took considerable effect upon one of the worst of them.

Those few Indians then present, who used to be my hearers in these parts; some having removed hence to Crossweeksung; seemed somewhat kindly disposed toward me, and glad to see me again. They had been so much attacked, however, by some of the opposing Pagans, that they were almost ashamed or afraid to manifest their friendship.

Feb. 17. After having spent much time in discoursing to the Indians in their respective houses, I got them together and repeated and inculcated what I had before taught them. Afterwards discoursed to them from Acts viii. 5–8. A divine influence seemed to attend the word. Several of the Indians here appeared to be somewhat awakened, and manifested earnest tears and sobs. My people of Crossweeksung continued with them day and night repeating and inculcating the truths I had taught them; and sometimes prayed and sung Psalms among them; discoursing with each other in their hearing, of the great things God had done for them and for the Indians from whence they came. This seemed, as my people told me, to have more effect upon them, than when they directed their discourse immediately to them.—I was refreshed and encouraged, and found a spirit of prayer in the evening, and earnest longings for the illumination and conversion of these poor Indians.

Feb. 18. Preached to an assembly of Irish people, nearly fifteen miles distant from the Indians.

Feb. 19. Preached to the Indians again, after having spent considerable time in conversing with them more privately. There appeared a great solemnity, and some concern and affection among the Indians belonging to these parts, as well as a sweet melting among those who came with me. Numbers of the Indians here seemed to have their prejudices and aversion to Christianity removed; and appeared well disposed and inclined to hear the word of God. My heart was comforted and refreshed, and my soul filled with longings for the conversion of these poor Indians.

Feb. 20. Preached to a small assembly of High Dutch people, who had seldom heard the gospel preached, and were some of them at least very ignorant; but numbers of them have lately been put upon an inquiry after the way of salvation with thoughtfulness. They gave wonderful attention; and some of them were much affected under the word, and afterwards said, as I was informed, that they never had been so much enlightened about the way of salvation in their whole lives before. They requested me to tarry with them, or come again and preach to them. It grieved me that I could not comply with their request. I could not but be affected with their circumstances; for they were as "sheep not having a shepherd," and some of them appeared under some degree of distress for sin; standing in peculiar need of the assistance of an experienced spiritual guide.

God was pleased to support and refresh my spirits, by affording me assistance this day, and so hopeful a prospect of success. I returned home rejoicing, and blessing the name of the Lord; found freedom and sweetness afterward in secret prayer, and had my soul drawn out for dear friends. Oh how blessed a thing it is to labour for God faithfully, and with encouragement of success! Blessed be the Lord for ever and ever for the assistance and comfort granted this day!

Feb. 21. Preached to a number of people, many of them Low Dutch. Several of the fore-mentioned High Dutch people attended the sermon, though eight or ten miles distant from their houses. Numbers of the Indians also belonging to these parts came of their own accord with my people from Crossweeksung, to the meetings. —There were two in particular, who, though the last Sabbath they opposed and ridiculed Christianity, now behaved soberly. May the present encouraging appearances continue!

My soul was refreshed and comforted; and I could not but bless God, who had enabled me in some good measure to be faithful the day past. Oh how sweet it is to be spent and worn out for God.

Feb. 22. Preached to the Indians. They appeared more free from prejudice and more cordial to Christianity than before; and some of them appeared affected with divine truths. My spirits were much supported, though my bodily strength was much wasted. Oh that God would be gracious to the souls of these poor Indians!

God has been very gracious to me this week. He has enabled me to preach every day; and has given me some assistance and encouraging prospect of success in almost every sermon.—Blessed be his name! Several of the white people have been awakened this week; and numbers of the Indians much cured of prejudices and jealousies, which they had conceived against Christianity, and seem to be really awakened.

Lord's day, Feb. 23. Preached to the Indians from John vi. 35–37. After public service discoursed particularly with several of them, and invited them to go down to Crossweeksung and tarry there at least for some time; knowing that they would then be free from the scoffs and temptations of the opposing Pagans, as well as in the way of hearing divine truths discoursed of both in public and private. Obtained a promise of some of them that they would speedily pay us a visit, and attend some farther instructions. They seemed to be considerably enlightened, and much freed from their prejudices against Christianity. But it is much to be feared that their prejudices will revive again, unless they can enjoy the means of instruction here, or be removed when they may be under such advantages, and out of the way of their Pagan acquaintances.

The next day BRAINERD left the Forks of Delaware to return to Crossweeksung, and spent the whole week till Saturday in his journey. He preached on the way every day except one; and was several times greatly assisted, and had much inward comfort and earnest longings to fill up all his time in the service of God.—He utters such expressions as these after preaching: "Oh that I may be enabled to plead the cause of God faithfully to my dying moment. Oh how sweet it would be to spend myself wholly for God, and in his cause, and to be freed from selfish motives in my labours."

Crossweeksung, March, 1746.

March 1. Catechised in my ordinary method. Was pleased and refreshed to see them answer the questions proposed to them with such remarkable readiness, discretion and knowledge. Toward the close of my discourse divine truths made considerable impressions upon the audience, and produced tears and sobs in some under concern; and more especially a sweet and humble melting in several, who, I have reason to hope, were truly gracious.

Lord's day, March 2. Preached from John xv. 16. The assembly appeared not so lively in their attention as usual, nor so much affected with divine truths in general as has been common. Some of my people who went up to the Forks of Delaware with me, being now returned, were accompanied by two of the Indians belonging to the Forks, who had promised me a speedy visit. May the Lord meet with them here. They can scarcely go into a house now but they will meet with christian conversation, whereby it is to be hoped they may be both instructed and awakened.

Discoursed to the Indians again in the afternoon, and observed among them some animation and engagedness in divine service, though not equal to what has often appeared here. I know of no assembly of christians, where there seems to be so much of the presence of God, where brotherly love so much prevails, and where I should take so much delight in the public worship of God in general, as in my own congregation; although not more than nine months ago, they were worshipping devils and dumb idols under the power of Pagan darkness and superstition. Amazing change this! effected by nothing less than divine power and grace. This is the doing of the Lord, and it is justly marvellous in our eyes.

The four next days were spent in great bodily weakness, but he speaks of some seasons of considerable inward comfort.

March 5. Spent some time just at evening in prayer, singing, and discoursing to my people upon divine things; and observed some agreeable tenderness and affection among them.—Their present situation is so compact and commodious, that they are easily and quickly called together with only the sound of a conk-shell (a shell like that of a periwinkle), so that they have frequent opportunities of attending religious exercises publicly.—This seems to be a great means under God of keeping alive the impressions of divine things in their minds.

March 6. I walked alone in the evening, and enjoyed sweetness and comfort in prayer beyond what I have of late enjoyed. My soul rejoiced in my pilgrim state; and I was delighted with the thoughts of labouring and enduring hardness for God; felt some longing desires to preach the gospel to dear immortal souls; and confided in God, that he would be with me in my work, and that he never would leave nor forsake me to the end of my race. Oh may I obtain mercy of God to be faithful to my dying moment!

March 7. In the afternoon went on with my work with freedom and cheerfulness; God assisting me; and enjoyed comfort in the evening.

March 8. Catechised in the evening. My people answered the questions proposed to them well. I can perceive their knowledge in religion increases daily. And, what is still more desirable, the divine influence, which has been so remarkable among them, appears still to continue in some good measure. The divine presence seemed to be in the assembly this evening. Some, who I have good reason to think are christians indeed, were melted with a sense of divine goodness and their own barrenness and ingratitude, and seemed to have themselves, as one of them afterwards expressed it. Convictions also appeared to be revived in several instances; and divine truths were attended with such influence upon the assembly in general, that it might justly be called an evening of divine power.

Lord's day, March 9. Preached from Luke x. 38–42. The word of God was attended with power and energy upon the audience. Numbers were affected, and concerned to obtain the one thing needful. Several, who have given good evidence of being truly gracious, were much affected with a want of spirituality, and saw the need they stood in of growing in grace. The greater part of those, who had been under any impressions of divine things in times past, seemed now to have those impressions revived.

In the afternoon proposed to have catechised in my usual method. But, while we were engaged in the first prayer in the Indian language, as usual, a great part of the assembly was so much moved and affected with divine things, that I thought it seasonable and proper to omit the proposing of questions for that time, and to insist upon the most practical truths. I accordingly did so; making a further improvement of the passage of scripture on which I had discoursed in the former part of the day. There appeared to be a powerful divine influence in the congregation. Several, who, as I have reason to think, are truly pious, were so deeply affected with a sense of their own barrenness, and their unworthy treatment of the blessed Redeemer, that they looked on him as pierced by themselves, and mourned, yea some of them were in bitterness as for a first-born.

Some poor awakened sinners, also, appeared to be in anguish of soul to obtain an interest in Christ; so that there was a great mourning in the assembly: many heavy groans, sobs and tears! and one or two, newly come among us, were considerably awakened.

Methinks it would have refreshed the heart of any, who truly love Zion's interests, to have been in the midst of this divine influence, and seen the effects of it upon saints and sinners. The place of divine worship appeared both solemn and sweet; and was so endeared by a display of the divine presence and grace, that those who had any relish for divine things could not but cry, "How amiable are thy tabernacles, O Lord of Hosts!" After public worship was over, numbers came to my house; where we sang and discoursed of divine things; and the presence of God seemed here also to be in the midst of us.

While we were singing there was one individual, the woman mentioned in my journal of February 9, who, I may venture to say, if I may be allowed to say so much of any person I ever saw, was "filled with joy unspeakable and full of glory"; and could not but burst forth in prayer and praises to God before us all, with many tears; crying sometimes in English, and sometimes in Indian, "O blessed Lord! do come, do come! O do take me away; do let me die, and go to Jesus Christ! I am afraid if I live I shall sin again. O do let me die now! O dear Jesus, do come! I cannot stay, I cannot stay! O how can I live in this world; do take my soul away from this sinful place! O let me never sin any more! O what shall I do, what shall I do, dear Jesus! O dear Jesus!" In this ecstacy she continued some time, uttering these and similar expressions incessantly. The grand argument she used with God to take her away immediately was, that "if she lived, she should sin against him." When she had a little recovered herself, I asked her, if Christ was now sweet to her soul? Whereupon, turning to me with tears in her eyes, and with all the tokens of deep humility I ever saw in any person, she said, "I have many times heard you speak of the goodness and the sweetness of Christ, that he was better than all the world. But O I knew nothing what you meant. I never believed you, I never believed you! But now I know it is true"; or words to that effect. I answered, "And do you see enough in Christ for the greatest of sinners?" She replied, "O enough, enough for all the sinners in the world, if they would but come." When I asked her, "If she could not tell them of the goodness of Christ." Turning herself about to some christless souls, who stood by, and were much affected, she said, "Oh there is enough in Christ for you if you would but come. O strive, strive to give up your hearts to him," &c. On hearing something of the glory of heaven mentioned, that there was no sin in that world; she again fell into the same ecstacy of joy and desire of Christ's coming; repeating her former expressions, "O dear Lord, do let me go! O what shall I do; what shall I do. I want to go to Christ. I cannot live. O do let me die," &c.

She continued in this sweet frame for more than two hours, before she was able to get home. I am very sensible that there may be great joys, arising even to an ecstacy, where there is still no substantial evidence of their being well grounded. But, in the present case, there seemed to be no evidence wanting in order to prove this joy to be divine; either in regard to its preparatives, attendants, or consequents.

Of all the persons, whom I have seen under spiritual exercise, I scarcely ever saw one appear more bowed and broken under convictions of sin and misery, or what is usually called a preparatory work, than this woman; nor scarcely any, who seemed to have a greater acquaintance with her own heart than she had. She would frequently complain to me of the hardness and rebellion of her heart. Would tell me that her heart rose and quarrelled with God, when she thought he would do with her as he pleased, and send her to hell, notwithstanding her prayers, good frames, &c. and that her heart was not willing to come to Christ for salvation, but tried every where else for help. As she seemed to be remarkably sensible of her stubbornness and contrariety to God, under conviction, so she appeared to be no less remarkably bowed and reconciled to his sovereignty, before she obtained any relief or comfort; something of which I have noticed in my journal of Feb. 9. Since that time she has seemed constantly to breathe the temper and spirit of the new creature; crying after Christ, not through fear of hell as before, but with strong desires after him as her only satisfying portion; and has many times wept and sobbed bitterly because, as she apprehended, she did not and could not love him. When I have sometimes asked her why she appeared so sorrowful, and whether it was because she was afraid of hell; she would answer "No, I be not distressed about that; but my heart is so wicked, I cannot love Christ"; and thereupon burst into tears. But although this has been the habitual frame of her mind for several weeks together, so that the exercise of grace appeared evident to others; yet she seemed wholly insensible to it herself, and never had any remarkable comfort and sensible satisfaction until this evening.

This sweet and surprising ecstacy, appeared to spring from a true spiritual discovery of the glory, ravishing beauty, and excellency of Christ; and not from any gross imaginary notions of his human nature, such as that of seeing him in such a place, or pasture, as hanging on the cross, as bleeding and dying, as gently smiling, and the like; which delusions some have been carried away with. Nor did it rise from sordid selfish apprehensions of her having any benefit whatsoever conferred on her; but from a view of his personal excellency and transcendant loveliness; which drew forth those vehement desires of enjoying him which she now manifested, and made her long "to be absent from the body, that she might be present with the Lord."

The attendants of this ravishing comfort were such, as abundantly discovered its spring to be divine; and that it was truly "a joy in the Holy Ghost." Now she viewed divine truths as living realities, and could say, "I know these things are so; I feel that they are true!" Now her soul was resigned to the divine will in the most tender point; so that when I said to her, "What if God should take away your husband from you, who was then very sick, how do you think you could bear that?" She replied, "He belongs to God, and not to me; he may do with him just as he pleases." Now she had the most tender sense of the evil of sin, and discovered the utmost aversion to it, and longing to die, that she might be delivered from it. Now she could freely trust her all with God for time and eternity. When I questioned her, "How she would be willing to die and leave her little infant; and what she thought would become of it in that case?" she answered, "God will take care of it." Now she appeared to have the most humbling sense of her own meanness and unworthiness, her weakness and inability to preserve herself from sin, and to persevere in the way of holiness, crying, "If I live I shall sin." I then thought that I had never seen such an appearance of ecstacy and humility meeting in any one person in all my life before.

The consequents of this joy are no less desirable and satisfactory than its attendants. She since appears to be a most tender, brokenhearted, affectionate, devout, and humble christian; as exemplary in life and conversation as any person in my congregation. May she still "grow in grace and in the knowledge of Christ."

March 10. Towards night the Indians met together, of their own accord, and sang, prayed, and discoursed of divine things among themselves; at which time there was much affection among them.

Some who are hopefully gracious, appeared to be melted with divine things; and some others seemed much concerned for their souls. Perceiving their engagement and affection in religious exercises, I went among them, and prayed, and gave a word of exhortation; and observed two or three somewhat affected and concerned, who scarce ever appeared to be under any religious impressions before. It seemed to be a day and evening of divine power. Numbers retained the warm impressions of divine things which had been made upon their minds the day before.

My soul was refreshed with freedom and enlargement, and, I hope, the lively exercise of faith in secret prayer this night. My will was sweetly resigned to the divine will; my hopes respecting the enlargement of the kingdom of Christ somewhat raised; and I could commit Zion's cause to God as his own.

On Tuesday he speaks of some sweetness and spirituality in Christian conversation. On Wednesday complains that he enjoyed not much comfort and satisfaction through the day, because without salutary religious conversation.

March 14. Was visited by a considerable number of my people and spent some time in religious exercises with them.

March 15. In the evening catechised. My people answered the questions put to them with surprising readiness and judgment. There appeared some warmth, and a feeling sense of divine things among those who I have reason to hope are real christians, while I was discoursing upon peace of conscience and joy in the Holy Ghost. These seemed quickened and enlivened in divine service, though there was not so much appearance of concern among those whom I have reason to think in a christless state.

In the former part of the week following he was very ill, and under great dejection; being rendered unserviceable by his illness, and fearing that he should never be serviceable any more; and therefore exceedingly longed for death. But afterwards he was more encouraged, and life appeared more desirable; because, as he says, he "had a little dawn of hope that he might be useful in the world." In the latter part of this week he was somewhat relieved of his illness, in the use of means prescribed by his physician.

Lord's day, March 16. Preached to my congregation from Hebrews ii. 1–3. Divine truths seemed to have some considerable influence upon some of the hearers, and produced many tears, as well as heavy sighs and sobs, among those who have given evidence of being real christians, and others also. The impressions made upon the audience appeared in general deep and heart-affecting; not superficial, noisy and affected.

Towards night discoursed again on the Great Salvation. The word was again attended with some power upon the audience. Numbers wept affectionately, and to appearance unfeignedly; so that the Spirit of God seemed to be moving upon the face of the assembly. Baptized the woman particularly mentioned in my journal of last Lord's day; who now, as well as then, appeared to be in a devout, humble, and excellent frame of mind.

My house being thronged with my people in the evening; I spent the time in religious exercises with them, until my nature was almost spent. They are so unwearied in religious exercises and insatiable in their thirsting after christian knowledge, that I can sometimes scarcely avoid labouring so as greatly to exhaust my strength and spirits.

March 19. Several of the persons who went with me to the Forks of Delaware in February last, having been detained there by the dangerous illness of one of their company, returned home this day. Whereupon my people generally met together of their own accord, in order to spend some time in religious exercises; and especially to give thanks to God for his preserving goodness to those who had been absent from them for several weeks, and recovering mercy to him who had been sick; and that he had now returned them all in safety. As I was then absent; they desired my school-master to assist them in carrying on their religious solemnity; who tells me that they appeared engaged and affectionate in repeated prayer, singing, &c.

March 22. Catechised in my usual method in the evening. My people answered questions to my great satisfaction. There appeared nothing very remarkable in the assembly, considering what has been common among us. Although I may justly say the strict attention, the tenderness and affection, the many tears and heart affecting sobs, appearing in numbers in the assembly, would have been very remarkable, were it not that God has made these things common with us, and even with strangers soon after their coming among us, from time to time. I am far from thinking that every appearance and particular instance of affection that has been among us has been truly genuine, and purely from a divine influence. I am sensible of the contrary; and doubt not but that there has been some corrupt mixture, some chaff as well as wheat; especially since religious concern appeared so common and prevalent here.

Lord's day, March 23. There being about fifteen strangers, adult persons, come among us in the week past, several of whom had never been in any religious meeting till now; I thought it proper to discourse this day in a manner peculiarly suited to their circumstances and capacities; and accordingly attempted it from Hosea xiii. 9. "O Israel, thou hast destroyed thyself," &c. In the forenoon, I opened in the plainest manner I could, man's apostasy and ruined state, after having spoken some things respecting the being and perfections of God, and his creation of man in a state of uprightness and happiness. In the afternoon, endeavoured to open the glorious provision which God has made for the redemption of apostate creatures, by giving his own dear Son to suffer for them and satisfy divine justice on their behalf. There was not that affection and concern in the assembly which has been common among us; although there was a desirable attention appearing in general, and even in most of the strangers.

Near sun-set I felt an uncommon concern upon my mind, especially for the poor strangers; that God had so much withheld his presence and the powerful influence of his Spirit from the assembly in the exercises of the day; and thereby withheld from them that degree of conviction which I hoped they might have had. In this frame I visited several houses and discoursed with some concern and affection to several persons particularly; but without much appearance of success, till I came to a house where several of the strangers were. There the solemn truths on which I discoursed appeared to take effect; first upon some children; then upon several adult persons who had been somewhat awakened before; and afterwards upon several of the Pagan strangers.

I continued my discourse, with some fervency, until almost everyone in the house was melted into tears, and divers wept aloud, and appeared earnestly concerned to obtain an interest in Christ. Upon this, numbers soon gathered from all the houses round about; and so thronged the place, that we were obliged to remove to the house where we usually met for public worship. The congregation gathering immediately, and many appearing remarkably affected, I discoursed some time from Luke xix. 10. For the Son of man is come to seek, &c.; endeavouring to open the mercy, compassion, and concern of Christ for lost, helpless, and undone sinners. There was much visible concern and affection in the assembly; and I doubt not but that a divine influence accompanied what was spoken to the hearts of many. There were five or six of the strangers, men and women, who appeared to be considerably awakened; and, in particular, one very rugged young man, who seemed as if nothing would move him, was now brought to tremble like the jailer, and weep for a long time.

The Pagans who were awakened, seemed at once to put off their savage roughness and Pagan manners, and became sociable, orderly, and humane in their carriage. When they first came, I exhorted my religious people to take pains with them as they had done with other strangers from time to time, to instruct them in Christianity. But when some of them attempted something of that nature, the strangers would soon rise up and walk to other houses to avoid the hearing of such discourses. Whereupon some of the serious persons agreed to disperse themselves into the several parts of the settlement; so that wherever the strangers went, they met with some instructive discourse, and warm addresses respecting their salvation. But now, there was no need of using policy in order to get an opportunity of conversing with some of them about their spiritual concerns; for they were so far touched with a sense of their perishing state, as made them voluntarily yield to the closest addresses which were made them respecting their sin and misery, their need of an acquaintance with and interest in the great Redeemer.

March 24. Numbered the Indians, to see how many souls God had gathered together here since my coming into these parts; and found there were now about an hundred and thirty persons together, old and young. Sundry of those, who are my stated hearers, perhaps to the number of fifteen or twenty, were absent at this season. If all had been together, the number would now have been very considerable; especially considering how few were together at my first coming into this part of the country: the whole number, then, not amounting to ten persons at that time.

My people were out this day with the design of clearing some of their land, above fifteen miles distant from this settlement, in order to their settling there in a compact form, where they might be under the advantages of attending the public worship of God, of having their children taught in a school, and at the same time have a conveniency for planting: their land, in the place of our present residence, being of little or no value for that purpose. The design of their settling thus in a body, and cultivating their lands, of which they have done very little in their Pagan state, being of such necessity and importance to their religious interest, as well as worldly comfort; I thought it proper to call them together, and shew them the duty of labouring with faithfulness and industry, and that they must not now "be slothful in business," as they had ever been in their Pagan state. I endeavoured to press the importance of their being laborious, diligent, and vigorous in the prosecution of their business; especially at the present juncture, the season of planting being now near, in order to their being in a capacity of living together, and enjoying the means of grace and instruction. Having given them directions for their work, which they very much wanted, as well as for their behaviour in divers respects; I explained, sang, and endeavoured to inculcate upon them the 127th Psalm, common metre, Dr. Watt's version; and having recommended them, and the design of their going forth, to God, by prayer with them, I dismissed them to their business.

After the Indians were gone to their work, to clear their lands, I retired by myself, and poured out my soul to God, that he would smile on their feeble beginnings, and that he would settle an Indian town, which might be a mountain of holiness. I found my soul much refreshed in these petitions and much enlarged for Zion's interest, and for numbers of dear friends in particular. My sinking spirits were revived and raised; and I felt animated in the service to which God has called me.

This was the dearest hour I have enjoyed for many days, if not weeks. I found an encouraging hope that something would be done for God; and that God would use and help me in his work. O, how sweet were the thoughts of labouring for God, when I felt any spirit and courage, and had any hope that I ever should be succeeded.

In the evening, read and expounded to those of my people who were yet at home, and to the strangers newly come, the substance of the 3d chapter of the Acts. Numbers seemed to melt under the word; especially while I was discoursing upon ver. 19. "Repent ye, therefore, and be converted," &c. Several of the strangers also were affected. When I asked them afterwards, whether they did not now feel that their hearts were wicked as I had taught them; one of them replied, "Yes, she felt it now." Although, before she came here, upon hearing that I taught the Indians that their hearts were all bad by nature, and needed to be changed and made good by the power of God; she had said, "Her heart was not wicked, and she had never done any thing that was bad in her life." This, indeed, seems to be the case with them, I think universally, in their Pagan State. They seem to have no consciousness of sin and guilt, unless they can charge themselves with some gross acts of sin contrary to the commands of the second table.

The next day his schoolmaster was taken sick with a pleurisy, and he spent a great part of the remainder of this week in attending him. In his weak state, this was an almost overbearing burden; he being obliged constantly to wait upon him from day to day, and to lie on the floor at night. His spirits sunk in a considerable degree, with his bodily strength, under this burden.

March 27. Discoursed to a number of my people in one of their houses in a more private manner. Inquired particularly into their spiritual states, in order to see what impressions they were under. Laid before them the marks of a regenerate, as well as of an unregenerate state: and endeavoured to suit and direct my discourse to them severally, according as I apprehended their states to be. There was a considerable number gathered together before I finished my discourse; and several seemed much affected, while I was urging the necessity and infinite importance of getting into a renewed state. I find particular and close dealing with souls in private, is often very successful.

March 29. In the evening, catechised, as usual upon Saturday. Treated upon the benefits which believers receive from Christ at death. The questions were answered with great readiness and propriety; and those who I have reason to think, are the dear people of God, were in general sweetly melted. There appeared such a liveliness and vigour in their attendance upon the word of God, and such eagerness to be made partakers of the benefits mentioned; that they seemed not only to be "looking for," but "hasting to, the coming of the day of God." Divine truths seemed to distil upon the audience with a gentle, but melting efficacy, as the refreshing "showers upon the new mown grass." The assembly in general, as well as those who appear truly religious, were affected with some brief accounts of the blessedness of the godly at death; and most of them then discovered an affectionate inclination to cry, "Let me die the death of the righteous, and let my last end be like his": although many were not duly engaged to obtain the change of heart that is necessary to that blessed end.

Lord's day, March 30. Discoursed from Matt. xxv. 31–40. There was a very considerable moving, and affectionate melting, in the assembly. I hope that there were some real, deep, and abiding impressions of divine things made upon the minds of many. There was one aged man, newly come among us, who appeared to be considerably awakened, that never was touched with any concern for his soul before. In the evening, catechised. There was not that tenderness and melting engagement among God's people, which appeared the evening before, and many other times. They answered the questions distinctly, and well, and were devout and attentive in divine service.

March 31. Called my people together, as I had done the Monday evening before, and discoursed to them again on the necessity and importance of labouring industriously in order to their living together, and enjoying the means of grace, &c. Having engaged in a solemn prayer to God among them for a blessing upon their attempts, I dismissed them to their work. Numbers of them, both men and women, seemed to offer themselves willingly to this service; and some appeared affectionately concerned that God might go with them, and begin their little town for them; that by his blessing it might be a place comfortable for them and theirs, with regard both to procuring the necessaries of life, and to attending on the worship of God.

Towards night, I enjoyed some sweet meditations on these words: "It is good for me to draw near to God." My soul, I think, had some sweet sense of what is intended in those words.

The next day he was extremely busy in taking care of the schoolmaster, and in some other necessary affairs, which greatly diverted him from

what he looked upon as his proper business; but yet he speaks of com-
fort and refreshment at some time of the day.

April 2. I was somewhat exercised with a spiritual frame of mind;
but was a little relieved and refreshed in the evening with meditation alone in the woods. But alas! my days pass away as the chaff! it
is but little I do, or can do, that turns to any account; and it is my
constant misery and burden, that I am so fruitless in the vineyard
of the Lord. Oh that I were a pure spirit; that I might be active for
God! This, I think, more than any thing else, makes me long that
this corruptible might put on incorruption, and this mortal put on
immortality. God deliver me from clogs, fetters, and a body of
death, which impede my service from him.

The next day he complains bitterly of some exercises by corruption,
which he found in his own heart.

April 4. Spent the most of the day in writing on Revelation xxii.
17. "And whosoever will," &c. Enjoyed some freedom and encouragement in my work; and found some comfort in prayer.

April 5. Catechised in the evening. There appeared to be some
affection and fervent engagement in divine service through the assembly in general; especially towards the conclusion of my discourse. After public worship, a number of those, who I have reason
to think, are truly religious, came to my house, and seemed eager
for some farther entertainment upon divine things. While I was
conversing with them about their spiritual exercises: observing to
them, that God's work in the hearts of all his children, was for substance the same; and that their trials and temptations were also
alike; and shewing the obligations such were under to love one another in a peculiar manner; they seemed to be melted into tenderness and affection towards each other. I thought that that particular token of their being the disciples of Christ, viz. of their having
love one towards another, had scarcely ever appeared more evident
than at this time.

After public worship, a number of my dear christian Indians
came to my house; with whom I felt a sweet union of soul. My
heart was knit to them; and I cannot say I have felt such a sweet
and fervent love to the brethren, for some time past. I saw in them
appearances of the same love. This gave me somewhat of a view of
the heavenly state; and particularly of that part of the happiness of

heaven which consists in the communion of saints; and this was affecting to me.

Lord's day, April 6. Preached from Matt. vii. 21–23. Not every one that saith unto me, Lord, Lord, &c. There were considerable effects of the word visible in the audience, and such as were very desirable; an earnest attention, a great solemnity, many tears and heavy sighs, which were modestly suppressed in a considerable measure, and appeared unaffected and without any indecent commotion of the passions. Numbers of the religious people were put upon serious and close examination of their spiritual state, by hearing that "not every one that saith to Christ, Lord, Lord, shall enter into his kingdom." Some expressed fears lest they had deceived themselves, and taken up a false hope, because they found they had done so little of the will of his Father who is in heaven.

There was one man brought under very great and pressing concern for his soul; which appeared more especially after his retirement from public worship. That, which, he says, gave him his great uneasiness, was, not so much any particular sin, as that he had never done the will of God at all, but had sinned continually, and so had no claim to the kingdom of Heaven. In the afternoon, I opened to them the discipline of Christ in his Church, and the method in which offenders are to be dealt with. At which time the religious people were much affected; especially when they heard that the offender continuing obstinate, must finally be esteemed and treated "as an Heathen man," and Pagan, who has no part nor lot among God's visible people. Of this they seemed to have the most awful apprehensions; a state of Heathenism, out of which they were so lately brought, appeared very dreadful to them.

After public worship, I visited several houses, to see how they spent the remainder of the sabbath, and to treat with them solemnly on the great concerns of their souls. The Lord seemed to smile upon my private endeavours, and to make these particular and personal addresses more effectual upon some, than my public discourses.

April 7. Discoursed to my people in the evening, from 1 Cor. xi. 23–26. "For I have received of the Lord," &c. Endeavoured to open to them the institution, nature, and ends of the Lord's supper, as well as of the qualifications and preparations necessary to the right participation of that ordinance. Numbers appeared much affected with the love of Christ, manifested in his making this provision for the comfort of his people, at a season when himself was just entering upon his sharpest sufferings.

On Tuesday he went to the meeting of the Presbytery appointed at Elizabethtown. In his way thither he enjoyed some sweet meditations: but after he came there, he was, as he expresses it, "very vapoury and melancholy, and under an awful gloom which oppressed his mind." This continued until Saturday evening; when he began to have some relief and encouragement. He spent the Sabbath at Staten Island; where he preached to an assembly of Dutch and English, and enjoyed considerable refreshment and comfort, both in public and private. In the evening, he returned to Elizabethtown.

April 14. My spirits, this day, were raised and refreshed, and my mind composed; so that I was in a comfortable frame of soul most of the day. In the evening, my head was clear, my mind serene; I enjoyed sweetness in secret prayer and meditation on Psalm lxxiii. 28. "But it is good for me to draw near to God"; &c. O how free, how comfortable, cheerful, and yet solemn, do I feel when I am in a good measure freed from those damps and melancholy glooms under which I often labour. Blessed be the Lord, I find myself relieved in this respect.

April 15. My soul longed for more spirituality; and it was my burden that I could do no more for God. O, my barrenness in my daily affliction and heavy load! O how precious is time and how it pains me to see it slide away, while I do so little to any good purpose. O that God would make me more fruitful and spiritual.

The next day he speaks of his being almost overwhelmed with vapoury disorders: but yet not so, as wholly to destroy the composure of his mind.

April 17. Enjoyed some comfort in prayer, some freedom in meditation, and composure in my studies. Spent some time in writing in the forenoon. In the afternoon spent some time in conversation with several dear ministers. In the evening preached from Psalm lxxiii. 28. "But it is good for me to draw near to God." God helped me to feel the truths of my texts both in the first prayer and in the sermon. I was enabled to pour out my soul to God with great freedom, fervency and affection; and, blessed be the Lord, it was a comfortable season to me. I was enabled to speak with tenderness, and yet with faithfulness: and divine truths seemed to fall with weight and influence upon the hearers. My heart was melted for the dear assembly; and I loved every body in it; and scarcely ever felt more love to immortal souls in my life. My soul cried, "Oh that the dear creatures might be saved! Oh that God would have mercy upon them!"

He seems to have been in a very comfortable frame of mind the two next days.

Lord's day, April 20. Discoursed, both forenoon and afternoon, from Luke xxiv: explaining most of the chapter, and making remarks upon it. There was a desirable attention in the audience; though there was not so much appearance of affection and tenderness among them as had been usual. Our meeting was very full; there being sundry strangers present who had never been with us before. Enjoyed some freedom and, I hope, exercise of faith, in prayer in the morning, especially when I came to pray for Zion. I was free from that gloomy discouragement which so often oppresses my mind; and my soul rejoiced in the hopes of Zion's prosperity, and the enlargement of the dear kingdom of the great Redeemer. O that his kingdom might come!

In the evening catechised. My people answered the questions proposed to them readily and distinctly; and I could perceive that they advanced in their knowledge of the principles of Christianity. There appeared an affectionate melting in the assembly at this time. Several, who I trust are truly religious, were refreshed and quickened, and seemed by their discourse and behaviour after public worship to have their "hearts knit together in love." This was a sweet and blessed season, like many others with which my poor people have been favored in months past. God has caused this little fleece to be repeatedly wet with the blessed dew of his divine grace, while all the earth around has been comparatively dry.

April 21. Was composed and comfortable in mind most of the day; and was mercifully freed from those gloomy damps with which I am frequently exercised. Had freedom and comfort in prayer several times; and especially had some rising hopes of Zion's enlargement and prosperity. Oh how refreshing were those hopes to my soul! Oh that the kingdom of the dear Lord might come. Oh that the poor Indians might quickly be gathered in great numbers!

April 22. My mind was remarkably free this day from melancholy damps and glooms, and animated in my work. I found such fresh vigour and resolution in the service of God, that the mountains seemed to become a plain before me. O blessed be God for an interval of refreshment and fervent resolution in my Lord's work! In the evening, my soul was refreshed in secret prayer, and my heart drawn out for divine blessings; especially for the Church of God, and his interest among my own people, and for dear friends in remote places. Oh that Zion might prosper and precious souls be brought home to God!

In this comfortable fervent frame of mind he remained the two next days.

April 25. Of late I apprehended that a number of persons in my congregation were proper subjects of the ordinance of the Lord's supper; and that it might be seasonable speedily to administer it to them; and having taken advice of some of the reverend correspondents in this solemn affair; I accordingly proposed and appointed the next Lord's day, with leave of divine providence, for the administration of this ordinance; and this day as preparatory thereto was set apart for solemn fasting and prayer.

The design of this preparatory solemnity was to implore the blessings of God upon our renewing covenant with him, and with one another, to walk together in the fear of God, in love and christian fellowship, and to entreat that his presence might be with us in our designed approach to his table; as well as to humble ourselves before God on account of the apparent withdrawment, at least in a measure of that blessed influence, which has been so prevalent upon persons of all ages among us; as also on account of the rising appearance of carelessness, and vanity, and vice among some, who some time since appeared to be touched and affected with divine truths, and brought to some sensibility of their miserable and perishing state by nature. It was also designed that he might importunately pray for the peaceable settlement of the Indians together in a body; that they might be a commodious congregation for the worship of God; and that God would blast and defeat all the attempts that were, or might be, made against that pious design.

The solemnity was observed and seriously attended, not only by those who proposed at the Lord's table, but by the whole congregation universally. In the former part of the day, I endeavoured to open to my people the nature and design of a fast, as I had attempted more briefly to do before, and to instruct them in the duties of such a solemnity. In the afternoon I insisted upon the special reasons there were for our engaging in these solemn exercises at this time; both in regard of the need we stood in of divine assistance, in order to a due preparation for that sacred ordinance upon which some of us were proposing, with leave of divine Providence speedily to attend; and also in respect of the manifest decline of God's work here, as to the effectual conviction and conversion of sinners; there having been few of late deeply awakened with great solemnity and reverence, with much tenderness and many tears, by those who appeared to be truly religious; and there was some appearance of divine power upon those who had been awakened some time before, and who were still under concern.

After repeated prayer, and attendance upon the word of God, I proposed to the religious people, with as much brevity and plainness as I could, the substance of the doctrine of the christian faith, as I had formerly done previous to their baptism; and had their renewed cheerful assent to it. I then led them to a solemn renewal of their baptismal covenant; wherein they had explicitly and publicly given up themselves to God the Father, Son and Holy Ghost, avouching him to be their God; and at the same time renouncing their heathenish vanities, their idolatrous and superstitious practices; solemnly engaging to take the Word of God, so far as it was or might be made known to them, for the rule of their lives; promising to walk together in love, to watch over themselves and one another, to lead lives of seriousness and devotion, and to discharge the relative duties incumbent on them respectively, &c. This solemn transaction was attended with much gravity and seriousness; and at the same time with the utmost readiness, freedom and cheerfulness; and a religious union and harmony of soul seemed to crown the whole solemnity. I could not but think in the evening, that there had been manifest tokens of the divine presence with us in all the several services of the day; though it was also manifest that there was not that concern among Christless souls which has often appeared there.

April 26. Toward noon prayed with a dying child, and gave a word of exhortation to the bystanders to prepare for death; which seemed to take effect upon some. In the afternoon discoursed to my people from Matt. xxvi. 26–30 of the author, the nature, and designs of the Lord's supper; and endeavoured to point out the worthy receivers of that ordinance.

The religious people were affected, and even melted, with divine truths,—with a view of the dying love of Christ. Several others, who had been for some months under convictions of their perishing state, appeared now to be much moved with concern, and afresh engaged in seeking after an interest in Christ; although I cannot say that the word of God appeared so quick and powerful, so sharp and piercing to the assembly as it had sometimes formerly done. Baptized two adult persons; both serious and exemplary in their lives, and I hope truly religious. One of them was the man particularly mentioned in my journal of the 6th instant; who, although he was greatly distressed, because "he had never done the will of God," has since, it is hoped, obtained spiritual comfort upon good grounds.

In the evening I catechised those, who were designed to partake of the Lord's supper the next day, upon the institution, nature and end of that ordinance; and had abundant satisfaction respecting their doctrinal knowledge and fitness in that respect for an attendance upon it. They likewise appeared in general to have an affecting sense of the solemnity of this sacred ordinance, and to be humbled under a sense of their own unworthiness to approach to God in it; and to be earnestly concerned that they might be duly prepared for an attendance upon it.—Their hearts were full of love one toward another, and that was the frame of mind which they seemed concerned to maintain and bring to the Lord's table with them. In the singing and prayer after catechising, there appeared an agreeable tenderness and melting among them; and such tokens of brotherly love and affection, as would even constrain one to say "Lord, it is good to be here"; it is good to dwell where such an heavenly influence distils.

Lord's day, April 27. Preached from Tit. ii. 14, "Who gave himself for us," &c. The word of God, at this time, was attended with some appearance of divine power upon the assembly; so that the attention and gravity of the audience were remarkable; and especially towards the conclusions of the exercise, divers persons were much affected. Administered the sacrament of the Lord's supper to twenty three persons of the Indians, the number of the men and women being nearly equal; several others, to the number of five or six, being now absent at the Forks of Delaware, who would otherwise have communed with us. The ordinance was attended with great solemnity, and with a most desirable tenderness and affection. It was remarkable that in the season of the performance of the sacramental actions, especially in the distribution of the bread, they seemed to be affected in a most lively manner, as if Christ had been really crucified before them. The words of the institution, when repeated and enlarged upon in the season of the administration, seemed to meet with the same reception, to be entertained with the same free and full belief and affectionate engagement of soul, as if the Lord Jesus Christ himself had been present, and had personally spoken to them. The affections of the communicants, although considerably raised, were, notwithstanding, agreeably regulated and kept within proper bounds. So that there was a sweet, gentle, and affectionate melting without any indecent or boisterous commotion of the passions.

Having rested sometime after the administration of the sacrament, being extremely tired with the necessary prolixity of the work, I walked from house to house, and conversed particularly with most of the communicants, and found they had been almost universally refreshed at the Lord's table, "as with new wine." Never did I see such an appearance of Christian love among any people in all my life. It was so remarkable, that one might well have cried with an agreeable surprise, "Behold how they love one another." I think there could be no greater tokens of mutual affection among the people of God, in the early days of Christianity, than what now appeared here. The sight was so desirable, and so well becoming the gospel, that nothing less could be said of it than that it was "the doing of the Lord," the genuine operation of Him, "who is Love."

Towards night discoursed again on the forementioned text, Tit. ii. 14; and insisted on the immediate end and design of Christ's death: viz. That he might redeem his people from all iniquity, &c. This appeared to be a season of divine power among us. The religious people were much refreshed, and seemed remarkably tender and affectionate, full of love, joy, and peace, and desirous of being completely "redeemed from all iniquity"; so that some of them afterwards told me that "they had never felt the like before." Convictions also appeared to be revived in many instances; and several persons were awakened, whom I had never observed under any religious impressions before.

Such was the influence which attended our assembly, and so unspeakably desirable the frame of mind which many enjoyed in divine service, that it seemed almost grievous to conclude the public worship. The congregation, when dismissed, although it was then almost dark, appeared loth to leave the place, and employments which had been rendered so dear to them by the benefits enjoyed, while a blessed quickening influence distilled upon them. Upon the whole, I must say, I had great satisfaction relative to the administration of this ordinance in various respects. I have abundant reason to think, that those who came to the Lord's table had a good degree of doctrinal knowledge of the nature and design of the ordinance, and that they acted with understanding in what they did.

In the preparatory services, I found, I may justly say, uncommon freedom in opening to their understandings and capacities, the covenant of grace, and in shewing them the nature of this ordinance as a seal of that covenant; although many of them knew of no such thing as a seal, before my coming among them, or at least, of the use and design of it in the common affairs of life. They were likewise thoroughly sensible, that it was no more than a seal, or sign, and not the real body and blood of Christ; that it was designed for the refreshment and edification of the soul, and not for the feasting of the body. They were also acquainted with the end of the ordinance, that they were therein called to commemorate the dying love of Christ.

This competency of doctrinal knowledge, together with their grave and decent attendance upon the ordinance, their affectionate melting under it, and the sweet and christian frame of mind which they discovered after it, gave me great satisfaction respecting my administration of it to them. O, what a sweet and blessed season was this! God himself, I am persuaded, was in the midst of his people, attending on his own ordinance. I doubt not but many, in the conclusion of the day, could say with their whole hearts, "Verily, a day thus spent in God's house, is better than a thousand elsewhere." There seemed to be but one heart among the pious people. The sweet union, harmony and endearing love and tenderness subsisting among them was, I thought, the most lively emblem of the heavenly world, which I had ever seen.

April 28. Concluded the sacramental solemnity with a discourse upon John xiv. 15. "If ye love me, keep my commandments." At this time there appeared a very agreeable tenderness in the audience in general, but especially in the communicants. O, how free, how engaged and affectionate did these appear in the service of God! they seemed willing to have their ears bored to the door posts of God's house, and to be his servants forever.

Observing numbers in this excellent frame, and the assembly in general affected, and that by a divine influence, I thought it proper to improve this advantageous season as Hezekiah did the desirable season of his great passover, 2 Chron. 31, in order to promote the blessed reformation begun among them; and to engage those that appeared serious and religious to persevere therein. Accordingly I proposed to them, that they should renewedly enter into covenant before God, that they would watch over themselves and one another, lest they should dishonour the name of Christ, by falling into sinful and unbecoming practices; and especially that they would watch against the sin of drunkenness, "the sin that most easily besets them," and the temptations leading thereto, as well as the appearance of evil in that respect. They cheerfully complied with the proposal, and explicitly joined in that covenant: whereupon I proceeded in the most solemn manner of which I was capable, to call God to witness respecting their sacred engagements, and reminded them of the greatness of the guilt they would contract to themselves in the violation of it, as well as observed to them that God would be a terrible witness against those who should presume to do so in the great and notable day of the Lord. It was a season of amazing solemnity; and a divine awe appeared upon the face of the whole assembly in this transaction. Affectionate sobs, sighs and tears were now frequent in the audience; and I doubt not but that many silent cries were then sent up to the Fountain of grace for supplies of grace sufficient for the fulfillment of these solemn engagements. Baptized six children this day.

On Tuesday, April 29, he went to Elizabeth Town to attend the meeting of the Presbytery; and seemed to spend the time while absent from his people on this occasion, in a free and comfortable state of mind.

Cranberry, N. J. May, 1746.

May 3. Rode from Elizabeth Town home to my people at or near Cranberry; wither they are now removed, and where I hope God will settle them as a christian congregation. Was refreshed in lifting up my heart to God, while riding, and enjoyed a thankful frame of spirit for divine favours received the week past.

Was somewhat uneasy and dejected in the evening; having no house of my own to go to in this place; but God was my support.

Lord's day, May 4. My people being now removed to their lands, mentioned in my diary of March 24, where they were then and have since been making provision for a compact settlement, in order to their more convenient enjoyment of the gospel and other means of instruction, as well as of the comforts of life; I this day visited them; being now obliged to board with an English family at some distance from them; and preached to them in the forenoon from Mark iv. 5. "And some fell upon stony ground." &c. Endeavoured to shew them the reason there was to fear, lest many promising appearances and hopeful beginnings in religion, might prove abortive, like the seed dropped upon stony places.

In the afternoon discoursed upon Rom. viii. 9. "Now, if any man have not the spirit of Christ, he is none of his." I have reason to think this discourse was peculiarly seasonable, and that it had a good effect upon some of the hearers. Spent some hours afterwards in private conference with my people, and laboured to regulate some things which I apprehended amiss among some of them.

May 5. Visited my people again, and took care of their worldly concerns; giving them directions relating to their business. I daily discover more and more of what importance it is likely to be to their religious interests, that they become laborious and industrious, acquainted with the affairs of husbandry, and able in a good measure to raise the necessaries and comforts of life within themselves; for their present method of living greatly exposes them to temptations of various kinds.

May 6. Enjoyed some spirit and courage in my work; was in a good measure free from melancholy: blessed be God for freedom from this death.

May 7. Spent most of the day in writing as usual. Enjoyed some freedom in my work. Was favoured with some comfortable meditations this day. In the evening was in a sweet composed frame of mind: was pleased and delighted to leave all with God respecting myself, for time and eternity, and respecting the people of my charge, and dear friends. Had no doubt but that God would take care of me and of his own interest among my people; and was enabled to use freedom in prayer as a child with a tender father. O how sweet is such a frame!

May 8. In the evening, was somewhat refreshed with divine things, and enjoyed a tender melting frame in secret prayer; wherein my soul was drawn out for the interests of Zion, and comforted with the lively hope of the appearing of the great Redeemer. These were sweet moments; I felt almost loth to go to bed, and grieved that sleep was necessary. However, I lay down with a tender reverential fear of God, sensible that his favour is life, and his smiles better than all that earth can boast of, infinitely better than life itself.

May 9. Preached from John v. 40. "And ye will not come to me," &c. in the open wilderness; the Indians having as yet no house for public worship in this place, nor scarcely any shelters for themselves. Divine truths made considerable impressions upon the audience, and it was a season of great solemnity, tenderness and affection.

Baptized one man this day, the conjurer, murderer, &c. mentioned in my diary of Aug. 8, 1745, and Feb. 1, 1746, who appears to be such a remarkable instance of divine grace, that I cannot omit to give some brief account of him here. He lived near, and sometimes attended my meeting, at the Forks of Delaware, for more than a year together; but was, like many others of them, extremely attached to strong drink, and seemed to be in no degree reformed by the means which I used with them for their instruction and conversion. At this time he likewise murdered a likely young Indian, which threw him into some kind of horror and desperation, so that he kept at a distance from me, and refused to hear me preach for several months together, until I had an opportunity of conversing freely with him, and giving him encouragement, that his sin might be forgiven, for Christ's sake. After this he again attended my meeting sometimes.

But that which was the worst of all his conduct, was his conjuration. He was one of those who are sometimes called powaws, among the Indians; and, notwithstanding his frequent attendance upon my preaching, he still followed his old charms and juggling tricks, "giving out that himself was some great one, and to him they gave heed," supposing him to be possessed of great power. When I have instructed them respecting the miracle wrought by Christ in healing the sick, and mentioned them as evidence of his divine mission, and the truths of his doctrine; they have quickly observed the wonders of that kind, which this man had performed by his magic charms. Hence they had a high opinion of him and his superstitious notions; which seemed to be a fatal obstruction to some of them in regard to their receiving the Gospel. I have often thought that it would be a great favour to the design of evangelizing these Indians, if God would take that wretch out of the world; for I had scarcely any hope of his ever becoming good. But God, whose thoughts are not as man's thoughts, has been pleased to take a much more desirable method with him; a method agreeable to his own merciful nature, and I trust advantageous to his own interest among the Indians, as well as effectual to the salvation of his poor soul. To God be the glory of it. The first genuine concern for his soul, that ever appeared in him, was excited by seeing my interpreter and his wife baptised at the Forks of Delaware, July 21, 1745. Which so prevailed upon him, that with the invitation of an Indian who was a friend to Christianity, he followed me down to Crossweeksung, in the beginning of August, following in order, to hear me preach; and there continued for several weeks in the season of the most remarkable and powerful awakening among the Indians; at which time he was more effectually awakened, and brought under great concern for his soul. And then he says, upon his "feeling the word of God in his heart," as he expresses it, his spirit of conjuration left him entirely, so that he has had no more power of that nature since, than any other man living. He also declares, that he does not now so much as know, how he used to charm and conjure, and that he could not now do any thing of that nature if he were ever so desirous of it.

He continued under convictions of his sinful and perishing state, and a considerable degree of concern for his soul, all the fall and former part of the winter past; but was not so deeply exercised until some time in January. Then the word of God took such hold upon him, that he was brought into deep distress, and knew not what to do, nor where to turn himself. He then told me, that when he used to hear me preach from time to time in the fall of the year, my preaching pricked his heart, and made him very uneasy, but did not bring him to so great distress, because he still hoped he could do something for his own relief; but now he said, I drove him up in such a sharp corner, that he had no way to turn and could not avoid being in distress. He continued constantly under the heavy burden and pressure of a wounded spirit, until at length he was brought into the acute anguish and utmost agony of soul, mentioned in my Journal of Feb. 1st, which continued that night and part of the next day. After this he was brought to the utmost calmness and composure of mind; his trembling and heavy burden were removed; and he appeared perfectly sedate, although he had to his apprehensions scarcely any hope of salvation.

I observed him to appear remarkably composed; and thereupon asked him how he did? He replied, "It is done, it is done, it is all done now." I asked him what he meant? He answered, "I can never do any more to save myself; it is all done forever. I can do no more." I queried with him, whether he could not do a little more, rather than go to hell? He replied, "My heart is dead. I can never help myself." I asked him what he thought would become of him then? He answered, "I must go to hell." I asked him if he thought it was right, that God should send him to hell? He replied, "O it is right. The devil has been in me ever since I was born." I asked him if he felt this when he was in such great distress the evening before? He answered, "No; I did not then think it was right. I thought God would send me to hell, and that I was then dropping into it; but my heart quarrelled with God, and would not say it was right he should send me there. But now I know it is right; for I have always served the devil; and my heart has no goodness in it now; but it is as bad as ever it was," &c. I thought I had scarcely ever seen any person more effectually brought off from a dependance upon his own contrivances and endeavours for salvation, or more apparently to lie at the foot of sovereign mercy, than this man did under these views of things.

In this frame of mind he continued for several days, passing sentence of condemnation upon himself, and constantly owning that it would be right he should be damned, and that he expected this would be his portion for the greatness of his sins. Yet it was plain that he had a secret hope of mercy, though imperceptible to himself, which kept him not only from despair but from any pressing distress: so that, instead of being sad and dejected, his very countenance appeared pleasant and agreeable.

While he was in this frame, he several times asked me, "When I would preach again?" and seemed desirous to hear the word of God every day. I asked, "Why he wanted to hear me preach, seeing his heart was dead, and all was done; that he could never help himself, and expected that he must go to hell?" He replied, "I love to hear you speak about Christ for all." I added, "But what good will that do you, if you must go to hell at last?"—using now his own language with him, having before from time to time laboured in the best manner I could to represent to him the excellency of Christ, his all-sufficiency and willingness to save lost sinners, and persons just in his case; although to no purpose, as to yielding him any special comfort. He answered, "I would have others come to Christ, if I must go to hell myself." It was remarkable, that he seemed to have a great love for the people of God; and nothing affected him so much as being separated from them. This seemed to be a very dreadful part of the hell to which he saw himself doomed. It was likewise remarkable, that in this season he was most diligent in the use of all the means for the soul's salvation; although he had the clearest view of the insufficiency of means to afford him help. He would frequently say, That all he did signified nothing at all; and yet was never more constant in doing; attending secret and family prayer daily; and surprisingly diligent and attentive in hearing the word of God; so that he neither despaired of mercy, nor yet presumed to hope upon his own doings, but used means because appointed of God in order to salvation; and because he would wait upon God in his own way.

After he had continued in this frame of mind more than a week, while I was discoursing publicly, he seemed to have a lively soul-refreshing view of the excellency of Christ and the way of salvation by him; which melted him into tears, and filled him with admiration, comfort, satisfaction and praise to God. Since then, he has appeared to be a humble, devout and affectionate christian; serious and exemplary in his conversation and behaviour, frequently complaining of his barrenness, his want of spiritual warmth, life and activity, and yet frequently favoured with quickening and refreshing influences. In all respects, so far as I am capable of judging, he bears the marks of one "created anew in Christ Jesus to good works."

His zeal for the cause of God was pleasing to me, when he was with me at the Forks of Delaware in February last. There being an old Indian at the place where I preached, who threatened to bewitch me, and my religious people who accompanied me there; this man presently challenged him to do his worst; telling him that himself had been as great a conjuror as he; and that not withstanding, as soon as he felt that word to his heart which these people loved, meaning the word of God, his power of conjuring immediately left him. "And so it would you," said he, "if you did but once feel it in your heart; and you have no power to hurt them, nor so much as to touch one of them." &c. So that I may conclude my account of him, by observing, in allusion to what was said of St. Paul, that he now zealously "defends and practically preaches the faith which he once destroyed," or at least was instrumental in obstructing. May God have the glory of the amazing change which he has wrought in him!

May 10. Rode to Allen's-town to assist in the administration of the Lord's supper. In the afternoon, preached from Titus ii. 14. Who gave himself for us, &c. God was pleased to carry me through, and to grant me some freedom; and yet to deny me that enlargement and power for which I longed. In the evening my soul mourned and could not but mourn, that I had treated so excellent a subject in so defective a manner; that I had borne so broken a testimony for so worthy and glorious a Redeemer. If my discourse had met with the utmost applause from all the world, it would not have given me any satisfaction. Oh, it grieved me to think, that I had no more holy warmth and fervency, that I have been no more melted in discoursing of Christ's death and the end and design of it! Afterwards enjoyed some freedom and fervency in family and secret prayer, and longed much for the presence of God to attend his word and ordinances the next day.

Lord's day, May 11. Assisted in the administration of the Lord's supper; but enjoyed but little enlargement: was grieved and sunk with some things, which I thought undesirable, &c. In the afternoon went to the house of God, weak and sick in soul, as well as feeble in body, and longed that the people might be entertained and edified with divine truths, and that an honest, fervent testimony might be borne for God; but knew not how it was possible for me to do any thing of that kind to any good purpose. Yet God, who is rich in mercy, was pleased to give me assistance both in prayer and preaching. God helped me to wrestle for his presence in prayer, and to tell him that he had promised, "Where two or three are met together in his name, there he would be in the midst of them"; and that we were, at least some of us, so met; and pleaded that for his truth's sake he would be with us. Blessed be God, it was sweet to my soul, thus to plead and rely on God's promises. Discoursed upon Luke ix. 30, 31. And behold there talked with him two men, which were Moses and Elias, who appeared in glory, and spake of his decease, which he should accomplish at Jerusalem. Enjoyed special freedom from the beginning to the end of my discourse without interruption. Things pertinent to the subject were abundantly presented to my view, and such a fulness of matter, that I scarce knew how to dismiss the various heads and particulars I had occasion to touch upon. Blessed be the Lord, I was favoured with some fervency and power, as well as freedom; so that the word of God seemed to awaken the attention of a stupid audience to a considerable degree. I was inwardly refreshed with the consolations of God and could with my whole heart say, "Though there be no fruit in the vine, &c. yet will I rejoice in the Lord." After public service, was refreshed with the sweet conversation of some christian friends.

The four next days seem to have been mostly spent with spiritual comfort and profit.

May 16. Near night enjoyed some agreeable and sweet conversation with a dear minister; which was, I trust, blessed to my soul. My heart was warmed, and my soul engaged to live to God; so that I longed to exert myself with more vigour than ever I had done in his cause; and those words were quickening to me, "Herein is my Father glorified, that ye bring forth much fruit." Oh, my soul longed, and wished, and prayed to be enabled to live to God with the utmost constancy and ardour! In the evening, God was pleased to shine upon me in secret prayer, and draw out my soul after himself; and I had freedom in supplication for myself, but much more in intercession for others: so that I was sweetly constrained to say, "Lord, use me as thou wilt; do as thou wilt with me: but, O, promote thine own cause! Zion is thine; Oh, visit thine heritage! Let thy kingdom come! Oh, let thy blessed interest be advanced in the world." When I attempted to look to God respecting my worldly circumstances, and his providential dealings with me relative to my settling down in my congregation; which seems to be necessary, and yet very difficult and contrary to my fixed intentions for years past, as well as to my disposition, which has been and still is, at times especially, to go forth, and spend my life in preaching the gospel from place to place, and gathering souls afar off to Jesus the great Redeemer; I could only say, with the utmost calmness and composure, "Lord, if it be most for thy glory, let me proceed in it; but, if thou seest it will in any wise hinder my usefulness in thy cause, Oh prevent me from proceeding; for all I want respecting this world is such circumstances as may best capacitate me to do service for God in the world." But, blessed be God! I enjoyed liberty in prayer for my dear flock, and was enabled to pour out my soul into the bosom of a tender Father. My heart within me was melted, when I came to plead for my dear people and for the kingdom of Christ in general. Oh, how sweet was this evening to my soul! I knew not how to go to bed; and when I got to bed, longed for some way to improve time for God to some excellent purpose. Bless the Lord, O my soul!

May 17. Walked out in the morning, and felt much of the same frame which I enjoyed the evening before; had my heart enlarged in praying for the advancement of the kingdom of Christ and found the utmost freedom in leaving all my concerns with God.

I find discouragement to be an exceeding hindrance to my spiritual fervency and affection; but, when God enables me sensibly to find that I have done something for him, this refreshes and animates me, so that I could break through all hardships, and undergo any labours, and nothing seems too much either to do or to suffer. But Oh, what a death it is to strive and strive; to be always in a hurry, and yet do nothing, or at least, nothing for God! Alas, alas, that time flies away, and I do so little for God!

Lord's day, May 18th. I felt my own utter insufficiency for my work: God made me to see, that I was a child; yea that I was a fool. I discoursed both parts of the day from Rev. iii. 20, "Behold I stand at the door and knock." God gave me freedom and power in the latter part of my forenoon's discourse: although, in the former part of it I felt peevish and provoked with the unmannerly behaviour of the white people, who crowded in between my people and me; which proved a great temptation to me. But, blessed be God! I got these shackles off, before the middle of my discourse, and was favoured with a sweet frame of spirit in the latter part of the exercise; was full of love, warmth and tenderness in addressing my dear people. There appears some affectionate melting towards the conclusion of the forenoon exercise, and one or two instances of fresh awakening. In the intermission of public worship I took occasion to discourse to numbers, in a more private way, on the kindness and patience of the blessed Redeemer in standing and knocking, in continuing his gracious calls to sinners, who had long neglected and abused his grace; which seemed to take some effect upon several.

In the afternoon divine truths were attended with solemnity, and with some tears; although there was not that powerful awakening and quickening influence, which in times past has been common in our assemblies. The appearance of the audience under divine truths was comparatively discouraging; and I was ready to fear that God was about to withdraw the blessed influence of his spirit from us.

In the evening, I was grieved that I had done so little for God. Oh that I could be "a flame of fire" in the service of my God!

May 19. Visited and preached to my people from Acts xx. 18, 19, "And when they were come to him, he said unto them, Ye know from the first day," &c. and endeavoured to rectify their notions about religious affections; shewing them on the one hand the desirableness of religious affection, tenderness and fervent engagement in the worship and service of God, when such affection flows from a true spiritual discovery of divine glories from a just sense of the transcendant excellence and perfections of the blessed God;— and a view of the glory and loveliness of the great Redeemer; and that such views of divine things will naturally excite us to "serve the Lord with many tears, with much affection and fervency, and yet with all humility of mind." On the other hand I observed the sinfulness of seeking after high affections immediately and for their own sakes; that is, of making them the object which our eye and heart is first and principally set upon, when the glory of God ought to be that object. Shewed them that, if the heart be directly and chiefly fixed on God, and the soul engaged to glorify him, some degree of religious affection will be the effect and attendant of it. But to seek after affection directly and chiefly; to have the heart principally set upon that; is to place it in the room of God and his glory. If it be sought, that others may take notice of it, and admire us for our spirituality and forwardness in religion, it is then abominable pride; if for the sake of feeling the pleasure of being affected, it is then idolatry and self-gratification. Laboured also to expose the disagreeableness of those affections, which are sometimes wrought up in persons by the power of fancy, and their own attempts for that purpose, while I still endeavoured to recommend to them that religious affection, fervency and devotion which ought to attend all our religious exercises, and without which religion will be but an empty name and lifeless carcase. This appeared to be a seasonable discourse, and proved very satisfactory to some of the religious people, who before were exercised with some difficulties relating to this point. Afterwards took care of, and gave my people directions about, their worldly affairs.

On Tuesday, he complains of want of freedom and comfort; but had some returns of these on Wednesday.

May 22. In the evening was in a frame somewhat remarkable. I had apprehended for some days before, that it was the design of Providence that I should settle among my people here, and had in my own mind begun to make provision for it, and to contrive means to hasten it; and found my heart somewhat engaged in it; hoping that I might then enjoy more agreeable circumstances of life in several respects: and yet was never fully determined, never quite pleased with the thoughts of being settled and confined to one place. Nevertheless I seemed to have some freedom in that respect, because the congregation, with which I thought of settling, was one which God had enabled me to gather from among the Pagans. For I never, since I began to preach, could feel any freedom to enter into other men's labours, and settle down in the ministry where the gospel was preached before. I never could make that appear to be my province. When I felt any disposition to consult my worldly ease and comfort, God has never given me any liberty in this respect, either since, or for some years before, I began to preach. But God having succeeded my labours, and made me instrumental in gathering a church for him among these Indians, I was ready to think it might be his design to give me a quiet settlement, and a stated home of my own. This, considering the late frequent sinking and failure of my spirits, and the need I stood in of some agreeable society, and my great desire of enjoying conveniences and opportunities for profitable studies, was not altogether disagreeable to me. Although I still wanted to go about far and wide, in order to spread the blessed gospel among the benighted souls far remote, yet I never had been so willing to settle in any one place, for more than five years past, as I was in the preceding part of this week. But now these thoughts seemed to be wholly dashed to pieces, not by necessity, but of choice; for it appeared to me that God's dealings towards me had fitted me for a life of solitariness and hardship, and that I had nothing to lose, nothing to do with earth, and consequently nothing to lose by a total renunciation of it. It appeared to me just right that I should be destitute of house and home, and many of the comforts of life, which I rejoiced to see others of God's people enjoy. At the same time, I saw so much of the excellency of Christ's kingdom and the infinite desirableness of its advancement in the world, that it swallowed up all my other thoughts, and made me willing, yea, even rejoice, to be made a pilgrim or hermit in the wilderness to my dying moment; if I might thereby promote the blessed interest of the great Redeemer. If ever my soul presented itself to God for his service, without any reserve of any kind, it did so now. The language of my thoughts and disposition now was, "Here I am, Lord, send me; send me to the ends of the Earth: send me to the rough, the savage Pagans of the wilderness; send me from all that is called comfort in earth, or earthly comfort; send me even to death itself, if it be but in thy service, and to promote thy kingdom." At the same time, I had as quick and lively a sense of the value of worldly comforts, as I ever had; but only saw them infinitely overmatched by the worth of Christ's kingdom, and the propagation of his blessed gospel. The quiet settlement, the certain place of abode, the tender friendship, which I thought I might be likely to enjoy in consequence of such circumstances, appeared as valuable to me, considered absolutely and in themselves, as ever before; but considered comparatively, they appeared nothing. Compared with the value and preciousness of an enlargement of Christ's kingdom, they vanished as stars before the rising sun. Sure I am, that, although the comfortable accommodations of life appeared valuable and dear to me, yet I did surrender and resign myself, soul and body, to the service of God, and to the promotion of Christ's kingdom; though it should be in the loss of them all I could not do any other, because I could not will or choose any other. I was constrained, and yet chose, to say, "Farewell friends and earthly comforts, the dearest of them all, the very dearest, if the Lord calls for it: adieu, adieu; I will spend my life, to my latest moments, in caves, and dens of the earth, if the kingdom of Christ may thereby be advanced. I found extraordinary freedom at this time in pouring out my soul to God for his cause; and especially that his kingdom might be extended among the Indians, far remote; and I had a great and strong hope that God would do it. I continued wrestling with God in prayer for my dear little flock here; and more especially for the Indians elsewhere; as well as for dear friends in one place and another until it was bed time, and I feared I should hinder the family, &c. But, O, with what reluctancy did I feel myself obliged to consume time in sleep! I longed to be as a flame of fire, continually glowing in the divine service, and building up Christ's kingdom, to my latest, my dying moment.

May 23. In the morning, was in the same frame of mind as in the evening before. The glory of Christ's kingdom so much outshone the pleasure of earthly accommodations and enjoyments, that they appeared comparatively nothing, though in themselves good and desirable. My soul was melted in secret meditation and prayer; and I found myself divorced from any part or portion in this world; so that in those affairs which seemed of the greatest importance to me with respect to the present life, and in those with [which] the tenderest feelings of the heart are most sensibly connected; I could only say, "the will of the Lord be done." But just the same things, which I felt the evening before, I felt now, and found the same freedom in prayer for the people of my charge, for the propagation of the gospel among the Indians, and for the enlargement and spiritual welfare of Zion in general, and my dear friends in particular now, as I did then; and longed to burn out in one continued flame for God. Retained much of the same frame through the day. In the evening I was visited by my brother JOHN BRAINERD; the first visit which I have ever received from any near relative since I have been a missionary. Felt the same flame of spirit in the evening, as in the morning; and found that it was good for me to draw near to God, and leave all my concerns and burdens with him. Was enlarged and refreshed in pouring out my soul for the propagation of the gospel of the Redeemer among the distant tribes of Indians. Blessed be God. If ever I filled up a day with study and devotion, I was enabled so to fill up this day.

May 24. Visited the Indians, and took care of their secular business; which they are not able to manage themselves, without the constant care and advice of others. Afterwards discoursed to some of them particularly about their spiritual concerns.—Enjoyed this day somewhat of the same frame of mind which I felt the day before.

Lord's day, May 25. Discoursed both parts of the day from John xii. 44–48. "Jesus cried and said, He that believeth on me," &c. There was some degree of divine power attending the word of God. Several wept, and appeared considerably affected, and one, who had long been under spiritual trouble, now obtained clearness and comfort, and appeared to rejoice in God her Saviour. It was a day of grace and divine goodness; a day wherein something I trust was done for the cause of God among my people; a season of comfort and sweetness to numbers of the religious people; although there was not that influence upon the congregation which was common some months ago.

This week, at least the former part of it, he was in a very weak state, but yet seems to have been free from melancholy, which often had attended the failing of his bodily strength. He from time to time speaks of comfort and inward refreshment this week.

Lord's day, June 1, 1746. Preached both forenoon and afternoon from Matt. xi. 27, 28. The presence of God seemed to be in the assembly; and numbers were considerably melted and affected under divine truths. There was a desirable appearance in the congregation in general, an earnest attention and an agreeable tenderness; and it seemed as if God designed to visit us with further showers of divine grace. I then baptized ten persons: five adults, and five children; and was not a little refreshed with this addition made to the church of such as I hope will be saved. I have reason to hope that God has lately, at and since our celebration of the Lord's supper, brought to himself several persons who had long been under spiritual trouble and concern; although there have been few instances of persons lately awakened out of a state of security. Those comforted of late seem to be brought in, in a more silent way; neither their concern, nor consolation being so powerful and remarkable, as appeared among those more suddenly wrought upon in the beginning of this work of grace.

June 2. In the evening, enjoyed some freedom in secret prayer and meditation.

June 3. My soul rejoiced, early in the morning, to think that all things were at God's disposal. Oh, it pleased me to leave them there! Felt afterwards much as I did on Thursday evening last May 22, and continued in that frame for several hours. Walked out in the wilderness, and enjoyed freedom, fervency, and comfort in prayer, and again enjoyed the same in the evening.

June 4. Spent the day in writing, and enjoyed some comfort, satisfaction and freedom in my work. In the evening, I was favoured with a sweet refreshing frame of soul in secret prayer and meditation. Prayer was now wholly turned into praise, and I could do little else but try to adore and bless the living God. The wonders of his grace displayed in gathering to himself a church among the poor Indians here, were the subject matter of my meditation, and the occasion of exciting my soul to praise and bless his name. My soul was scarcely ever more disposed to inquire, What I should render to God for all his benefits, than at this time. Oh, I was brought into a strait, a sweet and happy strait, to know what to do! I longed to make some returns to God; but found I had nothing to return: I could only rejoice that God had done the work himself; and that none in heaven or earth might pretend to share the honour of it with him. I could only be glad that God's declarative glory was advanced by the conversion of these souls, and that it was to the enlargement of his kingdom in the world; but saw I was so poor that I had nothing to offer him. My soul and body, through grace, I could cheerfully surrender to him; but it appeared to me this was rather a burden than a gift; and nothing could I do to glory his dear and blessed name. Yet I was glad at heart, that he was unchangeably possessed of glory and blessedness. Oh that he might be adored and praised by all his intelligent creatures to the utmost extent of their capacities! My soul would have rejoiced to see others praise him, though I could do nothing towards it myself.

The next day he speaks of his being subject to some degree of melancholy; but of being somewhat relieved in the evening.

June 6. Discoursed to my people from part of Is. liii. The divine presence appeared to be among us in some measure.—Several persons were much melted and refreshed; and one man in particular, who had long been under concern for his soul, was now brought to see and feel, in a very lively manner, the impossibility of his doing any thing to help himself, or to bring him into the favour of God, by his tears, prayers and other religious performances; and found himself undone as to any power or goodness of his own, and that there was no way left him but to leave himself with God, to be disposed of as he pleased.

June 7. Being desired by the REV. WILLIAM TENNENT to be his assistant in the administration of the Lord's supper, I this morning rode to Freehold to render that assistance. My people also being invited to attend the sacramental solemnity; they cheerfully embraced the opportunity, and this day attended the preparatory services with me.

In the afternoon I preached from Psalm lxxiii. 28. "But it is good for me to draw near to God," &c. God gave me some freedom and warmth in my discourse: and I trust his presence was in the assembly. Was comfortably composed, enjoyed a thankful frame of spirit, and my soul was grieved, that I could not render something to God for his benefits bestowed. O that I could be swallowed up in his praise!

Lord's day, June 8. Spent much time in the morning in secret duties, between hope and fear respecting the enjoyment of God in the business of the day then before us. Was agreeably entertained in the forenoon by a discourse from MR. TENNENT, and felt somewhat melted and refreshed. In the season of communion, enjoyed some comfort; and especially in serving one of the tables. Blessed be the Lord! it was a time of refreshing to me, and I trust to many others.

Most of my people, who had been communicants at the Lord's table, before being present at this sacramental occasion, communed with others in the holy ordinance, at the desire, and I trust to the satisfaction and comfort of numbers of God's people, who had longed to see this day, and whose hearts had rejoiced in this work of grace among the Indians, which prepared the way for what appeared so agreeable at this time. Those of my people who communed, seemed in general, agreeably affected at the Lord's table, and some of them considerably melted with the love of Christ, although they were not so remarkably refreshed and feasted at this time, as when I administered this ordinance to them in our own congregation only. A number of my dear people sat down by themselves at the last table; at which time God seemed to be in the midst of them. Some of the by-standers were affected with seeing those who had been "aliens from the common wealth of Israel, and strangers to the covenant of promise," who of all men had lived "without hope and without God in the world," now brought near to God, as his professing people, and sealing their covenant with him, by a solemn and devout attendance upon this sacred ordinance. As numbers of God's people were refreshed with this sight, and thereby excited to bless God for the enlargement of his kingdom in the world; so some others, I was told, were awakened by it, apprehending the danger they were in of being themselves finally cast out; while they saw others from the east and west preparing, and hopefully prepared in some good measure, to sit down in the kingdom of God. At this season others of my people also, who were not communicants, were considerably affected; convictions were revived in several instances; and one, the man particularly mentioned in my journal of the 6th instant, obtained comfort and satisfaction; and has since given me such an account of his spiritual exercises, and the manner in which he obtained relief, as appears very hopeful. It seems as if He, who commanded the light to shine out of darkness, had now "shined into his heart, and given him the light of," and experimental "knowledge of the glory of God in the face of Jesus Christ."

In the afternoon God enabled me to preach with uncommon freedom, from 2 Cor. v. 20, "Now then we are ambassadors for Christ," &c. Through the great goodness of God, I was favoured with a constant flow of pertinent matter, and proper expressions, from the beginning to the end of my discourse. In the evening I could not but rejoice in God, and bless him in the manifestations of grace in the day past. Oh it was a sweet and solemn day and evening! a season of comfort to the godly, and of awakening to some souls! O that I could praise the Lord.

June 9. Enjoyed some sweetness in secret duties. A considerable number of my people met together early in a retired place in the woods, and prayed, sang and conversed of divine things; and were seen by some religious persons of the white people to be affected and engaged, and divers of them in tears in these religious exercises. Preached the concluding sermon from Gen. v. 24, "And Enoch walked with God," &c. God gave me enlargement and fervency in my discourse, so that I was enabled to speak with plainness and power; and God's presence seemed to be in the assembly. Praised be the Lord, it was a sweet meeting, a desirable assembly. I found my strength renewed, and lengthened out even to a wonder, so that I felt much stronger at the conclusion than in the beginning of this sacramental solemnity. I have great reason to bless God for this solemnity; wherein I have found assistance in addressing others, and sweetness in my own soul.

After my people had attended the concluding exercises of the sacramental solemnity, they returned home; many of them rejoicing for all the goodness of God which they had seen and felt; so that this appeared to be a profitable as well as comfortable season to numbers of my congregation. Their being present at this occasion, and a number of them communing at the Lord's table with other christians, was, I trust, for the honour of God and the interest of religion in these parts; as numbers I have reason to think, were quickened by means of it.

On Tuesday, he found himself spent, and his spirits exhausted, by his late labours; and on Wednesday complains of vapoury disorders and dejection of spirits, and of enjoying but little comfort and spirituality.

June 12. In the evening, enjoyed freedom of mind and some sweetness in secret prayer. It was a desirable season to me; my soul was enlarged in prayer for my own dear people, and for the enlargement of Christ's kingdom, and especially for the propagation of the Gospel among the Indians, far back in the wilderness. Was refreshed in prayer for dear friends in New-England and elsewhere. I found it sweet to pray at this time; and could, with all my heart, say, "It is good for me to draw near to God."

June 13. Preached to my people upon the new creature, from 2 Cor. v. 17, "If any man be in Christ," &c. The presence of God appeared to be in the assembly. It was a sweet and agreeable meeting, wherein the people of God were refreshed and strengthened; beholding their faces in the glass of God's word, and finding in themselves the works and lineaments of the new creature. Some sinners under concern were also renewedly affected; and afresh engaged for the securing of their eternal interests.

Baptised five persons at this time, three adults, and two children. One of these was the very aged woman, of whose exercises I gave an account in my diary, of Dec. 26. She now gave me a very punctual, rational, and satisfactory account of the remarkable change which she experienced some months after the beginning of her concern, which I must say, appeared to be the genuine operations of the Divine Spirit, so far as I am capable of judging. Although she was become so childish through age, that I could do nothing in a way of questioning with her, nor scarcely make her understand any thing that I asked her; yet when I let her alone to go on with her own story, she could give a very distinct and particular relation of the many and various exercises of soul, which she had experienced; so deep were the impressions left upon her mind by that influence and those exercises which she had experienced. I have great reason to think, that she is born anew in her old age: she being, I presume, upwards of eighty. I had good hopes of the other adults, and trust they are such as God will own "in the day when he makes up his jewels."

I came away from the meeting of the Indians, this day, rejoicing and blessing God for his grace manifested at this season.

June 14. Rode to Kingston to assist the REV. MR. WALES in the administration of the Lord's supper. In the afternoon, preached; but almost fainted in the pulpit. Yet God strengthened me when I was just gone, and enabled me to speak his word with freedom, fervency, and application to the conscience.—Praised be the Lord, "out of weakness I was made strong." I enjoyed some sweetness in and after public worship, but was extremely tired. Oh, how many are the mercies of the Lord! "To them that have no might he increaseth strength."

Lord's day, June 15. Was in a dejected, spiritless frame, so that I could not hold up my head, nor look any body in the face. Administered the Lord's supper at MR. WALE's desire, and found myself in good measure unburdened and relieved of my pressing load, when I came to ask a blessing on the elements. Here God gave me enlargement and a tender affectionate sense of spiritual things, so that it was a season of comfort, in some measure to me, and I trust, more so to others. In the afternoon, preached to a vast multitude, from Rev. xxii. 17—"And whoever will," &c. God helped me to offer a testimony for himself, and to leave sinners inexcusable in neglecting his grace. I was enabled to speak with such freedom, fluency and clearness, as commanded the attention of the great. Was extremely tired in the evening, but enjoyed composure and sweetness.

June 16. Preached again; and God helped me amazingly, so that this was a sweet refreshing season to my soul and others. Oh, forever blessed be God for help afforded at this time, when my body was so weak, and while there was so large an assembly to hear. Spent the afternoon in a comfortable agreeable manner.

The next day was spent comfortably. On Wednesday, he went to a meeting of ministers at Hopewell.

June 19. Visited my people with two of the Reverend correspondents. Spent some time in conversation with some of them upon spiritual things; and took some care of their worldly concerns.

This day makes up a complete year from the first time of my preaching to these Indians in New-Jersey. What amazing things God has wrought, in this space of time, for this poor people! What a surprising change appears in their tempers and behaviour! How are morose and savage Pagans, in this short period, transformed into agreeable, affectionate, and humble christians! and their drunken and Pagan howlings turned into devout and fervent praises to God! They "who were sometimes in darkness are now become light in the Lord." May they "walk as children of the light and of the day"! And now to Him that is of power to establish them according to the gospel, and the preaching of Christ—to God only wise, be glory through Jesus Christ, for ever and ever, Amen.

CHAPTER IX

General Remarks on the preceding Narrative of a work of Grace at Crossweeksung. I. On the Doctrines preached to the Indians. II. On the Moral Effects of preaching Christ Crucified. III. On the Continuance, Renewal and Quickness of the Work. IV. On the little appearance of False Religion.

CHAPTER X

*General Remarks on the Work of Grace at Cross-
weeksung continued.—Introduction.—Method of learning the Indian Language.—Method of Instructing the
Indians.—Difficulties in the way of converting them
to Christianity.—Attestations of neighbouring Minis-
isters, Elders and Deacons to the Display of Divine
grace at Crossweeksung.*

CHAPTER XI

*From the close of his Journal, June 19, 1746, to the
termination of his Missionary Labours, March 20, 1747.*

The hardships, which BRAINERD had endured, had now obviously
affected his constitution; and unfitted him for a life of so much toil
and exposure. Of this, he appears not to have been aware, until the
case had become hopeless; and, unfortunately, the circumstances, in
which he was placed, were calculated, instead of retarding, to hasten
the ravages of disease. He lived alone, in the midst of a wilderness;
in a miserable hut, built by Indians; with few of the necessaries, and
none of the comforts of life; at a distance from civilized society; without
even a nurse or a physician. His labours, also, were sufficient, to have
impaired a vigorous constitution. It is not surprising, therefore, that
his health was gradually, but fatally undermined.

On Friday, June 20th, as well as on the next day, he was very ill;
though, with great effort, he was enabled to preach to his people on
Saturday. His illness continued on the Sabbath, but he preached, notwithstanding, to his people both parts of the day; and after the public
worship was ended, he endeavoured to apply divine truths to the consciences of some, and addressed them personally for that end; several
were in tears, and some appeared much affected. But he was extremely
wearied with the services of the day, and so ill at night, that he could

have no bodily rest; but remarks, that "God was his support, and that
he was not left destitute of comfort in him." On Monday, he contin-
ued very ill; but speaks of his mind being calm and composed, resigned
to the divine dispensations, and content with his feeble state. By the
account which he gives of himself, the remaining part of this week,
he continued very feeble, and for the most part dejected in mind. He
enjoyed no great freedom nor sweetness in spiritual things; except that
for some very short spaces of time he had refreshment and encourage-
ment, which engaged his heart on divine things; and sometimes his
heart was melted with spiritual affection.

Lord's day, June 29. Preached, both parts of the day from John
xiv. 19. "Yet a little while, and the world seeth me no more," &c.
God was pleased to assist me, to afford me both freedom and
power, especially towards the close of my discourse, both forenoon
and afternoon. God's power appeared in the assembly, in both exercises. Numbers of God's people were refreshed and melted with divine things; one or two comforted, who had been long under distress: convictions, in divers instances, powerfully revived; and one
man in years much awakened, who had not long frequented our
meeting, and appeared before as stupid as a stock. God amazingly
renewed and lengthened out my strength. I was so spent at noon,
that I could scarce walk, and all my joints trembled; so that I could
not sit, nor so much as hold my hand still; and yet God
strengthened me to preach with power in the afternoon; although I
had given out word to my people, that I did not expect to be able
to do it. Spent some time afterwards in conversing, particularly,
with several persons, about their spiritual state; and had some satisfaction concerning one or two. Prayed afterwards with a sick child,
and gave a word of exhortation. Was assisted in all my work.
Blessed be God. Returned home with more health, than I went out
with; although my linen was wringing wet upon me, from a little
after ten in the morning, till past five in the afternoon. My spirits
also were considerably refreshed; and my soul rejoiced in hope,
that I had through grace done something for God. In the evening,
walked out, and enjoyed a sweet season in secret prayer and praise.
But Oh, I found the truth of the Psalmist's words, "My goodness
extendeth not to thee"! I could not make any returns to God; I
longed to live only to him, and to be in tune for his praise and serv-

ice for ever. Oh, for spirituality and holy fervency, that I might spend and be spent for God to my latest moment!

June 30. Spent the day in writing; but under much weakness and disorder. Felt the labours of the preceding day; although my spirits were so refreshed the evening before, that I was not then sensible of my being spent.

July 1. In the afternoon, visited, and preached to my people, from Heb. ix. 27. And as it is appointed unto men once to die, &c. on occasion of some person's lying at the point of death, in my congregation. God gave me some assistance; and his word made some impressions on the audience, in general. This was an agreeable and comfortable evening to my soul: my spirits were somewhat refreshed, with a small degree of freedom and help enjoyed in my work.

On Wednesday he went to Newark, to a meeting of the Presbytery; complains of lowness of spirits; and greatly laments his spending his time so unfruitfully. The remaining part of the week he spent there, and at Elizabethtown; and speaks of comfort and divine assistance, from day to day; but yet greatly complains for want of more spirituality.

Lord's day, July 6. [At Elizabethtown.] Enjoyed some composure and serenity of mind, in the morning: heard Mr. Dickinson preach, in the forenoon, and was refreshed with his discourse; was in a melting frame, some part of the time of sermon: partook of the Lord's supper, and enjoyed some sense of divine things in that ordinance. In the afternoon, I preached from Ezek. xxxiii. 11. "As I live, saith the Lord God," &c. God favoured me with freedom and fervency, and helped me to plead his cause, beyond my own power.

July 7. My spirits were considerably refreshed and raised, in the morning. There is no comfort, I find, in any enjoyment, without enjoying God, and being engaged in his service. In the evening, had the most agreeable conversation which I remember in all my life, upon God's being all in all, and all enjoyments being just that to us which God makes them, and no more. It is good to begin and end with God. O how does a sweet solemnity lay a foundation for true pleasure and happiness!

July 8. Rode home, and enjoyed some agreeable meditations by the way.

July 9. Spent the day in writing, enjoyed some comfort and refreshment of spirit in my evening retirement.

July 10. Spent most of the day in writing. Towards night rode to Mr. Tennent's; enjoyed some agreeable conversation: went home, in the evening, in a solemn, sweet frame of mind; was refreshed in secret duties, longed to live wholly and only for God, and saw plainly, there was nothing in the world worthy of my affection; so that my heart was dead to all below; yet not through dejection, as at some times, but from views of a better inheritance.

July 11. Was in a calm, composed frame, in the morning, especially in the season of my secret retirement. I think, that I was well pleased with the will of God, whatever it was, or should be, in all respects of which I had then any thought. Intending to administer the Lord's supper the next Lord's day, I looked to God for his presence and assistance upon that occasion; but felt a disposition to say, "The will of the Lord be done," whether it be to give me assistance, or not. Spent some little time in writing: visited the Indians, and spent some time in serious conversation with them; thinking it not best to preach, many of them being absent.

July 12. This day was spent in fasting and prayer by my congregation, as preparatory to the sacrament. I discoursed, both parts of the day, from Rom. iv. 25. "Who was delivered for our offences," &c. God gave me some assistance in my discourses, and something of divine power attended the word; so that this was an agreeable season. Afterwards led them to a solemn renewal of their covenant, and fresh dedication of themselves to God. This was a season both of solemnity and sweetness, and God seemed to be "in the midst of us." Returned to my lodgings, in the evening, in a comfortable frame of mind.

Lord's day, July 13. In the forenoon, discoursed on the bread of life, from John vi. 35. God gave me some assistance, in part of my discourse especially; and there appeared some tender affection in the assembly under divine truths; my soul also was somewhat refreshed. Administered the sacrament of the Lord's supper to thirty-one persons of the Indians. God seemed to be present in this ordinance; the communicants were sweetly melted and refreshed, most of them. O how they melted, even when the elements were first uncovered! There was scarcely a dry eye among them, when I took off the linen, and shewed them the symbols of Christ's broken body.—Having rested a little, after the administration of the sacrament, I visited the communicants, and found them generally in a sweet loving frame; not unlike what appeared among them on the former sacramental occasion, on April 27. In the afternoon, discoursed upon coming to Christ, and the satisfaction of those who do so, from the same verse I insisted on in the forenoon. This was likewise an agreeable season, a season of much tenderness, affection, and enlargement in divine service: and God, I am persuaded, crowned our assembly with his divine presence. I returned home much spent, yet rejoicing in the goodness of God.

July 14. Went to my people, and discoursed to them from Psalm cxix. 106. "I have sworn, and I will perform it." &c. Observed, 1. That all God's judgments or commandments are righteous. 2. That God's people have sworn to keep them; and this they do especially at the Lord's table. There appeared to be a powerful divine influence on the assembly, and considerable melting under the word. Afterwards, I led them to a renewal of their covenant before God, that they would watch over themselves and one another, lest they should fall into sin and dishonour the name of Christ, just as I did on Monday, April 28. This transaction was attended with great solemnity: and God seemed to own it by exciting in them a fear and jealousy of themselves, lest they should sin against God; so that the presence of God seemed to be amongst us in this conclusion of the sacramental solemnity.

The next day, he set out on a journey towards Philadelphia; from whence he did not return till Saturday. He went this journey, and spent the week, under a great degree of illness of body, and dejection of mind.

Lord's day, July 20. Preached twice to my people from John xvii. 24. "Father, I will that they also whom thou hast given me, be with me, where I am, that they may behold my glory, which thou hast given me." Was helped to discourse with great clearness and plainness in the forenoon. In the afternoon, enjoyed some tenderness, and spake with some influence. Numbers were in tears; and some, to appearance, in distress.

July 21. Preached to the Indians, chiefly for the sake of some strangers; proposed my design of taking a journey speedily to the Susquehannah; exhorted my people to pray for me, that God would be with me in that journey; and then chose divers persons of the congregation to travel with me. Afterwards, spent some time in discoursing to the strangers, and was somewhat encouraged with them. Took care of my people's secular business, and was not a little exercised with it. Had some degree of composure and comfort in secret retirement.

July 22. Was in a dejected frame, most of the day; wanted to wear out life, and have it at an end; but had some desires of living to God, and wearing out life for him. Oh that I could indeed do so!

The next day he went to Elizabeth-Town, to a meeting of the Presbytery; and spent this, and Thursday, and the former part of Friday, under a very great degree of melancholy, and gloominess of mind; not through any fear of future punishment, but as being distressed with a senselessness of all good, so that the whole world appeared empty and gloomy to him. In the latter part of Friday he was greatly relieved and comforted.

July 26. Was comfortable in the morning, my countenance and heart were not sad, as in days past; enjoyed some sweetness in lifting up my heart to God. Rode home to my people, and was in a comfortable, pleasant frame by the way; my spirits were much relieved of their burden, and I felt free to go through all difficulties and labours in my Master's service.

Lord's day, July 27. Discoursed to my people in the forenoon, from Luke xii. 37, on the duty and benefit of watching. God helped me in the latter part of my discourse, and the power of God appeared in the assembly. In the afternoon, discoursed from Luke xiii. 25. When once the master of the house is risen up, &c. Here also I enjoyed some assistance; and the Spirit of God seemed to attend what was spoken, so that there was a great solemnity, and some tears among Indians and others.

July 28. Was very weak, and scarce able to perform any business at all; but enjoyed sweetness and comfort in prayer, both morning and evening; and was composed and comfortable through the day. My mind was intense, and my heart fervent, at least in some degree, in secret duties, and I longed to spend and be spent for God.

July 29. My mind was cheerful, and free from the melancholy, with which I am often exercised; had freedom in looking up to God, at various times in the day. In the evening, I enjoyed a comfortable season in secret prayer; was helped to plead with God for my own dear people, that he would carry on his own blessed work among them; was assisted also in praying for the divine presence to attend me in my intended journey to the Susquehannah; and was helped to remember dear brethren and friends in New-England. I scarce knew how to leave the throne of grace, and it grieved me that I was obliged to go to bed; I longed to do something for God, but knew not how. Blessed be God for this freedom from dejection.

July 30. Was uncommonly comfortable, both in body and mind; in the forenoon especially, my mind was solemn; I was assisted in my work; and God seemed to be near to me; so that the day was as comfortable as most I have enjoyed for some time. In the evening, was favoured with assistance in secret prayer, and felt much as I did the evening before. Blessed be God for that freedom I then enjoyed at the throne of grace, for myself, my people, and my dear friends. It is good for me to draw near to God.

He seems to have continued very much in the same free, comfortable state of mind the next day.

Aug. 1. In the evening, enjoyed a sweet season in secret prayer; clouds of darkness and perplexing care were sweetly scattered, and nothing anxious remained. O how serene was my mind at this season! how free from that distracting concern I have often felt! "Thy will be done," was a petition sweet to my soul; and if God had bidden me choose for myself in any affair, I should have chosen rather to have referred the choice to him; for I saw he was infinitely wise, and could not do any thing amiss, as I was in danger of doing. Was assisted in prayer for my dear flock, that God would promote his own work among them, and that God would go with me in my intended journey to the Susquehannah; was helped to remember my dear friends in New England, and my dear brethren in the ministry. I found enough in the sweet duty of prayer to have engaged me to continue it in the whole night, would my bodily state have admitted of it. O how sweet it is, to be enabled heartily to say, Lord, not my will, but thine be done.

Aug. 2. Near night, preached from Matt. xi. 29. Take my yoke upon you, &c. Was considerably helped; and the presence of God seemed to be somewhat remarkably in the assembly; divine truths made powerful impressions, both upon saints and sinners. Blessed be God for such a revival among us. In the evening was very weary, but found my spirits supported and refreshed.

Lord's day, Aug. 3. Discoursed to my people, in the forenoon, from Col. iii. 4, and observed, that Christ is the believer's Life. God helped me, and gave me his presence in this discourse; and it was a season of considerable power to the assembly. In the afternoon, preached from Luke xix. 41, 42. And when he was come near, he beheld the city, &c. I enjoyed some assistance; though not so much as in the forenoon. In the evening I enjoyed freedom and sweetness in secret prayer; God enlarged my heart, freed me from melancholy damps, and gave me satisfaction in drawing near to himself. Oh that my soul could magnify the Lord, for these seasons of composure and resignation to his will.

Aug. 4. Spent the day in writing; enjoyed much freedom and assistance in my work; was in a composed and comfortable frame, most of the day; and in the evening enjoyed some sweetness in prayer. Blessed be God, my spirits were yet up, and I was free from sinking damps; as I have been in general ever since I came from Elizabeth-Town last. O what a mercy is this!

Aug. 5. Towards night, preached at the funeral of one of my christians, from Is. lvii. 2. He shall enter into peace, &c. I was oppressed with the nervous head-ache, and considerably dejected; however, had a little freedom, some part of the time I was discoursing. Was extremely weary in the evening; but notwithstanding, enjoyed some liberty and cheerfulness of mind in prayer; and found the dejection that I feared, much removed, and my spirits considerably refreshed.

He continued in a very comfortable, cheerful frame of mind the next day, and his heart enlarged in the service of God.

Aug. 7. Rode to my house, where I spent the last winter, in order to bring some things I needed for my Susquehannah journey; was refreshed to see that place, which God so marvelously visited with the showers of his grace. O how amazing did the power of God often appear there! Bless the Lord, O my soul, and forget not all his benefits.

The next day, he speaks of liberty, enlargement, and sweetness of mind, in prayer and religious conversation.

Aug. 9. In the afternoon, visited my people; set their affairs in order, as much as possible, and contrived for them the management of their worldly business; discoursed to them in a solemn manner, and concluded with prayer. Was composed and comfortable in the evening, and somewhat fervent in secret prayer; had some sense and view of the eternal world; and found a serenity of mind. O that I could magnify the Lord for any freedom which he affords me in prayer!

Lord's day, Aug. 10. Discoursed to my people, both parts of the day, from Acts iii. 19. Repent ye therefore, &c. In discoursing of repentance, in the forenoon, God helped me, so that my discourse was searching; some were in tears, both of the Indians and white people, and the word of God was attended with some power. In the intermission, I was engaged in discoursing to some in order to their baptism; as well as with one who had then lately met with some comfort, after spiritual trouble and distress. In the afternoon, was somewhat assisted again, though weak and weary. Afterwards baptized six persons; three adults and three children. Was in a comfortable frame in the evening, and enjoyed some satisfaction in secret prayer. I scarce ever in my life felt myself so full of tenderness, as this day.

Aug. 11. Being about to set out on a journey to the Susquehannah the next day, with leave of Providence, I spent some time this day in prayer with my people, that God would bless and succeed my intended journey, that he would send forth his blessed Spirit with his word, and set up his kingdom among the poor Indians in the wilderness. While I was opening and applying part of the cxth and iid Psalms, the power of God seemed to descend on the assembly in some measure; and while I was making the first prayer, numbers were melted, and found some affectionate enlargement of soul myself. Preached from Acts iv. 31. And when they had prayer, the place was shaken, &c. God helped me, and my interpreter also; there was a shaking and melting among us; and divers, I doubt not, were in some measure "filled with the Holy Ghost." Afterwards, Mr. Macnight prayed; and I then opened the two last stanzas of the lxxiid Psalm; at which time God was present with us; especially while I insisted upon the promise of all nations blessing the great Redeemer. My soul was refreshed, to think, that this day, this blessed glorious season, should surely come; and I trust, numbers of my dear people were also refreshed. Afterwards prayed; had some freedom, but was almost spent; then walked out, and left my people to carry on religious exercises among themselves. They prayed repeatedly, and sung, while I rested and refreshed myself. Afterwards, went to the meeting, prayed with, and dismissed the assembly. Blessed be God, this has been a day of grace. There were many tears and affectionate sobs among us this day. In the evening, my soul was refreshed in prayer; enjoyed liberty at the throne of grace, in praying for my people and friends, and the Church of God in general. Bless the Lord, O my soul.

The next day he set out on his journey towards the Susquehannah, and six of his Christian Indians with him, whom he had chosen out of his congregation, as those he judged most fit to assist him in the business he was going upon. He took his way through Philadelphia; intending to go to the Susquehannah river, far down, where it is settled by the white people, below the country inhabited by the Indians; and so to travel up the river to the Indian habitations. For although this was much farther about, yet hereby he avoided the huge mountains, and hideous wilderness, that must be crossed in the nearer way; which in time past he found to be extremely difficult and fatiguing. He rode this week as far as Charlestown, about thirty miles westward of Philadelphia; where he arrived on Friday: and in his way hither, was for the most part, in a composed, comfortable state of mind.

Aug. 16. [At Charlestown.] It being a day kept by the people of the place where I now was, as preparatory to the celebration of the Lord's supper, I tarried; heard Mr. Treat preach; and then preached myself. God gave me some good degree of freedom, and helped me to discourse with warmth and application, to the conscience. Afterwards, I was refreshed in spirit, though much tried; and spent the evening agreeably, having some freedom in prayer, as well as christian conversation.

Lord's day, Aug. 17. Enjoyed liberty, composure, and satisfaction, in the secret duties of the morning; had my heart somewhat enlarged in prayer for dear friends, as well as for myself. In the forenoon attended Mr. Treat's preaching, partook of the Lord's supper, five of my people also communicating in this holy ordinance; I enjoyed some enlargement and outgoing of soul in this season. In the afternoon preached from Ezek. xxxiii. 11. Say unto them, as I live, saith the Lord God, &c. Enjoyed not so much sensible assistance as the day before; however, was helped to some fervency in addressing immortal souls. Was somewhat confounded in the evening, because I thought I had done little or nothing for God; yet enjoyed some refreshment of spirit in christian conversation and prayer. Spent the evening, till near midnight, in religious exercises; and found my bodily strength which was much spent when I came from the public worship, something renewed before I went to bed.

Aug. 18. Rode on my way towards Paxton, upon Susquehannah river. Felt my spirits sink towards night, so that I had little comfort.

Aug. 19. Rode forward still; and at night lodged by the side of the Susquehannah. Was weak and disordered both this and the preceding day, and found my spirits considerably damped, meeting with none that I thought godly people.

Aug. 20. Having lain in a cold sweat all night, I coughed much bloody matter this morning, and was under great disorder of body, and not a little melancholy; but what gave me some encouragement, was, I had a secret hope that I might speedily get a dismission from earth, and all its toils and sorrows. Rode this day to one Chamber's, upon the Susquehannah, and there lodged. Was much afflicted in the evening, with an ungodly crew, drinking, swearing, &c. O what a hell would it be, to be numbered with the ungodly! Enjoyed some agreeable conversation with a traveller who seemed to have some relish of true religion.

Aug. 21. Rode up the river about fifteen miles and there lodged, in a family which appeared quite destitute of God. Laboured to discourse with the man about the life of religion, but found him very artful in evading such conversation. O what a death it is to some, to hear of the things of God! Was out of my element; but was not so dejected as at some times.

Aug. 22. Continued my course up the river; my people now being with me, who were before parted from me; travelled about all the English settlements; at night lodged in the open woods; and slept with more comfort than while among the ungodly company of white people. Enjoyed some liberty in secret prayer, this evening; and was helped to remember dear friends, as well as my dear flock, and the Chuch of God in general.

Aug. 23. Arrived at the Indian town, called Shaumoking, near night, was not so dejected as formerly; but yet somewhat exercised. Felt somewhat composed in the evening; enjoyed some freedom in leaving my all with God. Through the great goodness of God, I enjoyed some liberty of mind; and was not distressed with a despondency, as frequently heretofore.

Lord's day, Aug. 24. Towards noon, visited some of the Delawares, and discoursed with them about Christianity. In the afternoon discoursed to the King, and others, upon divine things; who seemed disposed to hear. Spent most of the day in these exercises. In the evening enjoyed some comfort and satisfaction; and especially had some sweetness in secret prayer. This duty was made so agreeable to me, that I loved to walk abroad, and repeatedly engage in it. Oh, how comfortable is a little glimpse of God!

Aug. 25. Spent most of the day in writing. Sent out my people that were with me, to talk with the Indians, and contract a friendship and familiarity with them, that I might have a better opportunity of treating with them about Christianity. Some good seemed to be done by their visit this day, divers appeared willing to hearken to Christianity. My spirits were a little refreshed, this evening; and I found some liberty and satisfaction in prayer.

Aug. 26. About noon, discoursed to a considerable number of Indians. God helped me, I am persuaded; for I was enabled to speak with much plainness, and some warmth and power; and the discourse had impression upon some, and made them appear very serious. I thought things now appeared as encouraging, as they did at Crossweeks. At the time of my first visit to those Indians, I was a little encouraged; I pressed things with all my might; and called out my people, who were then present, to give in their testimony for God; which they did. Towards night, was refreshed; had a heart to pray for the setting up of God's kingdom here; as well as for my dear congregation below, and my dear friends elsewhere.

Aug. 27. There having been a thick smoke in the house where I lodged all the night before, whereby I was almost choaked, I was this morning distressed with pains in my head and neck, and could have no rest. In the morning, the smoke was still the same; and a cold easterly storm gathering, I could neither live within doors, nor without, a long time together. I was pierced with the rawness of the air abroad, and in the house distressed with the smoke. I was this day very vapoury, and lived in great distress, and had not health enough to do any thing to any purpose.

Aug. 28. In the forenoon, I was under great concern of mind

about my work. Was visited by some who desired to hear me preach; discoursed to them, in the afternoon, with some fervency, and laboured to persuade them to turn to God. Was full of concern for the kingdom of Christ, and found some enlargement of soul in prayer, both in secret and in my family. Scarce ever saw more clearly, than this day, that it is God's work to convert souls, and especially poor Heathens. I knew, I could not touch them; I saw I could only speak to dry bones, but could give them no sense of what I said. My eyes were up to God for help: I could say the work was his; and if done, the glory would be his.

Aug. 29. Felt the same concern of mind, as the day before. Enjoyed some freedom in prayer, and a satisfaction to leave all with God. Travelled to the Delawares, found few at home, felt poorly; but was able to spend some time alone in reading God's word and in prayer, and enjoyed some sweetness in these exercises. In the evening, was assisted repeatedly in prayer, and found some comfort in coming to the throne of grace.

Aug. 30. Spent the forenoon in visiting a trader, who came down the river sick; and who appeared as ignorant as any Indian. In the afternoon, spent some time in reading, writing and prayer.

Lord's day, Aug. 31. Spent much time, in the morning, in secret duties; found a weight upon my spirits, and could not but cry to God with concern and engagement of soul. Spent some time also in reading and expounding God's word to my dear family which was with me, as well as in singing and prayer with them. Afterwards spake the word of God, to some few of the Susquehannah Indians. In the afternoon, felt very weak and feeble. Near night, was somewhat refreshed in mind, with some views of things relating to my great work. O how heavy is my work, when faith cannot take hold of an almighty arm, for the performance of it! Many times have I been ready to sink in this case. Blessed be God, that I may repair to a full fountain!

Sept. 1. Set out on a journey towards a place called The Great Island, about fifty miles distant from Shaumoking, in the north-western branch of the Susquehannah. Travelled some part of the way, and at night lodged in the woods. Was exceedingly feeble this day, and sweat much the night following.

Sept. 2. Rode forward; but no faster than my people went on foot. Was very weak, on this as well as the preceding days. I was so feeble and faint, that I feared it would kill me to lie out in the open air; and some of our company being parted from us, so that we had now no axe with us, I had no way to climb into a young pine tree, and with my knife to lop the branches, and so made a shelter from the dew. But the evening being cloudy, and very likely for rain, I was still under fears of being extremely exposed: sweat much in the night, so that my linen was almost wringing wet all night. I scarcely ever was more weak and weary, than this evening, when I was able to sit up at all. This was a melancholy situation I was in; but I endeavoured to quiet myself with considerations of the possibility of my being in much worse circumstances, amongst enemies, &c.

Sept. 3. Rode to the Delaware-town; found divers drinking and drunken. Discoursed with some of the Indians about Christianity; observed my interpreter much engaged and assisted in his work; some few persons seemed to hear with great earnestness and engagement of soul. About noon, rode to a small town of Shauwaunoes, about eight miles distant; spent an hour or two there, and returned to the Delaware-town, and lodged there. Was scarce ever more confounded with a sense of my own unfruitfulness and unfitness for my work, than now. O what a dead, heartless, barren, unprofitable wretch did I now see myself to be! My spirits were so low, and my bodily strength so wasted, that I could do nothing at all. At length, being much overdone, lay down on a buffalo-skin; but sweat much the whole night.

Sept. 4. Discoursed with the Indians, in the morning, about Christianity; my interpreter, afterwards, carrying on the discourse to a considerable length. Some few appeared well-disposed, and somewhat affected. Left this place, and returned towards Shaumoking; and at night lodged in the place where I lodged the Monday-night before: was in very uncomfortable circumstances in the evening, my people being belated, and not coming to me till past ten at night; so that I had no fire to dress any victuals, or to keep me warm, or keep off wild beasts; and I was scarce ever more weak and worn out in all my life. However, I lay down and slept before my people came up, expecting nothing else but to spend the whole night alone, and without fire.

Sept. 5. Was exceeding weak, so that I could scarcely ride; it seemed sometimes as if I must fall off from my horse, and lie in the open woods: however, got to Shaumoking, towards night: felt somewhat of a spirit of thankfulness, that God had so far returned me: was refreshed to see one of my christians, whom I left here in my late excursion.

Sept. 6. Spent the day in a very weak state; coughing and spitting blood, and having little appetite for any food I had with me; was able to do very little, except discourse a while of divine things to my own people, and to some few I met with. Had, by this time, very little life or heart to speak for God, through feebleness of body, and flatness of spirits. Was scarcely ever more ashamed and confounded in myself, than now. I was sensible, that there were numbers of God's people, who knew I was then out upon a design, or at least the pretence, of doing something for God, and in his cause, among the poor Indians; and they were ready to suppose, that I was fervent in spirit; but O the heartless frame of mind that I felt, filled me with confusion! O methought if God's people knew me, as God knows, they would not think so highly of my zeal and resolution for God, as perhaps now they do! I could not but desire they should see how heartless and irresolute I was, that they might be undeceived, and "not think of me above what they ought to think." And yet I thought, if they saw the utmost of my flatness and unfaithfulness, the smallness of my courage and resolution for God, they would be ready to shut me out of their doors, as unworthy of the company or friendship of christians.

Lord's day, Sept. 7. Was much in the same weak state of body, and afflicted frame of mind, as in the preceding day: my soul was grieved, and mourned that I could do nothing for God. Read and expounded some part of God's word to my own dear family, and spent some time in prayer with them; discoursed also a little to the Pagans; but spent the Sabbath with a little comfort.

Sept. 8. Spent the forenoon among the Indians; in the afternoon, left Shaumoking, and returned down the river, a few miles. Had proposed to have tarried a considerable time longer among the Indians upon the Susquehannah; but was hindered from pursuing my purpose by the sickness that prevailed there, the weakly circumstances of my own people that were with me, and especially my own extraordinary weakness, having been exercised with great nocturnal sweats, and a coughing up of blood, almost the whole of the journey. I was a great part of the time so feeble and faint, that it seemed as though I never should be able to reach home; and at the same time very destitute of the comforts, and even the necessaries of life; at least, what was necessary for one in so weak a state. In this journey I sometimes was enabled to speak the word of God with some power, and divine truths made some impressions on divers who heard me; so that several, both men and women, old and young, seemed to cleave to us, and be well disposed towards Christianity; but others mocked and shouted, which damped those who before seemed friendly, at least some of them. Yet God, at times, was evidently present, assisting me, my interpreter, and other dear friends who were with me. God gave, sometimes a good degree of freedom in prayer for the ingathering of souls there; and I could not but entertain a strong hope, that the journey should not be wholly fruitless. Whether the issue of it would be the setting up of Christ's kingdom there, or only the drawing of some few persons down to my congregation in New-Jersey; or whether they were now only being prepared for some further attempts, that might be made among them, I did not determine; but I was persuaded, the journey would not be lost. Blessed be God, that I had any encouragement and hope.

Sept. 9. Rode down the river, near thirty miles. Was extremely weak, much fatigued, and wet with a thunder storm. Discoursed with some warmth and closeness to some poor ignorant souls, on the life and power of religion; what were, and what were not the evidences of it. They seemed much astonished, when they saw my Indians ask a blessing, and give thanks, at dinner; concluding that a very high evidence of grace in them; but were astonished, when I insisted, that neither that, nor yet secret prayer, was any sure evidence of grace. O the ignorance of the world! How are some empty outward forms, that may all be entirely selfish, mistaken for true religion, infallible evidences of it! The Lord pity a deluded world!

Sept. 10. Rode near twenty miles homeward. Was much solicited to preach, but was utterly unable, through bodily weakness. Was extremely overdone with the heat and showers this day, and coughed up a considerable quantity of blood.

Sept. 11. Rode homeward; but was very weak, and sometimes scarce able to ride. Had a very importunate invitation to preach at a meeting-house I came by, the people being then gathering; but could not, by reason of weakness. Was resigned and composed under my weakness; but was much exercised with concern for my companions in travel, whom I had left with much regret, some lame, and some sick.

Sept. 12. Rode about fifty miles; and came, just at night, to a christian friend's house, about twenty-five miles westward from Philadelphia. Was courteously received, and kindly entertained, and found myself much refreshed in the midst of my weakness and fatigues.

Sept. 13. Was still agreeably entertained with christian friendship, and all things necessary for my weak circumstances. In the afternoon, heard Mr. Treat preach; and was refreshed in conversation with him, in the evening.

Lord's day, Sept. 14. At the desire of Mr. Treat and the people, I preached both parts of the day (but short) from Luke xiv. 23. And the Lord said unto the servant, go out, &c. God gave me some freedom and warmth in my discourse; and I trust, helped me in some measure to labour in singleness of heart.—Was much tired in the evening, but was comforted with the most tender treatment I ever met with in my life. My mind, through the whole of this day, was exceeding calm; and I could ask for nothing in prayer, with any encouragement of soul, but that "the will of God might be done."

Sept. 15. Spent the whole day, in concert with Mr. Treat, in endeavours to compose a difference, subsisting between certain persons in the congregation where we now were: and there seemed to be a blessing on our endeavours. In the evening, baptized a child; was in a calm, composed frame; and enjoyed, I trust, a spiritual sense of divine things, while administering the ordinance. Afterwards, spent the time in religious conversation, till late in the night. This was indeed a pleasant agreeable evening.

Sept. 16. Continued still at my friend's house, about twenty-five miles westward of Philadelphia. Was very weak, unable to perform any business, and scarcely able to sit up.

Sept. 17. Rode into Philadelphia. Still very weak, and my cough and spitting of blood continued. Enjoyed some agreeable conversation with friends, but wanted more spirituality.

Sept. 18. Went from Philadelphia to Mr. Treat's; was agreeably entertained on the road; and was in a sweet composed frame, in the evening.

Sept. 19. Rode from Mr. Treat's to Mr. Stockston's, at Princeton:

was extremely weak, but kindly received and entertained. Spent the evening with some degree of satisfaction.

Sept. 20. Arrived among my own people, near Cranberry, just at night: found them praying together; went in, and gave them some account of God's dealings with me and my companions in the journey; which seemed affecting to them. I then prayed with them, and thought the divine presence was amongst us; divers were melted into tears, and seemed to have a sense of divine things. Being very weak, I was obliged soon to repair to my lodgings, and felt much worn out, in the evening. Thus God has carried me through the fatigues and perils of another journey to the Susquehannah, and returned me again in safety, though under a great degree of bodily indisposition. Oh that my soul were truly thankful for renewed instances of mercy! Many hardships and distresses I endured in this journey! But the Lord supported me under them all.

Hitherto BRAINERD had kept a constant diary, giving an account of what passed from day to day, with very little interruption; but henceforward his diary is very much interrupted by his illness; under which he was often brought so low, as either not to be capable of writing, or not well able to bear the burden of a care so constant, as was requisite, to recollect, every evening, what had passed in the day, and digest it, and set down an orderly account of it in writing. However, his diary was not wholly neglected; but he took care, from time to time, to take some notice in it of the most material things concerning himself and the state of his mind, even till within a few days of his death, as the reader will see afterwards.

Lord's day, Sept. 21, 1746. I was so weak I could not preach, nor pretend to ride over to my people in the forenoon. In the afternoon, rode out; sat in my chair, and discoursed to my people from Rom. xiv. 7, 8. For none of us liveth to himself, &c. I was strengthened and helped in my discourse; and there appeared something agreeable in the assembly. I returned to my lodgings extremely tired, but thankful, that I had been enabled to speak a word to my poor people, from whom I had been so long absent. Was enabled to sleep very little this night, through weariness and pain. O how blessed should I be, if the little I do were all done with right views! Oh that, "whether I live, I might live to the Lord; or whether I die, I might die unto the Lord; that, whether living or dying, I might be the Lord's"!

Sept. 27. Spent this day, as well as the whole week past, under a great degree of bodily weakness, exercised with a violent cough, and a considerable fever. I had no appetite for any kind of food; and frequently brought up what I ate, as soon as it was down; oftentimes had little rest in my bed, owing to pains in my breast and back. I was able, however, to ride over to my people, about two miles, every day, and take some care of those who were then at work upon a small house for me to reside in among the Indians. I was sometimes scarce able to walk, and never able to sit up the whole day, through the week. Was calm and composed, and but little exercised with melancholy, as in former seasons of weakness. Whether I should ever recover or no, seemed very doubtful; but this was many times a comfort to me, that life and death did not depend upon my choice. I was pleased to think, that He who is infinitely wise, had the determination of this matter; and that I had no trouble to consider and weigh things upon all sides, in order to make the choice, whether I should live or die. Thus my time was consumed; I had little strength to pray, none to write or read, and scarce any to meditate; but through divine goodness, I could with great composure look death in the face, and frequently with sensible joy. O how blessed it is, to be habitually prepared for death! The Lord grant, that I may be actually ready also!

Lord's day, Sept. 28. Rode to my people; and, though under much weakness, attempted to preach from 2 Cor. xiii. 5. Examine yourselves, &c. Discoursed about half an hour; at which season divine power seemed to attend the word: but being extremely weak, I was obliged to desist; and after a turn of faintness, with much difficulty rode to my lodgings; where betaking myself to my bed, I lay in a burning fever, and almost delirious, for several hours; till towards morning, my fever went off with a violent sweat. I have often been feverish, and unable to rest quietly after preaching; but this was the most severe, distressing turn, that ever preaching brought upon me. Yet I felt perfectly at rest in my own mind, because I had made my utmost attempts to speak for God, and knew I could do no more.

Sept. 30. Yesterday and to-day, was in the same weak state, or rather weaker than in days past; was scarce able to sit up half the day. Was in a composed frame of mind, remarkably free from dejection and melancholy; as God has been pleased, in a great measure, to deliver me from these unhappy glooms, in the general course of my present weakness hitherto, and also from a peevish froward spirit. And O how great a mercy is this! Oh that I might always be perfectly quiet in seasons of greatest weakness, although nature should sink and fail! Oh that I may always be able with the utmost sincerity to say, "Lord, not my will but thine be done!" This, through grace, I can say at present, with regard to life or death, "The Lord do with me as seems good in his sight"; that whether I live or die, I may glorify Him, who is "worthy to receive blessing, and honour, and dominion for ever. Amen."

Oct. 4. Spent the former part of this week under a great degree of infirmity and disorder, as I had done several weeks before; was able, however, to ride a little every day, although unable to sit up half the day, till Thursday. Took some care daily of some persons at work upon my house. On Friday afternoon, found myself wonderfully revived and strengthened. Having some time before given notice to my people, and those of them at the Forks of Delaware in particular, that I designed, with the leave of Providence, to administer the sacrament of the Lord's supper upon the first Sabbath in October, on Friday afternoon I preached preparatory to the sacrament, from 2 Cor. xiii. 5; finishing what I had proposed to offer upon the subject the Sabbath before. The sermon was blessed of God to the stirring up religious affection, and a spirit of devotion, in the people of God; and to greatly affecting one who had backslidden from God, which caused him to judge and condemn himself. I was surprisingly strengthened in my work, while I was speaking; but was obliged immediately after to repair to bed, being now removed into my own house among the Indians; which gave me such speedy relief and refreshment, as I could not have well lived without. Spent some time on Friday night in conversing with my people about divine things, as I lay upon my bed; and found my soul refreshed, though my body was weak. This being Saturday, I discoursed particularly with divers of the communicants; and this afternoon preached from Zech. xii. 10. And I will pour on the house of David, &c. There seemed to be a tender melting, and hearty mourning for sin, in numbers in the congregation. My soul was in a comfortable frame, and I enjoyed freedom and assistance in public service; was myself as well as most of the congregation, much affected with the humble confession, and apparently broken-heartedness of the forementioned backslider; and could not but rejoice, that God had given him such a sense of his sin and unworthiness. Was extremely tired in the evening; but lay on my bed, and discoursed to my people.

Lord's day, Oct. 5. Was still very weak; and in the morning considerably afraid I should not be able to go through the work of the day; having much to do, both in private and public. Discoursed before the administration of the sacrament, from John i. 29. "Behold the Lamb of God, that taketh away the sins of the world." Where I considered I. In what respects Christ is called the Lamb of God; and observed that he is so called (1) From the purity and innocency of his nature. (2) From his meekness and patience under sufferings. (3) From his being that atonement which was pointed out in the sacrifice of the lambs, and in particular by the paschal lamb. II. Considered how and in what sense he "takes away the sin of the world": and observed, that the means and manner, in and by which he takes away the sins of men, was his "giving himself for them," doing and suffering in their room and stead, &c. And he is said to take away the sin of the world, not because all the world shall actually be redeemed from sin by him; but because (1) He has done and suffered sufficient to answer for the sins of the world, and so to redeem all mankind. (2) He actually does take away the sins of the elect world. And, III. Considered how we are to behold him, in order to have our sins taken away (1) Not with our bodily eyes. Nor (2) By imagining him on the cross, &c. But by a spiritual view of his glory and goodness, engaging the soul to rely on him, &c.—The divine presence attended this discourse; and the assembly was considerably melted with divine truths. After sermon, baptized two persons. Then administered the Lord's supper to near forty communicants, of the Indians, besides divers dear christians of the white people. It seemed to be a season of divine power and grace; and numbers seemed to rejoice in God. O the sweet union and harmony then appearing among the religious people! My soul was refreshed, and my religious friends, of the white people, with me. After the sacrament, could scarcely get home, though it was not more than twenty roods; but was supported and led by my friends, and laid on my bed; where I lay in pain till some time in the evening; and then was able to sit up and discourse with friends. O how was this day spent in prayers and praises among my dear people!

One might hear them, all the morning before public worship, and in the evening, till near midnight, praying and singing praises to God, in one or other of their houses. My soul was refreshed, though my body was weak.

This week, in two days, though in a very low state, he went to Elizabeth-Town, to attend the meeting of the Synod there: but was disappointed by its removal to New-York. He continued in a very composed, comfortable frame of mind.

Oct. 11. Towards night was seized with an ague, which was followed with a hard fever, and considerable pain; was treated with great kindness and was ashamed to see so much concern about so unworthy a creature, as I knew myself to be. Was in a comfortable frame of mind, wholly submissive, with regard to life or death. It was indeed a peculiar satisfaction to me, to think, that it was not my concern or business to determine whether I should live or die. I likewise felt peculiarly satisfied, while under this uncommon degree of disorder; being now fully convinced of my being really weak, and unable to perform my work. Whereas at other times my mind was perplexed with fears, that I was a misimprover of time, by conceiting I was sick, when I was not in reality so. O how precious is time! And how guilty it makes me feel, when I think that I have trifled away and misimproved it, or neglected to fill up each part of it with duty, to the utmost of my ability and capacity!

Lord's day, Oct. 12. Was scarcely able to sit up in the forenoon: in the afternoon, attended public worship, and was in a composed comfortable frame.

Lord's day, Oct. 19. Was scarcely able to do any thing at all in the week past except that on Thursday I rode out about four miles; at which time I took cold. As I was able to do little or nothing, so I enjoyed not much spirituality, or lively religious affection; though at times I longed much to be more fruitful and full of heavenly affection; and was grieved to see the hours slide away, while I could do nothing for God.—Was able this week to attend public worship. Was composed and comfortable, willing either to die or live; but found it hard to be reconciled to the thoughts of living useless. Oh that I might never live to be a burden to God's creation; but that I might be allowed to repair home, when my sojourning work is done!

This week, he went back to his Indians at Cranberry, to take some care of their spiritual and temporal concerns; and was much spent with riding; though he rode but a little way in a day.

Oct. 23. Went to my own house, and set things in order. Was very weak, and somewhat melancholy; laboured to do something, but had no strength; and was forced to lie down on my bed, very solitary.

Oct. 24. Spent the day in overseeing and directing my people, about mending their fence, and securing their wheat. Found that all their concerns of a secular nature depended upon me.—Was somewhat refreshed in the evening, having been able to do something valuable in the day time. O how it pains me, to see time pass away, when I can do nothing to any purpose!

Oct. 25. Visited some of my people; spent some time in writing, and felt much better in body, than usual. When it was near night, I felt so well, that I had thoughts of expounding; but in the evening was much disordered again, and spent the night in coughing, and spitting blood.

Lord's day, Oct. 26. In the morning was exceedingly weak: spent the day, till near night, in pain, to see my poor people wandering as sheep not having a shepherd, waiting and hoping to see me able to preach to them before night. It could not but distress me, to see them in this case, and to find myself unable to attempt any thing for their spiritual benefit. But towards night, finding myself a little better, I called them together to my house, and sat down, and read and expounded Matt. v. 1-16. This discourse, though delivered in much weakness, was attended with power to many of the hearers; especially what was spoken upon the last of these verses; where I insisted on the infinite wrong done to religion, by having our light become darkness, instead of shining before men. Many in the congregation were now deeply affected with a sense of their deficiency with respect to a spiritual conversation, which might recommend religion to others, and a spirit of concern and watchfulness seemed to be excited in them. One, in particular, who had fallen in the sin of drunkenness some time before, was now deeply convinced of his sin, and the great dishonour done to religion by his misconduct, and discovered a great degree of grief and concern on that account. My soul was refreshed to see this. And though I had no strength to speak so much as I would have done, but was obliged to lie down on the bed; yet I rejoiced to see such an humble melting in the congregation; and that divine truths, though faintly delivered, were attended with so much efficacy upon the auditory.

Oct. 27. Spent the day in overseeing and directing the Indians, about mending the fence round their wheat: was able to walk with them, and contrive their business, all the forenoon. In the afternoon, was visited by two dear friends, and spent some time in conversation with them. Towards night, I was able to walk out, and take care of the Indians again. In the evening, enjoyed a very peaceful frame.

Oct. 28. Rode to Princeton, in a very weak state; had such a violent fever, by the way, that I was forced to alight at a friend's house, and lie down for some time. Near night, was visited by Mr. Treat, Mr. Beaty, and his wife, and another friend. My spirits were refreshed to see them; but I was surprised, and even ashamed, that they had taken so much pains as to ride thirty or forty miles to see me. Was able to sit up most of the evening; and spent the time in a very comfortable manner with my friends.

Oct. 29. Rode about ten miles with my friends who came yesterday to see me; and then parted with them all but one, who stayed on purpose to keep me company, and cheer my spirits. Was extremely weak, and very feverish, especially towards night; but enjoyed comfort and satisfaction.

Oct. 30. Rode three or four miles, to visit Mr. Wales; spent some time, in an agreeable manner, in conversation; and though extremely weak, enjoyed a comfortable, composed frame of mind.

Oct. 31. Spent the day among friends, in a comfortable frame of mind, though exceedingly weak, and under a considerable fever.

Nov. 1. Took leave of friends, after having spent the forenoon with them, and returned home to my own house. Was much disordered in the evening, and oppressed with my cough; which has now been constant for a long time, with a hard pain in my breast, and fever.

Lord's day, Nov. 2. Was unable to preach, and scarcely able to sit up, the whole day. Was grieved, and almost sunk, to see my poor people destitute of the means of grace; especially as they could not read, and so were under great disadvantages for spending the Sabbath comfortably. O methought, I could be contented to be sick, if my poor flock had a faithful pastor to feed them with spiritual knowledge! A view of their want of this was more afflictive to me, than all my bodily illness.

Nov. 3. Being now in so weak and low a state, that I was utterly incapable of performing my work, and having little hope of recovery, unless by much riding, I thought it my duty to take a long journey into New-England, and to divert myself among my friends, whom I had not now seen for a long time. Accordingly I took leave of my congregation this day.—Before I left my people, I visited them all in their respective houses, and discoursed to each one, as I thought most proper and suitable for their circumstances, and found great freedom and assistance in so doing. I scarcely left one house but some were in tears; and many were not only affected with my being about to leave them, but with the solemn addresses I made them upon divine things; for I was helped to be fervent in spirit, while I discoursed to them.—When I had thus gone through my congregation, which took me most of the day, and had taken leave of them, and of the school, I left home, and rode about two miles, to the house where I lived in the summer past, and there lodged. Was refreshed, this evening, because I had left my congregation so well-disposed, and affected, and had been so much assisted in making my farewell addresses to them.

Nov. 4. Rode to Woodbridge, and lodged with Mr. Pierson; continuing still in a very weak state.

Nov. 5. Rode to Elisabeth-Town; intending, as soon as possible, to prosecute my journey into New-England. But was, in an hour or two after my arrival, taken much worse.

After this, for near a week, I was confined to my chamber, and most of the time to my bed: and then so far revived as to be able to walk about the house; but was still confined within doors.

In the beginning of this extraordinary turn of disorder, after my coming to Elisabeth-Town, I was enabled through mercy to maintain a calm, composed, and patient spirit, as I had been before from the beginning of my weakness. After I had been in Elisabeth-Town about a fortnight, and had so far recovered that I was able to walk about the house, upon a day of thanksgiving kept in this place, I was enabled to recall and recount over the mercies of God, in such a manner as greatly affected me, and filled me with thankfulness and praise. Especially my soul praised God for his work of grace among the Indians, and the enlargement of his dear kingdom. My soul blessed God for what he is in himself, and adored him, that he ever would display himself to creatures. I rejoiced, that he was God, and longed that all should know it, and feel it, and rejoice in it. "Lord, glorify thyself," was the desire and cry of my soul. O that all people might love and praise the blessed God; that he might have all possible honour and glory from the intelligent world!

After this comfortable thanksgiving-season, I frequently enjoyed freedom, enlargement, and engagedness of soul in prayer, and was enabled to intercede with God for my dear congregation, very often for every family, and every person, in particular. It was often a great comfort to me, that I could pray heartily to God for those, to whom I could not speak, and whom I was not allowed to see. But at other times, my spirits were so flat and low, and my bodily vigour so much wasted, that I had scarce any affections at all.

During his confinement at Elizabethtown, Brainerd wrote the following letter to his youngest brother.

To his Brother Israel, then a Student at Yale-College, New-Haven

Elizabeth-Town, New-Jersey, Nov. 24, 1746.
DEAR BROTHER,

I had determined to make you and my other friends in New-England a visit, this fall; partly from an earnest desire I had to see you and them, and partly with a view to the recovery of my health; which has, for more than three months past, been much impaired. In order to prosecute this design, I set out from my own people about three weeks ago, and came as far as to this place; where, my disorder greatly increasing, I have been obliged to keep house ever since, until the day before yesterday; when I was able to ride about half a mile, but found myself much tired with the journey. I have now no hopes of prosecuting my journey into New-England this winter; my present state of health will by no means admit of it. Although I am, through divine goodness, much better than I was some days ago; yet I have not strength now to ride more than ten miles a day, if the season were warm, and fit for me to travel in. My disorder has been attended with several symptoms of consumption; and I have been at times apprehensive, that my great change was at hand: yet blessed be God, I have never been affrighted; but, on the contrary, at times much delighted with a view of its approach.

O the blessedness of being delivered from the clogs of flesh and sense, from a body of sin and spiritual death! O the unspeakable sweetness of being translated into a state of complete purity and perfection! believe me, my brother, a lively view and hope of these things, will make the king of terrors himself appear agreeable. Dear brother, let me intreat you, to keep eternity in your view, and behave yourself as becomes one that must shortly "give an account of all things done in the body." That God may be your God, and prepare you for his service here, and his kingdom of glory hereafter, is the desire and daily prayer of

Your affectionate loving brother,
DAVID BRAINERD.

In December, I had revived so far as to be able to walk abroad, and visit my friends, and seemed to be on the gaining hand with regard to my health, in the main, until Lord's day, December 21. At which time I went to the public worship; and it being sacrament day, I laboured much at the Lord's table to bring forth a certain corruption, and have it slain, as being an enemy to God and my own soul; and could not but hope, that I had gained some strength against this, as well as other corruptions; and felt some brokenness of heart for my sin.

After this, having perhaps taken some cold, I began to decline as to bodily health; and continued to do so, till the latter end of January 1747. Having a violent cough, a considerable fever, an asthmatic disorder, and no appetite for any manner of food, nor any power of digestion, I was reduced to so low a state, that my friends, I believe, generally despaired of my life; and some of them, for some time together, thought I could scarce live a day. At this time, I could think of nothing, with any application of mind, and seemed to be in a great measure void of all affection, and was exercised with great temptations; but yet was not, ordinarily, afraid of death.

Lord's day, Feb. 1. Though in a very weak and low state, I enjoyed a considerable degree of comfort and sweetness in divine things; and was enabled to plead and use arguments with God in prayer, I think, with a child-like spirit. That passage of scripture occurred to my mind, and gave me great assistance, "If ye, being evil, know how to give good gifts to your children, how much more will your heavenly Father give the holy Spirit to them that ask him?" This text I was helped to plead, and insist upon; and saw the divine faithfulness engaged for dealing with me better than any earthly parent can do with his child. This season so refreshed my soul, that my body seemed also to be a gainer by it. From this time, I began gradually to amend. As I recovered some strength, vigour and spirit, I found at times some freedom and life in the exercises of devotion, and some longings after spirituality and a life of usefulness to the interests of the great Redeemer. At other times, I was awfully barren and lifeless, and out of frame for the things of God; so that I was ready often to cry out, "Oh that it were with me as in months past!" Oh that God had taken me away in the midst of my usefulness, with a sudden stroke, that I might not have been under a necessity of trifling away time in diversions! Oh that I had never lived to spend so much precious time, in so poor a manner, and to so little purpose! Thus I often reflected, was grieved, ashamed, and even confounded, sunk and discouraged.

Feb. 24. I was able to ride as far as Newark (having been confined within Elizabeth-Town almost four months), and the next day returned to Elizabeth-Town. My spirits were somewhat refreshed with the ride, though my body was weary.

Feb. 28. Was visited by an Indian of my own congregation; who brought me letters, and good news of the sober and good behaviour of my people in general. This refreshed my soul. I could not but soon retire, and bless God for his goodness; and found, I trust, a truly thankful frame of spirit, that God seemed to be building up that congregation for himself.

March 4. I met with reproof from a friend, which, although I thought I did not deserve it from him, yet was, I trust, blessed of God to make me more tenderly afraid of sin, more jealous over myself, and more concerned to keep both heart and life pure and unblameable. It likewise caused me to reflect on my past deadness and want of spirituality, and to abhor myself and look on myself as most unworthy. This frame of mind continued the next day; and for several days after, I grieved to think, that in my necessary diversions I had not maintained more seriousness, solemnity, heavenly affection and conversation. Thus my spirits were often depressed and sunk; and yet, I trust, that reproof was made to be beneficial to me.

March 11, being kept in Elizabeth-Town as a day of fasting and prayer, I was able to attend public worship; which was the first time I had been able so to do since December 21. O, how much weakness and distress did God carry me through in this space of time! But having obtained help from him, I yet live. Oh that I could live more to his glory!

Lord's day, March 15. Was able again to attend public worship, and felt some earnest desires of being restored to the ministerial work: felt, I think, some spirit and life, to speak for God.

March 18. Rode out with a design to visit my people; and the next day arrived among them: but was under great dejection in my journey.

On Friday morning, I rose early, walked about among my people, and enquired into their state and concerns; and found an additional weight and burden on my spirits, upon hearing some things disagreeable. I endeavoured to go to God with my distresses, and made some kind of lamentable complaint; and in a broken manner spread my difficulties before God; but notwithstanding, my mind continued very gloomy. About ten o'clock, I called my people together, and after having explained and sung a psalm, I prayed with them. There was a considerable deal of affection among them; I doubt not, in some instances, that which was more than merely natural.

This was the last interview which he ever had with his people.

CHAPTER XII

From the termination of his Missionary Labours to his Death.

On Friday, March 20, 1747, about 11 A.M. he left Cranberry; little suspecting that he saw it and his beloved people for the last time. On Saturday, he came to Elizabeth-Town, enfeebled in health, and oppressed with melancholy. Here he continued a considerable time, la-

bouring under the ravages of disease, and suffering from extreme depression of spirit.

March 28. Was taken this morning with violent griping pains. These pains were extreme, and constant, for several hours; so that it seemed impossible for me, without a miracle, to live twenty-four hours in such distress. I lay confined to my bed, the whole day, and in distressing pain, all the former part of it; but it pleased God to bless means for the abatement of my distress. Was exceedingly weakened by this pain, and continued so for several days following; being exercised with a fever, cough, and nocturnal sweats. In this distressed case, so long as my head was free of vapoury confusions, death appeared agreeable to me. I looked on it as the ends of toils, and an entrance into a place "where the weary are at rest"; and think I had some relish for the entertainments of the heavenly state; so that by these I was allured and drawn, as well as driven by the fatigues of life. O, how happy it is, to be drawn by desires of a state of perfect holiness!

April 4. Was sunk and dejected, very restless and uneasy, by reason of the misimprovement of time; and yet knew not what to do. I longed to spend time in fasting and prayer, that I might be delivered from indolence and coldness in the things of God; but, alas, I had not bodily strength for these exercises! O, how blessed a thing it is to enjoy peace of conscience! but how dreadful is a want of inward peace and composure of soul! It is impossible, I find, to enjoy this happiness without redeeming time, and maintaining a spiritual frame of mind.

Lord's day, April 5. It grieved me to find myself so inconceivably barren. My soul thirsted for grace: but, alas, how far was I from obtaining what appeared to me so exceeding excellent! I was ready to despair of ever being a holy creature and yet my soul was desirous of following hard after God; but never did I see myself so far from having apprehended, or being already perfect, as at this time. The Lord's supper being this day administered, I attended the ordinance: and though I saw in myself a dreadful emptiness, and want of grace, and saw myself as it were at an infinite distance from that purity which becomes the gospel, yet at the communion, especially at the distribution of the bread, I enjoyed some warmth of affection, and felt a tender love to the brethren; and, I think, to the glorious Redeemer, the first-born among them. I endeavoured then to bring forth mine and his enemies and slay them before him; and found great freedom in begging deliverance from this spiritual death, as well as in asking divine favours for my friends and congregation, and the church of Christ in general.

April 7. In the afternoon rode to Newark, to marry the Rev. Mr. Dickinson; and in the evening, performed that service. Afterwards, rode home to Elisabeth-Town, in a pleasant frame, full of composure and sweetness.

April 9. Attended the ordination of Mr. Tucker, and afterwards the examination of Mr. Smith: was in a comfortable frame of mind this day, and felt my heart, I think, sometimes in a spiritual frame.

April 10. Spent the forenoon in Presbyterial business. In the afternoon, rode to Elizabethtown; found my brother, John there: spent some time in conversation with him; but was extremely weak and outdone, my spirits considerably sunk, and my mind dejected.

April 13. Assisted in examining my brother. In the evening, was in a solemn devout frame; but was much overdone and oppressed with a violent head-ache.

April 14. Was able to do little or nothing: spent some time with Mr. Byram and other friends. This day my brother went to my people.

April 15. Found some freedom at the throne of grace several times this day. In the afternoon, was very weak, and spent the time to very little purpose; yet, in the evening, had, I thought, some religious warmth and spiritual desires in prayer. My soul seemed to go forth after God, and take complacence in his divine perfections. But, alas! afterwards awfully let down my watch, and grew careless and secure.

April 16. Was in bitter anguish of soul, in the morning, such as I have scarce ever felt, with a sense of sin and guilt. I continued in distress the whole day, attempting to pray wherever I went; and indeed could not help so doing; but looked upon myself so vile, that I dared not look any body in the face; and was even grieved, that any body should shew me any respect, or that they should be so deceived as to think I deserved it.

April 17. In the evening, could not but think, that God helped me to "draw near to the throne of grace," though most unworthy, and gave me a sense of his favour; which gave me inexpressible support and encouragement. Though I scarcely dared to hope that the mercy was real, it appeared so great; yet could not but rejoice, that ever God should discover his reconciled face to such a vile sinner. Shame and confusion, at times, covered me; and then hope, and joy, and admiration of divine goodness gained the ascendant. Sometimes I could not but admire the divine goodness, that the Lord had not let me fall into all the grossest, vilest acts of sins and open scandal, that could be thought of; and felt so much necessitated to praise God, that this was ready for a little while to swallow up my shame and pressure of spirit on account of my sins.

After this, his dejection and pressure of spirit returned; and he remained under it the two next days.

April 20. Was in a very disordered state, and kept my bed most of the day. I enjoyed a little more comfort, than in several of the preceding days. This day I arrived at the age of twenty-nine years.

April 21. I set out on my journey for New-England, in order (if it might be the will of God) to recover my health by riding; travelled to New-York, and there lodged.

This proved his final departure from New-Jersey.—He traveled slowly, and arrived among his friends at East-Haddam, about the beginning of May. There is very little account in his diary of the time that passed from his setting out on his journey to May 10. He speaks of his sometimes finding his heart rejoicing in the glorious perfections of God, and longing to live to him; but complains of the unfixedness of his thoughts, and their being easily diverted from divine subjects, and cries out of his leanness, as testifying against him, in the loudest manner. Concerning those diversions which he was obliged to use for his health, he says, that he sometimes found he could use diversions with "singleness of heart," aiming at the glory of God; but that he also found there was a necessity of great care and watchfulness, lest he should lose that spiritual temper of mind in his diversions, and lest they should degenerate into what was merely selfish, without any supreme aim at the glory of God in them.

Lord's day, May 10. (At Had-Lime) I could not but feel some measure of gratitude to God at this time, wherein I was much exercised, that he had always disposed me, in my ministry, to insist on the greatest doctrines of regeneration, the new creature, faith in Christ, progressive sanctification, supreme love to God, living entirely to the glory of God, being not our own, and the like. God thus helped me to see, in the surest manner, from time to time, that these, and the like doctrines necessarily connected with them, are the only foundation of safety and salvation for perishing sinners; and that those divine dispositions, which are consonant hereto, are that holiness, "without which no man shall see the Lord." The exercise of these God-like tempers—wherein the soul acts in a kind of concert with God, and would be and do every thing that is pleasing to him—I saw, would stand by the soul in a dying hour; for God must, I think, deny himself, if he cast away his own image, even the soul that is one in desires with himself.

Lord's day, May 17. (At Millington) Spent the forenoon at home, being unable to attend public worship. At this time, God gave me such an affecting sense of my own vileness, and the exceeding sinfulness of my heart, that there seemed to be nothing but sin and corruption within me. "Innumerable evils compassed me about"; my want of spirituality and holy living, my neglect of God, and living to myself.—All the abominations of my heart and life seemed to be open to my view; and I had nothing to say, but, "God be merciful to me a sinner."—Towards noon, I saw, that the grace of God in Christ, is infinitely free towards sinners, and such sinners as I was. I also saw, that God is the supreme good, that in his presence is life; and I began to long to die, that I might be with him, in a state of freedom from all sin. O how a small glimpse of his excellency refreshed my soul! O how worthy is the blessed God to be loved, adored, and delighted in, for himself, for his own divine excellencies!

Though I felt much dulness, and want of a spirit of prayer, this week; yet I had some glimpses of the excellency of divine things; and especially one morning, in secret meditation and prayer, the excellency and beauty of holiness, as a likeness to the glorious God, was so discovered to me, that I began to long earnestly to be in that world where holiness dwells in perfection. I seemed to long for this perfect holiness, not so much for the sake of my own happiness, although I saw clearly that this was the greatest, yea, the only happiness of the soul, as that I might please God, live entirely to him, and glorify him to the utmost stretch of my rational powers and capacities.

Lord's day, May 24. (At Long-Meadow) Could not but think, as I have often remarked to others, that much more of true religion consists in deep humility, brokenness of heart, and an abasing sense of barrenness and want of grace and holiness, than most who are called christians, imagine; especially those who have been esteemed the converts of the late day. Many seem to know of no other religion but elevated joys and affections, arising only from some flights of imagination, or some suggestion made to their mind, of Christ being theirs, God loving them, and the like.

On Thursday, May 28, he came from Long-Meadow to Northampton; appearing vastly better than, by his account, he had been in the winter; indeed so well, that he was able to ride twenty-five miles in a day, and to walk half a mile; and appeared cheerful, and free from melancholy: but yet undoubtedly, at that time, in a confirmed, incurable consumption.

I had much opportunity, before this, of particular information concerning him, from many who were well acquainted with him; and had myself once an opportunity of considerable conversation and some acquaintance with him, at New-Haven, near four years before, at the time of the commencement, when he offered that confession to the rector of the college, which has been already mentioned in this history; having been one whom he was pleased then several times to consult on that affair: but now I had opportunity for a more full acquaintance with him. I found him remarkably sociable, pleasant, and entertaining in his conversation; yet solid, savoury, spiritual, and very profitable. He appeared meek, modest, and humble; far from any stiffness, moroseness, superstitious demureness, or affected singularity in speech or behaviour, and seeming to dislike all such things. We enjoyed not only the benefit of his conversation, but had the comfort and advantage of hearing him pray in the family, from time to time.—His manner of praying was very agreeable; most becoming a worm of the dust, and a disciple of Christ, addressing an infinitely great and holy God, the Father of mercies; not with florid expressions, or a studied eloquence; not with any intemperate vehemence, or indecent boldness. It was at the greatest distance from any appearance of ostentation, and from every thing that might look as though he meant to recommend himself to those that were about him, or set himself off to their acceptance. It was free also from vain repetitions, without impertinent excursions, or needless multiplying of words. He expressed himself with the strictest propriety, with weight and pungency; and yet what his lips uttered seemed to flow from the fulness of his heart, as deeply impressed with a great and solemn sense of our necessities, unworthiness, and dependence, and of God's infinite greatness, excellency, and sufficiency, rather than

*merely from a warm and fruitful brain, pouring out good expressions.
I know not, that I ever heard him so much as ask a blessing or return
thanks at table, but there was something remarkable to be observed
both in the matter and manner of the performance. In his prayers, he
insisted much on the prosperity of Zion, the advancement of Christ's
kingdom in the world, and the flourishing and propagation of religion
among the Indians. And he generally made it one petition in his prayer,
"that we might not outlive our usefulness."*

Lord's day, May 31. [At Northampton,] I had little inward
sweetness in religion, most of the week past; not realizing and beholding spiritually the glory of God, and the blessed Redeemer;
from whence always arise my comforts and joys in religion, if I
have any at all: and if I cannot so behold the excellencies and perfections of God, as to cause me to rejoice in him for what he is in
himself, I have no solid foundation for joy. To rejoice, only because
I apprehend I have an interest in Christ, and shall be finally saved,
is a poor mean business indeed.

*This week, he consulted Dr. Mather, at my house concerning his ill-
ness; who plainly told him, that there were great evidences of his being
in a confirmed consumption, and that he could give him no encouragement, that he should ever recover. But it seemed not to occasion the
least discomposure in him, nor to make any manner of alteration as
to the cheerfulness and serenity of his mind, or the freedom or pleasant-
ness of his conversation.*

Lord's day, June 7. My attention was greatly engaged, and my
soul so drawn forth, this day, by what I heard of the "exceeding
preciousness of the saving grace of God's Spirit," that it almost
overcame my body, in my weak state. I saw that true grace is exceedingly precious indeed; that it is very rare; and that there is but
a very small degree of it, even where the reality of it is to be found;
at least, I saw this to be my case.

In the preceding week, I enjoyed some comfortable seasons of
meditation. One morning, the cause of God appeared exceedingly
precious to me. The Redeemer's kingdom is all that is valuable in
the earth, and I could not but long for the promotion of it in the
world. I saw also, that this cause is God's, that he has an infinitely
greater regard and concern for it, than I could possibly have; that if
I have any true love to this blessed interest it is only a drop derived
from that ocean. Hence I was ready to "lift up my head with joy";

and conclude, "Well, if God's cause be so dear and precious to him, he will promote it." Thus I did as it were, rest on God that he would surely promote that which was so agreeable to his own will; though the time when, must still be left to his sovereign pleasure.

He was advised by physicians still to continue riding; as what would tend, above any other means, to prolong his life. He was at a loss, for some time, which way to bend his course next; but finally determined to ride from hence to Boston; we having concluded that one of our family should go with him, and be helpful to him in his weak and low state.

June 9. I set out on a journey from Northampton to Boston. Travelled slowly, and got some acquaintance with divers ministers on the road.

Having now continued to ride for some considerable time together, I felt myself much better than I had formerly done; and found, that in proportion to the prospect I had of being restored to a state of usefulness, so I desired the continuance of life; but death appeared, inconceivably more desirable to me, than a useless life; yet blessed be God, I found my heart, at times fully resigned and reconciled to this greatest of afflictions, if God saw fit thus to deal with me.

June 12. I arrived in Boston this day, somewhat fatigued with my journey. Observed, that there is no rest, but in God; fatigues of body, and anxieties of mind, attend us both in town and country; no place is exempted.

Lord's day, June 14. I enjoyed some enlargement and sweetness in family prayer, as well as in secret exercises; God appeared excellent, his ways full of pleasure and peace, and all I wanted was a spirit of holy fervency, to live to him.

June 17. This and the two preceding days, I spent mainly in visiting the ministers of the town, and was treated with great respect by them.

June 18. I was taken exceedingly ill, and brought to the gates of death, by the breaking of small ulcers in my lungs, as my physician supposed. In this extremely weak state, I continued for several weeks, and was frequently reduced so low, as to be utterly speechless, and not able so much as to whisper a word. Even after I had so far revived, as to walk about the house, and to step out of doors,

I was exercised every day with a faint turn, which continued usually four or five hours; at which times, though I was not utterly speechless, but that I could say Yes, or No, yet I could not converse at all, nor speak one sentence, without making stops for breath; and divers times this season, my friends gathered round my bed, to see me breathe my last, which they expected every moment, as I myself also did.

How I was, that first day or two of my illness with regard to the exercise of reason, I scarcely know. I believe I was somewhat shattered with the violence of the fever at times; but the third day of my illness, and constantly afterwards, for four or five weeks together, I enjoyed as much serenity of mind, and clearness of thought, as perhaps I ever did in my life. I think that my mind never penetrated with so much ease and freedom into divine things, as at this time; and I never felt so capable of demonstrating the truth of many important doctrines of the gospel, as now. As I saw clearly the truth of those great doctrines, which are justly styled the doctrines of grace; so I saw with no less clearness, that the essence of religion consisted in the soul's conformity to God, and acting above all selfish views, for his glory, longing to be for him to live to him, and please and honour him in all things: and this from a clear view of his infinite excellency and worthiness in himself, to be loved, adored, worshipped, and served by all intelligent creatures. Thus I saw, that when a soul loves God with a supreme love, he therein acts like the blessed God himself, who most justly loves himself in that manner. So when God's interest and his are become one, and he longs that God should be glorified, and rejoices to think that he is unchangeably possessed of the highest glory and blessedness, herein also he acts in conformity to God. In like manner, when the soul is fully resigned to, and rests satisfied and content with the divine will, here it is also conformed to God.

I saw further, that as this divine temper, by which the soul exalts God, and treads self in the dust, is wrought in the soul by God's discovering his own glorious perfections in the face of Jesus Christ to it, by the special influences of the holy Spirit, so he cannot but have regard to it, as his own work; and as it is his image in the soul, he cannot but take delight in it. Then I saw again, that if God should slight and reject his own moral image, he must needs deny

himself; which he cannot do. And thus I saw the stability and infal-
libility of this religion; and that those who are truly possessed of it,
have the most complete and satisfying evidence of their being in-
terested in all the benefits of Christ's redemption, having their
hearts conformed to him; and that these, these only, are qualified
for the employments and entertainments of God's kingdom of glory;
as none but these have any relish for the business of heaven, which
is to ascribe glory to God, and not to themselves; and that God
(though I would speak it with great reverence of his name and perfection) cannot, without denying himself, finally cast such away.

The next thing I had then to do, was to inquire, whether this was
my religion: and here God was pleased to help me to the most easy
remembrance and critical review of what had passed in course, of a
religious nature, through several of the latter years of my life. Although I could discover much corruption attending my best duties,
many selfish views and carnal ends, much spiritual pride and self-
exaltation, and innumerable other evils which compassed me about;
yet God was pleased, as I was reviewing, quickly to put this question out of doubt, by shewing me, that I had, from time to time,
acted above the utmost influence of mere self-love; that I had
longed to please and glorify him, as my highest happiness, &c. This
review was through grace attended with a present feeling of the
same divine temper of mind. I felt now pleased, to think of the
glory of God, and longed for heaven, as a state wherein I might
glorify God perfectly, rather than a place of happiness for myself.
This feeling of the love of God in my heart, which I trust the Spirit
of God excited in me afresh, was sufficient to give me a full satisfaction, and make me long, as I had many times before done, to be
with Christ. I did not now want any of the sudden suggestions,
which many are so pleased with, "That Christ and his benefits are
mine; that God loves me," &c. in order to give me satisfaction about
my state. No, my soul now abhorred those delusions of Satan,
which are thought to be the immediate witness of the Spirit, while
there is nothing but an empty suggestion of a certain fact, without
any gracious discovery of the divine glory, or of the Spirit's work
in their own hearts. I saw the awful delusion of this kind of
confidence, as well as of the whole of that religion, from which they
usually spring, or at least of which they are the attendants. The
false religion of the late day, though a day of wondrous grace, the

imaginations, and impressions made only on the animal affections—together with the sudden suggestions made to the mind by Satan, transformed into an angel of light, of certain facts not revealed in scripture—and many such like things, I fear, have made up the greater part of the religious appearance in many places.

These things I saw with great clearness, when I was thought to be dying. God gave me great concern for his church and interest in the world, at this time; not so much because the late remarkable influence upon the minds of people was abated, as because that false religion—those hearts of imagination, and wild and selfish commotions of the animal affections—which attended the work of grace, had prevailed so far. This was that which my mind dwelt upon, almost day and night; and this, to me, was the darkest appearance, respecting religion, in the land; for it was this chiefly, that had prejudiced the world against inward religion. And I saw the great misery of all was, that so few saw any manner of difference between those exercises which are spiritual and holy, and those which have self-love only for their beginning, centre, and end.

As God was pleased to afford me clearness of thought, and composure of mind, almost continually, for several weeks together under my great weakness; so he enabled me, in some measure, to improve my time, as I hope, to valuable purposes. I was enabled to write a number of important letters, to friends in remote places: and sometimes I wrote when I was speechless, i.e. unable to maintain conversation with my body; though perhaps I was able to speak a word or two so as to be heard.

Among the letters written at this period, were the following. The reader will perceive that they were written by one, conscious that he was standing on the verge of the grace, and realizing in no ordinary degree, the infinite importance of eternity.

To his brother Israel, at College: written in the time of his extreme illness in Boston, a few months before his death.

Boston, June 30, 1747.

MY DEAR BROTHER,

It is on the verge of Eternity I now address you. I am heartily sorry, that I have so little strength to write what I long so much to communicate to you. But let me tell you, my brother, Eternity is another thing than we ordinarily take it to be in a healthful state. O, how vast and boundless! O, how fixed and unalterable! O, of what infinite importance is it, that we be prepared for Eternity! I have been just a dying, now for more than a week; and all around me have thought me so. I have had clear views of Eternity; have seen the blessedness of the godly, in some measure; and have longed to share their happy state; as well as been comfortably satisfied, that through grace, I shall do so: but O, what anguish is raised in my mind, to think of Eternity for those who are christless, for those who are mistaken, and who bring their false hopes to the grave with them! The sight was so dreadful, I could by no means bear it: my thoughts recoiled, and I said, under a more affecting sense than ever before, "Who can dwell with everlasting burnings!" O, methought, could I now see my friends, that I might warn them to see to it, that they lay their foundation for Eternity sure. And for you, my dear brother, I have been particularly concerned; and have wondered, I so much neglected conversing with you about your spiritual state at our last meeting. O, my brother, let me then beseech you now to examine, whether you are indeed a new creature? whether you have ever acted above self? whether the glory of God has ever been the sweetest and highest concern with you? whether you have ever been reconciled to all the perfections of God? in a word, whether God has been your portion, and a holy conformity to him your chief delight? If you cannot answer positively, consider seriously the frequent breathings of your soul; but do not however put yourself off with a slight answer. If you have reason to think you are graceless, O, give yourself and the throne of grace no rest, till God arise and save. But if the case should be otherwise, bless God for his grace, and press after holiness.

My soul longs, that you should be fitted for, and in due time go into the work of the ministry. I cannot bear to think of your going into any other business in life. Do not be discouraged, because you see your elder brothers in the ministry die early, one after another. I declare, now I am dying, I would not have spent my life otherwise for the whole world. But I must leave this with God.

If this line should come to your hands soon after the date, I should be almost desirous you should set out on a journey to me: it may be you may see me alive; which I should much rejoice in. But if you cannot come, I must commit you to the grace of God, where you are. May He be your guide and counsellor, your sanctifier and eternal portion!

O, my dear brother, flee fleshly lusts, and the enchanting amusements, as well as corrupt doctrines of the present day; and strive to live to God. Take this as the last line from

Your affectionate dying brother.
DAVID BRAINERD.

To his brother John, at Bethel, the town of Christian Indians, in New-Jersey; written likewise at Boston, when he was there on the brink of the grave, in the summer before his death.

DEAR BROTHER,

I am now just on the verge of Eternity, expecting very speedily to appear in the unseen world. I feel myself no more an inhabitant of earth, and sometimes earnestly long to "depart and be with Christ." I bless God, he has for some years given me an abiding conviction, that it is impossible for any rational creature to enjoy true happiness, without being entirely "devoted to him." Under the influence of this conviction I have in some measure acted. Oh that I had done more so. I saw both the excellency and necessity of holiness in life; but never in such a manner as now when I am just brought from the sides of the grave. O my brother, pursue after holiness; press towards this blessed mark; and let your thirsty soul continually say, "I shall never be satisfied till I awake in thy likeness." Although there has been a great deal of selfishness in my views; of which I am ashamed, and for which my soul is humbled at every view; yet, blessed be God, I find I have really had, for the most part, such a concern for his glory, and the advancement of his kingdom in the world, that it is a satisfaction to me to reflect upon these years.

And now, my dear brother, as I must press you to pursue after personal holiness, to be as much in fasting and prayer, as your health will allow, and to live above the rate of common christians; so I must entreat you solemnly to attend to your public work; labour to distinguish between true and false religion; and to that end, watch the motions of God's spirit upon your own heart—Look to him for help; and impartially compare your experiences with his word. Read Mr. Edwards on the affections; where the essence and soul of religion is clearly distinguished from false affections. Value religious joys according to the subject-matter of them: there are many who rejoice in their supposed justification; but what do these joys argue, but only that they love themselves? Whereas, in true spiritual joys, the soul rejoices in God for what he is in himself; blesses God for his holiness, sovereignty, power, faithfulness, and all his perfections; adores God, that he is what he is, that he is unchangeably possessed of infinite glory and happiness. Now, when men thus rejoice in the perfections of God, and in the infinite excellency of the way of salvation by Christ, and in the holy commands of God, which are a transcript of his holy nature; these joys are divine and spiritual. Our joys will stand by us at the hour of death, if we can be then satisfied, that we have thus acted above self; and in a disinterested manner, if I may so express it, rejoiced in the glory of the blessed God. I fear, you are not sufficiently aware how much false religion there is in the world; many serious christians and valuable ministers are too easily imposed upon by this false blaze. I likewise fear, you are not sensible of the dreadful effects and consequences of this false religion. Let me tell you, it is the devil transformed into an angel of light; it is a fiend of hell, that always springs up with every revival of religion, and stabs and murders the cause of God, while it passes current with multitudes of well meaning people for the height of religion. Set yourself, my brother, to crush all appearances of this nature, among the Indians, and never encourage any degrees of heat without light. Charge my people in the name of their dying minister, yea, in the name of Him who was dead and is alive, to live and walk as becomes the gospel. —Tell them, how great the expectations of God and his people are from them, and how awfully they will wound God's cause, if they fall into vice; as well as fatally prejudice other poor Indians.—Always insist, that their experiences are rotten, that their joys are delusive, although they may have been rapt up into the third heavens in their own conceit by them, unless the main tenour of their lives be spiritual, watchful, and holy. In pressing these things, "thou shalt both save thyself and those that hear thee."

God knows, I was heartily willing to have served him longer in the work of the ministry, although it had still been attended with all the labours and hardships of past years, if he had seen fit that it should be so: but as his will now appears otherwise, I am fully content, and can with the utmost freedom say, "The will of the Lord be done." It affects me, to think of leaving you in a world of sin; my heart pities you, that those storms and tempests are yet before you, from which I trust, through grace, I am almost delivered. But "God lives, and blessed be my Rock"; he is the same almighty Friend; and will, I trust, be your Guide and Helper, as he has been mine.

And now, my dear brother, "I commend you to God and to the word of his grace, which is able to build you up, and give you inheritance among all them that are sanctified. May you enjoy the divine presence both in private and public; and may "the arms of your hands be made strong, by the right hand of the mighty God of Jacob"! Which are the passionate desires and prayers of

> Your affectionate dying brother,
> DAVID BRAINERD.

At this season also, while I was confined at Boston, I read with care and attention some papers of old Mr. Shepard's, lately come to light, and designed for the press; and, as I was desired, and greatly urged, made some corrections, where the sense was left dark, for want of a word or two.—Besides this, I had many visitants; with whom, when I was able to speak, I always conversed of the things of religion; and was peculiarly assisted in distinguishing between the true and false religion of the times. There is scarcely any subject, which has been matter of controversy of late, but I was at one time or other compelled to discuss and shew my opinion respecting it; and that frequently before numbers of people. Especially, I discoursed repeatedly on the nature and necessity of that humiliation, self-emptiness, or full conviction of a person's being utterly undone in himself, which is necessary in order to a saving faith, and the extreme difficulty of being brought to this, and the great danger there is of persons taking up with some self-righteous appearances of it. The danger of this I especially dwelt upon, being persuaded that multitudes perish in this hidden way; and because so little is said from most pulpits to discover any danger here: so that persons being never effectually brought to die in themselves, are never truly united to Christ, and so perish. I also discoursed much on what I take to be the essence of true religion; endeavouring plainly to describe that god-like temper and disposition of soul, and that holy conversation and behaviour, which may justly claim the honour of having God for its original and patron. I have reason to hope God blessed my way of discoursing and distinguishing to some, both ministers and people; so that my time was not wholly lost.

He was much visited, while in Boston, by many persons of considerable note and character, and by some of the first rank; who showed him uncommon respect, and appeared highly pleased and entertained with his conversation. Besides being honoured with the company and respect of ministers of the town, he was visited by several ministers from various parts of the country. He took all opportunities to discourse on the peculiar nature, and distinguishing characteristics of true, spiritual, and vital religion; and to bear his testimony against the various false appearances of it, consisting in, or arising from impressions on the imagination, sudden and supposed immediate suggestions of truths not contained in the scripture, and that faith which consists primarily in a person believing that Christ died for him in particular, &c. What he said was, for the most part, heard with uncommon attention and regard: and his discourses and reasonings appeared manifestly to have great weight and influence with many with whom he conversed both ministers and others.

The honourable Commissioners in Boston, of the incorporated society in London for propagating the gospel in New-England and parts adjacent, having newly had committed to them a legacy of the late reverend and famous Dr. Daniel Williams, of London, for the support of two missionaries to the Heathen, were pleased while he was in Boston, to consult him about a mission to those Indians called the Six Nations, particularly about the qualifications requisite in a missionary to those Indians. They were so satisfied with his sentiments on this head, and had such confidence in his faithfulness, his judgement and discretion in things of this nature, that they desired him to undertake to find and recommend two persons fit to be employed in this business; and very much left the matter with him.

Several pious and generously disposed gentlemen in Boston, moved by the wonderful narrative of his labours and success among the Indians in New-Jersey, and more especially by their conversation with him on the same subject; took opportunity to inquire more particularly into the state and necessities of his congregation, and the school among them, with a charitable intention of contributing something to promote the excellent design of advancing the interests of Christianity among the Indians. Understanding that there was a want of Bibles for the school, three dozen Bibles were immediately procured, and 14 pounds in bills (of the old tenor) given over and above, besides more large benefactions made afterwards, which I shall have occasion to mention in their proper place.

BRAINERD's restoration from his extremely low state in Boston, so as to go abroad again and to travel, was very unexpected to him and his friends. My daughter, who was with him, writes thus concerning him, in a letter dated June 23.—"On Thursday, he was very ill with a violent fever, and extreme pain in his head and breast, and, at turns, delirious. So he remained till Saturday evening, when he seemed to be in the agonies of death; the family was up with him till one or two o'clock, expecting that every hour would be his last. On Sabbath day he was a little revived, his head was better, but very full of pain, and exceeding sore at his breast, much put to it for breath, &c. Yesterday he was better upon all accounts. Last night he slept but little. This morning he was much worse.—Dr. Pynchon says, he has no hopes of his life; nor does he think it likely that he will ever come out of the chamber; though he says he may be able to come to Northhampton.—"

In a letter dated June 29, she says as follows:—"Mr. BRAINERD has not so much pain, nor fever, since I last wrote, as before: yet he is extremely weak and low, and very faint, expecting every day will be his last. He says, it is impossible for him to live; for he has hardly vigour enough to draw his breath. I went this morning into town, and when I came home, Mr. Bromfield said, he never expected I should see him alive; for he lay two hours, as they thought, dying; one could scarcely tell, whether he was alive or not; he was not able to speak for some time: but now is much as he was before. The doctor thinks he will drop away in such a turn. Mr. BRAINERD says, he never felt any thing so much like dissolution, as that he felt to-day; and says, he never had any conception of its being possible for any creature to be alive, and yet so weak as he is from day to day.—Dr. Pynchon says, he should not be surprised, if he should so recover as to live half a year; nor would it surprise him, if he should die in half a day. Since I began to write, he is not so well, having had a faint turn again: yet patient and resigned, having no distressing fears, but the contrary."

His physician, the honourable Joseph Pynchon, Esq. when he visited him in his extreme illness in Boston, attributed his sinking so suddenly into a state so extremely low, and nigh unto death, to the breaking of ulcers, which had been long gathering in his lungs, as BRAINERD himself intimates in the forementioned passage in his diary, and there discharging and diffusing their purulent matter. This, while nature was labouring and struggling to throw it off, which could be done no other-

wise than by a gradual straining of it through the small vessels of those vital parts, occasioned a high fever and violent coughing, threw the whole frame of nature into the utmost disorder, and brought it near to a dissolution. But it was supposed, if the strength of nature held till the lungs had this way gradually cleared themselves of this putrid matter, he might revive, and continue better, till new ulcers gathered and broke; but that this would surely sink him again, and there was no hope of his recovery. He expressed himself to one of my neighbours, who at that time saw him in Boston, that he was as certainly a dead man, as if he was shot through the heart.

But so it was ordered in divine Providence, that the strength of nature held out through this great conflict, so as just to escape the grave at that turn; and then he revived, to the astonishment of all who knew his case. After he began to revive, he was visited by his youngest brother, Israel, a student at Yale College; who having heard of his extreme illness, went from thence to Boston, in order to see him; if he might find him alive, which he but little expected.

This visit was attended with a mixture of joy and sorrow to BRAINERD. He greatly rejoiced to see his brother; especially because he had desired an opportunity of some religious conversation with him before he died. But this meeting was attended with sorrow, as his brother brought to him the sorrowful tidings of his sister Spencer's death at Haddam; a sister, between whom and him had long subsisted a peculiarly dear affection, and much intimacy in spiritual matters, and whose house he used to make his own, when he went to Haddam, his native place. He had heard nothing of her sickness till this report of her death. But he had these comforts, together with the tidings, viz. a confidence of her being gone to heaven, and an expectation of his soon meeting her there.—His brother continued with him till he left the town, and came with him from thence to Northampton.—Concerning the last Sabbath Brainerd spent in Boston, he writes in his diary as follows:—

Lord's day, July 19. I was just able to attend public worship, being carried to the house of God in a chaise. Heard Dr. Sewall preach, in the forenoon: partook of the Lord's supper at this time. In this sacrament, I saw astonishing divine wisdom displayed; such wisdom, as I saw, required the tongues of angels and glorified saints to celebrate. It seemed to me that I never should do any thing at adoring the infinite wisdom of God, discovered in the contrivance of man's redemption, until I arrived at a world of perfection; yet I could not help striving "to call upon my soul, and all within me, to bless the name of God."—In the afternoon, heard Mr.

Prince preach.—I saw more of God in the wisdom discovered in the plan of man's redemption, than I saw of any other of his perfections, through the whole day.

He left Boston the next day. But before he came away, he had occasion to bear a very full, plain, and open testimony against that opinion, that the essence of saving faith lies in believing that Christ died for me in particular; and that this is the first act of faith in a true believer's closing with Christ. He did it in a long conference he had with a gentleman, who has very publicly and strenuously appeared to defend that tenet. He had this discourse with him in the presence of a number of respectable individuals who came to visit BRAINERD before he left the town, and to take their leave of him. In this debate, he made this plain declaration, at the same time confirming what he said by many arguments. That the essence of saving faith was wholly left out of the definition which that gentleman has published; and that the faith which he had defined, had nothing of God in it, nothing above nature, nor indeed above the power of the devils; and that all such as had this faith, and no better, though they might have this to never so high a degree, would surely perish. He declared also, that he never had greater assurance of the falseness of the principles of those who maintained such a faith, and of their dangerous and destructive tendency, or a more affecting sense of the great delusion and misery of those who depended on getting to heaven by such a faith, while they had no better, than he lately had when he was supposed to be at the point to die, and expected every minute to pass into eternity.—BRAINERD's discourse at this time, and the forcible reasonings by which he confirmed what he asserted, appeared to be greatly to the satisfaction of those present; as several of them took occasion expressly to manifest to him, before they took leave of him.

When this conversation was ended, having bid an affectionate farewell to his friends, he set out in the cool of the afternoon on his journey to Northampton, attended by his brother, and my daughter who went with him to Boston; and would have been accompanied out of the town by a number of gentlemen, besides that honourable person who gave him his company for some miles on that occasion, as a testimony of their esteem and respect, had not his aversion to any thing of pomp and shew prevented it.

July 25. I arrived here, at Northampton; having set out from Boston on Monday, about 4 o'clock P.M. In this journey, I rode about sixteen miles a day, one day with another. Was sometimes extremely tired and faint on the road, so that it seemed impossible for me to proceed any further: at other times I was considerably better, and felt some freedom both of body and mind.

Lord's day, July 26. This day I saw clearly, that I should never be happy; yea, that God himself could not make me happy, unless I could be in a capacity to "please and glorify him for ever." Take away this, and admit me in all the fine heavens that can be conceived of by men or angels, and I should still be miserable for ever.

Though he had so revived, as to be able to travel thus far, yet he manifested no expectation of recovery. He supposed as his physician did, that his being brought so near to death at Boston, was owing to the breaking of ulcers in his lungs. He told me that he had several such ill turns before, only not to so high a degree, but as he supposed, owing to the same cause, viz. the breaking of ulcers; that he was brought lower and lower every time; that it appeared to him, that in his last sickness he was brought as low as it was possible, and yet live; and that he had not the least expectation of surviving the next return of this breaking of ulcers; but still appeared perfectly calm in the prospect of death.

On Wednesday morning, the week after he came to Northampton, he took leave of his brother Israel, never expecting to see him again in this world; he now setting out from hence on his journey to New-Haven.

When Brainerd came hither, he had so much strength as to be able, from day to day, to ride out two or three miles, and to return; and sometimes to pray in the family: but from this time he gradually decayed, becoming weaker and weaker.

While he was here, his conversation from first to last was much on the same subjects as when in Boston. He spoke much of the nature of true religion in the heart and practice, as distinguished from its various counterfeits; expressing his great concern that the latter so much prevailed in many places. He often manifested his great abhorrence of all such doctrines and principles in religion, as had any tendency to Antinomianism; of all such notions, as seemed to diminish the necessity of holiness of life, or to abate men's regard to the commands of God, and a strict, diligent, and universal practice of virtue and piety, under a pretence of depreciating our works, and magnifying God's free grace. He spoke often, with much detestation, of such experiences and pretended discoveries and joys, as have nothing of the nature of sanctification in them as do not tend to strictness, tenderness, and diligence in religion, to meekness and benevolence towards mankind, and an humble behaviour. He also declared, that he looked on such pretended humility as worthy of no regard, which was not manifested by modesty of conduct and conversation. He spoke often with abhorrence of the spirit and practice which appear among the greater part of separatists at this day in the land, particularly those in the eastern parts of Connecticut; in their condemning, and separating from, the standing ministry and churches, their crying down learning and a learned ministry, their notion of an immediate call to the work of the ministry, and the forwardness of laymen to set up themselves as public teachers and preachers. He had been much conversant in the eastern part of Connecticut, it being near his native place, when the same principles, notion, and spirit began to operate, which have since prevailed to a greater height; and had acquaintance with some of those persons who are become heads and leaders of the separatists. He had also been conversant with persons of the same class elsewhere; and I heard him say, once and again, that he knew by his acquaintance with this sort of people, that what was chiefly and most generally in repute among them as the power of godliness, was an entirely different thing from that true vital piety recommended in the scriptures, and had nothing in it of that nature. He manifested a great dislike of a disposition in persons to much noise and show in religion, and affecting to be abundant in proclaiming and publishing their own experiences. Though at the same time he did not condemn, but approve of Christians speaking of their own experiences on some occasions, and to some persons, with due modesty and discretion. He himself sometimes, while at my house, spake of his own experiences; but it was always with apparent reserve, and in the exercise of care and judgement with respect to occasions, persons, and circumstances. He mentioned some remarkable things of his own religious experience to two young gentlemen, candidates for the ministry, who watched with him, each at different times, when he was very low, and not far from his end; but he desired both of them not to speak of what he had told them till after his death.

The subject of the debate already mentioned, which he had with a certain gentleman, the day he left Boston, seemed to lie with much weight on his mind after he came hither. He began to write a letter to that gentleman, expressing his sentiments concerning the dangerous tendency of some of the tenets he had expressed in conversation, and in the writings he had published; with the considerations by which the exceeding hurtful nature of those notions is evident; but he had not strength to finish his letter.

After he came hither, as long as he lived, he spoke much of that future prosperity of Zion, which is so often foretold and promised in the scripture. It was a theme upon which he delighted to dwell; and his mind seemed to be carried forth with earnest concern about it, and intense desires, that religion might speedily and abundantly revive and flourish. Though he had not the least expectation of recovery, yea, the nearer death advanced, and the more the symptoms of its approach increased, still the more did his mind seem to be taken up with this subject. He told me, when near his end, that "he never in all his life had his mind so led forth in desires and earnest prayers for the flourishing of Christ's kingdom on earth, as since he was brought so exceeding low at Boston." He seemed much to wonder, that there appeared no more of a disposition in ministers and people to pray for the flourishing of religion through the world; that so little a part of their prayers was generally taken up about it, in their families, and elsewhere. Particularly, he several times expressed his wonder, that there appeared no more forwardness to comply with the proposal lately made, in a Memorial from a number of ministers in Scotland, and sent over into America, for united extraordinary prayer, among Christ's ministers and people, for the coming of Christ's kingdom: and sent it as his dying advice to his own congregation, that they should practice agreeably to that proposal.

Though he was constantly exceeding weak; yet there appeared in him a continual care well to improve time, and fill it up with something that might be profitable, and in some respect for the glory of God or the good of men; either profitable conversation; or writing letters to absent friends; or noting something in his diary; or looking over his former writings, correcting them, and preparing them to be left in the hands of others at his death; or giving some directions concerning the future management of his people; or employment in secret devotions. He seemed never to be easy, however ill, if he was not doing something for God, or in his service. After he came hither, he wrote a preface to a diary of the famous MR. SHEPARD'S, in those papers before mentioned, lately found; having been much urged to it by those gentlemen in Boston who had the care of the publication; which diary, with his preface, has since been published.

In his diary for Lord's day, Aug. 9, he speaks of longing desires after death, through a sense of the excellency of a state of perfection.— In his diary for Lord's day, Aug. 16, he speaks of his having so much refreshment of soul in the house of God, that it seemed also to refresh his body. And this is not only noted in his diary, but was very observable to others; it was very apparent, not only, that his mind was exhilarated with inward consolation but also that his animal spirits and bodily strength seemed to be remarkably restored, as though he had

forgot his illness.—But this was the last time that ever he attended
public worship on the Sabbath.

On Tuesday morning that week, as I was absent on a journey, he
prayed with my family; but not without much difficulty, for want of
bodily strength; and this was the last family-prayer that he ever made.
—He had been wont, till now, frequently to ride out, two or three miles:
but this week, on Thursday, was the last time he ever did so.

Lord's day, Aug. 23. This morning, I was considerably refreshed
with the thought, yea, the hope and expectation of the enlargement
of Christ's kingdom; and I could not but hope, that the time was at
hand, when Babylon the great would fall, and rise no more. This
led me to some spiritual meditations, which were very refreshing to
me. I was unable to attend public worship, either part of the day;
but God was pleased to afford me fixedness and satisfaction in divine thoughts. Nothing so refreshes my soul, as when I can go to
God, yea, to God my exceeding joy. When he is so sensible, to my
soul, O how unspeakably delightful is this!

In the week past, I had divers turns of inward refreshing; though
my body was inexpressibly weak, followed continually with agues
and fevers. Sometimes my soul centred in God, as my only portion;
and I felt that I should be for ever unhappy, if He did not reign. I
saw the sweetness and happiness of being his subject, at his disposal. This made all my difficulties quickly vanish.

From this Lord's day, viz. Aug. 23. I was troubled very much
with vapoury disorders, and could neither write nor read, and
could scarcely live; although through mercy, was not so much
oppressed with heavy melancholy and gloominess, as at many other
times.

Till this week, he had been wont to lodge in a room above stairs;
but he now grew so weak, that he was no longer able to go up stairs
and down. Friday, Aug. 28, was the last time he ever went above stairs,
henceforward he betook himself to a lower room.

On Wednesday, Sept. 2, being the day of our public lecture, he
seemed to be refreshed with seeing the neighbouring ministers who
came hither to the lecture, and expressed a great desire once more
to go to the house of God on that day: and accordingly rode to the
meeting, and attended divine service, while the Reverend Mr. Wood-
bridge, of Hatfield, preached. He signified that he supposed it to be

the last time he should ever attend public worship; as it proved. Indeed it was the last time that he ever went out of our gate alive.

On the Saturday evening next following, he was unexpectedly visited by his brother, Mr. John Brainerd, who came to see him from New-Jersey. He was much refreshed by this unexpected visit; this brother being peculiarly dear to him; and he seemed to rejoice in a devout and solemn manner, to see him, and to hear the comfortable tidings which he brought concerning the state of his dear congregation of Christian Indians. A circumstance of this visit, of which he was exceedingly glad, was, that his brother brought him some of his private writings from New-Jersey, and particularly his diary which he had kept for many years past.

Lord's day, Sept. 6. I began to read some of my private writings, which my brother brought me; and was considerably refreshed with what I found in them.

Sept. 7. I proceeded further in reading my old private writings, and found that they had the same effect upon me as before. I could not but rejoice and bless God for what passed long ago, which without writing had been entirely lost.

This evening, when I was in great distress of body, my soul longed that God should be glorified: I saw there was no character but this. I could not but speak to the by-standers then of the only happiness, viz. pleasing God. O that I could for ever live to God! The day, I trust, is at hand, the perfect day. O the day of deliverance from all sin!

Lord's day, Sept. 13. I was much refreshed and engaged in meditation and writing, and found a heart to act for God. My spirits were refreshed and my soul delighted to do something for God.

On the evening following that Lord's day, his feet began to appear sensibly swollen; which thenceforward swelled more and more. A symptom of his dissolution coming on. The next day, his brother John left him, being obliged to return to New-Jersey on some business of great importance and necessity; intending to return again with all possible speed, hoping to see his brother yet once more in the land of the living.

BRAINERD having now, with much deliberation, considered of the important affair beforementioned, which was referred to him by the honourable commissioners in Boston, of the corporation in London for the propagation of the gospel in New-England, and parts adjacent, viz. the fixing upon and recommending of two persons proper to be employed as missionaries to the Six Nations; about this time wrote a letter, recommending two young gentlemen of his acquaintance to those commissioners, viz. Mr. Elihu Spencer of East-Haddam, and Mr. Job Strong of Northampton. The commissioners on the receipt of this letter, cheerfully and unanimously agreed to accept of and employ the persons whom he had recommended. They accordingly since have waited on the commissioners to receive their instructions; and pursuant to these have applied themselves to a preparation for the business of their mission. One of them, Mr. Spencer, has been solemnly ordained to that work, by several of the ministers of Boston, in the presence of an ecclesiastical council convened for that purpose; and is now gone forth to the nation of Oneidas, about a hundred and seventy miles beyond Albany.

On Wednesday, Sept. 16, he wrote a letter to a gentleman in Boston (one of those charitable persons beforementioned, who appeared so forward to contribute of their substance for promoting Christianity among the Indians), relating to the growth of the Indian school, and the need of another schoolmaster, or some person to assist the schoolmaster in instructing the Indian children. These gentlemen, on the receipt of this letter, had a meeting, and agreed with great cheerfulness to give 200 pounds (in bills of the old tenor) for the support of another schoolmaster; and desired the Rev. Mr. Pemberton of New-York (who was then at Boston, and was also, at their desire, present at their meeting), as soon as possible to procure a suitable person for that service; and also agreed to allow 74 pounds to defray some special charges which were requisite to encourage the mission to the Six Nations [besides the salary allowed by the commissioners], which was was also done on some intimations given by BRAINERD.

BRAINERD spent himself much in writing those letters, being exceedingly weak; but it seemed to be much to his satisfaction, that he had been enabled to do it; hoping that it was something done for God, and which might be for the advancement of Christ's kingdom and glory. In writing the last of these letters, he was obliged to use the hand of another, not being able to write himself.

On the Thursday of this week (Sept. 17), was the last time that ever he went out of his lodging room. That day, he was again visited by his brother Israel, who continued with him thenceforward till his death. On that evening he was taken with something of a diarrhea, which he looked upon as another sign of his approaching death; whereupon he expressed himself thus; "Oh the glorious time is now coming! I have longed to serve God perfectly: now God will gratify those desires!" And from time, to time, at the several steps and new symptoms

*of the sensible approach of his dissolution, he was so far from being
sunk or damped, that he seemed to be animated, and made more cheerful; as being glad at the appearance of death's approach. He often
used the epithet, glorious, when speaking of the day of his death, calling it that glorious day. And as he saw his dissolution gradually approaching, he talked much about it; and with perfect calmness spoke
of a future state. He also settled all his affairs, giving directions very
particularly and minutely, concerning what he would have done in
one respect and another after his decease. And the nearer death approached, the more desirous he seemed to be of it. He several times
spoke of the different kinds of willingness to die; and represented it
as an ignoble, mean kind, to be willing to leave the body, only to
get rid of pain; or to go to heaven, only to get honour and advancement there.*

Sept. 19. Near night, while I attempted to walk a little, my
thoughts turned thus; "How infinitely sweet it is, to love God, and
be all for him!" Upon which it was suggested to me, "You are not
an angel, not lively and active." To which my whole soul immediately replied, "I as sincerely desire to love and glorify God, as any
angel in heaven." Upon which it was suggested again, "But you are
filthy, not fit for heaven." Hereupon instantly appeared the blessed
robes of Christ's righteousness, in which I could not but exult and
triumph; and I viewed the infinite excellency of God, and my soul
even broke with longings, that God should be glorified. I thought of
dignity in heaven; but instantly the thought returned, "I do not go
to heaven to get honour, but to give all possible glory and praise."
O how I longed that God should be glorified on earth also! O I was
made—for eternity,—if God might be glorified! Bodily pains I cared
not for; though I was then in extremity, I never felt easier. I felt
willing to glorify God in that state of bodily distress, as long as he
pleased I should continue in it. The grave appeared really sweet,
and I longed to lodge my weary bones in it: but Oh, that God
might be glorified! this was the burden of all my cry. O I knew that
I should be active as an angel, in heaven; and that I should be
stripped of my filthy garments! so that there was no objection. But,
O to love and praise God more, to please him forever! this my soul
panted after, and even now pants for while I write. Oh that God
might be glorified in the whole earth! "Lord let thy kingdom
come." I longed for a spirit of preaching to descend and rest on

ministers, that they might address the consciences of men with closeness and power. I saw that God "had the residue of the Spirit; and my soul longed that it should be "poured from on high." I could not but plead with God for his great name to lose its glory in that work; my soul still longing, that God might be glorified.

The extraordinary frame he was in, that evening, could not be hid. "His mouth spake out of the abundance of his heart," expressing in a very affecting manner much the same things as are written in his diary. Among very many other extraordinary expressions, which he then uttered, were such as these:—"My heaven is to please God, and glorify him, and to give all to him, and to be wholly devoted to his glory: that is the heaven I long for; that is my religion, and that is my happiness, and always was ever since I suppose I had any true religion: and all those that are of that religion shall meet me in heaven. I do not go to heaven to be advanced, but to give honour to God. It is no matter where I shall be stationed in heaven, whether I have a high or low seat there; but to love, and please, and glorify God is all.—Had I a thousand souls, if they were worth any thing, I would give them all to God; but I have nothing to give, when all is done.—It is impossible for any rational creature to be happy without acting all for God: God himself could not make him happy any other way. I long to be in heaven, praising and glorifying God with the holy angels; all my desire is to glorify God.—My heart goes out to the burying place; it seems to me a desirable place: but O to glorify God! that is it; that is above all.—It is a great comfort to me, to think, that I have done a little for God in the world: Oh! it is but a very small matter; yet I have done a little; and I lament it, that I have not done more for him.—There is nothing in the world worth living for, but doing good, and finishing God's work, doing the work that Christ did. I see nothing else in the world, that can yield any satisfaction, besides living to God, pleasing him, and doing his whole will. —My greatest joy and comfort has been, to do something for promoting the interest of religion, and the souls of particular persons: and now, in my illness, while I am full of pain and distress, from day to day, all the comfort I have, is in being able to do some little service for God, either by something that I say, or by writing, or in some other way."

He intermingled with these and other like expressions, many pathetical counsels to those who were about him; particularly to my children and servants. He applied himself to some of my younger children at this time; calling them to him, and speaking to them one by one;

setting before them, in a very plain manner, the nature and essence of true piety, and its great importance and necessity; earnestly warning them not to rest in any thing short of a true and thorough change of heart, and a life devoted to God.—He counselled them not to be slack in the great business of religion, nor in the least to delay it; enforcing his counsels with this, that his words were the words of a dying man: said he, "I shall die here, and here I shall be buried, and here you will see my grave, and do you remember what I have said to you. I am going into eternity: and it is sweet for me to think of eternity: the endlessness of it makes it sweet: but O what shall I say to the eternity of the wicked! I cannot mention it, nor think of it; the thought is too dreadful. When you see my grave, then remember what I said to you while I was alive; then think with yourself, how the man who lies in that grave, counselled and warned me to prepare for death."

His body seemed to be marvellously strengthened, through the inward vigour and refreshment of his mind; so that, although before he was so weak that he could hardly utter a sentence, yet now he continued his most affecting and profitable discourse to us for more than an hour, with scarce any intermission; and said of it, when he had done, "it was the last sermon that ever he should preach."—This extraordinary frame of mind continued the next day; of which he says in his diary as follows.

Lord's day, Sept. 20. Was still in a sweet and comfortable frame: and was again melted with desires that God might be glorified, and with longings to love and live to him. Longed for the influences of the divine Spirit to descend on ministers, in a special manner. And O I longed to be with God, to behold his glory, and to bow in his presence!

It appears by what is noted in his diary, both of this day and the evening preceding, that his mind at this time was much impressed with a sense of the importance of the work of the ministry, and the need of the grace of God, and his special spiritual assistance in this work. It also appeared in what he expressed in conversation: particularly in his discourse to his brother Israel, who was then a member of Yale-College at New-Haven, prosecuting his studies for the work of the ministry. He now, and from time to time, in this his dying state, recommended to his brother a life of self-denial, of weanedness from the world, and devotedness to God, and an earnest endeavour to obtain much of the grace of God's Spirit, and God's gracious influences on his heart; representing the great need which ministers stand in of

*them, and the unspeakable benefit of them from his own experience.
Among many other expressions, he said thus:—"When ministers feel
these special gracious influences on their hearts, it wonderfully assists
them to come at the consciences of men, and as it were to handle
them; whereas, without them, whatever reason and oratory we make
use of, we do but make use of stumps, instead of hands."*

Sept. 21. I began to correct a little volume of my private writings.
God, I believe, remarkably helped me in it; my strength was surprisingly lengthened out, my thoughts were quick and lively, and
my soul refreshed, hoping it might be a work for God.—O how
good, how sweet it is to labour for God!

Sept. 22. Was again employed in reading and correcting, and had
the same success, as the day before. I was exceeding weak; but it
seemed to refresh my soul, thus to spend time.

Sept. 23. I finished my corrections of the little piece beforementioned, and felt uncommonly peaceful; it seemed as if I had now
done all my work in this world, and stood ready for my call to a
better. As long as I see any thing to be done for God, life is worth
having: but O, how vain and unworthy it is, to live for any lower
end!—This day, I indited a letter, I think, of great importance, to
the Rev. Mr. Byram in New-Jersey. Oh that God would bless and
succeed that letter, which was written for the benefit of his church!
Oh that God would purify the sons of Levi, that his glory may be
advanced!—This night, I endured a dreadful turn, wherein my life
was expected scarce an hour or minute together. But blessed be
God, I have enjoyed considerable sweetness in divine things, this
week, both by night and day.

Sept. 24. My strength began to fail exceedingly; which looked
further as if I had done all my work: however, I had strength to
fold and superscribe my letter. About two I went to bed, being
weak and much disordered, and lay in a burning fever till night,
without any proper rest. In the evening, I got up, having lain down
in some of my clothes; but was in the greatest distress, that ever I
endured, having an uncommon kind of hiccough; which either
strangled me, or threw me into a straining to vomit; and at the
same time was distressed with griping pains. O the distress of this
evening! I had little expectation of my living the night through, nor
indeed had any about me: and I longed for the finished moment!—I
was obliged to repair to bed by six o'clock; and through mercy en-

joyed some rest; but was grievously distressed at turns with the hiccough.—My soul breathed after God,—"When shall I come to God, even to God, my exceeding joy?" Oh for his blessed likeness!

Sept. 25. This day, I was unspeakably weak, and little better than speechless all the day; however, I was able to write a little, and felt comfortably in some part of the day. O it refreshed my soul, to think of former things, of desires to glorify God, of the pleasures of living to him! O, blessed God, I am speedily coming to thee, I hope. Hasten the day, O Lord, if it be thy blessed will, O come, Lord Jesus, come quickly. Amen.

Sept. 26. I felt the sweetness of divine things this forenoon; and had the consolation of a consciousness that I was doing something for God.

Lord's day, Sept. 27. This was a very comfortable day to my soul; I think, I awoke with God. I was enabled to lift up my soul to God, early this morning; and while I had little bodily strength, I found freedom to lift up my heart to God for myself and others. Afterwards, was pleased with the thoughts of speedily entering into the unseen world.

Early this morning, as one of the family came into the room, he expressed himself thus: "I have had more pleasure this morning, than all the drunkards in the world enjoy."—So much did he esteem the joy of faith above the pleasures of sin.—He felt that morning, an unusual appetite to food, with which his mind seemed to be exhilarated, looking on it as a sign of the very near approach of death. At this time he also said, "I was born on a Sabbath-day; and I have reason to think I was new-born on a Sabbath-day; and I hope I shall die on this Sabbath-day. I shall look upon it as a favour, if it may be the will of God that it should be so: I long for the time. O, why is his chariot so long in coming? why tarry the wheels of his chariot? I am very willing to part with all: I am willing to part with my dear brother John, and never to see him again, to go to be for ever with the Lord. O, when I go there, how will God's dear church on earth be upon my mind!"

Afterwards, the same morning, being asked how he did, he answered, "I am almost in eternity; I long to be there. My work is done; I have done with all my friends; all the world is nothing to me. I long to be in heaven, praising and glorifying God with the holy angels. All my desire is to glorify God."

During the whole of these last two weeks of his life, he seemed to continue in this frame of heart; loose from all the world, as having finished his work, and done with all things here below. He had now nothing to do but to die, and to abide in an earnest desire and expectation of the happy moment, when his soul should take its flight, to a state of perfect holiness, in which he should be found perfectly glorifying and enjoying God. He said, "That the consideration of the day of death, and the day of judgment, had a long time been peculiarly sweet to him." From time to time he spake of his being willing to leave the body and the world immediately, that day, that night, that moment, if it was the will of God. He also was much engaged in expressing his longings that the church of Christ on earth might flourish, and Christ's kingdom here might be advanced, notwithstanding he was about to leave the earth, and should not with his eyes behold the desirable event, nor be instrumental in promoting it. He said to me, one morning, as I came into his room, "My thoughts have been employed on the old dear theme, the prosperity of God's church on earth. As I waked out of sleep, I was led to cry for the pouring out of God's Spirit, and the advancement of Christ's kingdom, for which the Redeemer did and suffered so much. It is that especially which makes me long for it."—He expressed much hope that a glorious advancement of Christ's kingdom was near at hand.

He once told me, that "he had formerly longed for the outpouring of the Spirit of God, and the glorious times of the church, and hoped they were coming; and should have been willing to have lived to promote religion at that time, if that had been the will of God; but, says he, I am willing it should be as it is; I would not have the choice to make for myself, for ten thousand worlds." He expressed on his death-bed a full persuasion that he should in heaven see the prosperity of the church on earth, and should rejoice with Christ therein; and the consideration of it seemed to be highly pleasing and satisfying to his mind.

He also still dwelt much on the great importance of the work of gospel ministers; and expressed his longings, that they might be filled with the Spirit of God. He manifested much desire to see some of the neighbouring ministers, with whom he had some acquaintance, and of whose sincere friendship he was confident, that he might converse freely with them on that subject, before he died. And it so happened, that he had opportunity with some of them according to his desire.

Another thing that lay much on his heart, from time to time, in these near approaches of death, was the spiritual prosperity of his own congregation of Christian Indians in New-Jersey; and when he spake of them, it was with peculiar tenderness; so that his speech would be presently interrupted and drowned with tears.

He also expressed much satisfaction in the disposals of Providence, with regard to the circumstances of his death; particularly that God had before his death given him an opportunity in Boston, with so many considerable persons, ministers and others, to give in his testimony for God against false religion, and many mistakes that lead to it, and promote it. He was much pleased that he had an opportunity there to lay before pious and charitable gentlemen the state of the Indians, and their necessities to so good effect; and that God had since enabled him to write to them further concerning these affairs; and to write other letters of importance, which he hoped might be of good influence with regard to the state of religion among the Indians, and elsewhere, after his death. He expressed great thankfulness to God for his mercy in these things. He also mentioned it as what he accounted a merciful circumstance of his death, that he should die here. When he was sick at Boston, nigh unto death, it was with reluctance he thought of dying in a place where funerals are often attended with a pomp and show, to any appearance of which he was very averse: and though it was with some difficulty he got his mind reconciled to the prospect then before him, yet at last he was brought to acquiesce in the divine will, with respect to this circumstance of his departure. However, it pleased God to order the event so as to gratify his desire, which he had expressed, of getting back to Northampton, with a view particularly to a more silent and private burial. And speaking of these things, he said, "God had granted him all his desire"; and signified, that now he could with the greater alacrity leave the world.

Sept. 28. I was able to read, and make some few corrections in my private writings; but found I could not write, as I had done; I found myself sensibly declined in all respects. It has been only from a little while before noon, till about one or two o'clock, that I have been able to do any thing for some time past: yet this refreshed my heart, that I could do any thing either public or private, that I hoped was for God.

This evening, he was supposed to be dying. He thought so himself, and was thought so by those who were about him. He seemed glad at the appearance of the near approach of death. He was almost speechless, but his lips appeared to move: and one that sat very near him, heard him utter such expressions as these, "Come, Lord Jesus, come quickly.—O why is his chariot so long in coming."—After he revived, he blamed himself for having been too eager to be gone. And in expressing what he found in the frame of his mind at that time, he said, he then found an inexpressibly sweet love to those whom he looked upon as belonging to Christ, beyond almost all that ever he felt before; so that it "seemed, to use his own words, like a little piece of heaven to have one of them near him." And being asked, whether he heard the prayer that was, at his desire, made with him; he said, "Yes, he heard every word, and had an uncommon sense of the things that were uttered in that prayer, and that every word reached his heart."

On the evening of Tuesday, Sept. 29, as he lay on his bed, he seemed to be in an extraordinary frame; his mind greatly engaged in sweet meditations concerning the prosperity of Zion. There being present here at that time two young gentlemen of his acquaintance, who were candidates for the ministry, he desired us all to unite in singing a Psalm on that subject, even Zion's prosperity. And on his desire we sung a part of the ciid Psalm. This seemed much to refresh and revive him, and gave him new strength; so that, though before he could scarcely speak at all, now he proceeded, with some freedom of speech, to give his dying counsels to those two young gentlemen beforementioned, relating to their preparation for, and prosecution of, that great work of the ministry for which they were designed; and in particular, earnestly recommended to them frequent secret fasting and prayer: and enforced his counsel with regard to this, from his own experience of the great comfort and benefit of it; which, said he, I should not mention, were it not that I am a dying person. After he had finished his counsel, he made a prayer, in the audience of us all; wherein, besides praying for this family, for his brethren, and those candidates for the ministry; and for his own congregation, he earnestly prayed for the reviving and flourishing of religion in the world.—Till now, he had every day sat up part of the day; but after this he never rose from his bed.

Sept. 30. I was obliged to keep my bed the whole day, through weakness. However, redeemed a little time, and with the help of my brother, read and corrected about a dozen pages of my MS. giving an account of my conversion.

Oct. 1. I endeavoured again to do something by way of writing, but soon found my powers of body and mind utterly fail. Felt now so sweetly, as when I was able to do something which I hoped would do some good. In the evening, was discomposed and wholly delirious; but it was not long before God was pleased to give me some sleep, and fully composed my mind. O blessed be God for his great goodness to me, since I was so low at Mr. Bromfield's on Thursday, June 18, last. He has, except those few minutes, given me the clear exercise of my reason, and enabled me to labour much for him, in things both of a public and private nature; and perhaps to do more good, than I should have done if I had been well; besides the comfortable influences of his blessed Spirit, with which he has been pleased to refresh my soul. May his name have all the glory for ever and ever. Amen.

Oct. 2. My soul was this day, at turns, sweetly set on God: I longed to be with him, that I might behold his glory. I felt sweetly disposed to commit all to him, even my dearest friends, my dearest flock, my absent brother, and all my concerns for time and eternity. O that his kingdom might come in the world; that they might all love and glorify him, for what he is in himself; and that the blessed Redeemer might "see of the travail of his soul, and be satisfied! Oh, come, Lord Jesus, come quickly! Amen."

The next evening, we very much expected his brother John from New-Jersey; it being about a week after the time that he proposed for his return, when he went away. Though our expectations were still disappointed, yet Brainerd seemed to continue unmoved, in the same calm and peaceful frame, which he had before manifested; as having resigned all to God, and having done with his friends, and with all things here below.

On the morning of the next day, being Lord's day, Oct. 4, as my daughter Jerusah, who chiefly attended him, came into the room, he looked on her very pleasantly, and said, "Dear Jerusah, are you willing to part with me?—I am quite willing to part with you: I am willing to part with all my friends: I am willing to part with my dear brother John, although I love him the best of any creature living: I have committed him and all my friends to God, and can leave them with God. Though, if I thought I should not see you, and be happy with you in another world, I could not bear to part with you. But we shall spend an happy eternity together." In the evening, as one came into the room with a Bible in her hand, he expressed himself thus: "O that dear book! that lovely book! I shall soon see it opened! the mysteries that are in it, and the mysteries of God's providence will all be unfolded!"

His distemper now very apparently preyed on his vitals in an extraordinary manner: not by a sudden breaking of ulcers in his lungs, as at Boston, but by a constant discharge of purulent matter, in great quantities: so that what he brought up by expectoration, seemed to be as it were mouthfuls of almost clear pus; which was attended with very inward pain and distress.

On Tuesday, Oct. 6, he lay, for a considerable time, as if he were dying. At which time, he was heard to utter, in broken whispers, such expressions as these, "He will come, he will not tarry.—I shall soon be in glory.—I shall soon glorify God with the angels."—But after some time he revived.

The next day, Wednesday, Oct. 7, his brother John arrived from New-Jersey; where he had been detained much longer than he intended, by a mortal sickness prevailing among the Christian Indians, and by some other circumstances that made his stay with them necessary. BRAINERD was affected and refreshed with seeing him, and appeared fully satisfied with the reasons of his delay; seeing the interest of religion and the souls of his people required it.

The next day, Thursday, Oct. 8, he was in great distress and agonies of body; and for the greater part of the day, was much disordered as to the exercise of his reason. In the evening, he was more composed, and had the use of his reason well; but the pain of his body continued and increased. He told me that it was impossible for any one to concieve of the distress which he felt in his breath. He manifested much concern lest he should dishonour God by impatience, under his extreme agony; which was such, that he said, the thought of enduring it one minute longer was almost insupportable. He desired that others would be much in lifting up their hearts continually to God for him, that God would support him, and give him patience. He signified, that he expected to die that night; but seemed to fear a longer delay: and the disposition of his mind with regard to death, appeared still the same that it had been all along. And notwithstanding his bodily agonies, yet the interest of Zion lay still with great weight on his mind; as appeared by some considerable discourse he had that evening with the Rev. Mr. Billing, one of the neighbouring ministers, who was then present, concerning the great importance of the work of the ministry. Afterwards, when it was very late in the night, he had much very proper and profitable discourse with his brother John, concerning his congregation in New-Jersey, and the interest of religion among the Indians. In the latter part of the night, his bodily distress seemed to rise to a greater height than ever; and he said to those then about him, that "it was another thing to die, than people imagined"; explaining himself to mean that they were not aware what bodily pain and anguish is undergone before death. Towards day, his eyes fixed; and he continued lying immovable, till about six o'clock, on Friday,

Oct. 9, 1747, when his soul, as we may well conclude, was received by his dear Lord and Master, as an eminently faithful servant, into that state of perfection of holiness, and fruition of God for which he had so often and so ardently longed; and was welcomed by the glorious assembly in the upper world, as one peculiarly fitted to join them in their blessed employ and enjoyment.

Much respect was shewn to his memory at his funeral; which was on the Monday following, after a sermon preached the same day, on that solemn occasion. His funeral was attended by eight of the neighbouring ministers, and seventeen other gentlemen of liberal education, and a great concourse of people.